Ford Fiesta
Owners Workshop Manual

John S. Mead & Martynn Randall

Models covered

(4907 - 384)

Ford Fiesta Hatchback & Van
Petrol: 1.25 litre (1242cc), 1.4 litre (1388cc) & 1.6 litre (1596cc) Duratec
Diesel: 1.4 litre (1399cc) & 1.6 litre (1560cc) Duratorq TDCi turbo

Does NOT cover models with Mountune conversion
Does NOT cover facelifted model range introduced for 2013

© Haynes Publishing 2017

ABCDE
FGHI

A book in the **Haynes Owners Workshop Manual Series**

ISBN **978 1 78521 357 1**

British Library Cataloguing in Publication Data
A catalogue record for this book is available from the British Library.

Printed in Malaysia

Haynes Publishing
Sparkford, Yeovil, Somerset BA22 7JJ, England

Haynes North America, Inc
859 Lawrence Drive, Newbury Park, California 91320, USA

Printed using NORBRITE BOOK 48.8gsm (CODE: 40N6533) from NORPAC; procurement system certified under Sustainable Forestry Initiative standard. Paper produced is certified to the SFI Certified Fiber Sourcing Standard (CERT - 0094271)

Contents

LIVING WITH YOUR FORD FIESTA

Roadside repairs

Weekly checks

Lubricants and fluids

Tyre pressures

MAINTENANCE

Routine maintenance and servicing – petrol models

Routine maintenance and servicing – diesel models

Contents

The Ford Fiesta (Mk 7) model range covered by this manual was introduced into the UK in October 2008, superseding the previous Fiesta range. It is available in 3- and 5-door Hatchback, and 3-door Van versions with 1.25, 1.4 and 1.6 litre Duretec petrol engines, and 1.4 and 1.6 litre Duratorq TDCi diesel engines. The Duratorq diesel engines were developed jointly by Ford and the Peugeot/Citroën group and feature state-of-the art common-rail injection. With the exception of the 1.4 litre and later 1.6 diesels, all other engines are of the four-cylinder double overhead camshaft (DOHC) configuration, in-line type. The 1.4 litre and post-2010 1.6 litre diesels are four-cylinder single overhead camshaft (SOHC) in-line types. All engines are mounted transversely at the front of the car.

All models have front-wheel-drive, with a five-speed manual transmission. A four-speed electronically-controlled automatic transmission is also optionally available on 1.4 litre petrol engine models. The front suspension is of conventional MacPherson strut type, incorporating lower arms, and an anti-roll bar; at the rear, a semi-independent beam axle is combined with compact under-floor springs to provide a more spacious load area.

A wide range of standard and optional equipment is available within the Fiesta range to suit most tastes, including electric power steering, air conditioning, remote central locking, electric windows, electric sunroof, anti-lock braking system, electronic alarm system and supplemental restraint systems.

For the home mechanic, the Fiesta is a relatively straightforward vehicle to maintain, and most of the items requiring frequent attention are easily accessible.

Your Ford Fiesta Manual

The aim of this manual is to help you get the best value from your car. It can do so in several ways. It can help you decide what work must be done (even should you choose to get it done by a garage). It will also provide information on routine maintenance and servicing, and give a logical course of action and diagnosis when random faults occur. However, it is hoped that you will use the manual by tackling the work yourself. On simpler jobs it may even be quicker than booking the car into a garage and going there twice, to leave and collect it. Perhaps most important, a lot of money can be saved by avoiding the costs a garage must charge to cover its labour and overheads.

The manual has drawings and descriptions to show the function of the various components so that their layout can be understood. Tasks are described and photographed in a clear step-by-step sequence.

References to the 'left' and 'right' of the car are in the sense of a person in the driver's seat facing forward.

Project vehicles

The main vehicle used in the preparation of this manual, and which appears in many of the photographic sequences, was a Ford Fiesta 5-door Hatchback with a 1.6 litre diesel engine. Additional work was carried out on a Fiesta 3-door Hatchback with a 1.4 litre petrol engine.

Acknowledgements

Thanks are due to Draper Tools Limited, who provided some of the workshop tools, and to all those people at Sparkford who helped in the production of this manual.

We take great pride in the accuracy of information given in this manual, but vehicle manufacturers make alterations and design changes during the production run of a particular vehicle of which they do not inform us. No liability can be accepted by the authors or publishers for loss, damage or injury caused by any errors in, or omissions from, the information given.

Ford Fiesta 5-door

Working on your car can be dangerous. This page shows just some of the potential risks and hazards, with the aim of creating a safety-conscious attitude.

General hazards

Scalding

• Don't remove the radiator or expansion tank cap while the engine is hot.
• Engine oil, transmission fluid or power steering fluid may also be dangerously hot if the engine has recently been running.

Burning

• Beware of burns from the exhaust system and from any part of the engine. Brake discs and drums can also be extremely hot immediately after use.

Crushing

• When working under or near a raised vehicle, always supplement the jack with axle stands, or use drive-on ramps. *Never venture under a car which is only supported by a jack.*
• Take care if loosening or tightening high-torque nuts when the vehicle is on stands. Initial loosening and final tightening should be done with the wheels on the ground.

Fire

• Fuel is highly flammable; fuel vapour is explosive.
• Don't let fuel spill onto a hot engine.
• Do not smoke or allow naked lights (including pilot lights) anywhere near a vehicle being worked on. Also beware of creating sparks (electrically or by use of tools).
• Fuel vapour is heavier than air, so don't work on the fuel system with the vehicle over an inspection pit.
• Another cause of fire is an electrical overload or short-circuit. Take care when repairing or modifying the vehicle wiring.
• Keep a fire extinguisher handy, of a type suitable for use on fuel and electrical fires.

Electric shock

• Ignition HT and Xenon headlight voltages can be dangerous, especially to people with heart problems or a pacemaker. Don't work on or near these systems with the engine running or the ignition switched on.

• Mains voltage is also dangerous. Make sure that any mains-operated equipment is correctly earthed. Mains power points should be protected by a residual current device (RCD) circuit breaker.

Fume or gas intoxication

• Exhaust fumes are poisonous; they can contain carbon monoxide, which is rapidly fatal if inhaled. Never run the engine in a confined space such as a garage with the doors shut.
• Fuel vapour is also poisonous, as are the vapours from some cleaning solvents and paint thinners.

Poisonous or irritant substances

• Avoid skin contact with battery acid and with any fuel, fluid or lubricant, especially antifreeze, brake hydraulic fluid and Diesel fuel. Don't syphon them by mouth. If such a substance is swallowed or gets into the eyes, seek medical advice.
• Prolonged contact with used engine oil can cause skin cancer. Wear gloves or use a barrier cream if necessary. Change out of oil-soaked clothes and do not keep oily rags in your pocket.
• Air conditioning refrigerant forms a poisonous gas if exposed to a naked flame (including a cigarette). It can also cause skin burns on contact.

Asbestos

• Asbestos dust can cause cancer if inhaled or swallowed. Asbestos may be found in gaskets and in brake and clutch linings. When dealing with such components it is safest to assume that they contain asbestos.

Special hazards

Hydrofluoric acid

• This extremely corrosive acid is formed when certain types of synthetic rubber, found in some O-rings, oil seals, fuel hoses etc, are exposed to temperatures above 4000C. The rubber changes into a charred or sticky substance containing the acid. *Once formed, the acid remains dangerous for years. If it gets onto the skin, it may be necessary to amputate the limb concerned.*
• When dealing with a vehicle which has suffered a fire, or with components salvaged from such a vehicle, wear protective gloves and discard them after use.

The battery

• Batteries contain sulphuric acid, which attacks clothing, eyes and skin. Take care when topping-up or carrying the battery.
• The hydrogen gas given off by the battery is highly explosive. Never cause a spark or allow a naked light nearby. Be careful when connecting and disconnecting battery chargers or jump leads.

Air bags

• Air bags can cause injury if they go off accidentally. Take care when removing the steering wheel and trim panels. Special storage instructions may apply.

Diesel injection equipment

• Diesel injection pumps supply fuel at very high pressure. Take care when working on the fuel injectors and fuel pipes.

⚠️ *Warning: Never expose the hands, face or any other part of the body to injector spray; the fuel can penetrate the skin with potentially fatal results.*

Remember...

DO

• Do use eye protection when using power tools, and when working under the vehicle.

• Do wear gloves or use barrier cream to protect your hands when necessary.

• Do get someone to check periodically that all is well when working alone on the vehicle.

• Do keep loose clothing and long hair well out of the way of moving mechanical parts.

• Do remove rings, wristwatch etc, before working on the vehicle – especially the electrical system.

• Do ensure that any lifting or jacking equipment has a safe working load rating adequate for the job.

DON'T

• Don't attempt to lift a heavy component which may be beyond your capability – get assistance.

• Don't rush to finish a job, or take unverified short cuts.

• Don't use ill-fitting tools which may slip and cause injury.

• Don't leave tools or parts lying around where someone can trip over them. Mop up oil and fuel spills at once.

• Don't allow children or pets to play in or near a vehicle being worked on.

The following pages are intended to help in dealing with common roadside emergencies and breakdowns. You will find more detailed fault finding information at the back of the manual, and repair information in the main chapters.

If your car won't start and the starter motor doesn't turn

- ☐ If it's a model with manual transmission, make sure that the clutch pedal is fully depressed. On models with automatic transmission, make sure the selector is in P or N and the brake pedal is fully depressed.
- ☐ Open the bonnet and make sure that the battery terminals are clean and tight.
- ☐ Switch on the headlights and try to start the engine. If the headlights go very dim when you're trying to start, the battery is probably flat. Get out of trouble by jump starting using a friend's car.

If your car won't start even though the starter motor turns as normal

- ☐ Is there fuel in the tank?
- ☐ Is there moisture on electrical components under the bonnet? Switch off the ignition, then wipe off any obvious dampness with a dry cloth. Spray a water-repellent aerosol product (WD-40 or equivalent) on engine and fuel system electrical connectors like those shown in the photos.

A Check the security and condition of the battery connections.

B With the ignition off, check that the spark plug HT leads are securely connected by pushing them onto the ignition coil (petrol models).

C With the ignition off, check that the spark plug HT leads are securely connected to their spark plugs (petrol models).

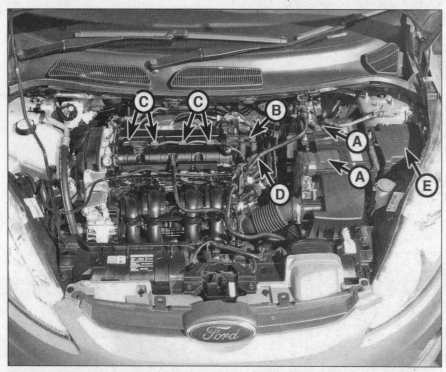

Check that electrical connections are secure (with the ignition switched off) and spray them with a water-dispersant spray like WD-40 if you suspect a problem due to damp.

D With the ignition off, check that the wiring connectors are securely connected to the ignition coil (petrol models).

E Check that all fuses are still in good condition and none have blown.

Jump starting

 Jump starting will get you out of trouble, but you must correct whatever made the battery go flat in the first place. There are three possibilities:

1 *The battery has been drained by repeated attempts to start, or by leaving the lights on.*

2 *The charging system is not working properly (alternator drivebelt slack or broken, alternator wiring fault or alternator itself faulty).*

3 *The battery itself is at fault (electrolyte low, or battery worn out).*

When jump-starting a car, observe the following precautions:

Caution: Remove the key in case the central locking engages when the jump leads are connected.

✓ Before connecting the booster battery, make sure that the ignition is switched off.
✓ Ensure that all electrical equipment (lights, heater, wipers, etc) is switched off.
✓ Take note of any special precautions printed on the battery case
✓ Make sure that the booster battery is the same voltage as the discharged one in the vehicle.

✓ If the battery is being jump-started from the battery in another vehicle, the two vehicles MUST NOT TOUCH each other.
✓ Make sure that the transmission is in neutral (or PARK, in the case of automatic transmission).

 Budget jump leads can be a false economy, as they often do not pass enough current to start large capacity or diesel engines. They can also get hot.

1 Connect one end of the red jump lead to the positive (+) terminal of the flat battery

2 Connect the other end of the red lead to the positive (+) terminal of the booster battery.

3 Connect one end of the black jump lead to the negative (-) terminal of the booster battery

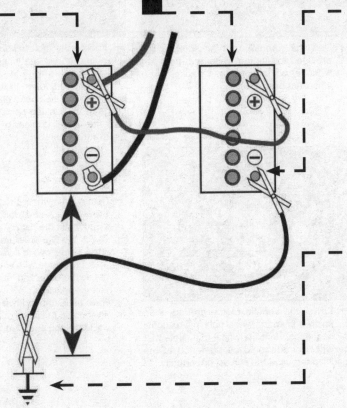

4 Connect the other end of the black jump lead to a bolt or bracket on the engine block, well away from the battery, on the vehicle to be started.

5 Make sure that the jump leads will not come into contact with the fan, drive-belts or other moving parts of the engine.

6 Start the engine using the booster battery and run it at idle speed. Switch on the lights, rear window demister and heater blower motor, then disconnect the jump leads in the reverse order of connection. Turn off the lights etc.

Wheel changing

Note: *Most Fiesta models are equipped with a puncture repair kit and do not have a spare wheel and jack*

Preparation

☐ When a puncture occurs, stop as soon as it is safe to do so.

☐ Park on firm level ground, if possible, and well out of the way of other traffic.

☐ Use hazard warning lights if necessary.

☐ If you have one, use a warning triangle to alert other drivers of your presence.

☐ Apply the handbrake and engage first or reverse gear (or Park on models with automatic transmission).

Changing the wheel

☐ Chock the wheel diagonally opposite the one being removed – a couple of large stones will do for this.

☐ If the ground is soft, use a flat piece of wood to spread the load under the jack.

Warning: Do not change a wheel in a situation where you risk being hit by other traffic. On busy roads, try to stop in a lay-by or a gateway. Be wary of passing traffic while changing the wheel – it is easy to become distracted by the job in hand.

1 Lift the floor covering and unscrew the spare wheel clamp bolt.

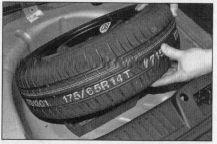

2 Lift out the spare wheel ...

3 ... then take out the jack and tools located in the spare wheel well.

4 Use the special tool or screwdriver provided to pull the wheel trim from the wheel or wheel nuts, then slacken each wheel nut by half a turn.

5 Locate the jack head below the jacking point nearest the wheel to be changed; the jacking point is indicated by a reinforced section in the sill. Ensure that the slot in the jack head engages with the sill flange at the jacking point. Raise the vehicle until the wheel is clear of the ground, then remove the wheel.

6 Fit the spare wheel and tighten the nuts moderately with the wheelbrace.

7 Lower the vehicle to the ground, then finally tighten the wheel nuts in a diagonal sequence. Refit the wheel trim. Note that the wheel nuts should be tightened to the specified torque at the earliest opportunity.

Finally . . .

☐ Remove the wheel chocks.

☐ Stow the jack and tools in the correct locations in the car.

☐ Check the tyre pressure on the wheel just fitted. If it is low, or if you don't have a pressure gauge with you, drive slowly to the next garage and inflate the tyre to the correct pressure.

☐ Have the damaged tyre or wheel repaired as soon as possible, or another puncture will leave you stranded.

Using the puncture repair kit

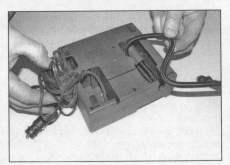

1 Lift the luggage compartment floor covering and take out the tyre repair kit. Remove the sealant bottle and compressor from the wrapping, then remove the air hose and electrical cable from the underside of the compressor.

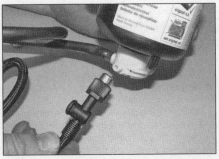

2 Screw the air hose onto the sealant bottle connection.

3 Fit the sealant bottle in the retainer on the compressor, then position the compressor near the punctured tyre.

4 Unscrew the dust cap from the punctured tyre, and screw the sealant bottle air hose onto the tyre valve.

5 Ensure that the switch on the compressor is set to O, then plug the compressor electrical cable into the accessory socket or cigarette lighter socket.

Important notes

- ☐ If the correct tyre pressure is not obtained within 10 minutes, it is likely that the tyre is too badly damaged to be repaired with the kit.
- ☐ The maximum speed sticker attached to the sealant bottle should be placed in the driver's field of view. Do not exceed the permitted maximum speed until an undamaged wheel and tyre have been fitted.
- ☐ On completion, disconnect the tyre repair kit and continue driving immediately so that the sealant is evenly distributed around the inside of the tyre.
- ☐ After driving approximately 6 miles (but no more than 10 minutes) stop and check the tyre pressure by connecting the air hose to the tyre valve. As long as the pressure indicated on the gauge is more than 1.0 bar (14.5 psi) it may be adjusted to the prescribed value using the compressor. If the pressure has fallen below 1.0 bar (14.5 psi) the repair has not been successful and the car should not be driven. It will therefore be necessary to seek roadside assistance.

6 Switch on the ignition, then set the compressor switch to I to start the compressor. To avoid discharging the battery when the compressor is running, it is advisable to start the engine. The pump will initially pump the sealant into the tyre which will take approximately 30 seconds, and then start to inflate the tyre. During the initial 30 second period, the pressure gauge on the pump will indicate up to 6 bar (87 psi) and then drop. The correct tyre pressure (see end of Weekly checks) should be obtained within 10 minutes. The compressor can then be switched off by returning the switch to the O position.

7 If it is necessary to release the pressure in the tyre, press the pressure relief valve button on the air hose.

Finally . . .

- ☐ Stow the puncture repair kit in the luggage compartment and refit the floor covering.
- ☐ Remember to obtain a new bottle of sealant at the earliest opportunity.

 Warning: Repair of a tyre using the puncture repair kit must be regarded as a 'get you home' emergency repair only. A new tyre must be fitted as soon as possible.

Towing

When all else fails, you may find yourself having to get a tow home – or of course you may be helping somebody else. Long-distance recovery should only be done by a garage or breakdown service. For shorter distances, DIY towing using another car is easy enough, but observe the following points:

☐ Use a proper tow-rope – they are not expensive. The vehicle being towed must display an ON TOW sign in its rear window.

☐ Always turn the ignition key to the 'on' position when the vehicle is being towed, so that the steering lock is released, and the direction indicator and brake lights work.

☐ A towing eye is provided with the tool kit in the luggage compartment. Only attach the tow-rope to the towing eyes.

☐ To fit the towing eye, remove the cover from the front or rear bumper, as required, then screw in the towing eye anti-clockwise as far as it will go using the handle of the wheel brace to turn the eye. Note that the towing eye has a left-hand thread.

☐ Before being towed, release the handbrake and select neutral on the transmission. On models with automatic transmission, special precautions apply – do not exceed 12 mph or travel further than 12 miles, and the wheels must always roll forward. If in doubt, do not tow, or transmission damage may result.

☐ Note that greater-than-usual pedal pressure will be required to operate the brakes, since the vacuum servo unit is only operational with the engine running.

☐ Greater-than-usual steering effort will also be required.

☐ The driver of the car being towed must keep the tow-rope taut at all times to avoid snatching.

☐ Make sure that both drivers know the route before setting off.

☐ Only drive at moderate speeds and keep the distance towed to a minimum. Drive smoothly and allow plenty of time for slowing down at junctions.

Identifying leaks

Puddles on the garage floor or drive, or obvious wetness under the bonnet or underneath the car, suggest a leak that needs investigating. It can sometimes be difficult to decide where the leak is coming from, especially if an engine undershield is fitted. Leaking oil or fluid can also be blown rearwards by the passage of air under the car, giving a false impression of where the problem lies.

⚠ *Warning: Most automotive oils and fluids are poisonous. Wash them off skin, and change out of contaminated clothing, without delay.*

HAYNES HiNT *The smell of a fluid leaking from the car may provide a clue to what's leaking. Some fluids are distinctively coloured. It may help to remove the engine undershield, clean the car carefully and to park it over some clean paper overnight as an aid to locating the source of the leak. Remember that some leaks may only occur while the engine is running.*

Sump oil

Engine oil may leak from the drain plug...

Oil from filter

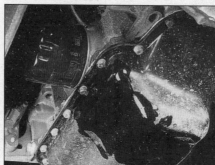

...or from the base of the oil filter.

Gearbox oil

Gearbox oil can leak from the seals at the inboard ends of the driveshafts.

Antifreeze

Leaking antifreeze often leaves a crystalline deposit like this.

Brake fluid

A leak occurring at a wheel is almost certainly brake fluid.

Power steering fluid

Power steering fluid may leak from the pipe connectors on the steering rack.

Introduction

There are some very simple checks which need only take a few minutes to carry out, but which could save you a lot of inconvenience and expense.

These checks require no great skill or special tools, and the small amount of time they take to perform could prove to be very well spent, for example:

☐ Keeping an eye on tyre condition and pressures, will not only help to stop them wearing out prematurely, but could also save your life.

☐ Many breakdowns are caused by electrical problems. Battery-related faults are particularly common, and a quick check on a regular basis will often prevent the majority of these.

☐ If your car develops a brake fluid leak, the first time you might know about it is when your brakes don't work properly. Checking the level regularly will give advance warning of this kind of problem.

☐ If the oil or coolant levels run low, the cost of repairing any engine damage will be far greater than fixing the leak, for example.

Underbonnet check points

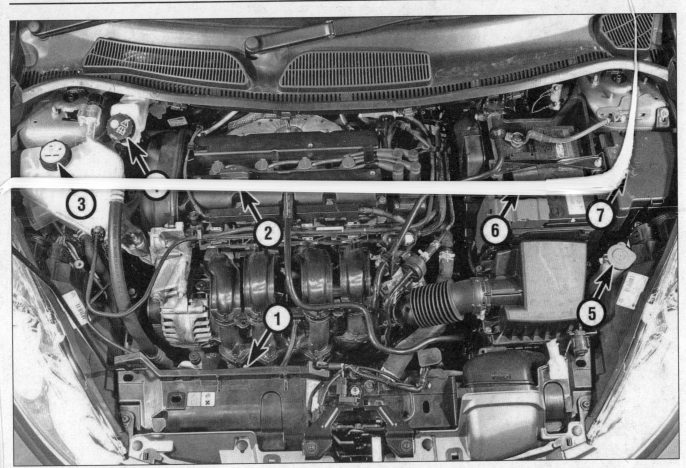

▲ Petrol engine models

1 Engine oil level dipstick
2 Engine oil filler cap
3 Coolant reservoir (expansion tank)
4 Brake and clutch fluid reservoir
5 Washer fluid reservoir
6 Battery
7 Engine compartment fuse/relay box

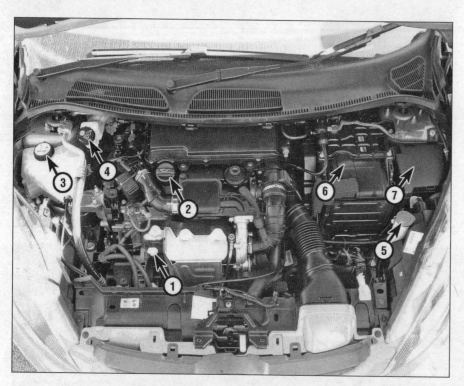

◄ 1.4 litre diesel engine (Stage IV emissions) models

1   *Engine oil level dipstick*
2   *Engine oil filler cap*
3   *Coolant reservoir (expansion tank)*
4   *Brake and clutch fluid reservoir*
5   *Washer fluid reservoir*
6   *Battery*
7   *Engine compartment fuse/relay box*

◄ 1.6 litre DOHC 16V diesel engine model shown – SOHC 8V (1.4 and 1.6 litre) models similar

1   *Engine oil level dipstick*
2   *Engine oil filler cap*
3   *Coolant reservoir (expansion tank)*
4   *Brake and clutch fluid reservoir*
5   *Washer fluid reservoir*
6   *Battery*
7   *Engine compartment fuse/relay box*

Tyre condition and pressure

It is very important that tyres are in good condition, and at the correct pressure – having a tyre failure at any speed is highly dangerous.

Tyre wear is influenced by driving style – harsh braking and acceleration, or fast cornering, will all produce more rapid tyre wear. As a general rule, the front tyres wear out faster than the rears. Interchanging the tyres from front to rear ("rotating" the tyres) may result in more even wear. However, if this is completely effective, you may have the expense of replacing all four tyres at once!

Remove any nails or stones embedded in the tread before they penetrate the tyre to cause deflation. If removal of a nail does reveal that the tyre has been punctured, refit the nail so that its point of penetration is marked. Then immediately change the wheel, and have the tyre repaired by a tyre dealer.

Regularly check the tyres for damage in the form of cuts or bulges, especially in the sidewalls. Periodically remove the wheels, and clean any dirt or mud from the inside and outside surfaces. Examine the wheel rims for signs of rusting, corrosion or other damage. Light alloy wheels are easily damaged by "kerbing" whilst parking; steel wheels may also become dented or buckled. A new wheel is very often the only way to overcome severe damage.

New tyres should be balanced when they are fitted, but it may become necessary to re-balance them as they wear, or if the balance weights fitted to the wheel rim should fall off. Unbalanced tyres will wear more quickly, as will the steering and suspension components. Wheel imbalance is normally signified by vibration, particularly at a certain speed (typically around 50 mph). If this vibration is felt only through the steering, then it is likely that just the front wheels need balancing. If, however, the vibration is felt through the whole car, the rear wheels could be out of balance. Wheel balancing should be carried out by a tyre dealer or garage.

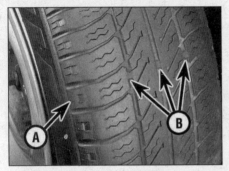

1 ***Tread Depth - visual check***
The original tyres have tread wear safety bands (B), which will appear when the tread depth reaches approximately 1.6 mm. The band positions are indicated by a triangular mark on the tyre sidewall (A).

2 ***Tread Depth - manual check***
Alternatively, tread wear can be monitored with a simple, inexpensive device known as a tread depth indicator gauge.

3 ***Tyre Pressure Check***
Check the tyre pressures regularly with the tyres cold. Do not adjust the tyre pressures immediately after the vehicle has been used, or an inaccurate setting will result.

Tyre tread wear patterns

Shoulder Wear

Underinflation (wear on both sides)
Under-inflation will cause overheating of the tyre, because the tyre will flex too much, and the tread will not sit correctly on the road surface. This will cause a loss of grip and excessive wear, not to mention the danger of sudden tyre failure due to heat build-up.
Check and adjust pressures
Incorrect wheel camber (wear on one side)
Repair or renew suspension parts
Hard cornering
Reduce speed!

Centre Wear

Overinflation
Over-inflation will cause rapid wear of the centre part of the tyre tread, coupled with reduced grip, harsher ride, and the danger of shock damage occurring in the tyre casing.
Check and adjust pressures

If you sometimes have to inflate your car's tyres to the higher pressures specified for maximum load or sustained high speed, don't forget to reduce the pressures to normal afterwards.

Uneven Wear

Front tyres may wear unevenly as a result of wheel misalignment. Most tyre dealers and garages can check and adjust the wheel alignment (or "tracking") for a modest charge.
Incorrect camber or castor
Repair or renew suspension parts
Malfunctioning suspension
Repair or renew suspension parts
Unbalanced wheel
Balance tyres
Incorrect toe setting
Adjust front wheel alignment
Note: *The feathered edge of the tread which typifies toe wear is best checked by feel.*

Lubricants, fluids and tyre pressures

Engine . . . . Multigrade engine oil, viscosity SAE 5W/30 Ford specification WSS-M2C913-C

Cooling system . . . . Motorcraft SuperPlus pink/red antifreeze Ford specification WSS-M97B44-D

Manual transmission . . . . SAE 75W/90 gear oil Ford specification WSD-M2C200-C

Automatic transmission . . . . Automatic transmission fluid Ford specification WSS-M2C938-A

Brake and clutch hydraulic system . . . . Super DOT 4, paraffin-free hydraulic fluid Ford specification ESD-M6C57-A

Tyre pressures (cold)

Note: *Pressures apply to original-equipment tyres, and may vary if any other make or type of tyre is fitted; check with the tyre manufacturer or supplier for correct pressures if necessary.*

Normal load (up to 3 passengers)	Front	Rear
175/65 R14 tyres:		
All except 1.6 litre diesel engine models	2.1 bar (30 psi)	1.8 bar (26 psi)
1.6 litre diesel engine models	2.3 bar (33 psi)	1.8 bar (26 psi)
195/50 R15 tyres:		
All except 1.6 litre diesel engine models	2.1 bar (30 psi)	1.8 bar (26 psi)
1.6 litre diesel engine models	2.3 bar (33 psi)	1.8 bar (26 psi)
195/60 R15 tyres	2.1 bar (30 psi)	2.1 bar (30 psi)
195/45 R16 tyres:		
All except 1.6 litre diesel engine models	2.2 bar (32 psi)	1.8 bar (26 psi)
1.6 litre diesel engine models	2.3 bar (33 psi)	1.8 bar (26 psi)
205/40 R17 tyres:		
All except 1.6 litre diesel engine models	2.2 bar (32 psi)	1.8 bar (26 psi)
1.6 litre diesel engine models	2.3 bar (33 psi)	1.8 bar (26 psi)

Fully laden		
175/65 R14 tyres	2.4 bar (35 psi)	3.2 bar (46 psi)
195/50 R15 tyres	2.4 bar (35 psi)	3.2 bar (46 psi)
195/60 R15 tyres	2.4 bar (35 psi)	2.6 bar (38 psi)
195/45 R16 tyres	2.4 bar (35 psi)	3.2 bar (46 psi)
205/40 R17 tyres	2.4 bar (35 psi)	2.8 bar (41 psi)

Temporary spare tyre		
All models	3.0 bar (44 psi)	3.0 bar (44 psi)

Chapter 1A
Routine maintenance and servicing – petrol models

Contents

Degrees of difficulty

| **Easy,** suitable for novice with little experience | 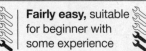 | **Fairly easy,** suitable for beginner with some experience | 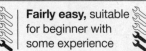 | **Fairly difficult,** suitable for competent DIY mechanic | 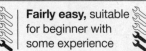 | **Difficult,** suitable for experienced DIY mechanic | 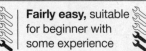 | **Very difficult,** suitable for expert DIY or professional | |

1   Servicing specifications – petrol models

Lubricants and fluids................................. Refer to end of prelims 'Lubricants and fluids'

Capacities
Engine oil (including oil filter)
    1.25 and 1.4 litre engines................................... 3.8 litres
    1.6 litre engine .... 4.0 litres
Cooling system (approximate)
    All models.. 5.5 litres
Transmission
    Manual transmission....................................... 2.3 litres
    Automatic transmission (total capacity)..................... 6.7 litres
Washer fluid reservoir
    All models.. 2.5 litres
Fuel tank
    All models.. 42.0 litres

Cooling system
Antifreeze mixture:
    50% antifreeze .... Protection down to -37°C
Note: *Refer to antifreeze manufacturer for latest recommendations.*

Ignition system
Spark plugs .... Motorcraft AYFS 22 C
Spark plug gap... 1.3 mm

Brakes
Friction material minimum thickness:
    Front brake pads .... 1.5 mm
    Rear brake shoes .... 1.0 mm

Remote control battery
Type CR2032, 3V

Torque wrench settings	Nm	lbf ft
Engine oil drain plug..	28	21
Manual transmission filler/level plug	35	26
Roadwheel nuts...	110	81
Spark plugs	15	11

2 Maintenance schedule – petrol models

1 The maintenance intervals in this manual are provided with the assumption that you, not the dealer, will be carrying out the work. These are the minimum maintenance intervals based on the standard service schedule recommended by the manufacturer for vehicles driven daily. If you wish to keep your vehicle in peak condition at all times, you may wish to perform some of these procedures more often. We encourage frequent maintenance, because it enhances the efficiency, performance and resale value of your vehicle.

2 If the vehicle is driven in dusty areas, used to tow a trailer, or driven frequently at slow speeds (idling in traffic) or on short journeys, more frequent maintenance intervals are recommended.

3 When the vehicle is new, it should be serviced by a dealer service department (or other workshop recognised by the vehicle manufacturer as providing the same standard of service) in order to preserve the warranty. The vehicle manufacturer may reject warranty claims if you are unable to prove that servicing has been carried out as and when specified, using only original equipment parts or parts certified to be of equivalent quality.

Every 250 miles or weekly

☐ Refer to *Weekly checks*

Every 6000 miles or 6 months, whichever comes first

☐ Renew the engine oil and filter (Section 6)

Note: *Ford recommend that the engine oil and filter are changed every 12 500 miles or 12 months. However, oil and filter changes are good for the engine, and we recommend that the oil and filter are renewed more frequently, especially if the car is used on a lot of short journeys.*

Every 12 500 miles or 12 months, whichever comes first

In addition to the items listed above, carry out the following:

☐ Renew the pollen filter, where applicable (Section 7)
☐ Check all components, pipes and hoses for fluid leaks (Section 8)
☐ Check the condition of the auxiliary drivebelt (Section 9)
☐ Check the antifreeze/inhibitor strength (Section 31)
☐ Check the condition and operation of the seat belts (Section 10)
☐ Check the front brake pads and discs for wear (Section 11)
☐ Check the condition of the driveshaft gaiters (Section 12)
☐ Check the steering and suspension components for condition and security (Section 13)
☐ Check the rear brake shoes and drums for wear (Section 14)
☐ Check and if necessary adjust the handbrake (Section 15)
☐ Check the condition of the exhaust system components (Section 16)
☐ Check the roadwheel nuts are tightened to the specified torque (Section 17)
☐ Lubricate all door, bonnet and tailgate hinges and locks (Section 18)
☐ Check the operation of the horn, all lights, and the wipers and washers (Section 19)
☐ Carry out a road test (Section 20)

Every 37 500 miles or 3 years, whichever comes first

In addition to the items listed above, carry out the following:

☐ Renew the spark plugs (Section 21)
☐ Renew the air filter (Section 22)
☐ Check the braking system rubber hoses (Section 23)

Every 62 500 miles

In addition to the items listed above, carry out the following:

☐ Renew the timing belt and tensioner (Section 24)

Note: *Although the normal interval for timing belt renewal is 100 000 miles or 8 years, it is strongly recommended that the interval suggested above is observed, especially on cars which are subjected to intensive use, ie, mainly short journeys or a lot of stop-start driving. The actual belt renewal interval is very much up to the individual owner, but bear in mind that severe engine damage will result if the belt breaks.*

Every 100 000 miles or 8 years, whichever comes first

☐ Adjust the valve clearances (Section 25)
☐ Renew the auxiliary drivebelt (Section 26)

Every 2 years, regardless of mileage

☐ Renew the brake fluid (Section 27)
☐ Check the manual transmission oil level (Section 28)
☐ Check the automatic transmission fluid level (Section 29)
☐ Renew the remote control battery (Section 30)
☐ Renew the coolant (Section 31)

Note: *Ford state that, if their Super Plus antifreeze is in the system from new, the coolant need only be changed every 10 years. If there is any doubt as to the type or quality of the antifreeze which has been used, we recommend this shorter interval be observed.*

3 Component location – petrol models

Front underbody view

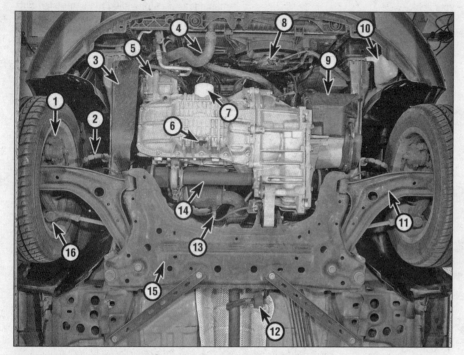

1 Brake caliper
2 Brake hose
3 Auxiliary drivebelt lower cover
4 Radiator bottom hose
5 Air conditioning compressor
6 Engine oil drain plug
7 Engine oil filter
8 Cooling fan
9 Gearchange cable front cover
10 Washer reservoir
11 Suspension lower arm
12 Exhaust front mounting
13 Oxygen sensor
14 Driveshaft
15 Subframe
16 Track rod end

Rear underbody view

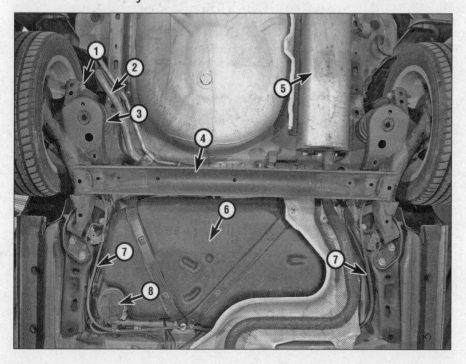

1 Shock absorber
2 Fuel filler pipe
3 Rear coil spring
4 Rear suspension beam
5 Exhaust rear silencer
6 Fuel tank
7 Handbrake cable
8 Charcoal canister

Underbonnet view of a 1.25 litre model (others similar)

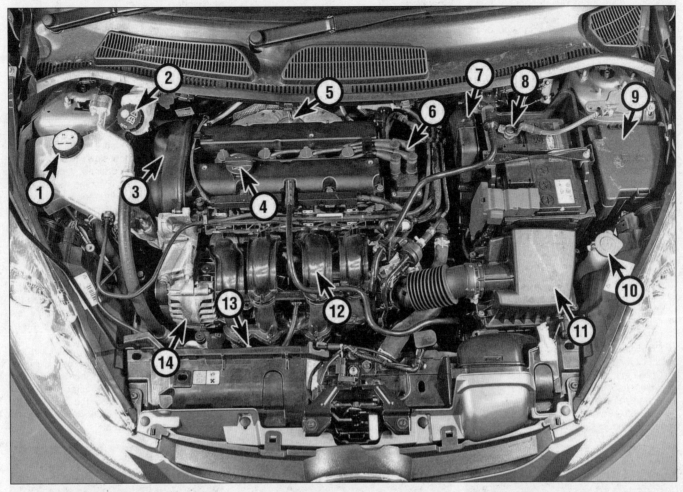

1 Coolant reservoir (expansion tank)
2 Brake and clutch fluid reservoir
3 Timing belt upper cover
4 Engine oil filler cap
5 Oxygen sensor

6 Ignition coil
7 Powertrain control module
8 Battery negative lead
9 Fuse/relay box
10 Windscreen washer fluid reservoir filler

11 Air cleaner
12 Inlet manifold
13 Engine oil level dipstick
14 Alternator

4   General Information

1 This Chapter is designed to help the home mechanic maintain his/her car for safety, economy, long life and peak performance.
2 The Chapter contains a master maintenance schedule, followed by Sections dealing specifically with each task in the schedule. Visual checks, adjustments, component renewal and other helpful items are included. Refer to the accompanying illustrations of the engine compartment and the underside of the car for the locations of the various components.
3 Servicing your car in accordance with the mileage/time maintenance schedule and the following Sections will provide a planned maintenance programme, which should result in a long and reliable service life. This is a comprehensive plan, so maintaining some items but not others at the specified service intervals, will not produce the same results.
4 As you service your car, you will discover that many of the procedures can – and should – be grouped together, because of the particular procedure being performed, or because of the proximity of two otherwise-unrelated components to one another. For example, if the car is raised for any reason, the exhaust can be inspected at the same time as the suspension and steering components.
5 The first step in this maintenance programme is to prepare yourself before the actual work begins. Read through all the Sections relevant to the work to be carried out, then make a list and gather all the parts and tools required. If a problem is encountered, seek advice from a parts specialist, or a dealer service department.

5   Regular maintenance

1 If, from the time the car is new, the routine maintenance schedule is followed closely, and frequent checks are made of fluid levels and high-wear items, as suggested throughout this manual, the engine will be kept in relatively good running condition, and the need for additional work will be minimised.
2 It is possible that there will be times when the engine is running poorly due to the lack

of regular maintenance. This is even more likely if a used car, which has not received regular and frequent maintenance checks, is purchased. In such cases, additional work may need to be carried out, outside of the regular maintenance intervals.

3 If engine wear is suspected, a compression test (refer to Chapter 2A Section 2) will provide valuable information regarding the overall performance of the main internal components. Such a test can be used as a basis to decide on the extent of the work to be carried out. If, for example, a compression test indicates serious internal engine wear, conventional maintenance as described in this Chapter will not greatly improve the performance of the engine, and may prove a waste of time and money, unless extensive overhaul work is carried out first.

4 The following series of operations are those most often required to improve the performance of a generally poor-running engine:

Primary operations

a) *Clean, inspect and test the battery (refer to 'Weekly checks ').*
b) *Check all the engine-related fluids (refer to 'Weekly checks ').*
c) *Check the condition of all hoses, and check for fluid leaks (Section 8).*
d) *Check the condition of the auxiliary drivebelt (Section 9).*
e) *Renew the spark plugs (Section 21).*
f) *Check the condition of the air filter, and renew if necessary (Section 22).*

5 If the above operations do not prove fully effective, carry out the following secondary operations:

Secondary operations

6 All items listed under Primary operations, plus the following:
a) *Check the charging system (Chapter 5A Section 5).*
b) *Check the ignition system (Chapter 5B Section 2).*
c) *Check the fuel system (Chapter 4A Section 10).*

6 Engine oil and filter renewal – petrol models

1 Frequent oil and filter changes are the most important preventative maintenance procedures which can be undertaken by the DIY owner. As engine oil ages, it becomes diluted and contaminated, which leads to premature engine wear.

2 Before starting this procedure, gather together all the necessary tools and materials. Also make sure that you have plenty of clean rags and newspapers handy, to mop-up any spills. Ideally, the engine oil should be warm, as it will drain more easily, and more built-up sludge will be removed with it. Take care not to touch the exhaust or any other hot parts of the engine when working under the car. To avoid any possibility of scalding, and to protect yourself from possible skin irritants and other

harmful contaminants in used engine oils, it is advisable to wear gloves when carrying out this work.

3 Firmly apply the handbrake, then jack up the front of the car and support it on axle stands (see *'Jacking and vehicle support'*).

4 Remove the oil filler cap **(see illustration)**.

5 Using a spanner, or preferably a socket and bar, slacken the drain plug about half a turn. Position the draining container under the drain plug, then remove the plug completely **(see illustrations)**.

6 Allow some time for the oil to drain, noting that it may be necessary to reposition the container as the oil flow slows to a trickle.

7 After all the oil has drained, wipe the drain plug with a clean rag. Examine the condition of the sealing O-ring, and renew it if it shows signs of damage which may prevent an oil-tight seal. Clean the area around the drain plug opening, then refit the plug complete with O-ring and tighten it securely.

8 Move the container into position under the oil filter, which is located on the front of the cylinder block **(see illustration)**.

9 Use an oil filter removal tool to slacken the filter initially, then unscrew it by hand the rest of the way **(see illustration)**. Empty the oil from the old filter into the container.

10 Use a clean rag to remove all oil, dirt and sludge from the filter sealing area on the engine.

11 Apply a light coating of clean engine oil to the sealing ring on the new filter, then screw the filter into position on the engine **(see illustration)**. Tighten the filter firmly by hand only – do not use any tools.

6.4 Removing the oil filler cap

6.5a Slacken the oil drain plug on the back of the sump with a socket ...

6.5b ... then unscrew it by hand, and allow the oil to drain

6.8 Oil filter cartridge (arrowed)

6.9 Using a strap wrench to slacken the filter cartridge

6.11 Apply a light coating of engine oil to the sealing ring on the new filter

12 Remove the old oil and all tools from under the car, then lower the car to the ground.

13 Fill the engine through the filler hole, using the correct grade and type of oil (refer to *Weekly checks* for details of topping-up). Pour in half the specified quantity of oil first, then wait a few minutes for the oil to drain into the sump. Continue to add oil, a small quantity at a time, until the level is up to the lower mark on the dipstick. Adding approximately a further 0.5 to 1.0 litre will bring the level up to the upper mark on the dipstick.

14 Start the engine and run it for a few minutes, while checking for leaks around the oil filter seal and the sump drain plug. Note that there may be a delay of a few seconds before the oil pressure warning light goes out when the engine is first started, as the oil circulates through the new oil filter and the engine oil galleries before the pressure builds-up.

15 Stop the engine, and wait a few minutes for the oil to settle in the sump once more. With the new oil circulated and the filter now completely full, recheck the level on the dipstick, and add more oil as necessary.

16 Dispose of the used engine oil and filter safely, with reference to General repair procedures in the Reference chapter14 of this manual. Do not discard the old filter with domestic household waste. The facility for waste oil disposal provided by many local council refuse tips and/or recycling centres generally has a filter receptacle alongside.

7 Pollen filter renewal

1 Working in the footwell on the driver's side, pull out the centre pin and extract the plastic rivet securing the inner trim panel to the base of the facia. Pull the panel away to release the three retaining clips at the rear and remove the trim panel **(see illustrations)**.

2 Undo the retaining screw securing the base pollen filter housing cover to the side of the air distribution housing. Disengage and remove the cover from the housing **(see illustrations)**.

3 Slide out the pollen filter, into the driver's footwell, and remove it **(see illustration)**.

7.1a Extract the plastic rivet ...

7.1b ... and remove the inner trim panel from the base of the facia

4 When fitting the new filter, note the direction-of-airflow arrow marked on its top edge – the arrow should point into the car.

5 Slide the filter fully into position, secure the cover with the retaining screw, then refit the facia inner trim panel.

8 Hose and fluid leak check

Note: *Also refer to Section 23.*

General

1 Visually inspect the engine joint faces, gaskets and seals for any signs of water or oil leaks. Pay particular attention to the areas around the cylinder head cover, cylinder head, oil filter and sump joint faces. Bear in mind that, over a period of time, some very slight seepage from these areas is to be expected – what you are really looking for is any indication of a serious leak. Should a leak be found, renew the offending gasket or oil seal by referring to the appropriate Chapters in this manual.

2 High temperatures in the engine compartment can cause the deterioration of the rubber and plastic hoses used for engine, accessory and emission systems operation. Periodic inspection should be made for cracks, loose clamps, material hardening and leaks.

3 When checking the hoses, ensure that all the cable-ties or clips used to retain the hoses are in place, and in good condition. Clips which are broken or missing can lead to chafing of the hoses, pipes or wiring, which could cause more serious problems in the future.

4 Carefully check the large top and bottom radiator hoses, along with the other smaller-diameter cooling system hoses and metal pipes; do not forget the heater hoses/pipes which run from the engine to the bulkhead. Inspect each hose along its entire length, renewing any that is cracked, swollen or shows signs of deterioration. Cracks may become more apparent if the hose is squeezed, and may often be apparent at the hose ends.

5 Make sure that all hose connections are tight. If the large-diameter air hoses from the air cleaner are loose, they will leak air, and upset the engine idle quality. If the spring clamps that are used to secure some of the hoses appear to be slackening, they should be updated with worm-drive clips to prevent the possibility of leaks.

6 Some other hoses are secured to their fittings with clamps. Where clamps are used, check to be sure they haven't lost their tension, allowing the hose to leak. If clamps aren't used, make sure the hose has not expanded and/or hardened where it slips over the fitting, allowing it to leak.

7 Check all fluid reservoirs, filler caps, drain plugs and fittings, etc, looking for any signs of leakage of oil, transmission and/or brake hydraulic fluid and coolant. Also check the clutch hydraulic fluid lines which lead from the

7.2a Undo the retaining screw (arrowed) ...

7.2b ... and take off the pollen filter housing cover

7.3 Slide out the pollen filter, into the driver's footwell, and remove it

fluid reservoir, master cylinder, and the slave cylinder (on the transmission).

8 If the vehicle is regularly parked in the same place, close inspection of the ground underneath it will soon show any leaks; ignore the puddle of water which will be left if the air conditioning system is in use. Place a clean piece of cardboard below the engine, and examine it for signs of contamination after the vehicle has been parked over it overnight – be aware, however, of the fire risk inherent in placing combustible material below the catalytic converter.

9 Remember that some leaks will only occur with the engine running, or when the engine is hot or cold. With the handbrake firmly applied, start the engine from cold, and let the engine idle while you examine the underside of the engine compartment for signs of leakage.

10 If an unusual smell is noticed inside or around the car, especially when the engine is thoroughly hot, this may point to the presence of a leak.

11 As soon as a leak is detected, its source must be traced and rectified. Where oil has been leaking for some time, it is usually necessary to use a steam cleaner, pressure washer or similar, to clean away the accumulated dirt, so that the exact source of the leak can be identified.

Vacuum hoses

12 It's quite common for vacuum hoses, especially those in the emissions system, to be colour-coded, or to be identified by coloured stripes moulded into them. Various systems require hoses with different wall thicknesses, collapse resistance and temperature resistance. When renewing hoses, be sure the new ones are made of the same material.

13 Often the only effective way to check a hose is to remove it completely from the vehicle. If more than one hose is removed, be sure to label the hoses and fittings to ensure correct installation.

14 When checking vacuum hoses, be sure to include any plastic T-fittings in the check. Inspect the fittings for cracks, and check the hose where it fits over the fitting for distortion, which could cause leakage.

15 A small piece of vacuum hose (approximately 6 mm inside diameter) can be used as a stethoscope to detect vacuum leaks. Hold one end of the hose to your ear, and probe around vacuum hoses and fittings, listening for the 'hissing' sound characteristic of a vacuum leak.

 Warning: When probing with the vacuum hose stethoscope, be very careful not to come into contact with moving engine components such as the auxiliary drivebelt, radiator electric cooling fan, etc.

Fuel hoses

 Warning: There are certain precautions which must be taken when inspecting or servicing

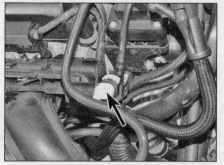

8.16 Check the security of the fuel hose where it joins the fuel rail (arrowed)

fuel system components. Work in a well-ventilated area, and do not allow open flames (cigarettes, appliance pilot lights, etc) or bare light bulbs near the work area. Mop-up any spills immediately, and do not store fuel-soaked rags where they could ignite.

16 Check all fuel hoses for deterioration and chafing. Check especially for cracks in areas where the hose bends, and also just before fittings, such as where a hose attaches to the fuel rail (see illustration).

17 High-quality fuel line, usually identified by the word 'Fluoroelastomer' printed on the hose, should be used for fuel line renewal. Never, under any circumstances, use non-reinforced vacuum line, clear plastic tubing or water hose as a substitute for fuel lines.

18 Spring-type clamps may be used on fuel lines. These clamps often lose their tension over a period of time, and can be 'sprung' during removal. Renew all spring-type clamps with proper petrol pipe clips whenever a hose is renewed.

Metal pipes

19 Sections of metal piping are often used for fuel line between the fuel tank and the engine, and for most air conditioning applications. Check carefully to be sure the piping has not been bent or crimped, and that cracks have not started in the line; also check for signs of excessive corrosion.

20 If a section of metal fuel line must be renewed, only seamless steel piping should be used, since copper and aluminium piping don't have the strength necessary to withstand normal engine vibration.

21 Check the metal lines where they enter the brake master cylinder, ABS hydraulic unit or clutch master/slave cylinders (as applicable) for cracks in the lines or loose fittings. Any sign of brake fluid leakage calls for an immediate and thorough inspection.

Air conditioning refrigerant

 Warning: Refer to the safety information given in 'Safety first!' and Chapter 3, regarding the dangers of disturbing any of the air conditioning system components.

22 The air conditioning system is filled with a liquid refrigerant, which is retained under high pressure. If the air conditioning system is opened and depressurised without the aid of specialised equipment, the refrigerant will immediately turn into gas and escape into the atmosphere. If the liquid comes into contact with your skin, it can cause severe frostbite. In addition, the refrigerant contains substances which are environmentally damaging; for this reason, it should not be allowed to escape into the atmosphere.

23 Any suspected air conditioning system leaks should be immediately referred to a Ford dealer or air conditioning specialist. Leakage will be shown up as a steady drop in the level of refrigerant in the system.

24 Note that water may drip from the condenser drain pipe, underneath the car, immediately after the air conditioning system has been in use. This is normal, and should not be cause for concern.

9 Auxiliary drivebelt check – petrol models

1 A single auxiliary drivebelt is fitted at the right-hand side of the engine. The length of the drivebelt varies according to whether air conditioning is fitted. A tensioner is not used – the belt is 'elastic' and self-tensioning.

2 Due to their function and material makeup, drivebelts are prone to failure after a long period of time, and should therefore be inspected regularly.

3 Since the drivebelt is located very close to the right-hand side of the engine compartment, it is possible to gain better access by raising the front of the car and removing the right-hand wheel. Undo the two screws and remove the drivebelt lower cover.

4 With the engine stopped, inspect the full length of the drivebelt for cracks and separation of the belt plies. It will be necessary to turn the engine (using a spanner or socket and bar on the crankshaft pulley bolt) in order to move the belt from the pulleys so that the belt can be inspected thoroughly. Twist the belt between the pulleys so that both sides can be viewed. Also check for fraying, and glazing which gives the belt a shiny appearance. Check the pulleys for nicks, cracks, distortion and corrosion.

5 Small cracks in the belt ribs are not usually serious, but look closely to see whether the crack has extended into the belt plies. If the belt is in any way suspect, or is known to have seen long service, renew it as described in Section 26.

6 If the belt appears to be too slack (or has actually been slipping in service), this indicates that the 'elastic' belt is over-stretched – possibly as a result of incorrect fitting. Any slipping may also be due to external contamination of the belt (eg by oil or water).

11.2 With the wheel removed, the pad thickness can be seen through the front of the caliper

12.1a Check the outer constant velocity (CV) joint gaiters ...

12.1b ... and, though less prone to wear, check the inner gaiters too

10 Seat belt check

1 Check the seat belts for satisfactory operation and condition. Pull sharply on the belt to check that the locking mechanism engages correctly. Inspect the webbing for fraying and cuts. Check that they retract smoothly and without binding into their reels.
2 Check the accessible seat belt mountings, ensuring that all bolts are securely tightened.

11 Front brake pad and disc wear check

1 Apply the handbrake, then jack up the front of the car and support it securely on axle stands (see 'Jacking and vehicle support'). Remove the front roadwheels.
2 The brake pad thickness, and the condition of the disc, can be assessed roughly with just the wheels removed **(see illustration)**. For a comprehensive check, the brake pads should be removed and cleaned. The operation of the caliper can then also be checked, and the condition of the brake disc itself can be fully examined on both sides. Refer to Chapter 9 for further information.
3 On completion, refit the roadwheels and lower the car to the ground.

12 Driveshaft gaiter check

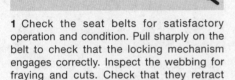

1 With the car raised and securely supported on stands, turn the steering onto full lock, then slowly rotate the roadwheel. Inspect the condition of the outer constant velocity (CV) joint rubber gaiters while squeezing the gaiters to open out the folds. Check for signs of cracking, splits or deterioration of the rubber which may allow the grease to escape and lead to water and grit entry into the joint. Also check the security and condition of the retaining clips. Repeat these checks on the

inner CV joints **(see illustrations)**. If any damage or deterioration is found, the gaiters should be renewed as described in Chapter 8.
2 At the same time, check the general condition of the CV joints themselves by first holding the driveshaft and attempting to rotate the wheel. Repeat this check by holding the inner joint and attempting to rotate the driveshaft. Any appreciable movement indicates wear in the joints, wear in the driveshaft splines, or a loose driveshaft retaining nut.

13 Steering and suspension check

Front suspension and steering

1 Raise the front of the car, and securely support it on axle stands (see 'Jacking and vehicle support').
2 Visually inspect the balljoint dust covers and the steering rack-and-pinion gaiters for splits, chafing or deterioration **(see illustration)**. Any wear of these components will cause loss of lubricant, together with dirt and water entry, resulting in rapid deterioration of the balljoints or steering gear.
3 Grasp the roadwheel at the 12 o'clock and 6 o'clock positions, and try to rock it **(see illustration)**. Very slight free play may be felt, but if the movement is appreciable, further investigation is necessary to determine the

source. Continue rocking the wheel while an assistant depresses the footbrake. If the movement is now eliminated or significantly reduced, it is likely that the hub bearings are at fault. If the free play is still evident with the footbrake depressed, then there is wear in the suspension joints or mountings.
4 Now grasp the wheel at the 9 o'clock and 3 o'clock positions, and try to rock it as before. Any movement felt now may again be caused by wear in the hub bearings or the steering track rod balljoints. If the outer balljoint is worn, the visual movement will be obvious. If the inner joint is suspect, it can be felt by placing a hand over the rack-and-pinion rubber gaiter and gripping the track rod. If the wheel is now rocked, movement will be felt at the inner joint if wear has taken place.
5 Using a large screwdriver or flat bar, check for wear in the suspension mounting bushes by levering between the relevant suspension component and its attachment point. Some movement is to be expected, as the mountings are made of rubber, but excessive wear should be obvious. Also check the condition of any visible rubber bushes, looking for splits, cracks or contamination of the rubber.
6 With the car standing on its wheels, have an assistant turn the steering wheel back-and-forth, about an eighth of a turn each way. There should be very little, if any, lost movement between the steering wheel and roadwheels. If this is not the case, closely

13.2 Check the steering gaiters for signs of splitting

13.3 Check for wear in the front suspension and hub bearings

13.9 Check for signs of fluid leakage from the shock absorbers

16.2 Check the condition of the exhaust rubber mountings

observe the joints and mountings previously described. In addition, check the steering column universal joints for wear, and also check the rack-and-pinion steering gear itself.

Rear suspension

7 Chock the front wheels, then jack up the rear of the car and support securely on axle stands (see 'Jacking and vehicle support').
8 Working as described previously for the front suspension, check the rear hub bearings, the suspension bushes and the shock absorber mountings for wear.

Shock absorber

9 Check for any signs of fluid leakage around the shock absorber body, or from the rubber gaiter around the piston rod **(see illustration)**. Should any fluid be noticed, the shock absorber is defective internally, and should be renewed. Shock absorbers should always be renewed in pairs on the same axle.
10 The efficiency of the shock absorber may be checked by bouncing the car at each corner. Generally speaking, the body will return to its normal position and stop after being depressed. If it rises and returns on a rebound, the shock absorber is probably suspect. Also examine the shock absorber upper and lower mountings for any signs of wear.

14 Rear brake shoe and drum wear check

1 Remove the rear brake drums, and check the brake shoes for signs of wear or contamination. At the same time, also inspect the wheel cylinders for signs of leakage, and the brake drum for signs of wear. Refer to the relevant Sections of Chapter 9 for further information.

15 Handbrake check and adjustment

1 The handbrake should be fully applied (and capable of holding the car on a slope) after approximately three to five clicks of the ratchet. Should adjustment be necessary, refer to Chapter 9 for the full adjustment procedure.

16 Exhaust system check

1 With the engine cold (at least three hours after the vehicle has been driven), check the complete exhaust system, from its starting point at the engine to the end of the tailpipe. Ideally, this should be done on a hoist, where unrestricted access is available; if a hoist is not available, raise and support the vehicle on axle stands (see 'Jacking and vehicle support').
2 Make sure that all brackets and rubber mountings are in good condition, and tight; if any of the mountings are to be renewed, ensure that the new ones are of the correct type – in the case of the rubber mountings, their colour is a good guide. Those nearest to the catalytic converter are more heat-resistant than the others **(see illustration)**.
3 Check the pipes and connections for evidence of leaks, severe corrosion, or damage. One of the most common points for a leak to develop is around the welded joints between the pipes and silencers. Leakage at any of the joints or in other parts of the system will usually show up as a black sooty stain in the vicinity of the leak. **Note:** *Exhaust sealants should not be used on any part of the exhaust system upstream of the catalytic converter (between the converter and engine) – even if the sealant does not contain additives harmful to the converter, pieces of it may break off and foul the element, causing local overheating.*
4 At the same time, inspect the underside of the body for holes, corrosion, open seams, etc, which may allow exhaust gases to enter the passenger compartment. Seal all body openings with silicone or body putty.
5 Rattles and other noises can often be traced to the exhaust system, especially the rubber mountings. Try to move the system, silencer(s), heat shields and catalytic converter. If any components can touch the body or suspension parts, secure the exhaust system with new mountings.

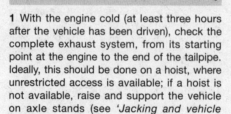

6 Check the running condition of the engine by inspecting inside the end of the tailpipe; the exhaust deposits here are an indication of the engine's state of tune. The inside of the tailpipe should be dry, and should vary in colour from dark grey to light grey/brown; if it is black and sooty, or coated with white deposits, this may indicate the need for a full fuel system inspection.

17 Roadwheel nut tightness check

1 Remove the wheel trims or alloy wheel centre covers, and slacken the roadwheel nuts slightly.
2 Tighten the nuts to the specified torque, using a torque wrench.

18 Hinge and lock lubrication

1 Work around the car and lubricate the hinges of the bonnet, doors and tailgate with light oil.
2 Lightly lubricate the bonnet release mechanism with a smear of grease.
3 Check carefully the security and operation of all hinges, latches and locks, adjusting them where required. Check the operation of the central locking system.
4 Check the condition and operation of the tailgate struts, renewing them both if either is leaking or no longer able to support the tailgate securely when raised.

19 Electrical systems check

1 Check the operation of all the electrical equipment, ie, lights, direction indicators, horn, etc. Refer to the appropriate sections of Chapter 13 for details if any of the circuits are found to be inoperative.
2 Check all accessible wiring connectors, harnesses and retaining clips for security, and for signs of chafing or damage. Rectify any faults found.

20 Road test

Instruments and electrical equipment

1 Check the operation of all instruments and electrical equipment.
2 Make sure that all instruments read correctly, and switch on all electrical equipment in turn, to check that it functions properly.

Steering and suspension

3 Check for any abnormalities in the steering, suspension, handling or road 'feel'.

4 Drive the car, and check that there are no unusual vibrations or noises.

5 Check that the steering feels positive, with no excessive 'sloppiness', or roughness, and check for any suspension noises when cornering and driving over bumps.

Drivetrain

6 Check the performance of the engine, clutch, transmission and driveshafts.

7 Listen for any unusual noises from the engine, clutch and transmission.

8 Make sure that the engine runs smoothly when idling, and that there is no hesitation when accelerating.

9 Check that, where applicable, the clutch action is smooth and progressive, that the drive is taken up smoothly, and that the pedal travel is not excessive. Also listen for any noises when the clutch pedal is depressed.

10 Check that all gears can be engaged smoothly without noise, and that the gear lever action is smooth and not abnormally vague or 'notchy'.

11 Listen for a metallic clicking sound from the front of the car, as the car is driven slowly in a circle with the steering on full-lock. Carry out this check in both directions. If a clicking noise is heard, this indicates wear in a driveshaft joint (see Chapter 8 Section 5).

Braking system

12 Make sure that the car does not pull to one side when braking, and that the wheels do not lock prematurely when braking hard. They should not lock at all on models with ABS.

13 Check that there is no vibration through the steering when braking.

14 Check that the handbrake operates correctly, without excessive movement of the lever, and that it holds the car stationary on a slope.

15 Test the operation of the brake servo unit as follows. Depress the footbrake four or five times to exhaust the vacuum, then start the engine. As the engine starts, there should be a noticeable 'give' in the brake pedal as vacuum builds-up. Allow the engine to run for at least two minutes, and then switch it off. If the brake pedal is now depressed again, it should be possible to detect a hiss from the servo as the pedal is depressed. After about four or five applications, no further hissing should be heard, and the pedal should feel considerably harder.

21 Spark plug renewal and ignition system check – petrol models	

Spark plug renewal

1 The correct functioning of the spark plugs is vital for the correct running and efficiency of the engine. It is essential that the plugs fitted are appropriate for the engine.

2 If the correct type is used and the engine is in good condition, the spark plugs should not need attention between scheduled intervals. Spark plug cleaning is rarely necessary, and should not be attempted unless specialised equipment is available, as damage can easily be caused to the firing ends.

3 Spark plug removal and refitting requires a spark plug socket, with an extension which can be turned by a ratchet handle or similar. This socket is lined with a rubber sleeve, to protect the porcelain insulator of the spark plug, and to hold the plug while you insert it into the spark plug hole. You will also need feeler blades and/or a spark plug gap checking gauge to check and adjust the spark plug electrode gap, and (ideally) a torque wrench to tighten the new plugs to the specified torque.

4 To remove the spark plugs, first open the bonnet; the plugs are easily reached at the top of the engine.

5 Note how the spark plug (HT) leads are routed and secured by the clips on the cylinder head cover; unclip the leads as necessary, to provide enough slack in the lead. To prevent the possibility of mixing up spark plug (HT) leads, it is a good idea to try to work on one spark plug at a time.

6 If the marks on the original-equipment spark plug (HT) leads cannot be seen, mark the leads 1 to 4, to correspond to the cylinder the lead serves (No 1 cylinder is at the timing belt end of the engine). Pull the leads from the plugs by gripping the rubber boot sealing the cylinder head cover opening, not the lead, otherwise the lead connection may be fractured **(see illustration)**.

7 It is advisable to soak up any water in the spark plug recesses with a rag, and to remove any dirt from them using a clean brush, vacuum cleaner or compressed air before removing the plugs, to prevent any dirt or water from dropping into the cylinders.

 Warning: Wear eye protection when using compressed air.

8 Unscrew the spark plugs, ensuring that the socket is kept in alignment with each plug – if the socket is forcibly moved to either side, the porcelain top of the plug may be broken off **(see illustration)**. Remove the plug.

9 If any undue difficulty is encountered when unscrewing any of the spark plugs, carefully check the cylinder head threads and sealing surfaces for signs of wear, excessive corrosion or damage; if any of these conditions is found, seek the advice of a Ford dealer as to the best method of repair.

10 As each plug is removed, examine it as follows – this will give a good indication of the condition of the engine:

a) If the insulator nose of the spark plug is clean and white, with no deposits, this is indicative of a weak mixture.

b) If the tip and insulator nose are covered with hard black-looking deposits, then this is indicative that the mixture is too rich.

21.6 Pull the HT leads from the spark plugs by gripping the rubber boot

21.8 Unscrew the spark plugs using a suitable socket

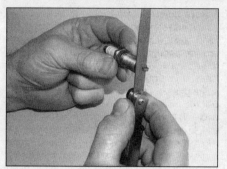

21.13a Measure the spark plug gap with a feeler blade …

21.13b … or with a checking/adjusting tool

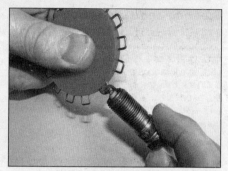

21.13c To change the gap, bend the outer electrode only

c) *Should the plug be black and oily, then it is likely that the engine is fairly worn, as well as the mixture being too rich.*

d) *If the insulator nose is covered with light tan to greyish-brown deposits, then the mixture is correct, and it is likely that the engine is in good condition.*

11 If you are renewing the spark plugs, purchase the new plugs, then check each of them first for faults such as cracked insulators or damaged threads.

12 The spark plug electrode gap is of considerable importance as, if it is too large or too small, the size of the spark and its efficiency will be seriously impaired. However, certain models covered by this manual may use spark plugs with multiple earth electrodes – unless there is clear information to the contrary, no attempt should be made to adjust the plug gap on a spark plug with more than one earth electrode.

13 To set the electrode gap on plugs with one earth electrode, measure the gap with a feeler gauge or gap checking/adjusting tool, and then bend open, or closed, the outer plug electrode until the correct gap is achieved

HAYNES HiNT

It's often difficult to insert spark plugs into their holes without cross-threading them. To avoid this possibility, fit a short length of rubber or plastic hose over the end of the spark plug. The flexible hose acts as a universal joint, to help align the plug with the plug hole. Should the plug begin to cross thread, the hose will slip on the spark plug, preventing thread damage to the aluminium cylinder head.

(see illustrations). The centre electrode should never be bent, as this may crack the insulation and cause plug failure, if nothing worse. If the outer electrode is not exactly over the centre electrode, bend it gently to align them.

14 Before fitting the spark plugs, check that the threaded connector sleeves at the top of the plugs are tight (where fitted), and that the plug exterior surfaces and threads are clean. Brown staining on the porcelain, immediately above the metal body, is quite normal, and does not necessarily indicate a leak between the body and insulator.

15 On installing the spark plugs, first check that the cylinder head thread and sealing surface are as clean as possible; use a clean rag wrapped around a paintbrush to wipe clean the sealing surface. Apply a smear of copper-based grease or anti-seize compound to the threads of each plug, and screw them in by hand where possible. Take extra care to enter the plug threads correctly, as the cylinder head is made of aluminium alloy – it's often difficult to insert spark plugs into their holes without cross-threading them (see **Haynes Hint**).

16 When each spark plug is started correctly on its threads, screw it down until it just seats lightly, then tighten it to the specified torque wrench setting. If a torque wrench is not available – and this is one case where the use of a torque wrench is strongly recommended – tighten each spark plug through no more than 1/16th of a turn. Do not exceed the specified torque setting, and NEVER overtighten spark plugs.

21.22 Check the HT lead connections at the ignition coil

17 Reconnect the spark plug (HT) leads in their correct order, using a twisting motion on the boot until it is firmly seated on the end of the spark plug and on the cylinder head cover.

Ignition system check

⚠️ *Warning: Due to the high voltages produced by the electronic ignition system, extreme care must be taken when working on the system with the ignition switched on. Persons with surgically-implanted cardiac pacemaker devices should keep well clear of the ignition circuits, components and test equipment.*

18 The spark plug (HT) leads should be checked whenever new spark plugs are fitted.

19 Ensure that the leads are numbered before removing them, to avoid confusion when refitting. Pull the leads from the plugs by gripping the rubber boot end fitting, not the lead, otherwise the lead connection may be fractured.

20 Check inside the end fitting for signs of corrosion, which will look like a white crusty powder. Push the end fitting back onto the spark plug, ensuring that it is a tight fit on the plug. If not, remove the lead again, and use pliers to carefully crimp the metal connector inside the end fitting until it fits securely on the end of the spark plug.

21 Using a clean rag, wipe the entire length of the lead to remove any built-up dirt and grease. Once the lead is clean, check for burns, cracks and other damage. Do not bend the lead excessively, nor pull the lead lengthwise – the conductor inside might break.

22 Disconnect the other end of the lead from the ignition coil (see illustration). Check for corrosion and a tight fit in the same manner as the spark plug end.

23 Check the remaining leads one at a time, in the same way.

24 If new spark plug (HT) leads are required, purchase a set for your car and engine.

25 Even with the ignition system in first-class condition, some engines may still occasionally experience poor starting attributable to damp ignition components. To disperse moisture, a water-dispersant aerosol can be very effective.

22.2 Remove the four bolts (arrowed) securing the cover to the air cleaner housing

22.3 Lift up the cover and take out the filter element

23.2 Rubber brake hose fitted to the front caliper

22 Air filter element renewal – petrol models

Caution: Never drive the vehicle with the air cleaner filter element removed. Excessive engine wear could result, and backfiring could even cause a fire under the bonnet.

1 The air filter element is located in the air cleaner assembly on the left-hand side of the engine compartment.

2 Remove the four bolts securing the cover to the air cleaner housing **(see illustration)**.

3 The cover can now be lifted, and the filter element removed **(see illustration)**.

4 If carrying out a routine service, the element must be renewed regardless of its apparent condition.

5 If you are checking the element for any other reason, inspect its lower surface; if it is oily or very dirty, renew the element. If it is only moderately dusty, it can be re-used by blowing it clean from the upper to the lower surface with compressed air. Because it is a pleated-paper type filter, it cannot be washed or re-oiled. If it cannot be cleaned satisfactorily with compressed air, discard and renew it.

 Warning: Wear eye protection when using compressed air.

23 Braking system rubber hose check

1 Position the car over an inspection pit, on car ramps, or jack it up one wheel at a time (see *'Jacking and vehicle support'*).

2 Inspect the braking system rubber hoses fitted to each front caliper, and on each side of the rear axle **(see illustration)**. Look for perished, swollen or hardened rubber, and any signs of cracking, especially at the metal end fittings. If there's any doubt as to the condition of any hose, renew it as described in Chapter 9.

24 Timing belt renewal

1 Refer to the procedures contained in Chapter 2A Section 8.

25 Valve clearance check and adjustment – petrol models

1 Refer to the procedures contained in Chapter 2A Section 5.

26 Auxiliary drivebelt renewal

Note: *No tensioner is fitted on these engines, so the only way to remove an old belt is to cut it off. Even if the old belt could be prised off without damaging it or the pulleys, a belt which has already been fitted has stretched, and may slip if re-used.*

Removal

1 Firmly apply the handbrake, then jack up the front of the vehicle and support it securely on axle stands (see *'Jacking and vehicle support'*). Remove the right-hand front wheel.

2 Undo the two screws and remove the drivebelt lower cover **(see illustrations)**.

3 Cut off the old drivebelt – take care that no

26.2a Undo the screws ...

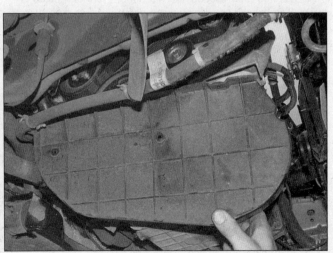

26.2b ... and take off the drivebelt lower cover

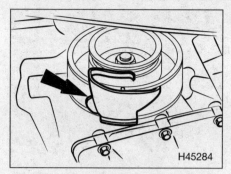

26.8 Fit the first installation tool, centrally on the pulley mark

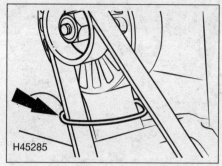

26.11 The second tool fits round the belt and alternator mounting bracket

damage is caused to surrounding components as this is done.

4 Due to the fitting method required for this unusual type of belt, it is essential that all the belt pulleys are as clean as possible before installing the new belt.

5 Wipe all the pulleys over with a suitable solvent, to ensure any traces of oil are removed. It's important that the new belt doesn't slip round the pulleys as it is stretched into place.

Refitting

6 The fitting procedure for the 'elastic' drive- belt is quite lengthy, and involves the use of several plastic tools (which should be provided with a new, genuine Ford belt). Ford state that, if the fitting procedure is not followed, a new belt may suffer premature failure.

7 Using a dab of paint or typist's correction fluid, mark the crankshaft pulley at the 6 o'clock position. It doesn't matter where the engine is positioned (ie, relative to TDC) before starting.

8 Fit the first installation tool to the crankshaft pulley, fitted centrally on the pulley mark you just made **(see illustration)**.

9 Fit the new belt around the alternator pulley, then the air conditioning pump pulley, the coolant pump pulley, and finally, around the plastic installation tool. Make sure the drivebelt is seated properly in the pulley grooves.

10 Turn the engine slowly in the normal direction of rotation (clockwise, as seen from the pulley itself). The engine should only be turned so that the mark made earlier moves from the 6 o'clock to the 8 o'clock position. As the engine is turned, guide the belt onto the crankshaft pulley, with the help of the plastic tool.

11 Now fit the second plastic tool to the alternator mounting bracket. The tool clips round the bracket and the new belt, and keeps the belt on the pulley as it is stretched fully over the crankshaft pulley **(see illustration)**.

12 Start turning the engine slowly again, as before. Guide the belt gradually onto the crankshaft pulley, keeping an eye on the other

pulleys as this is done. Make sure that the belt goes in to its grooves properly – 'help' it into place if necessary, using a blunt tool.

13 Once the pulley mark comes round to the 3 o'clock position, the belt should be fully fitted onto the crankshaft pulley, and the belt guide tools can be removed.

14 Turn the engine through a full 360°, and check that the belt is sitting correctly in the pulley grooves.

15 Refit the crankshaft pulley lower cover, then refit the roadwheel and lower the car to the ground.

27 Brake fluid renewal

Caution: Brake hydraulic fluid can harm your eyes and damage painted surfaces, so use extreme caution when handling and pouring it. Do not use fluid that has been standing open for some time, as it absorbs moisture from the air. Excess moisture can cause a dangerous loss of braking effectiveness.

1 The procedure is similar to that for bleeding the hydraulic system as described in Chapter 9 Section 2, except that allowance should be made for the old fluid to be expelled when bleeding each section of the circuit.

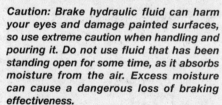

2 Working as described in Chapter 9 Section 2, open the first bleed screw in the sequence, and pump the brake pedal gently until the level in the reservoir is approaching the MIN mark. Top-up to the MAX level with new fluid, and continue pumping until only new fluid remains in the reservoir, and new fluid can be seen emerging from the bleed screw. Tighten the screw, and top the reservoir level up to the MAX level line.

3 Work through all the remaining bleed screws in the sequence until new fluid can be seen at all of them. Be careful to keep the master cylinder reservoir topped-up above the MIN level at all times, or air may enter the system. If this happens, further bleeding will be required, to remove the air.

4 When the operation is complete, check that all bleed screws are securely tightened, and that their dust caps are refitted. Wash off all traces of spilt fluid, and recheck the master cylinder reservoir fluid level.

5 Check the operation of the brakes before taking the car on the road.

28 Manual transmission oil level check

1 Position the car over an inspection pit, on car ramps, or jack it up and support it on axle stands, but make sure that it is level.

2 Unclip the plastic cover fitted over the gearchange cables at the front of the transmission **(see illustration)**.

3 Remove all traces of dirt, then unscrew the filler/level plug from the front face of the transmission. This will probably be very tight, and a large Allen key or bit will be needed – access is made awkward by the plastic shroud around the gearchange cables **(see illustration)**.

4 The level must be just below the bottom edge of the filler/level plug hole (use a cranked tool such as an Allen key to check the level). If necessary, top-up the level with the specified grade of oil (see Lubricants and fluids0,6) until

28.2 Unclip the plastic cover from the front of the transmission

28.3 Unscrew and remove the filler/level plug

the oil just starts to run out. Allow any excess oil to flow out until the level stabilises (see illustrations).

5 When the level is correct, clean and refit the filler/level plug (check the condition of the O-ring seal, and renew if necessary), then tighten it to the specified torque.

6 Lower the car to the ground.

29 Automatic transmission fluid level check

1 The fluid level must be checked with the engine/transmission at operating temperature. This can be achieved by checking the level after a journey of at least 10 miles. If the level is checked when cold, follow this up with a level check when the fluid is hot.

2 Park the car on level ground, and apply the handbrake very firmly. As an added precaution, chock the front and rear wheels, so that the car cannot move.

3 With the engine idling, apply the footbrake, then move the selector lever gently from position P to position 1 and back to P.

4 The fluid level dipstick is located on the rear of the transmission. Before removing the dipstick, thoroughly clean the area around it – no dirt or debris must be allowed to enter the transmission.

5 Extract the dipstick, and wipe it clean using a clean piece of rag or tissue. Re-insert the dipstick completely, then pull it out once more. The fluid level should be between the reference marks on the side of the dipstick (see illustrations). Note: If the level is checked when cold, the reading obtained will appear to be low – recheck the level when hot before topping-up, as the transmission must not be overfilled.

6 If topping-up is required, this is done via the dipstick tube. It is most important that no dirt or debris enters the transmission as this is done – use a clean funnel (preferably with a filter) and fresh fluid from a clean container.

7 Pour the fresh fluid a little at a time down the dipstick tube, checking the level

28.4a Top-up the oil level …

28.4b … then allow any excess to flow out before refitting the plug

29.5a Pull out the automatic transmission fluid dipstick

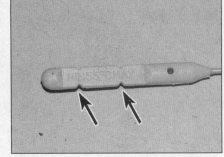

29.5b Dipstick fluid level upper and lower markings (arrowed)

frequently. The difference between the MIN and MAX marks is 0.4 litres.

8 When the level is correct, refit the dipstick and switch off the engine.

9 The need for regular topping-up of the transmission fluid indicates a leak, which should be found and rectified without delay.

30 Remote control battery renewal – petrol models

Note: All the remote control units described below are fitted with a type CR 2032, 3 volt battery.

1 Although not in the Ford maintenance schedule, we recommend that the battery

is changed every 2 years, regardless of the vehicle's mileage. However, if the door locks repeatedly fail to respond to signals from the remote control at the normal distance, change the battery in the remote control before attempting to troubleshoot any of the vehicle's other systems.

Control with a folding key

2 Insert a small flat-bladed screwdriver fully into the slot on the side of the transmitter unit, push the screwdriver towards the key blade and remove the key blade (see illustrations).

3 Use the screwdriver, inserted at the side and front of the transmitter unit, to separate the two halves of the unit (see illustration).

4 Note the fitted position of the battery (positive side down), then prise the battery

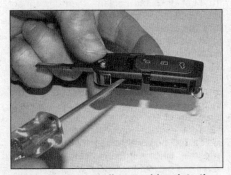

30.2a Insert a small screwdriver into the slot on the side of the transmitter unit …

30.2b … then push the screwdriver towards the key blade and remove the key blade

30.3 Insert the screwdriver at the side and front of the transmitter unit to separate the two halves

30.4 Note the fitted position of the battery, then prise it out and insert the new one

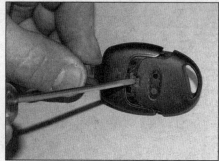

30.6 Insert a small screwdriver into the slot provided and slide the transmitter unit from the key blade

30.7 Release the clip each side and open the transmitter unit

30.8 Note the fitted position of the battery, then prise it out and insert the new one

from its location, and insert the new one **(see illustration)**. Avoid touching the battery or the terminals with bare fingers.

5 Snap the two halves of the transmitter together, and re-attach it to the key blade.

Control without a folding key

Type 1

6 Insert a small flat-bladed screwdriver into the slot provided and slide the transmitter unit from the key blade **(see illustration)**.

7 Use the screwdriver to release the clip each side and open the transmitter unit **(see illustration)**.

8 Note the fitted position of the battery (positive side up), then prise the battery from its location, and insert the new one **(see illustration)**. Avoid touching the battery or the terminals with bare fingers.

9 Snap the two halves of the transmitter together, and re-attach it to the key blade.

Type 2

10 Depress the two tabs on the side of the transmitter unit and carefully lift off the cover.

11 Remove the key blade from the transmitter unit.

12 Use a small flat-bladed the screwdriver, inserted at the side of the transmitter unit, to separate the two halves of the unit.

13 Note the fitted position of the battery (positive side down), then prise the battery from its location, and insert the new one. Avoid touching the battery or the terminals with bare fingers.

14 Snap the two halves of the transmitter together, place the key blade in position and refit the cover.

31 Coolant strength check and renewal

⚠️ **Warning: Do not allow antifreeze to come in contact with your skin or painted surfaces of the vehicle. Flush contaminated areas immediately with plenty of water. Don't store new coolant, or leave old coolant lying around, where it's accessible to children or pets – they're attracted by its sweet smell. Ingestion of even a small amount of coolant can be fatal. Wipe up garage-floor and drip-pan spills immediately. Keep antifreeze containers covered, and repair cooling system leaks as soon as they're noticed.**

⚠️ **Warning: Never remove the expansion tank filler cap when the engine is running, or has just been switched off, as the cooling system will be hot, and the consequent escaping steam and scalding coolant could cause serious injury.**

⚠️ **Warning: Wait until the engine is cold before starting these procedures.**

Strength check

1 Use a hydrometer to check the strength of the antifreeze. Follow the instructions provided with your hydrometer. The antifreeze strength should be approximately 50%. If it is significantly less than this, drain a little coolant from the radiator (see this Section), add antifreeze to the coolant expansion tank, then recheck the strength.

Coolant draining

2 To drain the system, first remove the expansion tank filler cap.

3 Firmly apply the handbrake, then jack up the front of the vehicle and support it securely on axle stands (see 'Jacking and vehicle support').

4 Place a suitable container beneath the right-hand side of the radiator.

5 Release the retaining clamp and disconnect the bottom hose from the radiator. Allow the coolant to drain into the container.

6 Once the coolant has stopped draining from the radiator, reconnect the bottom hose and secure with the retaining clamp.

System flushing

7 With time, the cooling system may gradually lose its efficiency, as the radiator core becomes choked with rust, scale deposits from the water, and other sediment. To minimise this, as well as using only good-quality antifreeze and clean soft water, the system should be flushed as follows whenever any part of it is disturbed, and/or when the coolant is renewed.

8 With the coolant drained, refit the radiator bottom hose and refill the system with fresh water. Refit the expansion tank filler cap, start the engine and warm it up to normal operating temperature, then stop it and (after allowing it to cool down completely) drain the system again. Repeat as necessary until only clean water can be seen to emerge, then refill finally with the specified coolant mixture.

9 If only clean, soft water and good-quality antifreeze (even if not to Ford's specification) has been used, and the coolant has been renewed at the suggested intervals, the above procedure will be sufficient to keep the system clean for a considerable length of time. If, however, the system has been neglected, a more thorough operation will be required, as follows.

10 First drain the coolant, then disconnect the radiator top hose. Insert a garden hose into the radiator top hose connection, and allow water to circulate through the radiator until it runs clean from the bottom outlet.

11 To flush the engine, insert the garden hose into the radiator bottom hose, wrap a piece of rag around the garden hose to seal the connection, and allow water to circulate until it runs clear.

12 Try the effect of repeating this procedure in the top hose, although this may not be effective, since the thermostat will probably close and prevent the flow of water.

13 In severe cases of contamination, reverse-flushing of the radiator may be necessary. This may be achieved by inserting the garden hose

into the bottom outlet, wrapping a piece of rag around the hose to seal the connection, then flushing the radiator until clear water emerges from the top hose outlet.

14 If the radiator is suspected of being severely choked, remove the radiator (Chapter 3 Section 3), turn it upside-down, and repeat the procedure described in paragraph 13.

15 Flushing the heater matrix can be achieved using a similar procedure to that described in paragraph 13, once the heater inlet and outlet hoses have been identified. These two hoses will be of the same diameter, and pass through the engine compartment bulkhead (refer to the procedures contained in Chapter 3 for more details).

16 The use of chemical cleaners is not recommended, and should be necessary only as a last resort; the scouring action of some chemical cleaners may lead to other cooling system problems. Normally, regular renewal of the coolant will prevent excessive contamination of the system.

Coolant filling

17 With the cooling system drained and flushed, ensure that all disturbed hose unions are correctly secured. If it was raised, lower the vehicle to the ground.

18 Set the heater temperature control to maximum heat, but ensure the blower is turned off.

19 Prepare a sufficient quantity of the specified coolant mixture (see below); allow for a surplus, so as to have a reserve supply for topping-up.

20 Slowly fill the system through the expansion tank. Since the tank is the highest point in the system, all the air in the system should be displaced into the tank by the rising liquid. Slow pouring reduces the possibility of air being trapped and forming airlocks.

21 Continue filling until the coolant level reaches the expansion tank MAX level line (see *Weekly checks*), then refit the filler cap.

22 Start the engine and run it at 2500 rpm for 15 minutes. If the level in the expansion tank drops significantly, top-up to the MAX level line, to minimise the amount of air circulating in the system.

23 Increase the engine speed to 5000 rpm, then allow it to return to idle. Repeat this sequence 6 times.

24 Increase the engine speed to 4000 rpm, maintain this speed for 10 seconds, then reduce the engine speed to 2500 rpm and maintain this speed for 10 minutes.

25 Stop the engine, then leave the car to cool down completely (overnight, if possible).

26 With the system cool, open the expansion tank, and top-up the tank to the MAX level line. Refit the filler cap, tightening it securely, and clean up any spillage.

27 After refilling, always check carefully all components of the system (but especially any unions disturbed during draining and flushing) for signs of coolant leaks. Fresh antifreeze has a searching action, which will rapidly expose any weak points in the system.

Antifreeze type and mixture

Caution: Do not use engine antifreeze in the windscreen/tailgate washer system, as it will damage the vehicle's paintwork. A screenwash additive should be added to the washer system in its maker's recommended quantities.

28 If the vehicle's history (and therefore the quality of the antifreeze in it) is unknown, owners are advised to drain and thoroughly reverse-flush the system, before refilling with fresh coolant mixture.

29 If the antifreeze used is to Ford's specification, the levels of protection it affords are indicated in the coolant packaging.

30 To give the recommended standard mixture ratio for antifreeze, 50% (by volume) of antifreeze must be mixed with 50% of clean, soft water; if you are using any other type of antifreeze, follow its manufacturer's instructions to achieve the correct ratio.

31 You are unlikely to fully drain the system at any one time (unless the engine is being completely stripped), and the capacities quoted in the Specifications are therefore slightly academic for routine coolant renewal. As a guide, only two-thirds of the system's total capacity is likely to be needed for coolant renewal.

32 As the drained system will be partially filled with flushing water, in order to establish the recommended mixture ratio, measure out 50% of the system capacity in antifreeze and pour it into the hose/expansion tank as described above, then top-up with water. Any topping-up while refilling the system should be done with water – for *Weekly checks* use a suitable mixture.

33 Before adding antifreeze, the cooling system should be drained, preferably flushed, and all hoses checked for condition and security. As noted earlier, fresh antifreeze will rapidly find any weaknesses in the system.

34 After filling with antifreeze, a label should be attached to the expansion tank, stating the type and concentration of antifreeze used, and the date installed. Any subsequent topping-up should be made with the same type and concentration of antifreeze.

General cooling system checks

35 The engine should be cold for the cooling system checks, so perform the following procedure before driving the vehicle, or after it has been shut off for at least three hours.

36 Remove the expansion tank filler cap, and clean it thoroughly inside and out with a rag. Also clean the filler neck on the expansion tank. The presence of rust or corrosion in the filler neck indicates that the coolant should be changed. The coolant inside the expansion tank should be relatively clean and transparent. If it is rust-coloured, drain and flush the system, and refill with a fresh coolant mixture.

37 Carefully check the radiator hoses and heater hoses along their entire length; renew any hose which is cracked, swollen or deteriorated.

38 Inspect all other cooling system components (joint faces, etc) for leaks. A leak in the cooling system will usually show up as white- or antifreeze-coloured deposits on the area adjoining the leak. Where any problems of this nature are found on system components, renew the component or gasket with reference to Chapter 3.

Airlocks

39 If, after draining and refilling the system, symptoms of overheating are found which did not occur previously, then the fault is almost certainly due to trapped air at some point in the system, causing an airlock and restricting the flow of coolant; usually, the air is trapped because the system was refilled too quickly.

40 If an airlock is suspected, first try gently squeezing all visible coolant hoses. A coolant hose which is full of air feels quite different to one full of coolant when squeezed. After refilling the system, most airlocks will clear once the system has cooled, and been topped-up.

41 While the engine is running at operating temperature, switch on the heater and heater fan, and check for heat output. Provided there is sufficient coolant in the system, lack of heat output could be due to an airlock in the system.

42 Airlocks can have more serious effects than simply reducing heater output – a severe airlock could reduce coolant flow around the engine. Check that the radiator top hose is hot when the engine is at operating temperature – a top hose which stays cold could be the result of an airlock (or a non-opening thermostat).

43 If the problem persists, stop the engine and allow it to cool down completely, before unscrewing the expansion tank filler cap or loosening the hose clips and squeezing the hoses to bleed out the trapped air. In the worst case, the system will have to be at least partially drained (this time, the coolant can be saved for re-use) and flushed to clear the problem. If all else fails, have the system evacuated and vacuum filled by a suitably-equipped garage.

Expansion tank cap check

44 Wait until the engine is completely cold – perform this check before the engine is started for the first time in the day.

45 Place a wad of cloth over the expansion tank cap, then unscrew it slowly and remove it.

46 Examine the condition of the rubber seal on the underside of the cap. If the rubber appears to have hardened, or cracks are visible in the seal edges, a new cap should be fitted.

47 If the car is several years old, or has covered a large mileage, consider renewing the cap regardless of its apparent condition – they are not expensive. If the pressure relief valve built into the cap fails, excess pressure in the system will lead to puzzling failures of hoses and other cooling system components.

Chapter 1B
Routine maintenance and servicing – diesel models

Contents

Degrees of difficulty

Easy, suitable for novice with little experience	**Fairly easy,** suitable for beginner with some experience	**Fairly difficult,** suitable for competent DIY mechanic	**Difficult,** suitable for experienced DIY mechanic 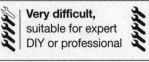	**Very difficult,** suitable for expert DIY or professional

1 Servicing specifications – diesel models

Lubricants and fluids . . . . Refer to end of Prelims - *'Lubricants and fluids'*

Capacities

Engine oil (including oil filter)
    1.4 litre engines . . . . 3.8 litres
    1.6 litre engines . . . . 3.9 litres
Cooling system (approximate)
    All models . . . . 6.1 litres
Manual transmission
    All models . . . . 2.3 litres
Washer fluid reservoir
    All models . . . . 2.5 litres
Fuel tank
    All models . . . . 40.0 litres

Cooling system

Antifreeze mixture:
    50% antifreeze . . . . Protection down to -37°C
Note: *Refer to antifreeze manufacturer for latest recommendations.*

Brakes

Friction material minimum thickness:
    Front brake pads . . . . 1.5 mm
    Rear brake shoes . . . . 1.0 mm

Remote control battery

Type CR2032, 3V

Torque wrench settings

	Nm	lbf ft
Engine oil drain plug	35	25
Engine oil filter cover	25	18
Manual transmission filler/level plug	35	26
Roadwheel nuts	110	81

2 Maintenance schedule – diesel models

1 The maintenance intervals in this manual are provided with the assumption that you, not the dealer, will be carrying out the work. These are the minimum maintenance intervals based on the standard service schedule recommended by the manufacturer for vehicles driven daily. If you wish to keep your vehicle in peak condition at all times, you may wish to perform some of these procedures more often. We encourage frequent maintenance, because it enhances the efficiency, performance and resale value of your vehicle.
2 If the vehicle is driven in dusty areas, used to tow a trailer, or driven frequently at slow speeds (idling in traffic) or on short journeys, more frequent maintenance intervals are recommended.
3 When the vehicle is new, it should be serviced by a dealer service department (or other workshop recognised by the vehicle manufacturer as providing the same standard of service) in order to preserve the warranty. The vehicle manufacturer may reject warranty claims if you are unable to prove that servicing has been carried out as and when specified, using only original equipment parts or parts certified to be of equivalent quality.

Every 250 miles or weekly
☐ Refer to *Weekly checks*

Every 6000 miles or 6 months, whichever comes first
☐ Renew the engine oil and filter (Section 6)

Note: *Ford recommend that the engine oil and filter are changed every 12 500 miles or 12 months. However, oil and filter changes are good for the engine, and we recommend that the oil and filter are renewed more frequently, especially if the car is used on a lot of short journeys.*

Every 12 500 miles or 12 months, whichever comes first
In addition to the items listed above, carry out the following:
☐ Renew the pollen filter, where applicable (Section 7)
☐ Drain any water from the fuel filter (Section 8)
☐ Check all components, pipes and hoses for fluid leaks (Section 9)
☐ Check the condition of the auxiliary drivebelt (Section 10)
☐ Check the antifreeze/inhibitor strength (Section 30)
☐ Check the condition and operation of the seat belts (Section 11)
☐ Check the front brake pads and discs for wear (Section 12)
☐ Check the condition of the driveshaft gaiters (Section 13)
☐ Check the steering and suspension components for condition and security (Section 14)
☐ Check the rear brake shoes and drums for wear (Section 15)
☐ Check and if necessary adjust the handbrake (Section 16)
☐ Check the condition of the exhaust system components (Section 17)
☐ Check the roadwheel nuts are tightened to the specified torque (Section 18)
☐ Lubricate all door, bonnet and tailgate hinges and locks (Section 19)
☐ Check the operation of the horn, all lights, and the wipers and washers (Section 20)
☐ Carry out a road test (Section 21)

Every 37 500 miles or 3 years, whichever comes first
In addition to the items listed above, carry out the following:
☐ Renew the fuel filter (Section 22)
☐ Renew the air filter (Section 23)
☐ Check the braking system rubber hoses (Section 24)

Every 62 500 miles
In addition to the items listed above, carry out the following:
☐ Renew the timing belt and tensioner (Section 25)

Note: *Although the normal interval for timing belt renewal is 125 000 miles or 10 years, it is strongly recommended that the interval suggested above is observed, especially on cars which are subjected to intensive use, ie, mainly short journeys or a lot of stop-start driving. The actual belt renewal interval is very much up to the individual owner, but bear in mind that severe engine damage will result if the belt breaks.*

Every 100 000 miles or 8 years, whichever comes first
☐ Renew the auxiliary drivebelt (Section 26)

Every 2 years, regardless of mileage
☐ Renew the brake fluid (Section 27)
☐ Check the manual transmission oil level (Section 28)
☐ Renew the remote control battery (Section 29)
☐ Renew the coolant (Section 30)

Note: *Ford state that, if their Super Plus antifreeze is in the system from new, the coolant need only be changed every 10 years. If there is any doubt as to the type or quality of the antifreeze which has been used, we recommend this shorter interval be observed.*

3 Component location – diesel models

Front underbody view

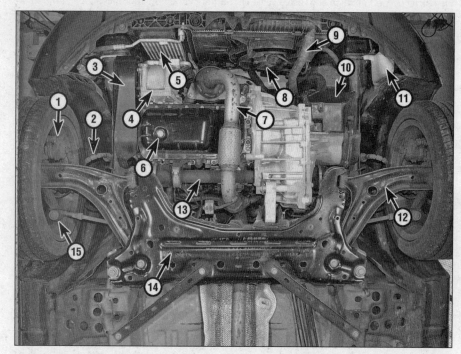

1 Brake caliper
2 Brake hose
3 Auxiliary drivebelt lower cover
4 Air conditioning compressor
5 Intercooler
6 Engine oil drain plug
7 Exhaust system
8 Cooling fan
9 Radiator bottom hose
10 Gearchange cable front cover
11 Washer reservoir
12 Suspension lower arm
13 Driveshaft
14 Subframe
15 Track rod end

Rear underbody view

1 Shock absorber
2 Fuel filler pipe
3 Rear coil spring
4 Rear suspension beam
5 Exhaust rear silencer
6 Fuel tank
7 Handbrake cable

Underbonnet view of a 1.4 litre model (Stage IV emissions)

1 Coolant reservoir (expansion tank)
2 Brake and clutch fluid reservoir
3 Engine oil filler cap
4 Air cleaner
5 Fuel filter
6 Powertrain control module
7 Battery negative lead
8 Fuse/relay box
9 Windscreen washer fluid reservoir filler
10 Airflow sensor
11 Turbocharger
12 Intake air resonator
13 Engine oil level dipstick

Underbonnet view of a 1.4 litre models (Stage V emissions)

1 Engine oil filler cap
2 Engine oil level dipstick
3 Coolant reservoir (expansion tank)
4 Brake and clutch fluid reservoir
5 Fuel filter
6 Power train control module (PCM)
7 Battery negative lead
8 Fuse/relay box
9 Windscreen washer fluid reservoir filler
10 Air cleaner
11 Turbocharger
12 Throttle body

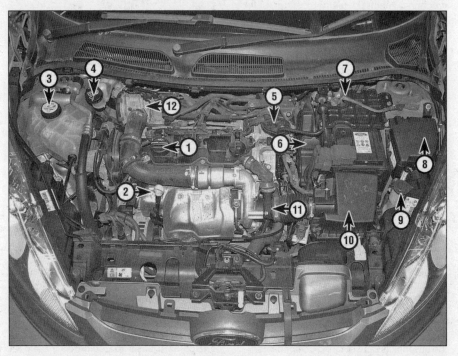

Underbonnet view of a 1.6 litre DOHC 16V model – SOHC 8V engine similar

1 Engine oil filler cap
2 Engine oil level dipstick
3 Coolant reservoir (expansion tank)
4 Brake and clutch fluid reservoir
5 Fuel filter
6 Powertrain control module
7 Battery negative lead
8 Fuse/relay box
9 Windscreen washer fluid reservoir filler
10 Air cleaner
11 Airflow sensor
12 Turbocharger
13 Turbocharger/exhaust manifold heat
   shields
14 Throttle housing

4 General Information

1 This Chapter is designed to help the home mechanic maintain his/her car for safety, economy, long life and peak performance.
2 The Chapter contains a master maintenance schedule, followed by Sections dealing specifically with each task in the schedule. Visual checks, adjustments, component renewal and other helpful items are included. Refer to the accompanying illustrations of the engine compartment and the underside of the car for the locations of the various components.
3 Servicing your car in accordance with the mileage/time maintenance schedule and the following Sections will provide a planned maintenance programme, which should result in a long and reliable service life. This is a comprehensive plan, so maintaining some items but not others at the specified service intervals, will not produce the same results.
4 As you service your car, you will discover that many of the procedures can – and should – be grouped together, because of the particular procedure being performed, or because of the proximity of two otherwise-unrelated components to one another. For example, if the car is raised for any reason, the exhaust can be inspected at the same time as the suspension and steering components.
5 The first step in this maintenance programme is to prepare yourself before the

actual work begins. Read through all the Sections relevant to the work to be carried out, then make a list and gather all the parts and tools required. If a problem is encountered, seek advice from a parts specialist, or a dealer service department.

5 Regular maintenance

1 If, from the time the car is new, the routine maintenance schedule is followed closely, and frequent checks are made of fluid levels and high-wear items, as suggested throughout this manual, the engine will be kept in relatively good running condition, and the need for additional work will be minimised.
2 It is possible that there will be times when the engine is running poorly due to the lack of regular maintenance. This is even more likely if a used car, which has not received regular and frequent maintenance checks, is purchased. In such cases, additional work may need to be carried out, outside of the regular maintenance intervals.
3 If engine wear is suspected, a compression test or leakdown test (refer to Chapter 2B Section 2, Chapter 2D Section 2 or Chapter 2E Section 2) will provide valuable information regarding the overall performance of the main internal components. Such a test can be used as a basis to decide on the extent of the work to be carried out. If, for example, the test indicates serious internal engine

wear, conventional maintenance as described in this Chapter will not greatly improve the performance of the engine, and may prove a waste of time and money, unless extensive overhaul work is carried out first.
4 The following series of operations are those most often required to improve the performance of a generally poor-running engine:

Primary operations

a) Clean, inspect and test the battery (refer to 'Weekly checks').
b) Check all the engine-related fluids (refer to 'Weekly checks').
c) Check the condition of all hoses, and check for fluid leaks (Section 9).
d) Check the condition of the auxiliary drivebelt (Section 10).
e) Renew the fuel filter (Section 22).
f) Check the condition of the air filter, and renew if necessary (Section 23).

5 If the above operations do not prove fully effective, carry out the following secondary operations:

Secondary operations

6 All items listed under Primary operations, plus the following:
a) Check the charging system (Chapter 5A Section 5).
b) Check the preheating system (Chapter 5A Section 11).
c) Check the fuel system (Chapter 4B Section 12).

6.5 Unscrew the drain plug from the base of the sump

6 Engine oil and filter renewal – diesel models

1 Frequent oil and filter changes are the most important preventative maintenance procedures which can be undertaken by the DIY owner. As engine oil ages, it becomes diluted and contaminated, which leads to premature engine wear.

2 Before starting this procedure, gather together all the necessary tools and materials. Also make sure that you have plenty of clean rags and newspapers handy, to mop-up any spills. Ideally, the engine oil should be warm, as it will drain better, and more built-up sludge will be removed with it. Take care, however, not to touch the exhaust or any other hot parts of the engine when working under the vehicle. To avoid any possibility of scalding, and to protect yourself from possible skin irritants and other harmful contaminants in used engine oils, it is advisable to wear gloves when carrying out this work.

3 Firmly apply the handbrake, then jack up the front of the car and support it on axle stands (see 'Jacking and vehicle support').

4 Undo the retaining bolts and remove the engine undertray (where fitted).

5 Slacken the drain plug about half a turn, position the draining container under the drain plug, then remove the plug completely **(see illustration)**. If possible, try to keep the plug pressed into the sump while unscrewing it by hand the last couple of turns (see **Haynes Hint**). Recover the sealing ring from the drain plug.

6 Allow some time for the old oil to drain, noting that it may be necessary to reposition the container as the oil flow slows to a trickle.

7 After all the oil has drained, wipe off the drain plug with a clean rag, and fit a new sealing washer. Clean the area around the drain plug opening, and refit the plug. Tighten the plug securely.

8 If the filter is also to be renewed, move the container into position under the oil filter, which is located on the front side of the cylinder block.

9 The filter element is contained within a filter cover. Using a socket or spanner, slacken and remove the filter cover from above (see

As the drain plug releases from the threads, move it away sharply so the stream of oil issuing from the sump runs into the container, not up your sleeve.

illustration). Be prepared for oil spillage, and recover the O-ring seal from the cover. If improved access to the filter is required, remove the air filter housing as described in Chapter 4B Section 4.

10 Pull the filter element from the filter housing.

11 Use a clean rag to remove all oil, dirt and sludge from the inside and outside of the filter cover.

12 Fit the new O-ring to the filter cover, then insert the new filter element into the housing, ensuring that the element locating peg engages correctly with the corresponding hole in the housing **(see illustrations)**.

6.12a Fit the new O-ring to the cover

6.15a Remove the oil filler cap ...

6.9 Engine oil filter cover (arrowed)

13 Apply a little clean engine oil to the O-ring seal, then refit the filter/cover to the housing and tighten the cover to the specified torque.

14 Remove the old oil and all tools from under the car, refit the engine undertray (where applicable), then lower the car to the ground.

15 Remove the dipstick, then unscrew the oil filler cap. Fill the engine, using the correct grade and type of oil (see Lubricants and fluids0,6). An oil can spout or funnel may help to reduce spillage **(see illustrations)**. Pour in half the specified quantity of oil first, then wait a few minutes for the oil to run to the sump. Continue adding oil a small quantity at a time until the level is up to the lower mark on the dipstick. Adding approximately 1.0 litre will bring the level up to the upper mark on the dipstick. Refit the filler cap.

16 Start the engine and run it for a few minutes; check for leaks around the oil filter

6.12b Ensure the filter locating peg (arrowed) locates into the corresponding hole in the housing (arrowed)

6.15b ... and start filling the engine with oil

7.1a Extract the plastic rivet …

7.1b … and remove the inner trim panel from the base of the facia

7.2a Undo the retaining screw (arrowed) …

7.2b … and take off the pollen filter housing cover

7.3 Slide out the pollen filter, into the driver's footwell, and remove it

seal and the sump drain plug. Note that there may be a delay of a few seconds before the oil pressure warning light goes out when the engine is first started, as the oil circulates through the engine oil galleries and the new oil filter (where fitted) before the pressure builds-up.

17 Switch off the engine, and wait a few minutes for the oil to settle in the sump once more. With the new oil circulated and the filter completely full, recheck the level on the dipstick, and add more oil as necessary.

18 Dispose of the used engine oil and filter safely, with reference to General repair procedures in the Reference chapter14 of this manual. Do not discard the old filter with domestic household waste. The facility for waste oil disposal provided by many local council refuse tips and/or recycling centres generally has a filter receptacle alongside.

7   Pollen filter renewal

1 Working in the footwell on the driver's side, pull out the centre pin and extract the plastic rivet securing the inner trim panel to the base of the facia. Pull the panel away to release the three retaining clips at the rear and remove the trim panel **(see illustrations)**.

2 Undo the retaining screw securing the base pollen filter housing cover to the side of the air distribution housing. Disengage and remove the cover from the housing **(see illustrations)**.

3 Slide out the pollen filter, into the driver's footwell, and remove it **(see illustration)**.

4 When fitting the new filter, note the direction-of-airflow arrow marked on its top edge – the arrow should point into the car.

5 Slide the filter fully into position, secure the cover with the retaining screw, then refit the facia inner trim panel.

8   Fuel filter water draining – diesel models

Note: *Various types of fuel filters are fitted to these engines depending on model year and territory. The following procedures depict a typical example.*

1 The fuel filter is located at the rear of the engine compartment between the air cleaner housing and the battery **(see illustrations)**. Access to the filter is extremely limited and it is recommended that the windscreen cowl panel and bulkhead closure panel are removed as described in Chapter 11 to provide additional working clearance.

1.4 litre engines (Stage IV emissions)

2 A water drain outlet is provided at the base of the fuel filter housing, to which a suitable piece of tubing may be fitted.

3 Place a suitable container beneath the drain tube, and cover the surrounding area with rags.

4 Open the drain plug, and allow fuel and water to drain until water-free fuel emerges from the end of the tube **(see illustration)**. Close the drain plug.

5 Dispose of the drained fuel safely.

6 If removed, refit the bulkhead closure panel

8.1a Fuel filter location (arrowed) on 1.4 litre (Stage IV emissions) engines…

8.1b … 1.4 litre (Stage V emissions) and 1.6 litre engines (arrowed)

8.4 Fit a tube to the drain plug, then unscrew the plug

8.8 Attach a tube to the water drain outlet

8.9 Slacken the vent screw on top of the filter and allow fuel and water to drain

8.15 Rotate the centre fitting clockwise and lift it a little

and windscreen cowl panel as described in Chapter 11 Section 20.

7 Start the engine. If difficulty is experienced, bleed the fuel system (Chapter 4B Section 3).

1.6 litre DOHC engines

8 A water drain outlet is provided at the base of the fuel filter housing, to which a suitable piece of tubing may be fitted. To gain access to the drain outlet, refer to Section 22 and release the vacuum hoses from the support bracket above the fuel filter. Undo the three bolts and move the wiring harness support bracket and vacuum hose support bracket clear of the filter. Unbolt and remove the filter retaining bracket, lift the filter from its location and attach the drain tube to the water drain outlet (see illustration).

9 Slacken the vent screw on top of the filter and allow fuel and water to drain until water-free fuel emerges from the end of the tube (see illustration). Close the vent screw.

10 Dispose of the drained fuel safely.

11 Refit the filter retaining bracket, vacuum hose support bracket and wiring harness support bracket with reference to Section 22.

12 If removed, refit the bulkhead closure panel and windscreen cowl panel as described in Chapter 11 Section 20.

1.6 litre SOHC engines and 1.4 litre (Stage V emissions) engines

13 Pull up the front edge and remove the plastic cover from the top of the engine.

14 On these engines, a drain pipe is attached to the underside of the filter housing, which exits at the back of the engine. To prevent fuel spillage, position a suitable container under the back of the engine, on the left-hand side.

15 Rotate the centre fitting on the top of the filter clockwise slightly and lift it (see illustration). This opens the drain tap, and allows the fuel/water to drain from the filter. As soon as water-free fuel emerges from the pipe, press down the fitting and rotate it anti-clockwise to secure it.

All engines

16 Start the engine. If difficulty is experienced, bleed the fuel system (Chapter 4B Section 3).

9 Hose and fluid leak check

Note: Also refer to Section 24.

General

1 Visually inspect the engine joint faces, gaskets and seals for any signs of water or oil leaks. Pay particular attention to the areas around the cylinder head cover, cylinder head, oil filter and sump joint faces. Bear in mind that, over a period of time, some very slight seepage from these areas is to be expected – what you are really looking for is any indication of a serious leak. Should a leak be found, renew the offending gasket or oil seal by referring to the appropriate Chapters in this manual.

2 High temperatures in the engine compartment can cause the deterioration of the rubber and plastic hoses used for engine, accessory and emission systems operation. Periodic inspection should be made for cracks, loose clamps, material hardening and leaks.

3 When checking the hoses, ensure that all the cable-ties or clips used to retain the hoses are in place, and in good condition. Clips which are broken or missing can lead to chafing of the hoses, pipes or wiring, which could cause more serious problems in the future.

4 Carefully check the large top and bottom radiator hoses, along with the other smaller-diameter cooling system hoses and metal pipes; do not forget the heater hoses/pipes which run from the engine to the bulkhead. Inspect each hose along its entire length, renewing any that is cracked, swollen or shows signs of deterioration. Cracks may become more apparent if the hose is squeezed, and may often be apparent at the hose ends.

5 Make sure that all hose connections are tight. If the large-diameter air hoses from the air cleaner are loose, they will leak air, and upset the engine idle quality. If the spring clamps that are used to secure some of the hoses appear to be slackening, they should be updated with worm-drive clips to prevent the possibility of leaks.

6 Some other hoses are secured to their fittings with clamps. Where clamps are used, check to be sure they haven't lost their tension, allowing the hose to leak. If clamps aren't used, make sure the hose has not expanded and/or hardened where it slips over the fitting, allowing it to leak.

7 Check all fluid reservoirs, filler caps, drain plugs and fittings, etc, looking for any signs of leakage of oil, transmission and/or brake hydraulic fluid and coolant. Also check the clutch hydraulic fluid lines which lead from the fluid reservoir, master cylinder, and the slave cylinder (on the transmission).

8 If the vehicle is regularly parked in the same place, close inspection of the ground underneath it will soon show any leaks; ignore the puddle of water which will be left if the air conditioning system is in use. Place a clean piece of cardboard below the engine, and examine it for signs of contamination after the vehicle has been parked over it overnight – be aware, however, of the fire risk inherent in placing combustible material below the catalytic converter.

9 Remember that some leaks will only occur with the engine running, or when the engine is hot or cold. With the handbrake firmly applied, start the engine from cold, and let the engine idle while you examine the underside of the engine compartment for signs of leakage.

10 If an unusual smell is noticed inside or around the car, especially when the engine is thoroughly hot, this may point to the presence of a leak.

11 As soon as a leak is detected, its source must be traced and rectified. Where oil has been leaking for some time, it is usually necessary to use a steam cleaner, pressure washer or similar, to clean away the accumulated dirt, so that the exact source of the leak can be identified.

Vacuum hoses

12 It's quite common for vacuum hoses, especially those in the emissions system, to be colour-coded, or to be identified by coloured stripes moulded into them. Various systems require hoses with different wall thicknesses, collapse resistance and temperature resistance. When renewing

hoses, be sure the new ones are made of the same material.

13 Often the only effective way to check a hose is to remove it completely from the vehicle. If more than one hose is removed, be sure to label the hoses and fittings to ensure correct installation.

14 When checking vacuum hoses, be sure to include any plastic T-fittings in the check. Inspect the fittings for cracks, and check the hose where it fits over the fitting for distortion, which could cause leakage.

15 A small piece of vacuum hose (approximately 6 mm inside diameter) can be used as a stethoscope to detect vacuum leaks. Hold one end of the hose to your ear, and probe around vacuum hoses and fittings, listening for the 'hissing' sound characteristic of a vacuum leak.

 Warning: When probing with the vacuum hose stethoscope, be very careful not to come into contact with moving engine components such as the auxiliary drivebelt, radiator electric cooling fan, etc.

Fuel pipes/hoses

 Warning: Refer to the safety information given in 'Safety first!' and Chapter 4B before disturbing any of the fuel system components.

16 Check all fuel lines at their connections to the injection pump, accumulator rail, injectors and fuel filter housing.

17 Examine each fuel hose/pipe along its length for splits or cracks. Check for leakage from the union nuts and examine the unions between the metal fuel lines and the fuel filter housing. Also check the area around the fuel injectors for signs of leakage.

18 To identify fuel leaks between the fuel tank and the engine bay, the vehicle should raised and securely supported on axle stands. Inspect the fuel tank and filler neck for punctures, cracks and other damage. The connection between the filler neck and tank is especially critical. Sometimes a rubber filler neck or connecting hose will leak due to loose retaining clamps or deteriorated rubber.

19 Carefully check all rubber hoses and metal fuel lines leading away from the fuel tank. Check for loose connections, deteriorated hoses, kinked lines, and other damage. Pay particular attention to the vent pipes and hoses, which often loop up around the filler neck and can become blocked or kinked, making tank filling difficult. Follow the fuel supply and return lines to the front of the vehicle, carefully inspecting them all the way for signs of damage or corrosion. Renew damaged sections as necessary.

Air conditioning refrigerant

 Warning: Refer to the safety information given in 'Safety first!' and Chapter 3, regarding the dangers of disturbing any of the air conditioning system components.

20 The air conditioning system is filled with a liquid refrigerant, which is retained under high pressure. If the air conditioning system is opened and depressurised without the aid of specialised equipment, the refrigerant will immediately turn into gas and escape into the atmosphere. If the liquid comes into contact with your skin, it can cause severe frostbite. In addition, the refrigerant contains substances which are environmentally damaging; for this reason, it should not be allowed to escape into the atmosphere.

21 Any suspected air conditioning system leaks should be immediately referred to a Ford dealer or air conditioning specialist. Leakage will be shown up as a steady drop in the level of refrigerant in the system.

22 Note that water may drip from the condenser drain pipe, underneath the car, immediately after the air conditioning system has been in use. This is normal, and should not be cause for concern.

10 Auxiliary drivebelt check – diesel models

1 A single auxiliary drivebelt is fitted at the right-hand side of the engine. The length of the drivebelt varies according to whether air conditioning is fitted. An automatic tensioner is fitted so setting the drivebelt tension is unnecessary.

2 Due to their function and material makeup, drivebelts are prone to failure after a long period of time, and should therefore be inspected regularly.

3 Since the drivebelt is located very close to the right-hand side of the engine compartment, it is possible to gain better access by raising the front of the car and removing the right-hand wheel. Where fitted, undo the retaining bolts and remove the engine undertray, then undo the two screws and remove the drivebelt lower cover.

4 With the engine stopped, inspect the full length of the drivebelt for cracks and separation of the belt plies. It will be necessary to turn the engine (using a spanner or socket and bar on the crankshaft pulley bolt) in order to move the belt from the pulleys so that the belt can be inspected thoroughly. Twist the belt between the pulleys so that both sides can be viewed. Also check for fraying, and glazing which gives the belt a shiny appearance. Check the pulleys for nicks, cracks, distortion and corrosion.

5 Small cracks in the belt ribs are not usually serious, but look closely to see whether the crack has extended into the belt plies. If the belt is in any way suspect, or is known to have seen long service, renew it as described in Section 26.

6 If the belt appears to be too slack (or has actually been slipping in service), this may indicate a problem with the belt tensioner, or external contamination of the belt (eg, by oil or water).

12.2 With the wheel removed, the pad thickness can be seen through the front of the caliper

11 Seat belt check

1 Check the seat belts for satisfactory operation and condition. Pull sharply on the belt to check that the locking mechanism engages correctly. Inspect the webbing for fraying and cuts. Check that they retract smoothly and without binding into their reels.

2 Check the accessible seat belt mountings, ensuring that all bolts are securely tightened.

12 Front brake pad and disc wear check

1 Apply the handbrake, then jack up the front of the car and support it securely on axle stands (see 'Jacking and vehicle support'). Remove the front roadwheels.

2 The brake pad thickness, and the condition of the disc, can be assessed roughly with just the wheels removed **(see illustration)**. For a comprehensive check, the brake pads should be removed and cleaned. The operation of the caliper can then also be checked, and the condition of the brake disc itself can be fully examined on both sides. Refer to Chapter 9 for further information.

3 On completion, refit the roadwheels and lower the car to the ground.

13 Driveshaft gaiter check

1 With the car raised and securely supported on stands, turn the steering onto full lock, then slowly rotate the roadwheel. Inspect the condition of the outer constant velocity (CV) joint rubber gaiters while squeezing the gaiters to open out the folds. Check for signs of cracking, splits or deterioration of the rubber which may allow the grease to escape and lead to water and grit entry into the joint. Also check the security and condition of the retaining clips. Repeat these checks on the inner CV joints (see illustrations). If any damage or deterioration is found, the gaiters should be renewed as described in Chapter 8.

2 At the same time, check the general condition of the CV joints themselves by first holding the driveshaft and attempting to rotate the wheel. Repeat this check by holding the inner joint and attempting to rotate the driveshaft. Any appreciable movement indicates wear in the joints, wear in the driveshaft splines, or a loose driveshaft retaining nut.

14 Steering and suspension check

Front suspension and steering

1 Raise the front of the car, and securely support it on axle stands (see 'Jacking and vehicle support').

2 Visually inspect the balljoint dust covers and the steering rack-and-pinion gaiters for splits, chafing or deterioration (see illustration). Any wear of these components will cause loss of lubricant, together with dirt and water entry, resulting in rapid deterioration of the balljoints or steering gear.

3 Grasp the roadwheel at the 12 o'clock and 6 o'clock positions, and try to rock it (see illustration). Very slight free play may be felt, but if the movement is appreciable, further investigation is necessary to determine the source. Continue rocking the wheel while an assistant depresses the footbrake. If the movement is now eliminated or significantly reduced, it is likely that the hub bearings are at fault. If the free play is still evident with the footbrake depressed, then there is wear in the suspension joints or mountings.

4 Now grasp the wheel at the 9 o'clock and 3 o'clock positions, and try to rock it as before. Any movement felt now may again be caused by wear in the hub bearings or the steering track rod balljoints. If the outer balljoint is worn, the visual movement will be obvious. If the inner joint is suspect, it can be felt by placing a hand over the rack-and-pinion rubber gaiter and gripping the track rod. If the wheel is now rocked, movement will be felt at the inner joint if wear has taken place.

13.1a Check the outer constant velocity (CV) joint gaiters ...

13.1b ... and, though less prone to wear, check the inner gaiters too

5 Using a large screwdriver or flat bar, check for wear in the suspension mounting bushes by levering between the relevant suspension component and its attachment point. Some movement is to be expected, as the mountings are made of rubber, but excessive wear should be obvious. Also check the condition of any visible rubber bushes, looking for splits, cracks or contamination of the rubber.

6 With the car standing on its wheels, have an assistant turn the steering wheel back-and-forth, about an eighth of a turn each way. There should be very little, if any, lost movement between the steering wheel and roadwheels. If this is not the case, closely observe the joints and mountings previously described. In addition, check the steering column universal joints for wear, and also check the rack-and-pinion steering gear itself.

Rear suspension

7 Chock the front wheels, then jack up the rear of the car and support securely on axle stands (see 'Jacking and vehicle support').

8 Working as described previously for the front suspension, check the rear hub bearings, the suspension bushes and the shock absorber mountings for wear.

Shock absorber

9 Check for any signs of fluid leakage around the shock absorber body, or from the rubber gaiter around the piston rod (see illustration). Should any fluid be noticed, the shock absorber is defective internally, and should

be renewed. Note: Shock absorbers should always be renewed in pairs on the same axle.

10 The efficiency of the shock absorber may be checked by bouncing the car at each corner. Generally speaking, the body will return to its normal position and stop after being depressed. If it rises and returns on a rebound, the shock absorber is probably suspect. Also examine the shock absorber upper and lower mountings for any signs of wear.

15 Rear brake shoe and drum wear check

1 Remove the rear brake drums, and check the brake shoes for signs of wear or contamination. At the same time, also inspect the wheel cylinders for signs of leakage, and the brake drum for signs of wear. Refer to the relevant Sections of Chapter 9 for further information.

16 Handbrake check and adjustment

1 The handbrake should be fully applied (and capable of holding the car on a slope) after approximately three to five clicks of the ratchet. Should adjustment be necessary, refer to Chapter 9 Section 14 for the full adjustment procedure.

14.2 Check the steering gaiters for signs of splitting

14.3 Check for wear in the front suspension and hub bearings

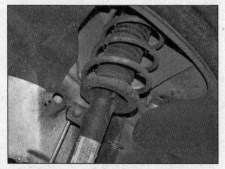

14.9 Check for signs of fluid leakage from the shock absorbers

17.2 Check the condition of the exhaust rubber mountings

17 Exhaust system check

1 With the engine cold (at least three hours after the vehicle has been driven), check the complete exhaust system, from its starting point at the engine to the end of the tailpipe. Ideally, this should be done on a hoist, where unrestricted access is available; if a hoist is not available, raise and support the vehicle on axle stands (see *'Jacking and vehicle support'*).
2 Make sure that all brackets and rubber mountings are in good condition, and tight; if any of the mountings are to be renewed, ensure that the new ones are of the correct type – in the case of the rubber mountings, their colour is a good guide. Those nearest to the catalytic converter are more heat-resistant than the others **(see illustration)**.
3 Check the pipes and connections for evidence of leaks, severe corrosion, or damage. One of the most common points for a leak to develop is around the welded joints between the pipes and silencers. Leakage at any of the joints or in other parts of the system will usually show up as a black sooty stain in the vicinity of the leak. **Note:** *Exhaust sealants should not be used on any part of the exhaust system upstream of the catalytic converter (between the converter and engine) – even if the sealant does not contain additives harmful to the converter, pieces of it may break off and foul the element, causing local overheating.*
4 At the same time, inspect the underside of the body for holes, corrosion, open seams, etc, which may allow exhaust gases to enter the passenger compartment. Seal all body openings with silicone or body putty.
5 Rattles and other noises can often be traced to the exhaust system, especially the rubber mountings. Try to move the system, silencer(s), heat shields and catalytic converter. If any components can touch the body or suspension parts, secure the exhaust system with new mountings.
6 Check the running condition of the engine by inspecting inside the end of the tailpipe; the exhaust deposits here are an indication of the engine's state of tune. The inside of

the tailpipe should be dry, and should vary in colour from dark grey to light grey/brown; if it is black and sooty, or coated with white deposits, this may indicate the need for a full fuel system inspection.

18 Roadwheel nut tightness check

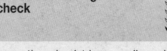

1 Remove the wheel trims or alloy wheel centre covers, and slacken the roadwheel nuts slightly.
2 Tighten the nuts to the specified torque, using a torque wrench.

19 Hinge and lock lubrication

1 Work around the car and lubricate the hinges of the bonnet, doors and tailgate with light oil.
2 Lightly lubricate the bonnet release mechanism with a smear of grease.
3 Check carefully the security and operation of all hinges, latches and locks, adjusting them where required. Check the operation of the central locking system.
4 Check the condition and operation of the tailgate struts, renewing them both if either is leaking or no longer able to support the tailgate securely when raised.

20 Electrical systems check

1 Check the operation of all the electrical equipment, ie, lights, direction indicators, horn, etc. Refer to the appropriate sections of Chapter 13 for details if any of the circuits are found to be inoperative.
2 Note that the brake light switch is described in Chapter 9 Section 17.
3 Check all accessible wiring connectors, harnesses and retaining clips for security, and for signs of chafing or damage. Rectify any faults found.

21 Road test

Instruments and electrical equipment

1 Check the operation of all instruments and electrical equipment.
2 Make sure that all instruments read correctly, and switch on all electrical equipment in turn, to check that it functions properly.

Steering and suspension

3 Check for any abnormalities in the steering, suspension, handling or road 'feel'.

4 Drive the car, and check that there are no unusual vibrations or noises.
5 Check that the steering feels positive, with no excessive 'sloppiness', or roughness, and check for any suspension noises when cornering and driving over bumps.

Drivetrain

6 Check the performance of the engine, clutch, transmission and driveshafts.
7 Listen for any unusual noises from the engine, clutch and transmission.
8 Make sure that the engine runs smoothly when idling, and that there is no hesitation when accelerating.
9 Check that the clutch action is smooth and progressive, that the drive is taken up smoothly, and that the pedal travel is not excessive. Also listen for any noises when the clutch pedal is depressed.
10 Check that all gears can be engaged smoothly without noise, and that the gear lever action is smooth and not abnormally vague or 'notchy'.
11 Listen for a metallic clicking sound from the front of the car, as the car is driven slowly in a circle with the steering on full-lock. Carry out this check in both directions. If a clicking noise is heard, this indicates wear in a driveshaft joint (see Chapter 8 Section 5).

Braking system

12 Make sure that the car does not pull to one side when braking, and that the wheels do not lock prematurely when braking hard. They should not lock at all on models with ABS.
13 Check that there is no vibration through the steering when braking.
14 Check that the handbrake operates correctly, without excessive movement of the lever, and that it holds the car stationary on a slope.
15 Test the operation of the brake servo unit as follows. Depress the footbrake four or five times to exhaust the vacuum, then start the engine. As the engine starts, there should be a noticeable 'give' in the brake pedal as vacuum builds-up. Allow the engine to run for at least two minutes, and then switch it off. If the brake pedal is now depressed again, it should be possible to detect a hiss from the servo as the pedal is depressed. After about four or five applications, no further hissing should be heard, and the pedal should feel considerably harder.

22 Fuel filter renewal

Note: *Various types of fuel filters are fitted to these engines depending on model year and territory. The following procedures depict a typical example.*
Note: *After renewing the filter it will be necessary to prime and bleed the fuel system,*

22.3a Remove the two bolts on top ...

22.3b ... then work the cover out between the hoses

which can prove troublesome on these engines. Refer to the procedures contained in Chapter 4B and ensure you have the necessary equipment before proceeding.

1 The fuel filter is located at the rear of the engine compartment between the air cleaner housing and the battery **(see illustrations 8.1a and 8.1b)**. To gain sufficient working clearance to allow removal and refitting of the filter, remove the windscreen cowl panel and bulkhead closure panel as described in Chapter 11 Section 20.

1.4 litre engines (Stage IV emissions)

2 Owing to the extreme difficulty which may be experienced removing the filter, we found it was far easier to remove the air cleaner first, as described in Chapter 4B Section 4.

3 Remove the two bolts securing the fuel filter metal cover, then hold the fuel and brake servo vacuum hoses out of the way, and manoeuvre the cover out of position **(see illustrations)**.

4 Depress the tabs on the quick-release fittings and disconnect the fuel pipes from the filter – one on the front, and one at the rear **(see illustration)**. Plug or tape over the pipes to prevent dirt ingress and fuel loss.

5 Undo the single filter retaining screw, and manoeuvre the filter from the bracket – this may prove to be quite tricky, as there is very limited room. The filter will only lift up so far, as there is a wiring plug for the fuel heater and water detector at the base **(see illustrations)**. Even this plug is difficult to disconnect, if the air cleaner has not been removed.

6 Unscrew the fuel heater and water detector (where fitted) from the filter. Discard the O-ring seals – new ones must be fitted.

7 Fitting a new filter is a reversal of removal, noting the following points:

a) *Ensure that the fuel hose connections are securely remade.*

b) *Refit the bulkhead closure panel and windscreen cowl panel as described in Chapter 11 Section 20.*

c) *If removed, refit the air cleaner as described in Chapter 4B Section 4.*

d) *On completion, prime and bleed the*

22.4 Depress the tabs on the quick-release fittings and disconnect the fuel pipes from the filter

fuel system as described in Chapter 4B Section 3.

e) *When the engine is running, check for any sign of leakage from the disturbed pipes.*

1.6 litre DOHC engines

8 Release the vacuum hoses from the support bracket above the fuel filter. Undo the three bolts and move the wiring harness

22.5a Undo the filter retaining screw in front ...

22.5b ... then lift the filter, and disconnect the wiring plug (arrows) underneath

22.8a Release the vacuum hoses (arrowed) from the support bracket above the fuel filter

22.8b Undo the bolt at the front (arrowed) …

22.8c … the two bolts at the rear (arrowed) …

22.8d … and move the wiring harness support bracket …

22.8e … and vacuum hose support bracket clear of the filter

support bracket and vacuum hose support bracket clear of the filter (see illustrations).

9 Disconnect the fuel filter wiring connector, then undo the three bolts and lift the retaining bracket off the top of the filter (see illustrations).

10 Depress the tabs on the quick-release fittings and disconnect the two fuel pipes from the top of the filter (see illustrations).

11 Lift the fuel filter up and out of the mounting bracket (see illustration).

1.6 litre SOHC engines and 1.4 litre (Stage V emissions) engines

12 Undo the 3 bolts and remove the engine cover bracket from above the filter (see illustration).

22.9a Disconnect the fuel filter wiring connector (A), then undo the three bolts (B) …

22.9b … and lift the retaining bracket off the top of the filter

22.10a Depress the tabs on the quick-release fittings and disconnect the fuel pipe to the fuel pump …

22.10b … and the fuel supply pipe to the filter

22.11 Lift the fuel filter up and out of the mounting bracket

22.12 Undo the bolts and remove the bracket

22.13 Depress the clip and disconnect the wiring plug

22.14 Depress the buttons and disconnect the pipes

22.15 Fuel filter retaining bolts

22.16 Rotate the fitting clockwise and lift it slightly

22.17 Remove the Torx screws

22.19 Ensure the seal is in place on the top of the filter element

13 Disconnect the wiring plug from the top of the filter **(see illustration)**.

14 Depress the release buttons and disconnect the fuel pipes from the filter **(see illustration)**. Plug the openings to prevent contamination.

15 Undo the 2 retaining bolts and lift the filter from the housing **(see illustration)**.

16 Hold the filter over a suitable container, then gentle rotate the fitting on the top of the filter clockwise slightly, lift it slightly and allow the fuel to drain from the base **(see illustration)**.

17 Undo the 3 Torx screws and separate the top of the filter from the element **(see illustration)**.

18 Press down the centre fitting on the filter top, then rotate it clockwise slightly to secure it.

19 Ensure the new seal is in place, and locate the filter top onto the new filter element **(see illustration)**.

20 Refit and tighten the 3 Torx screws securing the filter top.

21 Locate the filter into the housing, and tighten the retaining bolts.

22 Reconnect the fuel pipes to their original locations, and reconnect the wiring plug.

23 Refit the bracket above the filter and tighten the retaining bolts securely.

All engines

24 Fitting a new filter is a reversal of removal, noting the following points:

a) *Ensure that the fuel hose connections are securely remade.*

b) *Refit the bulkhead closure panel and windscreen cowl panel as described in Chapter 11 Section 20.*

c) *On completion, prime and bleed the fuel system as described in Chapter 4B Section 3.*

d) *When the engine is running, check for any sign of leakage from the disturbed pipes.*

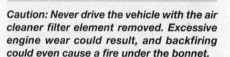

23 Air filter element renewal – diesel models

Caution: Never drive the vehicle with the air cleaner filter element removed. Excessive engine wear could result, and backfiring could even cause a fire under the bonnet.

1.4 litre engines (Stage IV emissions)

1 The air cleaner is located on top of the engine.

2 Undo the three screws at the front of the filter cover, then lift the cover and withdraw the filter element. Note which way up the element was fitted **(see illustrations)**.

3 Position the new element in the filter housing and refit the filter cover. Note the

23.2a On 1.4 litre models, undo the three screws along the front ...

23.2b ... then lift the cover at the front, unhook at the back ...

23.2c ... and remove the air filter element

23.5 Disconnect the wiring connector from the airflow sensor on the air cleaner cover

23.6 Undo the four bolts securing the cover to the air cleaner housing

23.7 The cover can now be lifted, and the filter element removed

three lugs at the rear of the cover which engage with the housing. Tighten the retaining screws securely.

1.6 litre engines and 1.4 litre (Stage V emissions) engines

4 The air filter element is located in the air cleaner assembly on the left-hand side of the engine compartment.
5 Disconnect the wiring connector from the airflow sensor on the air cleaner cover (see illustration).
6 Undo the four bolts securing the cover to the air cleaner housing (see illustration).
7 The cover can now be lifted, and the filter element removed (see illustration).
8 Position the new element in the filter housing and refit the filter cover. Tighten the retaining screws securely.

24 Braking system rubber hose check

1 Position the car over an inspection pit, on car ramps, or jack it up one wheel at a time (see 'Jacking and vehicle support').
2 Inspect the braking system rubber hoses fitted to each front caliper, and on each side of the rear axle (see illustration). Look for perished, swollen or hardened rubber, and any signs of cracking, especially at the metal end fittings. If there's any doubt as to the condition of any hose, renew it as described in Chapter 9.

24.2 Rubber brake hose fitted to the front caliper

25 Timing belt renewal

1 Refer to the procedures contained in Chapter 2B Section 7, Chapter 2D Section 7 or Chapter 2E Section 7.

26 Auxiliary drivebelt renewal

Removal

1 Firmly apply the handbrake, then jack up the front of the vehicle and support it securely on axle stands (see 'Jacking and vehicle support'). Remove the right-hand roadwheel.
2 Where fitted, undo the retaining bolts and remove the engine undertray, then undo the two screws and remove the drivebelt lower cover.
3 Engage an open-ended spanner with the lug at the top of the tensioner arm, then rotate the tensioner arm clockwise to release the belt tension. Insert a 3 mm diameter drill bit or rod into the hole in the tensioner body, so that the tensioner arm rests against it and locks it in this position (see illustration). It is useful to have a small mirror available to enable the alignment of the locking holes to be more easily seen in the limited space available.

26.3 Turn the tensioner clockwise and lock with a 3 mm diameter rod or drill inserted in the hole provided

4 Note how the drivebelt is routed, then remove the belt from the pulleys. Note that if the belt is to be re-used, mark the direction of rotation. The belt must be refitted the same way round.

Refitting

5 Fit the belt around the pulleys, ensuring that the ribs on the belt are correctly engaged with the grooves in the pulleys and the drivebelt is correctly routed.
6 Using an open-ended spanner, hold the tensioner arm so that the locking drill bit/rod can be removed, then release the pressure on the spanner so that the automatic tensioner takes up the slack in the drivebelt.
7 Refit the drivebelt lower cover and, where applicable, the engine undertray. Refit the roadwheel then lower the vehicle to the ground and tighten the wheel nuts to the specified torque.

27 Brake fluid renewal

⚠ *Warning: Brake hydraulic fluid can harm your eyes and damage painted surfaces, so use extreme caution when handling and pouring it. Do not use fluid that has been standing open for some time, as it absorbs moisture from the air. Excess moisture can cause a dangerous loss of braking effectiveness.*

1 The procedure is similar to that for bleeding the hydraulic system as described in Chapter 9 Section 2, except that allowance should be made for the old fluid to be expelled when bleeding each section of the circuit.
2 Working as described in Chapter 9 Section 2, open the first bleed screw in the sequence, and pump the brake pedal gently until the level in the reservoir is approaching the MIN mark. Top-up to the MAX level with new fluid, and continue pumping until only new fluid remains in the reservoir, and new fluid can be seen emerging from the bleed screw. Tighten the screw, and top the reservoir level up to the MAX level line.
3 Work through all the remaining bleed screws in the sequence until new fluid can

28.2 Unclip the plastic cover from the front of the transmission

28.3 Unscrew and remove the filler/level plug

be seen at all of them. Be careful to keep the master cylinder reservoir topped-up above the MIN level at all times, or air may enter the system. If this happens, further bleeding will be required, to remove the air.

4 When the operation is complete, check that all bleed screws are securely tightened, and that their dust caps are refitted. Wash off all traces of spilt fluid, and recheck the master cylinder reservoir fluid level.

5 Check the operation of the brakes before taking the car on the road.

28 Manual transmission oil level check

1 Position the car over an inspection pit, on car ramps, or jack it up and support it on axle stands, but make sure that it is level. Where fitted, undo the retaining bolts and remove the engine undertray.

2 Unclip the plastic cover fitted over the gearchange cables at the front of the transmission **(see illustration)**.

3 Remove all traces of dirt, then unscrew the filler/level plug from the front face of the transmission. This will probably be very tight, and a large Allen key or bit will be needed – access is made awkward by the plastic shroud around the gearchange cables **(see illustration)**.

4 The level must be just below the bottom edge of the filler/level plug hole (use a cranked tool such as an Allen key to check the level). If necessary, top-up the level with the specified grade of oil (see Lubricants and fluids0,6) until the oil just starts to run out. Allow any excess oil to flow out until the level stabilises **(see illustrations)**.

5 When the level is correct, clean and refit the filler/level plug (check the condition of the O-ring seal, and renew if necessary), then tighten it to the specified torque. Clip the plastic cover back into position.

6 Where applicable, refit the engine undertray,

28.4a Top-up the oil level …

then lower the car to the ground.

29 Remote control battery renewal – diesel models

Note: *All the remote control units described below are fitted with a type CR 2032, 3 volt battery.*

1 Although not in the Ford maintenance schedule, we recommend that the battery is changed every 2 years, regardless of the vehicle's mileage. However, if the door locks

29.2a Insert a small screwdriver into the slot on the side of the transmitter unit …

28.4b … then allow any excess to flow out before refitting the plug

repeatedly fail to respond to signals from the remote control at the normal distance, change the battery in the remote control before attempting to troubleshoot any of the vehicle's other systems.

Control with a folding key

2 Insert a small flat-bladed screwdriver fully into the slot on the side of the transmitter unit, push the screwdriver towards the key blade and remove the key blade **(see illustrations)**.

3 Use the screwdriver, inserted at the side and front of the transmitter unit, to separate the two halves of the unit **(see illustration)**.

29.2b … then push the screwdriver towards the key blade and remove the key blade

29.3 Insert the screwdriver at the side and front of the transmitter unit to separate the two halves

29.4 Note the fitted position of the battery, then prise it out and insert the new one

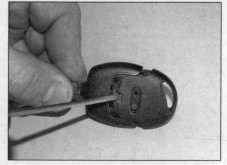

29.6 Insert a small screwdriver into the slot provided and slide the transmitter unit from the key blade

4 Note the fitted position of the battery (positive side down), then prise the battery from its location, and insert the new one **(see illustration)**. Avoid touching the battery or the terminals with bare fingers.
5 Snap the two halves of the transmitter together, and re-attach it to the key blade.

Control without a folding key

Type 1

6 Insert a small flat-bladed screwdriver into the slot provided and slide the transmitter unit from the key blade **(see illustration)**.
7 Use the screwdriver to release the clip each side and open the transmitter unit **(see illustration)**.
8 Note the fitted position of the battery (positive side up), then prise the battery from its location, and insert the new one **(see illustration)**. Avoid touching the battery or the terminals with bare fingers.
9 Snap the two halves of the transmitter together, and re-attach it to the key blade.

Type 2

10 Depress the two tabs on the side of the transmitter unit and carefully lift off the cover.
11 Remove the key blade from the transmitter unit.
12 Use a small flat-bladed the screwdriver, inserted at the side of the transmitter unit, to separate the two halves of the unit.
13 Note the fitted position of the battery (positive side down), then prise the battery

from its location, and insert the new one. Avoid touching the battery or the terminals with bare fingers.
14 Snap the two halves of the transmitter together, place the key blade in position and refit the cover.

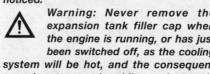

30 Coolant strength check and renewal

⚠️ *Warning: Do not allow antifreeze to come in contact with your skin or painted surfaces of the vehicle. Flush contaminated areas immediately with plenty of water. Don't store new coolant, or leave old coolant lying around, where it's accessible to children or pets – they're attracted by its sweet smell. Ingestion of even a small amount of coolant can be fatal. Wipe up garage-floor and drip-pan spills immediately. Keep antifreeze containers covered, and repair cooling system leaks as soon as they're noticed.*

⚠️ *Warning: Never remove the expansion tank filler cap when the engine is running, or has just been switched off, as the cooling system will be hot, and the consequent escaping steam and scalding coolant could cause serious injury.*

⚠️ *Warning: Wait until the engine is cold before starting these procedures.*

Strength check

1 Use a hydrometer to check the strength of the antifreeze. Follow the instructions provided with your hydrometer. The antifreeze strength should be approximately 50%. If it is significantly less than this, drain a little coolant from the radiator (see this Section), add antifreeze to the coolant expansion tank, then recheck the strength.

Coolant draining

2 To drain the system, first remove the expansion tank filler cap.
3 Firmly apply the handbrake, then jack up the front of the vehicle and support it securely on axle stands (see 'Jacking and vehicle support'). Where fitted, undo the retaining bolts and remove the engine undertray.
4 Place a suitable container beneath the right-hand side of the radiator.
5 Release the retaining clamp and disconnect the bottom hose from the radiator. Allow the coolant to drain into the container.
6 Once the coolant has stopped draining from the radiator, reconnect the bottom hose and secure with the retaining clamp.

System flushing

7 With time, the cooling system may gradually lose its efficiency, as the radiator core becomes choked with rust, scale deposits from the water, and other sediment. To minimise this, as well as using only good-quality antifreeze and clean soft water, the system should be flushed as follows whenever any part of it is disturbed, and/or when the coolant is renewed.
8 With the coolant drained, refit the radiator bottom hose and refill the system with fresh water. Refit the expansion tank filler cap, start the engine and warm it up to normal operating temperature, then stop it and (after allowing it to cool down completely) drain the system again. Repeat as necessary until only clean water can be seen to emerge, then refill finally with the specified coolant mixture.
9 If only clean, soft water and good-quality

29.7 Release the clip each side and open the transmitter unit

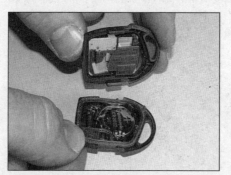

29.8 Note the fitted position of the battery, then prise it out and insert the new one

antifreeze (even if not to Ford's specification) has been used, and the coolant has been renewed at the suggested intervals, the above procedure will be sufficient to keep the system clean for a considerable length of time. If, however, the system has been neglected, a more thorough operation will be required, as follows.

10 First drain the coolant, then disconnect the radiator top hose. Insert a garden hose into the radiator top hose connection, and allow water to circulate through the radiator until it runs clean from the bottom outlet.

11 To flush the engine, insert the garden hose into the radiator bottom hose, wrap a piece of rag around the garden hose to seal the connection, and allow water to circulate until it runs clear.

12 Try the effect of repeating this procedure in the top hose, although this may not be effective, since the thermostat will probably close and prevent the flow of water.

13 In severe cases of contamination, reverse-flushing of the radiator may be necessary. This may be achieved by inserting the garden hose into the bottom outlet, wrapping a piece of rag around the hose to seal the connection, then flushing the radiator until clear water emerges from the top hose outlet.

14 If the radiator is suspected of being severely choked, remove the radiator (Chapter 3 Section 3), turn it upside-down, and repeat the procedure described in paragraph 13.

15 Flushing the heater matrix can be achieved using a similar procedure to that described in paragraph 13, once the heater inlet and outlet hoses have been identified. These two hoses will be of the same diameter, and pass through the engine compartment bulkhead (refer to the procedures contained in Chapter 3 for more details).

16 The use of chemical cleaners is not recommended, and should be necessary only as a last resort; the scouring action of some chemical cleaners may lead to other cooling system problems. Normally, regular renewal of the coolant will prevent excessive contamination of the system.

Coolant filling

17 With the cooling system drained and flushed, ensure that all disturbed hose unions are correctly secured. Where applicable, refit the engine undertray, then lower the vehicle to the ground.

18 Set the heater temperature control to maximum heat, but ensure the blower is turned off.

19 Prepare a sufficient quantity of the specified coolant mixture (see below); allow for a surplus, so as to have a reserve supply for topping-up.

20 Slowly fill the system through the expansion tank. Since the tank is the highest point in the system, all the air in the system should be displaced into the tank by the rising liquid. Slow pouring reduces the possibility of air being trapped and forming airlocks.

Continue filling until the coolant level reaches the top of the expansion tank.

21 With the help of an assistant, start the engine and run it at 2500 rpm until the coolant level stabilises. If the level in the expansion tank drops significantly, top-up to the MAX level line, to minimise the amount of air circulating in the system.

22 Once the coolant level has stabilised, refit the expansion tank filler cap and continue running the engine at 2500 rpm for a further 15 minutes.

23 Increase the engine speed to 5000 rpm, then allow it to return to idle. Repeat this sequence 6 times.

24 Increase the engine speed to 4000 rpm, maintain this speed for 10 seconds, then reduce the engine speed to 2500 rpm and maintain this speed for 15 minutes.

25 Stop the engine, then leave the car to cool down completely (overnight, if possible).

26 With the system cool, open the expansion tank, and top-up the tank to the MAX level line. Refit the filler cap, tightening it securely, and clean up any spillage.

27 After refilling, always check carefully all components of the system (but especially any unions disturbed during draining and flushing) for signs of coolant leaks. Fresh antifreeze has a searching action, which will rapidly expose any weak points in the system.

Antifreeze type and mixture

Note: *Do not use engine antifreeze in the windscreen/tailgate washer system, as it will damage the vehicle's paintwork. A screenwash additive should be added to the washer system in its maker's recommended quantities.*

28 If the vehicle's history (and therefore the quality of the antifreeze in it) is unknown, owners are advised to drain and thoroughly reverse-flush the system, before refilling with fresh coolant mixture.

29 If the antifreeze used is to Ford's specification, the levels of protection it affords are indicated in the coolant packaging.

30 To give the recommended standard mixture ratio for antifreeze, 50% (by volume) of antifreeze must be mixed with 50% of clean, soft water; if you are using any other type of antifreeze, follow its manufacturer's instructions to achieve the correct ratio.

31 You are unlikely to fully drain the system at any one time (unless the engine is being completely stripped), and the capacities quoted in the Specifications are therefore slightly academic for routine coolant renewal. As a guide, only two-thirds of the system's total capacity is likely to be needed for coolant renewal.

32 As the drained system will be partially filled with flushing water, in order to establish the recommended mixture ratio, measure out 50% of the system capacity in antifreeze and pour it into the hose/expansion tank as described above, then top-up with water. Any topping-up while refilling the system should

be done with water – for *Weekly checks* use a suitable mixture.

33 Before adding antifreeze, the cooling system should be drained, preferably flushed, and all hoses checked for condition and security. As noted earlier, fresh antifreeze will rapidly find any weaknesses in the system.

34 After filling with antifreeze, a label should be attached to the expansion tank, stating the type and concentration of antifreeze used, and the date installed. Any subsequent topping-up should be made with the same type and concentration of antifreeze.

General cooling system checks

35 The engine should be cold for the cooling system checks, so perform the following procedure before driving the vehicle, or after it has been shut off for at least three hours.

36 Remove the expansion tank filler cap, and clean it thoroughly inside and out with a rag. Also clean the filler neck on the expansion tank. The presence of rust or corrosion in the filler neck indicates that the coolant should be changed. The coolant inside the expansion tank should be relatively clean and transparent. If it is rust-coloured, drain and flush the system, and refill with a fresh coolant mixture.

37 Carefully check the radiator hoses and heater hoses along their entire length; renew any hose which is cracked, swollen or deteriorated.

38 Inspect all other cooling system components (joint faces, etc) for leaks. A leak in the cooling system will usually show up as white- or antifreeze-coloured deposits on the area adjoining the leak. Where any problems of this nature are found on system components, renew the component or gasket with reference to Chapter 3.

Airlocks

39 If, after draining and refilling the system, symptoms of overheating are found which did not occur previously, then the fault is almost certainly due to trapped air at some point in the system, causing an airlock and restricting the flow of coolant; usually, the air is trapped because the system was refilled too quickly.

40 If an airlock is suspected, first try gently squeezing all visible coolant hoses. A coolant hose which is full of air feels quite different to one full of coolant when squeezed. After refilling the system, most airlocks will clear once the system has cooled, and been topped-up.

41 While the engine is running at operating temperature, switch on the heater and heater fan, and check for heat output. Provided there is sufficient coolant in the system, lack of heat output could be due to an airlock in the system.

42 Airlocks can have more serious effects than simply reducing heater output – a severe airlock could reduce coolant flow around the engine. Check that the radiator top hose is hot when the engine is at operating temperature

– a top hose which stays cold could be the result of an airlock (or a non-opening thermostat).

43 If the problem persists, stop the engine and allow it to cool down completely, before unscrewing the expansion tank filler cap or loosening the hose clips and squeezing the hoses to bleed out the trapped air. In the worst case, the system will have to be at least partially drained (this time, the coolant can be saved for re-use) and flushed to clear the problem. If all else fails, have the system evacuated and vacuum filled by a suitably-equipped garage.

Expansion tank cap check

44 Wait until the engine is completely cold – perform this check before the engine is started for the first time in the day.

45 Place a wad of cloth over the expansion tank cap, then unscrew it slowly and remove it.

46 Examine the condition of the rubber seal on the underside of the cap. If the rubber appears to have hardened, or cracks are visible in the seal edges, a new cap should be fitted.

47 If the car is several years old, or has covered a large mileage, consider renewing the cap regardless of its apparent condition – they are not expensive. If the pressure relief valve built into the cap fails, excess pressure in the system will lead to puzzling failures of hoses and other cooling system components.

Chapter 2 Part A
Petrol engine in-car repair procedures

Contents

Degrees of difficulty

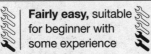

| **Easy,** suitable for novice with little experience | **Fairly easy,** suitable for beginner with some experience | **Fairly difficult,** suitable for competent DIY mechanic | **Difficult,** suitable for experienced DIY mechanic | **Very difficult,** suitable for expert DIY or professional |

Specifications

General

Engine type.	Four-cylinder, in-line, double overhead camshafts, variable valve timing on 1.6 litre engines only
Designation:	
1.25 and 1.4 litre engines	Duratec 16V
1.6 litre engines	Duratec 16V Ti-VCT
Engine codes:	
1.25 litre engines	SNJA, SNJB, STJA and STJB
1.4 litre engines	SPJA and SPJC
1.6 litre engines	HXJA, HXJB and U5JA
Capacity:	
1.25 litre engine	1242 cc
1.4 litre engine	1388 cc
1.6 litre engines	1596 cc
Bore:	
1.25 litre engines	71.9 mm
1.4 litre engines	75.9 mm
1.6 litre engines	79.0 mm
Stroke:	
1.25 and 1.4 litre engines	76.5 mm
1.6 litre engines	81.4 mm
Compression ratio:	
1.25 litre engines	10.0: 1
1.4 and 1.6 litre engines	11.0: 1
Firing order	1-3-4-2 (No 1 cylinder at timing belt end)
Direction of crankshaft rotation	Clockwise (seen from right-hand side of car)

Valve clearances (cold)

Inlet	0.17 to 0.23 mm
Exhaust:	
1.25 and 1.4 litre engines	0.27 to 0.33 mm
1.6 litre engines	0.31 to 0.37 mm

Camshafts

Camshaft bearing journal diameter	Unavailable at time of writing
Camshaft bearing journal-to-cylinder head running clearance	Unavailable at time of writing
Camshaft endfloat (typical).	0.05 to 0.13 mm

Lubrication

Oil pressure (minimum, warm engine):	
Idling (800 rpm).	1.0 bar
At 2000 rpm	2.5 bars
Pressure relief valve opens at.	4.0 bars
Oil pump clearances	Not specified

Torque wrench settings

	Nm	lbf ft
Air conditioning compressor mounting bolts	25	18
Alternator mounting bracket bolts	42	31
Camshaft bearing cap:		
1.25 and 1.4 litre engines:		
Stage 1	7	5
Stage 2	Angle-tighten a further 45°	
1.6 litre engines:		
Stage 1	10	7
Stage 2:		
Timing belt end bearing cap outer bolts	Angle-tighten a further 53°	
Timing belt end bearing cap inner bolts	Angle-tighten a further 70°	
All other bearing cap bolts	Angle-tighten a further 45°	
Camshaft position sensor (1.6 litre engines)	9	7
Camshaft sensor ring (1.6 litre engines)	21	15
Camshaft sprocket bolt (1.25 and 1.4 litre engines)*	60	44
Coolant outlet to cylinder head	20	15
Coolant pump pulley bolts	27	20
Crankcase breather to cylinder block	9	7
Crankshaft position sensor	9	7
Crankshaft oil seal carrier.	9	7
Crankshaft pulley/vibration damper: *		
M12 bolt:		
Stage 1	40	30
Stage 2	Angle-tighten a further 90°	
M14 bolt:		
Stage 1	100	74
Stage 2	Angle-tighten a further 90°	
Stage 3	Angle-tighten a further 15°	
Cylinder head bolts: *		
Stage 1	5	4
Stage 2	15	11
Stage 3	35	26
Stage 4	Angle-tighten a further 75°	
Cylinder head cover	10	7
Driveplate bolts:		
Stage 1	30	22
Stage 2	Angle-tighten a further 80°	
Engine mountings:		
Right-hand mounting bracket to cylinder head	55	41
Right-hand mounting to cylinder head bracket*	80	59
Right-hand mounting to body	48	35
Left-hand mounting to transmission	80	59
Left-hand mounting to body.	80	59
Roll restrictor/rear mounting bolts	48	35
Engine-to-transmission bolts	48	35
Exhaust flexible section-to-catalytic converter nuts	48	35
Exhaust manifold heat shield bolts	10	7
Exhaust manifold nuts/bolts.	54	40
Flywheel bolts:		
Stage 1	30	22
Stage 2	Angle-tighten a further 80°	
Inlet manifold bolts.	18	13
Oil baffle to cylinder block	9	7
Oil drain plug	28	21
Oil filter connector	45	33

Torque wrench settings (continued)

	Nm	lbf ft
Oil intake pipe to oil baffle	9	7
Oil pressure switch.	15	11
Oil pump to cylinder block	9	7
Spark plugs	15	11
Sump bolts:		
Sump-to-block bolts:		
Stage 1	10	7
Stage 2	20	15
Sump-to-transmission bolts.	48	35
TDC pin hole blanking plug	20	15
Timing belt cover bolts.	9	7
Timing belt tensioner bolt.	20	15
Torque converter to driveplate*	37	27
VCT solenoid	8	6
VCT unit blanking plugs	16	12
VCT unit retaining bolts:		
Stage 1	25	18
Stage 2	Angle-tighten a further 75°	

Use new fasteners

1 General Information

How to use this Chapter

1 This Part of Chapter 2 is devoted to in-car repair procedures on the 1.25, 1.4 and 1.6 litre Duratec 16V petrol engines. All procedures concerning engine removal, refitting, and overhaul can be found in Chapter 2F.

2 Refer to Vehicle identification numbers in the Reference Section at the end of this manual for details of engine code locations.

3 Most of the operations included in this Chapter are based on the assumption that the engine is still installed in the car. Therefore, if this information is being used during a complete engine overhaul, with the engine already removed, many of the steps included here will not apply.

Engine description

4 The Duratec engine (formerly the Zetec-SE), is a sixteen-valve, double overhead camshaft (DOHC), four-cylinder, in-line unit, mounted transversely at the front of the car, with the transmission on its left-hand end.

5 Apart from the plastic timing belt covers, plastic cylinder head cover, plastic inlet manifold, and the cast-iron cylinder liners, the main engine components (including the sump) are manufactured entirely of aluminium alloy.

Caution: When tightening bolts into aluminium castings, it is important to adhere to the specified torque wrench settings, to avoid stripping threads.

6 The crankshaft runs in five main bearings, the centre main bearing's upper half incorporating thrustwashers to control crankshaft endfloat.

Note: *On all petrol engines covered by this manual, it is not possible to remove the intermediate/main bearing section or to remove the crankshaft or pistons. No separate parts are available, and replacement/exchange units are supplied with crankshaft, pistons, connecting rods, etc, already fitted. Consult a Ford dealer or parts specialist for further information.*

7 The connecting rods rotate on horizontally-split bearing shells at their big-ends, however the big-ends are of unusual design in that the caps are sheared from the rods during manufacture thus making each cap individually matched to its own connecting rod. The pistons are attached to the connecting rods by gudgeon pins which are an interference fit in the connecting rod small-end bores. The aluminium alloy pistons are fitted with three piston rings: two compression rings and an oil control ring.

8 The inlet and exhaust valves are each closed by coil springs; they operate in guides which are shrink-fitted into the cylinder head, as are the valve seat inserts.

9 Both camshafts are driven by the same toothed timing belt, each operating eight valves via bucket tappets. Each camshaft rotates in five bearings that are line-bored directly in the cylinder head and the (bolted-on) bearing caps; this means that the bearing caps are not available separately from the cylinder head, and must not be interchanged with caps from another engine.

10 1.6 litre engines are available with variable valve timing on the both the inlet and exhaust camshafts – this engine is known as the Ti-VCT (Twin independent Variable Camshaft Timing). Engine oil pressure is used to vary the positions of the camshaft sprocket in relation to the camshafts, thus varying the valves' opening and closing times. Control of the oil flow is achieved using solenoid valves, which in turn are controlled by the engine management powertrain control module (PCM). Varying the valve timing is this manner results in improved driveability and output, whist reducing fuel consumption and exhaust emissions.

11 The coolant pump is bolted to the right-hand end of the cylinder block, beneath the front run of the timing belt, and is driven by the auxiliary drivebelt from the crankshaft pulley.

12 Lubrication is by means of an eccentric-rotor trochoidal pump, which is mounted on the crankshaft right-hand end, and draws oil through a strainer located in the sump. The pump forces oil through an externally-mounted full-flow cartridge-type filter.

Operations with engine in car

13 The following work can be carried out with the engine in the car:

a) *Cylinder head cover – removal and refitting.*
b) *Timing belt – renewal.*
c) *Timing belt tensioner and sprockets – removal and refitting.*
d) *Camshaft oil seals – renewal.*
e) *Camshafts, tappets and shims – removal and refitting.*
f) *Cylinder head – removal and refitting.*
g) *Sump – removal and refitting.*
h) *Crankshaft oil seals – renewal.*
i) *Oil pump – removal and refitting.*
j) *Flywheel/driveplate – removal and refitting.*
k) *Engine/transmission mountings – removal and refitting.*

2 Compression test – description and interpretation

1 When engine performance is down, or if misfiring occurs which cannot be attributed to the ignition or fuel systems, a compression test can provide diagnostic clues as to the engine's condition. If the test is performed regularly, it can give warning of trouble before any other symptoms become apparent.

2 The engine must be fully warmed-up to operating temperature, the oil level must be correct and the battery must be fully-charged. The help of an assistant will also be required.

3 Note that it is necessary to remove the fuel pump relay to allow the compression test to be performed. This will log a fault code in the engine management powertrain control module when the engine is turned over on the starter, and the fault code will have to be cleared, using Ford diagnostic equipment or a compatible alternative, on completion of the test. Unless you have access to the necessary diagnostic equipment it may be preferable to have the compression test carried out by a Ford dealer or suitably-equipped garage. Should you wish to proceed, the procedure is as follows.

4 Refer to Chapter 12 Section 3 and remove the fuel pump relay from the engine compartment fusebox. Now start the engine and allow it to run until it stalls.

5 Disable the ignition system by disconnecting the multiplug from the DIS ignition coil. Remove all the spark plugs with reference to Chapter 1A Section 21.

6 Fit a compression tester to the No 1 cylinder spark plug hole – the type of tester which screws into the spark plug thread is preferable.

7 Arrange for an assistant to hold the accelerator pedal fully depressed to the floor, while at the same time cranking the engine over for several seconds on the starter motor. Observe the compression gauge reading. The compression will build-up fairly quickly in a healthy engine. Low compression on the first stroke, followed by gradually-increasing pressure on successive strokes, indicates worn piston rings. A low compression on the first stroke which does not rise on successive strokes, indicates leaking valves or a blown head gasket (a cracked cylinder head could also be the cause). Deposits on the underside of the valve heads can also cause low compression. Record the highest gauge reading obtained, then repeat the procedure for the remaining cylinders.

8 Due to the variety of testers available, and the fluctuation in starter motor speed when cranking the engine, different readings are often obtained when carrying out the compression test. For this reason, actual compression pressure figures are not quoted by Ford. However, the most important factor is that the compression pressures are uniform in all cylinders, and that is what this test is mainly concerned with.

9 Add some engine oil (about three squirts from a plunger type oil can) to each cylinder through the spark plug holes, and then repeat the test.

10 If the compression increases after the oil is added, the piston rings are probably worn. If the compression does not increase significantly, the leakage is occurring at the valves or the head gasket. Leakage past the valves may be caused by burned valve seats and/or faces, or warped, cracked or bent valves.

11 If two adjacent cylinders have equally low compressions, it is most likely that the head gasket has blown between them. The appearance of coolant in the combustion chambers or on the engine oil dipstick would verify this condition.

12 If one cylinder is about 20 percent lower than the other, and the engine has a slightly rough idle, a worn lobe on the camshaft could be the cause.

13 On completion of the checks, refit the spark plugs and reconnect the HT leads and the DIS ignition coil multiplug. Refit the fuel pump relay to the fusebox, then clear the fault code from the powertrain control module.

3 Top Dead Centre (TDC) for No 1 piston – locating

1 Top dead centre (TDC) is the highest point of the cylinder that each piston reaches as the crankshaft turns. Each piston reaches its TDC position at the end of its compression stroke, and then again at the end of its exhaust stroke. For the purpose of engine timing, TDC on the compression stroke for No 1 piston is used. No 1 cylinder is at the timing belt end of the engine. Proceed as follows.

2 Disconnect the battery negative terminal (refer to 'Disconnecting the battery'), then remove the spark plugs as described in Chapter 1A Section 21.

3 Firmly apply the handbrake, then jack up the front of the vehicle and support it securely on axle stands (see 'Jacking and vehicle support'). If the engine is to be turned using the right-hand front roadwheel with top gear engaged (manual transmission models only), it is only necessary to raise the right-hand front roadwheel off the ground.

4 Where necessary, undo the fasteners, remove the engine undershield, then remove the auxiliary drivebelt lower cover for access to the crankshaft pulley and bolt.

1.25 and 1.4 litre engines

5 Remove the cylinder head cover as described in Section 4.

6 The piston of No 1 cylinder must now be positioned just before top dead centre (TDC). To do this, have an assistant turn the crankshaft until the slots in the left-hand ends of the camshafts are parallel with the upper surface of the cylinder head. Note that the slots are slightly offset so make sure that the lower edges of the slots are aligned with cylinder head. Turn the crankshaft slightly anti-clockwise (viewed from the right-hand end of the engine).

7 Unscrew the blanking plug from the right-hand rear side of the engine cylinder block. A TDC timing pin must now be inserted and tightened into the hole. It is highly recommended that the special Ford timing pin 303-748 is obtained, or alternatively, a timing pin from a reputable tool manufacturer (see illustrations).

8 With the timing pin in position, turn the crankshaft slowly clockwise until the specially-machined surface on the crank web just touches the timing pin. No 1 piston is now at TDC on its compression stroke. To confirm this, check that the camshaft lobes for No 4 cylinder are 'rocking' (ie, exhaust valves closing and inlet valves opening).

9 It should now be possible to insert the camshaft setting bar into the slots in the left-hand ends of the camshafts. If the Ford setting tool 303-376B is unavailable, a home-made tool can be fabricated out of a length of flat metal bar 5.00 mm thick. The bar must be a good fit in the slots and should be

3.7a Undo the blanking plug from the right-hand rear corner of the cylinder block ...

3.7b ... and screw-in the timing pin

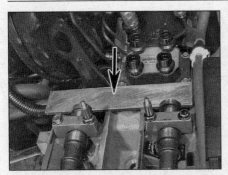

3.9 Locate the home-made camshaft setting tool (arrowed) in the slots

3.14 Undo the nuts/bolts (arrowed) and remove the right-hand engine mounting

3.15a The inlet camshaft sprocket is marked with a dot (arrowed) …

3.15b … and the exhaust camshaft sprocket with a groove (arrowed)

3.18a Fit the special tool over the VCT units

3.18b The tool is marked with a dot (2) for the inlet camshaft, a line (1) for the exhaust camshaft, and an arrow (3) which must point upwards

approximately 180 to 230 mm long by 20 to 30 mm wide **(see illustration)**.
10 If the bar cannot be inserted in the slots with the crankshaft at TDC, the valve timing must be adjusted as described in Section 8 of this Chapter.
11 Once the work requiring the engine to be set at TDC has been completed, remove the metal bar from the camshaft slots then unscrew the timing pin and refit the blanking plug. Refit the spark plugs (Chapter 1A), cylinder head cover (Section 4), auxiliary drivebelt lower cover, and where necessary the engine undershield. Lower the vehicle to the ground and reconnect the battery negative terminal.

1.6 litre engines

12 Remove the upper timing belt cover as described in Section 7.
13 Position a trolley jack under the engine. Use a block of wood on the jack head to prevent damage to the sump. Take the weight of the engine.
14 Pull the coolant expansion tank upwards and move it to one side. With the engine securely supported, remove the nuts/bolts securing the right-hand engine mounting to the body and engine bracket, then lift off the mounting **(see illustration)**. New nuts should be obtained for refitting the mounting.
15 Rotate the crankshaft pulley clockwise until the marks (dot on the inlet sprocket groove on the exhaust sprocket) of the

camshaft VCT units are approaching the 11 o'clock position **(see illustrations)**.
16 Undo the blanking plug from the right-hand rear side of the engine cylinder block **(see illustration 3.7a)**. A TDC timing pin must now be inserted and tightened into the hole. It is highly recommended that the Ford timing pin 303-748 is obtained, or alternatively, a timing pin from a reputable tool manufacturer **(see illustration 3.7b)**. The diameter of the pin is critical as it determines the TDC point where the machined flat on the crankshaft web contacts the shank of the tool – note that the web does not contact the end of the tool.
17 With the timing pin in position, turn the crankshaft slowly clockwise until the specially machined surface on the crank web just touches the timing pin. No 1 piston is now at TDC on its compression stroke.
18 Now it is necessary to fit Ford special tool 303-1097 over the VCT units on the ends of the camshafts. Note that the tool is marked with a line to indicate the exhaust side, a dot to indicate the inlet side, and an arrow which must point upwards **(see illustrations)**.
19 Once the work requiring the engine to be set at TDC has been completed, remove the special tool from the camshaft VCT units then unscrew the timing pin and refit the blanking plug. Refit the spark plugs (Chapter 1A Section 21), upper timing belt cover, auxiliary drivebelt lower cover, and where necessary the engine undershield. Lower the vehicle to the ground and reconnect the battery negative terminal.

4 Cylinder head cover – removal and refitting

Removal

1 Disconnect the battery negative terminal (refer to 'Disconnecting the battery').
2 Disconnect the breather pipe from the front of the cover **(see illustration)**.
3 Disconnect the HT leads from the spark plugs, unclip them from the cover, and position them to the left-hand side of the engine compartment.
4 On 1.6 litre engines, disconnect the wiring

4.2 Disconnect the breather pipe (arrowed)

4.4a Disconnect the camshaft position sensors wiring plugs

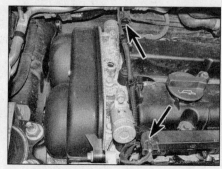

4.4b Disconnect the VCT solenoid wiring plugs (arrowed)

4.4c Then undo the bolt (arrowed) …

4.4d … and pull the solenoids from their locations

plugs from the camshaft position sensors and VCT solenoids on the cylinder head cover, clean around the area, then undo the retaining bolts and remove both VCT oil control solenoids from the top, right-hand end of the cylinder head **(see illustrations)**. Plug the openings to prevent contamination. Examine the O-ring seals, and renew if necessary.

5 Where fitted, undo the nut and bolt and move the wiring connector bracket at the left-hand rear corner of the cylinder head cover to one side.

6 On all engines, the cylinder head cover is secured by a total of twelve bolts. Note their fitted locations and remove the bolts. On 1.6 litre engines, the bolts are integral with the cover.

7 On 1.25 and 1.4 litre engines, remove the centre top bolt from the timing belt upper cover **(see illustration)**. This bolt secures the timing belt cover to the cylinder head cover.

8 Carefully lift the cover from the top of the cylinder head, unclipping any wiring as necessary. Recover the gasket – this may be re-used if it is not damaged.

Refitting

9 Clean the mating surfaces of the cylinder head and the cover gasket.

10 Lower the cover onto the cylinder head, ensuring that the gasket stays in place.

11 Progressively tighten all bolts to the specified torque.

12 The remainder of refitting is a reversal of removal.

5 Valve clearances – checking and adjustment

1 Remove the cylinder head cover as described in Section 4. **Note:** *If checking the valve clearances with the timing belt removed (eg, after refitting the camshafts), rotate the crankshaft 90° anti-clockwise back from TDC on No 1 cylinder so the pistons are halfway down the cylinder bores. Verify this by inserting a long screwdriver down the spark plug holes.*

2 Remove the spark plugs (Chapter 1A Section 21) in order to make turning the engine easier. The engine may be turned using a spanner on the crankshaft pulley bolt

or by raising the front right-hand roadwheel clear of the ground, engaging top gear and turning the wheel (manual transmission models only). If the former method is used, jack up and support the front of the car (see *'Jacking and vehicle support'*) then unbolt the lower cover for access to the pulley bolt; if the latter method is used, apply the handbrake then jack up the front right-hand side of the car until the roadwheel is clear of the ground and support with an axle stand.

3 Draw the valve positions on a piece of paper, numbering them 1 to 8 inlet and exhaust, from the timing belt (right-hand) end of the engine (ie, 1E, 1I, 2E, 2I and so on). As there are two inlet and two exhaust valves for each cylinder, draw the cylinders as large circles and the four valves as smaller circles. The inlet valves are at the front of the cylinder head, and the exhaust valves are at the rear. As the valve clearances are adjusted, cross them off.

4 Turn the engine in a clockwise direction until both inlet valves of No 1 cylinder are fully shut and the apex of the camshaft lobes are pointing upwards away from the valve positions.

5 Insert a feeler blade of the correct thickness (see Specifications) between the heel of the camshaft lobe and the tappet **(see illustration)**. It should be a firm sliding fit. If this is the case, the clearance is correct and the valve position can be crossed off. If the clearance is not correct, use feeler blades to determine the exact clearance and record this on the drawing. From this clearance it will be possible to calculate the thickness of the new tappet to be fitted. Note that no shims are fitted between the camshaft and tappet – the complete tappet must be renewed.

6 Check the clearance of the second inlet valve for No 1 cylinder, and if necessary record the existing clearance on the drawing.

7 Now turn the engine until the inlet valves of No 2 cylinder are fully shut and the camshaft lobes pointing away from the valve positions. Check the clearances as described previously, and record any that are incorrect.

8 After checking all of the inlet valve clearances, check the exhaust valve clearances in the same way, but note that the clearances are different.

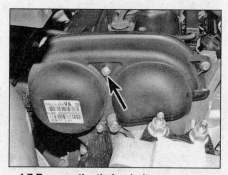

4.7 Remove the timing belt upper cover centre top bolt (arrowed)

5.5 Insert a feeler gauge between the heel of the camshaft lobe and the tappet

5.10a Measure the thickness of the tappets with a micrometer

5.10b The thickness of each tappet should be etched on its underside

9 Where adjustment is required, the procedure is to remove the camshafts as described in Section 11.

10 If the recorded clearance was too small, a thinner tappet must be fitted, and conversely if the clearance was too large, a thicker tappet must be fitted. To calculate the thickness of the new tappet, first use a micrometer to measure the thickness of the existing tappet (C) and add this to the measured clearance (B) **(see illustrations)**. Deduct the desired clearance (A) to provide the thickness (D) of the new tappet. The thickness of the tappet should be etched on the downward facing surface, however use the micrometer to verify this. The formula is as follows.

New tappet thickness D
= Existing tappet thickness C
+ Measured clearance B
– Desired clearance A

Sample calculation

Desired clearance (A) = 0.20
Measured clearance (B) = 0.15
Existing tappet thickness (C) = 2.725
Tappet thickness required (D) =
    C+B-A = 2.675
All measurements in mm

11 The tappets are available in varying thicknesses in increments of 0.025 mm.

12 It will be helpful for future adjustment if a record is kept of the thickness of tappet fitted at each position so it is possible to identify which new tappets will be needed before removing the camshafts.

13 When all the clearances have been checked and adjusted, refit the lower cover (where removed), lower the car to the ground and refit the cylinder head cover as described in Section 4.

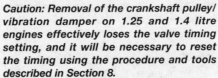

6 Crankshaft pulley/ vibration damper – removal and refitting

Caution: Removal of the crankshaft pulley/ vibration damper on 1.25 and 1.4 litre engines effectively loses the valve timing setting, and it will be necessary to reset the timing using the procedure and tools described in Section 8.
Note: *The crankshaft pulley/vibration damper retaining bolt may only be used once. Obtain a new bolt for the refitting procedure. On 1.25 and 1.4 litre engines, it will also be necessary to obtain new camshaft sprocket retaining bolts.*

Removal

1 Remove the auxiliary drivebelt as described in Chapter 1A Section 26.

2 Set the engine to the top dead centre (TDC) position as described in Section 3.

3 Remove the starter motor as described in Chapter 5A Section 9, then use Ford tool 303-393 and 303-393-02 to lock the crankshaft in position. This tool bolts across the starter motor aperture in the transmission bellhousing, and engages with the teeth of the starter ring gear on the flywheel/driveplate **(see illustrations)**.

4 Using a suitable socket and extension bar, undo and remove the crankshaft pulley/ vibration damper retaining bolt, then slide the pulley/damper off the end of the crankshaft.

5 Note that three different crankshaft pulley/ vibration damper retaining bolts may be fitted: M12 x 29 mm, M12 x 44.5 mm or M14 x 80 mm. In order to determine which bolt is required, use a Vernier caliper to measure the depth of the hole in the end of the crankshaft. A 42 mm depth requires a 29 mm bolt, a 52 mm depth requires a 44.5 mm bolt and an 81 mm depth requires an 80 mm bolt. Obtain the correct size of new bolt prior to refitting.

Refitting

1.25 and 1.4 litre engines

6 Unbolt and remove the upper timing cover (see Section 7). While holding each of the camshaft sprockets stationary in turn, loosen

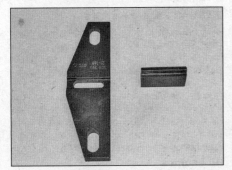

6.3a Ford tool No 303-393 and 303-393-02

6.3b The assembled tools bolt across the starter motor aperture ...

6.3c ... and engages with the teeth on the flywheel ring gear

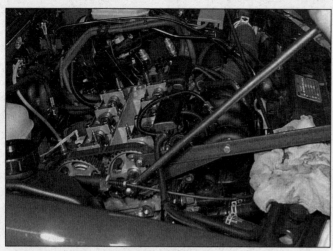

6.6 Slacken the camshaft sprocket retaining bolts whilst holding the sprockets with a home-made tool

7.5 Timing belt upper cover bolts (arrowed)

the sprocket retaining bolts until they are just finger-tight, to enable the sprockets to turn on the camshafts. To hold the sprockets stationary, make up a sprocket-holding tool using two lengths of steel strip (one long, the other short), and three nuts and bolts; one nut and bolt forms the pivot of a forked tool, with the remaining two nuts and bolts at the tips of the 'forks' to engage with the sprocket spokes (see illustration). Alternatively, the camshafts can be held stationary using a spanner on the special hexagon flats.

All engines

7 Temporarily remove the crankshaft timing pin.
8 Clean the end of the crankshaft and the crankshaft pulley/vibration damper.
9 Locate the crankshaft pulley/vibration damper on the end of the crankshaft, and press it fully home.
10 Insert the new crankshaft pulley/vibration damper retaining bolt and tighten it to the specified Stage 1 torque setting.
11 Now angle-tighten the bolt through the Stage 2 angle specified using an angle-tightening gauge. Where an M14 bolt is used, tighten it further through the specified Stage 3 angle.

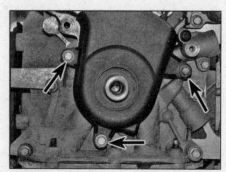

7.9 Timing belt lower cover bolts (arrowed)

1.25 and 1.4 litre engines

12 The valve timing must now be set and the camshaft sprocket bolts tightened as described in Section 8.
13 Refit the timing belt upper cover.

1.6 litre engines

14 Remove the crankshaft and camshaft locking tools, then refit the timing belt cover, and engine mounting in the reverse of the procedure described in Section 3.

All engines

15 Fit a new auxiliary drivebelt as described in Chapter 1A Section 26.

7 Timing belt covers – removal and refitting

Upper cover

Removal

1 Pull the coolant expansion tank upwards and move it to one side.
2 Slacken the coolant pump pulley bolts, then remove the auxiliary drivebelt as described in Chapter 1A Section 26.
3 Unscrew the 4 bolts and remove the coolant pump pulley.
4 On 1.25 and 1.4 litre engines, undo the single bolt securing the upper timing belt cover to the cylinder head cover (see illustration 4.7).
5 On all engines, unscrew the timing belt upper cover retaining bolts (see illustration).
6 Manoeuvre the timing cover from the engine compartment.

Refitting

7 Refitting is a reversal of removal. Fit a new auxiliary drivebelt as described in Chapter 1A Section 26.

Lower cover

Removal

8 The timing belt lower cover is located around the crankshaft. First remove the crankshaft pulley/vibration damper as described in Section 6.
9 Working beneath the right-hand wheel arch, unscrew the retaining bolts and withdraw the timing cover (see illustration).

Refitting

10 Refitting is a reversal of removal.

8 Timing belt – removal and refitting

Caution: The camshaft sprockets are made from a type of plastic. Care must be taken to avoid damage to the sprockets during the following procedure.

Removal

1 Loosen the four bolts securing the coolant pump pulley.
2 Remove the crankshaft pulley/vibration damper as described in Section 6.
3 Remove the coolant pump pulley.

1.25 and 1.4 litre engines

4 Unbolt and remove the upper timing cover (see Section 7). While holding each of the camshaft sprockets stationary in turn, loosen the sprocket retaining bolts until they are just finger-tight, to enable the sprockets to turn on the camshafts. To hold the sprockets stationary, make up a sprocket-holding tool as described in Section 6. Alternatively, the camshafts can be held stationary using a spanner on the special hexagon flats.

All engines

5 Where fitted, remove the timing belt guide disc from the end of the crankshaft.

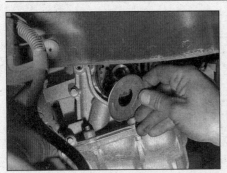

8.5 Remove the timing belt guide disc (where fitted)

8.7 Support the engine with a trolley jack and block of wood under the sump

8.10 Insert a 4 mm drill bit or rod into the tensioner arms (arrowed)

Note which way round the disc is fitted – the concave side faces outwards (see illustration).

6 Remove the alternator as described in Chapter 5A Section 7.

7 The engine must now be supported, as the right-hand mounting (right as seen from the driver's seat) must be removed. Supporting the engine should ideally be done from above, using an engine crane or a special engine lifting beam. However, in the absence of these tools, the engine can be supported from below, on the cast-aluminium sump, providing a piece of wood is used to spread the load (see illustration).

8 With the engine securely supported, remove the nuts/bolts securing the right-hand mounting to the body and engine bracket, then lift off the mounting (see illustration 3.14). New nuts should be obtained for refitting the mounting.

9 Unbolt the lower half of the engine right-hand mounting bracket from the engine.

10 Push the timing belt eccentric tensioner pulley rearwards to detension the belt, then insert Ford tool No 303-1054 or a suitable equivalent into the pulley arm to lock it in position (see illustration).

11 If the timing belt is to be re-used (this is not recommended), use white paint or similar to mark its direction of rotation, and note from the manufacturer's markings which way round it is fitted. Withdraw the belt from the sprockets and from over the tensioner

(see illustration). Do not attempt to turn the crankshaft or camshafts until the timing belt is refitted.

Inspection

12 If the belt is being removed for reasons other than routine renewal, check it carefully for any signs of uneven wear, splitting, cracks (especially at the roots of the belt teeth) or contamination with oil or coolant. Renew the belt if there is the slightest doubt about its condition. As a safety measure, the belt should be renewed irrespective of its apparent condition whenever the engine is overhauled.

13 Check the sprockets for signs of wear or damage, and ensure that the tensioner pulley rotates smoothly on its bearings; renew any worn or damaged components. Ford dealers (and many motor factors) now supply 'cambelt kits', consisting of the belt itself and a new tensioner – for peace of mind, it is recommended that one of these is purchased.

14 If signs of oil or coolant contamination are found on the old belt, trace the source of the leak and rectify it, then wash down the engine timing belt area and related components to remove all traces of oil or coolant.

Refitting

1.25 and 1.4 litre engines

15 Ensure that the engine is still set to TDC

on No 1 cylinder (Section 3). Remove the camshaft sprocket bolts and renew. Only finger-tighten the bolts at this stage, the camshaft sprockets must be free to rotate on their shafts.

16 Locate the timing belt on the crankshaft sprocket, then feed it over the two camshaft sprockets and finally, around the tensioner. If the original belt is being refitted, make sure that it is the correct way round as noted during removal (see illustrations).

17 Where applicable, refit the timing belt guide disc on the end of the crankshaft, making sure that the concave side faces outwards.

18 Remove the locking pin from the tensioner, and allow it to tension the belt.

19 Refit the engine mounting bracket to the cylinder block, and tighten the bolts to the specified torque.

20 Refit the upper engine mounting bracket tightening the bolts and the new nuts to the specified torque. Remove the jack from under the engine, or remove the hoist from above, as applicable.

21 Refit the timing belt lower cover, and tighten the bolts to the specified torque.

22 Refit the crankshaft pulley/vibration damper as described in Section 6.

23 Tighten the camshaft sprocket retaining bolts to the specified torque while holding the sprockets using the tool described in Section 6, or using a spanner

8.11 Note the belt may be marked with direction-of-rotation arrows

8.16a Fit the belt around the camshaft sprockets ...

8.16b ... and the crankshaft sprocket

8.23a Tighten the camshaft sprocket retaining bolts

8.23b Use an open-ended spanner on the hexagon section of the camshaft

8.27 Timing belt routing

on the hexagon flats provided **(see illustrations)**.

24 Remove the camshaft setting bar, the crankshaft timing pin and flywheel/driveplate locking tool.

25 Rotate the crankshaft clockwise 1¾ turns approximately. Refit the crankshaft TDC timing pin then rotate the crankshaft clockwise until it stops against the timing pin. Check to see whether the setting bar will fit in the camshaft slots. If necessary, loosen the camshaft sprocket bolts, turn the camshafts slightly (without moving the timing belt) so the setting bar can be fitted, then retighten the camshaft sprocket bolts. On completion, remove the timing pin and bar and refit the blanking plug.

26 Refit the timing belt upper cover, and the alternator. Refit the coolant pump pulley, and tighten the bolts as far as possible for now – once the auxiliary drivebelt has been fitted it will be easier to tighten the bolts to the specified torque.

1.6 litre engines

27 Ensure the engine's still set to TDC on No 1 cylinder (Section 3), then working clockwise, locate the timing belt on the crankshaft sprocket, then over the camshaft VCT units, then around the tensioner. If the original belt is being refitted, make sure that it is the correct way round as noted during removal **(see illustration)**.

28 Where applicable, refit the timing belt guide disc on the end of the crankshaft, making sure that the concave side faces outwards.

29 Remove the locking pin from the tensioner, and allow it to tension the belt.

30 Refit the lower timing belt cover and tighten the bolts to the specified torque.

31 Refit the crankshaft pulley/vibration damper as described in Section 6.

32 Remove the locking tool from the camshaft VCT units, the crankshaft timing pin, and the flywheel/driveplate locking tool.

33 Rotate the crankshaft clockwise approximately 1¾ turns, until the marks on the camshaft VCT units are in the 11 o'clock position **(see illustrations 3.15a and 3.15b)**.

34 Refit the crankshaft timing pin, and rotate the crankshaft clockwise until it stops against the timing pin. Refit the VCT units locking tool

to check their positions. If the tool cannot be fitted, remove the belt, and carry out the fitting/tensioning procedure again. If the timing is correct, remove the timing pin and VCT locking tool. Refit the cylinder block blanking plug.

35 Refit the engine mounting bracket to the cylinder block, and tighten the bolts to the specified torque.

36 Refit the upper engine mounting bracket tightening the bolts and the new nuts to the specified torque. Remove the jack from under the engine, or remove the hoist from above, as applicable.

37 Refit the timing belt upper cover, and the alternator. Refit the coolant pump pulley, and tighten the bolts as far as possible for now – once the auxiliary drivebelt has been fitted it will be easier to tighten the bolts to the specified torque.

All engines

38 The remainder of refitting is a reversal of removal.

9 Timing belt tensioner and sprockets – removal, inspection and refitting

Tensioner pulley

1 Remove the auxiliary drivebelt as described in Chapter 1A Section 26.

2 Remove the timing belt upper cover as described in Section 7.

3 As a precaution against losing the valve timing, use string to tie the front and rear runs of the timing belt together. This will ensure that the belt remains engaged with the camshaft sprockets while the tensioner pulley is removed.

4 Push the tensioner pulley rearwards to detension the belt, then insert Ford tool No 303-1054 or a suitable equivalent into the pulley arm to lock it in position **(see illustration 8.10)**.

5 Undo the tensioner pulley centre mounting bolt and withdraw the unit from the engine.

6 While the tensioner pulley is removed, make sure that the timing belt remains fully engaged with the camshaft and crankshaft sprockets.

7 Spin the tensioner pulley, and check that

it turns freely without any roughness or tightness. Do not attempt to clean the pulley by immersing in any cleaning fluid. **Note:** *It is recommended that a new tensioner is fitted, regardless of the apparent condition of the old one. If the tensioner were to seize or break up in service, the resulting damage to the timing belt could lead to serious engine damage.*

8 Clean the cylinder block in the area of the tensioner.

9 Locate the tensioner pulley in position ensuring that the lug on the tensioner mounting plate engages with the square hole on the cylinder block **(see illustration)**. Insert the mounting bolt and tighten it to the specified torque.

10 Remove the locking pin from the tensioner, and allow it to tension the belt.

11 Remove the string used to tie the front and rear runs of the timing belt together.

12 Provided that the timing belt has remained fully engaged with the camshaft and crankshaft sprockets, it should not be necessary to check the valve timing. However, if there is any doubt, check the valve timing as described in Section 3.

13 Refit the timing belt upper cover as described in Section 7.

14 Fit a new auxiliary drivebelt as described in Chapter 1A Section 26.

Camshaft sprockets

Caution: The camshaft sprockets are made from a type of plastic. Care must be taken to avoid damage to the sprockets during the following procedure.

9.9 The lug on the tensioner mounting plate (arrowed) must locate in the square hole (arrowed) in the cylinder block

9.16a Unscrew the bolt …

9.16b … and remove the camshaft sprocket

9.18 Counterhold the camshaft with a spanner on the hexagonal section, then unscrew the blanking plug from the VCT unit

15 Remove the timing belt as described in Section 8.

1.25 and 1.4 litre engines

16 Unscrew the bolts and remove the sprockets from the camshafts (see illustrations).

1.6 litre engines

17 Remove the cylinder head cover as described in Section 4.
18 Counterhold the camshafts using an open-ended spanner on the hexagonal sections, then unscrew the blanking plugs from the centre of the VCT units (see illustration).
19 Still counterholding the camshafts, slacken and remove the VCT units' centre Torx bolts (see illustrations). Remove the VCT units from the ends of the camshafts.

All engines

20 Examine the teeth of the sprockets for wear and damage, and renew them if necessary.

9.19a Unscrew the Torx bolt …

9.19b … and pull the VCT unit from the camshaft

1.25 and 1.4 litre engines

21 Locate the sprockets on the camshafts, and screw in the retaining bolts loosely.
22 Fit the timing belt as described in Section 8.

1.6 litre engines

23 Insert Ford tool No 303-376B into the slots in the left-hand ends of the camshafts. If the Ford setting tool 303-376B is unavailable, a home-made tool can be fabricated out of a length of flat metal bar 20 mm thick (see illustrations).
24 Locate the VCT units on the ends of the camshafts, but only finger-tighten the retaining bolts at this stage. Ensure the timing marks on the VCT units (dot on the inlet sprocket, groove on the exhaust sprocket) are at the 12 o'clock position (see illustration).
25 Fit the VCT locking tool (No 303-1097) over the units (see illustrations 3.18a and 3.18b). Note how the dots/holes on the VCT units align with the groove/dot on the sprockets (see illustration).

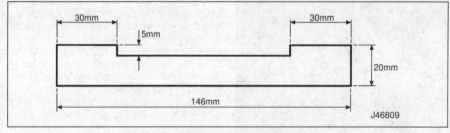

9.23a Camshaft setting tool dimensions

Drawing not to scale

9.23b Fit the setting tool into the slots in the end of the camshafts

9.24 Ensure the groove (1) on the exhaust VCT unit and the dot (2) on the inlet unit are at the 12 o'clock position

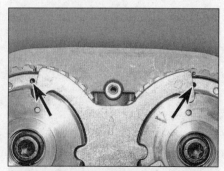

9.25 Note how the dots/holes on the VCT units align with the groove/dot on the sprockets (arrowed)

9.29a Renew the seal if necessary ...

9.29b ... then refit the plugs to the VCT units

9.32 Slide the sprocket from the end of the crankshaft

26 Tighten each VCT unit retaining bolt to the specified Stage 1 torque.

27 Remove the camshaft setting bar and the VCT locking tool, then counterhold the camshafts using a spanner on the hexagonal section, and tighten each VCT unit retaining bolt to the specified Stage 2 angle setting using an angle-tightening gauge. Do not allow the camshafts to rotate.

28 Refit the VCT locking tool, and check the marks on the sprockets align with the marks on the VCT units **(see illustration 9.25)**. If not, repeat the VCT unit refitting procedure.

29 If the timing is correct, counterhold the camshafts using a spanner on the hexagonal section, and fit the each VCT unit blanking plug. Tighten each plug to the specified

torque. Renew the plug seal if necessary **(see illustrations)**.

30 Fit the timing belt as described in Section 8, and the cylinder head cover as described In Section 4.

Crankshaft sprocket

31 Remove the timing belt as described in Section 8.

32 Slide the sprocket off the end of the crankshaft **(see illustration)**.

33 Examine the teeth of the sprocket for wear and damage, and renew if necessary.

34 Wipe clean the end of the crankshaft, then slide on the sprocket.

35 Refit the timing belt as described in Section 8.

10 Camshaft oil seals – renewal

1 Remove the camshaft sprockets or VCT units as described in Section 9.

2 Note the fitted depths of the oil seals as a guide for fitting the new ones.

3 Using a screwdriver or similar tool, carefully prise the oil seals from the cylinder head/camshaft bearing caps. Take care not to damage the oil seal contact surfaces on the ends of the camshafts or the oil seal seatings. An alternative method of removing the seals is to drill a small hole, then insert a self-tapping screw and use pliers to pull out the seal **(see illustrations)**.

4 Wipe clean the oil seal seatings and also the ends of the camshafts.

5 Apply a little clean engine oil to the seal lip, then locate it over the camshaft and into the cylinder head/camshaft bearing cap. Make sure that the closed end of the oil seal faces outwards **(see illustration)**.

6 Using a socket or length of metal tubing, drive the oil seals squarely into position to the previously-noted depths. Wipe away any excess oil **(see illustration)**.

7 Refit the camshaft sprockets or VCT units as described in Section 9.

10.3a Drill a small hole and insert a self-tapping screw ...

10.3b ... then pull out the oil seal using a pair of pliers

11 Camshafts and tappets – removal, inspection and refitting

Removal

1 Before removing the camshafts, it may be useful to check and record the valve clearances as described in Section 5. If any clearance is not within limits, new tappets can be obtained and fitted.

2 Remove the camshaft oil seals as described in Section 10.

3 The camshaft bearing caps are marked for position – the inlet caps have the letter I and exhaust caps have the letter E. On the project car these were not very clear, and if this is the case, mark them using paint or a marker

10.5 Locate the new oil seal into the cylinder/camshaft bearing cap

10.6 Drive the new seal into position with a socket

11.3a No 3 inlet camshaft bearing cap

11.3b No 3 exhaust camshaft bearing cap

11.3c Number the bearing caps with paint if they are not clearly marked

pen. Make sure they are identified for inlet and exhaust camshafts (see illustrations).

4 Position the crankshaft so that No 1 piston is approximately 25 mm before TDC. This can be done by starting from the TDC position; carefully insert a large screwdriver down No 1 cylinder spark plug hole until the tip touches the top of the piston, and turn the engine anti-clockwise until the screwdriver shaft has descended 25 mm.

5 Position the camshafts so that none of the valves are at full lift (ie, fully-open, being heavily pressed down by the cam lobes). To do this, turn each camshaft using a spanner on the hexagon flats provided.

6 Progressively loosen the camshaft bearing cap retaining bolts, working in a diagonal sequence. Work gradually and evenly to release the pressure of the valve springs on the caps (see illustration).

7 Withdraw the caps, keeping them in order to aid refitting, then lift the camshafts from the cylinder head. The exhaust camshaft can be identified by the reference lobe for the camshaft position sensor on 1.25 and 1.4 litre engines, therefore, there is no need to mark the camshafts; on 1.6 litre engines, the inlet camshaft is marked 7A and the exhaust marked 3A (see illustrations). Note: On 1.6 litre engines, renew the O-ring between the right-hand bearing cap and the cylinder head (see illustration).

8 Obtain sixteen small, clean containers, and number them 1 to 8 for both the inlet and exhaust camshafts. Lift the tappets one by one from the cylinder head.

Inspection

9 With the camshafts and tappets removed, check each for signs of obvious wear (scoring, pitting, etc) and for ovality, and renew if necessary.

10 Visually examine the camshaft lobes for score marks, pitting, and evidence of overheating (blue, discoloured areas). Look for flaking away of the hardened surface layer of each lobe. If any such signs are evident, renew the component concerned.

11 Examine the camshaft bearing journals and the cylinder head bearing surfaces for signs of obvious wear or pitting. If any such signs are evident, renew the component concerned.

12 To check camshaft endfloat, remove the tappets, clean the bearing surfaces carefully, and refit the camshafts and bearing caps. Tighten the bearing cap bolts to the specified

torque wrench setting, then measure the endfloat using a dial gauge mounted on the cylinder head so that its tip bears on the camshaft right-hand end.

13 Tap the camshaft fully towards the gauge, zero the gauge, then tap the camshaft fully away from the gauge, and note the gauge reading. If the endfloat measured is found to be more than the typical value given, fit a new camshaft and repeat the check; if the clearance is still excessive, the cylinder head must be renewed.

Refitting

14 Lubricate the cylinder head tappet bores and the tappets with engine oil. Carefully refit the tappets to the cylinder head, ensuring each tappet is refitted to its original bore. Some care will be needed to enter the tappets squarely into their bores.

11.6 Undo the camshaft bearing cap bolts ...

11.7a ... withdraw the caps ...

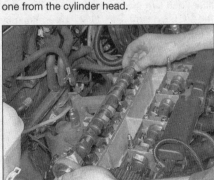
11.7b ... then remove the camshafts

11.7c The exhaust camshaft is marked 3A – 1.6 litre engines

11.7d On 1.6 litre engines, recover the O-ring seal under the right-hand (No 1) bearing cap

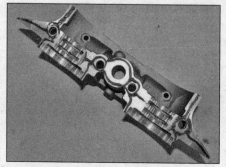

11.15 The slots in the end of the camshafts should be just above, and approximately parallel to the cylinder head upper surface

11.17 Apply a thin bead of sealant (see text) to the underside of the bearing cap(s) at the timing belt end of the engine as shown

11.18 Oil the camshaft bearing surfaces

15 Liberally oil the camshaft bearings and lobes. Ensuring that each camshaft is in its original location, refit the camshafts, locating each so that the slot in its left-hand end is approximately parallel to, and just above, the cylinder head mating surface. At this stage, position the camshafts so that none of the valves are at full lift – see paragraph 5 **(see illustration)**.
16 Clean the mating faces of the cylinder head and camshaft bearing caps.
17 Apply a thin smear of suitable sealant (Ford recommend WSK-M2G348-A5 or Loctite 518) to the camshaft bearing caps at the timing belt end of the engine only **(see illustration)**. On 1.6 litre engines, renew the O-ring seal beneath the timing belt end bearing cap **(see illustration 11.7d)**.
18 Oil the bearing surfaces, then locate the camshaft bearing caps on the camshafts and insert the retaining bolts loosely. Make sure that each cap is located in its previously-noted position **(see illustration)**.
19 Ensuring each cap is kept square to the cylinder head as it is tightened down, and working in a diagonal sequence, tighten the camshaft bearing cap bolts slowly and by one turn at a time, until each cap touches the cylinder head. Next, go round again in the same diagonal sequence, tightening the bolts to the specified Stage 1 torque wrench setting. Note that on 1.6 litre engines, the torque wrench setting for the bearing cap bolts at the timing belt end of the engine are different to all the other caps.

12.17 Check the cylinder head gasket face for distortion using a straight-edge

20 Still working in a diagonal sequence, tighten the bolts further to the specified Stage 2 angle. It is recommended that an angle gauge is used for this, to ensure accuracy. Again, note that on 1.6 litre engines, the angle settings for the bearing cap bolts at the timing belt end of the engine are different to all the other caps.
21 Wipe off all surplus sealant, and check the valve clearances as described in Section 5.
22 Fit new camshaft oil seals as described in Section 10.

12 Cylinder head – removal, inspection and refitting

Removal

1 Depressurise the fuel system as described in Chapter 4A Section 2.
2 Drain the cooling system as described in Chapter 1A Section 31.
3 Disconnect the battery negative terminal (refer to 'Disconnecting the battery').
4 Remove the inlet manifold and exhaust manifold as described in Chapter 4A.
5 Remove the camshafts and tappets as described in Section 11.
6 Remove the inlet manifold support bolt from the front of the engine at the timing belt end. Lower the car to the ground.
7 Make a note of their fitted locations and the harness routing, then disconnect any wiring plugs attached to components on the cylinder head. Label the plugs if necessary to aid refitting.
8 Unbolt the timing belt rear cover, which is secured by three bolts.
9 Release the spring-type clip and disconnect the coolant pipe from the left-hand rear of the cylinder head.
10 Undo the 4 bolts and detach the coolant housing from the left-hand end of the cylinder head.
11 Make a last check round the cylinder head, to ensure that nothing remains connected or attached which would prevent the head from being lifted off. Prepare a clean surface to lay the head down on once it has been removed.

12 Working in the reverse of the tightening sequence **(see illustration 12.26a or 12.26b)**, slacken the ten cylinder head bolts progressively and by half a turn at a time; a Torx key (TX 55 size) will be required. Remove all the bolts.
13 Lift the cylinder head away; use assistance if possible, as it is a heavy assembly. Remove the gasket, noting the two dowels. Although the gasket cannot be re-used, it is advisable to retain it for comparison with the new one, to confirm that the right part has been supplied.

Inspection

14 The mating faces of the cylinder head and cylinder block must be perfectly clean before refitting the head. Use a hard plastic or wood scraper to remove all traces of gasket and carbon; also clean the piston crowns. Take particular care during the cleaning operations, as aluminium alloy is easily damaged.
15 Make sure that the carbon is not allowed to enter the oil and coolant passages – this is particularly important for the lubrication system, as carbon could block the oil supply to the engine's components. Using adhesive tape and paper, seal the coolant, oil and bolt holes in the cylinder block. To prevent carbon entering the gap between the pistons and bores, smear a little grease in the gap. After cleaning each piston, use a small brush to remove all traces of grease and carbon from the gap, then wipe away the remainder with a clean rag. Note that 1.6 litre engines have a filter fitted into the oil supply galleries feeding the VCT system. This filter is permanently installed and cannot be removed.
16 Check the mating surfaces of the cylinder block and the cylinder head for nicks, deep scratches and other damage. If slight, they may be removed carefully with a file, but if excessive, renewal is necessary as it is not permissible to machine the surfaces.
17 If warpage of the cylinder head gasket surface is suspected, use a straight-edge to check it for distortion **(see illustration)**. Refer to Part D of this Chapter if necessary.
18 If possible, clean out the bolt holes in the block using compressed air, to ensure no oil or coolant is present. Screwing a bolt into an oil- or coolant-filled hole can (in extreme

12.23 Locate the new cylinder head gasket over the dowels

cases) cause the block to fracture, due to the hydraulic pressure created.

19 Although not essential, if a suitable tap-and-die set is available, it's worth running the correct-size tap down the bolt threads in the cylinder block. This will clean the threads of any debris, and go some way to restoring any damaged threads. Make absolutely sure the tap is the right size and thread pitch, and lightly oil the tap before starting.

20 Ford insist that the cylinder head bolts must be renewed.

Refitting

21 Wipe clean the mating surfaces of the cylinder head and cylinder block, and check that the two locating dowels are in position in the block.

22 Turn the crankshaft anti-clockwise so that pistons 1 and 4 are approximately 25 mm before TDC, in order to avoid the risk of valve/piston contact. Turn the crankshaft using a spanner on the pulley bolt.

23 If the old gasket is still available, check that it is identical to the new one – for instance, there are several different thicknesses of gasket, indicated by the number of small holes on one side. Position the new gasket

over the dowels on the cylinder block surface. It can only be fitted one way round – check carefully that the holes in the gasket align with the holes in the block surface, and that none are blocked **(see illustration)**.

24 It is useful when refitting a cylinder head to have an assistant on hand to help guide the head onto the dowels. Take care that the gasket does not get moved as the head is lowered into position. To confirm that the head is aligned correctly, once it is in place, temporarily slide in two or more of the head bolts, and check that they fit into the block holes.

25 Fit the new head bolts carefully, and screw them in by hand only until finger-tight.

26 Working progressively and in sequence, tighten the cylinder head bolts to their Stage 1 torque setting **(see illustrations)**.

27 Next, go around again in the same sequence, and tighten the bolts to the Stage 2 setting, then to the Stage 3 setting.

28 Finally, the bolts should be angle-tightened further, by the specified Stage 4 amount, using an angle-tightening gauge **(see illustration)**.

29 The remainder of refitting is a reversal of removal, noting the following points:

a) Refit the camshafts and tappets as described in Section 11, and the timing belt as described in Section 8.
b) Refit the inlet and exhaust manifolds as described in Chapter 4A.
c) Tighten all fasteners to the specified torque, where given.
d) Ensure that all hoses and wiring are correctly routed, and that hose clips and wiring connectors are securely refitted.
e) Refill the cooling system as described in Chapter 1A Section 31.
f) Check all disturbed joints for signs of oil or coolant leakage once the engine has been restarted and warmed-up to normal operating temperature.

13 Sump – removal and refitting

Removal

1 Apply the handbrake, then jack up the front of the car and support it on axle stands (see 'Jacking and vehicle support').

2 Drain the engine oil, then check the drain plug sealing washer and renew if necessary. Clean and refit the engine oil drain plug together with the washer, and tighten it to the specified torque wrench setting. Although not strictly necessary, as the oil is being drained, it makes sense to fit a new oil filter at the same time (see Chapter 1A Section 6).

3 Release the clip, undo the retaining bolt, and pull the engine oil level dipstick guide tube from the sump. Check the condition of the seal at the base of the tube, and renew it if necessary.

4 Unscrew the bolts securing the transmission to the sump, then progressively unscrew the sump-to-block bolts.

5 On these models, a sump gasket is not used, and sealant is used instead. Unfortunately, the use of sealant makes removal of the sump more difficult. If care is taken not to damage the surfaces, the sealant can be cut around using a sharp knife.

6 On no account lever between the mating faces, as this will almost certainly damage them, resulting in leaks when finished. Ford technicians have a tool comprising a metal rod which is inserted through the sump drain hole, and a handle to pull the sump downwards. Providing care is taken not to damage the threads, a large screwdriver could be used in the drain hole to prise down the sump.

7 While the sump is removed, take the opportunity to remove the oil pump pick-up/strainer pipe, and clean it with reference to Section 14.

Refitting

8 Thoroughly clean the contact surfaces of the sump and crankcase. Take care not to damage the oil pump gasket or the crankshaft oil seal, both of which are partially exposed

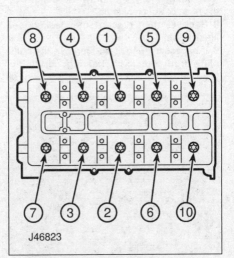

12.26a Cylinder head bolt tightening sequence – 1.25 and 1.4 litre engines

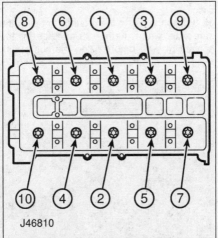

12.26b Cylinder head bolt tightening sequence – 1.6 litre engines

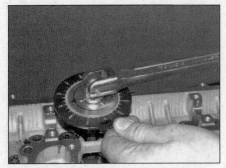

12.28 Use an angle-gauge for the final stage

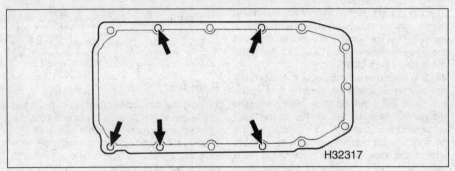

13.9 Sump alignment stud positions (arrowed)

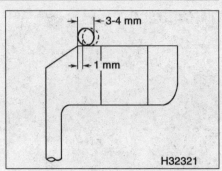

13.10 Apply the bead of sealant to the sump mating surface as shown

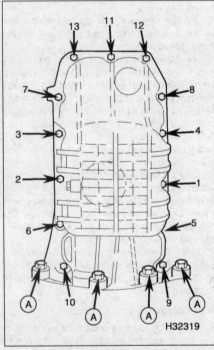

13.13 Sump bolt tightening sequence. Also shows sump-to-transmission bolts (A)

when the sump is removed. If necessary, use a cloth rag to clean inside the sump and crankcase. If the oil pump pick-up/strainer pipe was removed, fit a new O-ring and refit the pipe with reference to Section 14.

9 Ford state that, to refit the sump, five M8x20 studs must be screwed into the base of the engine **(see illustration)**. This not only helps to align the sump, ensuring that the bead of sealant is not displaced as the sump is fitted, but also ensures that the sealant does not enter the blind holes. Cut a slot across the end of each stud, to make removal easier when the sump is in place.

10 Apply a 3 to 4 mm diameter bead of sealant (Ford recommend WSE M4G323-A4, or equivalent) to the sump pan, to the inside of the bolt holes **(see illustration)**. The sump bolts must be fitted and tightened within 10 minutes of applying the sealant.

11 Offer the sump up into position over the studs, and fully refit the remaining bolts by hand. Unscrew the studs, and refit the sump bolts in their place. The sump should be fitted flush with the block at the transmission end.

12 Insert the four sump-to-transmission bolts and tighten them to the specified torque.

13 The sump-to-crankcase bolts are tightened in two stages. Working in sequence **(see illustration)**, tighten all the sump bolts to the specified Stage 1 torque, then go around again in sequence, and tighten them to the Stage 2 setting.

14 Refit the engine oil level dipstick guide tube, with a new seal where necessary, and tighten the retaining bolt securely. Replace the clip.

15 Lower the car to the ground. To be on the safe side, wait a further 30 minutes for the sealant to cure before filling the sump with fresh oil, as described in Chapter 1A Section 6.

16 Finally start the engine and check for signs of oil leaks.

14 Oil pump – removal, inspection and refitting

Removal

1 Remove the crankshaft right-hand oil seal as described in Section 16.

2 Remove the sump as described in Section 13.

3 Undo the timing belt rear cover lower 2 bolts.

4 On models with air conditioning, remove the four bolts securing the air conditioning compressor, and tie it up clear of the engine without disconnecting any of the hoses.

5 Unscrew the bolts securing the oil pump pick-up/strainer pipe to the baffle plate/main bearing cap.

6 Unscrew the bolt securing the oil pump pick-up/strainer pipe to the oil pump, then withdraw the pipe and recover the sealing O-ring **(see illustration)**. Discard the O-ring.

7 Unscrew the bolts securing the oil pump to the cylinder block/crankcase, noting the locations of the three different lengths of bolt **(see illustration)**. Withdraw the pump over the nose of the crankshaft.

8 Recover then discard the gasket **(see illustration)**.

9 If necessary, unbolt and remove the baffle plate from the main bearing cap/ladder **(see illustration)**. Thoroughly clean all

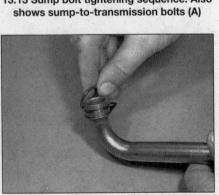

14.6 Remove the O-ring seal from the oil pump pick-up/strainer pipe

14.7 Remove the oil pump-to cylinder block/crankcase bolts

14.8 Remove the oil pump gasket

14.9 Unbolt the baffle plate from the main bearing cap/ladder

15.4 Oil pressure switch (arrowed)

16.6 Locate the new right-hand oil seal over the crankshaft

components, particularly the mating surfaces of the pump, the sump, and the cylinder block/crankcase.

Inspection

10 It is not possible to obtain individual components of the oil pump, furthermore, there are no torque settings available for tightening the pump cover plate bolts. However, the following procedure is provided for owners wishing to dismantle the oil pump for examination.

11 Take out the bolts, and remove the pump cover plate; noting any identification marks on the rotors, withdraw the rotors.

12 Inspect the rotors for obvious signs of wear or damage, and renew if necessary; if either rotor, the pump body, or its cover plate are scored or damaged, the complete oil pump assembly must be renewed.

13 The oil pressure relief valve can be dismantled as follows.

14 Unscrew the threaded plug, and recover the valve spring and plunger. If the plug's sealing O-ring is worn or damaged, a new one must be obtained, to be fitted on reassembly.

15 Reassembly is the reverse of the dismantling procedure; ensure the spring and valve are refitted the correct way round, and tighten the threaded plug securely.

Refitting

16 If removed, refit the oil baffle plate to the crankcase and tighten the bolts.

17 The oil pump must be primed on installation, by pouring clean engine oil into it and rotating its inner rotor a few turns.

18 Use a little grease to stick the new gasket in place on the cylinder block/crankcase.

19 Offer the oil pump over the nose of the crankshaft, and turn the inner rotor as necessary to align its flats with the flats on the crankshaft. Locate the pump on the dowels, then insert the retaining bolts in their previously-noted locations and progressively tighten them to the specified torque.

20 Locate a new O-ring (dipped in oil) on the pick-up/strainer pipe, then locate the pipe in the oil pump and insert the retaining bolts. Insert the bolts retaining the pipe on the baffle plate/main bearing cap. Tighten the bolts to the specified torque.

21 Where removed, refit the air conditioning compressor, tightening the bolts to the specified torque.

22 Refit the sump as described in Section 13.

23 Fit a new crankshaft oil seal as described in Section 16.

15 Oil pressure switch – removal and refitting

1 The oil pressure switch is a vital early warning of low oil pressure. The switch operates the oil warning light on the instrument panel – the light should come on with the ignition, and go out almost immediately when the engine starts.

2 If the light does not come on, there could be a fault on the instrument panel, the switch wiring, or the switch itself. If the light does not go out, low oil level, worn oil pump (or sump pick-up blocked), blocked oil filter, or worn main bearings could be to blame – or again, the switch may be faulty.

3 If the light comes on while driving, the best advice is to turn the engine off immediately, and not to drive the car until the problem has been investigated – ignoring the light could mean expensive engine damage.

Removal

4 The oil pressure switch is located on the front face of the engine, above the oil filter (see illustration).

5 Disconnect the wiring plug from the switch.

6 Unscrew the switch from the block, and remove it. There should only be a very slight loss of oil when this is done.

Inspection

7 Examine the switch for signs of cracking or splits. If the top part of the switch is loose, this is an early indication of impending failure.

8 Check that the wiring terminals at the switch are not loose, then trace the wire from the switch connector until it enters the main loom – any wiring defects will give rise to apparent oil pressure problems.

Refitting

9 Refitting is the reverse of the removal procedure, noting the following points:

a) Tighten the switch securely.
b) Reconnect the switch connector, making sure it clicks home properly. Ensure that the wiring is routed away from any hot or moving parts.
c) Check the engine oil level and top-up if necessary (see ' Weekly checks0,5 ').
d) Check for signs of oil leaks once the engine has been restarted and warmed-up to normal operating temperature.

16 Crankshaft oil seals – renewal

Right-hand oil seal

1 Remove the crankshaft sprocket as described in Section 9.

2 As a safety precaution, refit the engine right- hand mounting upper section and mounting bracket, and tighten the mounting bolts/nuts.

3 Note the fitted depth of the oil seal as a guide for fitting the new one.

4 Using a screwdriver, prise the old oil seal from the oil pump housing. Take great care not to damage the seal contact surface on the nose of the crankshaft, or the seating in the housing.

5 Wipe clean the seating and the nose of the crankshaft.

6 Apply a little clean engine oil to the inner lip of the seal, then locate it over the crankshaft and into the oil pump housing. Make sure that the closed end of the oil seal faces outwards (see illustration).

7 Using a socket or length of metal tubing, drive the oil seal squarely into position to the previously-noted depth. The Ford installation tool (303-395) is used together with an old crankshaft pulley bolt to press the oil seal into position. The same idea may be used with metal tubing and a large washer – do not use a new crankshaft pulley bolt, as it is only permissible to use the bolt once. With the oil seal in position, wipe away any excess oil.

8 With the weight of the engine once more supported, unscrew the nuts and bolts and remove the engine right-hand mounting upper section and mounting bracket.

16.15 Locate the new oil seal housing (complete with fitting sleeve) over the end of the crankshaft

9 Refit the crankshaft sprocket with reference to Section 9.

Left-hand oil seal

10 Remove the flywheel/driveplate as described in Section 17.
11 Remove the sump as described in Section 13.
12 Unscrew the six bolts and withdraw the oil seal carrier from the end of the crankshaft. Note that the seal and carrier are made as one unit – it is not possible to obtain the seal separately.
13 Clean the carrier contact surface on the cylinder block, and the end of the crankshaft.
14 The new oil seal carrier is supplied complete with a fitting sleeve, which ensures that the oil seal lips are correctly located on the crankshaft. Ford state that neither the crankshaft nor the new oil seal should be lubricated before fitting.
15 Locate the oil seal carrier and fitting sleeve over the end of the crankshaft. Press the carrier into position, noting that the centre bolt holes are formed into locating dowels **(see illustration)**.
16 Insert the retaining bolts and progressively tighten them to the specified torque.
17 Remove the fitting sleeve and check that the oil seal lips are correctly located **(see illustration)**.
18 Refit the sump as described in Section 13.
19 Refit the flywheel/driveplate as described in Section 17.

17.2 Home-made flywheel locking tool

16.17 With the oil seal housing bolted into position, remove the fitting ring

17 Flywheel/driveplate – removal, inspection and refitting

Removal

1 Remove the transmission as described in Chapter 7A or 7B, and the clutch as described in Chapter 6 Section 6 on manual transmission models.
2 Hold the flywheel/driveplate stationary using one of the following methods:
a) If an assistant is available, insert one of the transmission mounting bolts into the cylinder block and have the assistant engage a wide-bladed screwdriver with the starter ring gear teeth while the bolts are loosened. Alternatively, a piece of angle-iron can be engaged with the ring gear and located against the transmission mounting bolt.
b) A further method is to fabricate a piece of flat metal bar with a pointed end to engage the ring gear – fit the tool to the transmission bolt and use washers and packing to align it with the ring gear, then tighten the bolt to hold it in position **(see illustration)**.
3 Unscrew and remove the bolts, then lift the flywheel/driveplate off the locating dowel on the crankshaft **(see illustration)**.

Inspection

4 Clean the flywheel/driveplate to remove grease and oil. Inspect the surface for cracks,

17.3 Remove the flywheel retaining bolts. Note the dowel (arrowed) in the end of the crankshaft

rivet grooves, burned areas and score marks. Light scoring can be removed with emery cloth. Check for cracked and broken ring gear teeth. Lay the flywheel/driveplate on a flat surface, and use a straight-edge to check for warpage.
5 Clean and inspect the mating surfaces of the flywheel/driveplate and the crankshaft. If the crankshaft oil seal is leaking, renew it (see Section 16) before refitting the flywheel/driveplate. In fact, given the large amount of work needed to remove the flywheel/driveplate, it's probably worth fitting a new seal anyway, as a precaution.
6 While the flywheel/driveplate is removed, clean carefully its inner face, particularly the recesses which serve as the reference points for the crankshaft speed/position sensor. Clean the sensor's tip, and check that the sensor is securely fastened. The sensor mounting may be removed if necessary by first removing the sensor, then unscrewing the bolt and withdrawing the mounting from the cylinder block **(see illustration)**.

Refitting

7 Make sure that the mating faces of the flywheel/driveplate and crankshaft are clean, then locate the flywheel/driveplate on the crankshaft and engage it with the locating dowel.
8 Insert the retaining bolts finger-tight.
9 Lock the flywheel/driveplate (see paragraph 2), then tighten the bolts in a diagonal sequence to the specified Stage 1 torque setting. Again, working in a diagonal sequence, tighten the bolts through the specified Stage 2 angle using an angle-tightening gauge.
10 Refit the clutch with reference to Chapter 6 Section 6, and the transmission as described in Chapter 7A or 7B.

18 Engine/transmission mountings – inspection and renewal

General

1 The engine/transmission mountings seldom require attention, but broken or deteriorated

17.6 Crankshaft position sensor mounting and retaining bolt

mountings should be renewed immediately, or the added strain placed on the driveline components may cause damage or wear.

2 While separate mountings may be removed and refitted individually, if more than one is disturbed at a time – such as if the engine/transmission unit is removed from its mountings – they must be reassembled and their fasteners tightened in the position marked on removal.

3 On reassembly, the complete weight of the engine/transmission unit must not be taken by the mountings until all are correctly aligned with the marks made on removal. Tighten the engine/transmission mounting fasteners to their specified torque wrench settings.

Inspection

4 During the check, the engine/transmission unit must be raised slightly, to remove its weight from the mountings.

5 Raise the front of the vehicle, and support it securely on axle stands. Position a jack under the sump, with a large block of wood between the jack head and the sump, then carefully raise the engine/transmission just enough to take the weight off the mountings.

 Warning: DO NOT place any part of your body under the engine when it is supported only by a jack.

6 Check the mountings to see if the rubber is cracked, hardened or separated from the metal components. Sometimes the rubber will split right down the centre.

7 Check for relative movement between each mounting's brackets and the engine/transmission or body (use a large screwdriver or lever to attempt to move the mountings). If movement is noted, lower the engine and check-tighten the mounting fasteners.

Renewal

Note: *The following paragraphs assume the engine is supported beneath the sump as described earlier.*

Right-hand mounting

8 Lift up the coolant expansion tank and

18.9 Right-hand engine mounting retaining nuts/bolts (arrowed)

position it to one side. Note there is no need to disconnect the coolant pipes.

9 Mark the position of the mounting on the vehicle, right-hand inner wing panel, then undo the two nuts securing the mounting to the engine bracket **(see illustration)**. Discard the nuts, new ones must be fitted.

10 Where fitted, undo the bolt securing the wiring harness to the engine mounting.

11 Undo the three retaining bolts securing the mounting to the inner wing panel and withdraw the mounting from the vehicle.

12 On refitting, tighten all fasteners to the torque wrench settings specified. Re-align the marks made on removal, then tighten the new mounting bracket retaining nuts.

Left-hand mounting

13 Remove the air cleaner assembly as described in Chapter 4A Section 5.

14 Remove the battery and battery tray as described in Chapter 5A Section 4. Note that it is not necessary to remove the powertrain control module from the battery tray, just position the tray clear for access to the mounting.

15 Undo the three nuts securing the battery tray support bracket in position. Release the wiring loom from the support bracket and lift the support bracket out of the engine compartment **(see illustration)**.

18.15 Undo the retaining nuts and lift out the battery tray support bracket

16 With the transmission supported, mark the position of the mounting bracket on the transmission and on the body sidemember. Undo the three bolts securing the mounting bracket to the transmission and the two bolts securing the mounting to the body sidemember **(see illustrations)**. Remove the mounting from the engine compartment.

17 On refitting, re-align the mounting in the position noted on removal, then tighten all fasteners to the specified torque wrench settings. Refit the components disturbed for access using a reversal of the removal procedures.

Rear mounting (roll restrictor)

18 To remove the engine rear mounting, apply the handbrake, then jack up the front of the car and support it on axle stands (see *'Jacking and vehicle support'*). Unscrew the through-bolts and remove the engine rear mounting link from the bracket on the transmission and from the bracket on the subframe **(see illustration)**. Hold the engine stationary while the bolts are being removed, since the link will be under tension.

19 On refitting, ensure that the bolts are securely tightened to the specified torque wrench setting.

18.16a Left-hand engine mounting bracket-to-transmission retaining bolts (arrowed) ...

18.16b ... and mounting-to-body sidemember retaining bolts (arrowed)

18.18 Rear mounting/roll restrictor retaining bolts (arrowed)

Chapter 2 Part B
1.4 litre (Stage IV emissions) diesel engine in-car repair procedures

Contents

Degrees of difficulty

Easy, suitable for novice with little experience	Fairly easy, suitable for beginner with some experience	Fairly difficult, suitable for competent DIY mechanic	Difficult, suitable for experienced DIY mechanic	Very difficult, suitable for expert DIY or professional

Specifications

General

Engine type.	Four-cylinder, in-line, single overhead camshaft
Designation	Duratorq TDCi
Engine code	F6JD and F6JB
Capacity	1399 cc
Bore	73.7 mm
Stroke	82.0 mm
Compression ratio	18.0: 1
Firing order	1-3-4-2 (No 1 cylinder at timing belt end)
Direction of crankshaft rotation	Clockwise (seen from right-hand side of car)
Emissions level	Stage IV

Compression pressures (engine hot, at cranking speed)

Normal	25 to 30 bar
Minimum	18 bar
Maximum difference between any two cylinders	5 bar

Camshaft

Endfloat	0.195 to 0.300 mm
Bearing journal diameter	23.959 to 23.980 mm

Lubrication system

Oil pump type	Gear type, driven directly by the right-hand end of the crankshaft, by two flats machined along the crankshaft journal

Oil pressure:
Idle	1.0 to 2.0 bar
2000 rpm	2.3 to 3.7 bar
Oil pressure warning switch operating pressure	0.8 bar

Torque wrench settings

	Nm	lbf ft
Auxiliary drivebelt tensioner	25	18
Big-end bolts: *		
Stage 1	10	7
Stage 2	Slacken 180°	
Stage 3	10	7
Stage 4	Angle-tighten a further 130°	
Camshaft bearing upper and lower housings	10	7
Camshaft position sensor bolt	5	4
Camshaft sprocket bolt	45	33
Coolant outlet housing bolts	10	7
Crankshaft position sensor bolt	5	4
Crankshaft pulley/sprocket bolt: *		
Stage IV emissions level models:		
Stage 1	30	22
Stage 2	Angle-tighten a further 180°	
Stage V emissions level models:		
Stage 1	35	25
Stage 2	Angle-tighten a further 190°	
Cylinder head bolts: *		
Stage 1	20	15
Stage 2	40	30
Stage 3	Angle-tighten a further 180°	
Cylinder head cover bolts	10	7
Engine mountings:		
Left-hand mounting to transmission	80	59
Left-hand mounting to body	80	59
Right-hand mounting bracket to engine	60	44
Right-hand mounting to engine bracket*	48	35
Right-hand mounting to body	48	35
Roll restrictor/rear mounting bolts	48	35
Engine-to-transmission bolts	48	35
Flywheel bolts: *		
Stage 1	30	22
Stage 2	Angle-tighten a further 90°	
Fuel pump mounting bracket	20	15
Fuel pump sprocket nut	50	37
High-pressure fuel pipe unions	25	18
Intermediate shaft centre bearing cap locknuts	25	18
Main bearing ladder outer (smaller) bolts	8	6
Main bearing ladder to cylinder block (M11 bolts): *		
Stage 1	10	7
Stage 2	Slacken 180°	
Stage 3	30	22
Stage 4	Angle-tighten a further 140°	
Piston oil jet spray tube bolt	20	15
Oil filter cover	25	18
Oil filter housing	10	7
Oil pick-up pipe	10	7
Oil pressure switch	25	18
Oil pump to cylinder block	10	7
Sump bolts/nuts	10	7
Sump drain plug	34	25
Timing belt covers	10	7
Timing belt idler pulley	37	27
Timing belt tensioner pulley	30	22
Vacuum pump	20	15

*Use new fasteners

1   General Information

How to use this Chapter

1 This Part of Chapter 2 is devoted to in-car repair procedures on the 1.4 litre Duratorq (68ps/67bhp) diesel engine. All procedures concerning engine removal, refitting, and overhaul can be found in Chapter 2F.

2 This engine is easily identified by the air filter assembly at the rear of the engine compartment. Refer to Vehicle identification numbers in the Reference Section at the end of this manual for details of engine code locations.

3 Most of the operations included in this Chapter are based on the assumption that the engine is still installed in the car. Therefore, if this information is being used during a complete engine overhaul, with the engine already removed, many of the steps included here will not apply.

Engine description

4 The Duratorq TDCi turbo-diesel engine was developed jointly by Ford and the Peugeot/Citroën group, and appears in several of the latest small Peugeot and Citroën models, where it is known as the 1.4 HDi engine. The engine is a single overhead camshaft eight-valve design, with four cylinders in-line, mounted transversely in the car, with the transmission on the left-hand side.

5 A toothed timing belt drives the camshaft, high-pressure fuel pump and coolant pump. The camshaft operates the inlet and exhaust valves via rocker arms, which are supported at their pivot ends by hydraulic self-adjusting tappets. The camshaft is supported by bearings machined directly in the cylinder head and camshaft bearing housing.

6 The high-pressure fuel pump supplies fuel to the fuel accumulator rail, and subsequently to the electronically-controlled injectors which inject the fuel directly into the combustion chambers. This 'common-rail' design differs from previous diesel engines, where an injection pump supplies the fuel at high pressure to each injector. The earlier, conventional type injection pump required fine calibration and timing, and these functions are now undertaken by the high-pressure pump, electronic injectors and engine management powertrain control module (PCM).

7 The crankshaft runs in five main bearings of the usual shell type. Endfloat is controlled by thrustwashers either side of No 2 main bearing.

8 The pistons are selected to be of matching weight, and incorporate fully-floating gudgeon pins retained by circlips.

9 The gear-type oil pump is fitted over the end of the crankshaft, and is driven by interlocking machined flats on the crankshaft and pump gear.

Precautions

10 The engine is a complex unit, with numerous accessories and ancillary components. The design of the engine compartment is such that every conceivable space has been utilised, and access to virtually all of the engine components is extremely limited. In many cases, ancillary components will have to be removed, or moved to one side, and wiring, pipes and hoses will have to be disconnected or removed from various cable clips and support brackets.

11 When working on this engine, read through the entire procedure first, look at the car and engine at the same time, and establish whether you have the necessary tools, equipment, skill and patience to proceed. Allow considerable time for any operation, and be prepared for the unexpected. Any major work on these engines is not for the faint-hearted!

12 Because of the limited access, many of the engine photographs appearing in this Chapter were, by necessity, taken with the engine removed from the car.

⚠️ *Warning: It is essential to observe strict precautions when working on the fuel system components of the engine, particularly the high-pressure side of the system. Before carrying out any engine operations that entail working on, or near, any part of the fuel system, refer to the special information given in Chapter 4B, Section 2.*

Operations with engine in car

a) Compression pressure – testing.
b) Cylinder head cover – removal and refitting.
c) Crankshaft pulley – removal and refitting.
d) Timing belt covers – removal and refitting.
e) Timing belt – removal, refitting and adjustment.
f) Timing belt tensioner and sprockets – removal and refitting.
g) Camshaft oil seal – renewal.
h) Camshaft, rocker arms and hydraulic tappets – removal, inspection and refitting.
i) Sump – removal and refitting.
j) Oil pump – removal and refitting.
k) Crankshaft oil seals – renewal.
l) Engine/transmission mountings – inspection and renewal.
m) Flywheel – removal, inspection and refitting.

2   Compression and leakdown tests – description and interpretation

Compression test

1 When engine performance is down, or if misfiring occurs which cannot be attributed to the fuel system, a compression test can provide diagnostic clues as to the engine's condition. If the test is performed regularly, it can give warning of trouble before any other symptoms become apparent.

2 The cause of poor compression is less easy to establish on a diesel engine than on a petrol one. The effect of introducing oil into the cylinders ('wet' testing) is not conclusive, because there is a risk that the oil will sit in the swirl chamber or in the recess on the piston crown instead of passing to the rings. However, the following can be used as a rough guide to diagnosis.

3 All cylinders should produce very similar pressures; any difference greater than that specified indicates the existence of a fault. Note that the compression should build-up quickly in a healthy engine; low compression on the first stroke, followed by gradually-increasing pressure on successive strokes, indicates worn piston rings. A low compression reading on the first stroke, which does not build-up during successive strokes, indicates leaking valves or a blown head gasket (a cracked head could also be the cause). Deposits on the undersides of the valve heads can also cause low compression.

4 A low reading from two adjacent cylinders is almost certainly due to the head gasket having blown between them; the presence of coolant in the engine oil will confirm this.

5 If the compression reading is unusually high, the cylinder head surfaces, valves and pistons are probably coated with carbon deposits. If this is the case, the cylinder head should be removed and decarbonised (see Part E).

6 A compression tester specifically intended for diesel engines must be used, because of the higher pressures involved. The tester is connected to an adapter which screws into the glow plug hole.

7 Note that It is necessary to disconnect certain wiring connectors in the engine management system to allow the compression test to be performed. This will log a fault code in the powertrain control module when the engine is turned over on the starter, and the fault code will have to be cleared, using Ford diagnostic equipment or a compatible alternative, on completion of the test. It may not be possible to start the engine until the fault code is cleared. For this reason primarily, but also due to the cost of purchasing a compression tester for occasional use, it is advisable to have the compression test carried out by a Ford dealer or suitably-equipped garage.

Leakdown test

8 A leakdown test measures the rate at which compressed air fed into the cylinder is lost. It is an alternative to a compression test, and in many ways it is better, since the escaping air provides easy identification of where pressure loss is occurring (piston rings, valves or head gasket).

9 The equipment needed for leakdown testing is unlikely to be available to the home mechanic. If poor compression is suspected, have the test performed by a Ford dealer or suitably-equipped garage.

3.8 Insert an 8 mm drill through the camshaft sprocket hole, into the corresponding hole in the cylinder head

3.9 Insert a 5 mm drill through the crankshaft sprocket flange hole, into the corresponding oil pump hole

into engagement with the cylinder head **(see illustration)**.

9 Insert a 5 mm diameter bolt, rod or drill through the hole in crankshaft sprocket flange and into the corresponding hole in the oil pump **(see illustration)**, if necessary, carefully turn the crankshaft either way until the rod enters the timing hole in the block.

10 The crankshaft and camshaft are now locked in position, preventing unnecessary rotation.

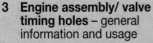

3 Engine assembly/ valve timing holes – general information and usage

Note: *Do not attempt to rotate the engine whilst the crankshaft and camshaft are locked in position. If the engine is to be left in this state for a long period of time, it is a good idea to place suitable warning notices inside the car, and in the engine compartment. This will reduce the possibility of the engine being accidentally cranked on the starter motor, which is likely to cause damage with the locking pins in place.*

1 Timing holes are located in the crankshaft sprocket flange, and in the camshaft sprocket hub. The holes are used to align the crankshaft and camshaft with the pistons halfway up the cylinder bores. This ensures that the valve timing is maintained during operations that require removal and refitting of the timing belt. When the holes are aligned with their corresponding holes in the cylinder block/head and flywheel, suitable-diameter bolts/pins can be inserted to lock the crankshaft and camshaft in position, preventing rotation.

2 Note that the fuel system on these engines uses a high-pressure fuel pump that does not have to be timed. The alignment of the fuel pump sprocket (and hence the fuel pump itself) with respect to crankshaft and camshaft position, is therefore less critical than on a conventional diesel engine.

3 To align the engine assembly/valve timing holes, proceed as follows.

4 Apply the handbrake, then jack up the front of the car and support it on axle stands (see *'Jacking and vehicle support'*). Remove the right-hand front roadwheel.

5 To gain access to the crankshaft pulley, to enable the engine to be turned, the wheel arch plastic liner must be removed. The liner is secured by several plastic expanding rivets. To remove the rivets, push in the centre pins a little, then prise the clips from place. Remove the liner from under the front wing. Where necessary, unclip the coolant hoses from under the wing to improve access further. The crankshaft can then be turned using a suitable socket and extension bar fitted to the pulley bolt.

6 Remove the timing belt upper and lower covers as described in Section 6.

7 Temporarily refit the crankshaft pulley bolt, remove the crankshaft locking tool, then turn the crankshaft until the timing hole in camshaft sprocket hub is aligned with the corresponding hole, in approximately the 2 o'clock position, in the cylinder head. Note that the crankshaft must always be turned in a clockwise direction (viewed from the right-hand side of vehicle). Use a small mirror so that the position of the sprocket hub timing slot can be observed. When the slot is aligned with the corresponding hole in the cylinder head, the camshaft is positioned correctly.

8 Insert an 8 mm bolt, rod or drill through the hole in the camshaft sprocket hub and

4 Cylinder head cover – removal and refitting

> ⚠️ **Warning: Refer to the precautionary information contained in Section 1 before proceeding.**

Removal

1 Disconnect the battery negative terminal (refer to *'Disconnecting the battery'*).

2 Remove the air cleaner assembly as described in Chapter 4B Section 4.

3 Slacken the retaining clip and disconnect the turbocharger outlet hose from the outlet flange adjacent to the oil filler cap **(see illustration)**.

4 Disconnect the wiring connector, then undo the retaining bolts, lift up the right-hand end and remove the resonator **(see illustrations)**. Recover the O-ring seal.

5 Remove the diesel fuel filter as described in Chapter 1B Section 22, then undo the three bolts securing the diesel filter support bracket.

6 Thoroughly clean the fuel return pipe connections on each injector. Prise out the retaining clips and disconnect the fuel return pipes from the injectors. Plug the openings to prevent dirt ingress.

7 Thoroughly clean the fuel hose quick-release connections on the high-pressure fuel pump. Plug the openings to prevent dirt ingress. Release the fuel feed and return pipes/hoses from the various clips on the cylinder head cover/inlet manifold and move the pipes/hoses to one side.

8 Disconnect the wiring plugs from the top of each injector, then make sure all wiring harnesses are freed from any retaining

4.3 Slacken the retaining clamps and disconnect the turbo outlet hose

4.4a Undo the bolts (arrowed) and lift up the right-hand end ...

4.4b ... to disengage the resonator box from the turbocharger

4.11a Undo the 8 bolts (arrowed) at the front …

4.11b … and the two bolts (arrowed) at the rear

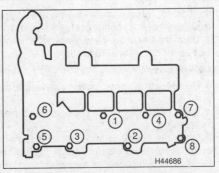

4.12 Cylinder head cover tightening sequence

brackets on the cylinder head cover/inlet manifold. Disconnect any vacuum pipes as necessary, having first noted their fitted positions.

9 Remove the timing belt upper cover, as described in Section 6.

10 Undo the two screws securing the EGR pipe to the cylinder head cover.

11 Undo the eight bolts securing the cylinder head cover and inlet manifold at the front, and the two retaining bolts along the rear edge of the cover. Lift the assembly away **(see illustrations)**. Recover the manifold rubber seals.

Refitting

12 Refitting is a reversal of removal, bearing in mind the following points:

a) *Examine the cover seal(s) for signs of damage and deterioration, and renew if necessary. Smear a little clean engine oil on the manifold seals.*

b) *Tighten the cylinder head cover bolts to the specified torque, in the order shown* **(see illustration)**.

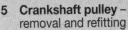

5 Crankshaft pulley – removal and refitting

Removal

1 Remove the auxiliary drivebelt as described in Chapter 1B Section 26. Turn the tensioner anti-clockwise, and insert a 3 mm diameter rod or drill bit to hold it away from the drivebelt **(see illustration)**.

2 To lock the crankshaft, working underneath the engine, insert a 12 mm rod or drill bit into the hole in the right-hand face of the engine block casting over the lower section of the flywheel. Rotate the crankshaft until the tool engages in the corresponding hole in the flywheel **(see illustration)**. **Note:** *The hole in the casting and the hole in the flywheel are provided purely to lock the crankshaft whilst the pulley bolt is undone. It does not position the crankshaft at TDC.*

3 Using a suitable socket and extension bar, unscrew the retaining bolt, remove the washer, then slide the pulley off the end of the crankshaft **(see illustration)**. If the pulley is tight fit, it can be drawn off the crankshaft

using a suitable puller. If a puller is being used, refit the pulley retaining bolt without the washer, to avoid damaging the crankshaft as the puller is tightened.

Caution: Do not touch the outer magnetic sensor ring of the sprocket with your fingers, or allow metallic particles to come into contact with it.

Refitting

4 Refit the pulley onto the crankshaft sprocket face, ensuring that the notch on the back of the pulley aligns with the key on the sprocket **(see illustration)**.

5 Thoroughly clean the threads of the pulley retaining bolt, then apply a coat of locking compound to the bolt threads.

6 Refit the crankshaft pulley retaining bolt and washer. Tighten the bolt to the specified torque, then through the specified angle,

5.1 Insert a drill or pin to lock the auxiliary drivebelt tensioner in position

5.3 Undo the crankshaft pulley retaining bolt

preventing rotation of the crankshaft using the locking rod method employed on removal.

7 Refit the auxiliary drivebelt as described in Chapter 1B Section 26.

6 Timing belt covers – removal and refitting

⚠ *Warning: Refer to the precautionary information contained in Section 1 before proceeding.*

Removal

Upper cover

1 Release the clips, move the coolant expansion tank to one side, then where

5.2 The locking pin/bolt (arrowed) must locate in the hole in the flywheel (arrowed) to prevent rotation

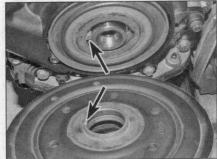

5.4 The notch in the pulley (arrowed) must align with the key in the sprocket (arrowed)

applicable, release the wiring harness from the upper cover – cut any cable-ties used.

2 Undo the five screws and remove the timing belt upper cover **(see illustration)**.

Lower cover

3 Remove the upper cover as described previously.

4 Remove the crankshaft pulley as described in Section 5.

5 Undo the five bolts and remove the lower cover **(see illustration)**. Detach the wiring harness from the cover as necessary.

Refitting

6 Refitting is a reversal of removal, ensuring that each cover section is correctly located, and that the cover retaining bolts are securely tightened. Ensure that all disturbed hoses are reconnected and retained by their relevant clips.

---

7 Timing belt –
removal and refitting

General

1 The timing belt drives the camshaft, high-pressure fuel pump and coolant pump from a toothed sprocket on the end of the crankshaft. If the belt breaks or slips in service, the pistons are likely to hit the valve heads, resulting in expensive damage.

2 The timing belt should be renewed at the specified intervals, or earlier if it is contaminated with oil or at all noisy in operation (a 'scraping' noise due to uneven wear).

3 If the timing belt is being removed, it is a wise precaution to check the condition of the coolant pump at the same time (check for signs of coolant leakage). This may avoid the need to remove the timing belt again at a later stage, should the coolant pump fail.

Removal

4 Disconnect the battery negative terminal (refer to 'Disconnecting the battery').

5 Lift the coolant expansion tank from its location and position it to one side.

7.11 Timing belt guide retaining bolt (arrowed)

6.2 Undo the five screws (arrowed) and remove the upper timing belt cover

6 Apply the handbrake, then jack up the front of the car and support it on axle stands (see 'Jacking and vehicle support'). Remove the front right-hand roadwheel, wheel arch liner (to expose the crankshaft pulley) and the engine undershield.

7 Remove the auxiliary drivebelt as described in Chapter 1B Section 26.

8 Remove the crankshaft pulley as described in Section 5.

9 Remove the timing belt upper and lower covers as described in Section 6.

10 Undo the bolt and remove the crankshaft position sensor adjacent to the crankshaft sprocket flange, and move it to one side.

11 Undo the retaining screw and remove the timing belt guide, again adjacent to the crankshaft sprocket flange **(see illustration)**.

12 Lock the crankshaft and camshaft in the correct position as described in Section 3. If necessary, temporarily refit the crankshaft pulley bolt to enable the crankshaft to be rotated.

13 Insert an Allen key into the hexagonal hole on the timing belt tensioner pulley. Slacken the tensioner pulley retaining bolt and allow the tensioner to rotate, relieving the belt tension **(see illustration)**. With the belt slack, temporarily tighten the pulley bolt. If the tensioner is being renewed with the belt, it can be removed completely.

14 Undo the crankshaft pulley bolt, and remove the crankshaft sprocket, recovering the Woodruff key.

Caution: Do not touch the outer magnetic sensor ring of the sprocket with your

7.13 Insert an Allen key into the hole (arrowed), slacken the pulley bolt and allow the tensioner to rotate

6.5 Lower cover retaining bolts (arrowed)

fingers, or allow metallic particles to come into contact with it.

15 Position a trolley jack under the engine, and using a block of wood on the jack head, take the weight of the engine.

16 Remove the locking tool from the camshaft sprocket.

17 With the engine securely supported, remove the three nuts and three bolts securing the right-hand mounting, and lift it off. Three new nuts should be obtained for refitting the mounting.

18 Unbolt the engine right-hand mounting bracket from the engine (four bolts).

19 Note its routing, then remove the timing belt from the sprockets.

Inspection

20 Renew the belt as a matter of course, regardless of its apparent condition. The cost of a new belt is nothing compared with the cost of repairs, should the belt break in service.

21 Check the old belt for signs of oil or coolant contamination – if any are found, trace the source of the leak and rectify it, then wash down the engine timing belt area and related components, to remove all traces of oil or coolant.

22 Check the sprockets for signs of wear or damage, and ensure that the tensioner and idler pulleys rotate smoothly; renew any worn or damaged components. Ford dealers (and many motor factors) now supply 'cambelt kits', consisting of the belt itself, a new tensioner and a new idler pulley – for peace of mind, it is recommended that one of these is purchased.

23 As stated previously, since the coolant pump is also driven by the timing belt, it pays to check its condition while the belt is off. If the pump pulley does not rotate freely and quietly, if there is the slightest sign of coolant leakage, or simply if the pump is known to have seen long service, it would make sense to fit a new pump at the same time (see Chapter 3 Section 7).

Refitting

24 Refit the Woodruff key to the crankshaft nose, then fit the crankshaft sprocket. Ensure that the crankshaft and camshaft timing holes are aligned, and refit the locking pins.

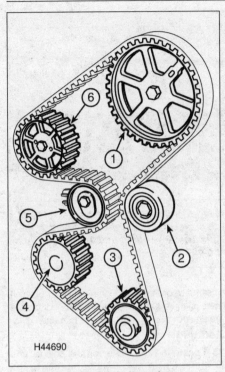

7.26 Timing belt routing

1 Camshaft sprocket
2 Idler pulley
3 Crankshaft sprocket
4 Coolant pump sprocket
5 Tensioner pulley
6 High-pressure fuel pump sprocket

25 Turn the fuel pump sprocket so that the two holes at the centre of the hub are aligned vertically.
26 Locate the timing belt on the crankshaft sprocket then, keeping it taut, locate it around the idler pulley, camshaft sprocket, fuel pump sprocket, coolant pump sprocket, and the tensioner roller (see illustration).
27 Refit the timing belt guide below the crankshaft sprocket, and tighten the retaining bolt securely.
28 Slacken the tensioner pulley bolt and, using an Allen key, rotate the tensioner anti-clockwise to tension the belt. As the belt is tensioned in this way, the tensioner's index

8.3 Undo the retaining bolt and remove the camshaft sprocket

7.28 Align the index arm (A) with the locating stud (B)

arm will move clockwise, until the index arm is aligned (see illustration).
29 Refit the engine right-hand mounting bracket, and tighten the bolts to the specified torque.
30 Refit the top section of the engine right-hand mounting bracket, using new nuts, and tightening the nuts and bolts to the specified torque. Now the trolley jack can be removed from under the car.
31 Remove the camshaft and crankshaft timing pins and temporarily refit the crankshaft pulley bolt to enable the crankshaft to be rotated. Using a socket on the crankshaft pulley bolt, rotate the engine clockwise ten complete revolutions. Refit the crankshaft and camshaft locking pins, and check that the fuel pump sprocket holes are aligned as described in paragraph 25.
32 Check that the tensioner index arm is still aligned between the sides of the 'window' behind it, and in line with the locating stud. If it is not, reset the tension as necessary, then repeat paragraph 31.
33 With the belt correctly fitted and tensioned, refit the crankshaft position sensor and tighten its retaining bolt securely.
34 Refit the timing belt lower and upper covers as described in Section 6, then refit the crankshaft pulley as described in Section 5.
35 Place the coolant expansion tank back in position, then refit the auxiliary drivebelt as described in Chapter 1B Section 26.

8.5 Align the sprocket lug with the notch in the end of the camshaft (arrowed)

A sprocket holding tool can be made from two lengths of steel strip bolted together to form a forked end. Bend the end of the strip through 90° to form the fork 'prongs'.

8 Timing belt sprockets and tensioner – removal and refitting

Camshaft sprocket

Removal

1 Remove the timing belt as described in Section 7.
2 Remove the locking tool from the camshaft sprocket. Slacken the sprocket retaining bolt – to prevent the camshaft rotating as the bolt is slackened, a sprocket-holding tool will be required (see Tool Tip 1). Do not try to use the tool in the timing hole to prevent the sprocket from rotating while the bolt is slackened.
3 Remove the sprocket retaining bolt, then slide the sprocket off the end of the camshaft (see illustration). Examine the camshaft oil seal for signs of oil leakage and, if necessary, renew it as described in Section 14.
4 Clean the camshaft sprocket thoroughly, and renew it if there are any signs of wear, damage or cracks.

Refitting

5 Refit the camshaft sprocket, aligning the lug on the back of the sprocket with the notch in the camshaft (see illustration).
6 Refit the sprocket retaining bolt, and tighten it to the specified torque, preventing the camshaft from turning as during removal.
7 Align the engine assembly/valve timing hole in the camshaft sprocket with the hole in the cylinder head, and refit the timing pin to lock the camshaft in position.
8 Refit the timing belt as described in Section 7.

Crankshaft sprocket

Removal

9 Remove the timing belt as described in Section 7.
10 Check that the engine assembly/valve timing holes are still aligned as described in Section 3.

8.17 Insert a suitable drill bit through the sprocket into the hole in the backplate

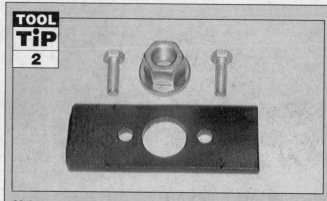

Make a sprocket releasing tool from a short strip of steel. Drill two holes in the strip to correspond with the two holes in the sprocket. Drill a third hole just large enough to accept the flats of the sprocket retaining nut.

11 Slide the sprocket off the end of the crankshaft, and recover the Woodruff key if it is loose.
12 Examine the crankshaft oil seal for signs of oil leakage and, if necessary, renew it as described in Section 14.
13 Clean the crankshaft sprocket thoroughly, and renew it if there are any signs of wear, damage or cracks.

Refitting

14 Refit the crankshaft sprocket, locating it over the Woodruff key.
15 Refit the timing belt as described in Section 7.

Fuel pump sprocket

Removal

16 Remove the timing belt as described in Section 7.
17 Using a suitable socket, undo the pump sprocket retaining nut. The sprocket can be held stationary by inserting a suitably-sized locking pin, drill or rod through the hole in the sprocket, and into the corresponding hole in the backplate (see illustration), or by using a suitable forked tool engaged with the holes in the sprocket (see Tool Tip 1).
18 The pump sprocket is a taper fit on the pump shaft, and it will be necessary to make up another tool to release it from the taper (see Tool Tip 2).
19 Partially unscrew the sprocket retaining nut, fit the home-made tool, and secure it to the sprocket with two suitable bolts. Prevent the sprocket from rotating as before, and unscrew the sprocket retaining nut. The nut will bear against the tool as it is undone, forcing the sprocket off the shaft taper. Once the taper is released, remove the tool, unscrew the nut fully, and remove the sprocket from the pump shaft.
20 Clean the sprocket thoroughly, and renew it if there are any signs of wear, damage or cracks.

Refitting

21 Refit the pump sprocket and retaining nut, and tighten the nut to the specified torque. Prevent the sprocket rotating using the sprocket holding tool as the nut is tightened.
22 Refit the timing belt as described in Section 7.

Coolant pump sprocket

23 The coolant pump sprocket is integral with the pump, and cannot be removed. Coolant pump removal is described in Chapter 3 Section 7.

Tensioner pulley

Removal

24 Remove the timing belt as described in Section 7.
25 Remove the tensioner pulley retaining bolt, and lift off the pulley.
26 Clean the tensioner pulley, but do not use any strong solvent which may enter the pulley bearings. Check that the pulley rotates freely, with no sign of stiffness or free play. Renew the pulley if there is any doubt about its condition, or if there are any obvious signs of wear or damage.
27 Examine the pulley mounting stud for signs of damage and if necessary, renew it.

Refitting

28 Refit the tensioner pulley ensuring that the pulley arm engages over the locating peg.
29 Refit and tension the timing belt as described in Section 7.

Idler pulley

Removal

30 Remove the timing belt as described in Section 7.
31 Undo the retaining nut and withdraw the idler pulley from the engine.
32 Clean the idler pulley, but do not use any strong solvent which may enter the bearings. Check that the pulley rotates freely, with no sign

of stiffness or free play. Renew the idler pulley if there is any doubt about its condition, or if there are any obvious signs of wear or damage.

Refitting

33 Locate the idler pulley on the engine, and fit the retaining nut. Tighten the nut to the specified torque.
34 Refit the timing belt as described in Section 7.

 9 Camshaft, rocker arms and hydraulic tappets – removal, inspection and refitting

Removal

1 Drain the cooling system as described in Chapter 1B Section 30.
2 Remove the cylinder head cover as described in Section 4.
3 Remove the camshaft sprocket as described in Section 8.
4 Refit the right-hand engine mounting, but only tighten the bolts moderately; this will keep the engine supported during the camshaft removal.
5 Undo the bolts and remove the vacuum pump. Recover the pump O-ring seals (see illustration).

9.5 Undo the vacuum pump bolts (arrowed)

9.7 Upper camshaft bearing housing bolts (arrowed)

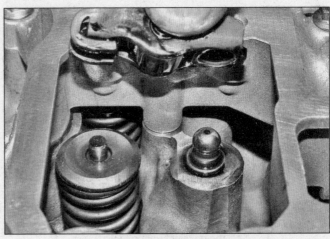

9.11 Remove the rocker arms

6 Disconnect the wiring plug, unscrew the retaining bolt, and remove the camshaft position sensor from the cylinder head.

7 Working in a spiral pattern, progressively and evenly unscrew the twelve camshaft upper bearing housing bolts **(see illustration)**. Carefully lift the housing away.

8 Note the orientation of the camshaft, then lift it upwards from the housing and slide off and discard the oil seal.

9 To remove the rocker arms and hydraulic tappets, undo the thirteen bolts and remove the lower half of the camshaft bearing housing.

10 Obtain eight small, clean plastic containers, and number them 1 to 8; alternatively, divide a larger container into eight compartments.

11 Lift out each rocker arm. Place the rocker arms in their respective positions in the box or containers **(see illustration)**.

12 A compartmentalised container filled with engine oil is now required to retain the hydraulic tappets while they are removed from the cylinder head (plastic egg boxes might be suitable). Withdraw each hydraulic tappet and place it in the container, keeping them each identified for correct refitting. The tappets must be totally submerged in the oil to prevent air entering them **(see illustration)**.

13 Recover the five O-ring seals between the housing and the cylinder head.

Inspection

14 Inspect the cam lobes and the camshaft bearing journals for scoring or other visible evidence of wear. Once the surface hardening of the cam lobes has been eroded, wear will occur at an accelerated rate. **Note:** *If these symptoms are visible on the tips of the camshaft lobes, check the corresponding rocker arm, as it will probably be worn as well.*

15 Examine the condition of the bearing surfaces in the cylinder head and camshaft bearing housing. If wear is evident, the cylinder head and bearing housing will both have to be renewed, as they are a matched assembly.

16 Inspect the rocker arms and tappets for scuffing, cracking or other damage and renew any components as necessary. Also check the condition of the tappet bores in the cylinder head. As with the camshafts, any wear in this area will necessitate cylinder head renewal.

Refitting

17 Thoroughly clean the sealant from the mating surfaces of the cylinder head and camshaft bearing housing. Use a suitable liquid gasket dissolving agent (available from motor factors) together with a soft putty knife; do not use a metal scraper, or the faces will be damaged. As there is no conventional gasket

used, the cleanliness of the mating faces is of the utmost importance.

18 Clean off any oil, dirt or grease from both components and dry with a clean lint-free cloth. Ensure that all the oilways are completely clean.

19 Ensure that the timing marks are aligned as described in Section 3 – in this position, the pistons are halfway down the cylinder bores.

20 Liberally lubricate the hydraulic tappet bores in the cylinder head with clean engine oil.

21 Insert the hydraulic tappets into their original bores in the cylinder head unless they have been renewed.

22 Lubricate the rocker arms, and place them over their respective tappets and valve stems.

23 Sparingly apply a bead of RTV sealant (such as Ford sealant WSE-M4G323-A4) to the mating face of the cylinder head-to-camshaft lower bearing housing, and position the five new O-ring seals **(see illustration)**. Make sure the sealant does not enter the blind holes in the cylinder head and housing, or damage may result. The housing should be fitted within four minutes of applying the sealant.

24 Insert two 12 mm rods or drill bits into the locating holes in the cylinder head to guide the bearing housing into position (Ford special tool number 303-034). Refit the lower bearing housing over the tools, insert the bolts and finger-tighten them in order **(see illustration)**.

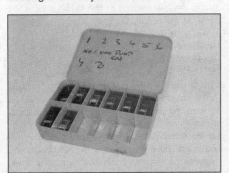

9.12 Place all the components in the respective positions in a box

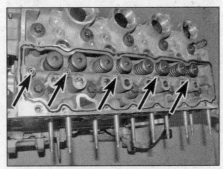

9.23 Apply a bead of sealant, and fit the new O-rings (arrowed)

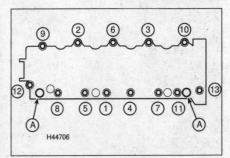

9.24 Insert guide pins/rods into the guide holes (A), fit the housing and tighten the bolts in sequence

9.27 Lay the camshaft in position, and apply a bead of sealant to the housing mating face

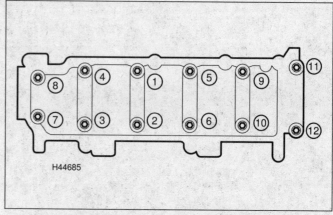

9.29 Upper camshaft housing bolts tightening sequence

25 Remove the guide pins/rods, and tighten the housing bolts in the previous sequence to the specified torque.
26 Lubricate the camshaft bearing journals with clean engine oil, and lay the camshaft in position.
27 Sparingly apply a bead of RTV sealant to the mating face of the camshaft lower bearing housing (see illustration).
28 Insert two 12 mm rods or drill bits into the locating holes in the lower camshaft bearing housing to guide the upper housing into position.
29 Lower the upper housing over the guide pins/rods, and finger-tighten the bolts gradually and evenly, in sequence, until the housing makes firm contact with the lower housing (see illustration).
30 Remove the guides pins/rods, and tighten the housing to the specified torque in the same sequence.
31 Fit a new camshaft oil seal as described in Section 14.
32 Refit the camshaft sprocket to the camshaft, and tighten the bolt to the specified torque.
33 Refit the camshaft position sensor to the camshaft housing. If necessary, turn the camshaft so that the sensor tip aligns with one of the three webs on the signal ring. Position the sensor so that the gap between

the sprocket signal ring and the sensor end is 1.2 mm for a used sensor. If fitting a new sensor, the small tip of the sensor must be just touching one of the three webs of the signal ring (see illustration). Tighten the bolt to the specified torque.
34 Turn the camshaft sprocket to the position where the timing tool can be inserted, then refit the timing belt as described in Section 7.
35 The remainder of refitting is a reversal of removal.

10 Cylinder head –
removal and refitting

Note: This is an involved procedure, and it is suggested that this Section is read thoroughly before starting work. To aid refitting, make notes on the locations of all relevant brackets and the routing of hoses and cables before removal.

Removal

1 Apply the handbrake, then jack up the front of the car and support it on axle stands (see 'Jacking and vehicle support'). Remove the front right-hand roadwheel, the engine undershield, and the front wheel arch liner. The undershield is secured by several screws,

and the wheel arch liner is secured by several plastic expanding rivets. Push the centre pins in a little, then prise the rivet from place.
2 Remove the cylinder head cover as described in Section 4.
3 Remove the timing belt as described in Section 7.
4 Remove the alternator (see Chapter 5A Section 7) and mounting bracket.
5 Disconnect the vacuum pipe from the brake vacuum pump.
6 Undo the five bolts and remove the heat shield from the catalytic converter.
7 Remove the turbocharger heat shield.
8 Remove the camshaft, rocker arms and hydraulic tappets as described in Section 9.
9 Disconnect either the vacuum hose or wiring plug from the EGR valve, as applicable.
10 Take out the four bolts securing the thermostat housing to the cylinder head, and remove the housing (see illustration).
11 Undo the union bolts and remove the oil feed pipe from the engine block and the turbocharger. Recover the union sealing washers.
12 Slacken the retaining clamp and disconnect the turbocharger oil return hose from the engine block.
13 Working from underneath, remove the four bolts securing the catalytic converter to the turbocharger, and separate the joint. Note: Do not allow any strain to be placed on the flexible section of the exhaust pipe, as damage will result. Support the system using axle stands, bricks, etc.
14 Remove the injectors as described in Chapter 4B Section 11.
15 Undo the nut and the bolt securing the high-pressure fuel pump mounting bracket to the cylinder head. Using a stud extractor, remove the pump mounting bracket retaining stud.
16 Working in the reverse of the tightening sequence (see illustration 10.33), undo the cylinder head bolts by half a turn at a time, until they are all loose and can be removed. Discard the bolts once they're removed – new ones should be used when refitting.

9.33 When fitting a used sensor, the gap between the sensor end and the sensor ring web should be 1.2 mm

10.10 Thermostat housing bolts (arrowed)

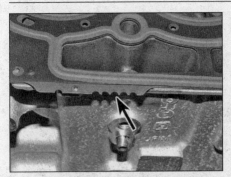

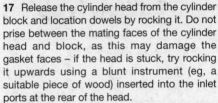

10.26 Cylinder head gasket thickness identification notches (arrowed)

10.29 Ensure the gasket fits correctly over the locating dowels

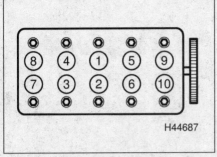

H44687

10.33 Cylinder head bolt tightening sequence

17 Release the cylinder head from the cylinder block and location dowels by rocking it. Do not prise between the mating faces of the cylinder head and block, as this may damage the gasket faces – if the head is stuck, try rocking it upwards using a blunt instrument (eg, a suitable piece of wood) inserted into the inlet ports at the rear of the head.

18 Lift the cylinder head from the block, and recover the gasket. Although the gasket cannot be re-used, it should be retained so that a new one of identical type can be obtained for refitting.

Inspection

19 The mating faces of the cylinder head and cylinder block must be perfectly clean before refitting the head. Use a hard plastic or wood scraper to remove all traces of gasket and carbon; also clean the piston crowns. Take particular care during the cleaning operations, as aluminium alloy is easily damaged.

20 Make sure that the carbon is not allowed to enter the oil and water passages – this is particularly important for the lubrication system, as carbon could block the oil supply to the engine's components. Using adhesive tape and paper, seal the water, oil and bolt holes in the cylinder block. To prevent carbon entering the gap between the pistons and bores, smear a little grease in the gap. After cleaning each piston, use a small brush to remove all traces of grease and carbon from the gap, then wipe away the remainder with a clean rag.

21 Check the mating surfaces of the cylinder block and the cylinder head for nicks, deep scratches and other damage. If slight, they may be removed carefully with a file, but if excessive, renewal is necessary as it is not permissible to machine the surfaces.

22 If warpage of the cylinder head gasket surface is suspected, use a straight-edge to check it for distortion. Refer to Part E of this Chapter if necessary.

23 If possible, clean out the bolt holes in the block using compressed air, to ensure no oil or water is present. Screwing a bolt into an oil- or water-filled hole can (in extreme cases) cause the block to fracture, due to the hydraulic pressure created.

24 Although not essential, if a suitable tap-and-die set is available, it's worth running the correct-size tap down the bolt threads in the cylinder block. This will clean the threads of any debris, and go some way to restoring any damaged threads. Make absolutely sure the tap is the right size and thread pitch, and lightly oil the tap before starting.

25 New head bolts must be used when refitting – re-using the old ones isn't worth the risk. If the bolts or their threads 'let go' when they're tightened, the bottom half of the engine could be reduced to scrap very quickly.

26 The head gasket has a series of notches along one edge, which denote its thickness (see illustration). Ford state that the new gasket should have the same number of notches as the old one.

Refitting

27 Before fitting the head, make sure that the crankshaft sprocket timing holes are still aligned (check that the timing pin can be fitted). In this position, the pistons are halfway down the bores, which avoids the possibility of piston-to-valve contact when the head is fitted.

28 Wipe clean the mating surfaces of the cylinder head and cylinder block, and check that the two locating dowels are in position in the block.

29 Fit the new head gasket the right way round on the cylinder block (see illustration).

30 Carefully lower the cylinder head onto the gasket and block, making sure that it locates correctly onto the dowels.

31 It is useful when refitting a cylinder head to have an assistant on hand, to help guide the head onto the dowels. Take care that the gasket does not get moved as the head is lowered into position. To confirm that the head is aligned correctly, once it is in place, temporarily slide in two or more of the head bolts, and check that they fit into the block holes.

32 Though it is not required by Ford, there is no harm in lightly oiling the threads of the head bolts before fitting them. This is particularly recommended if the block threads have not been cleaned with a tap-and-die set. Fit the head bolts carefully, and screw them in by hand only until finger-tight.

33 Working progressively and in sequence, tighten the cylinder head bolts to their Stage 1 torque setting, using a torque wrench and suitable socket (see illustration).

34 Once all the bolts have been tightened to their Stage 1 torque setting, working again in the specified sequence, tighten each bolt to the specified Stage 2 setting. Finally, angle-tighten the bolts through the specified Stage 3 angle. It is recommended that an angle-measuring gauge is used during this stage of tightening, to ensure accuracy. Note: Retightening of the cylinder head bolts after running the engine is not required.

35 Refit the hydraulic tappets, rocker arms, and camshaft housing (complete with camshaft) as described in Section 9.

36 Refit the timing belt as described in Section 7.

37 The remainder of refitting is a reversal of removal, noting the following points:

a) Use new sealing washers when refitting the turbocharger oil feed pipe, and make sure the pipe is routed so that it is at least 15 mm away from the turbocharger housing.

b) When refitting a cylinder head, it is good practice to renew the thermostat.

c) Refit the camshaft position sensor and set the air gap with reference to Section 9.

d) Tighten all fasteners to the specified torque where given.

e) Refill the cooling system as described in Chapter 1B Section 30.

f) The engine may run erratically for the first few miles, until the engine management PCM relearns its stored values.

11 Sump – removal and refitting

Removal

1 Drain the engine oil, then clean and refit the engine oil drain plug, tightening it securely. If the engine is nearing its service interval when the oil and filter are due for renewal, it is recommended that the filter is also removed, and a new one fitted. After reassembly, the engine can then be refilled with fresh oil. Refer to Chapter 1B Section 6 for further information.

11.8 Apply a bead of sealant to the sump or crankcase mating surface

11.9 Refit the sump and tighten the bolts

2 Apply the handbrake, then jack up the front of the car and support it on axle stands (see 'Jacking and vehicle support'). Undo the screws and remove the engine undershield.
3 To improve access, remove the exhaust front pipe as described in Chapter 4B Section 18.
4 Progressively slacken and remove the sixteen sump retaining bolts, and two nuts. Since the sump bolts vary in length, remove each bolt in turn, and store it in its correct fitted order by pushing it through a clearly-marked cardboard template. This will avoid the possibility of installing the bolts in the wrong locations on refitting.
5 Try to break the joint by striking the sump with the palm of your hand, then lower and withdraw the sump from under the car. If the sump is stuck (which is quite likely) use a putty knife, or similar, carefully inserted between the sump and block. Ease the knife along the joint until the sump is released, taking care not to damage the mating faces.
6 While the sump is removed, take the opportunity to check the oil pump pick-up/strainer for signs of clogging or splitting. If necessary, remove the pump as described in Section 12, and clean or renew the strainer.

Refitting

7 Clean all traces of sealant from the mating surfaces of the cylinder block/crankcase and sump, then use a clean rag to wipe out the sump and the engine's interior.
8 Ensure that the sump mating surfaces are clean and dry, then apply a thin coating of suitable RTV sealant (such as Ford WSE-M4G323-A4) to the sump or crankcase mating surface (see illustration). The sump should be fitted within four minutes of applying the sealant.
9 Offer up the sump to the cylinder block/crankcase. Refit its retaining nuts and bolts, ensuring that each bolt is screwed into its original location. Tighten the nuts and bolts evenly and progressively to the specified torque setting (see illustration).
10 Lower the car to the ground, then refill the engine with oil as described in Chapter 1B Section 6.

12 Oil pump – removal, inspection and refitting

Removal

1 Remove the sump as described in Section 11.

2 Unscrew and remove the sump stud nearest the crankshaft sprocket end of the engine.
3 Remove the crankshaft sprocket as described in Section 8. Make sure the Woodruff key is removed from its slot in the crankshaft nose.
4 Disconnect the wiring plug, undo the bolts and remove the crankshaft position sensor, located on the right-hand end of the cylinder block.
5 Undo the three Allen bolts and remove the oil pump pick-up tube from the pump/block, complete with the dipstick guide tube (see illustration). Discard the oil seal, a new one must be fitted.
6 Undo the eight bolts, and remove the oil pump (see illustration).

Inspection

7 Undo and remove the Torx screws securing the cover to the oil pump (see illustration). Examine the pump rotors and body for signs of wear and damage. If worn, the complete pump must be renewed.
8 Remove the circlip, and extract the cap, valve piston and spring, noting which way

12.5 Undo the three Allen bolts (arrowed) and remove the oil pick-up tube

12.6 Undo the eight bolts (arrowed) and remove the oil pump

12.7 Undo the Torx screws and remove the pump cover

12.8a Remove the circlip …

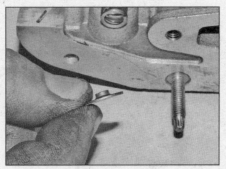

12.8b … cap …

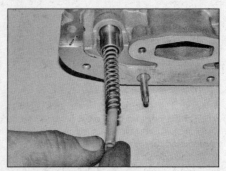

12.8c … spring …

12.8d … and piston

12.12 Apply a bead of sealant to the cylinder block mating surface

around they are fitted **(see illustrations)**. The condition of the relief valve spring can only be measured by comparing it with a new one; if there is any doubt about its condition, it should also be renewed.

9 Refit the relief valve piston and spring, then secure them in place with the circlip.

10 Refit the cover to the oil pump, and tighten the Torx screws securely.

Refitting

11 Remove all traces of sealant, and thoroughly clean the mating surfaces of the oil pump and cylinder block.

12 Apply a 4 mm wide bead of RTV sealant (such as Ford WSE-M4G323-A4) to the mating face of the cylinder block **(see illustration)**. Ensure that no sealant enters any of the holes in the block. The pump should be fitted within four minutes of applying the sealant.

13 With a new oil seal fitted, refit the oil pump over the end of the crankshaft, aligning the flats in the pump drivegear with the flats machined in the crankshaft **(see illustrations)**. Note that new oil pumps are supplied with the

oil seal already fitted, and a seal protector sleeve. The sleeve fits over the end of the crankshaft to protect the seal as the pump is fitted.

14 Install the oil pump bolts, and tighten them to the specified torque.

15 Refit the oil pick-up tube to the pump/ cylinder block using a new O-ring seal. Ensure the oil dipstick guide tube is correctly refitted.

16 Refit the Woodruff key to the crankshaft, and slide the crankshaft sprocket into place.

17 The remainder of refitting is a reversal of removal.

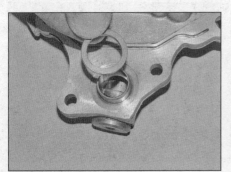

12.13a Fit a new oil seal …

12.13b … align the pump gear flats (arrowed) …

12.13c … with those of the crankshaft (arrowed)

13 Oil cooler –
removal and refitting

Removal

1 Apply the handbrake, then jack up the front of the car and support it on axle stands (see *'Jacking and vehicle support'*). Undo the screws and remove the engine undershield.

2 The oil cooler is fitted to the front of the oil filter housing. Drain the coolant as described in Chapter 1B Section 30.

3 Drain the engine oil as described in Chapter 1B Section 6, or be prepared for fluid spillage.

4 Undo the bolts and remove the oil cooler. Recover the O-ring seals **(see illustrations)**.

Refitting

5 Fit new O-ring seals into the recesses in the oil filter housing, and refit the cooler. Tighten the bolts securely.

6 Refill or top-up the cooling system and engine oil level as described in Chapter 1B Section 6 or Weekly checks0,5 (as applicable). Start the engine, and check the oil cooler for signs of leakage.

14 Oil seals – renewal

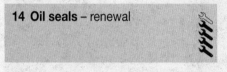

Crankshaft right-hand oil seal

1 Remove the crankshaft sprocket as described in Section 8.

2 Measure and note the fitted depth of the oil seal.

3 Pull the oil seal from the housing using a hooked instrument. Alternatively, drill a small hole in the oil seal, and use a self-tapping screw and a pair of pliers to remove it **(see illustration)**.

4 Clean the oil seal housing and the crankshaft sealing surface.

5 The new seal has a Teflon lip, and must not be oiled or marked. The new seal should be supplied with a protector sleeve, which fits over the end of the crankshaft to prevent

13.4a Undo the bolts (arrowed), remove the oil cooler …

any damage to the seal lip. With the sleeve in place, press the seal (open end first) into the pump to the previously-noted depth, using a suitable tube or socket.

6 Refit the crankshaft sprocket as described in Section 8.

Crankshaft left-hand oil seal

7 Remove the flywheel as described in Section 16.

8 Measure and note the fitted depth of the oil seal.

9 Pull the oil seal from the housing using a hooked instrument. Alternatively, drill a small hole in the oil seal, and use a self-tapping screw and a pair of pliers to remove it **(see illustration 14.3)**.

10 Clean the oil seal housing and the crankshaft sealing surface.

11 The new seal has a Teflon lip, and must not be oiled or marked. The new seal should be supplied with a protector sleeve, which fits over the end of the crankshaft to prevent any damage to the seal lip **(see illustration)**. With the sleeve in place, press the seal (open end first) into the housing to the previously-noted depth, using a suitable tube or socket.

12 Refit the flywheel as described in Section 16.

Camshaft oil seal

13 Remove the camshaft sprocket as described in Section 8. In principle, there is no need to remove the timing belt completely, but remember that if the belt has been

13.4b … and recover the O-ring seals

contaminated with oil from a leaking seal, it must be renewed.

14 Pull the oil seal from the housing using a hooked instrument. Alternatively, drill a small hole in the oil seal and use a self-tapping screw and a pair of pliers to remove it **(see illustration 14.3)**.

15 Clean the oil seal housing and the camshaft sealing surface.

16 The seal has a Teflon lip, and must not be oiled or marked. The new seal should be supplied with a protector sleeve. which fits over the end of the camshaft to prevent any damage to the seal lip **(see illustration)**. With the sleeve in place, press the seal (open end first) into the housing to the previously-noted depth, using a suitable tube or socket which bears only of the outer edge of the seal.

17 Refit the camshaft sprocket as described in Section 8.

18 Where necessary, fit a new timing belt with reference to Section 7.

15 Oil pressure switch –
removal and refitting

1 The oil pressure switch is a vital early warning of low oil pressure. The switch operates the oil warning light on the instrument panel – the light should come on with the ignition, and go out almost immediately when the engine starts.

2 If the light does not come on, there could

14.3 Drill a hole then use a self-tapping screw and pliers to extract the oil seal

14.11 The new oil seal comes with a protective sleeve (arrowed) which fits over the end of the crankshaft

14.16 The new oil seal comes with a protective sleeve (arrowed) which fits over the end of the camshaft

be a fault on the instrument panel, the switch wiring, or the switch itself. If the light does not go out, low oil level, worn oil pump (or sump pick-up blocked), blocked oil filter, or worn main bearings could be to blame – or again, the switch may be faulty.

3 If the light comes on while driving, the best advice is to turn the engine off immediately, and not to drive the car until the problem has been investigated – ignoring the light could mean expensive engine damage.

Removal

4 The oil pressure switch is located at the front of the cylinder block, adjacent to the oil dipstick guide tube. If preferred, access to the switch may be gained from below, with the car jacked up and the engine undershield removed (see *'Jacking and vehicle support'*).

5 Remove the protective sleeve from the wiring plug (where applicable), then disconnect the wiring from the switch.

6 Unscrew the switch from the cylinder block, and recover the sealing washer **(see illustration)**. Be prepared for oil spillage (as the switch is well above the oil level in the sump, this should be virtually nil). If the switch is to be left removed from the engine for any length of time, plug the hole in the cylinder block.

Inspection

7 Examine the switch for signs of cracking or splits. If the top part of the switch is loose, this is an early indication of impending failure.

8 Check that the wiring terminals at the switch are not loose, then trace the wire from the switch connector until it enters the main loom – any wiring defects will give rise to apparent oil pressure problems.

Refitting

9 Refitting is the reverse of the removal procedure, noting the following points:
a) *Use a new sealing washer, and tighten the switch securely.*
b) *Reconnect the switch connector, making sure it clicks home properly. Ensure that the wiring is routed away from any hot or moving parts.*
c) *Check the engine oil level and top-up if necessary (see 'Weekly checks0,5 ').*
d) *Check for signs of oil leaks once the engine has been restarted and warmed-up to normal operating temperature.*

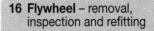

16 Flywheel – removal, inspection and refitting

Removal

1 Remove the transmission as described in Chapter 7A Section 6, then remove the clutch assembly as described in Chapter 6 Section 6.

2 To lock the crankshaft and stop the flywheel turning as the bolts are undone,

15.6 The oil pressure switch is on the front face of the cylinder block

working underneath the engine, insert a 12 mm diameter rod or drill bit into the hole in the right-hand face of the engine block casting over the lower section of the flywheel. Rotate the crankshaft until the tool engages in the corresponding hole in the flywheel **(see illustration 5.2)**.

3 Make alignment marks between the flywheel and crankshaft to aid refitment. Slacken and remove the flywheel retaining bolts, and remove the flywheel from the end of the crankshaft. Be careful not to drop it; it is heavy. If the flywheel locating dowel (where fitted) is a loose fit in the crankshaft end, remove it and store it with the flywheel for safe-keeping. Discard the flywheel bolts; new ones must be used on refitting.

Inspection

4 Examine the flywheel for scoring of the clutch face, and for wear or chipping of the ring gear teeth. If the clutch face is scored, the flywheel may be surface-ground, but renewal is preferable. Seek the advice of a Ford dealer or engine reconditioning specialist to see if machining is possible. If the ring gear is worn or damaged, the flywheel must be renewed, as it is not possible to renew the ring gear separately.

Refitting

5 Clean the mating surfaces of the flywheel and crankshaft. Remove any remaining locking compound from the threads of the crankshaft holes, using the correct-size tap, if available.

6 If the new flywheel retaining bolts are not supplied with precoated threads, apply a suitable thread-locking compound to the threads of each bolt **(see illustration)**.

7 Ensure that the locating dowel is in position. Offer up the flywheel, locating it on the dowel (where fitted) and fit the new retaining bolts. Where no locating dowel is fitted, align the previously-made marks to ensure the flywheel is refitted in its original position.

8 Lock the flywheel using the method employed on dismantling, and tighten the retaining bolts to the specified torque, then through the specified angle.

9 Refit the clutch as described in Chapter 6

16.6 If the new bolts are not supplied with their threads precoated, apply thread-locking compound

Section 6. Remove the flywheel locking tool, and refit the transmission as described in Chapter 7A Section 6.

17 Engine/transmission mountings – inspection and renewal

General

1 The engine/transmission mountings seldom require attention, but broken or deteriorated mountings should be renewed immediately, or the added strain placed on the driveline components may cause damage or wear.

2 While separate mountings may be removed and refitted individually, if more than one is disturbed at a time – such as if the engine/transmission unit is removed from its mountings – they must be reassembled and their fasteners tightened in the position marked on removal.

3 On reassembly, the complete weight of the engine/transmission unit must not be taken by the mountings until all are correctly aligned with the marks made on removal. Tighten the engine/transmission mounting fasteners to their specified torque wrench settings.

Inspection

4 During the check, the engine/transmission unit must be raised slightly, to remove its weight from the mountings.

5 Raise the front of the vehicle, and support it securely on axle stands. Position a jack under the sump, with a large block of wood between the jack head and the sump, then carefully raise the engine/transmission just enough to take the weight off the mountings.

 Warning: DO NOT place any part of your body under the engine when it is supported only by a jack.

6 Check the mountings to see if the rubber is cracked, hardened or separated from the metal components. Sometimes the rubber will split right down the centre.

7 Check for relative movement between each mounting's brackets and the engine/transmission or body (use a large screwdriver or lever to attempt to move the mountings).

17.10 Right-hand engine mounting-to-engine bracket retaining nuts (arrowed)

17.11 Right-hand engine mounting-to-inner wing panel retaining bolts (arrowed)

17.14 Undo the retaining nuts and lift out the battery tray support bracket

If movement is noted, lower the engine and check-tighten the mounting fasteners.

Renewal

8 Note: *The following paragraphs assume the engine is supported beneath the sump as described earlier.*

Right-hand mounting

9 Lift up the coolant expansion tank and position it to one side. Note there is no need to disconnect the coolant pipes.

10 Mark the position of the mounting on the vehicle, right-hand inner wing panel, then undo the three nuts securing the mounting to the engine bracket **(see illustration)**. Discard the nuts, new ones must be fitted.

11 Undo the three retaining bolts securing the mounting to the inner wing panel and withdraw the mounting from the vehicle **(see illustration)**.

12 On refitting, tighten all fasteners to the

torque wrench settings specified. Re-align the marks made on removal, then tighten the new mounting bracket retaining nuts.

Left-hand mounting

13 Remove the battery and battery tray as described in Chapter 5A Section 4. Note that it is not necessary to remove the powertrain control module from the battery tray, just position the tray clear for access to the mounting.

14 Undo the three nuts securing the battery tray support bracket in position. Release the wiring loom from the support bracket and lift the support bracket out of the engine compartment **(see illustration)**.

15 With the transmission supported, mark the position of the mounting bracket on the transmission and on the body sidemember. Undo the three bolts securing the mounting bracket to the transmission and the two bolts securing the mounting to the body

sidemember **(see illustrations)**. Remove the mounting from the engine compartment.

16 On refitting, re-align the mounting in the position noted on removal, then tighten all fasteners to the specified torque wrench settings. Refit the components disturbed for access using a reversal of the removal procedures.

Rear mounting (roll restrictor)

17 To remove the engine rear mounting, apply the handbrake, then jack up the front of the car and support it on axle stands (see *'Jacking and vehicle support'*). Unscrew the through-bolts and remove the engine rear mounting link from the bracket on the transmission and from the bracket on the subframe **(see illustration)**. Hold the engine stationary while the bolts are being removed, since the link will be under tension.

18 On refitting, ensure that the bolts are securely tightened to the specified torque wrench setting.

17.15a Left-hand engine mounting bracket-to-transmission retaining bolts (arrowed) ...

17.15b ... and mounting-to-body sidemember retaining bolts (arrowed)

17.17 Rear mounting/roll restrictor retaining bolts (arrowed)

Chapter 2 Part C
1.4 litre (Stage V emissions) diesel engine in-car repair procedures

Contents

Degrees of difficulty

Easy, suitable for novice with little experience	Fairly easy, suitable for beginner with some experience	Fairly difficult, suitable for competent DIY mechanic	Difficult, suitable for experienced DIY mechanic	Very difficult, suitable for expert DIY or professional

Specifications

General

Designation	Duratorq-TDCi
Engine code*	KVJA
Capacity	1399 cc
Bore	73.7 mm
Stroke	82.0 mm
Direction of crankshaft rotation	Clockwise (viewed from the right-hand side of vehicle)
No 1 cylinder location.	At the transmission end of block
Compression ratio	16: 1
Emissions level.	Stage V

The engine code is stamped on a plate attached to the front of the cylinder block, next to the oil filter

Compression pressures (engine hot, at cranking speed)

Normal	20 ± 5 bar
Minimum	15 bar
Maximum difference between any two cylinders.	5 bar

Camshaft

Camshaft end float.	0.195 – 0.3 mm

Lubrication system

Oil pump type...	Gear-type, driven directly by the right-hand end of the crankshaft, by two flats machined along the crankshaft journal.

Minimum oil pressure at 80°C:
Idle speed..	1.0 to 2.0 bar
2000 rpm	2.3 to 3.7 bar

Torque wrench settings

	Nm	lbf ft
Ancillary drivebelt tensioner roller	20	15
Big-end bolts: *		
Stage 1..	10	7
Stage 2..	Slacken 180°	
Stage 3..	10	7
Stage 4..	Angle-tighten a further 130°	
Camshaft bearing caps	10	7
Camshaft bearing ladder:		
Studs	10	7
Bolts	10	7
Camshaft position sensor bolt...........................	5	4
Camshaft sprocket bolt		
Stage 1..	20	15
Stage 2..	Angle-tighten a further 50°	
Coolant outlet housing bolts	8	6
Crankshaft position/speed sensor bolt	10	7
Crankshaft pulley/sprocket bolt: *		
Stage 1..	35	26
Stage 2..	Angle-tighten a further 190°	
Cylinder head bolts: *		
Stage 1..	20	15
Stage 2..	40	30
Stage 3..	Angle-tighten a further 260°	
Cylinder head cover	10	7
EGR valve...	10	7
Engine-to-transmission fixing bolts	47	35
Flywheel bolts: *		
Stage 1..	30	22
Stage 2..	Angle-tighten a further 90°	
Fuel pump sprocket	50	37
Left-hand engine/transmission mounting:		
Mounting-to-bracket centre nut.......................	148	109
Mounting-to-bracket outer nuts.......................	48	35
Mounting bracket to transmission	80	59
Main bearing ladder outer seam bolts:		
Stage 1..	5	4
Stage 2..	10	7
Main bearing ladder to cylinder block:		
Stage 1..	10	7
Stage 2..	Slacken 180°	
Stage 3..	30	22
Stage 4..	Angle-tighten a further 140°	
Piston oil jet spray tube bolt............................	20	15
Oil cooler retaining bolts................................	10	7
Oil filter cover	25	18
Oil pick-up pipe	10	7
Oil pressure switch.....................................	30	22
Oil pump to cylinder block:		
Stage 1..	5	4
Stage 2..	9	7
Rear engine/transmission mounting......................	25	18
Right-hand engine mounting:		
Mounting to Inner wing (nuts/bolts)	48	35
Mounting bracket to engine block	55	41
Sump drain plug.......................................	35	26
Sump bolts/nuts.......................................	10	7
Timing belt idler pulley.................................	37	27
Timing belt tensioner pulley	30	22
Vacuum pump bolts....................................	20	15

*Do not re-use

1 General Information

How to use this Chapter

1 This Part of Chapter 2 describes the repair procedures that can reasonably be carried out on the engine while it remains in the vehicle. If the engine has been removed from the vehicle and is being dismantled as described in Part F, any preliminary dismantling procedures can be ignored.

2 Note that, while it may be possible physically to overhaul items such as the piston/connecting rod assemblies while the engine is in the car, such tasks are not usually carried out as separate operations. Usually, several additional procedures are required (not to mention the cleaning of components and oilways); for this reason, all such tasks are classed as major overhaul procedures, and are described in Part F of this Chapter.

3 Part F describes the removal of the engine/transmission from the car, and the full overhaul procedures that can then be carried out.

DV series engines

4 The 1.4 litre DV series of engines are the result of development collaboration between Citroën/Peugeot and Ford. The latest version fitted to the Ford Fiesta is a single overhead cam (SOHC), 8-valve variant. The direct injection, turbocharged, four-cylinder engine is mounted transversely, with the transmission mounted on the left-hand side.

5 To distinguish this engine from the earlier 1.4 litre TDCi engine, identify the air cleaner housing in the engine compartment. On earlier engines the housing is located at the rear of the engine compartment, whereas on the later engines (covered by this Chapter), the air cleaner housing is located at the front, left-hand corner of the engine compartment.

6 A toothed timing belt drives the camshaft, high-pressure fuel pump and coolant pump. The camshaft operates the inlet and exhaust valves via rocker arms which are supported at their pivot ends by hydraulic self-adjusting tappets. The camshaft is supported by bearings machined directly in the cylinder head and camshaft bearing housing.

7 The high-pressure fuel pump supplies fuel to the fuel rail, and subsequently to the electronically-controlled injectors which inject the fuel direct into the combustion chambers. This design differs from the previous type where an injection pump supplies the fuel at high pressure to each injector. The earlier, conventional type injection pump required fine calibration and timing, and these functions are now completed by the high-pressure pump, electronic injectors and engine management ECM.

8 The crankshaft runs in five main bearings of the usual shell type. Endfloat is controlled by thrustwashers either side of No 2 main bearing.

9 The pistons are selected to be of matching weight, and incorporate fully-floating gudgeon pins retained by circlips.

Repair operations precaution

10 The engine is a complex unit with numerous accessories and ancillary components. The design of the engine compartment is such that every conceivable space has been utilised, and access to virtually all of the engine components is extremely limited. In many cases, ancillary components will have to be removed, or moved to one side, and wiring, pipes and hoses will have to be disconnected or removed from various cable clips and support brackets.

11 When working on this engine, read through the entire procedure first, look at the car and engine at the same time, and establish whether you have the necessary tools, equipment, skill and patience to proceed. Allow considerable time for any operation, and be prepared for the unexpected.

12 Because of the limited access, many of the engine photographs appearing in this Chapter were, by necessity, taken with the engine removed from the vehicle.

⚠️ **Warning: It is essential to observe strict precautions when working on the fuel system components of the engine, particularly the high-pressure side of the system. Before carrying out any engine operations that entail working on, or near, any part of the fuel system, refer to the special information given in Chapter 4B Section 2.**

13 Operations with engine in vehicle
a) Compression pressure – testing.
b) Cylinder head cover – removal and refitting.
c) Crankshaft pulley – removal and refitting.
d) Timing belt covers – removal and refitting.
e) Timing belt – removal, refitting and adjustment.
f) Timing belt tensioner and sprockets – removal and refitting.
g) Camshaft oil seal – renewal.
h) Camshaft, rocker arms and hydraulic tappets – removal, inspection and refitting.
i) Sump – removal and refitting.
j) Oil pump – removal and refitting.
k) Crankshaft oil seals – renewal.
l) Engine/transmission mountings – inspection and renewal.
m) Flywheel – removal, inspection and refitting.

2 Compression and leakdown tests – description and interpretation

Compression test

Note: A compression tester specifically designed for diesel engines must be used for this test.

1 When engine performance is down, or if misfiring occurs which cannot be attributed to the fuel system, a compression test can provide diagnostic clues as to the engine's condition. If the test is performed regularly, it can give warning of trouble before any other symptoms become apparent.

2 A compression tester specifically intended for diesel engines must be used, because of the higher pressures involved. The tester is connected to an adapter which screws into the glow plug or injector hole. On this engine, an adapter suitable for use in the glow plug holes will be required, so as not to disturb the fuel system components. It is unlikely to be worthwhile buying such a tester for occasional use, but it may be possible to borrow or hire one – if not, have the test performed by a garage.

3 Unless specific instructions to the contrary are supplied with the tester, observe the following points:
a) The battery must be in a good state of charge, the air filter must be clean, and the engine should be at normal operating temperature.
b) All the glow plugs should be removed as described in Chapter 5A Section 12 before starting the test.
c) Disconnect the fuel injector wiring plugs.

4 The compression pressures measured are not so important as the balance between cylinders. Values are given in the Specifications.

5 The cause of poor compression is less easy to establish on a diesel engine than on a petrol one. The effect of introducing oil into the cylinders ('wet' testing) is not conclusive, because there is a risk that the oil will sit in the swirl chamber or in the recess on the piston crown instead of passing to the rings. However, the following can be used as a rough guide to diagnosis.

6 All cylinders should produce very similar pressures; any difference greater than that specified indicates the existence of a fault. Note that the compression should build-up quickly in a healthy engine; low compression on the first stroke, followed by gradually-increasing pressure on successive strokes, indicates worn piston rings. A low compression reading on the first stroke, which does not build-up during successive strokes, indicates leaking valves or a blown head gasket (a cracked head could also be the cause). Deposits on the undersides of the valve heads can also cause low compression.

7 A low reading from two adjacent cylinders is almost certainly due to the head gasket having blown between them; the presence of coolant in the engine oil will confirm this.

8 If the compression reading is unusually high, the cylinder head surfaces, valves and pistons are probably coated with carbon deposits. If this is the case, the cylinder head should be removed and decarbonised. **Note:** After performing this test, a fault code may be generated and stored in the PCM memory. Have the PCM self-diagnosis facility interrogated by a Ford dealer or suitably-equipped specialist, and the fault code erased.

Leakdown test

9 A leakdown test measures the rate at which compressed air fed into the cylinder is lost. It is

an alternative to a compression test, and in many ways it is better, since the escaping air provides easy identification of where pressure loss is occurring (piston rings, valves or head gasket).
10 The equipment needed for leakdown testing is unlikely to be available to the home mechanic. If poor compression is suspected, have the test performed by a suitably-equipped garage.

3 Engine assembly/valve timing holes – general information and usage

Note: *Do not attempt to rotate the engine whilst the crankshaft and camshaft are locked in position. If the engine is to be left in this state for a long period of time, it is a good idea to place suitable warning notices inside the vehicle, and in the engine compartment. This will reduce the possibility of the engine being accidentally cranked on the starter motor, which is likely to cause damage with the locking pins in place.*
1 Timing holes or slots are located only in the crankshaft pulley flange and camshaft sprocket hub. The holes/slots are used to position the pistons halfway up the cylinder bores. This will ensure that the valve timing is maintained during operations that require removal and refitting of the timing belt. When the holes/slots are aligned with their corresponding holes in the cylinder block and cylinder head, suitable diameter bolts/pins can be inserted to lock the crankshaft and camshaft in position, preventing rotation.

3.9 Insert a 5.0 mm drill bit/bolt through the round hole in the sprocket flange into the hole in the oil pump housing (lower timing belt removed for clarity)

2 Note that the fuel system used on these engines does not have a conventional diesel injection pump, but instead uses a high-pressure fuel pump. However, the fuel pump sprocket must be pegged in position in a similar fashion to the camshaft sprocket.
3 To align the engine assembly/valve timing holes, proceed as follows.
4 Apply the handbrake, then jack up the front of the vehicle and support it on axle stands (see *'Jacking and vehicle support'*). Remove the right-hand front roadwheel.
5 To gain access to the crankshaft pulley, to enable the engine to be turned, the wheel arch plastic liner must be removed. The liner is secured by several plastic expanding rivets/nut/bolts. To remove the rivets, push in the centre pins a little, then prise the clips from place. Remove the liner from under the front wing.

3.10 Insert an 8.0 mm bolt through the hole in the camshaft sprocket into the corresponding hole in the cylinder head

6 Remove the starter motor and remove the crankshaft pulley as described in Section 5.
7 Remove the upper and lower timing belt covers as described in Section 6.
8 Temporarily refit the crankshaft pulley bolt (without the crankshaft pulley) and then remove the crankshaft locking tool.
9 Turn the crankshaft until the timing hole in the crankshaft sprocket aligns with the hole in the oil pump casing (this is at the 12 o'clock position). Fit the special tool 303-732, or a suitable alternative and lock the crankshaft in position **(see illustration)**.
10 With the crankshaft locked in position fit the camshaft locking tool (303-735 or similar). The hole in the camshaft sprocket should be at approximately the 1 o'clock position **(see illustration)**. If this is not the case remove the crankshaft locking pin and rotate the engine one revolution. Note that the crankshaft must always be turned in a clockwise direction (viewed from the right-hand side of vehicle).
11 When refitting the timing belt, insert Ford tool No 303-732 through the slot in the fuel pump sprocket and into the corresponding hole in the fuel pump mounting bracket. In the absence of this tool use a 5 mm bolt or drill bit.
12 The crankshaft and camshaft are now locked in position, preventing unnecessary rotation.

4 Cylinder head cover – removal and refitting

4.2 Pull up the front edge of the cover

4.3 Release the clamp and disconnect the hose

Removal

1 Disconnect the battery negative lead as described in Chapter 5A Section 4.
2 Pull up the front edge and remove the plastic cover from the top of the engine **(see illustration)**.
3 Release the hose clamp and disconnect the hose from the throttle body **(see illustration)**.
4 Slacken the clamp at the turbocharger end of the hose, then undo the support bracket nut and remove the hose **(see illustrations)**. Plug the openings to prevent contamination.

4.4a Release the clamp at the turbocharger end of the hose...

4.4b ... then undo the bracket nut and remove the hose

4.5a Remove the bolt ...

4.5b ... unclip the wiring harness duct and move it to one side

4.8 Throttle body retaining bolts

4.9 Prise up the fuel pipe clip, and release the wiring harness

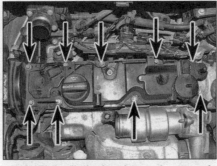

4.10a The cylinder head cover is secured by 9 bolts on the top ...

4.10b ... one bolt in the end behind the camshaft sprocket ...

5 Disconnect the wiring plugs from the fuel injectors, then undo the retaining bolt and unclip the wiring harness duct from the top of the engine (see illustrations).
6 Release the clips and disconnect the breather hose from the cylinder head cover.
7 Unclip the wiring harness, then unbolt and then remove the timing belt upper cover as described in Section 6.
8 Disconnect the wiring plug, undo the 4 retaining bolts and remove the throttle body (see illustration). One of the bolts is accessed

from the and access is limited. A new throttle body-to-manifold seal will be required.
9 Unclip the fuel pipe assembly and wiring harness from the rear of the cover (see illustration).
10 Remove the 11 bolts and then remove the cover (see illustrations). Recover the rubber seal.

Refitting

11 Refitting is a reversal of removal, but ensure that the seal is correctly located (see illustration).

4.10c ... and one at the rear of the cover

4.10d Carefully manoeuvre the cover from place

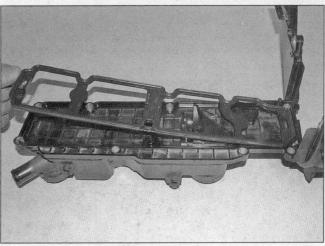

4.11 Renew the seal

5.4 Install the flywheel locking tool
(arrowed)

5.5a Where fitted remove the cover

5.5b Remove the bolt and...

5.5c ...then the pulley

sensor ring of the sprocket with your fingers, or allow metallic particles to come into contact with it.

Refitting

6 Refit the pulley to the end of the crankshaft.
7 Refit the crankshaft pulley. Fit a new bolt and retaining washer. Tighten the bolt to the specified torque, then through the specified angle.
8 Remove the locking tool.
9 Refit and tension the auxiliary drivebelt as described in Chapter 1B Section 26.
10 Refit the remaining components in reverse order of removal.

6 Timing belt covers –
removal and refitting

⚠ **Warning: Refer to the precautionary information contained in Section 1 before proceeding.**

Removal

Upper cover

1 Remove the engine cover from the top of the engine.
2 Unclip the wiring loom from the cover **(see illustration)**.
3 Undo the 4 bolts and remove the timing belt upper cover **(see illustration)**.

Lower cover

4 Remove the crankshaft pulley as described in Section 5.
5 Position a trolley/workshop jack under the engine. Place a block of wood on the jack head (to help spread the load on the sump), then take the weight of the engine.
6 Prise up the coolant expansion tank and move it to one side – there is no need to drain the coolant.
7 Undo the nuts/bolts, and remove the right-hand engine mounting **(see illustration)**.
8 Remove the engine mounting bracket from the engine.
9 Undo the 3 retaining bolts and move the wiring harness guide away from the engine

5 Crankshaft pulley –
removal and refitting

Removal

1 Jack up and support the front of the vehicle (see 'Jacking and vehicle support').
2 Disconnect the battery (Chapter 5A Section 1) and remove the engine undershield.
3 Remove the auxiliary drivebelt as described in Chapter 1B Section 26.
4 To lock the crankshaft, working underneath the engine, insert a 12 mm diameter rod or bolt into the hole in the engine block casting over the lower section of the flywheel **(see**

illustration). Note that the hole in the casting and flywheel is provided purely to lock the crankshaft whilst the pulley bolt it undone – it does not position the crankshaft at TDC. Rotate the crankshaft clockwise until the tool engages in the hole in the flywheel – don't rotate the crank pulley anti-clockwise.
5 Using a suitable socket and extension bar, unscrew the retaining bolt, remove the washer, then slide the pulley off the end of the crankshaft **(see illustrations)**. If the pulley is tight fit, it can be drawn off the crankshaft using a suitable puller. If a puller is being used, refit the pulley retaining bolt without the washer, to avoid damaging the crankshaft as the puller is tightened.
Caution: Do not touch the outer magnetic

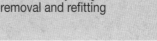

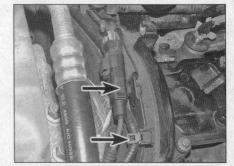

6.2 Release the clips securing the wiring loom

6.3 Upper cover bolts

6.7 Engine mounting nuts/bolt

6.9a Remove the two bolts at the front of the harness guide ...

6.9b ... and the bolt at the rear

(see illustrations). The rear bolt is accessible from underneath the vehicle.

10 Undo the 4 bolts and remove the lower cover.

Refitting

11 Refitting of all the covers is a reversal of the relevant removal procedure, ensuring that each cover section is correctly located, and that the cover retaining bolts are securely tightened. Ensure that all disturbed hoses are reconnected and retained by their relevant clips.

7 Timing belt – removal, inspection, refitting and tensioning

General

1 The timing belt drives the camshaft, high-pressure fuel pump, and coolant pump from a toothed sprocket on the end of the crankshaft. If the belt breaks or slips in service, the pistons are likely to hit the valve heads, resulting in expensive damage.

2 The timing belt should be renewed at the specified intervals, or earlier if it is contaminated with oil, or at all noisy in operation (a 'scraping' noise due to uneven wear).

3 If the timing belt is being removed, it is a wise precaution to renew the coolant pump at the same time. This may avoid the need to remove the timing belt again at a later stage, should the coolant pump fail. The timing belt tensioner should always be replaced when a new timing belt is fitted.

Removal

4 Unclip the coolant expansion tank and move it to one side (see illustration).

5 Remove the upper and lower timing belt covers, as described in Section 6.

6 Undo the bolt and remove the crankshaft position sensor adjacent to the crankshaft

sprocket flange, and move it to one side (see illustration).

7 Undo the retaining bolt and remove the timing belt protection bracket, again, adjacent to the crankshaft sprocket flange (see illustration).

8 Lock the crankshaft and camshaft in the correct position as described in Section 3. If necessary, temporarily refit the crankshaft pulley bolt to enable the crankshaft to be rotated.

9 Insert a hexagon key into the belt tensioner pulley centre, slacken the pulley bolt, and

allow the tensioner to rotate, relieving the belt tension (see illustration). With belt slack, temporarily tighten the pulley bolt.

10 Note its routing, then remove the timing belt from the sprockets.

Inspection

11 Renew the belt as a matter of course, regardless of its apparent condition. The cost of a new belt is nothing compared with the cost of repairs should the belt break in service. If signs of oil contamination are found, trace the source of the oil leak and rectify it.

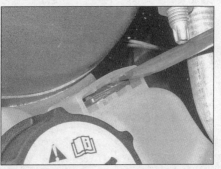

7.4 Carefully spread the coolant tank lug to release the clips

7.6 Undo the bolt (arrowed) and remove the crankshaft position sensor

7.7 Remove the timing belt protection bracket

7.9 Slacken the bolt and allow the tensioner to rotate, relieving the tension on the belt

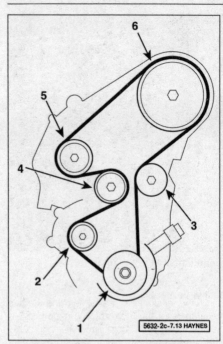

7.13 Timing belt routing

1 Crankshaft   4 Tensioner
2 Waterpump   5 Fuel pump
3 Idler   6 Camshaft

Wash down the engine timing belt area and all related components, to remove all traces of oil. The tensioner must always be replaced. Check that the idler pulleys rotate freely without any sign of roughness, and also check that the coolant pump pulley rotates freely. It is highly recommended that both the coolant pump and the idler pulley are replaced at the same time as the timing belt and tensioner.

Refitting and tensioning

12 Commence refitting by ensuring that the crankshaft, camshaft and fuel pump sprocket

7.15 The index arm must align with the lug (arrowed)

timing pins are in position as described in Section 3.
13 Locate the timing belt on the crankshaft sprocket, then keeping it taut, locate it around the idler pulley, camshaft sprocket, high-pressure pump sprocket, coolant pump sprocket, and the tensioner roller **(see illustration)**.
14 Refit the timing belt protection bracket and tighten the retaining bolt securely.
15 Slacken the tensioner pulley bolt, and using a hexagonal key, rotate the tensioner anti-clockwise, which moves the index arm clockwise, until the index arm is aligned as shown **(see illustration)**.
16 Remove the camshaft, crankshaft and fuel pump sprocket (where applicable) timing pins and, using a socket on the crankshaft pulley bolt, rotate the crankshaft clockwise 10 complete revolutions. Refit the crankshaft and camshaft locking pins.
17 Check that the tensioner index arm is still aligned between the edges of the area shown **(see illustration 7.15)**. If it is not, remove and belt and begin the refitting process again, starting at Paragraph 12.
18 The remainder of refitting is a reversal of removal. Tighten all fasteners to the specified torque where given.

8 Timing belt sprockets and tensioner – removal and refitting

Camshaft sprocket
Removal
1 Remove the timing belt as described in Section 7.
2 Remove the locking tool from the camshaft sprocket/hub. Slacken the sprocket hub retaining bolt. To prevent the camshaft rotating as the bolt is slackened, a sprocket holding tool will be required. In the absence of the special Ford tool, an acceptable substitute can be fabricated at home **(see Tool Tip 1)**. Do not attempt to use the engine assembly/valve timing locking tool to prevent the sprocket from rotating whilst the bolt is slackened.
3 Remove the sprocket hub retaining bolt, and slide the sprocket and hub off the end of the camshaft.
4 Clean the camshaft sprocket thoroughly, and renew it if there are any signs of wear, damage or cracks.

Refitting
5 Refit the camshaft sprocket to the camshaft **(see illustration)**.
6 Refit the sprocket hub retaining bolt. Tighten the bolt to the specified torque, preventing the camshaft from turning as during removal.
7 Align the engine assembly/valve timing slot in the camshaft sprocket hub with the hole in the cylinder head and refit the timing pin to lock the camshaft in position.
8 Fit the timing belt around the pump sprocket and camshaft sprocket, and tension the timing belt as described in Section 7.

Crankshaft sprocket
Removal
9 Remove the timing belt as described in Section 7.

A sprocket holding tool can be made from two lengths of steel strip bolted together to form a forked end. Drill holes and insert bolts in the ends of the fork to engage with the sprocket spokes.

8.5 Ensure the lug on the sprocket hub engages with the slot on the end of the camshaft (arrowed)

8.11a Slide the sprocket from the crankshaft...

8.11b ...and recover the Woodruff key

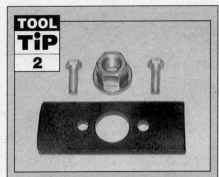

Make a sprocket releasing tool from a short strip of steel. Drill two holes in the strip to correspond with the two holes in the sprocket. Drill a third hole just large enough to accept the flats of the sprocket retaining nut.

10 Check that the engine assembly/valve timing holes are still aligned as described in Section 3, and the camshaft sprocket and flywheel are locked in position.
11 Slide the sprocket off the end of the crankshaft and collect the Woodruff key **(see illustrations)**.
12 Examine the crankshaft oil seal for signs of oil leakage and, if necessary, renew it as described in Section 14.
13 Clean the crankshaft sprocket thoroughly, and renew it if there are any signs of wear, damage or cracks. Recover the crankshaft locating key.

Refitting

14 Refit the key to the end of the crankshaft, then refit the crankshaft sprocket (with the flange facing the crankshaft pulley).
15 Fit the timing belt around the crankshaft sprocket, and tension the timing belt as described in Section 7.

Fuel pump sprocket

Removal

16 Remove the timing belt as described in Section 7.
17 Using a suitable socket, undo the pump sprocket retaining nut. The sprocket can be held stationary by inserting a suitably-sized locking pin, drill or rod through the slot in the sprocket, and into the corresponding hole in the backplate, or by using a suitable forked tool engaged with the holes in the sprocket **(see Tool Tip 1)**.
18 The pump sprocket is a taper fit on the

pump shaft and it will be necessary to make up another tool to release it from the taper **(see Tool Tip 2)**.
19 Partially unscrew the sprocket retaining nut, fit the home-made tool, and secure it to the sprocket with two suitable bolts. Prevent the sprocket from rotating as before, and unscrew the sprocket retaining nut. The nut will bear against the tool as it is undone, forcing the sprocket off the shaft taper. Once the taper is released, remove the tool, unscrew the nut fully, and remove the sprocket from the pump shaft.
20 Clean the sprocket thoroughly, and renew it if there are any signs of wear, damage or cracks.

Refitting

21 Refit the pump sprocket and retaining nut, and tighten the nut to the specified torque. Prevent the sprocket rotating as the nut is tightened using the sprocket holding tool.
22 Refit the timing belt as described in Section 7.

Coolant pump sprocket

23 The coolant pump sprocket is integral with the pump, and cannot be removed. Coolant pump removal is described in Chapter 3 Section 7.

Tensioner pulley

Removal

24 Remove the timing belt as described in Section 7.
25 Remove the tensioner pulley retaining

bolt, and then remove the tensioner **(see illustration)**.
26 Clean the tensioner pulley, but do not use any strong solvent which may enter the pulley bearings. Check that the pulley rotates freely, with no sign of stiffness or free play. The pulley should always be replaced when the timing belt is replaced.
27 Examine the pulley mounting stud for signs of damage and if necessary, renew it.

Refitting

28 Refitting is a reversal of removal.
29 Refit the timing belt as described in Section 7.

Idler pulley

Removal

30 Remove the timing belt as described in Section 7.
31 Undo the retaining bolt/nut and withdraw the idler pulley from the engine **(see illustration)**.
32 Clean the idler pulley, but do not use any strong solvent which may enter the bearings. Check that the pulley rotates freely, with no sign of stiffness or free play. Renew the idler pulley if there is any doubt about its condition, or if there are any obvious signs of wear or damage.

Refitting

33 Locate the idler pulley on the engine, and fit the retaining bolt/nut. Tighten the bolt/nut to the specified torque.
34 Refit the timing belt as described in Section 7.

9 Camshafts, rocker arms and hydraulic tappets – removal, inspection and refitting

Removal

1 Remove the cylinder head cover/manifold as described in Section 4.

8.25 Remove the tensioner

8.31 Timing belt idler pulley retaining nut (arrowed)

9.4 Remove the vacuum pump

9.6 Remove the camshaft position sensor (arrowed)

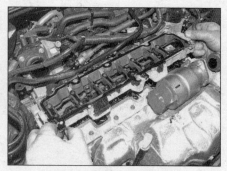

9.7 Remove the bearing ladder

2 Remove the timing belt (Section 7) and the camshaft sprocket as described in Section 8.

3 Refit the right-hand engine mounting, but only tighten the bolts moderately; this will keep the engine supported during the camshaft removal.

4 Undo the bolts and remove the vacuum pump (see Chapter 9 Section 21). Recover the pump O-ring seals (see illustration).

5 Unbolt the fuel filter (see Chapter 1B Section 22) and move it to one side.

6 Disconnect the wiring plug from the camshaft position sensor (see illustration). Unbolt and remove the sensor from the bearing ladder.

7 Working in reverse order to that shown (see illustration 9.22) remove the retaining bolts and then remove camshaft bearing cap ladder (see illustration).

8 Lift out the camshaft (see illustration) and dispose of the oil seal. A new one will be required.

9 Obtain 8 small, clean plastic containers, and number them 1 to 4 inlet and 1 to 4 exhaust; alternatively, divide a larger container into 8 compartments.

10 Lift out each rocker arm. Place the rocker arms in their respective positions in the box or containers (see illustration).

11 A compartmentalised container filled with engine oil is now required to retain the hydraulic tappets while they are removed from the cylinder head. Withdraw each hydraulic follower (see illustration) and place it in the container, keeping them each identified for correct refitting. The tappets must be totally submerged in the oil to prevent air entering them.

Inspection

12 Inspect the cam lobes and the camshaft bearing journals for scoring or other visible evidence of wear. Once the surface hardening of the cam lobes has been eroded, wear will occur at an accelerated rate. **Note:** *If these symptoms are visible on the tips of the camshaft lobes, check the corresponding rocker arm, as it will probably be worn as well.*

13 Examine the condition of the bearing surfaces in the cylinder head and camshaft bearing housing. If wear is evident, the cylinder head and bearing housing will both have to be renewed, as they are a matched assembly.

14 Inspect the rocker arms and tappets for scuffing, cracking or other damage and renew any components as necessary. Also check the condition of the tappet bores in the cylinder head. As with the camshafts, any wear in this area will necessitate cylinder head renewal.

Refitting

15 Thoroughly clean the sealant from the mating surfaces of the cylinder head and camshaft bearing housing. Use a suitable liquid gasket dissolving agent (available from Ford dealers) together with a soft putty knife; do not use a metal scraper or the faces will be damaged. As there is no conventional gasket used, the cleanliness of the mating faces is of the utmost importance.

16 Clean off any oil, dirt or grease from both components and dry with a clean lint-free cloth. Ensure that all the oilways are completely clean.

17 Liberally lubricate the hydraulic tappet bores in the cylinder head with clean engine oil.

18 Insert the hydraulic tappets into their original bores in the cylinder head unless they have been renewed.

19 Lubricate the rocker arms and place them over their respective tappets and valve stems. Lubricate the bearing surfaces (see illustration) and then refit the camshaft.

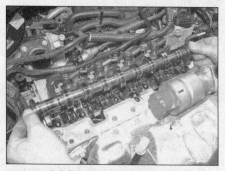

9.8 Remove the camshaft

9.10 Remove the rocker arms (cam followers)

9.11 Use long nose pliers to remove the hydraulic tappets

9.19 Lubricate the bearing surfaces

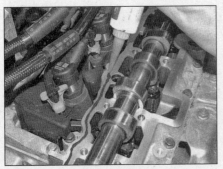

9.20 Apply sealant to the camshaft housing

9.21 Refit the bearing ladder

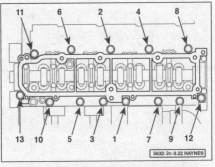

9.22 Tighten the bolts to the specified torque in the order shown

20 Apply a thin bead of silicone sealant (Ford part No WSE-M4G323-A4) to the mating surface of the camshaft cover/bearing ladder as shown (see illustration).
21 Assembly the bearing ladder within 10 minutes of applying the sealant (see illustration). Ford technicians use a special tool (303-245) to align the bearing ladder, however 2 suitable bolts (with their heads and threads cut off) can be used if the tool is not available.
22 Tighten the bolts to the specified torque in sequence (see illustration).
23 Fit a new camshaft oil seal as described in Section 14.
24 Refit the camshaft sprocket, and tighten the retaining bolt.
25 Refit the timing belt and temporarily refit the crankshaft pulley bolt – use the old bolt. Rotate the engine at least 20 revolutions to allow the oil pump to deliver oil to the camshaft and associated components. Refit the timing belt cover.
26 Refit the remainder of the components in the reverse order of removal.

10 Cylinder head – removal and refitting

Removal

1 Apply the handbrake, then jack up the front of the vehicle and support it on axle stands (see 'Jacking and vehicle support').

2 Disconnect the battery as described in Chapter 14 Section 6.
3 Drain the cooling system as described in Chapter 1B Section 30.
4 Remove the timing belt, camshaft, rocker arms and hydraulic tappets as described in Section 9.
5 Remove the turbocharger and exhaust manifold as described in Chapter 4B.
6 Unbolt the fuel filter assembly (and move it to one side) and the remove the glow plugs as described in Chapter 5A Section 12.
7 Undo the upper mounting bolts, and pivot the alternator away from the engine, undo the oil dipstick guide tube bolt, then undo the bolts securing the alternator mounting bracket to the cylinder head/block (see illustration).
8 Undo the coolant outlet housing (left-hand

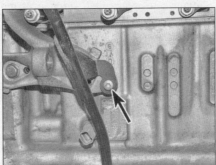

10.7 The engine oil level dipstick guide tube is secured to the alternator bracket by a Torx bolt (arrowed)

end of the cylinder head) retaining bolts, slacken the two bolts securing the housing support bracket to the top of the transmission bellhousing, and move the outlet housing away from the cylinder head a little (see illustration). There is no need to disconnect the hoses.
9 Remove the brake vacuum pump as described in Chapter 9 Section 21.
10 Disconnect the high-pressure fuel pipe from the common rail to the pump, and disconnect the fuel supply and return hoses. Where fitted, remove the bracket at the rear of the pump, then undo the bolt/nut and remove the pump and mounting bracket as an assembly (see illustrations). Immediately seal all the openings in the fuel system. Note that a new high-pressure pipe must be fitted – see Chapter 4B Section 9.

10.8 Access to the coolant outlet housing will be improved if the vacuum pump is removed first

10.10a Remove the high-pressure pipe (arrowed)

10.10b Lift up the green collars and...

10.10c ...remove the fuel bleed hoses from the injectors

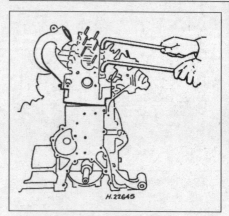

10.14 Free the cylinder head using angled rods

10.18a Pull the non-return valve from the cylinder head...

10.18b ...and push a new one into place

11 Unbolt the EGR pipe and inlet duct from the rear of the cylinder head.

12 Check that no components or electrical connectors are still fitted to the cylinder head.

13 Working in the reverse of the sequence shown **(see illustration 10.32)** undo the cylinder head bolts. Discard the bolts – new ones must be fitted.

14 Release the cylinder head from the cylinder block and location dowels by rocking it. The Ford tool for doing this consists simply of two metal rods with 90-degree angled ends **(see illustration)**. Do not prise between the mating faces of the cylinder head and block, as this may damage the gasket faces.

15 Lift the cylinder head from the block, and recover the gasket.

Preparation for refitting

16 The mating faces of the cylinder head and cylinder block must be perfectly clean before refitting the head. Ford recommend the use of a scouring agent for this purpose, but acceptable results can be achieved by using a hard plastic or wood scraper to remove all traces of gasket and carbon. The same method can be used to clean the piston crowns. Take particular care to avoid scoring or gouging the cylinder head/cylinder block mating surfaces during the cleaning operations, as aluminium alloy is easily

damaged. Make sure that the carbon is not allowed to enter the oil and water passages – this is particularly important for the lubrication system, as carbon could block the oil supply to the engine's components. Using adhesive tape and paper, seal the water, oil and bolt holes in the cylinder block. To prevent carbon entering the gap between the pistons and bores, smear a little grease in the gap. After cleaning each piston, use a small brush to remove all traces of grease and carbon from the gap, then wipe away the remainder with a clean rag.

17 Check the mating surfaces of the cylinder block and the cylinder head for nicks, deep scratches and other damage. If slight, they may be removed carefully with a file, but if excessive, machining may be the only alternative to renewal. If warpage of the cylinder head gasket surface is suspected, use a straight-edge to check it for distortion. Refer to Part E of this Chapter if necessary.

18 Thoroughly clean the threads of the cylinder head bolt holes in the cylinder block. Ensure that the bolts run freely in their threads, and that all traces of oil and water are removed from each bolt hole. If required, pull the oil feed non-return valve from the cylinder head, and check the ball moves freely. Push a new valve into place if necessary **(see illustrations)**.

Gasket selection

19 The gasket thickness is indicated by

10.23 Measure the piston protrusion using a DTI gauge

notches/holes on the front edge of the gasket. If the crankshaft or pistons/connecting rods have not been disturbed, fit a new gasket with the same number of notches/holes as the previous one. If the crankshaft/piston or connecting rods have been disturbed, it's necessary to work out the piston protrusion as follows:

20 Remove the crankshaft timing pin, then turn the crankshaft until pistons 1 and 4 are at TDC (Top Dead Centre). Position a dial test indicator (dial gauge) on the cylinder block adjacent to the rear of No 1 piston, and zero it on the block face. Transfer the probe to the crown of No 1 piston (10.0 mm in from the rear edge), then slowly turn the crankshaft back-and-forth past TDC, noting the highest reading on the indicator. Record this reading as protrusion A.

21 Repeat the check described in paragraph 18, this time 10.0 mm in from the front edge of the No 1 piston crown. Record this reading as protrusion B.

22 Add protrusion A to protrusion B, then divide the result by 2 to obtain an average reading for piston No 1.

23 Repeat the procedure described in paragraphs 20 to 22 on piston 4, then turn the crankshaft through 180° and carry out the procedure on the piston Nos 2 and 3 **(see illustration)**. Check that there is a maximum difference of 0.07 mm protrusion between any two pistons.

24 If a dial test indicator is not available, piston protrusion may be measured using a straight-edge and feeler blades or Vernier calipers. However, this is much less accurate, and cannot therefore be recommended.

25 Note the greatest piston protrusion measurement, and use this to determine the correct cylinder head gasket from the table below. The series of notches/holes on the side of the gasket are used for thickness identification **(see illustration)**.

Refitting

26 Turn the crankshaft and position Nos 1 and 4 pistons at TDC, then turn the crankshaft a quarter turn (90°) anti-clockwise.

27 Thoroughly clean the surfaces of the cylinder head and block.

28 Make sure that the locating dowels are in

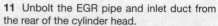

10.25 Cylinder head gasket thickness identification notches (arrowed)

10.28 Ensure the gasket locates over the dowels (arrowed)

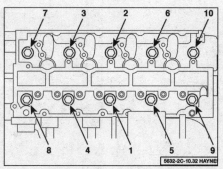

10.32 Cylinder head bolt tightening sequence

place, then fit the correct gasket the right way round on the cylinder block (see illustration).
29 Carefully lower the cylinder head onto the gasket and block, making sure that it locates correctly onto the dowels.
30 Apply a smear of grease to the threads, and to the underside of the heads of the new cylinder head bolts.
31 Carefully insert the cylinder head bolts into their holes (do not drop them in) and initially finger-tighten them.
32 Working progressively and in sequence, tighten the cylinder head bolts to their Stage 1 torque setting, using a torque wrench and suitable socket (see illustration).
33 Once all the bolts have been tightened to their Stage 1 torque setting, working again in the specified sequence, tighten each bolt to the specified Stage 2 setting. Finally, angle-tighten the bolts through the specified Stage 3 angle. It is recommended that an angle-measuring gauge is used during this stage of tightening, to ensure accuracy. **Note:** *Retightening of the cylinder head bolts after running the engine is not required.*
34 Refit the hydraulic tappets, rocker arms, and camshaft housing (complete with camshafts) as described in Section 9.
35 Refit the timing belt as described in Section 7.
36 The remainder of refitting is a reversal of removal, noting the following points.

a) *Use a new seal when refitting the coolant outlet housing.*
b) *When refitting a cylinder head, it is good practice to renew the thermostat.*
c) *Refit the camshaft position sensor and set the air gap with reference to Chapter 4B Section 12.*
d) *Tighten all fasteners to the specified torque where given.*
e) *Refill the cooling system as described in Chapter 1B Section 30.*
f) *The engine may run erratically for the first few miles, until the engine management ECM relearns its stored values.*

11 Sump – removal and refitting

Removal

1 Drain the engine oil, then clean and refit the engine oil drain plug, tightening it securely. If the engine is nearing its service interval when the oil and filter are due for renewal, it is recommended that the filter is also removed, and a new one fitted. After reassembly, the engine can then be refilled with fresh oil. Refer to Chapter 1B Section 6 for further information.
2 Apply the handbrake, then jack up the front of the vehicle and support it on axle stands (see 'Jacking and vehicle support'). Undo the bolts and remove the engine undershield.

3 Remove the exhaust front pipe as described in Chapter 4B Section 18.
4 Where necessary, disconnect the wiring connector from the oil temperature sender unit, which is screwed into the sump.
5 Progressively slacken and remove all the sump retaining bolts/nuts. Since the sump bolts vary in length, remove each bolt in turn, and store it in its correct fitted order by pushing it through a clearly-marked cardboard template. This will avoid the possibility of installing the bolts in the wrong locations on refitting.
6 Try to break the joint by striking the sump with the palm of your hand, then lower and withdraw the sump from under the car. If the sump is stuck (which is quite likely) use a putty knife or similar, carefully inserted between the sump and block. Ease the knife along the joint until the sump is released. While the sump is removed, take the opportunity to check the oil pump pick-up/strainer for signs of clogging or splitting. If necessary, remove the pump as described in Section 12, and clean or renew the strainer.

Refitting

7 Clean all traces of sealant from the mating surfaces of the cylinder block/crankcase and sump, then use a clean rag to wipe out the sump and the engine's interior.
8 Ensure that the sump mating surfaces are clean and dry, then apply a 3mm diameter bead of sealant (Ford part No WSE-M4G323-A4) to the sump mating surface (see illustration). The sealant must be applied to the Inside of the bolt holes. Note that the sump must be installed within 10 minutes of applying the sealant, and the bolts tightened within a further 5 minutes.
9 Offer up the sump to the cylinder block/crankcase. Refit its retaining bolts/nuts, ensuring that each bolt is screwed into its original location. Tighten the bolts evenly and progressively to the specified torque setting (see illustration).
10 Reconnect the wiring connector to the oil temperature sensor (where fitted).
11 Lower the vehicle to the ground, wait at least 30 minutes and then refill the engine with oil as described in Chapter 1B Section 6.

11.8 Apply a bead of sealant to the sump or crankcase mating surface. Ensure the sealant is applied to the inside of the retaining bolt holes

11.9 Refit the sump and tighten the bolts

12.4 Oil pick-up tube bolts (arrowed)

12.5 Oil pump retaining bolts (arrowed)

12 Oil pump – removal, inspection and refitting

Removal

1 Remove the sump as described in Section 11.

2 Remove the crankshaft sprocket as described in Section 8. Recover the locating key from the crankshaft.

3 Disconnect the wiring plug, undo the bolts and remove the crankshaft position sensor, located on the right-hand end of the cylinder block.

4 Undo the three Torx security bolts and remove the oil pump pick-up tube from the pump/block **(see illustration)**. Discard the oil seal, a new one must be fitted.

5 Undo the 8 bolts, and remove the oil pump **(see illustration)**.

Inspection

6 Undo and remove the Torx bolts securing the cover to the oil pump **(see illustration)**. Examine the pump rotors and body for signs of wear and damage. If worn, the complete pump must be renewed.

7 Remove the circlip, and extract the cap, valve piston and spring, noting which way around they are fitted **(see illustrations)**. The

condition of the relief valve spring can only be measured by comparing it with a new one; if there is any doubt about its condition, it should also be renewed.

8 Refit the relief valve piston and spring, then secure them in place with the circlip.

9 Refit the cover to the oil pump, and tighten the Torx bolts securely.

Refitting

10 Remove all traces of sealant, and thoroughly clean the mating surfaces of the oil pump and cylinder block.

11 Apply a 4 mm diameter bead of silicone sealant to the mating face of the cylinder block **(see illustration)**. Ensure that no

12.6 Undo the Torx bolts and remove the pump cover

12.7a Remove the circlip…

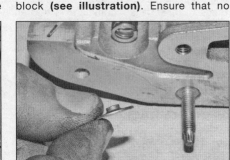

12.7b …cap…

12.7c …spring…

12.7d …and piston

12.11 Apply a bead of sealant to the cylinder block mating surface

12.12a Fit a new seal...

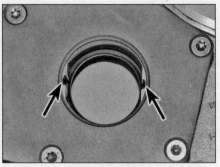

12.12b ...align the pump gear flats (arrowed)...

12.12c ...with those of the crankshaft (arrowed)

sealant enters any of the holes in the block.

12 With a new oil seal fitted, refit the oil pump over the end of the crankshaft, aligning the flats in the pump drive gear with the flats machined in the crankshaft **(see illustrations)**. Note that new oil pumps are supplied with the oil seal already fitted, and a seal protector sleeve. The sleeve fits over the end of the crankshaft to protect the seal as the pump is fitted.

13 Install the oil pump bolts and tighten them to the specified torque.

14 Refit the oil pick-up tube to the pump/ cylinder block using a new O-ring seal. Ensure the oil dipstick guide tube is correctly refitted.

15 Refit the woodruff key to the crankshaft, and slide the crankshaft sprocket into place.

16 The remainder of refitting is a reversal of removal.

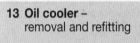

13 Oil cooler –
removal and refitting

Removal

1 Apply the handbrake, then jack up the front of the vehicle and support it on axle stands (see *'Jacking and vehicle support'*). Undo the fasteners and remove the engine undershield.

2 The oil cooler is fitted to the front of the oil filter housing. Drain the coolant as described in Chapter 1B Section 30.

3 Drain the engine oil as described in Chap-

ter 1B Section 6, or be prepared for fluid spillage.

4 Undo the bolts/stud and remove the oil cooler **(see illustration)**. Recover the gasket.

Refitting

5 Fit a new gasket into the recesses in the oil filter housing, and refit the cooler. Tighten the bolts securely.

6 Refill or top-up the cooling system and engine oil level as described in Chapter 1B or Weekly checks 0 Section 5 (as applicable). Start the engine, and check the oil cooler for signs of leakage.

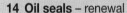

14 Oil seals – renewal

Crankshaft

Right-hand oil seal

1 Remove the crankshaft sprocket and Woodruff key as described in Section 8.

2 Measure and note the fitted depth of the oil seal.

3 Pull the oil seal from the housing using a screwdriver. Alternatively, drill a small hole in the oil seal, and use a self-tapping screw and a pair of pliers to remove it **(see illustration)**.

4 Clean the oil seal housing and the crankshaft sealing surface.

5 The new seal should be supplied with a protective sleeve, which fits over the end of the crankshaft to prevent any damage to

13.4 Undo the oil cooler bolts/stud (arrowed)

the seal lip. With the sleeve in place, press the seal (open end first) into the pump to the previously-noted depth, using a suitable tube or socket **(see illustrations)**.

6 Where applicable, remove the plastic sleeve from the end of the crankshaft.

7 Refit the crankshaft sprocket as described in Section 8.

Left-hand oil seal

8 Remove the flywheel, as described in Section 16.

9 Measure and note the fitted depth of the oil seal.

10 Pull the oil seal from the housing using a screwdriver. Alternatively, drill a small hole in the oil seal, and use a self-tapping screw and a pair of pliers to remove it **(see illustration 14.3)**.

11 Clean the oil seal housing and the crankshaft sealing surface.

14.3 Take great care not to mark the crankshaft whilst levering out the oil seal

14.5a Slide the seal and protective sleeve over the end of the crankshaft...

14.5b ...and press the seal into place

14.12 Slide the seal and protective sleeve over the left-hand end of the crankshaft

14.16 Drill a hole, insert a self-tapping screw, and pull the seal from place using pliers

14.18a Use the correct tool to fit the seal...

14.18b ...or a suitable socket

12 The new seal should be supplied with a protective sleeve, which fits over the end of the crankshaft to prevent any damage to the seal lip **(see illustration)**. With the sleeve in place, press the seal (open end first) into the housing to the previously-noted depth, using a suitable tube or socket.

13 Where applicable, remove the plastic sleeve from the end of the crankshaft.

14 Refit the flywheel, as described in Section 16.

Camshaft

15 Remove the camshaft sprocket as described in Section 8. In principle there is no need to remove the timing belt completely, but remember that if the belt has been contaminated with oil, it must be renewed.

16 Pull the oil seal from the housing using a hooked instrument. Alternatively, drill a small hole in the oil seal and use a self-tapping screw and a pair of pliers to remove it **(see illustration)**.

17 Clean the oil seal housing and the camshaft sealing surface.

18 Press the seal (open end first) into the housing to the previously-noted depth, using either the correct tool (303-684), a suitable tube or a socket which bears only of the outer edge of the seal **(see illustrations)**. If the seal was supplied with a protective sleeve, remove it.

19 Refit the camshaft sprocket as described in Section 8.

20 Where necessary, fit a new timing belt with reference to Section 7.

15.3 The oil pressure switch is located on the front face of the cylinder block (arrowed)

15.5 The oil level sensor is located on the rear face of the cylinder block (arrowed)

15 Oil pressure switch and level sensor – removal and refitting

Removal

Oil pressure switch

1 The oil pressure switch is located at the front of the cylinder block, adjacent to the oil dipstick guide tube. Note that on some models, access to the switch may be improved if the vehicle is jacked up and supported on axle stands, then undo the bolts and remove the engine undershield so that the switch can be reached from underneath (see *'Jacking and vehicle support'*).

2 Remove the protective sleeve from the wiring plug (where applicable), then disconnect the wiring from the switch.

3 Unscrew the switch from the cylinder block, and recover the sealing washer **(see illustration)**. Be prepared for oil spillage, and if the switch is to be left removed from the engine for any length of time, plug the hole in the cylinder block.

Oil level sensor

4 The oil level sensor is located at the rear of the cylinder block. Jack up the front of the vehicle and support it securely on axle stands (see *'Jacking and vehicle support'*). Undo the bolts and remove the engine undershield.

5 Reach up between the driveshaft and the cylinder block, and disconnect the sensor wiring plug **(see illustration)**.

6 Using an open-ended spanner, unscrew the sensor and withdraw it from position.

Refitting

Oil pressure switch

7 Examine the sealing washer for any signs of damage or deterioration, and if necessary renew.

8 Refit the switch, complete with washer, and tighten it to the specified torque where given.

9 Refit the engine undershield, and lower the vehicle to the ground.

Oil level sensor

10 Smear a little silicone sealant on the threads and refit the sensor to the cylinder block, tightening it securely.

11 Reconnect the sensor wiring plug.

12 Refit the engine undershield, and lower the vehicle to the ground.

16 Flywheel – removal, inspection and refitting

Removal

1 Remove the transmission as described in Chapter 7A Section 6, then remove the clutch assembly as described in Chapter 6 Section 6.

16.2 Lock the flywheel with a 12mm diameter rod or bolt (arrowed)

16.9 Flywheel retaining Torx bolts

2 Prevent the flywheel from turning. Do not attempt to lock the flywheel in position using the crankshaft pulley locking tool described in Section 3. Insert a 12 mm diameter rod or drill bit through the hole in the flywheel cover casting, and into a slot in the flywheel (see illustration)

3 Make alignment marks between the flywheel and crankshaft to aid refitment. Slacken and remove the flywheel retaining bolts, and remove the flywheel from the end of the crankshaft. Be careful not to drop it; it is heavy. If the flywheel locating dowel (where fitted) is a loose fit in the crankshaft end, remove it and store it with the flywheel for safe-keeping. Discard the flywheel bolts; new ones must be used on refitting.

Inspection

4 Examine the flywheel for scoring of the clutch face, and for wear or chipping of the ring gear teeth. If the clutch face is scored, the flywheel may be surface-ground, but renewal is preferable. Seek the advice of a Ford dealer or engine reconditioning specialist to see if machining is possible. If the ring gear is worn or damaged, the flywheel must be renewed, as it is not possible to renew the ring gear separately.

5 All engines are fitted with a dual-mass flywheel. The maximum travel of the primary mass in relation to the secondary must not exceed 15 teeth (or 20 degrees). If in doubt remove the flywheel and have a suitably equipped specialist check the flywheel. Inspect the flywheel for any grease or debris from the interface between the fixed part and the movable part of the flywheel. If any doubt to the condition of the flywheel exists, despite the expense we recommend replacing it.

Refitting

6 Clean the mating surfaces of the flywheel and crankshaft. Remove any remaining locking compound from the threads of the crankshaft holes, using the correct size of tap, if available.

7 If the new flywheel retaining bolts are not supplied with their threads already pre-coated, apply a suitable thread-locking compound to the threads of each bolt.

8 Ensure that the locating dowel is in position. Offer up the flywheel, locating it on the dowel

(where fitted), and fit the new retaining bolts. Where no locating dowel is fitted, align the previously-made marks to ensure the flywheel is refitted in its original position.

9 Lock the flywheel using the method employed on dismantling, and tighten the retaining bolts to the specified torque (see illustration).

10 Refit the clutch as described in Chapter 6 Section 6. Remove the flywheel locking tool, and refit the transmission as described in Chapter 7A Section 6.

17 Engine/transmission mountings – inspection and renewal

General

1 The engine/transmission mountings seldom require attention, but broken or deteriorated mountings should be renewed immediately, or the added strain placed on the driveline components may cause damage or wear.

2 While separate mountings may be removed and refitted individually, if more than one is disturbed at a time – such as if the engine/transmission unit is removed from its mountings – they must be reassembled and their fasteners tightened in the position marked on removal.

3 On reassembly, the complete weight of the engine/transmission unit must not be taken by the mountings until all are correctly aligned with the marks made on removal. Tighten the engine/transmission mounting fasteners to their specified torque wrench settings.

17.9 Right-hand engine mounting-to-engine bracket retaining nuts (arrowed)

Inspection

4 During the check, the engine/transmission unit must be raised slightly, to remove its weight from the mountings.

5 Raise the front of the vehicle, and support it securely on axle stands. Position a jack under the sump, with a large block of wood between the jack head and the sump, then carefully raise the engine/transmission just enough to take the weight off the mountings.

⚠ **Warning: DO NOT place any part of your body under the engine when it is supported only by a jack.**

6 Check the mountings to see if the rubber is cracked, hardened or separated from the metal components. Sometimes the rubber will split right down the centre.

7 Check for relative movement between each mounting's brackets and the engine/transmission or body (use a large screwdriver or lever to attempt to move the mountings). If movement is noted, lower the engine and check-tighten the mounting fasteners.

Renewal

Note: The following paragraphs assume the engine is supported beneath the sump as described earlier.

Right-hand mounting

8 Lift up the coolant expansion tank and position it to one side. Note there is no need to disconnect the coolant pipes.

9 Mark the position of the mounting on the vehicle, right-hand inner wing panel, then undo the three nuts securing the mounting to the engine bracket (see illustration). Discard the nuts, new ones must be fitted.

10 Undo the three retaining bolts securing the mounting to the inner wing panel and withdraw the mounting from the vehicle (see illustration).

11 On refitting, tighten all fasteners to the torque wrench settings specified. Re-align the marks made on removal, then tighten the new mounting bracket retaining nuts.

Left-hand mounting

12 Remove the battery and battery tray as described in Chapter 5A Section 4. Note that it is not necessary to remove the powertrain control module from the battery tray, just position the tray clear for access to the mounting.

17.10 Right-hand engine mounting-to-inner wing panel retaining bolts (arrowed)

17.13 Undo the retaining nuts and lift out the battery tray support bracket

17.14a Left-hand engine mounting bracket-to-transmission retaining bolts (arrowed) …

17.14b … and mounting-to-body sidemember retaining bolts (arrowed)

17.16 Rear mounting/roll restrictor retaining bolts (arrowed)

13 Undo the three nuts securing the battery tray support bracket in position. Release the wiring loom from the support bracket and lift the support bracket out of the engine compartment **(see illustration)**.

14 With the transmission supported, mark the position of the mounting bracket on the transmission and on the body side member. Undo the three bolts securing the mounting bracket to the transmission and the two bolts securing the mounting to the body side member **(see illustrations)**. Remove the mounting from the engine compartment.

15 On refitting, re-align the mounting in the position noted on removal, then tighten all fasteners to the specified torque wrench settings.

Refit the components disturbed for access using a reversal of the removal procedures.

Rear mounting (roll restrictor)

16 To remove the engine rear mounting, apply the handbrake, then jack up the front of the car and support it on axle stands (see *'Jacking and vehicle support'*). Unscrew the through-bolts and remove the engine rear mounting link from the bracket on the transmission and from the bracket on the subframe **(see illustration)**. Hold the engine stationary while the bolts are being removed, since the link will be under tension.

17 On refitting, ensure that the bolts are securely tightened to the specified torque wrench setting.

Chapter 2 Part D
1.6 litre DOHC diesel engine in-car repair procedures

Contents

Degrees of difficulty

Easy, suitable for novice with little experience	**Fairly easy,** suitable for beginner with some experience	**Fairly difficult,** suitable for competent DIY mechanic	**Difficult,** suitable for experienced DIY mechanic	**Very difficult,** suitable for expert DIY or professional

Specifications

General
Designation	Duratorq TDCi Double Overhead Camshaft (DOHC)
Engine codes	HHJD and HHJE
Capacity	1560 cc
Bore	75.0 mm
Stroke	88.3 mm
Compression ratio	18.0: 1
Firing order...	1-3-4-2 (No 1 cylinder at timing belt end)
Direction of crankshaft rotation	Clockwise (seen from right-hand side of car)

Compression pressures (engine hot, at cranking speed)
Normal	20 ± 5 bar
Minimum	15 bar
Maximum difference between any two cylinders...............	5 bar

Camshafts
Drive:
Inlet camshaft......................................	Toothed belt from crankshaft
Exhaust camshaft....................................	Chain-drive from inlet camshaft
Endfloat	0.195 to 0.300 mm

Lubrication system
Oil pump type...	Gear-type, driven directly by the right-hand end of the crankshaft, by two flats machined along the crankshaft journal

Minimum oil pressure at 80°C:
1000 rpm	1.3 bar
4000 rpm	3.5 bar

Torque wrench settings

	Nm	lbf ft
Auxiliary drivebelt tensioner	25	18
Big-end bearing cap bolts: *		
Stage 1	10	7
Stage 2	Slacken 180°	
Stage 3	10	7
Stage 4	Angle-tighten a further 130°	
Camshaft cover/bearing ladder:		
Studs	10	7
Bolts	10	7
Camshaft bearing caps	10	7
Camshaft position sensor bolt	5	4
Camshaft sprocket bolt:		
Stage 1	20	15
Stage 2	Angle-tighten a further 50°	
Coolant outlet housing bolts	10	7
Crankshaft position sensor bolt	5	4
Crankshaft pulley/sprocket bolt: *		
Stage 1	30	22
Stage 2	Angle-tighten a further 180°	
Cylinder head bolts: *		
Stage 1	20	15
Stage 2	40	30
Stage 3	Angle-tighten a further 260°	
Cylinder head cover/inlet manifold	10	7
EGR valve	10	7
Engine mountings:		
Left-hand mounting to transmission	80	59
Left-hand mounting to body	80	59
Right-hand mounting bracket to engine	60	44
Right-hand mounting to engine bracket*	48	35
Right-hand mounting to body	48	35
Roll restrictor/rear mounting bolts	48	35
Engine-to-transmission bolts	48	35
Flywheel bolts: *		
Stage 1	18	13
Stage 2	Angle-tighten a further 75°	
Fuel pump sprocket nut	43	32
High-pressure fuel pipe unions	25	18
Main bearing ladder outer seam bolts:		
Stage 1	5	4
Stage 2	10	7
Main bearing ladder to cylinder block (M11 bolts): *		
Stage 1	10	7
Stage 2	Slacken 180°	
Stage 3	30	22
Stage 4	Angle-tighten a further 140°	
Piston oil jet spray tube bolt	20	15
Oil filter cover	25	18
Oil pick-up pipe	10	7
Oil pressure switch	25	18
Oil pump to cylinder block	10	7
Oil separator	10	7
Sump drain plug	34	25
Sump bolts/nuts	10	7
Throttle housing to inlet manifold	8	6
Timing belt covers	10	7
Timing belt idler pulley	37	27
Timing belt tensioner pulley	30	22
Timing chain tensioner	10	7
Vacuum pump	20	15

*Use new fasteners

1   General Information

How to use this Chapter

1 This Part of Chapter 2 is devoted to in-car repair procedures on the 1.6 litre Duratorq diesel engine. All procedures concerning engine removal, refitting, and overhaul can be found in Chapter 2F.

2 Refer to Vehicle identification numbers in the Reference Section at the end of this manual for details of engine code locations.

3 Most of the operations included in this Chapter are based on the assumption that the engine is still installed in the car. Therefore, if this information is being used during a complete engine overhaul, with the engine already removed, many of the steps included here will not apply.

Engine description

4 The 1.6 litre Duratorq engine is the result of development collaboration between Citroën/Peugeot and Ford. The engine is of double overhead camshaft (DOHC) 16-valve design. The direct injection, turbocharged, four-cylinder engine is mounted transversely, with the transmission mounted on the left-hand side.

5 A toothed timing belt drives the inlet camshaft, high-pressure fuel pump and coolant pump. The inlet camshaft drives the exhaust camshaft via a chain. The camshafts operate the inlet and exhaust valves via rocker arms which are supported at their pivot ends by hydraulic self-adjusting tappets. The camshafts are supported by bearings machined directly in the cylinder head and camshaft bearing housing.

6 The high-pressure fuel pump supplies fuel to the fuel accumulator rail, and subsequently to the electronically-controlled injectors which inject the fuel direct into the combustion chambers. This design differs from the previous type where an injection pump supplies the fuel at high-pressure to each injector. The earlier, conventional type injection pump required fine calibration and timing, and these functions are now completed by the high-pressure pump, electronic injectors and engine management powertrain control module (PCM).

7 The crankshaft runs in five main bearings of the usual shell type. Endfloat is controlled by thrustwashers either side of No 2 main bearing.

8 The pistons are selected to be of matching weight, and incorporate fully-floating gudgeon pins retained by circlips.

9 The gear-type oil pump is fitted over the end of the crankshaft, and is driven by interlocking machined flats on the crankshaft and pump gear.

Repair operations precaution

10 The engine is a complex unit with numerous accessories and ancillary components. The design of the engine compartment is such that every conceivable space has been utilised, and access to virtually all of the engine components is extremely limited. In many cases, ancillary components will have to be removed, or moved to one side, and wiring, pipes and hoses will have to be disconnected or removed from various cable clips and support brackets.

11 When working on this engine, read through the entire procedure first, look at the car and engine at the same time, and establish whether you have the necessary tools, equipment, skill and patience to proceed. Allow considerable time for any operation, and be prepared for the unexpected.

12 Because of the limited access, many of the engine photographs appearing in this Chapter were, by necessity, taken with the engine removed from the vehicle.

⚠ **Warning: It is essential to observe strict precautions when working on the fuel system components of the engine, particularly the high-pressure side of the system. Before carrying out any engine operations that entail working on, or near, any part of the fuel system, refer to the special information given in Chapter 4B, Section 2.**

Operations with engine in car

a) *Compression pressure – testing.*
b) *Cylinder head cover/inlet manifold – removal and refitting.*
c) *Crankshaft pulley – removal and refitting.*
d) *Timing belt covers – removal and refitting.*
e) *Timing belt – removal, refitting and adjustment.*
f) *Timing belt tensioner and sprockets – removal and refitting.*
g) *Camshaft oil seal – renewal.*
h) *Camshaft, rocker arms and hydraulic tappets – removal, inspection and refitting.*
i) *Sump – removal and refitting.*
j) *Oil pump – removal and refitting.*
k) *Crankshaft oil seals – renewal.*
l) *Engine/transmission mountings – inspection and renewal.*
m) *Flywheel – removal, inspection and refitting.*

2   Compression and leakdown tests – description and interpretation

Compression test

1 When engine performance is down, or if misfiring occurs which cannot be attributed to the fuel system, a compression test can provide diagnostic clues as to the engine's condition. If the test is performed regularly, it can give warning of trouble before any other symptoms become apparent.

2 The cause of poor compression is less easy to establish on a diesel engine than on a petrol one. The effect of introducing oil into the cylinders ('wet' testing) is not conclusive, because there is a risk that the oil will sit in the swirl chamber or in the recess on the piston crown instead of passing to the rings. However, the following can be used as a rough guide to diagnosis.

3 All cylinders should produce very similar pressures; any difference greater than that specified indicates the existence of a fault. Note that the compression should build-up quickly in a healthy engine; low compression on the first stroke, followed by gradually-increasing pressure on successive strokes, indicates worn piston rings. A low compression reading on the first stroke, which does not build-up during successive strokes, indicates leaking valves or a blown head gasket (a cracked head could also be the cause). Deposits on the undersides of the valve heads can also cause low compression.

4 A low reading from two adjacent cylinders is almost certainly due to the head gasket having blown between them; the presence of coolant in the engine oil will confirm this.

5 If the compression reading is unusually high, the cylinder head surfaces, valves and pistons are probably coated with carbon deposits. If this is the case, the cylinder head should be removed and decarbonised (see Part D).

6 A compression tester specifically intended for diesel engines must be used, because of the higher pressures involved. The tester is connected to an adapter which screws into the glow plug hole.

7 Note that It is necessary to disconnect certain wiring connectors in the engine management system to allow the compression test to be performed. This will log a fault code in the powertrain control module when the engine is turned over on the starter, and the fault code will have to be cleared, using Ford diagnostic equipment or a compatible alternative, on completion of the test. It may not be possible to start the engine until the fault code is cleared. For this reason primarily, but also due to the cost of purchasing a compression tester for occasional use, it is advisable to have the compression test carried out by a Ford dealer or suitably-equipped garage.

Leakdown test

8 A leakdown test measures the rate at which compressed air fed into the cylinder is lost. It is an alternative to a compression test, and in many ways it is better, since the escaping air provides easy identification of where pressure loss is occurring (piston rings, valves or head gasket).

9 The equipment needed for leakdown testing is unlikely to be available to the home mechanic. If poor compression is suspected, have the test performed by a Ford dealer or suitably-equipped garage.

3.8 Insert a 5.0 mm diameter drill bit/bolt through the round hole in the sprocket flange, into the hole in the oil pump housing

3.9 Insert an 8.0 mm diameter drill bit/bolt through the hole in the camshaft sprocket into the corresponding hole in the cylinder head

3 Engine assembly/ valve timing holes – general information and usage

Note: *Do not attempt to rotate the engine whilst the crankshaft and camshaft are locked in position. If the engine is to be left in this state for a long period of time, it is a good idea to place suitable warning notices inside the vehicle, and in the engine compartment. This will reduce the possibility of the engine being accidentally cranked on the starter motor, which is likely to cause damage with the locking pins in place.*

1 Timing holes or slots are located in the crankshaft pulley flange, camshaft sprocket hub and high-pressure fuel pump sprocket. The holes/slots are used to position the pistons halfway up the cylinder bores. This will ensure that the valve timing is maintained during operations that require removal and refitting of the timing belt. When the holes/slots are aligned with their corresponding holes in the cylinder block and cylinder head, suitable diameter bolts/pins can be inserted to lock the crankshaft and camshaft in position, preventing rotation.

3.10 Insert a 5.0 mm drill bit/bolt through the round hole in the fuel pump sprocket into the cylinder head

2 Note that the type of fuel system used on these engines does not have a conventional diesel injection pump, but instead uses a high-pressure fuel pump. Although it may be argued that timing of the fuel pump is irrelevant because it merely pressurises the fuel in the fuel rail, Ford include this procedure using the same timing rod/pin used for crankshaft sprocket timing. In addition, note that the hole in the fuel pump sprocket only aligns correctly with the hole in the mounting bracket every 12 revolutions of the crankshaft (or every 6 revolutions of the camshaft sprocket).

3 To align the engine assembly/valve timing holes, proceed as follows.

4 Firmly apply the handbrake, then jack up the front of the vehicle and support it securely on axle stands (see *'Jacking and vehicle support'*). Remove the right-hand front roadwheel.

5 To gain access to the crankshaft pulley, to enable the engine to be turned, the lower wheel arch plastic liner must be removed. The liner is secured by several plastic expanding rivets/nut/screws. To remove the rivets, push in the centre pins a little, then prise the clips from place. Remove the liner from under the front wing. The crankshaft can then be turned using a suitable socket and extension bar fitted to the pulley bolt.

6 Remove the upper and lower timing belt covers as described in Section 6.

7 Temporarily refit the crankshaft pulley bolt, remove the crankshaft locking tool, then turn the crankshaft until the timing hole in the camshaft sprocket hub is aligned with the corresponding hole, in approximately the 2 o'clock position, in the cylinder head. Note that the crankshaft must always be turned in a clockwise direction (viewed from the right-hand side of vehicle). Use a small mirror so that the position of the sprocket hub timing slot can be observed. When the slot is aligned with the corresponding hole in

the cylinder head, the camshaft is positioned correctly.

8 Insert a 5 mm diameter bolt, rod or drill through the hole in crankshaft sprocket flange and into the corresponding hole in the oil pump **(see illustration)**, if necessary, carefully turn the crankshaft either way until the rod enters the timing hole in the block.

9 Insert an 8 mm bolt, rod or drill through the hole in the camshaft sprocket hub and into engagement with the cylinder head **(see illustration)**.

10 Insert a 5 mm diameter bolt, rod or drill through the hole in the fuel pump sprocket and into the corresponding hole, in approximately the 5 o'clock position, in the cylinder head **(see illustration)**. Note the comment in paragraph 2 – if the fuel pump sprocket holes are not aligned during removal of the timing belt, it is of no consequence, however, it is important to align the holes during the refitting procedure. If timing alignment is only being checked and the holes do not align at this stage, rotate the crankshaft one turn at a time (max 12 turns) until the holes do align.

11 The crankshaft and camshaft are now locked in position, preventing unnecessary rotation while working on the engine.

4 Cylinder head cover/ inlet manifold – removal and refitting

 Warning: Refer to the precautionary information contained in Section 1 before proceeding.

Removal

1 Disconnect the battery negative terminal (refer to *'Disconnecting the battery'*).

2 Remove the windscreen cowl panel and bulkhead closure panel as described in Chapter 11 Section 20.

3 Undo the two bolts securing the injector

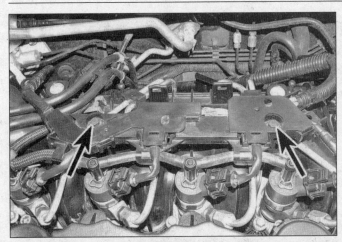

4.3 Undo the bolts (arrowed) securing the wiring harness trough to the inlet manifold

4.4a Disconnect the wiring connector from each injector ...

wiring harness trough to the top of the inlet manifold (see illustration).

4 Disconnect the wiring connector from the top of each injector, then lift off the wiring trough and move it to one side (see illustrations). Make sure the wiring harness is freed from any clips/brackets on the cylinder head cover/inlet manifold

5 Release the fuel hoses from the support bracket at the right-hand side of the cylinder head cover/inlet manifold.

6 Using a screwdriver, push in the retaining spring clip and disconnect the fuel return hose from the top of each injector. Plug the openings to prevent dirt ingress then move the return hose assembly to one side (see illustrations).

7 Unscrew the two bolts securing the EGR pipe to the right-hand end of the cylinder head cover/inlet manifold.

8 Disengage and release the retaining clamp securing the EGR pipe to the EGR valve at the rear of the engine. Undo the EGR pipe support bracket bolt and manipulate the EGR pipe up and out of the engine compartment (see illustrations).

9 Slacken the retaining clip and disconnect the intercooler hose from the resonator (see illustration).

10 Undo the bolt securing the resonator to

4.4b ... then lift off the wiring trough and move it to one side

4.6a Push in the retaining spring clip and disconnect the fuel return hose from the top of each injector ...

4.6b ... then move the return hose assembly to one side

4.8a Disengage and release the retaining clamp securing the EGR pipe to the EGR valve ...

4.8b ... undo the EGR pipe support bracket bolt ...

4.8c ... and manipulate the EGR pipe up and out of the engine compartment

4.9 Slacken the retaining clip and disconnect the intercooler hose from the resonator

4.10a Undo the bolt securing the resonator to the turbocharger flange

4.10b Pivot the resonator upwards and remove it from the engine ...

4.10c ... then recover the O-ring seal

4.11 Disengage the retaining clip tabs and disconnect the crankcase ventilation hose from the oil separator

4.12a Unbolt and remove the oil separator from the camshaft cover/bearing ladder ...

4.12b ... and recover the rubber seal

the turbocharger flange. Pivot the resonator upwards and remove it from the engine. Recover the O-ring seal **(see illustrations)**.

11 Disengage the retaining clip tabs and disconnect the crankcase ventilation hose from the oil separator **(see illustration)**.

12 Undo the 7 bolts and remove the oil separator from the camshaft cover/bearing ladder. Recover the rubber seal **(see illustrations)**.

13 Thoroughly clean the high-pressure fuel pipe unions at the fuel injectors and at the fuel accumulator rail at the rear of the engine.

14 Undo the union nuts and remove the high-pressure fuel pipes from the injectors and the fuel accumulator rail – counterhold the unions with a second spanner **(see illustration)**. Plug the openings to prevent dirt ingress. Note that new high-pressure fuel pipes will be required for refitting.

15 Release the vacuum hoses from the support bracket above the fuel filter. Undo the 3 bolts and move the wiring harness support bracket and vacuum hose support bracket clear of the inlet manifold **(see illustrations)**.

4.14 Use a second spanner to hold the injector port whilst slackening the fuel pipe unions

4.15a Undo the bolt at the front (arrowed) ...

4.15b ... the two bolts at the rear (arrowed) ...

4.15c ... and move the wiring harness support bracket ...

4.15d ... and vacuum hose support bracket clear of the inlet manifold

4.16 Undo the three bolts (arrowed) securing the throttle housing to the inlet manifold

4.17a Undo the remaining retaining bolt ...

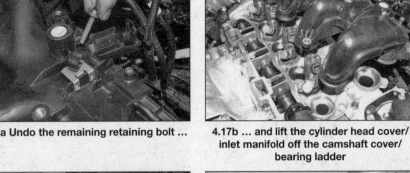

4.17b ... and lift the cylinder head cover/ inlet manifold off the camshaft cover/ bearing ladder

16 Undo the three bolts securing the throttle housing to the inlet manifold **(see illustration)**.
17 Make a final check that all wiring, hoses and brackets likely to impede removal of the cylinder head cover/inlet manifold are either disconnected or moved to one side. Undo the remaining retaining bolt and lift the cover/ manifold off the camshaft cover/bearing ladder. Recover the throttle housing flange seal and the manifold rubber seals **(see illustrations)**.

Refitting

18 Refitting is a reversal of removal, bearing in mind the following points:
a) *Examine the seals for signs of damage and deterioration, and renew if necessary. Smear a little clean engine oil on the manifold seals.*
b) *Renew the fuel injector high-pressure fuel pipes.*
c) *Tighten all retaining nuts, bolts and pipe unions to the specified torque, where given.*
d) *Refit the bulkhead closure panel and windscreen cowl panel as described in Chapter 11 Section 20.*
e) *On completion, prime and bleed the fuel system as described in Chapter 4B Section 3.*

4.17c Recover the throttle housing flange seal ...

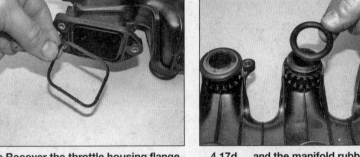

4.17d ... and the manifold rubber seals

the crankshaft. If the pulley is a tight fit, it can be drawn off the crankshaft using a suitable puller. If a puller is being used, refit the pulley retaining bolt without the washer, to avoid

damaging the crankshaft as the puller is tightened. With the pulley removed, note the cut-out which engages the tab on the nose of the crankshaft **(see illustrations)**.

5 Crankshaft pulley –
removal and refitting

Removal

1 Remove the auxiliary drivebelt as described in Chapter 1B Section 26.
2 To lock the crankshaft, working underneath the engine, insert a 12 mm diameter rod or bolt into the hole in the right-hand face of the engine block casting over the lower section of the flywheel **(see illustration)**. Note: *The hole in the casting and the hole in the flywheel are provided purely to lock the crankshaft whilst the pulley bolt is undone, it does not position the crankshaft at TDC. Rotate the crankshaft until the tool engages in the corresponding hole in the flywheel.*
3 Using a suitable socket and extension bar, unscrew the retaining bolt, remove the washer, then slide the pulley off the end of

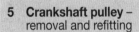

5.2 The locking pin/bolt (arrowed) must locate in the hole in the flywheel (arrowed) to prevent rotation

5.3a Undo the crankshaft pulley retaining bolt (arrowed)

5.3b Removing the crankshaft pulley – note the location cut-out and tab

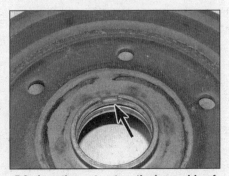

5.3c Location cut-out on the inner side of the crankshaft pulley

Caution: *Do not touch the outer magnetic sensor ring of the crankshaft sprocket with your fingers, or allow metallic particles to come into contact with it.*

Refitting

4 Refit the pulley to the end of the crankshaft, making sure the cut-out engages with the tab on the nose of the crankshaft.

5 Thoroughly clean the threads of the pulley retaining bolt, then apply a coat of locking compound to the bolt threads using Loctite (available from your Ford dealer); in the absence of this, any good-quality locking compound may be used. **Note:** *Ford recommend that a new bolt is fitted.*

6 Refit the crankshaft pulley retaining bolt and washer. Tighten the bolt to the specified

6.1 On models with air conditioning, undo the retaining nut (arrowed) and free the refrigerant pipe support bracket

6.3b … and remove the timing belt upper cover

6.6b Removing the lower timing belt cover

torque, then through the specified angle, preventing the crankshaft from turning using the method employed on removal.

7 Refit the auxiliary drivebelt as described in Chapter 1B Section 26.

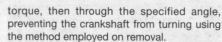

6 Timing belt covers – removal and refitting

⚠ **Warning:** *Refer to the precautionary information contained in Section 1 before proceeding.*

Removal

Upper cover

1 On models with air conditioning, undo

6.3a Undo the screws (arrowed) …

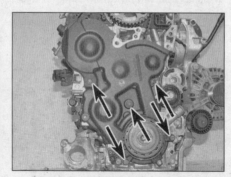

6.6a Lower timing belt cover screws (arrowed)

7.4 Removing the lower wheel arch liner

the retaining nut and free the refrigerant pipe support bracket from the stud on the suspension strut turret **(see illustration)**.

2 Lift the coolant expansion tank from its mountings and position it to one side as far as the hoses will allow.

3 Undo the 5 screws and remove the timing belt upper cover **(see illustrations)**.

Lower cover

4 Remove the upper cover as described previously.

5 Remove the crankshaft pulley as described in Section 5.

6 Unbolt and remove the auxiliary drivebelt tensioner, then undo the five bolts and remove the lower cover **(see illustrations)**.

Refitting

7 Refitting of all the covers is a reversal of the relevant removal procedure, ensuring that each cover section is correctly located, and that the cover retaining bolts are securely tightened.

7 Timing belt – removal, inspection, refitting and tensioning

General

1 The timing belt drives the inlet camshaft, high-pressure fuel pump, and coolant pump from a toothed sprocket on the end of the crankshaft. If the belt breaks or slips in service, the pistons are likely to hit the valve heads, resulting in expensive damage.

2 The timing belt should be renewed at the specified intervals, or earlier if it is contaminated with oil or at all noisy in operation (a 'scraping' noise due to uneven wear).

3 If the timing belt is being removed, it is a wise precaution to check the condition of the coolant pump at the same time (check for signs of coolant leakage). This may avoid the need to remove the timing belt again at a later stage, should the coolant pump fail.

Removal

4 Apply the handbrake, then jack up the front of the vehicle and support it on axle stands (see *'Jacking and vehicle support'*). Remove the front right-hand roadwheel, lower wheel arch liner (to expose the crankshaft pulley), and the engine undershield. The wheel arch liner is secured by several plastic expanding rivets/nuts/plastic clips **(see illustration)**.

5 Remove the auxiliary drivebelt as described in Chapter 1B Section 26.

6 Remove the upper and lower timing belt covers, as described in Section 6.

7 As a precaution against damage to the exhaust pipe flexible connection, refer to Chapter 4B Section 18 and disconnect the front exhaust pipe at the flange.

8 Position a trolley jack under the engine, and

7.8 Support the engine with a jack

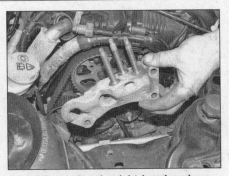

7.9 Removing the right-hand engine mounting support bracket

7.10 Undo the bolt (arrowed) and remove the crankshaft position sensor

using a block of wood on the jack head, take the weight of the engine **(see illustration)**.

9 Undo the bolts/nut and remove the right hand engine mounting – see Section 17. Also, unbolt and remove the mounting support bracket **(see illustration)**.

10 As a precaution against damage, undo the screw and remove the crankshaft position sensor adjacent to the crankshaft sprocket flange, and move it to one side **(see illustration)**.

11 Undo the retaining screw and remove the timing belt protection bracket, again, adjacent to the crankshaft sprocket flange.

12 Lock the crankshaft and camshaft sprockets in their correct timing positions as described in Section 3. If necessary, temporarily refit the crankshaft pulley bolt to enable the crankshaft to be rotated. At this stage, it is of no consequence that the fuel pump sprocket aligns correctly with the hole in the pump mounting bracket.

13 Insert a hexagon key into the belt tensioner pulley centre, slacken the pulley bolt, and allow the tensioner to rotate, relieving the belt tension **(see illustration)**. With the belt slack, temporarily tighten the pulley bolt.

14 Note its routing, then remove the timing belt from the sprockets.

Inspection

15 Renew the belt as a matter of course, regardless of its apparent condition. The cost of a new belt is nothing compared with the cost of repairs, should the belt break in service. If signs of oil contamination are found, trace the source of the oil leak and rectify it. Wash down the engine timing belt area and all related components, to remove all traces of oil. Check that the tensioner and idler pulleys rotate freely without any sign of roughness, and also check that the coolant pump pulley rotates freely. If necessary, renew these items.

Refitting and tensioning

16 Commence refitting by ensuring that the crankshaft and camshaft timing pins are still in position correctly. Also, locate and lock the fuel pump sprocket in its correct position as described in Section 3.

17 Locate the timing belt on the crankshaft sprocket, then keeping it taut, locate it around the idler pulley, camshaft sprocket, high-pressure pump sprocket, coolant pump sprocket, and the tensioner roller **(see illustration)**. If the timing belt has directional arrows on it, make sure that they point in the direction of normal engine rotation.

18 Refit the timing belt protection bracket and tighten the retaining bolt securely.

19 Slacken the tensioner pulley bolt, and using a hexagonal key, rotate the tensioner anti-clockwise, which moves the index arm clockwise, until the index arm is aligned as shown **(see illustration)**.

20 Remove the camshaft, crankshaft and fuel pump timing pins and, using a socket on the crankshaft pulley bolt, turn the crankshaft clockwise 10 complete revolutions. Align the camshaft and crankshaft timing holes and check that the timing pins can be inserted, then remove them. There is no requirement to check the fuel pump sprocket alignment, as it will only be aligned after 12 complete revolutions.

21 Check that the tensioner index arm is still aligned between the edges of the area shown **(see illustration 7.19)**. If it is not, remove and belt and begin the refitting process again, starting at paragraph 19.

22 The remainder of refitting is a reversal of removal. Tighten all fasteners to the specified torque where given.

8 Timing belt sprockets and tensioner – removal and refitting

Camshaft sprocket

Removal

1 Remove the timing belt as described in Section 7.

2 Remove the locking tool from the camshaft sprocket/hub. Slacken the sprocket hub

7.13 Slacken the bolt and allow the tensioner to rotate, relieving the tension on the belt

7.17 Timing belt routing

7.19 The index arm must align with the lug (arrowed)

A sprocket holding tool can be made from two lengths of steel strip bolted together to form a forked end. Drill holes and insert bolts in the ends of the fork to engage with the sprocket spokes.

8.5 Ensure the lug on the sprocket hub engages with the slot on the end of the camshaft (arrowed)

8.11a Slide the sprocket from the crankshaft ...

8.11b ... and recover the Woodruff key

retaining bolt. To prevent the camshaft rotating as the bolt is slackened, a sprocket holding tool will be required. In the absence of a special tool, an acceptable substitute can be fabricated at home **(see Tool Tip 1)**. Do not attempt to use the engine assembly/valve timing locking tool to prevent the sprocket from rotating whilst the bolt is slackened.

3 Remove the sprocket hub retaining bolt, and slide the sprocket and hub off the end of the camshaft.

4 Clean the camshaft sprocket thoroughly, and renew it if there are any signs of wear, damage or cracks.

Refitting

5 Refit the camshaft sprocket to the camshaft **(see illustration)**.

6 Refit the sprocket hub retaining bolt. Tighten the bolt to the specified torque, then through the specified angle, preventing the camshaft from turning as during removal.

7 Align the engine assembly/valve timing slot in the camshaft sprocket hub with the hole in the cylinder head and refit the timing pin to lock the camshaft in position.

8 Refit and tension the timing belt as described in Section 7.

Crankshaft sprocket

Caution: Do not touch the outer magnetic sensor ring of the crankshaft sprocket with your fingers, or allow metallic particles to come into contact with it.

Removal

9 Remove the timing belt as described in Section 7.

10 Check that the engine assembly/valve timing holes are still aligned as described in Section 3, and the camshaft sprocket and flywheel are locked in position.

11 Slide the sprocket off the end of the crankshaft and collect the Woodruff key **(see illustrations)**.

12 Examine the crankshaft oil seal for signs

of oil leakage and, if necessary, renew it as described in Section 14.

13 Clean the crankshaft sprocket thoroughly, and renew it if there are any signs of wear, damage or cracks. Recover the crankshaft locating key.

Refitting

14 Refit the key to the end of the crankshaft, then refit the crankshaft sprocket (with the flange facing the crankshaft pulley).

15 Refit and tension the timing belt as described in Section 7.

Fuel pump sprocket

Removal

16 Remove the timing belt as described in Section 7.

17 Using a suitable socket, slacken the pump sprocket retaining nut. The sprocket can be held stationary by using a suitable forked tool engaged with the holes in the sprocket **(see Tool Tip 1)**.

18 The pump sprocket is a taper fit on the pump shaft and it will be necessary to make up another tool to release it from the taper **(see Tool Tip 2)**.

19 Partially unscrew the sprocket retaining nut, fit the home-made tool, and secure it to

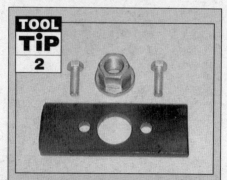

Make a sprocket releasing tool from a short strip of steel. Drill two holes in the strip to correspond with the two holes in the sprocket. Drill a third hole just large enough to accept the flats of the sprocket retaining nut.

the sprocket with two suitable bolts. Prevent the sprocket from rotating as before, and unscrew the sprocket retaining nut. The nut will bear against the tool as it is undone, forcing the sprocket off the shaft taper. Once the taper is released, remove the tool, unscrew the nut fully, and remove the sprocket from the pump shaft. Note that although the sprocket is on a taper, it incorporates a key so that it will only locate in one position.

20 Clean the sprocket thoroughly, and renew it if there are any signs of wear, damage or cracks.

Refitting

21 Refit the pump sprocket and retaining nut, and tighten the nut to the specified torque. Prevent the sprocket rotating as the nut is tightened using the sprocket holding tool.

22 Refit and tension the timing belt as described in Section 7.

Coolant pump sprocket

23 The coolant pump sprocket is integral with the pump, and cannot be removed. Coolant pump removal is described in Chapter 3 Section 7.

Tensioner pulley

Removal

24 Remove the timing belt as described in Section 7.

25 Undo the tensioner pulley retaining bolt, and lift off the pulley.

26 Clean the tensioner pulley, but do not

8.30 Timing belt idler pulley retaining nut (arrowed)

9.5 Vacuum pump bolts (arrowed)

9.7 Timing belt inner, upper cover bolts (arrowed)

use any strong solvent which may enter the pulley bearings. Check that the pulley rotates freely, with no sign of stiffness or free play. Renew the pulley if there is any doubt about its condition, or if there are any obvious signs of wear or damage.

Refitting

27 Refit the tensioner pulley ensuring that the pulley arm engages over the locating peg.
28 Refit and tension the timing belt as described in Section 7.

Idler pulley

Removal

29 Remove the timing belt as described in Section 7.
30 Undo the retaining nut and withdraw the idler pulley from the engine **(see illustration)**.
31 Clean the idler pulley, but do not use any strong solvent which may enter the bearings. Check that the pulley rotates freely, with no sign of stiffness or free play. Renew the idler pulley if

there is any doubt about its condition, or if there are any obvious signs of wear or damage.

Refitting

32 Locate the idler pulley on the engine, and fit the retaining nut. Tighten the nut to the specified torque.
33 Refit and tension the timing belt as described in Section 7.

9 Camshafts, rocker arms and hydraulic tappets – removal, inspection and refitting

Removal

1 Remove the cylinder head cover/inlet manifold as described in Section 4.
2 Remove the fuel injectors as described in Chapter 4B Section 11.
3 Remove the camshaft sprocket as described in Section 8.
4 Refit the right-hand engine mounting,

but only tighten the bolts moderately; this will keep the engine supported during the camshaft removal.
5 Undo the bolts and remove the vacuum pump. Recover the pump O-ring seals **(see illustration)**.
6 Remove the fuel filter (see Chapter 1B Section 22), then undo the bolts and remove the fuel filter mounting bracket.
7 Release the wiring harness clips, then undo the two bolts and remove the timing belt inner, upper cover **(see illustration)**.
8 Disconnect the wiring plug, unscrew the retaining bolt, and remove the camshaft position sensor from the camshaft cover/ bearing ladder.
9 Unbolt the turbocharger heat shields, then working gradually and evenly, slacken and remove the bolts securing the camshaft cover/bearing ladder to the cylinder head in sequence **(see illustration)**. Lift the cover/ ladder from position complete with the camshafts.
10 Undo the retaining bolts and remove the bearing caps. Note their fitted positions, as they must be refitted into their original positions **(see illustration)**. Note that the bearing caps are marked A for inlet, and E for exhaust, and 1 to 4 from the flywheel end of the cylinder head.
11 Undo the bolts securing the chain tensioner assembly to the camshaft cover/ bearing ladder, then lift the camshafts,

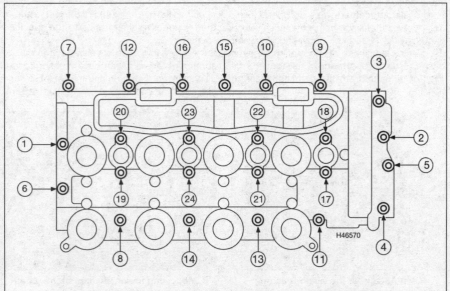

9.9 Camshaft cover/bearing ladder bolt slackening sequence

9.10 The camshaft bearing caps are numbered 1 to 4 from the flywheel end – A for inlet (arrowed) and E for exhaust

9.11a Undo the tensioner bolts (arrowed) …

9.11b … then lift the camshafts, chain and tensioner from the housing

9.21 Refit the hydraulic tappets …

chain and tensioner from the housing **(see illustrations)**. Discard the camshaft oil seal.
12 Obtain 16 small, clean plastic containers, and number them 1 to 8 inlet and 1 to 8 exhaust ; alternatively, divide a larger container into 16 compartments.
13 Lift out each rocker arm. Place the rocker arms in their respective positions in the box or containers.
14 A compartmentalised container filled with engine oil is now required to retain the hydraulic tappets while they are removed from the cylinder head. Withdraw each hydraulic tappet and place it in the container, keeping them each identified for correct refitting. The tappets must be totally submerged in the oil to prevent air entering them.

9.22 … and rocker arms to their original locations

Inspection

15 Inspect the cam lobes and the camshaft bearing journals for scoring or other visible evidence of wear. Once the surface hardening of the cam lobes has been eroded, wear will occur at an accelerated rate. **Note:** *If these symptoms are visible on the tips of the camshaft lobes, check the corresponding rocker arm, as it will probably be worn as well.*
16 Examine the condition of the bearing surfaces in the cylinder head and camshaft bearing housing. If wear is evident, the cylinder head and bearing housing will both have to be renewed, as they are a matched assembly.
17 Inspect the rocker arms and tappets for scuffing, cracking or other damage and renew any components as necessary. Also check the condition of the tappet bores in the cylinder head. As with the camshafts, any wear in this area will necessitate cylinder head renewal.

Refitting

18 Thoroughly clean the sealant from the mating surfaces of the cylinder head and camshaft bearing housing. Use a suitable liquid gasket dissolving agent (available from Ford dealers) together with a soft putty knife; do not use a metal scraper or the faces will be damaged. As there is no conventional gasket used, the cleanliness of the mating faces is of the utmost importance. Prise out the oil injector oil seals from the camshaft bearing housing.

19 Clean off any oil, dirt or grease from both components and dry with a clean lint-free cloth. Ensure that all the oilways are completely clean.
20 Liberally lubricate the hydraulic tappet bores in the cylinder head with clean engine oil.
21 Insert the hydraulic tappets into their original bores in the cylinder head unless they have been renewed **(see illustration)**.
22 Lubricate the rocker arms and place them over their respective tappets and valve stems **(see illustration)**.
23 Engage the timing chain around the camshaft sprockets, aligning the black-coloured links with the marked teeth on the camshaft sprockets **(see illustration)**. If the black colouring has been lost, there must be 12 chain link pins between the marks on the sprockets.
24 Fit the chain tensioner between the upper and lower runs of the chain, then lubricate the bearing surfaces with clean engine oil, and fit the camshafts into position on the underside of the camshaft cover/bearing ladder. Refit the bearing caps to their original positions and tighten the retaining bolts to the specified torque **(see illustrations)**. Tighten the tensioner retaining bolts to the specified torque.
25 Apply a thin bead of sealant to the mating surface of the camshaft cover/bearing ladder as shown. Ford recommend the use of silicone sealant WSE-M4G323-A4 **(see illustration)**.

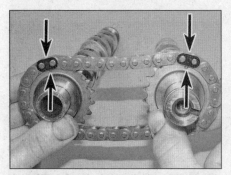

9.23 Align the marks on the sprockets with the centre of the black coloured chain links (arrowed). There must be 12 link pins between the sprocket marks

9.24a Assemble the chain tensioner between the upper and lower runs of the chain …

9.24b … and lower the camshafts, chain and tensioner into position

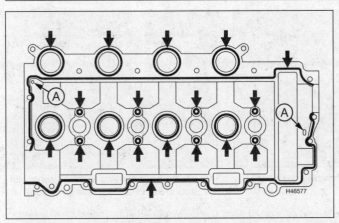

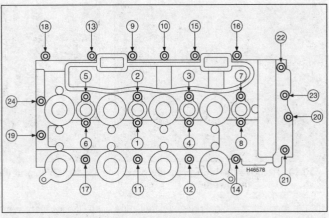

9.25 Apply sealant to the camshaft cover/bearing ladder as indicated by the heavy black lines. Ensure sealant does not enter the tensioner oil holes – marked A

9.26 Camshaft cover/bearing ladder bolt tightening sequence

Do not allow the sealant to obstruct the oil channels for the hydraulic chain tensioner.

26 Check that the black-coloured links on the chain are still aligned with the marks on the camshaft sprockets, then refit the camshaft cover/bearing ladder, and gradually and evenly tighten the retaining bolts until the cover/ladder is in contact with the cylinder head, then tighten the bolts to the specified torque in sequence **(see illustration)**. **Note:** *Ensure the cover/ladder is correctly located by checking the bores of the vacuum pump and camshaft oil seal at each end of the cover/ladder.*

27 Fit a new camshaft oil seal as described in Section 14.

28 Refit the camshaft sprocket, and tighten the retaining bolt finger tight.

29 Using a spanner on the camshaft sprocket bolt, rotate the camshafts approximately 40 complete revolutions clockwise. Check the black-coloured links on the chain still align with the marks on the camshaft sprockets.

30 If the marks still align, fully refit the camshaft sprocket as described in Section 8.

31 Refit and adjust the camshaft position sensor as described in Chapter 4B Section 12.

32 Press the new oil seals into the bearing housing, using a tube/socket of approximately 20 mm outside diameter, ensuring the inner lip of the seal fits around the injector guide tube **(see illustrations)**. Refit the injectors as described in Chapter 4B Section 11.

33 Refit the cylinder head cover/inlet manifold as described in Section 4.

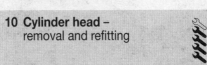

10 Cylinder head – removal and refitting

Removal

1 Apply the handbrake, then jack up the front of the vehicle and support it on axle stands (see *'Jacking and vehicle support'*).

9.32a Fit the new seal around a 20 mm outside diameter socket …

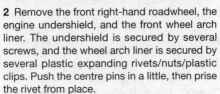

2 Remove the front right-hand roadwheel, the engine undershield, and the front wheel arch liner. The undershield is secured by several screws, and the wheel arch liner is secured by several plastic expanding rivets/nuts/plastic clips. Push the centre pins in a little, then prise the rivet from place.

3 Disconnect the battery negative terminal (refer to *'Disconnecting the battery'*).

4 Drain the cooling system as described in Chapter 1B Section 30.

5 Remove the camshafts, rocker arms and hydraulic tappets as described in Section 9.

6 Remove the turbocharger as described in Chapter 4B Section 16.

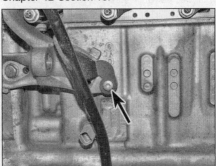

10.8 The engine oil level dipstick is secured to the alternator bracket by a Torx bolt (arrowed)

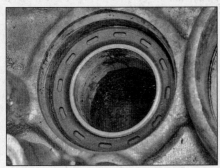

9.32b … and push it into place

7 Remove the glow plugs as described in Chapter 5A Section 12.

8 Undo the upper mounting bolts, and pivot the alternator away from the engine, undo the oil dipstick guide tube bolt, then undo the bolts securing the alternator mounting bracket to the cylinder head/block **(see illustration)**.

9 Undo the coolant outlet housing (left-hand end of the cylinder head) retaining bolts, slacken the two bolts securing the housing support bracket to the top of the transmission bellhousing, and move the outlet housing away from the cylinder head a little **(see illustration)**. There is no need to disconnect the hoses.

10.9 Undo the bolts (arrowed) and pull the coolant outlet housing from the left-hand end of the cylinderhead

10.10a Remove the high-pressure pipe (arrowed) ...

10.10b ... and the bracket (arrowed)

10.10c Pump mounting bracket upper nut and lower mounting bolt (arrowed)

10 Disconnect the high-pressure fuel pipe from the accumulator rail to the pump, and disconnect the fuel supply and return hoses. Remove the bracket at the rear of the pump, then undo the bolt/nut and remove the pump and mounting bracket as an assembly (see illustrations). Note that a new high-pressure fuel pipe must be fitted.

11 Working in the reverse of the sequence shown (see illustration 10.38) undo the cylinder head bolts.

12 Release the cylinder head from the cylinder block and location dowels by rocking it. A suitable tool for doing this consists simply of two metal rods with 90-degree angled ends (see illustration). Do not prise between the mating faces of the cylinder head and block, as this may damage the gasket faces.

13 Lift the cylinder head from the block, and recover the gasket.

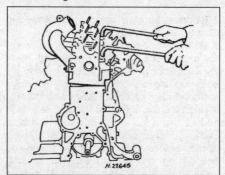

10.12 Free the cylinder head using angled rods

14 If necessary, remove the exhaust manifold with reference to Chapter 4B Section 14.

Preparation for refitting

15 The mating faces of the cylinder head and cylinder block must be perfectly clean before refitting the head. The use of a scouring agent is recommended for this purpose, but acceptable results can be achieved by using a hard plastic or wood scraper to remove all traces of gasket and carbon. The same method can be used to clean the piston crowns. Take particular care to avoid scoring or gouging the cylinder head/cylinder block mating surfaces during the cleaning operations, as aluminium alloy is easily damaged. Make sure that the carbon is not allowed to enter the oil and water passages – this is particularly important for the lubrication system, as carbon could block the oil supply to the engine's components. Using adhesive tape and paper, seal the water, oil and bolt holes in the cylinder block. To prevent carbon entering the gap between the pistons and bores, smear a little grease in the gap. After cleaning each piston, use a small brush to remove all traces of grease and carbon from the gap, then wipe away the remainder with a clean rag.

16 Check the mating surfaces of the cylinder block and the cylinder head for nicks, deep scratches and other damage. If slight, they may be removed carefully with a file, but if excessive, machining may be the only alternative to renewal. If warpage of the cylinder head gasket surface is suspected, use a straight-edge to check it for distortion. Refer to Part F of this Chapter if necessary.

17 Thoroughly clean the threads of the cylinder head bolt holes in the cylinder block. Ensure that the bolts run freely in their threads, and that all traces of oil and water are removed from each bolt hole. If required, pull the oil feed non-return valve from the cylinder head, and check that the ball moves freely. Push a new valve into place if necessary (see illustrations).

Gasket selection

18 Remove the crankshaft timing pin, then turn the crankshaft until pistons 1 and 4 are at TDC (Top Dead Centre). Position a dial test indicator (dial gauge) on the cylinder block adjacent to the rear of No 1 piston, and zero it on the block face. Transfer the probe to the crown of No 1 piston (10.0 mm in from the rear edge), then slowly turn the crankshaft back-and-forth past TDC, noting the highest reading on the indicator. Record this reading as protrusion A.

19 Repeat the check described in paragraph 18, this time 10.0 mm in from the front edge of the No 1 piston crown. Record this reading as protrusion B.

20 Add protrusion A to protrusion B, then divide the result by 2 to obtain an average reading for piston No 1.

21 Repeat the procedure described in paragraphs 18 to 20 on piston 4, then turn the crankshaft through 180° and carry out the procedure on the piston Nos 2 and 3 (see illustration). Check that there is a maximum

10.17a Pull the non-return valve from the cylinder head ...

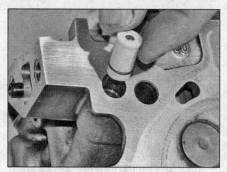

10.17b ... and push a new one into place

10.21 Measure the piston protrusion using a DTI gauge

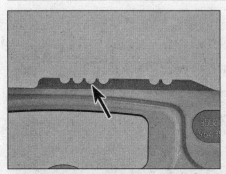

10.23 Cylinder head gasket thickness identification notches (arrowed)

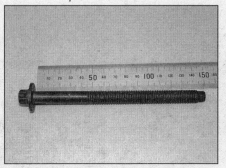

10.30 Measure the length from under the bolt head to its end

10.33 Ensure the gasket locates over the dowels (arrowed)

difference of 0.07 mm protrusion between any two pistons.

22 If a dial test indicator is not available, piston protrusion may be measured using a straight-edge and feeler blades or Vernier calipers. However, this is much less accurate, and cannot therefore be recommended.

23 Note the greatest piston protrusion measurement, and use this to determine the correct cylinder head gasket from the following table. The series of notches/holes on the side of the gasket are used for thickness identification **(see illustration)**.

Piston protrusion	Gasket identification
533 to 0.634 mm	2 notches
634 to 0.684 mm	3 notches
684 to 0.734 mm	1 notch
734 to 0.784 mm	4 notches
784 to 0.886 mm	5 notches

Head bolt examination

30 Carefully examine the cylinder head bolts for signs of damage to the threads or head, and for any sign of corrosion. If the bolts are in a satisfactory condition, measure the length of each bolt from the underside of the head to the end of the shank. According to the Citroën information for the identical engine, the bolts may be re-used providing that the measured length does not exceed 149.0 mm **(see illustration)**, however, Ford stipulate that they must be discarded and new ones fitted regardless of length. **Note:** *Considering the stress to which the cylinder head bolts are subjected, it is highly recommended that they are all renewed, regardless of their apparent condition.*

Refitting

31 Turn the crankshaft and position Nos 1 and 4 pistons at TDC, then turn the crankshaft a quarter turn (90°) anti-clockwise.

32 Thoroughly clean the surfaces of the cylinder head and block.

33 Make sure that the locating dowels are in place, then fit the correct gasket the right way round on the cylinder block **(see illustration)**.

34 If necessary, refit the exhaust manifold to the cylinder head as described in Chapter 4B Section 14.

35 Carefully lower the cylinder head onto the gasket and block, making sure that it locates correctly onto the dowels.

36 Apply a smear of high melting-point grease to the threads, and to the underside of the heads of the cylinder head bolts.

37 Carefully insert the cylinder head bolts into their holes (do not drop them in) and initially finger-tighten them.

38 Working progressively and in sequence, tighten the cylinder head bolts to their Stage 1 torque setting, using a torque wrench and suitable socket **(see illustration)**.

39 Once all the bolts have been tightened to their Stage 1 torque setting, working again in the specified sequence, tighten each bolt to the specified Stage 2 setting. Finally, angle-tighten the bolts through the specified Stage 3 angle. It is recommended that an angle-measuring gauge is used during this stage of tightening, to ensure accuracy. **Note:** *Retightening of the cylinder head bolts after running the engine is not required.*

40 Refit the hydraulic tappets, rocker arms, and camshaft housing (complete with camshafts) as described in Section 9.

41 Refit the timing belt as described in Section 7.

42 The remainder of refitting is a reversal of removal, noting the following points.

a) *Use a new seal when refitting the coolant outlet housing.*

b) *When refitting a cylinder head, it is good practice to renew the thermostat.*

c) *Refit the camshaft position sensor and set the air gap with reference to Chapter 4B Section 12.*

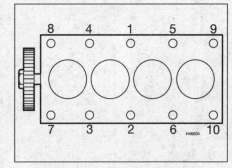

10.38 Cylinder head bolt tightening sequence

d) *Tighten all fasteners to the specified torque where given.*

e) *Refill the cooling system as described in Chapter 1B Section 30.*

f) *The engine may run erratically for the first few miles, until the engine management PCM relearns its stored values.*

11 Sump – removal and refitting

Removal

1 Apply the handbrake, then jack up the front of the vehicle and support it on axle stands (see *'Jacking and vehicle support'*).

2 Undo the screws and remove the engine undershield.

3 Drain the engine oil, then clean and refit the engine oil drain plug, tightening it securely. If the engine is nearing its service interval when the oil and filter are due for renewal, it is recommended that the filter is also removed, and a new one fitted. After reassembly, the engine can then be refilled with fresh oil. Refer to Chapter 1B Section 6 for further information.

4 Remove the exhaust front pipe as described in Chapter 4B Section 18.

5 Progressively slacken and remove all the sump retaining bolts/nuts. Since the sump bolts vary in length, remove each bolt in turn, and store it in its correct fitted order by pushing it through a clearly-marked cardboard template. This will avoid the possibility of installing the bolts in the wrong locations on refitting.

6 Try to break the joint by striking the sump with the palm of your hand, then lower and withdraw the sump from under the car. If the sump is stuck (which is quite likely) use a putty knife or similar, carefully inserted between the sump and block. Ease the knife along the joint until the sump is released. While the sump is removed, take the opportunity to check the oil pump pick-up/strainer for signs of clogging or splitting. If necessary, remove the pump as described in Section 12, and clean or renew the strainer.

11.8 Apply a bead of sealant to the sump or crankcase mating surface. Ensure the sealant is applied on the inside of the retaining bolt holes

11.9 Refit the sump and tighten the bolts

Refitting

7 Clean all traces of sealant from the mating surfaces of the cylinder block/crankcase and sump, then use a clean rag to wipe out the sump and the engine's interior.

8 Ensure that the sump mating surfaces are

12.4 Oil pick-up tube Allen bolts (arrowed)

clean and dry, then apply a thin coating of suitable sealant to the sump or crankcase mating surface (see illustration).

9 Offer up the sump to the cylinder block/crankcase. Refit its retaining bolts/nuts, ensuring that each bolt is screwed into its original location. Tighten the bolts evenly and progressively to the specified torque setting (see illustration).

10 Refit the engine undershield, then lower the vehicle to the ground. Refill the engine with oil as described in Chapter 1B Section 6.

12 Oil pump – removal, inspection and refitting

Removal

1 Remove the crankshaft sprocket as described in Section 8. Recover the locating key from the crankshaft.

2 Temporarily refit the right-hand engine mounting and support bracket, and remove the trolley jack, then remove the sump as described in Section 11.

3 Disconnect the wiring plug, undo the bolts and remove the crankshaft position sensor, located on the right-hand end of the cylinder block.

4 Undo the three Allen bolts and remove the oil pump pick-up tube from the pump/block (see illustration). Discard the oil seal, a new one must be fitted.

5 Undo the 8 bolts, and remove the oil pump (see illustration).

Inspection

6 Undo and remove the Torx screws securing the cover to the oil pump (see illustration). Examine the pump rotors and body for signs of wear and damage. If worn, the complete pump must be renewed.

7 Remove the circlip, and extract the cap, valve piston and spring, noting which way

12.5 Oil pump retaining bolts (arrowed)

12.6 Undo the Torx screws and remove the pump cover

around they are fitted **(see illustrations)**. The condition of the relief valve spring can only be measured by comparing it with a new one; if there is any doubt about its condition, it should also be renewed.

8 Refit the relief valve piston and spring, then secure them in place with the circlip.

9 Refit the cover to the oil pump, and tighten the Torx screws securely.

Refitting

10 Remove all traces of sealant, and thoroughly clean the mating surfaces of the oil pump and cylinder block.

11 Apply a 4 mm wide bead of silicone sealant to the mating face of the cylinder block **(see illustration)**. Ensure that no sealant enters any of the holes in the block.

12 With a new oil seal fitted, refit the oil pump over the end of the crankshaft, aligning the flats in the pump drivegear with the flats machined in the crankshaft **(see illustrations)**. Note that new oil pumps are supplied with the oil seal already fitted, and a seal protector sleeve. The sleeve fits over the end of the crankshaft to protect the seal as the pump is fitted.

13 Install the oil pump bolts and tighten them to the specified torque.

14 Refit the oil pick-up tube to the pump/ cylinder block using a new O-ring seal. Ensure the oil dipstick guide tube is correctly refitted.

15 Refit the woodruff key to the crankshaft, and slide the crankshaft sprocket into place.

16 The remainder of refitting is a reversal of removal.

13 Oil cooler – removal and refitting

Removal

1 Apply the handbrake, then jack up the front of the vehicle and support it on axle stands (see *'Jacking and vehicle support'*). Undo the screws and remove the engine undershield.

12.7a Remove the circlip …

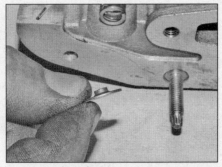
12.7b … cap …

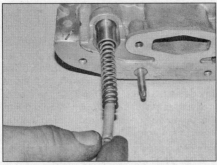
12.7c … spring …

12.7d … and piston

12.11 Apply a bead of sealant to the cylinder block mating surface

12.12a Fit a new seal …

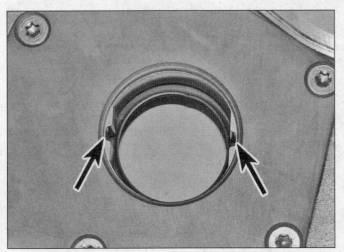
12.12b … align the pump gear flats (arrowed) …

12.12c … with those of the crankshaft (arrowed)

13.4a Undo the oil cooler bolts/stud (arrowed)

2 The oil cooler is fitted to the front of the oil filter housing. Drain the coolant as described in Chapter 1B Section 30.
3 Drain the engine oil as described in Chapter 1B Section 6, or be prepared for fluid spillage.
4 Undo the 5 bolts/stud and remove the oil cooler. Recover the O-ring seals **(see illustrations)**.

Refitting

5 Fit new O-ring seals into the recesses in the oil filter housing, and refit the cooler. Tighten the bolts securely.
6 Refill or top-up the cooling system and engine oil level as described in Chapter 1B or Weekly checks0,5 (as applicable). Start the engine, and check the oil cooler for signs of leakage.

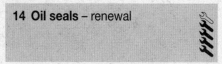

14 Oil seals – renewal

Crankshaft

Right-hand oil seal

1 Remove the crankshaft sprocket and Woodruff key as described in Section 8.
2 Measure and note the fitted depth of the oil seal.
3 Pull the oil seal from the housing using a screwdriver. Alternatively, drill a small hole in the oil seal, and use a self-tapping screw and a pair of pliers to remove it **(see illustration)**.

14.5b … and press the seal into place

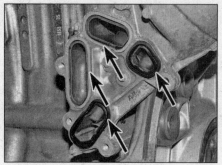

13.4b Renew the O-ring seals (arrowed)

4 Clean the oil seal housing and the crankshaft sealing surface.
5 The seal has a Teflon lip and must not be oiled or marked. The new seal should be supplied with a protector sleeve, which fits over the end of the crankshaft to prevent any damage to the seal lip. With the sleeve in place, press the seal (open end first) into the pump to the previously-noted depth, using a suitable tube or socket **(see illustrations)**.
6 Where applicable, remove the plastic sleeve from the end of the crankshaft.
7 Refit the crankshaft sprocket as described in Section 8.

Left-hand oil seal

8 Remove the flywheel, as described in Section 16.

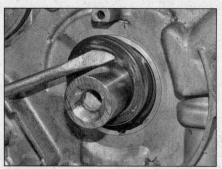

14.3 Take great care not to mark the crankshaft whilst levering out the oil seal

14.12 Slide the seal and protective sleeve over the left-hand end of the crankshaft

9 Measure and note the fitted depth of the oil seal.
10 Pull the oil seal from the housing using a screwdriver. Alternatively, drill a small hole in the oil seal, and use a self-tapping screw and a pair of pliers to remove it **(see illustration 14.3)**.
11 Clean the oil seal housing and the crankshaft sealing surface.
12 The seal has a Teflon lip and must not be oiled or marked. The new seal should be supplied with a protector sleeve, which fits over the end of the crankshaft to prevent any damage to the seal lip **(see illustration)**. With the sleeve in place, press the seal (open end first) into the housing to the previously-noted depth, using a suitable tube or socket.
13 Where applicable, remove the plastic sleeve from the end of the crankshaft.
14 Refit the flywheel, as described in Section 16.

Camshaft

15 Remove the camshaft sprocket as described in Section 8.
16 Pull the oil seal from the housing using a hooked instrument. Alternatively, drill a small hole in the oil seal and use a self-tapping screw and a pair of pliers to remove it **(see illustration)**.
17 Clean the oil seal housing and the camshaft sealing surface.
18 The seal has a Teflon lip and must not be oiled or marked. The new seal should be supplied with a protector sleeve. which fits

14.5a Slide the seal and protective sleeve over the end of the crankshaft …

14.16 Drill a hole, insert a self-tapping screw, and pull the seal from place using pliers

14.18 Fit the protective sleeve and seal over the end of the camshaft

15.3 The oil pressure switch is located on the front face of the cylinder block (arrowed)

15.5 The oil level sensor is located on the rear face of the cylinder block (arrowed)

over the end of the camshaft to prevent any damage to the seal lip **(see illustration)**. With the sleeve in place, press the seal (open end first) into the housing to the previously-noted depth, using a suitable tube or socket which bears only of the outer edge of the seal.

19 Refit the camshaft sprocket as described in Section 8.

15 Oil pressure switch and level sensor – removal and refitting

Removal

Oil pressure switch

1 The oil pressure switch is located at the front of the cylinder block, adjacent to the oil dipstick guide tube. Note that on some models, access to the switch may be improved if the vehicle is jacked up and supported on axle stands, then undo the screws and remove the engine undershield so that the switch can be reached from underneath (see *'Jacking and vehicle support'*).

2 Remove the protective sleeve from the wiring plug (where applicable), then disconnect the wiring from the switch.

3 Unscrew the switch from the cylinder block, and recover the sealing washer **(see illustration)**. Be prepared for oil spillage, and if the switch is to be left removed from the engine for any length of time, plug the hole in the cylinder block.

16.3 Flywheel retaining Torx bolts

Oil level sensor (where fitted)

4 The oil level sensor is located at the rear of the cylinder block. Firmly apply the handbrake, then jack up the front of the vehicle and support it securely on axle stands (see *'Jacking and vehicle support'*). Undo the screws and remove the engine undershield

5 Reach up between the driveshaft and the cylinder block, and disconnect the sensor wiring plug **(see illustration)**.

6 Using an open-ended spanner, unscrew the sensor and withdraw it from position.

Refitting

Oil pressure switch

7 Examine the sealing washer for any signs of damage or deterioration, and if necessary renew.

8 Refit the switch, complete with washer, and tighten it to the specified torque.

9 Refit the engine undershield, and lower the vehicle to the ground.

Oil level sensor

10 Smear a little silicone sealant on the threads and refit the sensor to the cylinder block, tightening it securely.

11 Reconnect the sensor wiring plug.

12 Refit the engine undershield, and lower the vehicle to the ground.

16 Flywheel – removal, inspection and refitting

Removal

1 Remove the transmission as described in Chapter 7A Section 6, then remove the clutch assembly as described in Chapter 6 Section 6.

2 Prevent the flywheel from turning by inserting a 12 mm diameter rod or drill bit through the hole in the flywheel cover casting, and into a slot in the flywheel **(see illustration 5.2)**. Alternatively, bolt a strap between the flywheel and the cylinder block/crankcase.

3 Make alignment marks between the flywheel and crankshaft to aid refitment. Slacken and remove the flywheel retaining

bolts, and remove the flywheel from the end of the crankshaft **(see illustration)**. Be careful not to drop it; it is heavy. If the flywheel locating dowel (where fitted) is a loose fit in the crankshaft end, remove it and store it with the flywheel for safe-keeping. Discard the flywheel bolts; new ones must be used on refitting.

Inspection

4 Examine the flywheel for scoring of the clutch face, and for wear or chipping of the ring gear teeth. If the clutch face is scored, the flywheel may be surface-ground, but renewal is preferable. Seek the advice of a Ford dealer or engine reconditioning specialist to see if machining is possible. If the ring gear is worn or damaged, the flywheel must be renewed, as it is not possible to renew the ring gear separately.

Refitting

5 Clean the mating surfaces of the flywheel and crankshaft. Remove any remaining locking compound from the threads of the crankshaft holes, using the correct size of tap, if available.

6 If the new flywheel retaining bolts are not supplied with their threads already precoated, apply a suitable thread-locking compound to the threads of each bolt.

7 Ensure that the locating dowel is in position. Offer up the flywheel, locating it on the dowel (where fitted), and fit the new retaining bolts. Where no locating dowel is fitted, align the previously-made marks to ensure the flywheel is refitted in its original position.

8 Lock the flywheel using the method employed on dismantling, and tighten the retaining bolts to the specified torque, then through the specified angle.

9 Refit the clutch as described in Chapter 6 Section 6. Remove the flywheel locking tool, and refit the transmission as described in Chapter 7A Section 6.

17 Engine/transmission mountings – inspection and renewal

1 Refer to Chapter 2B, Section 17.

Chapter 2 Part E
1.6 litre SOHC diesel engine in-car repair procedures

Contents

Degrees of difficulty

Easy, suitable for novice with little experience | **Fairly easy,** suitable for beginner with some experience | **Fairly difficult,** suitable for competent DIY mechanic | **Difficult,** suitable for experienced DIY mechanic | **Very difficult,** suitable for expert DIY or professional

Specifications

General

Designation	Duratorq-TDCi
Engine codes*	TZJA and TZLB
Capacity	1560 cc
Bore	75.0 mm
Stroke	88.3 mm
Direction of crankshaft rotation	Clockwise (viewed from the right-hand side of vehicle)
No 1 cylinder location	At the transmission end of block
Maximum power output	70 kW (95 PS) @ 3800 rpm
Maximum torque output	200 Nm @ 1750 – 3800 rpm
Compression ratio	16: 1

*The engine code is stamped on a plate attached to the front of the cylinder block, next to the oil filter

Compression pressures (engine hot, at cranking speed)

Normal	20 ± 5 bar
Minimum	15 bar
Maximum difference between any two cylinders	5 bar

Camshaft

Camshaft end float	0.195 – 0.3 mm

Lubrication system

Oil pump type . . . .   Gear-type, driven directly by the right-hand end of the crankshaft, by two flats machined along the crankshaft journal.

Minimum oil pressure at 80°C:
   Idle speed . . . .   1.0 to 2.0 bar
   2000 rpm . . . .   2.3 to 3.7 bar

Torque wrench settings

	Nm	lbf ft
Ancillary drivebelt tensioner roller	20	15
Big-end bolts: *		
Stage 1	10	7
Stage 2	Slacken 180°	
Stage 3	10	7
Stage 4	Angle-tighten a further 130°	
Camshaft bearing caps	10	7
Camshaft bearing ladder:		
Studs	10	7
Bolts	10	7
Camshaft position sensor bolt	5	4
Camshaft sprocket bolt		
Stage 1	20	15
Stage 2	Angle-tighten a further 50°	
Coolant outlet housing bolts	8	6
Crankshaft position/speed sensor bolt	10	7
Crankshaft pulley/sprocket bolt: *		
Stage 1	35	26
Stage 2	Angle-tighten a further 190°	
Cylinder head bolts: *		
Stage 1	20	15
Stage 2	40	30
Stage 3	Angle-tighten a further 260°	
Cylinder head cover	10	7
EGR valve	10	7
Engine-to-transmission fixing bolts	47	35
Flywheel bolts: *		
Stage 1	30	22
Stage 2	Angle-tighten a further 90°	
Fuel pump sprocket	50	37
Left-hand engine/transmission mounting:		
Mounting-to-bracket centre nut	148	109
Mounting-to-bracket outer nuts	48	35
Mounting bracket to transmission	80	59
Main bearing ladder outer seam bolts:		
Stage 1	5	4
Stage 2	10	7
Main bearing ladder to cylinder block:		
Stage 1	10	7
Stage 2	Slacken 180°	
Stage 3	30	22
Stage 4	Angle-tighten a further 140°	
Piston oil jet spray tube bolt	20	15
Oil cooler retaining bolts	10	7
Oil filter cover	25	18
Oil pick-up pipe	10	7
Oil pressure switch	30	22
Oil pump to cylinder block:		
Stage 1	5	4
Stage 2	9	7
Rear engine/transmission mounting	25	18
Right-hand engine mounting:		
Mounting to Inner wing (nuts/bolts)	48	35
Mounting bracket to engine block	55	41
Sump drain plug	35	26
Sump bolts/nuts	10	7
Timing belt idler pulley	37	27
Timing belt tensioner pulley	30	22
Vacuum pump bolts	20	15

*Do not re-use

1 General Information

How to use this Chapter

1 This Part of Chapter 2 describes the repair procedures that can reasonably be carried out on the engine while it remains in the vehicle. If the engine has been removed from the vehicle and is being dismantled as described in Part F, any preliminary dismantling procedures can be ignored.

2 Note that, while it may be possible physically to overhaul items such as the piston/connecting rod assemblies while the engine is in the car, such tasks are not usually carried out as separate operations. Usually, several additional procedures are required (not to mention the cleaning of components and oilways); for this reason, all such tasks are classed as major overhaul procedures, and are described in Part F of this Chapter.

3 Part F describes the removal of the engine/transmission from the car, and the full overhaul procedures that can then be carried out.

DV series engines

4 The 1.6 litre DV series of engines are the result of development collaboration between Citroën/Peugeot and Ford. Originally specified as a double overhead camshaft (DOHC) 16-valve design, the latest version fitted to the Ford Fiesta is a single overhead cam (SOHC), 8-valve variant. The direct injection, turbocharged, four-cylinder engine is mounted transversely, with the transmission mounted on the left-hand side.

5 A toothed timing belt drives the camshaft, high-pressure fuel pump and coolant pump. The camshaft operates the inlet and exhaust valves via rocker arms which are supported at their pivot ends by hydraulic self-adjusting tappets. The camshaft Is supported by bearings machined directly in the cylinder head and camshaft bearing housing.

6 The high-pressure fuel pump supplies fuel to the fuel rail, and subsequently to the electronically-controlled injectors which inject the fuel direct into the combustion chambers. This design differs from the previous type where an injection pump supplies the fuel at high pressure to each injector. The earlier, conventional type injection pump required fine calibration and timing, and these functions are now completed by the high-pressure pump, electronic injectors and engine management ECM.

7 The crankshaft runs in five main bearings of the usual shell type. Endfloat is controlled by thrustwashers either side of No 2 main bearing.

8 The pistons are selected to be of matching weight, and incorporate fully-floating gudgeon pins retained by circlips.

Repair operations precaution

9 The engine is a complex unit with numerous accessories and ancillary components. The design of the engine compartment is such that every conceivable space has been utilised, and access to virtually all of the engine components is extremely limited. In many cases, ancillary components will have to be removed, or moved to one side, and wiring, pipes and hoses will have to be disconnected or removed from various cable clips and support brackets.

10 When working on this engine, read through the entire procedure first, look at the car and engine at the same time, and establish whether you have the necessary tools, equipment, skill and patience to proceed. Allow considerable time for any operation, and be prepared for the unexpected.

11 Because of the limited access, many of the engine photographs appearing in this Chapter were, by necessity, taken with the engine removed from the vehicle.

⚠️ **Warning: It is essential to observe strict precautions when working on the fuel system components of the engine, particularly the high-pressure side of the system. Before carrying out any engine operations that entail working on, or near, any part of the fuel system, refer to the special information given in Chapter 4B Section 2.**

12 Operations with engine in vehicle
a) Compression pressure – testing.
b) Cylinder head cover – removal and refitting.
c) Crankshaft pulley – removal and refitting.
d) Timing belt covers – removal and refitting.
e) Timing belt – removal, refitting and adjustment.
f) Timing belt tensioner and sprockets – removal and refitting.
g) Camshaft oil seal – renewal.
h) Camshaft, rocker arms and hydraulic tappets – removal, inspection and refitting.
i) Sump – removal and refitting.
j) Oil pump – removal and refitting.
k) Crankshaft oil seals – renewal.
l) Engine/transmission mountings – inspection and renewal.
m) Flywheel – removal, inspection and refitting.

2 Compression and leakdown tests – description and interpretation

Compression test

Note: *A compression tester specifically designed for diesel engines must be used for this test.*

1 When engine performance is down, or if misfiring occurs which cannot be attributed to the fuel system, a compression test can provide diagnostic clues as to the engine's condition. If the test is performed regularly, it can give warning of trouble before any other symptoms become apparent.

2 A compression tester specifically intended for diesel engines must be used, because of the higher pressures involved. The tester is connected to an adapter which screws into the glow plug or injector hole. On this engine, an adapter suitable for use in the glow plug holes will be required, so as not to disturb the fuel system components. It is unlikely to be worthwhile buying such a tester for occasional use, but it may be possible to borrow or hire one – if not, have the test performed by a garage.

3 Unless specific instructions to the contrary are supplied with the tester, observe the following points:
a) The battery must be in a good state of charge, the air filter must be clean, and the engine should be at normal operating temperature.
b) All the glow plugs should be removed as described in Chapter 5A Section 12 before starting the test.
c) Disconnect the fuel injector wiring plugs.

4 The compression pressures measured are not so important as the balance between cylinders. Values are given in the Specifications.

5 The cause of poor compression is less easy to establish on a diesel engine than on a petrol one. The effect of introducing oil into the cylinders ('wet' testing) is not conclusive, because there is a risk that the oil will sit in the swirl chamber or in the recess on the piston crown instead of passing to the rings. However, the following can be used as a rough guide to diagnosis.

6 All cylinders should produce very similar pressures; any difference greater than that specified indicates the existence of a fault. Note that the compression should build-up quickly in a healthy engine; low compression on the first stroke, followed by gradually-increasing pressure on successive strokes, indicates worn piston rings. A low compression reading on the first stroke, which does not build-up during successive strokes, indicates leaking valves or a blown head gasket (a cracked head could also be the cause). Deposits on the undersides of the valve heads can also cause low compression.

7 A low reading from two adjacent cylinders is almost certainly due to the head gasket having blown between them; the presence of coolant in the engine oil will confirm this.

8 If the compression reading is unusually high, the cylinder head surfaces, valves and pistons are probably coated with carbon deposits. If this is the case, the cylinder head should be removed and decarbonised.

Note: *After performing this test, a fault code may be generated and stored in the PCM memory. Have the PCM self-diagnosis facility interrogated by a Ford dealer or suitably-equipped specialist, and the fault code erased.*

3.9 Insert a 5.0 mm drill bit/bolt through the round hole in the sprocket flange into the hole in the oil pump housing (lower timing belt removed for clarity)

3.10 Insert an 8.0 mm bolt through the hole in the camshaft sprocket into the corresponding hole in the cylinder head

Leakdown test

9 A leakdown test measures the rate at which compressed air fed into the cylinder is lost. It is an alternative to a compression test, and in many ways it is better, since the escaping air provides easy identification of where pressure loss is occurring (piston rings, valves or head gasket).
10 The equipment needed for leakdown testing is unlikely to be available to the home mechanic. If poor compression is suspected, have the test performed by a suitably-equipped garage.

3 Engine assembly/valve timing holes – general information and usage

Note: *Do not attempt to rotate the engine whilst the crankshaft and camshaft are locked in position. If the engine is to be left in this state for a long period of time, it is a good idea to place suitable warning notices inside the vehicle, and in the engine compartment. This will reduce the possibility of the engine being accidentally cranked on the starter motor, which is likely to cause damage with the locking pins in place.*

1 Timing holes or slots are located only in the crankshaft pulley flange and camshaft sprocket hub. The holes/slots are used to position the pistons halfway up the cylinder bores. This will ensure that the valve timing is maintained during operations that require removal and refitting of the timing belt. When the holes/slots are aligned with their corresponding holes in the cylinder block and cylinder head, suitable diameter bolts/pins can be inserted to lock the crankshaft and camshaft in position, preventing rotation.
2 Note that the fuel system used on these engines does not have a conventional diesel injection pump, but instead uses a high-pressure fuel pump. However, the fuel

pump sprocket must be pegged in position in a similar fashion to the camshaft sprocket.
3 To align the engine assembly/valve timing holes, proceed as follows.
4 Apply the handbrake, then jack up the front of the vehicle and support it on axle stands (see *'Jacking and vehicle support'*). Remove the right-hand front roadwheel.
5 To gain access to the crankshaft pulley, to enable the engine to be turned, the wheel arch plastic liner must be removed. The liner is secured by several plastic expanding rivets/nut/bolts. To remove the rivets, push in the centre pins a little, then prise the clips from place. Remove the liner from under the front wing.
6 Remove the starter motor and remove the crankshaft pulley as described in Section 5.
7 Remove the upper and lower timing belt covers as described in Section 6.
8 Temporarily refit the crankshaft pulley bolt (without the crankshaft pulley) and then remove the crankshaft locking tool.
9 Turn the crankshaft until the timing hole in the crankshaft sprocket aligns with the hole in the oil pump casing (this is at the 12 o'clock position). Fit the special tool 303-732, or a suitable alternative and lock the crankshaft in position **(see illustration)**.
10 With the crankshaft locked in position fit the camshaft locking tool (303-735 or similar).

The hole in the camshaft sprocket should be at approximately the 1 o'clock position **(see illustration)**. If this is not the case remove the crankshaft locking pin and rotate the engine one revolution. Note that the crankshaft must always be turned in a clockwise direction (viewed from the right-hand side of vehicle).
11 When refitting the timing belt, insert Ford tool No 303-732 through the slot in the fuel pump sprocket and into the corresponding hole in the fuel pump mounting bracket. In the absence of this tool use a 5 mm bolt or drill bit.
12 The crankshaft and camshaft are now locked in position, preventing unnecessary rotation.

4 Cylinder head cover – removal and refitting

Removal

1 Disconnect the battery negative lead as described in Chapter 5A Section 4.
2 Pull up the front edge and remove the plastic cover from the top of the engine **(see illustration)**.
3 Release the hose clamp and disconnect the hose from the throttle body **(see illustration)**.
4 Disconnect the wiring plug from the throttle

4.2 Pull up the front edge of the cover

4.3 Release the clamp and disconnect the hose

4.4a Release the clamp, then undo the nut and bolt at the front of the hose ...

4.4b ... and the nut underneath

4.5 Slacken the clamps and remove the elbow

4.6a Remove the bolt ...

4.6b ... unclip the wiring harness duct and move it to one side

4.9 Prise up the fuel pipe push-in clip, and release the wiring harness

body and then release the clamp, unbolt and remove the throttle body complete with the hose **(see illustrations)**. Plug the openings to prevent contamination.

5 Slacken the clamps, and remove the turbocharger to intercooler hose elbow **(see illustration)**. Seal the opening to the turbocharger.

6 Disconnect the wiring plugs from the fuel injectors, then undo the retaining bolt and unclip the wiring harness duct from the top of the engine **(see illustrations)**.

7 Release the clips and disconnect the breather hose from the cylinder head cover.

8 Unclip the wiring harness, then unbolt and then remove the timing belt upper cover as described in Section 6.

9 Unclip the fuel pipe assembly and wiring harness from the rear of the cover **(see illustration)**.

10 Undo the 4 retaining bolts and remove the air intake flange from the intake manifold **(see illustration)**. Renew the seal.

11 Remove the 11 bolts and then remove the cover **(see illustrations)**. Recover the rubber seal.

4.10 Undo the bolts and remove the intake flange

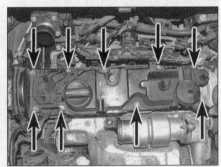

4.11a The cylinder head cover is secured by 9 bolts on the top ...

4.11b ... one bolt in the end behind the camshaft sprocket ...

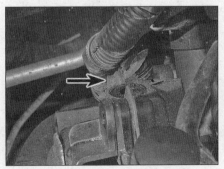

4.11c ... and one at the rear of the cover

4.11d Carefully manoeuvre the cover from place

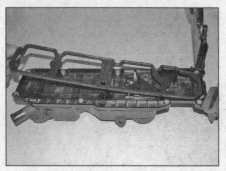

4.12 Renew the seal

5.4 Install the flywheel locking tool
(arrowed)

5.5a Where fitted remove the cover

Refitting

12 Refitting is a reversal of removal, but ensure that the seal is correctly located **(see illustration)**.

5 Crankshaft pulley – removal and refitting

Removal

1 Jack up and support the front of the vehicle (see *'Jacking and vehicle support'*).
2 Disconnect the battery (Chapter 5A Section 1) and remove the engine undershield.
3 Remove the auxiliary drivebelt as described in Chapter 1B Section 26.
4 To lock the crankshaft, working underneath the engine, insert a 12 mm diameter rod or bolt into the hole in the engine block casting over the lower section of the flywheel **(see illustration)**. Note that the hole in the casting and flywheel is provided purely to lock the crankshaft whilst the pulley bolt it undone – it does not position the crankshaft at TDC. Rotate the crankshaft clockwise until the tool engages in the hole in the flywheel – don't rotate the crank pulley anti-clockwise.
5 Using a suitable socket and extension bar, unscrew the retaining bolt, remove the washer, then slide the pulley off the end of the crankshaft **(see illustrations)**. If the pulley

5.5b Remove the bolt and...

5.5c ...then the pulley

is tight fit, it can be drawn off the crankshaft using a suitable puller. If a puller is being used, refit the pulley retaining bolt without the washer, to avoid damaging the crankshaft as the puller is tightened.
Caution: Do not touch the outer magnetic sensor ring of the sprocket with your fingers, or allow metallic particles to come into contact with it.

Refitting

6 Refit the pulley to the end of the crankshaft.
7 Refit the crankshaft pulley. Fit a new bolt and retaining washer. Tighten the bolt to the specified torque, then through the specified angle.
8 Remove the locking tool.

9 Refit and tension the auxiliary drivebelt as described in Chapter 1B Section 26.
10 Refit the remaining components in reverse order of removal.

6 Timing belt covers – removal and refitting

⚠ *Warning: Refer to the precautionary information contained in Section 1 before proceeding.*

Removal

Upper cover

1 Remove the engine cover from the top of the engine.
2 Unclip the wiring loom from the cover **(see illustration)**.
3 Undo the 4 bolts and remove the timing belt upper cover **(see illustration)**.

Lower cover

4 Remove the crankshaft pulley as described in Section 5.
5 Position a trolley/workshop jack under the engine. Place a block of wood on the jack head (to help spread the load on the sump), then take the weight of the engine.
6 Prise up the coolant expansion tank and move it to one side – there is no need to drain the coolant.

6.2 Release the clips securing the wiring loom

6.3 Upper cover bolts

6.7 Engine mounting nuts/bolt

6.9a Remove the two bolts at the front of the harness guide …

6.9b … and the bolt at the rear

7 Undo the nuts/bolts, and remove the right-hand engine mounting (see illustration).
8 Remove the engine mounting bracket from the engine.
9 Undo the 3 retaining bolts and move the wiring harness guide away from the engine (see illustrations). The rear bolt is accessible from underneath the vehicle.
10 Undo the 4 bolts and remove the lower cover.

Refitting

11 Refitting of all the covers is a reversal of the relevant removal procedure, ensuring that each cover section is correctly located, and that the cover retaining bolts are securely tightened. Ensure that all disturbed hoses are reconnected and retained by their relevant clips.

<table>
<tr><td>7</td><td>Timing belt – removal, inspection, refitting and tensioning</td></tr>
</table>

General

1 The timing belt drives the camshaft, high-pressure fuel pump, and coolant pump from a toothed sprocket on the end of the crankshaft. If the belt breaks or slips in service, the pistons are likely to hit the valve heads, resulting in expensive damage.
2 The timing belt should be renewed at the specified intervals, or earlier if it is contaminated with oil, or at all noisy in operation (a 'scraping' noise due to uneven wear).
3 If the timing belt is being removed, it is a wise precaution to renew the coolant pump at the same time. This may avoid the need to remove the timing belt again at a later stage, should the coolant pump fail. The timing belt tensioner should always be replaced when a new timing belt is fitted.

Removal

4 Unclip the coolant expansion tank and move it to one side (see illustration).
5 Remove the upper and lower timing belt covers, as described in Section 6.
6 Undo the bolt and remove the crankshaft position sensor adjacent to the crankshaft

sprocket flange, and move it to one side (see illustration).
7 Undo the retaining bolt and remove the timing belt protection bracket, again, adjacent to the crankshaft sprocket flange (see illustration).
8 Lock the crankshaft and camshaft in the correct position as described in Section 3. If necessary, temporarily refit the crankshaft pulley bolt to enable the crankshaft to be rotated.
9 Insert a hexagon key into the belt tensioner pulley centre, slacken the pulley bolt, and allow the tensioner to rotate, relieving the belt tension (see illustration). With belt slack, temporarily tighten the pulley bolt.
10 Note its routing, then remove the timing belt from the sprockets.

Inspection

11 Renew the belt as a matter of course, regardless of its apparent condition. The cost of a new belt is nothing compared with the cost of repairs should the belt break in service. If signs of oil contamination are found, trace the source of the oil leak and rectify it. Wash down the engine timing belt area and all related components, to remove all traces of oil. The tensioner must always be replaced. Check that the idler pulleys rotate freely without any sign of roughness, and also check that the coolant pump pulley rotates freely. It is highly recommended that both the coolant pump and the idler pulley are replaced at the same time as the timing belt and tensioner.

7.4 Carefully spread the coolant tank lug to release the clips

7.6 Undo the bolt (arrowed) and remove the crankshaft position sensor

7.7 Remove the timing belt protection bracket

7.9 Slacken the bolt and allow the tensioner to rotate, relieving the tension on the belt

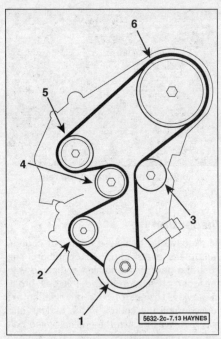

7.13 Timing belt routing

1 Crankshaft   4 Tensioner
2 Waterpump   5 Fuel pump
3 Idler   6 Camshaft

Refitting and tensioning

12 Commence refitting by ensuring that the crankshaft, camshaft and fuel pump sprocket timing pins are in position as described in Section 3.
13 Locate the timing belt on the crankshaft sprocket, then keeping it taut, locate it around the idler pulley, camshaft sprocket, high-pressure pump sprocket, coolant pump sprocket, and the tensioner roller (**see illustration**).
14 Refit the timing belt protection bracket and tighten the retaining bolt securely.
15 Slacken the tensioner pulley bolt, and using a hexagonal key, rotate the tensioner anti-clockwise, which moves the index arm clockwise, until the index arm is aligned as shown (**see illustration**).
16 Remove the camshaft, crankshaft and

8.5 Ensure the lug on the sprocket hub engages with the slot on the end of the camshaft (arrowed)

7.15 The index arm must align with the lug (arrowed)

fuel pump sprocket (where applicable) timing pins and, using a socket on the crankshaft pulley bolt, rotate the crankshaft clockwise 10 complete revolutions. Refit the crankshaft and camshaft locking pins.
17 Check that the tensioner index arm is still aligned between the edges of the area shown (**see illustration 7.15**). If it is not, remove and belt and begin the refitting process again, starting at Paragraph 12.
18 The remainder of refitting is a reversal of removal. Tighten all fasteners to the specified torque where given.

8 Timing belt sprockets and tensioner – removal and refitting

Camshaft sprocket
Removal
1 Remove the timing belt as described in Section 7.
2 Remove the locking tool from the camshaft sprocket/hub. Slacken the sprocket hub retaining bolt. To prevent the camshaft rotating as the bolt is slackened, a sprocket holding tool will be required. In the absence of the special Ford tool, an acceptable substitute can be fabricated at home (**see Tool Tip 1**). Do not attempt to use the engine assembly/valve timing locking tool to prevent the sprocket from rotating whilst the bolt is slackened.
3 Remove the sprocket hub retaining bolt,

8.11a Slide the sprocket from the crankshaft...

A sprocket holding tool can be made from two lengths of steel strip bolted together to form a forked end. Drill holes and insert bolts in the ends of the fork to engage with the sprocket spokes.

and slide the sprocket and hub off the end of the camshaft.
4 Clean the camshaft sprocket thoroughly, and renew it if there are any signs of wear, damage or cracks.
Refitting
5 Refit the camshaft sprocket to the camshaft (**see illustration**).
6 Refit the sprocket hub retaining bolt. Tighten the bolt to the specified torque, preventing the camshaft from turning as during removal.
7 Align the engine assembly/valve timing slot in the camshaft sprocket hub with the hole in the cylinder head and refit the timing pin to lock the camshaft in position.
8 Fit the timing belt around the pump sprocket and camshaft sprocket, and tension the timing belt as described in Section 7.

Crankshaft sprocket
Removal
9 Remove the timing belt as described in Section 7.
10 Check that the engine assembly/valve timing holes are still aligned as described in Section 3, and the camshaft sprocket and flywheel are locked in position.
11 Slide the sprocket off the end of the crankshaft and collect the Woodruff key (**see illustrations**).

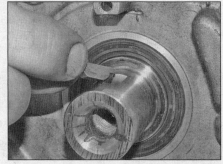

8.11b ...and recover the Woodruff key

Make a sprocket releasing tool from a short strip of steel. Drill two holes in the strip to correspond with the two holes in the sprocket. Drill a third hole just large enough to accept the flats of the sprocket retaining nut.

12 Examine the crankshaft oil seal for signs of oil leakage and, if necessary, renew it as described in Section 14.

13 Clean the crankshaft sprocket thoroughly, and renew it if there are any signs of wear, damage or cracks. Recover the crankshaft locating key.

Refitting

14 Refit the key to the end of the crankshaft, then refit the crankshaft sprocket (with the flange facing the crankshaft pulley).

15 Fit the timing belt around the crankshaft sprocket, and tension the timing belt as described in Section 7.

Fuel pump sprocket

Removal

16 Remove the timing belt as described in Section 7.

17 Using a suitable socket, undo the pump sprocket retaining nut. The sprocket can be held stationary by inserting a suitably-sized locking pin, drill or rod through the slot in the

sprocket, and into the corresponding hole in the backplate, or by using a suitable forked tool engaged with the holes in the sprocket **(see Tool Tip 1)**.

18 The pump sprocket is a taper fit on the pump shaft and it will be necessary to make up another tool to release it from the taper **(see Tool Tip 2)**.

19 Partially unscrew the sprocket retaining nut, fit the home-made tool, and secure it to the sprocket with two suitable bolts. Prevent the sprocket from rotating as before, and unscrew the sprocket retaining nut. The nut will bear against the tool as it is undone, forcing the sprocket off the shaft taper. Once the taper is released, remove the tool, unscrew the nut fully, and remove the sprocket from the pump shaft.

20 Clean the sprocket thoroughly, and renew it if there are any signs of wear, damage or cracks.

Refitting

21 Refit the pump sprocket and retaining nut, and tighten the nut to the specified torque. Prevent the sprocket rotating as the nut is tightened using the sprocket holding tool.

22 Refit the timing belt as described in Section 7.

Coolant pump sprocket

23 The coolant pump sprocket is integral with the pump, and cannot be removed. Coolant pump removal is described in Chapter 3 Section 7.

Tensioner pulley

Removal

24 Remove the timing belt as described in Section 7.

25 Remove the tensioner pulley retaining bolt, and then remove the tensioner **(see illustration)**.

26 Clean the tensioner pulley, but do not use any strong solvent which may enter the pulley

bearings. Check that the pulley rotates freely, with no sign of stiffness or free play. The pulley should always be replaced when the timing belt is replaced.

27 Examine the pulley mounting stud for signs of damage and if necessary, renew it.

Refitting

28 Refitting is a reversal of removal.

29 Refit the timing belt as described in Section 7.

Idler pulley

Removal

30 Remove the timing belt as described in Section 7.

31 Undo the retaining bolt/nut and withdraw the idler pulley from the engine **(see illustration)**.

32 Clean the idler pulley, but do not use any strong solvent which may enter the bearings. Check that the pulley rotates freely, with no sign of stiffness or free play. Renew the idler pulley if there is any doubt about its condition, or if there are any obvious signs of wear or damage.

Refitting

33 Locate the idler pulley on the engine, and fit the retaining bolt/nut. Tighten the bolt/nut to the specified torque.

34 Refit the timing belt as described in Section 7.

9 Camshafts, rocker arms and hydraulic tappets – removal, inspection and refitting

Removal

1 Remove the cylinder head cover/manifold as described in Section 4.

2 Remove the timing belt (Section 7) and the camshaft sprocket as described in Section 8.

3 Refit the right-hand engine mounting,

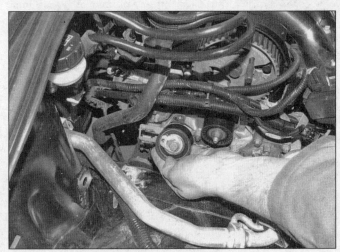
8.25 Remove the tensioner

8.31 Timing belt idler pulley retaining nut (arrowed)

9.4 Remove the vacuum pump

9.6 Remove the camshaft position sensor (arrowed)

9.7 Remove the bearing ladder

but only tighten the bolts moderately; this will keep the engine supported during the camshaft removal.

4 Undo the bolts and remove the vacuum pump (see Chapter 9 Section 21). Recover the pump O-ring seals (see illustration).

5 Unbolt the fuel filter (see Chapter 1B Section 22) and move it to one side.

6 Disconnect the wiring plug from the camshaft position sensor (see illustration). Unbolt and remove the sensor from the bearing ladder.

7 Working in reverse order to that shown (see illustration 9.22) remove the retaining bolts and then remove camshaft bearing cap ladder (see illustration).

8 Lift out the camshaft (see illustration) and dispose of the oil seal. A new one will be required.

9.8 Remove the camshaft

9.11 Use long nose pliers to remove the hydraulic tappets

9 Obtain 8 small, clean plastic containers, and number them 1 to 4 inlet and 1 to 4 exhaust; alternatively, divide a larger container into 8 compartments.

10 Lift out each rocker arm. Place the rocker arms in their respective positions in the box or containers (see illustration).

11 A compartmentalised container filled with engine oil is now required to retain the hydraulic tappets while they are removed from the cylinder head. Withdraw each hydraulic follower (see illustration) and place it in the container, keeping them each identified for correct refitting. The tappets must be totally submerged in the oil to prevent air entering them.

Inspection

12 Inspect the cam lobes and the camshaft

9.10 Remove the rocker arms (cam followers)

9.19 Lubricate the bearing surfaces

bearing journals for scoring or other visible evidence of wear. Once the surface hardening of the cam lobes has been eroded, wear will occur at an accelerated rate. Note: If these symptoms are visible on the tips of the camshaft lobes, check the corresponding rocker arm, as it will probably be worn as well.

13 Examine the condition of the bearing surfaces in the cylinder head and camshaft bearing housing. If wear is evident, the cylinder head and bearing housing will both have to be renewed, as they are a matched assembly.

14 Inspect the rocker arms and tappets for scuffing, cracking or other damage and renew any components as necessary. Also check the condition of the tappet bores in the cylinder head. As with the camshafts, any wear in this area will necessitate cylinder head renewal.

Refitting

15 Thoroughly clean the sealant from the mating surfaces of the cylinder head and camshaft bearing housing. Use a suitable liquid gasket dissolving agent (available from Ford dealers) together with a soft putty knife; do not use a metal scraper or the faces will be damaged. As there is no conventional gasket used, the cleanliness of the mating faces is of the utmost importance.

16 Clean off any oil, dirt or grease from both components and dry with a clean lint-free cloth. Ensure that all the oilways are completely clean.

17 Liberally lubricate the hydraulic tappet bores in the cylinder head with clean engine oil.

18 Insert the hydraulic tappets into their original bores in the cylinder head unless they have been renewed.

19 Lubricate the rocker arms and place them over their respective tappets and valve stems. Lubricate the bearing surfaces (see illustration) and then refit the camshaft.

20 Apply a thin bead of silicone sealant (Ford part No WSE-M4G323-A4) to the mating surface of the camshaft cover/bearing ladder as shown (see illustration).

21 Assembly the bearing ladder within 10 minutes of applying the sealant (see illustration). Ford technicians use a special tool (303-245) to align the bearing ladder, however 2 suitable bolts (with their heads and

9.20 Apply sealant to the camshaft housing

9.21 Refit the bearing ladder

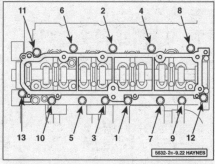

9.22 Tighten the bolts to the specified torque in the order shown

threads cut off) can be used if the tool is not available.

22 Tighten the bolts to the specified torque in sequence **(see illustration)**.

23 Fit a new camshaft oil seal as described in Section 14.

24 Refit the camshaft sprocket, and tighten the retaining bolt.

25 Refit the timing belt and temporarily refit the crankshaft pulley bolt – use the old bolt. Rotate the engine at least 20 revolutions to allow the oil pump to deliver oil to the camshaft and associated components. Refit the timing belt cover.

26 Refit the remainder of the components in the reverse order of removal.

10 Cylinder head – removal and refitting

Removal

1 Apply the handbrake, then jack up the front of the vehicle and support it on axle stands (see 'Jacking and vehicle support').

2 Disconnect the battery as described in Chapter 14 Section 6.

3 Drain the cooling system as described in Chapter 1B Section 30.

4 Remove the timing belt, camshaft, rocker arms and hydraulic tappets as described in Section 9.

5 Remove the turbocharger and exhaust manifold as described in Chapter 4B.

6 Unbolt the fuel filter assembly (and move it to one side) and the remove the glow plugs as described in Chapter 5A Section 12.

7 Undo the upper mounting bolts, and pivot the alternator away from the engine, undo the oil dipstick guide tube bolt, then undo the bolts securing the alternator mounting bracket to the cylinder head/block **(see illustration)**.

8 Undo the coolant outlet housing (left-hand end of the cylinder head) retaining bolts, slacken the two bolts securing the housing support bracket to the top of the transmission bellhousing, and move the outlet housing away from the cylinder head a little **(see illustration)**. There is no need to disconnect the hoses.

9 Remove the brake vacuum pump as described in Chapter 9 Section 21.

10 Disconnect the high-pressure fuel pipe from the common rail to the pump, and disconnect the fuel supply and return hoses. Where fitted, remove the bracket at the rear of the pump, then undo the bolt/nut and remove the pump and mounting bracket as an assembly **(see illustrations)**. Immediately seal all the openings in the fuel system. Note that a new high-pressure pipe must be fitted – see Chapter 4B Section 9.

11 Unbolt the EGR pipe and inlet duct from the rear of the cylinder head.

12 Check that no components or electrical connectors are still fitted to the cylinder head.

13 Working in the reverse of the sequence shown **(see illustration 10.32)** undo the cylinder head bolts. Discard the bolts – new ones must be fitted.

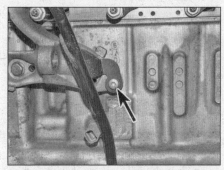

10.7 The engine oil level dipstick guide tube is secured to the alternator bracket by a Torx bolt (arrowed)

10.8 Access to the coolant outlet housing will be improved if the vacuum pump is removed first

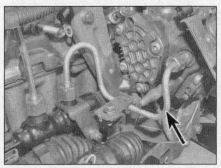

10.10a Remove the high-pressure pipe (arrowed)

10.10b Pull up the green collars and...

10.10c ...remove the fuel bleed hoses from the injectors

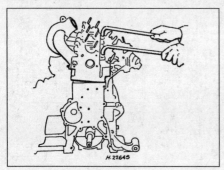

10.14 Free the cylinder head using angled rods

10.18a Pull the non-return valve from the cylinder head…

10.18b …and push a new one into place

14 Release the cylinder head from the cylinder block and location dowels by rocking it. The Ford tool for doing this consists simply of two metal rods with 90-degree angled ends **(see illustration)**. Do not prise between the mating faces of the cylinder head and block, as this may damage the gasket faces.
15 Lift the cylinder head from the block, and recover the gasket.

Preparation for refitting

16 The mating faces of the cylinder head and cylinder block must be perfectly clean before refitting the head. Ford recommend the use of a scouring agent for this purpose, but acceptable results can be achieved by using a hard plastic or wood scraper to remove all traces of gasket and carbon. The same method can be used to clean the piston crowns. Take particular care to avoid scoring or gouging the cylinder head/cylinder block mating surfaces during the cleaning operations, as aluminium alloy is easily damaged. Make sure that the carbon is not allowed to enter the oil and water passages – this is particularly important for the lubrication system, as carbon could block the oil supply to the engine's components. Using adhesive tape and paper, seal the water, oil and bolt holes in the cylinder block. To prevent carbon entering the gap between the pistons and bores, smear a little grease in the gap. After cleaning each piston, use a small brush to remove all traces of grease and carbon from the gap, then wipe away the remainder with a clean rag.

17 Check the mating surfaces of the cylinder block and the cylinder head for nicks, deep scratches and other damage. If slight, they may be removed carefully with a file, but if excessive, machining may be the only alternative to renewal. If warpage of the cylinder head gasket surface is suspected, use a straight-edge to check it for distortion. Refer to Part F of this Chapter if necessary.
18 Thoroughly clean the threads of the cylinder head bolt holes in the cylinder block. Ensure that the bolts run freely in their threads, and that all traces of oil and water are removed from each bolt hole. If required, pull the oil feed non-return valve from the cylinder head, and check the ball moves freely. Push a new valve into place if necessary **(see illustrations)**.

Gasket selection

19 The gasket thickness is indicated by notches/holes on the front edge of the gasket. If the crankshaft or pistons/connecting rods have not been disturbed, fit a new gasket with the same number of notches/holes as the previous one. If the crankshaft/piston or connecting rods have been disturbed, it's necessary to work out the piston protrusion as follows:
20 Remove the crankshaft timing pin, then turn the crankshaft until pistons 1 and 4 are at TDC (Top Dead Centre). Position a dial test indicator (dial gauge) on the cylinder block adjacent to the rear of No 1 piston, and zero it on the block face. Transfer the probe to the crown of No 1 piston (10.0 mm in from the

rear edge), then slowly turn the crankshaft back-and-forth past TDC, noting the highest reading on the indicator. Record this reading as protrusion A.
21 Repeat the check described in paragraph 18, this time 10.0 mm in from the front edge of the No 1 piston crown. Record this reading as protrusion B.
22 Add protrusion A to protrusion B, then divide the result by 2 to obtain an average reading for piston No 1.
23 Repeat the procedure described in paragraphs 20 to 22 on piston 4, then turn the crankshaft through 180° and carry out the procedure on the piston Nos 2 and 3 **(see illustration)**. Check that there is a maximum difference of 0.07 mm protrusion between any two pistons.
24 If a dial test indicator is not available, piston protrusion may be measured using a straight-edge and feeler blades or Vernier calipers. However, this is much less accurate, and cannot therefore be recommended.
25 Note the greatest piston protrusion measurement, and use this to determine the correct cylinder head gasket from the table below. The series of notches/holes on the side of the gasket are used for thickness identification **(see illustration)**.

Refitting

26 Turn the crankshaft and position Nos 1 and 4 pistons at TDC, then turn the crankshaft a quarter turn (90°) anti-clockwise.
27 Thoroughly clean the surfaces of the cylinder head and block.

10.23 Measure the piston protrusion using a DTI gauge

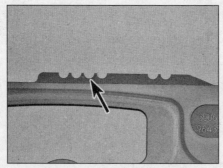

10.25 Cylinder head gasket thickness identification notches (arrowed)

10.28 Ensure the gasket locates over the dowels (arrowed)

28 Make sure that the locating dowels are in place, then fit the correct gasket the right way round on the cylinder block **(see illustration)**.

29 Carefully lower the cylinder head onto the gasket and block, making sure that it locates correctly onto the dowels.

30 Apply a smear of grease to the threads, and to the underside of the heads of the new cylinder head bolts.

31 Carefully insert the cylinder head bolts into their holes (do not drop them in) and initially finger-tighten them.

32 Working progressively and in sequence, tighten the cylinder head bolts to their Stage 1 torque setting, using a torque wrench and suitable socket **(see illustration)**.

33 Once all the bolts have been tightened to their Stage 1 torque setting, working again in the specified sequence, tighten each bolt to the specified Stage 2 setting. Finally, angle-tighten the bolts through the specified Stage 3 angle. It is recommended that an angle-measuring gauge is used during this stage of tightening, to ensure accuracy. **Note:** *Retightening of the cylinder head bolts after running the engine is not required.*

34 Refit the hydraulic tappets, rocker arms, and camshaft housing (complete with camshafts) as described in Section 9.

35 Refit the timing belt as described in Section 7.

36 The remainder of refitting is a reversal of removal, noting the following points.

a) *Use a new seal when refitting the coolant outlet housing.*

b) *When refitting a cylinder head, it is good practice to renew the thermostat.*

c) *Refit the camshaft position sensor and set the air gap with reference to Chapter 4B Section 12.*

d) *Tighten all fasteners to the specified torque where given.*

e) *Refill the cooling system as described in Chapter 1B Section 30.*

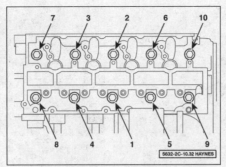

10.32 Cylinder head bolt tightening sequence

f) *The engine may run erratically for the first few miles, until the engine management ECM relearns its stored values.*

11 Sump – removal and refitting

Removal

1 Drain the engine oil, then clean and refit the engine oil drain plug, tightening it securely. If the engine is nearing its service interval when the oil and filter are due for renewal, it is recommended that the filter is also removed, and a new one fitted. After reassembly, the engine can then be refilled with fresh oil. Refer to Chapter 1B Section 6 for further information.

2 Apply the handbrake, then jack up the front of the vehicle and support it on axle stands (see 'Jacking and vehicle support'). Undo the bolts and remove the engine undershield.

3 Remove the exhaust front pipe as described in Chapter 4B Section 18.

4 Where necessary, disconnect the wiring connector from the oil temperature sender unit, which is screwed into the sump.

5 Progressively slacken and remove all the sump retaining bolts/nuts. Since the sump bolts vary in length, remove each bolt in turn, and store it in its correct fitted order by pushing it through a clearly-marked cardboard template. This will avoid the possibility of installing the bolts in the wrong locations on refitting.

6 Try to break the joint by striking the sump with the palm of your hand, then lower and withdraw the sump from under the car. If the sump is stuck (which is quite likely) use a putty knife or similar, carefully inserted between the sump and block. Ease the knife along the joint until the sump is released. While the sump is removed, take the opportunity to check the oil pump pick-up/strainer for signs of clogging or splitting. If necessary, remove the pump as described in Section 12, and clean or renew the strainer.

Refitting

7 Clean all traces of sealant from the mating surfaces of the cylinder block/crankcase and sump, then use a clean rag to wipe out the sump and the engine's interior.

8 Ensure that the sump mating surfaces are clean and dry, then apply a 3mm diameter bead of sealant (Ford part No WSE-M4G323-A4) to the sump mating surface **(see illustration)**. The sealant must be applied to the inside of the bolt holes. Note that the sump must be installed within 10 minutes of applying the sealant, and the bolts tightened within a further 5 minutes.

9 Offer up the sump to the cylinder block/crankcase. Refit its retaining bolts/nuts, ensuring that each bolt is screwed into its original location. Tighten the bolts evenly and progressively to the specified torque setting **(see illustration)**.

10 Reconnect the wiring connector to the oil temperature sensor (where fitted).

11 Lower the vehicle to the ground, wait at least 30 minutes and then refill the engine with oil as described in Chapter 1B Section 6.

11.8 Apply a bead of sealant to the sump or crankcase mating surface. Ensure the sealant is applied to the inside of the retaining bolt holes

11.9 Refit the sump and tighten the bolts

12.4 Oil pick-up tube bolts (arrowed)

12.5 Oil pump retaining bolts (arrowed)

12 Oil pump – removal, inspection and refitting

Removal

1 Remove the sump as described in Section 11.
2 Remove the crankshaft sprocket as described in Section 8. Recover the locating key from the crankshaft.
3 Disconnect the wiring plug, undo the bolts and remove the crankshaft position sensor, located on the right-hand end of the cylinder block.
4 Undo the three Torx security bolts and remove the oil pump pick-up tube from the pump/block (see illustration). Discard the oil seal, a new one must be fitted.
5 Undo the 8 bolts, and remove the oil pump (see illustration).

Inspection

6 Undo and remove the Torx bolts securing the cover to the oil pump (see illustration). Examine the pump rotors and body for signs of wear and damage. If worn, the complete pump must be renewed.
7 Remove the circlip, and extract the cap, valve piston and spring, noting which way around they are fitted (see illustrations). The condition of the relief valve spring can only be measured by comparing it with a new one; if there is any doubt about its condition, it should also be renewed.
8 Refit the relief valve piston and spring, then secure them in place with the circlip.
9 Refit the cover to the oil pump, and tighten the Torx bolts securely.

Refitting

10 Remove all traces of sealant, and thoroughly clean the mating surfaces of the oil pump and cylinder block.
11 Apply a 4 mm diameter bead of silicone sealant to the mating face of the cylinder block (see illustration). Ensure that no sealant enters any of the holes in the block.

12.6 Undo the Torx bolts and remove the pump cover

12.7a Remove the circlip…

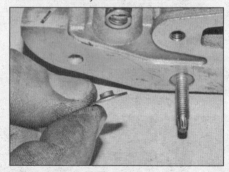

12.7b …cap…

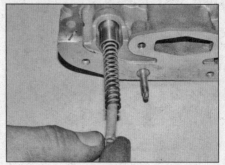

12.7c …spring…

12.7d …and piston

12.11 Apply a bead of sealant to the cylinder block mating surface

12.12a Fit a new seal...

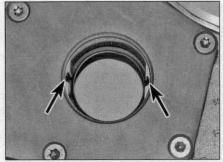

12.12b ...align the pump gear flats (arrowed)...

12.12c ...with those of the crankshaft (arrowed)

12 With a new oil seal fitted, refit the oil pump over the end of the crankshaft, aligning the flats in the pump drive gear with the flats machined in the crankshaft **(see illustrations)**. Note that new oil pumps are supplied with the oil seal already fitted, and a seal protector sleeve. The sleeve fits over the end of the crankshaft to protect the seal as the pump is fitted.

13 Install the oil pump bolts and tighten them to the specified torque.

14 Refit the oil pick-up tube to the pump/cylinder block using a new O-ring seal. Ensure the oil dipstick guide tube is correctly refitted.

15 Refit the woodruff key to the crankshaft, and slide the crankshaft sprocket into place.

16 The remainder of refitting is a reversal of removal.

13 Oil cooler –
removal and refitting

Removal

1 Apply the handbrake, then jack up the front of the vehicle and support it on axle stands (see *'Jacking and vehicle support'*). Undo the fasteners and remove the engine undershield.

2 The oil cooler is fitted to the front of the oil filter housing. Drain the coolant as described in Chapter 1B Section 30.

3 Drain the engine oil as described in Chapter 1B Section 6, or be prepared for fluid spillage.

4 Undo the bolts/stud and remove the oil cooler **(see illustration)**. Recover the gasket.

Refitting

5 Fit a new gasket into the recesses in the oil filter housing, and refit the cooler. Tighten the bolts securely.

6 Refill or top-up the cooling system and engine oil level as described in Chapter 1B or Weekly checks 0 Section 5 (as applicable). Start the engine, and check the oil cooler for signs of leakage.

14 Oil seals – renewal

Crankshaft

Right-hand oil seal

1 Remove the crankshaft sprocket and Woodruff key as described in Section 8.

2 Measure and note the fitted depth of the oil seal.

3 Pull the oil seal from the housing using a screwdriver. Alternatively, drill a small hole in the oil seal, and use a self-tapping screw and a pair of pliers to remove it **(see illustration)**.

4 Clean the oil seal housing and the crankshaft sealing surface.

5 The new seal should be supplied with a protective sleeve, which fits over the end of the crankshaft to prevent any damage to the seal lip. With the sleeve in place, press

13.4 Undo the oil cooler bolts/stud (arrowed)

the seal (open end first) into the pump to the previously-noted depth, using a suitable tube or socket **(see illustrations)**.

6 Where applicable, remove the plastic sleeve from the end of the crankshaft.

7 Refit the crankshaft sprocket as described in Section 8.

Left-hand oil seal

8 Remove the flywheel, as described in Section 16.

9 Measure and note the fitted depth of the oil seal.

10 Pull the oil seal from the housing using a screwdriver. Alternatively, drill a small hole in the oil seal, and use a self-tapping screw and a pair of pliers to remove it **(see illustration 14.3)**.

11 Clean the oil seal housing and the crankshaft sealing surface.

14.3 Take great care not to mark the crankshaft whilst levering out the oil seal

14.5a Slide the seal and protective sleeve over the end of the crankshaft...

14.5b ...and press the seal into place

14.12 Slide the seal and protective sleeve over the left-hand end of the crankshaft

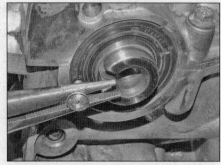

14.16 Drill a hole, insert a self-tapping screw, and pull the seal from place using pliers

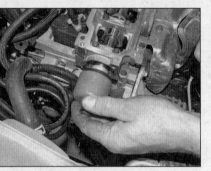

14.18a Use the correct tool to fit the seal...

14.18b ...or a suitable socket

12 The new seal should be supplied with a protective sleeve, which fits over the end of the crankshaft to prevent any damage to the seal lip **(see illustration)**. With the sleeve in place, press the seal (open end first) into the housing to the previously-noted depth, using a suitable tube or socket.
13 Where applicable, remove the plastic sleeve from the end of the crankshaft.
14 Refit the flywheel, as described in Section 16.

Camshaft

15 Remove the camshaft sprocket as described in Section 8. In principle there is no need to remove the timing belt completely, but remember that if the belt has been contaminated with oil, it must be renewed.
16 Pull the oil seal from the housing using a hooked instrument. Alternatively, drill a small hole in the oil seal and use a self-tapping screw and a pair of pliers to remove it **(see illustration)**.
17 Clean the oil seal housing and the camshaft sealing surface.
18 Press the seal (open end first) into the housing to the previously-noted depth, using either the correct tool (303-684), a suitable tube or a socket which bears only of the outer edge of the seal **(see illustrations)**. If the seal was supplied with a protective sleeve, remove it.
19 Refit the camshaft sprocket as described in Section 8.
20 Where necessary, fit a new timing belt with reference to Section 7.

15 Oil pressure switch and level sensor – removal and refitting

Removal

Oil pressure switch

1 The oil pressure switch is located at the front of the cylinder block, adjacent to the oil dipstick guide tube. Note that on some models, access to the switch may be improved if the vehicle is jacked up and supported on axle stands, then undo the bolts and remove the engine undershield so that the switch can be reached from underneath (see *'Jacking and vehicle support'*).
2 Remove the protective sleeve from the wiring plug (where applicable), then disconnect the wiring from the switch.

15.3 The oil pressure switch is located on the front face of the cylinder block (arrowed)

3 Unscrew the switch from the cylinder block, and recover the sealing washer **(see illustration)**. Be prepared for oil spillage, and if the switch is to be left removed from the engine for any length of time, plug the hole in the cylinder block.

Oil level sensor

4 The oil level sensor is located at the rear of the cylinder block. Jack up the front of the vehicle and support it securely on axle stands (see *'Jacking and vehicle support'*). Undo the bolts and remove the engine undershield.
5 Reach up between the driveshaft and the cylinder block, and disconnect the sensor wiring plug **(see illustration)**.
6 Using an open-ended spanner, unscrew the sensor and withdraw it from position.

Refitting

Oil pressure switch

7 Examine the sealing washer for any signs of damage or deterioration, and if necessary renew.
8 Refit the switch, complete with washer, and tighten it to the specified torque where given.
9 Refit the engine undershield, and lower the vehicle to the ground.

Oil level sensor

10 Smear a little silicone sealant on the threads and refit the sensor to the cylinder block, tightening it securely.
11 Reconnect the sensor wiring plug.
12 Refit the engine undershield, and lower the vehicle to the ground.

16 Flywheel – removal, inspection and refitting

Removal

1 Remove the transmission as described in Chapter 7A Section 6, then remove the clutch assembly as described in Chapter 6 Section 6.
2 Prevent the flywheel from turning. Do not attempt to lock the flywheel in position using the crankshaft pulley locking tool described in Section 3. Insert a 12 mm diameter rod or drill bit through the hole in the flywheel cover

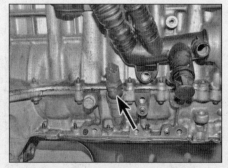

15.5 The oil level sensor is located on the rear face of the cylinder block (arrowed)

16.2 Lock the flywheel with a 12mm diameter rod or bolt (arrowed)

16.9 Flywheel retaining Torx bolts

casting, and into a slot in the flywheel **(see illustration)**

3 Make alignment marks between the flywheel and crankshaft to aid refitment. Slacken and remove the flywheel retaining bolts, and remove the flywheel from the end of the crankshaft. Be careful not to drop it; it is heavy. If the flywheel locating dowel (where fitted) is a loose fit in the crankshaft end, remove it and store it with the flywheel for safe-keeping. Discard the flywheel bolts; new ones must be used on refitting.

Inspection

4 Examine the flywheel for scoring of the clutch face, and for wear or chipping of the ring gear teeth. If the clutch face is scored, the flywheel may be surface-ground, but renewal is preferable. Seek the advice of a Ford dealer or engine reconditioning specialist to see if machining is possible. If the ring gear is worn or damaged, the flywheel must be renewed, as it is not possible to renew the ring gear separately.

5 All engines are fitted with a dual-mass flywheel. The maximum travel of the primary mass in relation to the secondary must not exceed 15 teeth (or 20 degrees). If in doubt remove the flywheel and have a suitably equipped specialist check the flywheel. Inspect the flywheel for any grease or debris from the interface between the fixed part and the movable part of the flywheel. If any doubt to the condition of the flywheel exists, despite the expense we recommend replacing it.

Refitting

6 Clean the mating surfaces of the flywheel and crankshaft. Remove any remaining locking compound from the threads of the crankshaft holes, using the correct size of tap, if available.

7 If the new flywheel retaining bolts are not supplied with their threads already pre-coated, apply a suitable thread-locking compound to the threads of each bolt.

8 Ensure that the locating dowel is in position. Offer up the flywheel, locating it on the dowel (where fitted), and fit the new retaining bolts. Where no locating dowel is fitted, align the previously-made marks to ensure the flywheel is refitted in its original position.

9 Lock the flywheel using the method employed on dismantling, and tighten the retaining bolts to the specified torque **(see illustration)**.

10 Refit the clutch as described in Chapter 6 Section 6. Remove the flywheel locking tool, and refit the transmission as described in Chapter 7A Section 6.

17 Engine/transmission mountings – inspection and renewal

General

1 The engine/transmission mountings seldom require attention, but broken or deteriorated mountings should be renewed immediately, or the added strain placed on the driveline components may cause damage or wear.

2 While separate mountings may be removed and refitted individually, if more than one is disturbed at a time – such as if the engine/transmission unit is removed from its mountings – they must be reassembled and their fasteners tightened in the position marked on removal.

3 On reassembly, the complete weight of the engine/transmission unit must not be taken by the mountings until all are correctly aligned with the marks made on removal. Tighten the engine/transmission mounting fasteners to their specified torque wrench settings.

Inspection

4 During the check, the engine/transmission

17.9 Right-hand engine mounting-to-engine bracket retaining nuts (arrowed)

unit must be raised slightly, to remove its weight from the mountings.

5 Raise the front of the vehicle, and support it securely on axle stands. Position a jack under the sump, with a large block of wood between the jack head and the sump, then carefully raise the engine/transmission just enough to take the weight off the mountings.

> ⚠ **Warning: DO NOT place any part of your body under the engine when it is supported only by a jack.**

6 Check the mountings to see if the rubber is cracked, hardened or separated from the metal components. Sometimes the rubber will split right down the centre.

7 Check for relative movement between each mounting's brackets and the engine/transmission or body (use a large screwdriver or lever to attempt to move the mountings). If movement is noted, lower the engine and check-tighten the mounting fasteners.

Renewal

Note: *The following paragraphs assume the engine is supported beneath the sump as described earlier.*

Right-hand mounting

8 Lift up the coolant expansion tank and position it to one side. Note there is no need to disconnect the coolant pipes.

9 Mark the position of the mounting on the vehicle, right-hand inner wing panel, then undo the three nuts securing the mounting to the engine bracket **(see illustration)**. Discard the nuts, new ones must be fitted.

10 Undo the three retaining bolts securing the mounting to the inner wing panel and withdraw the mounting from the vehicle **(see illustration)**.

11 On refitting, tighten all fasteners to the torque wrench settings specified. Re-align the marks made on removal, then tighten the new mounting bracket retaining nuts.

Left-hand mounting

12 Remove the battery and battery tray as described in Chapter 5A Section 4. Note that it is not necessary to remove the powertrain control module from the battery tray, just position the tray clear for access to the mounting.

17.10 Right-hand engine mounting-to-inner wing panel retaining bolts (arrowed)

17.13 Undo the retaining nuts and lift out the battery tray support bracket

17.14a Left-hand engine mounting bracket-to-transmission retaining bolts (arrowed) ...

17.14b ... and mounting-to-body sidemember retaining bolts (arrowed)

17.16 Rear mounting/roll restrictor retaining bolts (arrowed)

13 Undo the three nuts securing the battery tray support bracket in position. Release the wiring loom from the support bracket and lift the support bracket out of the engine compartment **(see illustration)**.

14 With the transmission supported, mark the position of the mounting bracket on the transmission and on the body side member. Undo the three bolts securing the mounting bracket to the transmission and the two bolts securing the mounting to the body side member **(see illustrations)**. Remove the mounting from the engine compartment.

15 On refitting, re-align the mounting in the position noted on removal, then tighten all fasteners to the specified torque wrench settings. Refit the components disturbed for access using a reversal of the removal procedures.

Rear mounting (roll restrictor)

16 To remove the engine rear mounting, apply the handbrake, then jack up the front of the car and support it on axle stands (see 'Jacking and vehicle support'). Unscrew the through-bolts and remove the engine rear mounting link from the bracket on the transmission and from the bracket on the subframe **(see illustration)**. Hold the engine stationary while the bolts are being removed, since the link will be under tension.

17 On refitting, ensure that the bolts are securely tightened to the specified torque wrench setting.

Chapter 2 Part F
Engine removal and overhaul procedures

Contents

Degrees of difficulty

Easy, suitable for novice with little experience 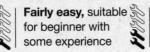	**Fairly easy,** suitable for beginner with some experience	**Fairly difficult,** suitable for competent DIY mechanic	**Difficult,** suitable for experienced DIY mechanic	**Very difficult,** suitable for expert DIY or professional

Specifications

Engine type

	Manufacturer's engine codes*
1.25 litre (1242 cc) DOHC 16-valve petrol engine	SNJA, SNJB, STJA and STJB
1.4 litre (1388 cc) DOHC 16-valve petrol engine	SPJA and SPJC
1.6 litre (1596 cc) DOHC 16-valve petrol engine	HXJA and HXJB
1.4 litre (1399 cc) SOHC 8-valve diesel engine	F6JD, F6JB and KVJA
1.6 litre (1560 cc) SOHC 8-valve diesel engine	TZJA, TZJB and T3JA
1.6 litre (1560 cc) DOHC 16-valve diesel engine	HHJD and HHJE

*For details of engine code location, see Vehicle identification 14 Section 3.

Petrol engines

Valves
Valve clearances (cold):
   Inlet . . . .   0.17 to 0.23 mm
   Exhaust:
      1.25 and 1.4 litre engines . . . .   0.27 to 0.33 mm
      1.6 litre engines. . . . .   0.31 to 0.37 mm
Valve length:
   1.25 and 1.4 litre engines:
      Inlet. . . . .   97.35 mm
      Exhaust. . . . .   99.40 mm
   1.6 litre engines:
      Inlet. . . . .   96.95 mm
      Exhaust. . . . .   99.40 mm
Valve springs
   Free length . . . .   53.2 mm
Cylinder head
   Maximum permissible gasket surface distortion . . . .   0.05 mm
Camshafts
   Camshaft bearing journal diameter . . . .   Unavailable at time of writing
   Camshaft bearing journal-to-cylinder head running clearance . . . . .   Unavailable at time of writing
   Camshaft endfloat (typical). . . . .   0.05 to 0.13 mm
Torque wrench settings . . . .   Refer to Chapter 2A Specifications

1.4 litre diesel engines (Stage IV emissions)

Cylinder head
  Maximum permissible gasket surface distortion . . . .   0.025 mm
Camshaft
  Endfloat . . . .   0.195 to 0.300 mm
  Bearing journal diameter . . . .   23.959 to 23.980 mm
Crankshaft
  Endfloat . . . .   0.100 to 0.300 mm
  Main bearing journal diameter . . . .   49.962 to 49.981 mm
  Connecting rod journal diameter . . . .   44.975 to 44.991 mm
Cylinder block
  Cylinder bore diameter (reboring not possible) . . . .   73.700 to 73.718 mm
  Main bearing radial clearance . . . .   0.017 to 0.043 mm
Connecting rods
  Big-end bore diameter . . . .   48.655 to 48.671 mm
  Small-end bore diameter . . . .   25.000 mm
  Connecting rod bearing clearance . . . .   0.024 to 0.070 mm
  Gudgeon pin length . . . .   59.700 to 60.000 mm
  Gudgeon pin diameter . . . .   24.995 to 25.000 mm
Pistons and piston rings
  Piston diameter . . . .   73.520 to 73.536 mm
  Piston-to-bore clearance . . . .   0.164 to 0.196 mm
  Piston ring end gaps – installed:
    Top compression ring . . . .   0.200 to 0.350 mm
    Second compression ring . . . .   0.200 to 0.400 mm
    Oil control ring . . . .   0.800 to 1.000 mm
  Piston ring gap arrangement . . . .   120° to each other
Torque wrench settings . . . .   Refer to Chapter 2B Specifications

1.4 litre diesel engines (Stage V emissions)

No information available

1.6 litre diesel engines

Valves

Valve stem diameter:
  Inlet 5.485 +0.0, -0.015 mm
  Exhaust . . . .   5.475 +0.0, -0.015 mm
Overall length:
  Inlet 96.43 ± 0.25 mm
  Exhaust . . . .   96.65 ± 0.2 mm
Cylinder head
  Maximum gasket face distortion . . . .   0.025 mm
Crankshaft
  Endfloat . . . .   0.100 to 0.300 mm
  Main bearing journal diameter . . . .   49.962 to 49.981mm
  Connecting rod journal diameter . . . .   44.975 to 44.991 mm
Cylinder block
  Cylinder bore diameter (reboring not possible) . . . .   75.000 to 75.018 mm
Pistons and piston rings
  Piston diameter . . . .   74.104 to 74.128 mm
  Piston-to-bore clearance . . . .   0.164 to 0.196 mm
  Piston ring end gaps – installed:
    Top compression ring . . . .   0.20 to 0.35 mm
    Second compression ring . . . .   0.20 to 0.40 mm
    Oil control ring . . . .   0.85 to 1.00 mm
  Piston ring gap arrangement . . . .   120° to each other
Torque wrench settings . . . .   Refer to Chapter 2C or 2D Specifications

1 General Information

Note: *On all petrol engines covered by this manual, it is not possible to remove the intermediate/main bearing section or to remove the crankshaft or pistons. No separate parts are available, and replacement/exchange units are supplied with crankshaft, pistons, connecting rods, etc, already fitted. Consult a Ford dealer or parts specialist for further information.*

1 Included in this Part of Chapter 2 are details of removing the engine/transmission from the car and general overhaul procedures for the cylinder head, cylinder block/crankcase and all other engine internal components.

2 The information given ranges from advice concerning preparation for an overhaul and the purchase of new parts, to detailed step-by-step procedures covering removal, inspection, renovation and refitting of engine internal components (where possible).

3 After Section 6, all instructions are based on the assumption that the engine has been removed from the car. For information concerning in-car engine repair, as well as the removal and refitting of those external components necessary for full overhaul, refer to Parts A to E of this Chapter (as applicable) and to Section 6. Ignore any preliminary dismantling operations described in Parts A to E that are no longer relevant once the engine has been removed from the car.

4 Apart from torque wrench settings, which are given at the beginning of Parts A to E (as applicable), all specifications relating to engine overhaul are at the beginning of this Part of Chapter 2.

2 Engine overhaul – general information

1 It is not always easy to determine when, or if, an engine should be completely overhauled, as a number of factors must be considered.

2 High mileage is not necessarily an indication that an overhaul is needed, while low mileage does not preclude the need for an overhaul. Frequency of servicing is probably the most important consideration. An engine which has had regular and frequent oil and filter changes, as well as other required maintenance, will most likely give many thousands of miles of reliable service. Conversely, a neglected engine may require an overhaul very early in its life.

3 Excessive oil consumption is an indication that piston rings, valve stem oil seals and/or valves and valve guides are in need of attention. Make sure that oil leaks are not responsible before deciding that the rings and/or guides are to blame. Perform a cylinder compression check to determine the likely cause of the problem.

4 Check the oil pressure with a gauge fitted in place of the oil pressure switch, and compare it with the value given in the Specifications. If it is extremely low, the main and big-end bearings and/or the oil pump are probably worn out.

5 Loss of power, rough running, knocking or metallic engine noises, excessive valve gear noise and high fuel consumption may also point to the need for an overhaul, especially if they are all present at the same time. If a complete tune-up does not remedy the situation, major mechanical work is the only solution.

6 An engine overhaul involves restoring the internal parts to the specifications of a new engine. During an overhaul, the pistons and rings are renewed, and the cylinder bores are reconditioned. New main bearings, connecting rod bearings and camshaft bearings are generally fitted, and if necessary, the crankshaft may be reground to restore the journals (note however that this work is not possible on petrol engines). The valves are also serviced as well, since they are usually in less-than-perfect condition at this point. While the engine is being overhauled, other components, such as the starter and alternator, can be overhauled as well. The end result should be a like-new engine that will give many trouble-free miles. **Note:** *Critical cooling system components such as the hoses, drivebelts, thermostat and coolant pump should be renewed when an engine is overhauled. The radiator should be checked carefully, to ensure that it is not clogged or leaking. Also, it is a good idea to renew the oil pump whenever the engine is overhauled.*

7 Before beginning the engine overhaul, read through the entire procedure to familiarise yourself with the scope and requirements of the job. Overhauling an engine is not difficult if you follow all of the instructions carefully, have the necessary tools and equipment, and pay close attention to all specifications; however, it can be time-consuming. Plan on the car being tied up for a minimum of two weeks, especially if parts must be taken to an engineering works for repair or reconditioning. Check on the availability of parts, and make sure that any necessary special tools and equipment are obtained in advance. Most work can be done with typical hand tools, although a number of precision measuring tools are required for inspecting parts to determine if they must be renewed. Often the engineering works will handle the inspection of parts, and offer advice concerning reconditioning and renewal.

8 Always wait until the engine has been completely dismantled, and all components, especially the engine block, have been inspected before deciding what service and repair operations must be performed by an engineering works. Since the condition of the block will be the major factor to consider when determining whether to overhaul the original engine or buy a reconditioned unit,

do not purchase parts or have overhaul work done on other components until the block has been thoroughly inspected. As a general rule, time is the primary cost of an overhaul, so it does not pay to fit worn or substandard parts.

9 As a final note, to ensure maximum life and minimum trouble from a reconditioned engine, everything must be assembled with care, and in a spotlessly-clean environment.

3 Engine removal – methods and precautions

1 If you have decided that an engine must be removed for overhaul or major repair work, several preliminary steps should be taken.

2 Locating a suitable place to work is extremely important. Adequate work space, along with storage space for the car, will be needed. If a garage is not available, at the very least a flat, level, clean work surface is required.

3 Cleaning the engine compartment and engine before beginning the removal procedure will help keep tools clean and organised.

4 The engine is removed complete with the transmission by lowering it out of the car; the car's body must be raised and supported securely sufficiently high that the engine/transmission can be unbolted as a single unit and lowered to the ground. An engine hoist will therefore be necessary. Make sure the equipment is rated in excess of the combined weight of the engine and transmission. Safety is of primary importance, considering the potential hazards involved in lifting the engine out of the car.

5 If the engine is being removed by a novice, an assistant should be available. Advice and aid from someone more experienced would also be helpful. There are many instances when one person cannot simultaneously perform all of the operations required when removing the engine from the car.

6 Plan the operation ahead of time. Arrange for, or obtain, all of the tools and equipment you will need, prior to beginning the job. Some of the equipment necessary to perform engine removal and installation safely and with relative ease are (in addition to an engine hoist) a heavy-duty trolley jack, complete sets of spanners and sockets as described at the end of this manual, wooden blocks, and plenty of rags and cleaning solvent for mopping-up spilled oil, coolant and fuel. If the hoist must be hired, make sure that you arrange for it in advance, and perform all of the operations possible without it beforehand. This will save you money and time.

7 Plan for the car to be out of use for quite a while. An engineering works will be required to perform some of the work which the do-it-yourselfer cannot accomplish without special equipment. These places often have a busy schedule, so it would be a good idea

to consult them before removing the engine, in order to accurately estimate the amount of time required to rebuild or repair components that may need work.

8 During the engine/transmission removal procedure, it is advisable to make notes of the locations of all brackets, cable-ties, earthing points, etc, as well as how the wiring harnesses, hoses and electrical connections are attached and routed around the engine and engine compartment. An effective way of doing this is to take a series of photographs of the various components before they are disconnected or removed; the resulting photographs will prove invaluable when the engine/transmission is refitted.

Caution: Always be extremely careful when removing and refitting the engine. Serious injury can result from careless actions. Plan ahead, take your time, and you will find that a job of this nature, although major, can be accomplished successfully.
Note: Such is the complexity of the power unit arrangement on these vehicles, and the variations that may be encountered according to model and optional equipment fitted, that the procedures given in Sections 4 and 5 should be regarded as a guide to the work involved, rather than an accurate step-by-step procedure. Where differences are encountered, or additional component disconnection or removal is necessary, make notes of the work involved as an aid to refitting.

4 Petrol engine – removal, separation and refitting

1 Depressurise the fuel system with reference to Chapter 4A Section 2.
2 Remove the windscreen cowl panel and bulkhead closure panel as described in Chapter 11 Section 20.
3 Remove the air cleaner assembly as described in Chapter 4A Section 5.
4 Remove the battery and battery tray as described in Chapter 5A Section 4.
5 Refer to Chapter 4A Section 11 and disconnect the three wiring connectors from the engine management PCM attached to the battery tray.
6 Undo the three nuts securing the battery tray support bracket in position. Release the wiring loom from the support bracket and lift the support bracket out of the engine compartment
7 Jack up the front of the car, and support it on axle stands (see *'Jacking and vehicle support'*). Although not essential immediately, it would pay at this stage to raise the car sufficiently to allow the engine and transmission to be withdrawn from underneath.
8 Drain the cooling system as described in Chapter 1A Section 31.
9 If the engine is being dismantled, drain the engine oil with reference to Chapter 1A Section 6.
10 Disconnect the fuel supply line quick-release connection from the fuel rail at the front of the engine.
11 Remove the alternator as described in Chapter 5A Section 7.
12 Disconnect the hoses from the coolant expansion tank, then release the two clips and remove the tank.
13 Disconnect the hose from the EVAP valve just below the fuel pressure regulator on the fuel rail.
14 Disconnect the brake servo vacuum hose from the inlet manifold.
15 Disconnect the two coolant hoses from the outlet elbow on the left-hand side of the engine, and also the two hoses from the thermostat housing on the front.
16 Disconnect the coolant hoses from the heater connections at the engine compartment bulkhead and from the oil cooler connection beneath the oil filter.
17 On automatic transmission models, disconnect the fluid cooling hoses at the quick-release connectors on the transmission.
18 Disconnect the following wiring plugs:
a) *Oxygen sensor wiring plug, located just behind the ignition coil, and the catalyst monitor wiring plug below it.*
b) *Camshaft position sensor wiring plug, which is located on the rear of the cylinder head, at the timing belt end.*
c) *Knock sensor wiring plug, located underneath the inlet manifold.*
d) *Starter motor wiring (refer to Chapter 5A Section 9 if necessary).*
e) *Where applicable, air conditioning compressor wiring plug.*
f) *Oil pressure switch, next to the oil filter.*
g) *Crankshaft position sensor, on the front of the engine, at the transmission end.*
h) *Reversing light switch, on the front of the transmission.*
i) *Coolant temperature sensor, below the ignition coil.*
j) *Ignition coil main wiring plug.*
19 Unbolt the engine earth strap just below the ignition coil, and the engine wiring harness support bracket just in front.
20 Where applicable, remove the four bolts securing the air conditioning compressor to the block, and secure the compressor to one side – do not disconnect any of the hoses.
21 Remove the radiator cooling fan and shroud – refer to Chapter 3 Section 5 if necessary.
22 Disconnect the transmission gearchange/selector cable(s) from the transmission as described in Chapter 7A or Chapter 7B, as applicable.
23 Loosen the three upper mounting nuts on both front suspension struts by three turns.
24 On both sides of the car, remove the lower arm balljoint clamp bolt from the swivel hub, and lever down the lower arm to separate it. Unclip the balljoint heat shields, and retain them for refitting.

25 Using the information in Chapter 8 Section 2, disconnect both driveshafts from the transmission, and also remove the intermediate shaft. There is no need to remove the driveshafts from the hubs, providing they can be supported clear so that the engine/transmission can drop down. The inner and outer joints should not be bent through more than 18° and 45° respectively.
26 To prevent damage to the exhaust flexible section, support it by attaching a pair of splints either side (two scrap strips of wood, plant canes, etc) using some cable-ties. Undo the nuts securing the flexible section to the exhaust manifold, and separate the joint. Recover the gasket, and discard it. Release the exhaust front rubber mounting block and move the system to one side.
27 Unbolt the engine rear mounting from under the car, referring to Chapter 2A Section 18 if necessary.
28 On manual transmission models, taking precautions against fluid spillage, prise up the spring clip and disconnect the clutch slave cylinder fluid pipe from on top of the transmission. Unclip the pipe, and tie it up to the bulkhead to reduce further fluid spillage.
29 Make a final check round the engine and transmission, to make sure nothing (apart from the left- and right-hand mountings) remains attached or in the way which will prevent it from being lowered out. Also make sure there is enough room under the front of the car for the engine/transmission to be lowered out and withdrawn.
30 Securely attach the engine/transmission unit to a suitable engine crane or hoist, and raise it so that the weight is just taken off the two remaining engine mountings. It is helpful at this stage to have an assistant available, either to work the crane or to guide the engine out.
31 With the engine securely supported, remove the three bolts from the engine left-hand mounting (on top of the transmission).
32 Similarly, remove the two nuts from the engine right-hand mounting, on the driver's side of the engine compartment.
33 With the help of an assistant, carefully lower the assembly from the engine compartment, making sure it clears the surrounding components and bodywork. Be prepared to steady the engine when it touches down, to stop it toppling over. Withdraw the assembly from under the car, and remove it to wherever it will be worked on.

Separation

34 To separate the transmission from the engine, first remove the starter motor with reference to Chapter 5A Section 9.

Manual transmission models

35 Remove the bolts securing the transmission to the engine. Note the fitted positions of any brackets.
36 With the aid of an assistant, draw the transmission off the engine. Once it is clear

of the dowels, do not allow it to hang on the input shaft.

Automatic transmission models

37 Rotate the crankshaft, using a socket on the pulley bolt, until one of the torque converter-to-driveplate retaining nuts becomes accessible through the starter motor opening. Working through the opening, undo the nut. Rotate the crankshaft as necessary and remove the remaining nuts in the same way. Note that new nuts will be required for refitting.

38 Remove the bolts securing the transmission to the engine. Note the fitted positions of any brackets.

39 With the aid of an assistant, draw the transmission squarely off the engine dowels making sure that the torque converter remains in position on the transmission.

Refitting

Manual transmission models

40 Make sure that the clutch is correctly centred and that the clutch release components are fitted to the bellhousing. Do not apply any grease to the transmission input shaft, the guide sleeve, or the release bearing itself, as these components have a friction-reducing coating which does not require lubrication.

41 Manoeuvre the transmission squarely into position, and engage it with the engine dowels. Refit the bolts securing the transmission to the engine, and tighten them to the specified torque. Refit the starter motor.

Automatic transmission models

42 Clean the contact surfaces on the torque converter and driveplate, and the transmission and engine mating faces. Lightly lubricate the torque converter guide projection and the engine/transmission locating dowels with grease.

43 Place a straight-edge across the bellhousing, and measure the distance between the torque converter spigot and the straight-edge. Position the torque converter so the distance is 15 mm **(see illustration)**.

44 Manoeuvre the transmission squarely into position, and engage it with the engine dowels. Refit the bolts securing the transmission to the engine and tighten lightly first in a diagonal sequence, then again to the specified torque.

45 Attach the torque converter to the drive-plate using new nuts. Rotate the crankshaft for access to the nuts as was done for removal. Fit and tighten all the nuts hand-tight first, then tighten again to the specified torque.

All models

46 The remainder of refitting is a reversal of removal, noting the following additional points:
a) Make sure that all mating faces are clean, and use new gaskets where necessary.
b) Tighten all nuts and bolts to the specified torque setting, where given.

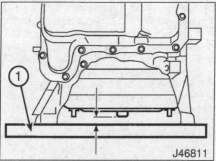

4.43 The distance between the straight-edge (1) and the torque converter spigot must be 15 mm

c) Use new nuts on the engine left- and right-hand mountings, but do not fully-tighten them until the car is resting on its wheels.
d) Use a new centre bearing cap and locknuts when refitting the intermediate shaft.
e) Fit new circlips to the grooves in the inner end of each driveshaft CV joint, and ensure that they fully engage as they are fitted into the transmission.
f) Check and if necessary adjust the gearchange cables as described in Chapter 7A or 7B, as applicable.
g) Refill the transmission with lubricant if necessary as described in Chapter 1A, 7A or 7B as applicable.
h) Top-up and bleed the clutch hydraulic system as described in Chapter 6.
i) Refill the engine with coolant and oil as described in Chapter 1A.
j) Tighten the suspension strut upper mounting nuts to the specified torque on completion (see Chapter 10).

5 Diesel engine – removal, separation and refitting

Warning: The diesel injection system operates at extremely high pressures when the pump is running. Wait at least one minute after stopping the engine before working on the fuel injection system components.

Removal

1 Remove the windscreen cowl panel and bulkhead closure panel as described in Chapter 11 Section 20.
2 Remove the air cleaner assembly as described in Chapter 4B Section 4.
3 Remove the battery and battery tray as described in Chapter 5A Section 4.
4 Refer to Chapter 4B Section 12 and disconnect the three wiring connectors from the engine management PCM attached to the battery tray.
5 Undo the three nuts securing the battery tray support bracket in position. Release the wiring loom from the support bracket and

lift the support bracket out of the engine compartment.
6 Jack up the front of the car, and support it on axle stands (see 'Jacking and vehicle support'). Although not essential immediately, it would pay at this stage to raise the car sufficiently to allow the engine and transmission to be withdrawn from underneath.
7 Undo the retaining bolts and remove the engine undertray.
8 Drain the cooling system as described in Chapter 1B Section 30.
9 If the engine is being dismantled, drain the engine oil with reference to Chapter 1B Section 6.
10 Remove the catalytic converter as described in Chapter 4B Section 18.
11 On 1.4 litre (Stage IV emissions) engines, release the retaining clips and cable-ties and remove the air inlet duct from the left-hand side of the engine.
12 Disconnect the fuel supply and return line quick-release connections from the fuel filter.
13 Disconnect the brake servo vacuum hose quick-release connection from the vacuum pump. Release the cable-ties and clips and move the fuel lines and vacuum hoses clear of the engine.
14 On 1.6 litre engines, slacken the retaining clips and disconnect the intercooler hoses from their engine attachments.
15 Remove the alternator as described in Chapter 5A Section 7.
16 Disconnect the hoses from the coolant expansion tank, then release the two clips and remove the tank.
17 Disconnect the coolant hoses from the thermostat housing at the left-hand side of the engine.
18 Disconnect the coolant hoses from the heater connections at the engine compartment bulkhead.
19 Trace the engine wiring harness from the transmission end of the engine, and cut any cable-ties securing it to parts of the engine.
20 Where applicable, remove the four bolts securing the air conditioning compressor to the block, and secure the compressor to one side – do not disconnect any of the hoses.
21 Remove the radiator cooling fan and shroud – refer to Chapter 3 Section 5 if necessary.
22 Disconnect the transmission gearchange cables from the transmission as described in Chapter 7A Section 3.
23 Loosen the three upper mounting nuts on both front suspension struts by three turns.
24 On both sides of the car, remove the lower arm balljoint clamp bolt from the swivel hub, and lever down the lower arm to separate it. Unclip the balljoint heat shields, and retain them for refitting.
25 Using the information in Chapter 8 Section 2, disconnect both driveshafts from the transmission, and also remove the intermediate shaft. There is no need to remove the driveshafts from the hubs, providing they

can be supported clear so that the engine/ transmission can drop down. The inner and outer joints should not be bent through more than 18° and 45° respectively.

26 Unbolt the engine rear mounting from under the car, referring to Chapter 2B Section 17, Chapter 2D Section 17, Chapter 2E Section 17 or Chapter 2C Section 17 if necessary.

27 Taking precautions against fluid spillage, prise up the spring clip and disconnect the clutch slave cylinder fluid pipe from on top of the transmission. Unclip the pipe, and tie it up to the bulkhead to reduce further fluid spillage.

28 Make a final check round the engine and transmission, to make sure nothing (apart from the left- and right-hand mountings) remains attached or in the way which will prevent it from being lowered out. Also make sure there is enough room under the front of the car for the engine/transmission to be lowered out and withdrawn.

29 Securely attach the engine/transmission unit to a suitable engine crane or hoist, and raise it so that the weight is just taken off the two remaining engine mountings. It is helpful at this stage to have an assistant available, either to work the crane or to guide the engine out.

30 With the engine securely supported, remove the three bolts from the engine left-hand mounting (on top of the transmission).

31 Similarly, remove the three nuts from the engine right-hand mounting, on the driver's side of the engine compartment.

32 With the help of an assistant, carefully lower the assembly from the engine compartment, making sure it clears the surrounding components and bodywork. Be prepared to steady the engine when it touches down, to stop it toppling over. Withdraw the assembly from under the car, and remove it to wherever it will be worked on.

Separation

33 To separate the transmission from the engine, first remove the starter motor with reference to Chapter 5A Section 9.

34 Remove the bolts securing the transmission to the engine. Note the fitted positions of any brackets.

35 With the aid of an assistant, draw the transmission off the engine. Once it is clear of the dowels, do not allow it to hang on the input shaft.

Refitting

36 Make sure that the clutch is correctly centred and that the clutch release components are fitted to the bellhousing. Do not apply any grease to the transmission input shaft, the guide sleeve, or the release bearing itself, as these components have a friction-reducing coating which does not require lubrication.

37 Manoeuvre the transmission squarely into position, and engage it with the engine dowels. Refit the bolts securing the transmission to the engine, and tighten them to the specified torque. Refit the starter motor.

38 The remainder of refitting is a reversal of removal, noting the following additional points:

a) Make sure that all mating faces are clean, and use new gaskets where necessary.

b) Tighten all nuts and bolts to the specified torque setting, where given.

c) Use new nuts on the engine left- and right-hand mountings, but do not fully-tighten them until the car is resting on its wheels.

d) Use a new centre bearing cap and lock-nuts when refitting the intermediate shaft.

e) Fit new circlips to the grooves in the inner end of each driveshaft CV joint, and ensure that they fully engage as they are fitted into the transmission.

f) Check and if necessary adjust the gearchange cables as described in Chapter 7A Section 2.

g) Refill the transmission with lubricant if necessary as described in Chapter 1B or 7A as applicable.

h) Top-up and bleed the clutch hydraulic system as described in Chapter 6 Section 4.

i) Refill the engine with coolant and oil as described in Chapter 1B.

j) Tighten the suspension strut upper mounting nuts to the specified torque on completion (see Chapter 10 Section 4).

6 Engine overhaul – dismantling sequence

Note: On all petrol engines covered by this manual, it is not possible to remove the intermediate/main bearing section or to remove the crankshaft or pistons. No separate parts are available, and replacement/exchange units are supplied with crankshaft, pistons, connecting rods, etc, already fitted. Consult a Ford dealer or parts specialist for further information.

1 It is much easier to dismantle and work on the engine if it is mounted on a portable engine stand. These stands can often be hired from a tool hire shop. Before the engine is mounted on a stand, the flywheel should be removed from the engine, so that the engine stand bolts can be tightened into the end of the cylinder block.

2 If a stand is not available, it is possible to dismantle the engine with it blocked up on a sturdy workbench or on the floor. Be extra careful not to tip or drop the engine when working without a stand.

3 If you're going to obtain a reconditioned ('recon') engine, all external components must be removed first, to be transferred to the new engine (just as they will if you are doing a complete engine overhaul yourself). **Note:** When removing the external components from the engine, pay close attention to details that may be helpful or important during refitting. Note the fitted position of gaskets, seals, spacers, pins, washers, bolts and other small items. These external components include the following:

Petrol engines

a) DIS ignition coil, HT leads and spark plugs.

b) All electrical switches and sensors.

c) Thermostat housing.

d) Fuel injection equipment.

e) Inlet and exhaust manifolds.

f) Oil filter.

g) Engine mountings and lifting brackets.

h) Ancillary component mounting brackets.

i) Oil filler tube and dipstick.

j) Coolant pipes and hoses.

k) Flywheel/driveplate.

Diesel engines

a) All electrical switches and sensors.

b) Fuel injection pump and mounting bracket, and fuel injectors and glow plugs.

c) Thermostat housing.

d) Inlet and exhaust manifolds.

e) Oil cooler.

f) Engine lifting brackets, hose brackets and wiring brackets.

g) Ancillary component mounting brackets.

h) Wiring harnesses and brackets.

i) Coolant pipes and hoses.

j) Oil filler tube and dipstick.

k) Flywheel.

4 If you are obtaining a 'short' motor (which consists of the engine cylinder block, crankshaft, pistons and connecting rods all assembled), then the timing belt, cylinder head, sump and oil pump will have to be removed also.

5 If you are planning a complete overhaul (diesel engines only) the engine can be disassembled and the internal components removed in the following order:

a) Engine external components (including inlet and exhaust manifolds).

b) Timing belt and sprocketst.

c) Cylinder head.

d) Flywheel.

e) Sump.

f) Oil pump.

g) Pistons and connecting rods.

h) Crankshaft and main bearings.

6 Before beginning the disassembly and overhaul procedures, make sure that you have all of the correct tools necessary. Refer to the reference section at the end of this manual for further information.

7 Cylinder head – dismantling

Note: New and reconditioned cylinder heads are available from the manufacturers and from engine overhaul specialists. Due to the fact that some specialist tools are required for the dismantling and inspection procedures, and new components may not be readily available, it may be more practical and economical for the home mechanic to purchase a reconditioned head rather than dismantle, inspect and recondition the original head.

1 Remove the cylinder head as described in Part A, B, C, D or E of this Chapter (as applicable).
2 If not already done, remove the inlet and exhaust manifolds with reference to the relevant Part of Chapter 4A or Chapter 4B. Also remove all external brackets and elbows.
3 Proceed as follows according to engine type.

Petrol engines

4 Remove the camshafts and tappets as described in Part A of this Chapter, being careful to store the components as described.
5 Using a valve spring compressor, compress each valve spring in turn until the split collets can be removed. A special valve spring compressor will be required, to reach into the deep wells in the cylinder head without risk of damaging the tappet bores; such compressors are now widely available from most good motor accessory shops. Release the compressor, and lift off the spring upper seat and spring **(see illustration)**.
6 If, when the valve spring compressor is screwed down, the spring upper seat refuses to free and expose the split collets, gently tap the top of the tool, directly over the upper seat, with a light hammer. This will free the seat.
7 Withdraw the valve through the combustion chamber. If it binds in the guide (won't pull through), push it back in, and de-burr the area around the collet groove with a fine file; take care not to mark the tappet bores.
8 Pull the valve stem seals from the valve guides using a pair of pliers. As the seals are removed, note whether they are of different colours for the inlet and exhaust valves – compare with the new parts, and note this for refitting. As a guide, the inlet valve seals are green, and the exhaust seals are red.
9 It is essential that the valves are kept together with their collets, spring seats and springs, and in their correct sequence (unless they are so badly worn that they are to be renewed). If they are going to be kept and used again, place them in a labelled polythene bag or similar small container **(see illustration)**. Note that No 1 valve is nearest to the timing belt end of the engine.

Diesel engines

10 Take off the glow plug wiring harness, noting how it is routed, then remove the glow plugs.
11 Unbolt and remove the EGR valve and recover the gasket.
12 Remove the oil pressure relief valve, which is located at the transmission end of the head.
13 Take off the fuel filter support nut (at the rear of the head, on the transmission end).
14 Lift out the hydraulic tappets and, on 1.4 litre (Stage V emissions) and 1.6 litre engines, the rocker arms – these must all be kept in their fitted order. There is no requirement by Ford to keep the hydraulic tappets in an oil bath while they're removed, but there's no

7.5 Removing the valve spring and upper seat

harm in doing so. The most important thing is that the tappets are stored (or marked) so they can be refitted to their original locations.
15 To remove the valve springs and valves from the cylinder head, a standard valve spring compressor will be required. Fit the spring compressor to the first valve and spring to be removed. Assuming that all of the valves and springs are to be removed, start by compressing the No 1 valve (nearest the timing cover end) and spring. Take care not to damage the valve stem with the compressor, and do not over-compress the spring, or the valve stem may bend.
16 When tightening the compressor, it may be found that the spring retainer does not release and the collets are then difficult to remove. In this instance, remove the compressor, then press a piece of tube (or a socket of suitable diameter) so that it does not interfere with the removal of the collets, against the retainer's outer rim. Tap the tube (or socket) with a hammer to unsettle the components.
17 Refit the compressor, and wind it in to enable the collets to be extracted.
18 Loosen off the compressor, and remove the retainer and spring. Withdraw the valve from the cylinder head.
19 Pull the valve stem seals from the valve guides using a pair of pliers. The valve stem oil seal also forms the spring seat and is deeply recessed in the cylinder head. It is also a tight fit on the valve guide making it difficult to remove with pliers or a conventional valve stem oil seal removal tool. It can be easily

7.19a Use a pair of pliers to remove the valve stem oil seal

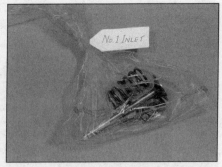

7.9 Use a labelled plastic bag to store and identify valve components

removed, however, using a self-locking nut of suitable diameter screwed onto the end of a bolt and locked with a second nut. Push the nut down onto the top of the seal; the locking portion of the nut will grip the seal allowing it to be withdrawn from the top of the valve guide **(see illustrations)**.
20 Repeat the removal procedure with each of the remaining seven valve assemblies in turn. As they are removed, keep the individual valves and their components together, and in their respective order of fitting, by placing them in a separate labelled bag **(see illustration 7.9)**.

8 Cylinder head and valves
– cleaning, inspection and renovation

1 Thorough cleaning of the cylinder head and valve components, followed by a detailed inspection, will enable you to decide how much valve service work must be carried out during the engine overhaul.

Cleaning

2 Scrape away all traces of old gasket material and sealing compound from the cylinder head. Take care not to damage the cylinder head surfaces.
3 Scrape away the carbon from the combustion chambers and ports, then wash the cylinder head thoroughly with paraffin or a suitable solvent.

7.19b Secure a self-locking nut of suitable diameter to a long bolt, then use the tool to remove the valve stem oilseal

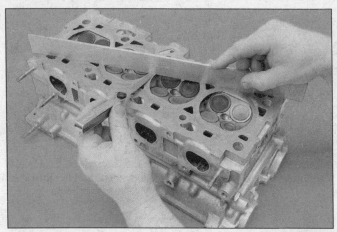

8.7 Check the head for warpage using a straight-edge and feeler blades

8.13 Measuring the diameter of a valve stem

4 Scrape off any heavy carbon deposits that may have formed on the valves, then use a power-operated wire brush to remove deposits from the valve heads and stems.

5 If the head is extremely dirty, it should be steam cleaned. On completion, make sure that all oil holes and oil galleries are cleaned.

Inspection and renovation

Note: *Be sure to perform all the following inspection procedures before concluding that the services of an engine overhaul specialist are required. Make a list of all items that require attention.*

Cylinder head

6 Inspect the head very carefully for cracks, evidence of coolant leakage and other damage. If cracks are found, a new cylinder head should be obtained.

7 Use a straight-edge and feeler blade to check that the cylinder head surface is not distorted **(see illustration)**. If the specified distortion limit is exceeded, machining of the gasket face is not recommended by the manufacturers, so the only course of action is to renew the cylinder head.

8 Examine the valve seats in each of the combustion chambers. If they are severely pitted, cracked or burned, then they will need to be renewed or recut by an engine overhaul specialist. If they are only slightly pitted, this

can be removed by grinding the valve heads and seats together with coarse, then fine, grinding paste as described below.

9 If the valve guides are worn, indicated by a side-to-side motion of the valve in the guide, new guides must be fitted. If necessary, insert a new valve in the guides to determine if the wear is on the guide or valve. If new guides are to be fitted, the valves must be renewed as a matter of course. Valve guides may be renewed using a press and a suitable mandrel, however, the work is best carried out by an engine overhaul specialist, since if it is not done skilfully, there is a risk of damaging the cylinder head.

10 Check the tappet bores in the cylinder head for wear. If excessive wear is evident, the cylinder head must be renewed.

11 Examine the camshaft bearing surfaces in the cylinder head as described in Chapter 2A, Chapter 2B, Chapter 2C, Chapter 2D or Chapter 2E as applicable.

Valves

12 Examine the head of each valve for pitting, burning, cracks and general wear, and check the valve stem for scoring and wear ridges. Rotate the valve, and check for any obvious indication that it is bent. Look for pits and excessive wear on the end of each valve stem.

13 If the valve appears satisfactory at this

stage, measure the valve stem diameter at several points using a micrometer **(see illustration)**. Any significant difference in the readings obtained indicates wear of the valve stem. Should any of these conditions be apparent, the valve(s) must be renewed.

14 If the valves are in satisfactory condition, or if new valves are being fitted, they should be ground (lapped) into their respective seats to ensure a smooth gas-tight seal.

15 Valve grinding is carried out as follows. Place the cylinder head upside-down on a bench, with a block of wood at each end to give clearance for the valve stems. Where applicable, take care to protect the camshaft bearing surfaces.

16 Smear a trace of coarse carborundum paste on the seat face, and press a suction grinding tool onto the valve head. With a semi-rotary action, grind the valve head to its seat, lifting the valve occasionally to redistribute the grinding paste **(see illustration)**.

17 When a dull, matt even surface is produced on both the valve seat and the valve, wipe off the paste and repeat the process with fine carborundum paste. A light spring placed under the valve head will greatly ease this operation.

18 When a smooth unbroken ring of light grey matt finish is produced on both the valve and seat, the grinding operation is complete. Be sure to remove all traces of grinding paste, using paraffin or a suitable solvent, before reassembly of the cylinder head.

Valve components

19 Examine the valve springs for signs of damage and discoloration, and also measure their free length using vernier calipers or a steel rule **(see illustration)** or by comparing the existing spring with a new component.

20 Stand each spring on a flat surface, and check it for squareness. If any of the springs are damaged, distorted or have lost their tension, obtain a complete new set of springs. It is normal to renew the springs as a matter of course during a major overhaul.

21 On petrol engines, inspect the tappet

8.16 Grinding-in a valve seat

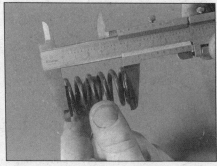

8.19 Checking the valve spring free length

9.1 Using a special tool to fit the valve stem oil seals

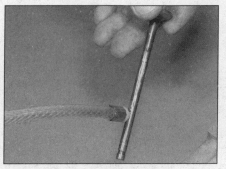

9.2a Oil the valve stems ...

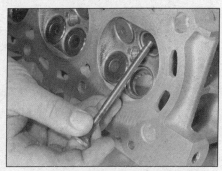

9.2b ... then insert the valves in their guides

buckets for scoring, pitting (especially on the shims), and wear ridges. Renew any components as necessary. Note that some scuffing is to be expected, and is acceptable provided that the tappets are not scored.

Rocker arms (1.6 litre DOHC 16-valve diesel engine)

22 Check the rocker arm contact surfaces for pits, wear, score marks or any indication that the surface-hardening has worn through. Check the components as described in Chapter 2D. Given that the rocker arms feature moving parts (the rollers), it may be wise to fit new parts as a matter of course if the engine has completed a very significant mileage.

Valve stem oil seals

23 The valve stem oil seals should be renewed as a matter of course.

9 Cylinder head – reassembly

1 Lubricate the valve stem oil seals with clean engine oil, then fit them by pushing into position in the cylinder head using a suitable socket or special tool **(see illustration)**. Ensure that the seals are fully engaged with the valve guide. Note that the inlet and exhaust seals are usually different colours – green for the inlet valves, red for the exhaust valves.
2 Lubricate the valve stems, then insert the

valves into their original locations. If new valves are being fitted, insert them into the locations to which they have been ground. Take care not to damage the valve stem oil seal as each valve is fitted **(see illustrations)**.
3 Locate the spring and cap over the valve stem.
4 Compress the valve spring and locate the split collets in the recess in the valve stem **(see illustrations)**. Release the compressor, then repeat the procedure on the remaining valves.
5 With all the valves installed, place the cylinder head on blocks on the bench and, using a hammer and interposed block of wood, tap the end of each valve stem to settle the components.
6 The previously-removed components can now be refitted with reference to Section 7.

10 Piston/connecting rod assemblies (diesel engines) – removal

1 Remove the cylinder head, sump, oil pump pick-up tube and baffle plate, as applicable, with reference to Chapter 2B, Chapter 2C, Chapter 2D or Chapter 2E.
2 Rotate the crankshaft so that No 1 big-end cap (timing end of the engine) is at the lowest point of its travel. If the big-end cap and rod are not already numbered, mark them with a marker pen. Mark both cap and rod to identify the cylinder they operate in.

3 Remove the main bearing ladder as described in Section 11.
4 Unscrew and remove the big-end bearing cap bolts, and withdraw the cap complete with shell bearing from the connecting rod. Make sure that the shell remains in the cap and if necessary identify it for position.
5 If only the bearing shells are being attended to, push the connecting rod up and off the crankpin, and remove the upper bearing shell. Keep the bearing shells and cap together in their correct sequence if they are to be refitted.
6 If the piston is being removed, push the connecting rod up and remove the piston and rod from the top of the bore. Note that if there is a pronounced wear ridge at the top of the bore, there is a risk of damaging the piston as the rings foul the ridge. However, it is reasonable to assume that a rebore and new pistons will be required in any case if the ridge is so pronounced.
7 Repeat the procedure for the remaining piston/connecting rod assemblies. Ensure that the caps and rods are marked before removal, as described previously, and keep all components in order.

11 Crankshaft (diesel engines) – removal

1 Remove the timing belt, crankshaft sprocket, sump, oil pick-up tube, flywheel and left-hand/flywheel end oil seal housing. The pistons/connecting rods must be free of the crankshaft journals, however it is not essential to remove them completely from the cylinder block.
2 Before the crankshaft is removed, check the endfloat. Mount a dial gauge with the probe in line with the crankshaft and just touching the crankshaft.
3 Push the crankshaft fully away from the gauge, and zero it. Next, lever the crankshaft towards the gauge as far as possible, and check the reading obtained. The distance that the crankshaft moved is its endfloat; if it is greater than specified, new thrustwashers will be required.
4 If no dial gauge is available, feeler blades can be used. Gently lever or push the crankshaft in

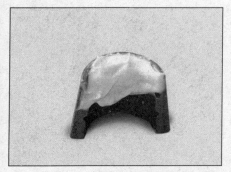

9.4a Apply a small dab of grease to each collet before installation – it will hold them in place on the valve stem

9.4b A dab of grease on a screwdriver will help to fit the collets

11.6 Prise up the two caps to expose the main bearing bolts at the flywheel end

one direction, then insert feeler blades between the crankshaft web and the main bearing with the thrustwashers to determine the clearance.

5 Work around the outside of the cylinder block, and unscrew all the small bolts securing the main bearing ladder to the base of the cylinder block. Note the correct fitted depth of the left-hand crankshaft oil seal in the cylinder block/main bearing ladder.

6 Working in a diagonal sequence, evenly and progressively slacken the large main bearing ladder retaining bolts by a turn at a time. Once all the bolts are loose, remove them from the ladder. **Note:** *Prise up the two caps at the flywheel end of the ladder to expose the two end main bearing bolts* **(see illustration)**. *The larger (M11) bolts should be discarded, and new bolts obtained for reassembly.*

7 With all the retaining bolts removed, carefully lift the main bearing ladder casting away from the base of the cylinder block. Recover the lower main bearing shells, and tape them to their respective locations in the casting. If the two locating dowels are a loose fit, remove them and store them with the casting for safe-keeping. Undo the big-end bolts and remove the pistons/connecting rods as described in Section 10.

8 Lift out the crankshaft, and discard both the oil seals.

9 Recover the upper main bearing shells, and store them along with the relevant lower bearing shell. Also recover the two thrustwashers (one fitted either side of No 2 main bearing) from the cylinder block.

12 Cylinder block/crankcase (diesel engines) – cleaning and inspection

Cleaning

1 For complete cleaning, the core plugs should be removed. Drill a small hole in them, then insert a self-tapping screw and pull out the plugs using pliers or a slide-hammer **(see illustration)**. Also remove all external components and senders (if not already done), noting their locations.

2 Scrape all traces of gasket or sealant from the cylinder block, taking care not to damage the head and sump mating faces.

3 If the block is extremely dirty, it should be steam-cleaned.

4 After the block has been steam-cleaned, clean all oil holes and oil galleries one more time. Flush all internal passages with warm water until the water runs clear, dry the block thoroughly and wipe all machined surfaces with a light rust-preventative oil. If you have access to compressed air, use it to speed up the drying process and to blow out all the oil holes and galleries.

 Warning: Wear eye protection when using compressed air.

5 If the block is not very dirty, you can do an adequate cleaning job with hot soapy water and a stiff brush. Take plenty of time, and do a thorough job. Regardless of the cleaning method used, be sure to clean all oil holes and galleries very thoroughly, dry the block completely and coat all machined surfaces with light oil.

6 The threaded holes in the block must be clean to ensure accurate torque wrench readings during reassembly. Run the proper-size tap into each of the holes to remove rust, corrosion, thread sealant or sludge, and to restore damaged threads. If possible, use compressed air to clear the holes of debris produced by this operation.

7 After coating the mating surfaces of the new core plugs with suitable sealant, refit them in the cylinder block. Make sure that they are driven in straight and seated properly,

or leakage could result. Special tools are available for this purpose, but a large socket, with an outside diameter that will just slip into the core plug, will work just as well **(see illustration)**.

8 Where applicable, remove the oil spray jets from their locations in the crankcase and clean them. After cleaning the cylinder block, refit the jets.

9 If the engine is not going to be reassembled right away, cover it with a large plastic bag to keep it clean and prevent it rusting.

Inspection

10 Visually check the block for cracks, rust and corrosion. Look for stripped threads in the threaded holes. It's also a good idea to have the block checked for hidden cracks by an engine reconditioning specialist that has the equipment to do this type of work, especially if the vehicle had a history of overheating or using coolant. If defects are found, have the block repaired, if possible, or renewed.

11 If in any doubt as to the condition of the cylinder block, have it inspected and measured by an engine reconditioning specialist. If the bores are worn or damaged, a new cylinder block will be required. If the bores are in a satisfactory condition, they will be able to carry out the necessary honing and supply appropriate oversized pistons, etc.

12 Refit all external components and senders in their correct locations, as noted before removal.

13 Piston/connecting rod assemblies (diesel engines) – inspection and reassembly

Inspection

1 Before the inspection process can begin, the piston/connecting rod assemblies must be cleaned, and the original piston rings removed from the pistons.

2 Carefully expand the old rings over the top of the pistons. The use of two or three old feeler blades will be helpful in preventing the rings dropping into empty grooves **(see illustration)**. Note that the oil control scraper ring is in two sections.

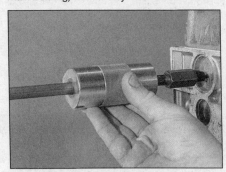

12.1 The core plugs should be removed with a slide hammer – don't drive them inwards

12.7 A large socket on an extension can be used to drive in new core plugs

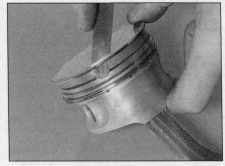

13.2 Using feeler blades to remove piston rings

3 Scrape away all traces of carbon from the top of the piston. A hand-held wire brush or a piece of fine emery cloth can be used once the majority of the deposits have been scraped away.

4 Remove the carbon from the ring grooves in the piston by cleaning them using an old ring. Break the ring in half to do this. Be very careful to remove only the carbon deposits; do not remove any metal, or scratch the sides of the ring grooves. Protect your fingers – piston rings are sharp.

5 Once the deposits have been removed, clean the piston/connecting rod assembly with paraffin or a suitable solvent, and dry thoroughly. Make sure the oil return holes in the ring grooves are clear.

6 If the pistons and cylinder bores are not damaged or worn excessively, the original pistons can be re-used. Normal piston wear appears as even vertical wear on the piston thrust surfaces, and slight looseness of the top ring in its groove. New piston rings, however, should always be used when the engine is reassembled.

7 Carefully inspect each piston for cracks around the skirt, at the gudgeon pin bosses, and at the piston ring lands (between the piston ring grooves).

8 Look for scoring and scuffing on the sides of the skirt, holes in the piston crown, and burned areas at the edge of the crown. If the skirt is scored or scuffed, the engine may have been suffering from overheating and/or abnormal combustion, which caused excessively-high operating temperatures. The cooling and lubricating systems should be checked thoroughly.

9 Scorch marks on the sides of the pistons show that blow-by has occurred and the rings are not sealing correctly. A hole in the piston crown is an indication that abnormal combustion (pre-ignition, knocking or detonation) has been occurring. If any of the above problems exist, the causes must be corrected, or the damage will occur again.

10 Corrosion of the piston, in the form of small pits, indicates that coolant is leaking into the combustion chamber and/or the crankcase. Again, the cause must be corrected, or the problem may persist in the rebuilt engine.

11 If in any doubt as to the condition of the pistons and connecting rods, have them inspected and measured by an engine reconditioning specialist. If new parts are required, they will be able to supply and fit appropriate-sized pistons/rings, and hone the cylinder block.

Reassembly

12 Before refitting the rings to the pistons, check their end gaps by inserting each of them in their cylinder bores. Use the piston to make sure that they are square. Using feeler blades, check that the gaps are within the tolerances given in the Specifications. Genuine rings are supplied pre-gapped; no attempt should be made to adjust the gaps by filing.

13 Install the new rings by fitting them over the top of the piston, starting with the oil control scraper ring sections. Use feeler blades in the same way as when removing the old rings. New rings generally have their top surfaces identified, and must be fitted the correct way round **(see illustration)**. Note that the first and second compression rings have different sections. Be careful when handling the compression rings; they will break if they are handled roughly or expanded too far. With all the rings in position, space the ring gaps at 120° to each other (unless otherwise specified). The oil control scraper ring expander must also be positioned opposite to the actual ring.

14 Crankshaft (diesel engines) – inspection

1 Clean the crankshaft using paraffin or a suitable solvent, and dry it, preferably with compressed air if available. Be sure to clean the oil holes with a pipe cleaner or similar probe, to ensure that they are not obstructed.

⚠️ **Warning: Wear eye protection when using compressed air.**

2 Check the main and big-end bearing journals for uneven wear, scoring, pitting and cracking.

3 Big-end bearing wear is accompanied by distinct metallic knocking when the engine is running (particularly noticeable when the engine is pulling from low revs), and some loss of oil pressure.

4 Main bearing wear is accompanied by severe engine vibration and rumble – getting progressively worse as engine revs increase – and again by loss of oil pressure.

5 Check the bearing journal for roughness by running a finger lightly over the bearing surface. Any roughness (which will be accompanied by obvious bearing wear) indicates that the crankshaft requires regrinding.

6 Have the crankshaft journals measured by an engine reconditioning specialist. If the crankshaft is worn or damaged, they may be able to regrind the journals and supply suitable

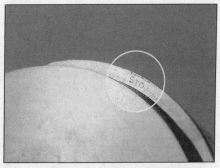
13.13 Look for etched markings identifying the piston ring top surface

undersize bearing shells. If no undersize shells are available and the crankshaft has worn beyond the specified limits, it will have to be renewed. Consult your Ford dealer or engine reconditioning specialist for further information on parts availability.

7 If the crankshaft has been reground, check for burrs around the crankshaft oil holes (the holes are usually chamfered, so burrs should not be a problem unless regrinding has been carried out carelessly). Remove any burrs with a fine file or scraper, and thoroughly clean the oil holes as described previously.

15 Main and big-end bearings (diesel engines) – inspection

1 Even though the main and big-end bearings should be renewed during the engine overhaul, the old bearings should be retained for close examination, as they may reveal valuable information about the condition of the engine. The size of the bearing shells is stamped on the back metal, and this information should be given to the supplier of the new shells.

2 Bearing failure occurs because of lack of lubrication, the presence of dirt or other foreign particles, overloading the engine, and corrosion. Regardless of the cause of bearing failure, it must be corrected before the engine is reassembled, to prevent it from happening again **(see illustration)**.

3 When examining the bearings, remove them from the engine block, the main bearing caps, the connecting rods and the rod caps, and lay them out on a clean surface in the same general position as their location in the engine. This will enable you to match any bearing problems with the corresponding crankshaft journal.

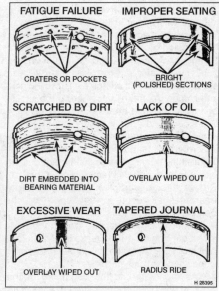
15.2 Typical bearing failures

4 Dirt and other foreign particles get into the engine in a variety of ways. Dirt may be left in the engine during assembly, or it may pass through filters or the crankcase ventilation system. It may get into the oil, and from there into the bearings. Metal chips from machining operations and normal engine wear are often present. Abrasives are sometimes left in engine components after reconditioning, especially when parts are not thoroughly cleaned using the proper cleaning methods.

5 Whatever the source, these foreign objects often end up embedded in the soft bearing material, and are easily recognised. Large particles will not embed in the bearing, and will score or gouge the bearing and journal. The best prevention for this cause of bearing failure is to clean all parts thoroughly, and keep everything spotlessly-clean during engine assembly. Frequent and regular engine oil and filter changes are also recommended.

6 Lack of lubrication (or lubrication breakdown) has a number of interrelated causes. Excessive heat (which thins the oil), overloading (which squeezes the oil from the bearing face) and oil leakage (from excessive bearing clearances, worn oil pump or high engine speeds) all contribute to lubrication breakdown. Blocked oil passages, which usually are the result of misaligned oil holes in a bearing shell, will also oil-starve a bearing and destroy it. When lack of lubrication is the cause of bearing failure, the bearing material is wiped or extruded from the steel backing of the bearing. Temperatures may increase to the point where the steel backing turns blue from overheating.

7 Driving habits can have a definite effect on bearing life. Full-throttle, low-speed operation (labouring the engine) puts very high loads on bearings, which tends to squeeze out the oil film. These loads cause the bearings to flex, which produces fine cracks in the bearing face (fatigue failure). Eventually, the bearing material will loosen in pieces and tear away from the steel backing. Short-trip driving leads to corrosion of bearings, because insufficient engine heat is produced to drive off the condensed water and corrosive gases. These products collect in the engine oil, forming acid and sludge. As the oil is carried to the engine bearings, the acid attacks and corrodes the bearing material.

8 Incorrect bearing installation during engine assembly will lead to bearing failure as well. Tight-fitting bearings leave insufficient bearing oil clearance, and will result in oil starvation. Dirt or foreign particles trapped behind a bearing shell result in high spots on the bearing which lead to failure.

9 Do not touch any shell's bearing surface with your fingers during reassembly; there is a risk of scratching the delicate surface, or of depositing particles of dirt on it.

10 As mentioned at the beginning of this Section, the bearing shells should be renewed as a matter of course during engine overhaul; to do otherwise is false economy.

16 Engine overhaul – reassembly sequence

1 Before reassembly begins, ensure that all new parts have been obtained and that all necessary tools are available. Read through the entire procedure to familiarise yourself with the work involved, and to ensure that all items necessary for reassembly of the engine are at hand. In addition to all normal tools and materials, jointing and thread-locking compound will be needed during engine reassembly. Do not use any kind of silicone-based sealant on any part of the fuel system or inlet manifold, and never use exhaust sealants upstream (on the engine side) of the catalytic converter.

2 In order to save time and avoid problems, engine reassembly can be carried out in the following order.
a) *Crankshaft and main bearings (diesel engines).*
b) *Pistons/connecting rods and main bearing ladder (diesel engines).*
c) *Oil pump.*
d) *Sump.*
e) *Flywheel/driveplate.*
f) *Cylinder head.*
g) *Timing sprockets and belt.*
h) *Engine external components (including inlet and exhaust manifolds).*

3 Ensure that everything is clean prior to reassembly. As mentioned previously, dirt and metal particles can quickly destroy bearings and result in major engine damage. Use clean engine oil to lubricate during reassembly.

17 Crankshaft (diesel engines) – refitting

Selection of new bearing shells

1 Have the crankshaft inspected and measured by a Ford dealer or engine reconditioning specialist. They will be able to carry out any regrinding/repairs, and supply suitable main and big-end bearing shells.

Refitting

2 It is assumed at this point that the cylinder block/crankcase and crankshaft have been cleaned and repaired or reconditioned as necessary. Position the engine upside-down.

3 Clean the backs of the bearing shells in both the cylinder block/crankcase and the main bearing ladder. If new shells are being fitted, ensure that all traces of protective grease are cleaned off using paraffin. Wipe dry the shells with a lint-free cloth.

4 Press the bearing shells into their locations, ensuring that the tab (where applicable) on each shell engages in the notch in the cylinder block/crankcase and bearing ladder. Take care not to touch any shell's bearing surface

with your fingers. Note that the upper bearing shells all have a grooved surface, whereas the lower shells have a plain bearing surface. It is essential that the lower bearing shell halves are centrally located in the ladder. To ensure this, a Ford special tool (303-737) is positioned over the ladder, and the bearing shells inserted through the slots in the tool **(see illustration)**. If this tool is not available, use a tape-measure or ruler to ensure the shells are perfectly central on their bearings.

5 Liberally lubricate each bearing shell in the cylinder block with clean engine oil, then lower the crankshaft into position.

6 Insert the thrustwashers to either side of No 2 main bearing upper location, and push them around the bearing journal until their edges are horizontal. Ensure that the oilway grooves on each thrustwasher face outwards (they should be visible).

7 Refit the piston and connecting rod assemblies as described in Section 18.

8 Thoroughly degrease the mating surfaces of the cylinder block/crankcase and the main bearing ladder. Apply a thin bead of RTV sealant to the main bearing ladder mating surface. Ford recommend the use of their WSE-M4G323-A4 sealant for this purpose. Use two aligning pins inserted into the main bearing ladder to ensure the correct positioning of the assembly. Make sure the sealant does not enter the blind holes in the cylinder block or ladder, or damage may result. The ladder should be fitted within four minutes of applying the sealant.

9 Lubricate the lower bearing shells with clean engine oil, then refit the main bearing ladder, ensuring that the shells are not displaced, and that the locating dowels engage correctly. Remove the aligning pins from the bearing ladder.

10 Install the large and small main bearing ladder retaining bolts, and screw them in until they are just making contact with the ladder. Note that the larger (M11) bolts must not be re-used – a new set should be obtained.

11 Tighten all the main bearing ladder bolts

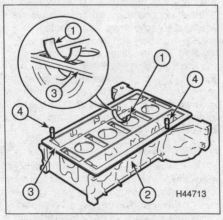

17.4 Main bearing shell refitment
1 Bearing shell   *3 Special tool*
2 Main bearing ladder   *4 Aligning pins*

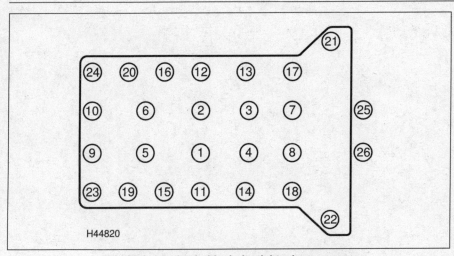

17.11 Main bearing ladder bolts tightening sequence

to their Stage 1 torque setting in sequence **(see illustration)**.

12 Slacken (Stage 2) the larger bolts half a turn (180°), then tighten them in sequence to the Stage 3 torque setting, followed by the Stage 4 angle-tightening setting. Apply sealant to the two new bearing ladder bolt caps, and tap them into place over the two flywheel end bolts.

13 Finally, tighten the smaller bearing ladder bolts to their Stage 2 setting.

14 Rotate the crankshaft a number of times by hand, to check for any obvious binding.

15 Check the crankshaft endfloat (refer to Section 11).

16 Fit new crankshaft oil seals as described in Chapter 2B, Chapter 2C, Chapter 2D or Chapter 2E (as applicable).

17 Refit the components removed in Section 11.

18 Piston/connecting rod assemblies (diesel engines) – refitting

1 Clean the backs of the big-end bearing shells, and the recesses in the connecting rods and big-end caps. If new shells are being fitted, ensure that all traces of the protective grease are cleaned off using paraffin. Wipe the shells and connecting rods dry with a lint-free cloth.

2 Lubricate No 1 piston and piston rings, and check that the ring gaps are spaced at 120° intervals to each other.

3 Fit a ring compressor to No 1 piston, then insert the piston and connecting rod into No 1 cylinder. Make sure that the mark or arrow on the piston crown is facing the timing belt

end of the engine. With No 1 crankpin at its lowest point, drive the piston carefully into the cylinder with the wooden handle of a hammer, at the same time guiding the connecting rod onto the crankpin **(see illustration)**.

4 On these engines, the connecting rod is made in one piece, then the big-end bearing cap is 'cracked' off. This ensures that the cap fits onto the connecting rod only in one position, and with maximum rigidity. Consequently, there are no locating notches for the bearing shells to fit into.

5 To ensure that the big-end bearing shells are centrally located in the connecting rod and cap, two special tools are available from Ford (303-736). These half-moon shaped tools are pressed in from either side of the rod/cap, and locate the shell exactly in the centre **(see illustration)**. Fit the shells into the connecting rods and big-end caps, and lubricate them with plenty of clean engine oil.

6 Tighten the bolts to the Stage 1 torque setting, then slacken them 180° (Stage 2). Tighten the bolts to the Stage 3 setting,

18.3 With the compressor fitted, use the handle of a hammer to gently drive the piston into the cylinder

followed by the Stage 4 angle-tightening setting.

7 Continue refitting the main bearing shells and ladder as described in Section 17.

8 On completion, refit the oil pump pick-up tube, sump and cylinder head as described in the relevant Chapter.

19 Engine – initial start-up after overhaul

1 With the engine refitted in the vehicle, double-check the engine oil and coolant levels. Make a final check that everything has been reconnected, and that there are no tools or rags left in the engine compartment.

2 On diesel engines, prime and bleed the fuel system as described in Chapter 4B Section 3.

3 Start the engine, noting that this may take a little longer than usual. Make sure that the oil pressure warning light goes out.

4 While the engine is idling, check for fuel, water and oil leaks. Don't be alarmed if there are some odd smells and smoke from parts getting hot and burning off oil deposits.

5 Assuming all is well, run the engine until it reaches normal operating temperature, then switch off the engine.

6 After a few minutes, recheck the oil and coolant levels as described in Weekly checks0,5, and top-up as necessary.

7 Note that there is no need to retighten the cylinder head bolts once the engine has first run after reassembly.

8 If new pistons, rings or crankshaft bearings have been fitted, the engine must be treated as new, and run-in for the first 600 miles. Do not operate the engine at full-throttle, or allow it to labour at low engine speeds in any gear. It is recommended that the oil and filter be changed at the end of this period.

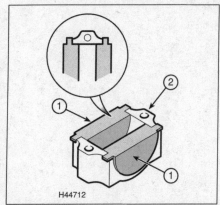

18.5 Big-end bearing shell positioning

1 Special tool   2 Bearing cap

Notes

Chapter 3
Cooling, heating and air conditioning systems

Contents

Degrees of difficulty

Easy, suitable for novice with little experience 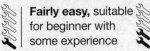	**Fairly easy,** suitable for beginner with some experience 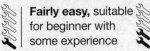	**Fairly difficult,** suitable for competent DIY mechanic 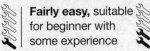	**Difficult,** suitable for experienced DIY mechanic 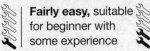	**Very difficult,** suitable for expert DIY or professional

Specifications

General

Maximum system pressure	1.4 bars
Thermostat start of opening temperature	88°C

Air conditioning system

Refrigerant	R134a
Refrigerant quantity:	
All except 1.6 litre diesel engine models	380 to 400 g
1.6 litre diesel engine models	540 to 560 g
Refrigerant oil	Ford WSH-M1C231-B
Refrigerant oil capacity	120 ml

Torque wrench settings

	Nm	lbf ft
Air conditioning compressor mounting bolts	25	18
Coolant pump bolts:		
Petrol engines	10	7
Diesel engines:		
Stage 1	3	2
Stage 2	10	7
Coolant pump pulley bolts (petrol engines)	27	20
Refrigerant pipe to compressor	20	15
Refrigerant pipe to expansion valve	10	7
Steering column shaft universal joint clamp bolt*	34	25
Thermostat cover bolts	10	7
Thermostat housing bolts:		
Petrol engines	10	7
Diesel engines:		
Stage 1	4	3
Stage 2	7	5

*Use a new bolt

1 General information and precautions

1 The cooling system is of pressurised type, comprising a pump driven by the auxiliary drivebelt (petrol engines) or the timing belt (diesel engines), an aluminium crossflow radiator, electric cooling fan, and a thermostat. The system functions as follows. Cold coolant from the radiator passes through the hose to the coolant pump, where it is pumped around the cylinder block and head passages. After cooling the cylinder bores, combustion surfaces and valve seats, the coolant reaches the underside of the thermostat, which is initially closed. The coolant passes through the heater, and is returned via the cylinder block to the coolant pump.

2 When the engine is cold, the thermostat is shut, and the coolant circulates only through the cylinder block, cylinder head and heater. When the coolant reaches a predetermined temperature, the thermostat opens and the coolant passes through to the radiator. As the coolant circulates through the radiator, it is cooled by the inrush of air when the car is in forward motion. Airflow is supplemented by the action of the electric cooling fan when necessary. Once the coolant has passed through the radiator, and has cooled, the cycle is repeated.

3 The electric cooling fan, mounted on the rear of the radiator, is controlled by a thermostatic switch. At a predetermined coolant temperature, the switch actuates the fan.

4 An expansion tank is fitted to allow for the expansion of the coolant when hot. On models fitted with an engine oil cooler or automatic transmission fluid cooler, the coolant is also passed through the oil/fluid cooler.

5 Refer to Section 10 for information on the air conditioning system.

Warning: Do not attempt to remove the expansion tank filler cap, or disturb any part of the cooling system, while the engine is hot; there is a high risk of scalding. If the expansion tank filler cap must be removed before the engine and radiator have fully cooled (even though this is not recommended) the pressure in the cooling system must first be relieved. Cover the cap with a thick layer of cloth, to avoid scalding, and slowly unscrew the filler cap until a hissing sound can be heard. When the hissing has stopped, indicating that the pressure has reduced, slowly unscrew the filler cap until it can be removed; if more hissing sounds are heard, wait until they have stopped before unscrewing the cap completely. At all times, keep well away from the filler cap opening and protect your hands.

Warning: Do not allow antifreeze to come into contact with skin, or with the painted surfaces of the car. Rinse off spills immediately, with plenty of water. Never leave antifreeze lying around in an open container, or in a puddle on the driveway or garage floor. Children and pets are attracted by its sweet smell, but antifreeze can be fatal if ingested.

Warning: If the engine is hot, the electric cooling fan may start rotating even if the engine is not running; be careful to keep hands, hair and loose clothing well clear when working in the engine compartment.

2 Cooling system hoses – disconnection and renewal

Note: Refer to the warnings given in Section 1 of this Chapter before proceeding. Do not attempt to disconnect any hose while the system is still hot.

1 If the checks described in the relevant part of Chapter 1A or Chapter 1B reveal a faulty hose, it must be renewed as follows.

2 First drain the cooling system (see Chapter 1A or 1B). If the coolant is not due for renewal, it may be re-used if it is collected in a clean container.

3 Before disconnecting a hose, first note its routing in the engine compartment, and whether it is secured by any clips or ties. Use a pair of pliers to release the spring clamps (or a screwdriver to slacken screw-type clamps) then move them along the hose, clear of the relevant inlet/outlet union. Carefully work the hose free **(see illustration)**.

4 Note that the coolant unions are fragile (most are made of plastic); do not use excessive force when attempting to remove the hoses. If a hose proves to be difficult to remove, try to release it by rotating the hose ends before attempting to free it – if this fails, try gently prising up the end of the hose with a small screwdriver to 'break' the seal.

5 When fitting a hose, first slide the clamps onto the hose, then work the hose into position. If spring-type clamps were originally fitted, it is a good idea to use screw-type clamps when refitting the hose (if only to make removal easier, next time). If the hose is stiff, use a little soapy water (washing-up liquid is ideal) as a lubricant, or soften the hose by soaking it in hot water.

6 Work the hose into position, checking that it is correctly routed and secured. Slide each clamp along the hose until it passes over the flared end of the relevant inlet/outlet union, before tightening the clamps securely.

7 Refill the cooling system with reference to Chapter 1A or Chapter 1B.

8 Check thoroughly for leaks as soon as possible after disturbing any part of the cooling system.

3 Radiator – removal, inspection and refitting

Note: If leakage is the reason for removing the radiator, bear in mind that minor leaks can often be cured using a radiator sealant with the radiator in situ.

Removal

1 Firmly apply the handbrake, then jack up the front of the vehicle and support it securely on axle stands (see 'Jacking and vehicle support'). Where fitted, remove the engine undershield.

2 Drain the cooling system as described in Chapter 1A or Chapter 1B.

3 On 1.6 litre diesel engine models, remove the intercooler as described in Chapter 4B Section 17.

4 On petrol engine, 1.4 litre (Stage V emissions) and 1.6 litre diesel engine models, remove the air cleaner assembly as described in Chapter 4A or Chapter 4B.

5 Release the retaining clip and disconnect the top hose from the radiator **(see illustration)**.

6 Depress the retaining tabs and disconnect the expansion tank hose from the top of the radiator.

7 On models with automatic transmission, remove the remaining fluid cooler hoses from the radiator.

8 Remove the radiator cooling fan as described in Section 5.

9 Working on one side at a time, lift up the forward edge of the radiator upper mounting retaining plate. Disengage the locating peg

2.3 Most of the coolant hoses are of the spring clamp type, which need large pliers to remove

3.5 Release the clip and disconnect the top hose from the radiator

3.9a Lift up the forward edge of the upper mounting retaining plate ...

3.9b ... disengage the locating peg and remove the retaining plate

3.9c Lift the mounting bush off the radiator mounting peg

3.10a Pull down the tab on the underside of the radiator ...

3.10b ... and disengage the condenser lower mounting lugs

3.10c Lift the radiator and disengage the upper brackets from the condenser

and remove the retaining plate. Lift the mounting bush off the radiator mounting peg **(see illustrations)**.

10 On models with air conditioning, pull down the tab on the underside of the radiator each side and disengage the condenser lower mounting lugs. Move the top of the radiator toward the engine, lift it slightly and disengage the upper brackets from the condenser **(see illustrations)**.

11 Lift the radiator upward off the lower mounting rubbers, then manipulate it up and out of the engine compartment. Recover the two mounting rubbers after removal **(see illustrations)**.

Inspection

12 If the radiator has been removed due to suspected blockage, reverse-flush it as described in Chapter 1A or Chapter 1B. Clean

3.11a Lift the radiator up then manipulate it up and out of the engine compartment ...

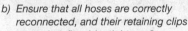

3.11b ... and recover the two lower mounting rubbers

dirt and debris from the radiator fins, using an airline (in which case, wear eye protection) or a soft brush. Be careful, as the fins are easily damaged, and are sharp.

13 If necessary, a radiator specialist can perform a 'flow test' on the radiator, to establish whether an internal blockage exists.

14 A leaking radiator must be referred to a specialist for permanent repair. Do not attempt to weld or solder a leaking radiator, as damage may result.

Refitting

15 Refitting is a reversal of removal, bearing in mind the following points:

a) *Refit the radiator cooling fan as described in Section 5.*

b) *Ensure that all hoses are correctly reconnected, and their retaining clips securely refitted (or tightened).*

c) *On 1.6 litre diesel engine models, refit the intercooler as described in Chapter 4B Section 17.*

d) *Where applicable, refit the air cleaner assembly as described in Chapter 4A or 4B.*

e) *On completion, refill the cooling system as described in Chapter 1A or 1B.*

4 Thermostat –
removal, testing and refitting

1 As the thermostat ages, it will become slower to react to changes in water temperature ('lazy'). Ultimately, the unit may stick in the open or closed position, and this causes problems. A thermostat which is stuck open will result in a very slow warm-up; a thermostat which is stuck shut will lead to rapid overheating.

2 Before assuming the thermostat is to blame for a cooling system problem, check the coolant level. If the system is draining due to a leak, or has not been properly filled, there may be an airlock in the system (refer to the coolant renewal procedure in the relevant Part of Chapter 1A or Chapter 1B).

3 If the engine seems to be taking a long time to warm up (based on heater output), the thermostat could be stuck open. Don't necessarily believe the temperature gauge reading – some gauges never seem to register very high in normal driving.

4 A lengthy warm-up period might suggest that the thermostat is missing – it may have been removed or inadvertently omitted by a previous owner or mechanic. Don't drive the car without a thermostat – the engine management system's PCM will then stay in warm-up mode for longer than necessary, causing emissions and fuel economy to suffer.

5 If the engine runs hot, use your hand to check the temperature of the radiator top hose. If the hose isn't hot, but the engine clearly is, the thermostat is probably stuck closed, preventing the coolant inside the engine from escaping to the radiator – renew the thermostat. Again, this problem may also be due to an airlock (refer to the coolant renewal procedure in the relevant Part of Chapter 1A or Chapter 1B).

6 If the radiator top hose is hot, it means that the coolant is flowing (at least as far as the radiator) and the thermostat is open. Consult the Fault diagnosis section at the end of this manual to assist in tracing possible cooling system faults, but a lack of heater output would now definitely suggest an airlock or a blockage.

7 To gain a rough idea of whether the thermostat is working properly when the engine is warming up, without dismantling the system, proceed as follows.

8 With the engine completely cold, start the engine and let it idle, while checking the temperature of the radiator top hose. Periodically check the temperature indicated on the coolant temperature gauge – if overheating is indicated, switch the engine off immediately.

9 The top hose should feel cold for some time as the engine warms up, and should then get warm quite quickly as the thermostat opens.

10 The above is not a precise or definitive test of thermostat operation, but if the system does not perform as described, remove and test the thermostat as described below. Note that it is not possible to test the thermostat fitted to the diesel engine.

Petrol engine models

Removal

11 Remove the alternator as described in Chapter 5A Section 7.

12 Drain the cooling system as described in Chapter 1A Section 31.

13 Loosen the clamps, and disconnect the two coolant hoses from the thermostat housing, located on the front of the engine, above the oil filter.

14 Unscrew the four securing bolts, and remove the thermostat housing from the engine. Recover the gasket.

15 Lift out the thermostat, and recover the sealing ring.

Refitting

16 Refitting is a reversal of removal, noting the following points:
a) Thoroughly clean the mating faces of the thermostat housing and the engine.
b) Use a new sealing ring when refitting the thermostat, and make sure the 'jiggle pin' (air bleed valve) is at the top.
c) Use a new gasket when refitting the housing, and tighten the bolts to the specified torque.
d) Refit the alternator as described in Chapter 5A Section 7.

e) On completion, refill the cooling system as described in Chapter 1A Section 31.

Diesel engine models

Removal

17 Drain the cooling system as described in Chapter 1B Section 30.

18 Remove the battery and battery tray as described in Chapter 5A Section 4.

19 On 1.4 litre engines (Stage IV emissions), disconnect the airflow sensor wiring connector. Undo the air intake duct retaining bolt, located adjacent to the airflow sensor, then detach the duct from the intake pipe at the rear of the engine and from the front body panel. Remove the duct from the engine compartment.

20 On 1.4 litre (Stage V emissions) and 1.6 litre engines, release the vacuum hoses from the support bracket above the fuel filter. Undo the three bolts and move the wiring harness support bracket and vacuum hose support bracket to one side (see illustrations).

21 Also on 1.4 litre (Stage V emissions) and 1.6 litre engines, undo the two bolts and move the fuel filter mounting bracket, complete with filter, to one side.

22 Disconnect the coolant temperature sensor wiring plug from the thermostat housing (see illustration).

23 Disconnect the four coolant hoses from the thermostat housing, noting their locations. Note that some of the hoses are disconnected after pressing down on the white-coloured release button.

24 At the base of the housing, loosen the screw and detach the mounting bracket for the bypass tube.

25 Remove the four mounting bolts and take off the thermostat housing.

Refitting

26 Refitting is a reversal of removal, noting the following points:
a) Thoroughly clean the mating faces of the thermostat housing and the engine.
b) Use a new gasket when refitting the housing, and tighten the bolts to the specified torque.
c) Refit the battery tray and battery as described in Chapter 5A Section 4.
d) On completion, refill the cooling system as described in Chapter 1B Section 30.

4.20a Undo the bolt at the front (arrowed)…

4.20b … the two bolts at the rear (arrowed) …

4.20c … and move the wiring harness support bracket …

4.20d … and vacuum hose support bracket to one side

4.22 Coolant temperature sensor wiring plug (arrowed) – diesel engines

Testing

Note: *DIY testing of the thermostat is not possible on the diesel engine, as the thermostat is an integral part of its housing. If there is good reason to suspect the thermostat is not working properly (read the introductory paragraphs in this Section), a new housing will have to be obtained.*

27 If the thermostat remains in the open position at room temperature, it is faulty, and must be renewed as a matter of course.

28 Check to see if there's an open temperature marking stamped on the thermostat.

29 Using a thermometer and container of water, heat the water until the temperature corresponds with the temperature marking stamped on the thermostat. If no marking is found, start the test with the water hot, and heat slowly until it boils.

30 Suspend the (closed) thermostat on a length of string in the water, and check that maximum opening occurs within two minutes, or before the water boils.

31 Remove the thermostat and allow it to cool down; check that it closes fully.

32 If the thermostat does not open and close as described, or if it sticks in either position, it must be renewed. Frankly, if there is any question about the operation of the thermostat, renew it – they are not expensive items.

5 Radiator cooling fan – testing, removal and refitting

Testing

1 On all models, the cooling fan is controlled by the engine management powertrain control module, using signals provided by the engine coolant temperature sensor.

2 The fan operation can be checked by connecting the fan motor directly to a 12 volt power supply. Disconnect the motor wiring plug, and apply 12 volts across the motor terminals (the black wire is the earth) – take great care not to short out the power supply wires.

3 If the fan fails to operate, the fan motor is almost certainly at fault.

4 Testing of the fan motor control circuit must be entrusted to a Ford dealer, who will have the necessary specialist diagnostic equipment to test the system – do not attempt to test the system using conventional test equipment, as the PCM may be damaged.

Removal

5 Disconnect the battery negative terminal (refer to *'Disconnecting the battery'*).

6 Firmly apply the handbrake, then jack up the front of the vehicle and support it securely on axle stands (see *'Jacking and vehicle support'*).

5.9 Unclip the transmission breather tube from the cooling fan mounting frame

5.11b ... then lift the motor and frame up to disengage the lower slide-in clips

7 On 1.6 litre diesel engine models, undo the three retaining bolts and remove the L-shaped intercooler support bracket situated over the right-hand side of the cooling fan.

8 Disconnect the cooling fan wiring plug from the fan motor and resistor, and unclip the wiring harness as necessary.

9 Unclip the transmission breather tube from the cooling fan mounting frame **(see illustration)**.

10 Using a suitable hose clamp, clamp the upper radiator hose, then release the clip and disconnect the hose from the radiator. If a hose clamp is not available, partially drain the cooling system as described in the relevant part of Chapter 1A or Chapter 1B.

11 Remove the cooling fan motor and mounting frame by releasing the two plastic catches either side at the top, then lift the motor and frame up to disengage the lower slide-in clips. Once released, the motor and frame can be removed **(see illustrations)**.

12 If desired, the fan motor can be removed from the frame after undoing the nut and removing the fan, then unscrewing the three motor securing bolts **(see illustration)**.

Refitting

13 Refitting is a reversal of removal. Reconnect the radiator fan wiring securely, and ensure the harness is routed clear of the fan blades or hot components. If the cooling system was drained, refill or top-up as described in the relevant Part of Chapter 1A, Chapter 1B and Weekly checks.

5.11a Release the two plastic catches either side at the top ...

5.12 Fan motor securing bolts (arrowed)

6 Coolant temperature sensor – removal and refitting

Warning: Do not attempt to remove the sensor while the cooling system is hot and/or pressurised, as there is a great risk of scalding.

1 Allow the engine to cool, then slowly remove the cap from the coolant expansion tank to depressurise the cooling system. To avoid any chance of coolant spillage, the system can be drained as described in Chapter 1A or 1B, but this is not essential if a new sensor is being fitted, and can quickly be substituted for the old one. Otherwise, if the system is not drained and the sensor will be left out for some time, a plug of some kind should be inserted to reduce coolant loss.

Petrol engine models

Removal

2 The sensor is located in the coolant outlet housing, beneath the ignition coil, at the transmission end of the cylinder head. To improve access, undo the four ignition coil mounting bolts, and move the coil to one side (the wiring can be left attached).

3 Two different types of sensor may be fitted. The first type is screwed into the coolant outlet housing, and the second type is clipped into place. Unscrew the sensor from the

6.3a Unscrew the engine coolant temperature sensor (arrowed) …

6.3b … or pull out the retaining clip (arrowed) followed by the sensor – petrol engines

housing, or pull out the clip as applicable (see illustrations).

Refitting

4 Refitting is a reversal of removal, noting the following points:
a) Renew the sensor seal if necessary.
b) Screw the sensor into position and tighten it securely, or refit the sensor and insert the clip, as applicable.
c) Either refill or top-up the cooling system as described in Chapter 1A or Weekly checks.

Diesel engine models

Removal

5 The sensor is clipped into the top of the thermostat housing, which is located at the transmission end of the engine.
6 To improve access on 1.4 litre engines (Stage IV emissions), disconnect the airflow sensor wiring connector. Undo the air intake duct retaining bolt, located adjacent to the airflow sensor, then detach the duct from the intake pipe at the rear of the engine and from the front body panel. Remove the duct from the engine compartment.
7 Release the sensor wiring plug, then pull out the spring clip used to retain the sensor, and remove the sensor from the housing (see illustration 4.22).

Refitting

8 Refitting is a reversal of removal, noting the following points:

a) Renew the sensor seal if necessary.
b) Push the sensor fully home, then retain it with the spring clip.
c) Either refill or top-up the cooling system as described in Chapter 1B or Weekly checks.

7 Coolant pump – removal and refitting

Petrol engine models

Removal

1 Remove the timing belt and tensioner as described in Chapter 2A Section 8.
2 Drain the cooling system as described in Chapter 1A Section 31.
3 Unscrew the bolts and remove the coolant pump from the cylinder block (see illustration). Remove and discard the gasket.

Refitting

4 Commence refitting by thoroughly cleaning the mating faces of the coolant pump and the cylinder block.
5 Refit the coolant pump, using a new gasket, and tighten the securing bolts to the specified torque.
6 Refit the timing belt tensioner and timing belt as described in Chapter 2A Section 8, then refill the cooling system (Chapter 1A Section 31).

Diesel engine models

Removal

7 Remove the timing belt as described in Chapter 2B, Chapter 2C, Chapter 2D or Chapter 2E.
8 If not already done, drain the cooling system as described in Chapter 1B Section 30.
9 Remove the bolts securing the coolant pump to the engine, and remove it (see illustrations). Recover the sealing ring or gasket.

Refitting

10 Commence refitting by thoroughly cleaning the mating faces of the coolant pump and the cylinder block. If the old coolant pump is being refitted, check the condition of the sealing ring. Obtain a new one if possible, but it appears that it may not be available separately.
11 Refit the coolant pump, and tighten the securing bolts to the specified torque, in two stages. The pump body is made of plastic, so care is required. The first stage of tightening is a very low torque, which in reality approximates to doing the bolts just up to the surface.
12 Refit the timing belt as described in Chapter 2B, Chapter 2C, Chapter 2D or Chapter 2E, then refill the cooling system (Chapter 1B Section 30).

8 Heating and ventilation system – general information

1 The heater/ventilation system consists of a four-speed blower motor (housed behind the facia), face-level vents in the centre and at each end of the facia, and air ducts to the front footwells.
2 The control unit is located in the facia, and the controls operate flap valves, to deflect and mix the air flowing through the various parts of the heater/ventilation system. The flap valves are contained in the air distribution housing, which acts as a central distribution unit, passing air to the various ducts and vents.

7.3 Coolant pump retaining bolts (arrowed) – petrol engines

7.9a Coolant pump retaining bolts (arrowed) – 1.4 litre (Stage IV emissions) and 1.6 litre DOHC diesel engines

7.9b Coolant pump retaining bolts – 1.4 litre (Stage V emissions) and 1.6 litre SOHC diesel engines

9.1 Unclip the gear lever trim from the base of the gear lever

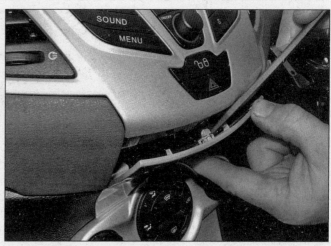

9.2a Carefully prise free the top of the blanking plate ...

3 Cold air enters the system through the grille at the rear of the engine compartment.

4 The air (boosted by the blower fan if required) then flows through the various ducts, according to the settings of the controls. Stale air is expelled through ducts at the rear of the car. If warm air is required, the cold air is passed through the heater matrix, which is heated by the engine coolant.

5 On models with air conditioning, a recirculation switch enables the outside air supply to be closed off, while the air inside the car is recirculated. This can be useful to prevent unpleasant odours entering from outside the car, but should only be used

briefly, as the recirculated air inside the car will soon deteriorate.

9 Heater/ventilation system components – removal and refitting

Heater/ventilation control panel

Removal

1 Unclip the gear lever or selector lever trim from the base of the gear/selector lever **(see illustration)**.

2 Using a plastic spatula or similar tool,

carefully prise free the top of the blanking plate located above the heater/ventilation control panel. Disengage the two lower pegs and remove the blanking plate **(see illustrations)**.

3 Carefully prise free the heater/ventilation control panel surround to release the three retaining clips each side. Disconnect the wiring connector at the rear and remove the control panel surround **(see illustrations)**.

4 Undo the four screws and withdraw the control panel from the facia **(see illustrations)**.

5 Disconnect the wiring connectors at the rear of the control panel **(see illustration)**. On models with manual temperature control,

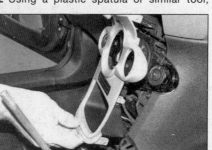

9.2b ... then disengage the two lower pegs and remove the blanking plate

9.3a Carefully prise free the heater/ ventilation control panel surround ...

9.3b ...then disconnect the wiring connector and remove the control panel surround

9.4a Undo the four screws (arrowed) ...

9.4b ... and withdraw the control panel from the facia

9.5 Disconnect the wiring connectors at the rear of the control panel

9.7a Extract the plastic rivet ...

9.7b ... and remove the inner trim panel from the base of the facia

it down and out from the footwell **(see illustration)**.

Refitting

14 Refitting is a reversal of removal, noting the following points:

a) *On automatic transmission models use a new clamp bolt when reconnecting the steering column shaft universal joint and tighten the clamp bolt to the specified torque.*

b) *On manual transmission models refit the clutch pedal as described in Chapter 6 Section 5.*

Heater blower motor resistor

Removal

15 Working in the footwell on the passenger's side, pull out the centre pin and extract the plastic rivet securing the inner trim panel to the base of the facia. Pull the panel away to release the three retaining clips at the rear and remove the trim panel **(see illustrations)**.

16 Disconnect the resistor wiring connector.

17 Unscrew the securing screws, and withdraw the resistor from the air distribution housing **(see illustration)**.

Refitting

18 Refitting is a reversal of removal.

Air distribution housing

Note: *On models with air conditioning, it is not possible to remove the air distribution*

release the two control cables from the clips at the rear of the panel, and disconnect the cable ends from the operating levers. Remove the panel from the car.

Refitting

6 Refitting is a reversal of removal.

Heater blower motor

Removal

7 Working in the footwell on the driver's side, pull out the centre pin and extract the plastic rivet securing the inner trim panel to the base of the facia. Pull the panel away to release the three retaining clips at the rear and remove the trim panel **(see illustrations)**.

8 On manual transmission models remove the clutch pedal as described in Chapter 6 Section 5.

9 On automatic transmission models, set the front wheels in the straight-ahead position, then lock the steering column in position by removing the ignition key. Working in the driver's footwell, undo the clamp bolt securing the steering column shaft lower universal joint to the steering gear pinion **(see illustration)**. Note that a new clamp bolt will be required for refitting. Pull the shaft upwards and off the pinion.

10 Unclip and remove the footwell air duct below the blower motor.

11 Disconnect the blower motor wiring connector.

12 Undo the retaining screw securing the blower motor to the air distribution housing **(see illustration)**.

13 Rotate the blower motor clockwise to release it from the housing then withdraw

9.9 Steering column shaft lower universal joint clamp bolt (arrowed)

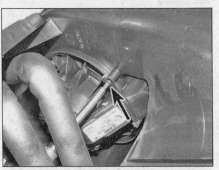

9.12 Undo the retaining screw (arrowed) securing the blower motor to the air distribution housing

9.13 Rotate the blower motor clockwise to release it from the housing

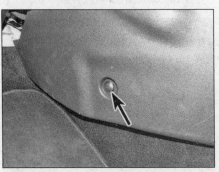

9.15a Extract the plastic rivet (arrowed) ...

9.15b ... and remove the inner trim panel from the base of the facia

9.17 Unscrew the securing screws, and withdraw the resistor from the air distribution housing

9.19 Turn the facia assembly upside down on the bench for access to the air distribution housing and attachments

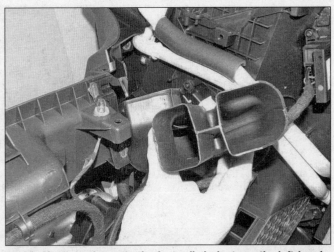

9.20a Unclip and remove the footwell air ducts on the left-hand side ...

housing without opening the refrigerant circuit (see Sections 10 and 11). Have the refrigerant discharged at a dealer service department or an automotive air conditioning repair facility before proceeding.

Note: *The air distribution housing is removed together with the complete facia assembly and is then separated from it on the bench. This is an involved and complex operation and it is suggested that the contents of this Section and the relevant Section in Chapter 11 are studied carefully to gain an understanding of the work involved, before proceeding.*

19 Remove the facia assembly as described in Chapter 11 Section 25. Turn the facia assembly upside down on the bench to improve access to the air distribution housing and attachments on the underside of the facia **(see illustration)**.

20 Unclip and remove the footwell air ducts on each side of the air distribution housing **(see illustrations)**.

21 On models with manual temperature control, release the two control cables from the clips on the air distribution housing, and disconnect the cable ends from the operating levers.

22 Disconnect the wiring connectors at the following components, where fitted **(see illustrations)**:

a) *Air inlet blend control motor.*
b) *Heater blower motor.*
c) *Sunlight sensor.*
d) *Heater blower motor resistor.*
e) *Air distribution control motor.*
f) *Temperature control motor.*
g) *Air temperature sensor.*

23 Release the disconnected wiring harness from the cable clips on the air distribution housing and move it to one side.

24 Remove the heater/ventilation control panel as described previously in paragraphs 2 to 6.

25 Undo the three nuts at the rear and the single bolt at the front securing the air

9.20b ... and right-hand side of the air distribution housing

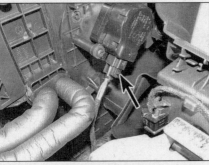

9.22a Disconnect the wiring connectors at the air inlet blend control motor (arrowed) ...

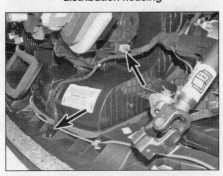

9.22b ... heater blower motor and sunlight sensor (arrowed) ...

9.22c ... heater blower motor resistor and air distribution control motor (arrowed) ...

9.22d ... temperature control motor (arrowed) ...

9.22e ... and air temperature sensor (arrowed)

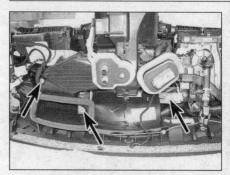

9.25a Undo the three nuts at the rear (arrowed) …

9.25b … and the single bolt at the front (arrowed) securing the air distribution housing to the facia andcrossmember

9.29 Lift off the foam insulation pad over the heater matrix pipe stubs

9.30 Undo the two screws (arrowed) securing the two halves of the bulkhead closure plate together

9.31a Cut through the foam sealing strip at the join of the bulkhead closure plate …

9.31b … and separate the two halves of the plate

distribution housing to the facia and cross-member **(see illustrations)**.

26 Make a final check that all wiring has been disconnected from the air distribution housing components, and that the harness has been released from the various cable clips and ties. Lift the housing up and off the retaining studs, and remove it from the facia.

Refitting

27 Refitting is a reversal of removal. On completion, refill the cooling system as described in Chapter 1A or 1B. On models with air conditioning, have the system evacuated, charged and leak-tested by the specialist who discharged it.

Heater matrix

Removal

28 Remove the air distribution housing as described previously in this Section.
29 Lift off the foam insulation pad over the heater matrix pipe stubs **(see illustration)**.
30 Undo the two screws securing the two halves of the bulkhead closure plate together **(see illustration)**.
31 Using a sharp knife, cut through the foam sealing strip at the join of the bulkhead closure plate and separate the two halves of the plate **(see illustrations)**.

32 Undo the securing screw and remove the heater matrix retainer **(see illustration)**.
33 Carefully slide out the heater matrix and heater pipe assembly from the air distribution housing **(see illustration)**.

Refitting

34 Refitting is a reversal of removal.

10 Air conditioning system – general information and precautions

1 Air conditioning is available on certain models. It enables the temperature of incoming air to be lowered, and also dehumidifies the air, which makes for rapid demisting and increased comfort.
2 The cooling side of the system works in the same way as a domestic refrigerator. Refrigerant gas is drawn into a belt-driven compressor, and passes into a condenser mounted in front of the radiator, where it loses heat and becomes liquid. The liquid passes through an expansion valve to an evaporator, where it changes from liquid under high pressure to gas under low pressure. This change is accompanied by a drop in temperature, which cools the evaporator. The refrigerant returns to the compressor, and the cycle begins again.
3 Air blown through the evaporator passes

9.32 Undo the securing screw (arrowed) and remove the heater matrix retainer

9.33 Carefully slide out the heater matrix and heater pipe assembly from the air distribution housing

10.6 Air conditioning service ports (arrowed)

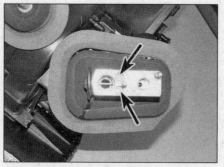

11.8a Undo the two retaining bolts (arrowed) ...

11.8b ... and remove the expansion valve from the refrigerant pipe stubs

to the heater assembly, where it is mixed with hot air blown through the heater matrix, to achieve the desired temperature in the passenger compartment.

4 The heating side of the system works in the same way as on models without air conditioning (see Section 8).

5 The operation of the system is controlled electronically. Any problems with the system should be referred to a Ford dealer or an air conditioning specialist.

Air conditioning service ports

Note: *The air conditioning service port location varies slightly according to model. The following is a general description of service port location.*

6 The high-pressure service port is the larger of the two service port connections and is located to the rear of the radiator on the right hand side **(see illustration)**.

7 The low-pressure service port is located at the rear right-hand side of the engine compartment **(see illustration 10.6)**.

Precautions

8 It is necessary to observe special precautions whenever dealing with any part of the system, its associated components, and any items which necessitate disconnection of the system.

⚠ *Warning: The refrigeration circuit contains a liquid refrigerant. This refrigerant is potentially dangerous, and should only be handled by qualified persons. If it is splashed onto the skin, it can cause frostbite. It is not itself poisonous, but in the presence of a naked flame it forms a poisonous gas; inhalation of the vapour through a lighted cigarette could prove fatal. Uncontrolled discharging of the refrigerant is dangerous, and potentially damaging to the environment. Do not disconnect any part of the system unless it has been discharged by a Ford dealer or an air conditioning specialist. Caution: Do not operate the air conditioning system if it is known to be short of refrigerant, as this may damage the compressor.*

11 Air conditioning system components – removal and refitting

⚠ *Warning: The air conditioning system is under high pressure. Do not loosen any fittings or remove any components until after the system has been discharged. Air conditioning refrigerant should be properly discharged into an approved type of container at a dealer service department or an automotive air conditioning repair facility capable of handling R134a refrigerant. Cap or plug the pipe lines as soon as they are disconnected, to prevent the entry of moisture. Always wear eye protection when disconnecting air conditioning system fittings.*
Note: *This Section refers to the components of the air conditioning system itself – refer to Sections 8 and 9 for details of components common to the heating/ventilation system.*

Compressor

Note: *If the compressor is being removed as part of another procedure, it may not be necessary to have the system discharged. Usually, the compressor can be unbolted and tied to one side without the need to disturb the refrigerant lines.*

Removal

1 Remove the auxiliary drivebelt as described in Chapter 1A Section 26 or Chapter 1B Section 26.

11.9a Remove the expansion valve retaining plate ...

2 Disconnect the compressor wiring plug.
3 With the system discharged, disconnect the refrigerant lines from the compressor. Discard the O-ring seals – new ones must be used when refitting.
4 Support the compressor, then remove the three mounting bolts (petrol engines) or four mounting bolts (diesel engines) and lower the compressor out of the engine bay.

Refitting

5 Refitting is a reversal of removal, noting the following points:
a) Use new O-rings, coated with refrigerant oil, when reconnecting the refrigerant lines.
b) Tighten the compressor mounting bolts to the specified torque.
c) Have the system evacuated, charged and leak-tested by the specialist that discharged it.

Evaporator

6 Have the refrigerant discharged at a dealer service department or an automotive air conditioning repair facility.
7 Remove the air distribution housing as described in Section 9.
8 Undo the two retaining bolts and remove the expansion valve from the refrigerant pipe stubs **(see illustrations)**. Note that new seals for the refrigerant pipes will be required for refitting. Suitably plug or cover the disconnected pipes.
9 Remove the expansion valve retaining plate, then lift off the foam pad **(see illustrations)**.

11.9b ... then lift off the foam pad

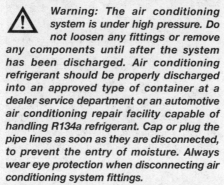

11.10 Undo the two screws (arrowed) securing the two halves of the bulkhead closure plate together

11.11a Cut through the foam sealing strip at the join of the bulkhead closure plate ...

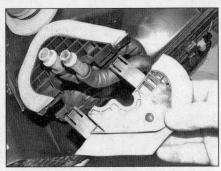

11.11b ... then release the retaining tabs and separate the two halves of the plate

11.12a Undo the retaining screw (arrowed) ...

11.12b ... lift off the pollen filter cover from the side of the air distribution housing ...

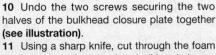
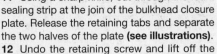

10 Undo the two screws securing the two halves of the bulkhead closure plate together **(see illustration)**.

11 Using a sharp knife, cut through the foam sealing strip at the join of the bulkhead closure plate. Release the retaining tabs and separate the two halves of the plate **(see illustrations)**.

12 Undo the retaining screw and lift off the pollen filter cover from the side of the air distribution housing, then slide out the filter **(see illustrations)**.

13 Undo the retaining screws and separate the two halves of the air distribution housing **(see illustrations)**.

14 Lift out the evaporator retaining plate, then carefully withdraw the evaporator and pipe assembly from the air distribution housing **(see illustrations)**.

Refitting

15 Refitting is a reversal of removal, ensuring that all disturbed pipe seals are renewed.

Condenser

Removal

16 Have the refrigerant discharged at a dealer service department or an automotive air conditioning repair facility.

17 Remove the radiator as described in Section 3.

18 Undo the retaining nuts and disconnect the upper and lower refrigerant pipe

11.12c ... then slide out the filter

11.13a Undo the retaining screws (arrowed) ...

11.13b ... and separate the two halves of the air distribution housing

11.14a Lift out the evaporator retaining plate ...

11.14b ... then carefully withdraw the evaporator and pipe assembly

connector blocks from the right-hand side of the condenser (see illustrations). Discard the seals – new ones must be used when refitting. Suitably cap the open fittings immediately to keep moisture and contamination out of the system.

19 Where applicable, disconnect the wiring connector from the pressure sensor on the right-hand side of the condenser.

20 Where fitted, undo the three retaining bolts and remove the support bracket from the right-hand side of the condenser.

21 Carefully lower the condenser and remove it from under the car.

Refitting

22 Refitting is the reverse of removal ensuring that all disturbed pipe seals are renewed.

23 Have the system evacuated, charged and leak-tested by the specialist who discharged it.

Receiver dryer

Note: *The following procedure is only applicable to 1.6 litre diesel engine models. On all other models, the receiver dryer is an integral part of the condenser.*

Removal

24 Have the refrigerant discharged at a dealer service department or an automotive air conditioning repair facility.

11.18a Undo the refrigerant pipe connector block upper retaining nut (arrowed) ...

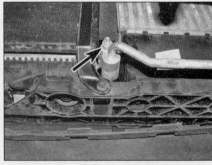

11.18b ... and lower retaining nut (arrowed), and disconnect the connector blocks

25 Remove the front bumper as described in Chapter 11 Section 6.

26 Undo the retaining nuts and disconnect the refrigerant pipe connector blocks from the base of the receiver dryer (see illustration). Discard the seals – new ones must be used when refitting. Suitably cap the open fittings immediately to keep moisture and contamination out of the system.

27 Disconnect the wiring plug from the air conditioning pressure switch (see illustration).

28 Undo the receiver dryer retaining clamp

nut and withdraw the receiver dryer from under the wheel arch.

Refitting

29 Refitting is a reversal of removal, noting the following points:

a) Use new O-rings, coated with refrigerant oil, when reconnecting the refrigerant lines.

b) Refit the front bumper as described in Chapter 11 Section 6.

c) Have the system evacuated, charged and leak-tested by the specialist who discharged it.

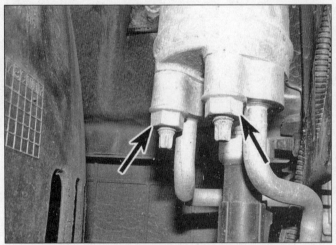

11.26 Undo the retaining nuts (arrowed) and disconnect the refrigerant pipe connector blocks from the receiver dryer

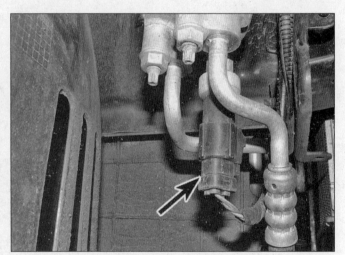

11.27 Disconnect the wiring plug (arrowed) from the air conditioning pressure switch

Chapter 4 Part A
Fuel and exhaust systems – petrol models

Contents

Degrees of difficulty

Easy, suitable for novice with little experience	Fairly easy, suitable for beginner with some experience	Fairly difficult, suitable for competent DIY mechanic	Difficult, suitable for experienced DIY mechanic	Very difficult, suitable for expert DIY or professional

Specifications

General

System type	Sequential multi-port fuel injection
Fuel octane requirement.	95 RON unleaded
Regulated fuel pressure (nominal)	3.6 to 4.0 bar

Torque wrench settings

	Nm	lbf ft
Catalytic converter support bracket (models from August 2009):		
Support bracket to cylinder block	51	38
Support bracket to catalytic converter.	24	18
Catalytic converter to cylinder block (models up to August 2009)	48	35
Exhaust centre section flange joint	48	35
Exhaust manifold heat shield bolts	10	7
Exhaust manifold to cylinder head:		
Stage 1	20	15
Stage 2	55	41
Fuel rail mounting bolts	8	6
Fuel tank strap retaining bolts	25	18
Inlet manifold nuts/bolts.	18	13
Intermediate shaft support bearing mounting bracket bolts	25	18
Variable camshaft timing oil control solenoids.	8	6

1 General information and precautions

1 The fuel system consists of a fuel tank (mounted under the floor, beneath the rear seats), fuel hoses, an electric fuel pump mounted in the fuel tank, and a sequential electronic fuel injection system controlled by an engine management electronic control unit (Powertrain Control Module).

2 The electric fuel pump supplies fuel under pressure to the fuel rail, which distributes fuel to the injectors. A pressure regulator controls the system pressure in relation to inlet tract depression. From the fuel rail, fuel is injected into the inlet ports, just above the inlet valves, by four fuel injectors. The fuel rail is mounted to the cylinder head, just above the plastic inlet manifold.

3 The amount of fuel supplied by the injectors is precisely controlled by the Powertrain Control Module (PCM). The module uses the signals from the crankshaft position sensor and the camshaft position sensor, to trigger each injector separately in cylinder firing order (sequential injection), with benefits in terms of better fuel economy and leaner exhaust emissions.

4 The Powertrain Control Module is the heart of the entire engine management system, controlling the fuel injection, ignition and emissions control systems. The module receives information from various sensors which is then computed and compared with preset values stored in its memory, to determine the required period of injection.

5 Information on crankshaft position and engine speed is generated by a crankshaft position sensor. The inductive head of the sensor runs just above the engine flywheel and scans a series of protrusions on the flywheel periphery. As the crankshaft rotates, the sensor transmits a pulse to the system's ignition module every time a protrusion passes it. There is one missing protrusion in the flywheel periphery at a point corresponding to 90° BTDC. The ignition module recognises the absence of a pulse from the crankshaft position sensor at this point to establish a reference mark for crankshaft position. Similarly, the time interval between absent pulses is used to determine engine speed. This information is then fed to the PCM for further processing.

6 The camshaft position sensor is located in the cylinder head so that it registers with a lobe on the camshaft. The camshaft position sensor functions in the same way as the crankshaft position sensor, producing a series of pulses; this gives the PCM a reference point, to enable it to determine the firing order, and operate the injectors in the appropriate sequence.

7 Engine temperature information is supplied by the coolant temperature sensor. The sensor is an NTC (Negative Temperature Coefficient) thermistor – that is, a semi-conductor whose electrical resistance decreases as its temperature increases. The sensor provides the PCM with a constantly-varying (analogue) voltage signal, corresponding to the temperature of the engine coolant. This is used to refine the calculations made by the module, when determining the correct amount of fuel required to achieve the ideal air/fuel mixture ratio.

8 On 1.25 and 1.4 litre engines, inlet air temperature and density information for air/ fuel mixture ratio calculations is provided by a temperature and manifold absolute pressure (TMAP) sensor. The TMAP sensor is located on the inlet manifold, and consists of a pressure transducer and a temperature sensor. The TMAP sensor provides information to the PCM relating to inlet manifold vacuum and barometric pressure, and the temperature of the air in the inlet manifold. When the ignition is switched on with the engine stopped, the sensor calculates barometric pressure and, when the engine is running, the sensor calculates inlet manifold vacuum. On 1.6 litre engines an airflow sensor located on the air cleaner is used instead of the TMAP sensor and performs in a similar fashion.

9 All engines features a throttle which is electronically-controlled – an accelerator cable is not fitted. Instead, a throttle position sensor fitted to the accelerator pedal provides the PCM with the throttle opening signal, and this is relayed to a motor-driven throttle valve. This system also enables the PCM to control the engine idle speed, varying the throttle opening as required by changes in engine temperature and load.

10 On models without ABS, roadspeed is monitored by the vehicle speed sensor. This component is a Hall-effect generator, mounted on the transmission, in place of the old speedometer drive. It supplies the module with a series of pulses corresponding to the car's roadspeed, enabling the module to control features such as the fuel shut-off on overrun. If ABS is fitted, roadspeed information is provided by the ABS wheel speed sensors, and the vehicle speed sensor is not fitted.

11 The clutch pedal position is monitored by a switch fitted to the pedal bracket. This sends a signal to the PCM.

12 An oxygen sensor in the exhaust system provides the module with constant feedback – ' closed-loop' control – which enables it to adjust the mixture to provide

the best possible operating conditions for the catalytic converter. A further sensor is fitted, downstream of the converter, to monitor the converter's operation, and this provides an even finer degree of emission control.

13 The air inlet side of the system consists of an air cleaner housing, the TMAP sensor or airflow sensor, an inlet hose and duct, and a throttle housing.

14 Both the idle speed and mixture are under the control of the PCM, and cannot be adjusted.

> ⚠ **Warning: Many of the procedures in this Chapter require the removal of fuel lines and connections, which may result in some fuel spillage. Before carrying out any operation on the fuel system, refer to the precautions given in 'Safety first!' at the beginning of this manual, and follow them implicitly. Petrol is a highly-dangerous and volatile liquid, and the precautions necessary when handling it cannot be overstressed. Residual pressure will remain in the fuel lines long after the car was last used. When disconnecting any fuel line, first depressurise the fuel system as described in Section 2. Before disconnecting any of the fuel injection system sensor wiring plugs, ensure at least that the ignition is switched off (ideally, disconnect the battery). If this is not done, it could result in a fault code being logged in the system memory, and may even cause damage to the component concerned.**

2 Fuel system – depressurisation

> ⚠ **Warning: The following procedure will merely relieve the pressure in the fuel system – remember that fuel will still be present in the system components, and take precautions accordingly before disconnecting any of them.**

Note: *Refer to the warnings in Section 1 before proceeding.*

1 The fuel system referred to in this Chapter is defined as the fuel tank and tank-mounted fuel pump/fuel gauge sender unit, the fuel injectors, fuel pressure regulator, and the metal pipes and flexible hoses of the fuel lines between these components. All these contain fuel, which will be under pressure while the engine is running and/or while the ignition is switched on.

2 The pressure will remain for some time after the ignition has been switched off, and must be relieved before any of these components is disturbed for servicing work.

3 The simplest depressurisation method is to disconnect the fuel pump electrical supply by removing the fuel pump fuse (refer to the wiring diagrams or the label on the relevant fusebox for exact location) and starting the engine; allow the engine to idle until it stops through lack of fuel. Turn the engine over

once or twice on the starter to ensure that all pressure is released, then switch off the ignition; do not forget to refit the fuse when work is complete.

4 Note that, once the fuel system has been depressurised and drained (even partially), it will take significantly longer to restart the engine – perhaps several seconds of cranking – before the system is refilled and pressure restored.

3 Unleaded petrol – general information and usage

1 All petrol models are designed to run on fuel with a minimum octane rating of 95 (RON). All models have a catalytic converter, and so must be run on unleaded fuel only. Under no circumstances should leaded fuel (UK '4-star' or LRP) be used, as this will damage the converter.

2 Super unleaded petrol (98 or 99 octane) can also be used in all models if wished, though there is no advantage in doing so.

4 Fuel pipes and fittings – general information and disconnection

1 Depressurise the fuel system (Section 2) and disconnect the cable from the negative battery terminal (Chapter 5A Section 1, 4) before proceeding.

2 The fuel supply pipe connects the fuel pump in the fuel tank to the fuel rail on the engine.

3 Whenever you're working under the vehicle, be sure to inspect all fuel and evaporative emission pipes for leaks, kinks, dents and other damage. Always replace a damaged fuel pipe immediately.

4 If you find signs of dirt in the pipes during disassembly, disconnect all pipes and blow them out with compressed air. Inspect the fuel strainer on the fuel pump pick-up unit for damage and deterioration.

Steel tubing

5 It is critical that the fuel pipes be replaced with pipes of equivalent type and specification.

6 Some steel fuel pipes have threaded fittings. When loosening these fittings, hold the stationary fitting with a spanner while turning the union nut.

Plastic tubing

> ⚠ **Warning: When removing or installing plastic fuel tubing, be careful not to bend or twist it too much, which can damage it. Also, plastic fuel tubing is NOT heat resistant, so keep it away from excessive heat.**

7 When replacing fuel system plastic tubing, use only original equipment replacement plastic tubing.

Flexible hoses

8 When replacing fuel system flexible hoses, use original equipment replacements, or hose to the same specification.

9 Don't route fuel hoses (or metal pipes) within 100 mm of the exhaust system or within 280 mm of the catalytic converter. Make sure that no rubber hoses are installed directly against the vehicle, particularly in places where there is any vibration. If allowed to touch some vibrating part of the vehicle, a hose can easily become chafed and it might start leaking. A good rule of thumb is to maintain a minimum of 8.0 mm clearance around a hose (or metal pipe) to prevent contact with the vehicle underbody.

Disconnecting Fuel pipe Fittings

10 Typical fuel pipe fittings:

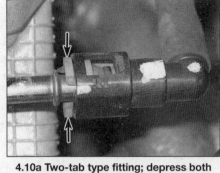
4.10a Two-tab type fitting; depress both tabs with your fingers, then pull the fuel pipe and the fitting apart

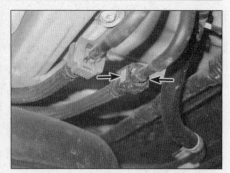
4.10b On this type of fitting, depress the two buttons on opposite sides of the fitting, then pull it off the fuel pipe

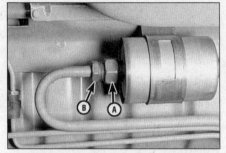
4.10c Threaded fuel pipe fitting; hold the stationary portion of the pipe or component (A) while loosening the union nut (B) with a flare-nut spanner

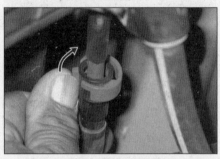
4.10d Plastic collar-type fitting; rotate the outer part of the fitting

4.10e Metal collar quick-connect fitting; pull the end of the retainer off the fuel pipe and disengage the other end from the female side of the fitting ...

4.10f ... insert a fuel pipe separator tool into the female side of the fitting, push it into the fitting and pull the fuel pipe off the pipe

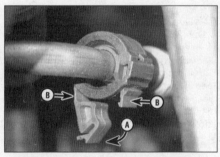
4.10g Some fittings are secured by lock tabs. Release the lock tab (A) and rotate it to the fully-opened position, squeeze the two smaller lock tabs (B) ...

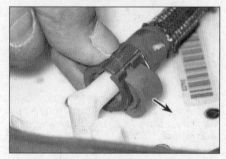
4.10h ... then push the retainer out and pull the fuel pipe off the pipe

4.10i Spring-lock coupling; remove the safety cover, install a coupling release tool and close the tool around the coupling ...

4.10j ... push the tool into the fitting, then pull the two pipes apart

4.10k Hairpin clip type fitting: push the legs of the retainer clip together, then push the clip down all the way until it stops and pull the fuel pipe off the pipe

5.1 Pull the collar away from the air cleaner assembly, and disconnect the crankcase ventilation hose

5.2 Prise up the red locking catch and disconnect the wiring plug

5.3 Slacken the retaining clip and disconnect the air outlet duct from the throttle housing

5.4 Depress the retaining tab and detach the air inlet duct from the front body panel

5.5 Pull the air cleaner upwards to remove it

5 Air cleaner assembly – removal and refitting

Removal

1 Pull the collar away from the air cleaner assembly, and disconnect the crankcase ventilation hose from the air cleaner (see illustration).
2 On 1.6 litre engines, disconnect the airflow sensor wiring plug, located in the outlet from the air cleaner cover (see illustration).
3 Slacken the retaining clip and disconnect

the air outlet duct from the throttle housing (see illustration).
4 Depress the retaining tab and detach the air inlet duct from the front body panel (see illustration).
5 Pull the air cleaner upwards to remove it (see illustration). The pegs on the base of the cleaner fit into rubber grommets. These pegs may prove troublesome to release, and some effort may be needed.

Refitting

6 Refitting is a reversal of the removal procedure. Locate the air cleaner pegs into the grommets and push down firmly to engage them in the grommets.

6 Accelerator pedal – removal and refitting

Removal

1 Disconnect the wiring plug from the accelerator pedal position sensor, then unscrew the two mounting nuts and remove the pedal/sensor assembly from the brake pedal mounting bracket studs (see illustration).

Refitting

2 Refitting is a reversal of the removal procedure.

7 Fuel tank – removal, inspection and refitting

Note: *Refer to the warnings in Section 1 before proceeding.*

Removal

1 Run the fuel level as low as possible prior to removing the tank.
2 Relieve the residual pressure in the fuel system (see Section 2), and equalise tank pressure by removing the fuel filler cap.
3 Disconnect the battery negative terminal (refer to Disconnecting the battery 14, 6).
4 Chock the front wheels, then jack up the rear of the vehicle, and support it securely on axle stands (see *'Jacking and vehicle support'*). Remove the rear roadwheels.
5 Unhook the exhaust system mounting rubbers from the rear hangers, and allow the exhaust system to rest on the rear axle.
6 Undo the five retaining nuts and remove the exhaust system heat shield from the fuel tank.
7 Release the handbrake cables from the underbody retaining clips on the fuel tank.
8 Release the fuel lines from the four underbody retaining clips nearest to the fuel tank.
9 Release the clips and disconnect the fuel tank filler and vent pipes (see illustration). Do not use any sharp-edged tools to release the pipes from their stubs, as the pipes are

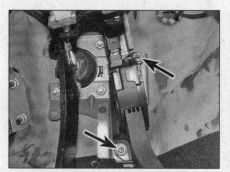

6.1 Accelerator pedal mounting nuts (arrowed)

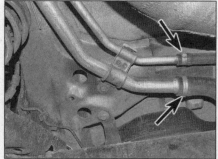

7.9 Release the clips (arrowed) and disconnect the fuel tank filler and vent pipes

7.12 Fuel tank strap rear retaining bolt (arrowed)

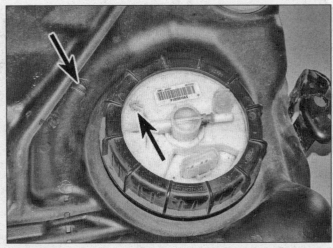

8.3 Alignment marks (arrowed) on the fuel pump/gauge sender unit and fuel tank

easily damaged. Discard the pipe clips and obtain worm-drive hose clips for refitting. Be prepared for fuel spillage and observe all relevant safety precautions.

10 Support the tank using a trolley jack and a large sheet of wood to spread the load.

11 Note exactly how the fuel tank retaining straps are arranged, to make refitting easier. In particular, note their fitted order under the retaining bolt head, at the front fixing.

12 Unbolt and remove the two fuel tank retaining straps (see illustration).

13 Partially lower the tank on the jack, taking care that no strain is placed on any fuel lines or wiring. As soon as the wiring connector for the fuel pump/gauge sender on top of the tank is accessible, reach in and disconnect it.

14 Squeeze the quick-release fitting, and disconnect the fuel tank vent pipe from the evaporative emissions charcoal canister at the side of the tank.

15 Disconnect the fuel supply line from the top of the tank, squeezing the quick-release connector and pulling off the line.

16 Lower the fuel tank to the ground, checking all the way down that no pipes or wiring are under any strain. Remove the tank from under the car.

17 If required the fuel pump/fuel gauge sender unit can be removed as described in Section 8, and the charcoal canister can be removed as described in Chapter 4C Section 2.

Inspection

18 Whilst removed, the fuel tank can be inspected for damage or deterioration. Removal of the fuel pump/fuel gauge sender unit (see Section 8) will allow a partial inspection of the interior. If the tank is contaminated with sediment or water, swill it out with clean fuel. Do not under any circumstances undertake any repairs on a leaking or damaged fuel tank; this work must be carried out by a professional who has experience in this critical and potentially-dangerous work.

19 Whilst the fuel tank is removed from the car, it should be placed in a safe area where sparks or open flames cannot ignite the fumes coming out of the tank. Be especially careful inside garages where a natural-gas type appliance is located, because the pilot light could cause an explosion.

Refitting

20 Refitting is a reversal of the removal procedure, noting the following points:

a) Ensure that all pipe and wiring connections are securely fitted.

b) When refitting the quick-release couplings, press them together until the locking lugs snap into their groove.

c) Tighten the tank strap retaining bolts to the specified torque.

d) If evidence of contamination was found, do not return any previously-drained fuel to the tank unless it is carefully filtered first.

8 Fuel pump/ fuel gauge sender unit – removal and refitting

Note: Refer to the warnings in Section 1 before proceeding. Ford specify the use of their service tool 310-069 (a large socket with projecting teeth to engage the fuel pump/ sender unit retaining ring's raised edges) for this task. Suitable alternatives to this tool are readily available from accessory stores and motor factor outlets.

Removal

1 A combined fuel pump and fuel gauge sender unit is located in the top face of the fuel tank. The combined unit can only be detached and withdrawn from the tank after the tank is released and lowered from under the car. Refer to Section 7 and remove the fuel tank, then proceed as follows.

2 Unscrew and remove the special retaining ring, by unscrewing it with the Ford tool or a suitable alternative.

3 Check that alignment marks are visible on the fuel pump/gauge sender unit and fuel tank. There should be an arrow on the sender unit aligned with three raised projections on the tank (see illustration). If no marks are visible, suitably mark the tank and sender unit with paint.

4 Carefully lift out the fuel pump/gauge sender unit from the tank. Take care that the sender unit float and arm are not damaged as the unit is removed.

5 Lift out the rubber seal and obtain a new seal for refitting.

6 If required, the fuel gauge sender unit can be removed from the pump by disconnecting the wiring connector, releasing the retaining catch and withdrawing the unit from the side of the pump.

Refitting

7 Refitting is a reversal of removal, but fit a new rubber seal and tighten the retaining ring securely. Refit the fuel tank as described in Section 7.

9 Fuel tank filler neck – removal and refitting

Note: Refer to the warnings in Section 1 before proceeding.

Removal

1 Chock the front wheels, then jack up the rear of the vehicle, and support it securely on axle stands (see 'Jacking and vehicle support'). Remove the left-hand rear wheel.

2 Remove the left-hand rear wheel arch liner, which is secured by a combination of screws and push-in clips.

3 Remove the single bolt securing the filler

9.3 Undo the bolt (arrowed) securing the filler neck and vent pipe support bracket to the wheel arch

9.5 Undo the bolt (arrowed) securing the filler pipe lower support bracket

neck and vent pipe support bracket to the wheel arch **(see illustration)**.

4 Release the clips and disconnect the fuel tank filler and vent pipes **(see illustration 7.9)**. Do not use any sharp-edged tools to release the pipes from their stubs, as the pipes are easily damaged. Discard the pipe clips and obtain worm-drive hose clips for refitting. Be prepared for fuel spillage and observe all relevant safety precautions.

5 Unscrew the single bolt securing the pipe lower support bracket **(see illustration)**, and remove the filler neck from under the car.

6 Check the condition of the filler neck and vent pipe, and renew if necessary.

Refitting

7 Refitting is a reversal of removal.

10 Fuel injection system – checking

Note: *Refer to the warnings in Section 1 before proceeding.*

1 If a fault appears in the fuel injection system, first ensure that all the system wiring connectors are securely connected and free of corrosion – also refer to paragraphs 5 to 8 below. Then ensure that the fault is not due to poor maintenance; ie, check that the air cleaner filter element is clean, the spark plugs are in good condition and correctly gapped, the cylinder compression pressures are correct, the ignition system wiring is in good condition and securely connected, and the engine breather

hoses are clear and undamaged, referring to Chapter 1A, Chapter 2A and Chapter 5B.

2 If these checks fail to reveal the cause of the problem, the car should be taken to a suitably-equipped Ford dealer for testing. A diagnostic connector is fitted under the facia on the driver's side into which dedicated electronic test equipment can be plugged. The test equipment is capable of 'interrogating' the engine management system powertrain control module (PCM) electronically and accessing its internal fault log (reading fault codes).

3 Fault codes can only be extracted from the PCM using a dedicated fault code reader. A Ford dealer will obviously have such a reader, but they are also available from other suppliers. It is unlikely to be cost-effective for the private owner to purchase a fault code reader, but a well-equipped local garage or auto-electrical specialist will have one.

4 Using this equipment, faults can be pinpointed quickly and simply, even if their occurrence is intermittent. Testing all the system components individually in an attempt to locate the fault by elimination is a time-consuming operation that is unlikely to be fruitful (particularly if the fault occurs dynamically), and carries a high risk of damage to the PCM's internal components.

Limited Operation Strategy

5 Certain faults, such as failure of one of the engine management system sensors, will cause the system to revert to a backup (or 'limp-home') mode, referred to by Ford as 'Limited Operation Strategy' (LOS). This is intended to be a 'get-you-home' facility only

– the engine management warning light will come on when this mode is in operation.

6 In this mode, the signal from the defective sensor is substituted with a fixed value (it would normally vary), which may lead to loss of power, poor idling, and generally-poor running, especially when the engine is cold.

7 However, the engine may in fact run quite well in this situation, and the only clue (other than the warning light) would be that the exhaust CO emissions (for example) will be higher than they should be.

8 Bear in mind that, even if the defective sensor is correctly identified and renewed, the engine will not return to normal running until the fault code is erased, taking the system out of LOS. This also applies even if the cause of the fault was a loose connection or damaged piece of wire – until the fault code is erased, the system will continue in LOS.

11 Fuel injection system components – removal and refitting

Note: *Refer to the warnings in Section 1 before proceeding.*

Throttle housing

1 Release the retaining clips and disconnect the air inlet duct from the air cleaner and throttle housing.

2 Undo the four mounting bolts, then disconnect the throttle control motor wiring plug, and remove the throttle housing **(see illustration)**. Recover the seal – a new one should be used when refitting.

3 Do not attempt to clean the inside of the throttle housing. The inner surfaces are specially coated during manufacture, and this coating should not be removed.

4 Refitting is a reversal of removal. Use a new seal, and tighten the mounting bolts securely, to prevent air leaks. On completion, switch on the ignition to position II, without touching any of the pedals and leave it switched on for one minute to initialise the throttle housing.

Fuel rail and injectors

5 Relieve the residual pressure in the fuel system (see Section 2), and equalise tank pressure by removing the fuel filler cap.

⚠️ **Warning: This procedure will merely relieve the increased pressure necessary for the engine to run – remember that fuel will still be present in the system components, and take precautions accordingly before disconnecting any of them.**

6 Disconnect the battery negative terminal (refer to 'Disconnecting the battery').

7 Remove the air cleaner as described in Section 5.

8 Disconnect the crankcase breather hose from the cylinder head cover.

9 Unclip the fuel supply pipe from the support bracket, then prise out the locking catch, depress the release button and disconnect the pipe from the fuel rail **(see illustration)**.

11.2 Throttle housing mounting bolts (arrowed)

11.9 Prise out the locking catch (arrowed) then depress the release button

11.10a Push the locking clips (arrowed) forwards …

11.10b … and gently pull the connector assembly from the injectors

11.12a Undo the fuel rail mounting bolts (arrowed) …

11.12b … and pull the fuel rail upwards from place

11.13a Release the retaining clips from the rail …

11.13b … and pull the injector from the rail

10 Depress the wire locking clips and pull the wiring connectors assembly up from the injectors **(see illustrations)**. If necessary, on 1.6 litre engines, disconnect the wiring plug from the camshaft position sensor to allow the harness assembly to be moved to one side.

11 Release the coolant hose and, where applicable, the fuel supply hose from the clips on the fuel rail.

12 Unscrew and remove the two fuel rail mounting bolts. Carefully pull the fuel rail upwards to release the injectors from place – there will be some resistance from the injector O-ring seals **(see illustrations)**.

13 Remove the retaining clips and carefully pull the injectors from the fuel rail **(see illustrations)**.

14 Using a screwdriver, prise the O-rings from the grooves at each end of the injectors

(see illustration). Discard the O-rings and obtain new ones.

15 If required, the fuel pulse damper can be removed after the retaining clip has been removed **(see illustration)**. When refitting the damper, lubricate the new O-ring seals with clean engine oil.

16 Refitting is the reverse of the removal procedure, noting the following points:

a) Fit new injector O-rings, and lubricate them with clean engine oil to aid refitting.

b) Tighten the fuel rail mounting bolts to the specified torque.

c) Ensure that the hoses and wiring are routed correctly, and secured on reconnection by any clips or ties provided.

d) On completion, switch the ignition on to activate the fuel pump and pressurise the system, without cranking the engine.

Check for signs of fuel leaks around all disturbed unions and joints before attempting to start the engine.

TMAP sensor

17 The TMAP sensor is only fitted to 1.25 and 1.4 litre engines and is located in the upper centre of the inlet manifold **(see illustration)**.

18 With the ignition switched off, disconnect the sensor wiring plug, then undo the mounting bolt and withdraw it from the manifold. Check the condition of the sensor O-ring seal, and obtain a new one if necessary.

19 Refitting is a reversal of removal. Use a new seal if necessary, and tighten the mounting bolt securely, to prevent air leaks.

Airflow sensor

20 The airflow sensor is only fitted to 1.6 litre engines and is located in the air cleaner cover.

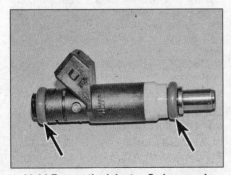

11.14 Renew the injector O-rings seals (arrowed)

11.15 Prise out the clip and remove the fuel pulse damper

11.17 TMAP sensor location (arrowed) on the inlet manifold

21 Disconnect the wiring plug from the airflow sensor **(see illustration 5.2)**.

22 Undo the two bolts and pull the sensor from the air cleaner cover.

23 Refitting is a reversal of removal. Note the arrow on the top of the sensor indicating airflow.

Powertrain Control Module (PCM)

Note: *The module is fragile. Take care not to drop it, or subject it to any other kind of impact. Do not subject it to extremes of temperature, or allow it to get wet.*

Note: *If a new PCM is to be fitted, the configuration information stored within the module must be uploaded to Ford diagnostic equipment prior to the module being removed, and downloaded to the new PCM once installed. Entrust this task to a Ford dealer or suitably-equipped specialist.*

24 Disconnect the battery negative terminal (refer to *'Disconnecting the battery'*).

25 Remove the cover over the PCM.

26 Drill out the shear-bolt securing the security shield over the PCM upper wiring connector **(see illustration)**. A 6 mm drill bit will be required, and the hole must be drilled centrally, to avoid damaging the PCM – Ford dealers use a special guide tool (418-537) to ensure this, which is a short tube with a 6 mm hole down the centre.

27 Remove the security shield, then disconnect the three wiring connectors from the PCM.

28 Undo the four retaining nuts and remove the PCM from the mounting plate.

29 Refitting is a reversal of removal. Strictly speaking, a new shear-bolt should be obtained for refitting, and tightened until the head shears off. However, as this is only a deterrent to 'chipping' the module, an ordinary bolt can be used instead.

Crankshaft position sensor

30 The sensor is located on the front left-hand side of the engine, close to the transmission. For improved access, apply the handbrake, then jack up the front of the car and support it on axle stands (see *'Jacking and vehicle support'*).

31 With the ignition switched off, disconnect the wiring plug, then unscrew the mounting bolt and withdraw the sensor **(see illustration)**.

32 Refitting is a reversal of removal. Ensure that the sensor is clean when refitting, and tighten the bolt securely.

Camshaft position sensor

33 On 1.25 and 1.4 litre engines, one sensor is fitted, located on the right-hand rear of the cylinder head. On 1.6 litre engines, there are two sensors fitted – one over each of the camshafts at the left-hand end of the cylinder head cover.

34 With the ignition switched off, disconnect the wiring from the camshaft position sensor(s) **(see illustrations)**.

35 Unscrew the mounting bolt(s) and withdraw the sensor(s) from the cylinder head or cylinder head cover (as applicable).

36 Refitting is a reversal of removal, but use a new seal. Smear a little engine oil on the seal before fitting the sensor, and tighten the bolt(s) securely.

Coolant temperature sensor

37 Refer to Chapter 3 Section 6.

Clutch pedal position switch

38 Working in the driver's footwell, disconnect the wiring connector from the clutch pedal position switch, located on the clutch pedal mounting bracket.

39 Rotate the switch anti-clockwise by a quarter-turn, and withdraw it from the pedal bracket **(see illustration)**. Do not depress the clutch pedal during the removal or refitting procedure – the pedal must be 'at rest'.

40 Refitting is a reversal of the removal procedure. The switch is automatically adjusted/calibrated by the vehicle system.

Variable camshaft timing oil control solenoids

41 The solenoids are only fitted to 1.6 litre engines and are located at the front, right-hand end of the cylinder head cover **(see illustration)**.

42 Disconnect the solenoid wiring plug, then

11.26 PCM security shield shear-bolt (arrowed)

11.31 Crankshaft position sensor (arrowed)

11.34a Disconnect the wiring from the camshaft position sensor – 1.25 and 1.4 litre engines

11.34b Disconnect the wiring from the camshaft position sensors – 1.6 litre engines

11.39 Turn the clutch pedal switch anti-clockwise to remove it

11.41 Camshaft timing oil control solenoids (arrowed)

11.42 Undo the bolt and pull the solenoid from place

12.6 Undo the bolt (arrowed) securing the support bracket to the manifold

undo the retaining bolt and pull the solenoid from place **(see illustration)**.

43 Refitting is a reversal of removal. Ensure the solenoid and aperture are scrupulously clean prior to refitting. Tighten the bolt to the specified torque.

Oxygen sensor

44 Refer to Chapter 4C Section 2.

Vehicle speed sensor

Note: *On models with ABS, vehicle speed information is derived from the ABS wheel speed sensors, and a vehicle speed sensor is not fitted. For more information on the ABS wheel sensors, refer to Chapter 9 Section 20.*

45 The sensor is mounted on top of the transmission, above the left-hand driveshaft.

46 With the ignition switched off, disconnect the sensor wiring plug, then pull the sensor retaining pin (at the base) out sideways, and lift the sensor out of the transmission.

47 Refitting is a reversal of removal. Check the condition of the O-ring seal, and fit a new one if necessary. Ensure the sensor is fully seated, and held securely by the retaining pin.

Knock sensor

48 Refer to Chapter 5B Section 6.

12 Manifolds – removal and refitting

Note: *Refer to the warnings in Section 1 before proceeding.*

Inlet manifold

1 Depressurise the fuel system as described in Section 2.

2 Disconnect the battery negative terminal (refer to *'Disconnecting the battery'*).

3 Remove the air cleaner as described in Section 5.

4 Remove the auxiliary drivebelt as described

in Chapter 1A Section 26.

5 Remove the throttle housing as described in Section 11.

6 Undo the bolt securing the vacuum hose and purge valve support bracket to the manifold **(see illustration)**.

7 Remove the fuel rail and injectors as described in Section 11.

8 Where applicable, disconnect the wiring plug from the TMAP sensor on top of the manifold **(see illustration 11.17)**.

9 Undo the bolt securing the engine oil level dipstick guide tube to the manifold.

10 Note their fitted locations and disconnect any remaining vacuum hoses/pipes/wiring harnesses attached to the manifold.

11 Undo the seven retaining bolts and remove the manifold. Renew the manifold-to-cylinder head seals/gasket **(see illustration)**.

12 Refitting is a reversal of removal, noting the following points:

a) *Ensure that the mating faces are clean, and use new manifold gaskets if necessary.*

b) *Tighten all fixings to the specified torque.*

c) *On completion, switch the ignition on to activate the fuel pump and pressurise the system, without cranking the engine. Check for signs of fuel leaks around all disturbed unions and joints before attempting to start the engine.*

Exhaust manifold

Models up to August 2009

13 Disconnect the battery negative terminal (refer to *'Disconnecting the battery'*).

14 Disconnect the oxygen sensor at the wiring connector behind the ignition coil **(see illustration)**.

15 Undo the four bolts at the top and the two bolts each side and remove the exhaust manifold upper heat shield.

16 Firmly apply the handbrake, then jack up the front of the vehicle and support it securely on axle stands (see *'Jacking and vehicle support'*).

17 Remove the right-hand driveshaft and intermediate shaft as described in Chapter 8 Section 2.

18 Disconnect the catalyst monitor sensor at the wiring connector on the transmission.

19 To prevent damage to the exhaust flexible section, support it by attaching a pair of splints either side (two scrap strips of wood, plant canes, etc) using some cable-ties.

20 Unscrew the two nuts securing the exhaust flexible section to the catalytic converter, and separate the joint. Recover the gasket.

21 Undo the two bolts and remove the catalytic converter heat shield.

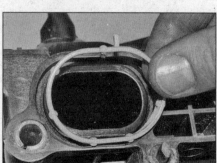

12.11 Renew the manifold-to-cylinder head seals

12.14 Oxygen sensor wiring connector (arrowed)

12.22a Unscrew the mounting bolts …

12.22b … and nuts …

12.22c … and withdraw the exhaust manifold from the cylinder head

12.22d Recover the gasket from the studs on the cylinder head

22 Undo the exhaust manifold mounting nuts and bolts (seven in total), then slide the manifold off the cylinder head studs and lower it down to remove it. Take care not to damage the sensors or their wiring. Recover the gasket and discard it **(see illustrations)**.

Models from August 2009

23 Disconnect the battery negative terminal (refer to *'Disconnecting the battery'*).
24 Disconnect the oxygen sensor at the wiring connector behind the ignition coil **(see illustration 12.14)**.
25 Undo the four bolts and remove the exhaust manifold upper heat shield.
26 Undo the bolt and four nuts securing the exhaust manifold to the cylinder head.
27 Firmly apply the handbrake, then jack up the front of the vehicle and support it securely on axle stands (see *'Jacking and vehicle support'*).
28 Remove the right-hand driveshaft and intermediate shaft as described in Chapter 8 Section 2.

29 Undo the three bolts and remove the intermediate shaft support bearing mounting bracket from the cylinder block.
30 Disconnect the catalyst monitor sensor at the wiring connector on the transmission.
31 Undo the four bolts and remove the catalytic converter lower support bracket.
32 To prevent damage to the exhaust flexible section, support it by attaching a pair of splints either side (two scrap strips of wood, plant canes, etc) using some cable-ties.
33 Unscrew the two nuts securing the exhaust flexible section to the catalytic converter. Unhook the rubber mounting block and separate the joint. Recover the gasket.
34 Slide the manifold off the cylinder head studs and lower it down to remove it. Take care not to damage the sensors or their wiring. Recover the gasket and discard it

All models

35 Refitting is a reversal of removal, noting the following points:
a) Ensure that the mating faces are clean,

and use a new manifold gasket.
b) Tighten all fixings to the specified torque.
c) Refit the right-hand driveshaft and intermediate shaft as described in Chapter 8 Section 2.

13 Exhaust system – general information, removal and refitting

Caution: Any work on the exhaust system should only be attempted once the system is completely cool – this may take several hours, especially in the case of the forward sections, such as the manifold and catalytic converter.

General information

1 The exhaust system consists of the exhaust manifold with integral catalytic converter, and the centre section incorporating the silencer. On 1.6 litre engine models, the centre section incorporates an additional silencer at the

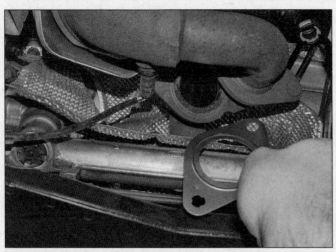

13.8 Separate the centre section from the catalytic converter, and recover the gasket

13.9 Unhook the rubber mountings and remove the centre section

front. A flexible ('mesh') section is fitted to allow for engine movement. On models up to August 2009, the flexible section is located in the centre section, downstream of the centre section-to-catalytic converter flange joint. On models from August 2009, the flexible section is located just after the catalytic converter, upstream of the centre section-to-catalytic converter flange joint.

2 When fitted in the factory, the exhaust system from the centre section flange joint to the end of the tail pipe is one piece. However, if the rear silencer is to be renewed, new silencers should be available – check with your parts supplier. It will be necessary to cut through the centre section using a hacksaw if a new rear silencer is to be fitted.

3 The system is suspended throughout its entire length by rubber mountings.

Removal

4 To remove a part of the system, first jack up the front or rear of the car, and support it on axle stands (see 'Jacking and vehicle support'). Alternatively, position the car over an inspection pit, or on car ramps.

Manifold and catalytic converter

5 Refer to Section 12.

Centre section

6 To prevent damage to the exhaust flexible section, support it by attaching a pair of splints either side (two scrap strips of wood, plant canes, etc) using some cable-ties. If a new centre section is being fitted, this precaution only applies to the new section of exhaust.

7 From under the car, undo the nuts and

remove the underfloor cross-brace beneath the exhaust centre section.

8 Unscrew the nuts securing the centre section to the catalytic converter, and separate the joint. Recover the gasket **(see illustration)**.

9 Unhook the centre section's rubber mountings, and remove it from under the car **(see illustrations)**.

Rear silencer

10 If the original one-piece exhaust system is still fitted, it will be necessary to cut off the old rear silencer to enable fitment of the new unit. Using the new rear silencer as a pattern, mark the exhaust centre section to determine the cut point. Ensure that the cut point will allow a sufficient length of centre section to fit into the new rear silencer.

11 Using a hacksaw, cut through the centre section at the marked cut point. Unhook the rear silencer's rubber mountings, and remove it from under the car.

12 If a replacement rear silencer has already been fitted, unbolt the clamp securing the silencer to the centre section, and separate the pipes. Usually, this will require some effort – the most successful method involves twisting the silencer from side to side, to break the joint. Unfortunately, if the pipe at the rear of the centre section has suffered from corrosion, it's very likely that the centre section will be damaged beyond repair in removing the silencer. A less-destructive method of removal involves heating the two pipes, but this carries the risk of damaging the underbody components, and even a risk of fire from the fuel tank and lines.

13 Unhook the silencer rubber mountings, and remove it from under the car.

Heat shields

14 The heat shields are secured to the underside of the body by special nuts. Each shield can be removed separately, but note that they may overlap, making it necessary to loosen another section first. If a shield is being removed to gain access to a component located behind it, it may prove sufficient in some cases to remove the retaining nuts and/or bolts, and simply lower the shield, without disturbing the exhaust system. Otherwise, remove the exhaust section as described earlier.

Refitting

15 In all cases, refitting is a reversal of removal, but note the following points:
a) *Always use new gaskets, nuts and clamps (as applicable), and coat all threads with copper grease. Make sure any new clamps are the same size as the original – over-tightening a clamp which is too big will not seal the joint.*
b) *On a sleeved joint (such as that between the centre section and rear silencer), use a smear of exhaust jointing paste to achieve a gas-tight seal.*
c) *If any of the exhaust mounting rubbers are in poor condition, fit new ones.*
d) *Make sure that the exhaust is suspended properly on its mountings, and will not come into contact with the floor or any suspension parts. The rear silencer especially must be aligned correctly before tightening the clamp nuts.*
e) *Tighten all nuts/bolts to the specified torque, where given.*

Notes

Chapter 4 Part B
Fuel and exhaust systems – diesel models

Contents

Degrees of difficulty

Easy, suitable for novice with little experience **Fairly easy,** suitable for beginner with some experience **Fairly difficult,** suitable for competent DIY mechanic **Difficult,** suitable for experienced DIY mechanic **Very difficult,** suitable for expert DIY or professional

Specifications

General
System type . . . . TDCi (Turbo-Diesel Common-rail injection) with full electronic control, direct injection and turbocharger. Intercooler on 1.6 litre engines
Firing order . . . . 1-3-4-2 (No 1 at flywheel end)
Fuel system operating pressure . . . . 200 to 1350 bars (according to engine speed)
Idle speed:
   1.4 litre engine . . . . 800 ± 20 rpm (controlled by PCM)
   1.6 litre engine . . . . 750 rpm (controlled by PCM)
Engine cut-off speed . . . . 5000 rpm (controlled by PCM)

High-pressure fuel pump
Type . . . . Bosch
Direction of rotation . . . . Clockwise, viewed from sprocket end

Injectors
Type . . . . Electromagnetic

Turbocharger
Type . . . . KKK
Boost pressure (approximate) . . . . 1 bar at 3000 rpm

Torque wrench settings

	Nm	lbf ft
Accumulator rail mounting bolts/nuts	22	16
Accumulator rail/injector fuel pipe unions: *		
Stage 1	20	15
Stage 2	25	18
Camshaft position sensor bolt	5	4
Catalytic converter lower mounting bolts	25	18
Catalytic converter-to-turbocharger bolts		
(1.4 litre engines (Stage IV emissions)	25	18
Catalytic converter-to-turbocharger clamp bolt nut		
(all other diesel engines)	15	11
Exhaust centre section flange joint	48	35
Exhaust manifold nuts:		
1.4 litre engines (Stage IV emissions)	25	18
All other engines	30	22
Fuel injector:		
1.4 litre engines (Stage IV emissions):		
Injector clamp retaining bolts: †		
Stage 1	15	11
Stage 2	Angle-tighten a further 70°	
1.6 litre DOHC 16-valve engines:		
Injector clamp retaining nuts: †		
Stage 1	4	3
Stage 2	Angle-tighten a further 75°	
1.6 litre SOHC 8-valve engines, and 1.4 litre (Stage V emissions) engines:		
Stage 1	7	5
Stage 2	Angle-tighten a further 85°	
High-pressure fuel pump:		
Front mounting bolts	22	16
Rear mounting bolts:		
M6	8	6
M8	20	15
Turbocharger mounting bolts/nuts†	25	18
Turbocharger oil feed pipe banjo bolts	30	22

*These torque settings are using special crow's-foot adapter – see Section 2
† Do not re-use

1 General information and system operation

1 The fuel system consists of a rear-mounted fuel tank, a fuel filter with integral water separator and fuel heater (to avoid fuel waxing in cold conditions), and an electronically-controlled high-pressure diesel injection system, together with a turbocharger.

2 The exhaust system is conventional, but to meet the latest emission levels, an unregulated catalytic converter and an exhaust gas recirculation system are fitted to all models. On certain 1.6 litre engines and 1.4 litre (Stage V emissions) engines, the catalytic converter incorporates a diesel particulate filter.

3 The high-pressure diesel injection system (generally known as a 'common-rail' system) derives its name from the fact that a common-rail (referred to as an accumulator rail), or fuel reservoir, is used to supply fuel to all the fuel injectors. Instead of an in-line or distributor type injection pump, which distributes the fuel directly to each injector, a high-pressure pump is used, which generates a very high fuel pressure (1500 bars at high engine speed) in the accumulator rail. The accumulator rail stores fuel, and maintains a constant fuel pressure with the aid of a pressure control valve. Each injector is supplied with high-pressure fuel from the accumulator rail, and the injectors are individually controlled via signals from the system electronic control unit (Powertrain Control Module, or PCM). The injectors are electromagnetically-operated.

4 In addition to the various sensors used on previous diesel engines with a conventional fuel injection pump, common-rail systems also have a fuel pressure sensor. The fuel pressure sensor allows the PCM to maintain the required fuel pressure, via the pressure control valve.

System operation

5 For the purposes of describing the operation of a common-rail injection system, the components can be divided into three sub-systems; the low-pressure fuel system, the high-pressure fuel system, and the electronic control system.

Low-pressure fuel system

6 The low-pressure fuel system consists of the following components:
a) Fuel tank.
b) Fuel transfer pump.
c) Fuel filter/water trap/heater.
d) Low-pressure fuel lines.

7 The low-pressure system (fuel supply system) is responsible for supplying clean fuel to the high-pressure fuel system.

High-pressure fuel system

8 The high-pressure fuel system consists of the following components:
a) High-pressure fuel pump with pressure control valve.
b) High-pressure fuel accumulator rail.
c) Fuel injectors.
d) High-pressure fuel lines.

9 Fuel is drawn from the fuel tank, through the fuel filter, by means of a fuel transfer pump incorporated into the high-pressure pump. After passing through the transfer pump, the fuel is supplied through internal passages to the high-pressure pump, which forces it into the accumulator rail. As diesel fuel has a certain elasticity, the pressure in the accumulator rail remains constant, even though fuel leaves the rail each time one of the injectors operates. Additionally, a pressure control valve mounted on the high-pressure pump ensures that the fuel pressure is maintained within preset limits.

10 The pressure control valve is operated by the PCM. When the valve is opened, fuel is returned from the high-pressure pump to the tank, via the fuel return lines, and the pressure in the accumulator rail falls. To enable the PCM to trigger the pressure control valve correctly, the pressure in the accumulator rail is measured by a fuel pressure sensor.

11 The electromagnetically-controlled fuel injectors are operated individually, via signals from the PCM, and each injector injects fuel directly into the relevant combustion chamber. The fact that high fuel pressure is always available allows very precise and highly flexible injection in comparison to a conventional injection pump: for example combustion during the main injection process can be improved considerably by the pre-injection of a very small quantity of fuel.

Electronic control system

12 The electronic control system consists of the following components:

a) *Electronic control unit (PCM).*
b) *Crankshaft speed/position sensor.*
c) *Camshaft position sensor.*
d) *Accelerator pedal position sensor.*
e) *Coolant temperature sensor.*
f) *Fuel temperature sensor.*
g) *Airflow sensor.*
h) *Fuel pressure sensor.*
i) *Fuel injectors.*
j) *Fuel pressure control valve.*
k) *EGR solenoid valve.*
l) *Vehicle speed sensor (or ABS wheel sensors).*
m) *Intake air shutoff throttle housing*
n) *Inlet manifold absolute pressure sensor*
o) *Brake and clutch pedal position switches*

13 The information from the various sensors is passed to the PCM, which evaluates the signals. The PCM contains electronic 'maps' which enable it to calculate the optimum quantity of fuel to inject, the appropriate start of injection, and even pre- and post-injection fuel quantities, for each individual engine cylinder under any given condition of engine operation.

14 Additionally, the PCM carries out monitoring and self-diagnostic functions. Any faults in the system are stored in the PCM memory, which enables quick and accurate fault diagnosis using appropriate diagnostic equipment (such as a suitable fault code reader).

System components

High-pressure pump

15 The high-pressure pump is mounted on the engine in the position normally occupied by the conventional distributor fuel injection pump. The pump is driven at half engine speed by the timing belt, and is lubricated by the fuel which it pumps.

16 The fuel transfer pump (integral with the high-pressure pump) forces the fuel into the high-pressure pump chamber, via a safety valve.

17 The high-pressure pump consists of three radially-mounted pistons and cylinders. The pistons are operated by an eccentric cam mounted on the pump drive spindle. As a piston moves down, fuel enters the cylinder through an inlet valve. When the piston reaches bottom dead centre (BDC), the inlet valve closes, and as the piston moves back up the cylinder, the fuel is compressed. When the pressure in the cylinder matches the pressure in the accumulator rail, an outlet valve opens, and fuel is forced into the accumulator rail. When the piston reaches top dead centre (TDC), the outlet valve closes, due to the pressure drop, and the pumping cycle is repeated. The use of multiple cylinders provides a steady flow of fuel, minimising pulses and pressure fluctuations.

18 As the pump needs to be able to supply sufficient fuel under full-load conditions, it will supply excess fuel during idle and part-load conditions. This excess fuel is returned from the high-pressure circuit to the low-pressure circuit (to the tank) via the pressure control valve.

19 The pump incorporates a facility to effectively switch off one of the cylinders to improve efficiency and reduce fuel consumption when maximum pumping capacity is not required. When this facility is operated, a solenoid-operated needle holds the inlet valve in the relevant cylinder open during the delivery stroke, preventing the fuel from being compressed.

Accumulator rail

20 As its name suggests, the accumulator rail acts as an accumulator, storing fuel and preventing pressure fluctuations. Fuel enters the rail from the high-pressure pump, and each injector has its own connection to the rail. The fuel pressure sensor is mounted in the rail, and the rail also has a connection to the fuel pressure control valve on the pump.

Pressure control valve

21 The pressure control valve is operated by the PCM, and controls the system pressure. The valve is integral with the high-pressure pump and cannot be separated.

22 If the fuel pressure is excessive, the valve opens, and fuel flows back to the tank. If the pressure is too low, the valve closes, enabling the high-pressure pump to increase the pressure.

23 The valve is an electromagnetically-operated ball valve. The ball is forced against its seat, against the fuel pressure, by a powerful spring, and also by the force provided by the electromagnet. The force generated by the electromagnet is directly proportional to the current applied to it by the PCM. The desired pressure can therefore be set by varying the current applied to the electromagnet. Any pressure fluctuations are damped by the spring.

Fuel pressure sensor

24 The fuel pressure sensor is mounted in the accumulator rail, and provides very precise information on the fuel pressure to the PCM.

Fuel injector

25 The injectors are mounted on the engine in a similar manner to conventional diesel fuel injectors. The injectors are electro-magnetically-operated via signals from the PCM, and fuel is injected at the pressure existing in the accumulator rail. The injectors are high-precision instruments and are manufactured to very high tolerances.

26 Fuel flows into the injector from the accumulator rail, via an inlet valve and an inlet throttle, and an electromagnet causes the injector nozzle to lift from its seat, allowing injection. Excess fuel is returned from the injectors to the tank via a return line. The injector operates on a hydraulic servo principle: the forces resulting inside the injector due to the fuel pressure effectively amplify the effects of the electromagnet, which does not provide sufficient force to open the injector nozzle directly. The injector functions as follows. Five separate forces are essential to the operation of the injector:

a) *A nozzle spring forces the nozzle needle against the nozzle seat at the bottom of the injector, preventing fuel from entering the combustion chamber.*
b) *In the valve at the top of the injector, the valve spring forces the valve ball against the opening to the valve control chamber. The fuel in the chamber is unable to escape through the fuel return.*
c) *When triggered, the electromagnet exerts a force which overcomes the valve spring force, and moves the valve ball away from its seat. This is the triggering force for the start of injection. When the valve ball moves off its seat, fuel enters the valve control chamber.*
d) *The pressure of the fuel in the valve control chamber exerts a force on the valve control plunger, which is added to the nozzle spring force.*
e) *A slight chamfer towards the lower end of the nozzle needle causes the fuel in the control chamber to exert a force on the nozzle needle.*

27 When these forces are in equilibrium, the injector is in its rest (idle) state, but when a voltage is applied to the electromagnet, the forces work to lift the nozzle needle, injecting fuel into the combustion chamber. There are four phases of injector operation as follows:

a) *Rest (idle) state – all forces are in equilibrium. The nozzle needle closes off the nozzle opening, and the valve spring forces the valve ball against its seat.*
b) *Opening – the electromagnet is triggered which opens the nozzle and triggers the injection process. The force from the electromagnet allows the valve ball to leave its seat. The fuel from the valve control chamber flows back to the tank via the fuel return line. When the valve opens, the pressure in the valve control chamber drops, and the force on the valve plunger is reduced. However, due to the*

effect of the input throttle, the pressure on the nozzle needle remains unchanged. The resulting force in the valve control chamber is sufficient to lift the nozzle from its seat, and the injection process begins.

c) *Injection – within a few milliseconds, the triggering current in the electromagnet is reduced to a lower holding current. The nozzle is now fully open, and fuel is injected into the combustion chamber at the pressure present in the accumulator rail.*

d) *Closing – the electromagnet is switched off, at which point the valve spring forces the valve ball firmly against its seat, and in the valve control chamber, the pressure is the same as that at the nozzle needle. The force at the valve plunger increases, and the nozzle needle closes the nozzle opening. The forces are now in equilibrium once more, and the injector is once more in the idle state, awaiting the next injection sequence.*

PCM and sensors

28 The PCM and sensors are described earlier in this Section – see Electronic control system.

Air inlet sensor and turbocharger

29 An airflow sensor is fitted downstream of the air filter to monitor the quantity of air supplied to the turbocharger. The turbocharger itself is a variable-nozzle geometry type.

Intake air shutoff throttle housing

30 The intake air shutoff throttle housing controls the volume of air drawn into the engine according to driving conditions, and thus influences the composition of the recirculated exhaust gases. It is activated by the PCM. In addition, the unit ensures that the engine does not run-on after switching off the ignition.

2 High-pressure diesel injection system – special information

Warnings and precautions

1 It is essential to observe strict precautions when working on the fuel system components, particularly the high-pressure side of the system. Before carrying out any operations on the fuel system, refer to the precautions given in Safety first0,2 ! at the beginning of this manual, and to the following additional information.

• Do not carry out any repair work on the high-pressure fuel system unless you are competent to do so, have all the necessary tools and equipment required, and are aware of the safety implications involved.

• Before starting any repair work on the fuel system, wait at least 30 seconds after switching off the engine to allow the fuel circuit pressure to reduce.

• Never work on the high-pressure fuel system with the engine running.

• Keep well clear of any possible source of fuel leakage, particularly when starting the engine after carrying out repair work. A leak in the system could cause an extremely high-pressure jet of fuel to escape, which could result in severe personal injury.

• Never place your hands or any part of your body near to a leak in the high-pressure fuel system.

• Do not use steam-cleaning equipment or compressed air to clean the engine or any of the fuel system components.

Procedures and information

2 Strict cleanliness must be observed at all times when working on any part of the fuel system. This applies to the working area in general, the person doing the work, and the components being worked on.

3 Before working on the fuel system components, they must be thoroughly cleaned with a suitable degreasing fluid. Specific cleaning products may be obtained from dealers. Alternatively, a suitable brake cleaning fluid may be used. Cleanliness is particularly important when working on the fuel system connections at the following components:

a) Fuel filter.
b) High-pressure fuel pump.
c) Accumulator rail.
d) Fuel injectors.
e) High-pressure fuel pipes.

4 After disconnecting any fuel pipes or components, the open union or orifice must be immediately sealed to prevent the entry of dirt or foreign material. Plastic plugs and caps in various sizes are available in packs from motor factors and accessory outlets, and are particularly suitable for this application (see illustration). Fingers cut from disposable rubber gloves should be used to protect components such as fuel pipes, fuel injectors and wiring connectors, and can be secured in place using elastic bands. Suitable gloves of this type are available at no cost from most filling station forecourts.

5 Whenever any of the high-pressure fuel pipes are disconnected or removed, new pipes must be obtained for refitting.

6 On the completion of any repair on the high-pressure fuel system, the use of a leak-detecting compound is recommended. This is a powder which is applied to the fuel pipe unions and connections, which is white when dry. Any leak in the system will cause the product to darken, indicating the source of the leak.

7 The torque wrench settings given in the Specifications must be strictly observed when tightening component mountings and connections. This is particularly important when tightening the high-pressure fuel pipe unions. To use a torque wrench on the fuel pipe unions, two crow's-foot adapters are required – these are available from motor factors and accessory outlets (see illustration).

3 Fuel system – priming and bleeding

1 After disconnecting any part of the fuel system or running out of fuel, it is necessary to prime the fuel system and bleed off any air which may have entered the system components.

2 In many circumstances, the system will self-bleed by operating the starter for a maximum of 30 seconds. If the engine does not start within this time, wait 5 seconds and repeat the procedure. If, after a reasonable number of attempts, the engine still will not start, proceed as follows.

3 It will be necessary to obtain the special Ford priming hose (kit No.310-110) or a suitable alternative with a hand-priming function, and temporarily connect it into the fuel supply line to the fuel filter (see illustration).

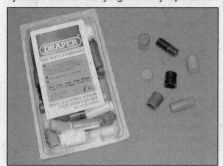

2.4 Typical plastic plug and cap set for sealing disconnected fuel pipes and components

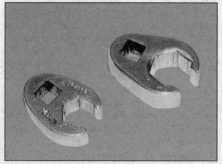

2.7 Two crow's-foot adapters will be necessary for tightening the fuel pipe unions

3.3 Using a hand priming kit to assist with fuel system bleeding

4.3 Disconnect the airflow sensor wiring plug

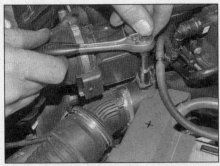

4.4 Remove the air inlet duct bolt near the battery

4.5 Slacken the hose clip and disconnect the turbo outlet duct

4.6 Prise off the breather pipe from the oil separator

4.7a Unscrew the two mounting screws …

4.7b … then lift the air cleaner off the engine, detaching the wiring harness and duct at the rear

4 On some models, a clear plastic fuel pipe is fitted in the fuel return line in the engine compartment, and the pump should be operated until fuel appears in the pipe – on other models, operate the pump until the fuel reaches the pump. Continue to squeeze the pump until it becomes firm, then squeeze and hold the pump for a further 10 seconds. Release the pump, then squeeze and hold it a further 10 seconds.

5 Where applicable, disconnect the temporary hand priming pump, and reconnect the supply pipe to the fuel filter.

6 Operate the starter until the engine starts.

---

4   Air cleaner assembly –
     removal and refitting

---

*1.4 litre engines
(Stage IV emissions)*

Air cleaner

1 Remove the windscreen cowl panel and bulk-head closure panel as described in Chapter 11 Section 20.

2 Disconnect the wiring connector from the manifold absolute pressure sensor, then release the wiring and hoses from the right-hand side of the air cleaner.

3 Unplug the wiring connector from the airflow sensor **(see illustration)**.

4 Undo the air inlet duct retaining bolt near

the battery, and unclip the upper pipe from the lower one **(see illustration)**.

5 Loosen the retaining clip at the base of the inlet air duct where it joins the turbocharger, and prise the duct off **(see illustration)**.

6 Prise off the breather pipe from the connection on the oil separator **(see illustration)**.

7 Undo the two air cleaner mounting screws at the rear, and the two screws at the front (not to be confused with the three screws securing the air filter lid), then pull up the air cleaner at the rear to release its mounting pegs. As the air cleaner is lifted, detach the wiring harness and the air inlet duct at the rear **(see illustrations)**.

8 To remove the air inlet ducting, release the retaining clips and remove the relevant section of ducting.

9 Refitting is a reversal of removal.

Intake air resonator

10 Slacken the retaining clip and disconnect the turbocharger outlet hose from the outlet flange adjacent to the oil filler cap.

11 Disconnect the wiring connector, then undo the retaining bolts, lift up the right- hand end and remove the resonator **(see illustrations)**. Recover the O-ring seal.

12 Refitting is a reversal of removal. Fit a new O-ring seal to the turbocharger end of the resonator if the old one is in poor condition.

4.11a Undo the retaining bolts (arrowed) …

4.11b … then pivot the right-hand end of the resonator up and disengage it from the turbocharger outlet stud

4.13 Disengage the retaining clip tabs and disconnect the crankcase ventilation hose

4.14 Slacken the clip and disconnect the air outlet duct from the turbocharger

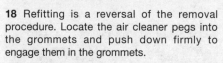

4.15a Detach the small-bore hose located in the air cleaner cover ...

1.4 litre (Stage V emissions) and 1.6 litre engines

Air cleaner

DOHC models

13 Disengage the retaining clip tabs and disconnect the crankcase ventilation hose from the oil separator **(see illustration)**.

14 Slacken the retaining clip and disconnect the air outlet duct from the turbocharger **(see illustration)**.

15 Detach the small-bore hose located in the outlet from the air cleaner cover, then disconnect the airflow sensor wiring plug **(see illustrations)**.

16 Depress the retaining tab and detach the air inlet duct from the front body panel **(see illustration)**.

17 Pull the air cleaner upwards to disengage the rubber mountings **(see illustration)**.

18 Refitting is a reversal of the removal procedure. Locate the air cleaner pegs into the grommets and push down firmly to engage them in the grommets.

SOHC models

19 Pull up the front edge, and remove the plastic cover from the top of the engine.

20 Slacken the clamp and disconnect the inlet ducting from the turbocharger **(see illustration)**.

21 Disconnect the wiring plug from the airflow sensor.

22 Pull the small bore rubber hose from the air cleaner cover.

23 Remove the bolt at the right-hand front corner securing the wiring plug bracket **(see illustration)**.

24 Release the clip and disconnect the air intake ducting at the bonnet slam panel **(see illustration)**.

4.15b ... then disconnect the airflow sensor wiring plug

25 Undo the retaining bolt at the front left-hand corner, then pull the air cleaner housing upwards from the rubber grommets **(see illustration)**.

26 Refitting is a reversal of removal.

4.16 Depress the retaining tab and detach the air inlet duct from the front body panel

4.17 Pull the air cleaner upwards to disengage the rubber mountings

4.20 Slacken the clamp and disconnect the ducting

4.23 Remove the bolt securing the bracket

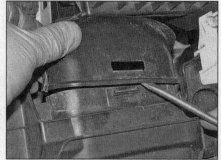

4.24 Disconnect the air intake ducting

4.25 Undo the Torx bolt at the front left-hand corner

Intake air resonator

27 Slacken the retaining clip and disconnect the intercooler hose from the resonator (see illustration).

28 Undo the bolt near the intercooler hose, and the bolt securing the resonator to the turbocharger flange. Pivot the resonator upwards and remove it from the engine. Recover the O-ring seal (see illustrations).

5 Accelerator pedal – removal and refitting

1 Refer to Chapter 4A Section 6.

6 Fuel tank – removal, inspection and refitting

1 Refer to the warnings and precautions in Section 2 before proceeding.
2 Refer to Chapter 4A Section 7. Fuel tank removal and refitting is the same as for petrol models, with the exception that an evaporative emissions charcoal canister is not fitted to diesel models. Note also that there is a fuel return line as well as a supply line on the top of the tank.

7 Fuel gauge sender unit – removal and refitting

Note: *Refer to the warnings in Section 2 before proceeding. Ford specify the use of their service tool 310-069 (a large socket with projecting teeth to engage the sender unit retaining ring's raised edges) for this task. Suitable alternatives to this tool are readily available from accessory stores and motor factor outlets.*

Removal

1 The fuel gauge sender unit is located in the top face of the fuel tank. The unit can only be detached and withdrawn from the tank after the tank is released and lowered from under the car. Refer to Section 6 and remove the fuel tank, then proceed as follows.

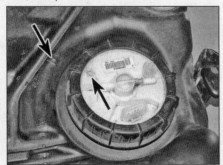

7.3 Alignment marks (arrowed) on the fuel gauge sender unit and fuel tank

4.27 Slacken the retaining clip and disconnect the intercooler hose from the resonator

4.28b ... pivot the resonator upwards and disengage it from the turbocharger outlet stud ...

2 Unscrew and remove the special retaining ring, by unscrewing it with the Ford tool or a suitable alternative.
3 Check that alignment marks are visible on the gauge sender unit and fuel tank. There should be an arrow on the sender unit aligned with three raised projections on the tank (see illustration). If no marks are visible, suitably mark the tank and sender unit with paint.
4 Carefully lift out the gauge sender unit housing from the tank. Take care that the sender unit float and arm are not damaged as the unit is removed.
5 Lift out the rubber seal and obtain a new seal for refitting.
6 If required, the fuel gauge sender unit can be removed from the housing by disconnecting the wiring connector, releasing the retaining catch and withdrawing the unit from the side of the housing.

Refitting

7 Refitting is a reversal of removal, but fit a new rubber seal and tighten the retaining ring securely. Refit the fuel tank as described in Section 6.

8 Fuel tank filler neck – removal and refitting

Note: *Refer to the warnings and precautions in Section 2 before proceeding.*
1 Refer to Chapter 4A Section 9.

4.28a Undo the resonator retaining bolts ...

4.28c ... then recover the O-ring seal

9 High-pressure fuel pump – removal and refitting

⚠ **Warning: Refer to the information contained in Section 2 before proceeding.**
Note: *A new fuel pump-to-accumulator rail high-pressure fuel pipe will be required for refitting.*

Removal

1 Disconnect the battery negative terminal (refer to 'Disconnecting the battery').
2 Remove the windscreen cowl panel and bulkhead closure panel as described in Chapter 11 Section 20.
3 Remove the timing belt as described in Chapter 2B Section 7, Chapter 2C Section 7, Chapter 2D Section 7 or Chapter 2E Section 7. After removing the timing belt, temporarily refit the right-hand engine mounting.
4 Remove the fuel pump sprocket as described in Chapter 2B Section 8, Chapter 2C Section 8, Chapter 2D Section 8 or Chapter 2E Section 7.

1.4 litre engines (Stage IV emissions)

5 Remove the air cleaner as described in Section 4.
6 Remove the two screws securing the EGR pipe elbow to the inlet manifold.
7 Disengage and release the retaining clamp securing the EGR cooler to the EGR valve

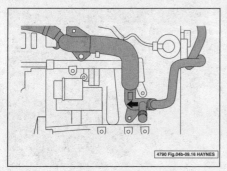

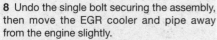

9.16 Remove the coolant pipe assembly to access the pump

9.17 Counterhold the pump union with a second spanner whilst slackening the accumulator-to-pump pipe union

9.18 High-pressure fuel pump front mounting bolts (arrowed)

8 Undo the single bolt securing the assembly, then move the EGR cooler and pipe away from the engine slightly.

9 Depress the quick-release connector buttons and disconnect the fuel supply and return hoses from the pump. Plug the end of the hoses to prevent dirt ingress.

10 Disconnect the wiring plugs from the fuel flow and pressure control valves, noting their locations for refitting. Detach the wiring loom as necessary.

11 Remove the two bolts securing the fuel pump support bracket, and remove the bracket from the engine.

1.4 litre (Stage V emissions) and 1.6 litre engines

12 Disconnect the wiring plugs from the fuel flow and pressure control valves, noting their locations for refitting. Detach the wiring loom as necessary.

13 Undo the three bolts and one nut securing the wiring loom support bracket to the top of the pump. Release the loom from the cable clips and remove the support bracket. Undo the bolt securing the lower rear support bracket to the pump.

14 Depress the quick-release connector buttons and disconnect the fuel supply and return hoses from the pump. Plug the end of the hoses to prevent dirt ingress.

15 On DOHC 16-valve engines, remove the EGR valve tube as described in Chapter 4C Section 3.

16 On SOHC 8-valve engines, partially drain the cooling system (Chapter 1B Section 30), then undo the bolts, release the hoses and remove the coolant pipe assembly from the rear of the engine **(see illustration)**.

All engines

17 Clean carefully around the unions at either end of the pump-to-accumulator rail metal pipe – it is very important that no dirt enters the system. Counterhold the pump union with a second spanner – the union screwed into the pump must not be allowed to unscrew **(see illustration)**. Keep the pipe in place until both unions have been fully loosened, and the pipe can be removed – this reduces the

chance of dirt getting in. Plug the open ends on the pump and accumulator rail – this is most important. Discard the pipe – a new one must be fitted.

18 Support the pump, then undo the three front mounting bolts, and remove the pump from its mounting bracket **(see illustration)**.

Caution: The high-pressure fuel pump is manufactured to extremely close tolerances, and must not be dismantled in any way. Do not unscrew the fuel pipe male union on the rear of the pump, or attempt to remove the sensor, piston de-activator switch, or the seal on the pump shaft. No parts for the pump are available separately, and if the unit is in any way suspect, it must be renewed.

Refitting

19 Locate the pump in the mounting bracket, and refit the three mounting bolts, hand-tight. Refit the pump rear support bracket, tightening the bolts to the specified torque, then tighten the three pump mounting bolts to the specified torque.

20 Fit a new metal fuel pipe between the pump and the accumulator rail. The unions at each end of the pipe must be tightened to the specified torque in two stages. Use a second spanner to counterhold the union screwed into the pump. Do not allow the union to move.

21 The remainder of refitting is a reversal of removal.

22 With everything reassembled and reconnected, prime the fuel system as described in Section 3. Observing the precautions listed in Section 2, start the engine and allow it to idle. Check for leaks at the high-pressure fuel pipe unions with the engine idling. If satisfactory, increase the engine speed to 4000 rpm and check again for leaks.

23 Take the car for a short road test, and check for leaks once again on return. If any leaks are detected, obtain and fit another new high-pressure fuel pipe. Do not attempt to cure even the slightest leak by further tightening of the pipe unions.

10 Accumulator rail – removal and refitting

⚠️ *Warning: Refer to the information contained in Section 2 before proceeding.*

Note: *A complete new set of high-pressure fuel pipes will be required for refitting.*

Removal

1 Disconnect the battery negative terminal (refer to 'Disconnecting the battery').

2 Remove the windscreen cowl panel and bulkhead closure panel as described in Chapter 11 Section 20.

1.4 litre engines (Stage IV emissions)

3 Remove the EGR cooler as described in Chapter 4C Section 3.

4 Remove the cylinder head cover as described in Chapter 2B Section 4.

5 Noting how it is routed, disconnect the glow plug wiring and move it to one side.

1.4 litre (Stage V emissions) and 1.6 litre engines

6 Remove the EGR valve tube as described in Chapter 4C Section 3.

DOHC 16-valve engines

7 Undo the two bolts securing the injector wiring harness trough to the top of the inlet manifold **(see illustration)**.

8 Disconnect the wiring connector from

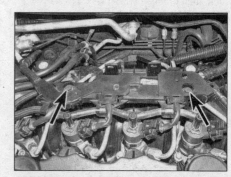

10.7 Undo the bolts (arrowed) securing the wiring harness trough to the inlet manifold

the top of each injector, then lift off the wiring trough and move it to one side **(see illustrations)**. Make sure the wiring harness is freed from any clips/brackets on the cylinder head cover/inlet manifold

9 Release the fuel hoses from the support bracket at the right-hand side of the cylinder head cover/inlet manifold.

10 Using a screwdriver, push in the retaining spring clip and disconnect the fuel return hose from the top of each injector. Plug the openings to prevent dirt ingress then move the return hose assembly to one side **(see illustrations)**.

11 Disconnect the wiring connector from each glow plug. Noting how it is routed, release the glow plug wiring from the clips and brackets and move it to one side.

12 Release the clips and brackets as necessary, and move the fuel hoses clear of the accumulator rail.

SOHC 8-valve engines

13 Remove the air cleaner as described in Section 4.

14 Slacken the clamps, undo the retaining bolts/nuts and remove the air intake ducting assembly from the top of the engine.

15 Remove the fuel filter as described in Chapter 1B Section 22.

16 Remove the EGR valve assembly as described in Chapter 4C Section 3.

17 Undo the bolts/nut and remove the throttle body/duct assembly from the intake manifold.

All engines

18 Clean the area around the high-pressure fuel pipes to and from the accumulator rail, then unscrew the pump-to-accumulator rail pipe unions. Use a second spanner to counterhold the union screwed in to the pump body as described in Section 9. The screwed-in union must not be allowed to move. Remove the pipe.

19 Repeat the procedure on the accumulator rail-to-injector fuel pipes. Use a second spanner to counterhold the unions screwed into the injectors **(see illustration)** – these unions must not be allowed to move. Note their fitted locations and remove the pipes.

10.8a Disconnect the wiring connector from each injector ...

10.8b ... then lift off the wiring trough and move it to one side

10.10a Push in the retaining spring clip and disconnect the fuel return hose from the top of each injector ...

10.10b ... then move the return hose assembly to one side

20 Plug the openings in the accumulator rail and fuel pump to prevent dirt ingress.

21 Disconnect the pressure sensor wiring plug from the accumulator rail **(see illustration)**.

22 Unscrew the two accumulator rail mounting bolts/nuts, and manoeuvre it out **(see illustration)**. **Note:** *The fuel pressure sensor on the accumulator rail must not be removed.*

Refitting

23 Locate the accumulator rail in position, refit and finger-tighten the mounting bolts.

24 Reconnect the accumulator pressure sensor wiring plug.

25 Fit the new pump-to-rail high-pressure pipe, and only finger-tighten the unions at

first, then tighten the unions to the Stage 1 torque setting, followed by the Stage 2 torque setting. Use a second spanner to counterhold the union screwed into the pump body.

26 Fit the new set of rail-to-injector high-pressure pipes, and finger-tighten the unions.

27 Tighten the accumulator mounting bolts to the specified torque.

28 Tighten the rail-to-injector pipe unions to the Stage 1 torque setting, followed by the Stage 2 setting. Use a second spanner to counterhold the injector unions.

29 The remainder of refitting is a reversal of removal, noting the following points:
a) *Ensure all wiring connectors and harnesses are correctly refitting and secured.*
b) *Prime and bleed the fuel system as described in Section 3.*

10.19 Use a second spanner to counterhold the fuel injector unions whilst slackening the pipe unions

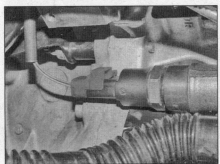
10.21 Disconnect the accumulator rail pressure sensor wiring plug

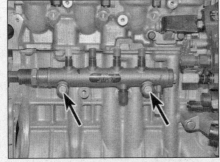
10.22 Remove the accumulator rail mounting bolts (arrowed)

c) *Observing the precautions listed in Section 2, start the engine and allow it to idle. Check for leaks at the high-pressure fuel pipe unions with the engine idling. If satisfactory, increase the engine speed to 4000 rpm and check again for leaks. Take the car for a short road test, and check for leaks once again on return. If any leaks are detected, obtain and fit additional new high-pressure fuel pipes as required. Do not attempt to cure even the slightest leak by further tightening of the pipe unions. During the road test, initialise the engine management PCM as follows – engage third gear and stabilise the engine at 1000 rpm, then accelerate fully up to 3500 rpm.*

11 Fuel injectors – removal and refitting

⚠ **Warning: Refer to the information contained in Section 2 before proceeding.**

Note: *The following procedure describes the removal and refitting of the injectors as a complete set. However, each injector may be removed individually if required. New copper washers, upper seals, injector clamp retaining nuts/bolts and a high-pressure fuel pipe will be required for each disturbed injector when refitting.*

1.4 litre engine (Stage IV emissions)

Removal

1 Remove the EGR cooler as described in Chapter 4C Section 3.
2 Remove the cylinder head cover as described in Chapter 2B Section 4.
3 Noting how it is routed, disconnect the glow plug wiring and move it to one side.
4 Clean the area around the high-pressure fuel pipes between the injectors and the accumulator rail, then unscrew the pipe unions. Use a second spanner to counterhold the union screwed in to the injector body **(see illustration 10.19)**. The injectors' screwed-in

unions must not be allowed to move. Remove the pipes. Plug the openings in the accumulator rail and injectors to prevent dirt ingress.
5 Thoroughly clean the fuel return pipe connections on each injector. Prise out the retaining clips and disconnect the fuel return pipes from the injectors **(see illustration)**. Plug the openings to prevent dirt ingress.
6 Unscrew the injector retaining bolt, and remove the clamp. If loose, recover the clamp's locating dowel from the cylinder head **(see illustrations)**.
7 Carefully pull or lever the injector out. Do not lever against or pull on the solenoid housing at the top of the injector.
8 Remove the copper washer and the upper seal from each injector, or from the cylinder head if they stayed in place **(see illustration)**. New copper washers and upper seals will be

required for refitting. Cover the injector hole in the cylinder head, to prevent dirt ingress.
9 Examine each injector visually for any signs of obvious damage or deterioration. If any defects are apparent, renew the injector(s).
Caution: The injectors are manufactured to extremely close tolerances, and must not be dismantled in any way. Do not unscrew the fuel pipe union on the side of the injector, or separate any parts of the injector body. Do not attempt to clean carbon deposits from the injector nozzle or carry out any form of ultrasonic or pressure testing.

Refitting

10 Locate a new upper seal on the body of each injector, and place a new copper washer on the injector nozzle **(see illustrations)**.

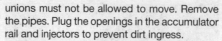
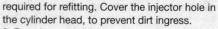

11.5 Prise out the circlip and disconnect the fuel return pipe

11.6a Undo the injector clamp bolt ...

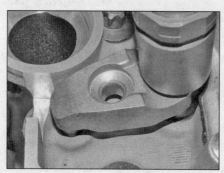

11.6b ... and remove the clamp

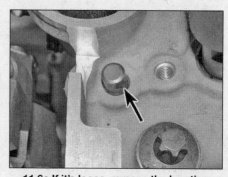

11.6c If it's loose, remove the locating dowel (arrowed)

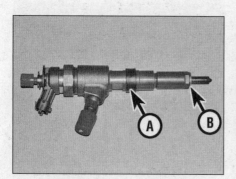

11.8 Fuel injector upper seal (A) and copper washer (B)

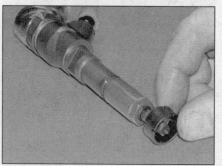

11.10a Locate a new upper seal on the body of each injector ...

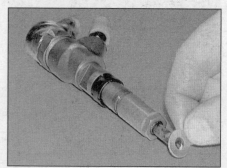

11.10b ... and place a new copper washer on the injector nozzle

11 Refit the injector clamp locating dowels to the cylinder head, if removed.

12 Place the injector clamp in the slot on each injector body, and refit the injectors to the cylinder head. Guide the clamp onto the locating dowel as each injector is inserted. Ensure the upper injector seals are correctly located in the cylinder head.

13 Fit the new injector clamp retaining bolts and tighten the bolts finger-tight only at this stage.

14 Working on one fuel injector at a time, remove the blanking plugs from the fuel pipe unions on the accumulator rail and the relevant injector. Locate a new high-pressure fuel pipe over the unions, and screw on the union nuts. Take care not to cross-thread the nuts or strain the fuel pipes as they are fitted. Once the union nut threads have started, finger-tighten the nuts only at this stage.

15 When all the fuel pipes are in place, tighten the injector clamp retaining bolts to the specified torque and through the specified angle.

16 Using an open-ended spanner, hold each fuel pipe union in turn, and tighten the union nut to the specified torque using a torque wrench and crow's-foot adapter **(see illustration)**. Tighten all the disturbed union nuts in the same way.

17 The remainder of refitting is a reversal of removal, following the points listed in paragraph 24 of the previous Section.

1.4 litre (Stage V emissions) and 1.6 litre engines

DOHC 16-valve engines

Removal

18 Disconnect the battery negative terminal (refer to *'Disconnecting the battery'*).

19 Remove the EGR valve tube as described in Chapter 4C Section 3.

20 Undo the two bolts securing the injector wiring harness trough to the top of the inlet manifold **(see illustration 10.7)**.

21 Disconnect the wiring connector from the top of each injector, then lift off the wiring trough and move it to one side **(see illustrations 10.8a and 10.8b)**. Make sure the wiring harness is freed from any clips/brackets on the cylinder head cover/inlet manifold

22 Release the fuel hoses from the support bracket at the right-hand side of the cylinder head cover/inlet manifold

23 Using a screwdriver, push in the retaining spring clip and disconnect the fuel return hose from the top of each injector. Plug the openings to prevent dirt ingress then move the return hose assembly to one side **(see illustrations 10.10a and 10.10b)**.

24 Disconnect the wiring connector from each glow plug. Noting how it is routed, release the glow plug wiring from the clips and brackets and move it to one side.

25 Release the clips and brackets as necessary, and move the fuel hoses clear of the accumulator rail.

26 Remove the intake air resonator as described in Section 4.

27 Disengage the retaining clip tabs and disconnect the crankcase ventilation hose from the oil separator **(see illustration)**.

28 Undo the seven bolts and remove the oil separator from the camshaft cover/bearing ladder. Recover the rubber seal **(see illustrations)**.

29 Clean the area around the high-pressure fuel pipe unions on the accumulator rail-to-injector fuel pipes then unscrew the pipe unions. Use a second spanner to counterhold the unions screwed into the injectors – these unions must not be allowed to move. Note their fitted locations and remove the pipes.

30 Plug the openings in the accumulator rail and fuel injectors to prevent dirt ingress.

31 Unscrew the injector retaining nuts, and carefully pull or lever the injector from place. If necessary, use an open-ended spanner and twist the injector to free it from position **(see illustrations)**. Do not lever against or pull on the solenoid housing at the top of the injector. Note down the injectors position – if the injectors are to be refitted, they must be refitted to their original locations.

32 Remove the copper washer and the upper seal from each injector, or from the cylinder head if they remained in place during injector removal. New copper washers and upper seals will be required for refitting. Cover the injector hole in the cylinder head to prevent dirt ingress.

33 Examine each injector visually for any

11.16 Using a torque wrench and crow's-foot adapter, tighten the fuel pipe union nuts

11.27 Disengage the retaining clip tabs and disconnect the crankcase ventilation hose from the oil separator

11.28a Unbolt and remove the oil separator from the camshaft cover/bearing ladder ...

11.28b ... and recover the rubber seal

11.31a Injector retaining nuts (arrowed)

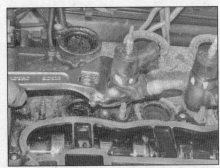
11.31b Use a spanner to twist the injector and free it from position

11.33 Note the injector classification number

11.34 Fit the injectors into their original locations

11.38 Tighten the high-pressure pipe union nuts using a crow's-foot adapter

signs of obvious damage or deterioration. If any defects are apparent, renew the injector(s). Note down the 8-digit injector classification number – this may be needed during the refitting procedure if the ECM has been renewed **(see illustration)**.

Caution: The injectors are manufactured to extremely close tolerances and must not be dismantled in any way. Do not unscrew the fuel pipe union on the side of the injector, or separate any parts of the injector body. Do not attempt to clean carbon deposits from the injector nozzle or carry out any form of ultrasonic or pressure testing.

Refitting

34 Ensure the injector clamps are in place over their respective circlips on the injector bodies, the fit the injectors into place in the cylinder head. If the original injectors are being refitted, ensure they are fitted into their original positions **(see illustration)**.

35 Fit the new injector retaining nuts, but only finger-tighten them at this stage. When tightening the nuts, ensure the clamps stay horizontal.

36 Working on one fuel injector at a time, remove the blanking plugs from the fuel pipe unions on the accumulator rail and the relevant injector. Locate a new high-pressure fuel pipe over the unions and screw on the union nuts. Take care not to cross-thread the nuts or strain the fuel pipes as they are fitted. Once the union nut threads have started, finger-tighten the nuts only at this stage, to the ends of the threads.

37 When all the fuel pipes are in place, tighten the injector clamp retaining nuts to the specified torque and through the specified angle.

38 Using an open-ended spanner, hold each fuel pipe union in turn and tighten the union nut to the specified torque using a

torque wrench and crow's-foot adapter **(see illustration)**. Tighten all the union nuts in the same way.

39 If new injectors have been fitted, their classification numbers must be programmed into the engine management PCM using dedicated diagnostic equipment/scanner. If this equipment is not available, entrust this task to a Ford dealer or suitably-equipped repairer. Note that it should be possible to drive the vehicle, albeit with reduced performance/increased emissions, to a repairer for the numbers to be programmed.

40 The remainder of refitting is a reversal of removal, following the points listed in paragraph 24 of the previous Section.

SOHC 8-valve engines

Removal

41 Disconnect the battery as described in Chapter 5A Section 4.

42 Release the clamp, undo the nuts/bolt and move the intake ducting/throttle body from above the cylinder head cover to one side.

43 Disconnect the wiring plugs from the injectors **(see illustration)**.

44 Undo the retaining bolt, then unclip the wiring harness tray and move it to one side for access to the injectors **(see illustrations)**.

45 Hold down the black central union, pull up the green collar, and pull the fuel return hose from the top of each injector. Plug the openings to prevent dirt ingress then move the return hose assembly to one side **(see illustrations)**. Plug the openings to prevent contamination.

11.43 Disconnect the wiring plugs

11.44a Undo the bolt ...

11.44b ... then unclip the wiring harness tray and move it to one side

11.45a Pull up the green collar ...

11.45b ... then pull the return union from each injector

11.47 Use a second spanner to prevent the injector port from rotating

11.49a Injector clamp retaining bolt

11.49b Carefully remove the injector

46 Remove the starter motor as described in Chapter 5A Section 9.
47 Clean the area around the high-pressure fuel pipe unions on the accumulator rail-to-injector fuel pipes then unscrew the pipe unions. Use a second spanner to counterhold the unions screwed into the injectors – these unions must not be allowed to move **(see illustration)**. Note their fitted locations and remove the pipes.
48 Plug the openings in the accumulator rail and fuel injectors to prevent dirt ingress.
49 Unscrew the injector retaining bolt, remove the clamp and carefully pull or lever the injector from place. If necessary, use an open-ended spanner and twist the injector to free it from position **(see illustrations)**. Do not lever against or pull on the solenoid housing at the top of the injector. Note down the injectors position – if the injectors are to be refitted, they must be refitted to their original locations.
50 Remove the copper washer from each injector, or from the cylinder head if they remained in place during injector removal. New copper washers will be required for refitting. Cover the injector hole in the cylinder head to prevent dirt ingress.
51 Remove the seal from each of the cylinder head injector recesses or injector body. New ones will be required.
52 Examine each injector visually for any signs of obvious damage or deterioration. If any defects are apparent, renew the injector(s). Note down the injector classification number – this may be needed during the refitting procedure if the injectors have been renewed.

Caution: The injectors are manufactured to extremely close tolerances and must not be dismantled in any way. Do not unscrew the fuel pipe union on the side of the injector, or separate any parts of the injector body. Do not attempt to clean carbon deposits from the injector nozzle or carry out any form of ultrasonic or pressure testing.
53 Use a vacuum cleaner to remove any debris from the cylinder head recesses, and the surrounding areas.

Refitting

54 Renew the copper seals on the injectors, and the seals in the cylinder head recesses **(see illustrations)**.
55 Insert the injectors into the cylinder head. If the injectors are being refitted, they must be inserted into their original locations.
56 Refit the injector clamps, but don't tighten the retaining bolts at this stage.
57 Working on one fuel injector at a time, remove the blanking plugs from the fuel pipe unions on the accumulator rail and the relevant injector. Locate a new high-pressure fuel pipe over the unions and screw on the union nuts. Take care not to cross-thread the nuts or strain the fuel pipes as they are fitted. Once the union nut threads have started, finger-tighten the nuts only at this stage, to the ends of the threads.
58 When all the fuel pipes are in place, tighten the injector clamp retaining bolts to the specified torque and through the specified angle.
59 Using an open-ended spanner, hold

each fuel pipe union in turn and tighten the union nut to the specified torque using a torque wrench and crow's-foot adapter **(see illustration 11.38)**. Tighten all the union nuts in the same way.
60 If new injectors have been fitted, their classification numbers must be programmed into the engine management PCM using dedicated diagnostic equipment/scanner. If this equipment is not available, entrust this task to a Ford dealer or suitably-equipped repairer. Note that it should be possible to drive the vehicle, albeit with reduced performance/increased emissions, to a repairer for the numbers to be programmed.
61 The remainder of refitting is a reversal of removal.

12 Electronic control system components – testing, removal and refitting

Testing

1 If a fault is suspected in the electronic control side of the system, first ensure that all the wiring connectors are securely connected and free of corrosion. Ensure that the suspected problem is not of a mechanical nature, or due to poor maintenance; ie, check that the air cleaner filter element is clean, the engine breather hoses are clear and undamaged, and that the cylinder compression pressures are correct, referring to Chapter 2B, Chapter 2D or Chapter 2E for further information.
2 If these checks fail to reveal the cause of the problem, the car should be taken to a suitably-equipped Ford dealer for testing. A diagnostic connector is fitted under the facia on the driver's side into which dedicated electronic test equipment can be plugged. The test equipment is capable of 'interrogating' the engine management system powertrain control module (PCM) electronically and accessing its internal fault log (reading fault codes). This will allow the fault to be quickly and simply traced, alleviating the need to test all the system components individually, which is a time-consuming operation that carries a risk of damaging the PCM.

11.54a Renew the copper seals on the injectors...

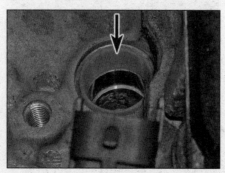
11.54b ...and the seals in the cylinder head

12.5 Drill out the shear-bolt (arrowed) securing the security shield over the PCM wiring connector

12.10 Crankshaft position sensor (arrowed)

12.20 Disconnect the camshaft position sensor wiring plug

Powertrain Control Module (PCM)

Caution: The module is fragile. Take care not to drop it, or subject it to any other kind of impact. Do not subject it to extremes of temperature, or allow it to get wet.

Note: *If a new PCM is to be fitted, the configuration information stored within the module must be uploaded to Ford diagnostic equipment prior to the module being removed, and downloaded to the new PCM once installed. Entrust this task to a Ford dealer or suitably-equipped specialist.*

3 Disconnect the battery negative terminal (refer to 'Disconnecting the battery').

4 Remove the cover over the PCM.

5 Drill out the shear-bolt securing the security shield over the PCM upper wiring connector **(see illustration)**. A 6 mm drill bit will be required, and the hole must be drilled centrally, to avoid damaging the PCM – Ford dealers use a special guide tool (418-537) to ensure this, which is a short tube with a 6 mm hole down the centre.

6 Remove the security shield, then disconnect the three wiring connectors from the PCM.

7 Undo the four retaining nuts and remove the PCM from the mounting plate.

8 Refitting is a reversal of removal. Strictly speaking, a new shear-bolt should be obtained for refitting, and tightened until the head shears off. However, as this is only a deterrent to 'chipping' the module, an ordinary bolt can be used instead.

Crankshaft position sensor

9 Disconnect the battery negative terminal (refer to 'Disconnecting the battery').

10 The crankshaft position sensor is located adjacent to the crankshaft pulley on the right-hand end of the engine **(see illustration)**.

11 Remove the timing belt upper cover as described in Chapter 2B Section 6, Chapter 2C Section 6, Chapter 2D Section 6 or Chapter 2E Section 6.

12 Disconnect the wiring plug from the crankshaft position sensor.

13 Remove the crankshaft pulley as described in Chapter 2B Section 5, Chapter 2C Section 5, Chapter 2D Section 5 or Chapter 2E Section 6.

14 Remove the timing belt lower cover as described in Chapter 2B Section 6, Chapter 2C Section 6, Chapter 2D Section 6 or Chapter 2E Section 6.

15 Unbolt and remove the crankshaft sensor from the engine.

16 Refitting is a reversal of removal. Ensure that the sensor is clean when refitting, and tighten its mounting bolt securely.

Camshaft position sensor

17 Disconnect the battery negative terminal (refer to 'Disconnecting the battery').

18 The camshaft position sensor is mounted on the right-hand end of the cylinder head cover, directly behind the camshaft sprocket.

19 Remove the upper timing belt cover as described in Chapter 2B Section 6, Chap-

ter 2C Section 6, Chapter 2D Section 6 or Chapter 2E Section 6.

20 Unplug the sensor wiring connector **(see illustration)**.

21 Undo the bolt and pull the sensor from position **(see illustration)**.

22 Upon refitting, position the sensor so that the air gap between the sensor end and the webs of the signal wheel is 1.2 mm, measured with feeler gauges, for a used sensor. If fitting a new sensor, the small tip of the sensor must be just touching one of the webs of the signal wheel. Tighten the sensor retaining bolt to the specified torque **(see illustration)**.

23 The remainder of refitting is a reversal of removal.

Accelerator pedal position sensor

24 The sensor is integral with the accelerator pedal assembly. Refer to Section 5 for the pedal removal procedure.

Coolant temperature sensor

25 Refer to Chapter 3 Section 6.

Fuel temperature sensor

⚠️ *Warning: Refer to the information contained in Section 2 before proceeding.*

26 Disconnect the battery negative terminal (refer to 'Disconnecting the battery').

27 The sensor is clipped in to the plastic fuel manifold at the right-hand rear end of the cylinder head. To remove the sensor, disconnect the wiring plug, then unclip the sensor from the manifold. Be prepared for fuel spillage **(see illustration)**.

12.21 Camshaft position sensor retaining bolt

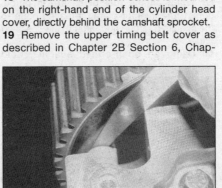

12.22 The gap between the end of the sensor and the webs of the signal wheel must be 1.2 mm (used sensor only)

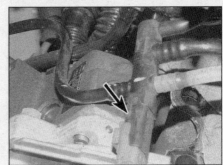

12.27 Fuel temperature sensor (arrowed)

28 Refitting is a reversal of removal.
29 Observing the precautions listed in Section 2, start the engine and allow it to idle. Check for leaks at the fuel temperature sensor with the engine idling. If satisfactory, increase the engine speed to 4000 rpm and check again for leaks. Take the car for a short road test and check for leaks once again on return. If any leaks are detected, obtain and fit a new sensor.

Airflow sensor

30 Disconnect the battery negative terminal (refer to 'Disconnecting the battery').
31 On the 1.4 litre engines (Stage IV emissions), the airflow sensor is located between the air cleaner housing and turbocharger outlet duct. On the 1.4 litre (Stage V emissions) and 1.6 litre engines, it is bolted to the air cleaner cover outlet, and an outlet duct connects it to the turbocharger (see illustrations).

1.4 litre engines (Stage IV emissions)

32 Disconnect the sensor wiring plug.
33 Release the retaining clip, and disconnect the air duct from the airflow sensor.
34 Undo the two retaining bolts and remove the sensor from the air cleaner housing.

1.4 litre (Stage V emissions) and 1.6 litre engines

35 Unplug the wiring connector from the airflow sensor.
36 Undo the two retaining bolts and withdraw the sensor from the air cleaner cover.

All engines

37 Suitably plug or cover the turbocharger air duct, using clean rag to prevent any dirt or foreign material from entering.
38 Refitting is a reverse of the removal procedure. On the 1.6 litre engine, check the condition of the O-ring seal, and fit a new one if necessary.

Fuel pressure sensor

39 The fuel pressure sensor is integral with the accumulator rail, and is not available separately. The sensor must not be removed from the rail.

12.31a Airflow sensor wiring plug (arrowed) – 1.4 litre engines (Stage IV emissions)

Fuel pressure control valve

40 The fuel pressure control valve is integral with the high-pressure fuel pump, and cannot be separated.

EGR valve

41 Refer to Chapter 4C Section 3.

Vehicle speed sensor

Note: On models with ABS, vehicle speed information is derived from the ABS wheel sensors, and a vehicle speed sensor is not fitted. For more information on the ABS wheel sensors, refer to Chapter 9 Section 20.
42 The sensor is mounted on top of the trans-mission, above the left-hand driveshaft.
43 With the ignition switched off, disconnect the sensor wiring plug, then pull the sensor retaining pin (at the base) out sideways, and lift the sensor out of the transmission.
44 Refitting is a reversal of removal. Check the condition of the O-ring seal, and fit a new one if necessary. Ensure the sensor is fully seated, and held securely by the retaining pin.

Intake air shutoff throttle

45 Disconnect the battery negative terminal (refer to 'Disconnecting the battery').
46 The intake air shutoff throttle is located on the right-hand front of the cylinder head, between the resonator and inlet manifold (1.4

12.31b Airflow sensor wiring plug (arrowed) – 1.4 litre (Stage V emissions) and 1.6 litre engines

litre engines) or in the inlet air duct between the intercooler and inlet manifold (1.6 litre engines) (see illustration). Its purpose is to prevent engine run-on when switching off, and to vary the volume air drawn into the engine in order to control the composition of recirculated exhaust gas.

1.4 litre engines

47 Slacken the retaining clip and disconnect the resonator air duct/air intake hose from the intake air shutoff throttle.
48 On Stage IV emissions engines, disconnect the wiring connector, then undo the retaining bolts, lift up the right-hand end and remove the resonator (see illustrations 4.11a and 4.11b). Recover the O-ring seal.
49 Disconnect the wiring plug from the shutoff throttle.
50 Undo the four bolts and remove the throttle from the inlet manifold.
51 Refitting is a reversal of removal, however, check the condition of the O-ring seal, and fit a new one if necessary.

1.6 litre engines

52 Disconnect the wiring connectors from the top and side of the intake air shutoff throttle (see illustration).
53 Slacken the clip and disconnect the intercooler air duct from the base of the intake air shutoff throttle (see illustration).
54 Undo the three flange retaining bolts and

12.46 Intake air shutoff throttle location (arrowed) – 1.6 litre engines

12.52 Disconnect the wiring connectors (arrowed) from the intake air shutoff throttle – 1.6 litre engines

12.53 Slacken the clip (arrowed) and disconnect the intercooler air duct – 1.6 litre engines

12.54 Undo the three retaining bolts (arrowed) and remove the intake air shutoff throttle – 1.6 litreengines

12.64 MAP sensor retaining bolt (arrowed) – 1.6 litre engines

12.67 Depress the clip and disconnect the wiring plug

remove the intake air shutoff throttle from the inlet manifold (see illustration).

55 If necessary, slacken the retaining clip and disconnect the upper air duct from the shutoff throttle.

56 Refitting is a reversal of removal, however, check the condition of the O-ring seal, and fit a new one if necessary.

Manifold absolute pressure (MAP) sensor

57 Disconnect the battery negative terminal (refer to 'Disconnecting the battery').

58 The MAP sensor is located at the right-hand rear of the air cleaner on 1.4 litre engines (Stage IV emissions), and on the top of the intake air shutoff throttle on 1.4 litre (Stage V emissions) and 1.6 litre engines.

1.4 litre engines (Stage IV emissions)

59 Remove the windscreen cowl panel and bulkhead closure panel as described in Chapter 11 Section 20.

60 Disconnect the wiring plug from the sensor.

61 Unscrew the mounting bolt and remove the sensor from the air cleaner.

62 Refitting is a reversal of removal.

1.4 litre (Stage V emissions) and 1.6 litre engines

DOHC engines

63 Disconnect the wiring plug from the sensor.

64 Unscrew the mounting bolt and remove the sensor from the top of the intake air shutoff throttle (see illustration).

65 Refitting is a reversal of removal.

SOHC engines

66 Pull up the front edge and remove the plastic cover from the top of the engine.

67 Disconnect the wiring plug from the MAP sensor located on the top of the intake manifold (see illustration).

68 Undo the retaining bolt and remove the MAP sensor.

69 Refitting is a reversal of removal.

13 Inlet manifold – removal and refitting

1.4L (Stage IV emissions) and 1.6L DOHC engines

1 The inlet manifold is integral with the cylinder head cover. Refer to Chapter 2B or 2D.

1.4L (Stage V emissions) and 1.6L SOHC engines

2 Pull up the front edge, then remove plastic cover from the top of the engine.

3 Slacken the clamp, undo the nuts/bolts and remove the air intake pipe from the top of the engine.

4 Remove the windscreen cowl panels as described in Chapter 11 Section 20.

5 Disconnect the wiring plug from the MAP sensor on the manifold.

6 Remove the EGR valve as described in Chapter 4C Section 3.

7 Undo the 3 retaining bolts/studs securing the manifold to the cylinder head, and manoeuvre it from place.

8 Refitting is a reversal of removal, Renew the manifold seals.

14 Exhaust manifold – removal and refitting

Removal

1 Remove the turbocharger as described in Section 16.

2 Undo the retaining nuts, recover the spacers, and remove the manifold. Recover the gasket (see illustrations).

Refitting

3 Refitting is a reverse of the removal procedure, bearing in mind the following points:

a) Ensure that the manifold and cylinder head mating faces are clean, with all traces of old gasket removed.

b) Use a new gasket when refitting the manifold to the cylinder head.

c) Tighten the exhaust manifold retaining nuts to the specified torque.

d) Refit the turbocharger as described in Section 16.

15 Turbocharger – description and precautions

Description

1 A turbocharger is fitted to increase engine efficiency by raising the pressure in the inlet manifold above atmospheric pressure. Instead of the air simply being sucked into the cylinders, it is forced in.

2 Energy for the operation of the turbocharger comes from the exhaust gas. The gas flows through a specially-shaped housing (the

14.2a Undo the exhaust manifold nuts, recover the spacers, and remove the manifold

14.2b Recover the manifold gasket

16.5a Undo the turbocharger oil supply
pipe banjo bolts from the cylinder block ...

16.5b ... and the turbocharger

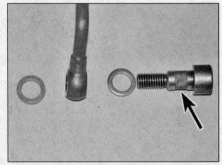

16.5c Note the filter (arrowed) incorporated
into the banjo bolt

turbine housing) and, in so doing, spins the
turbine wheel. The turbine wheel is attached
to a shaft, at the end of which is another vaned
wheel known as the compressor wheel. The
compressor wheel spins in its own housing,
and compresses the inlet air on the way to the
inlet manifold.

3 Boost pressure (the pressure in the inlet
manifold) is limited by a wastegate, which
diverts the exhaust gas away from the turbine
wheel in response to a pressure-sensitive
actuator. The turbocharger incorporates
a variable intake nozzle to improve boost
pressure at low engine speeds.

4 The turbo shaft is pressure-lubricated by
an oil feed pipe from the main oil gallery. The
shaft 'floats' on a cushion of oil. A drain pipe
returns the oil to the sump.

Precautions

5 The turbocharger operates at extremely
high speeds and temperatures. Certain
precautions must be observed, to avoid
premature failure of the turbo, or injury to the
operator.

*Do not operate the turbo with any of its
parts exposed, or with any of its hoses
removed. Foreign objects falling onto
the rotating vanes could cause excessive
damage, and (if ejected) personal injury.*

*Do not race the engine immediately after
start-up, especially if it is cold. Give the oil
a few seconds to circulate.*

*Always allow the engine to return to idle
speed before switching it off – do not blip*

*the throttle and switch off, as this will leave
the turbo spinning without lubrication.*

*Allow the engine to idle for several minutes
before switching off after a high-speed
run.*

*Observe the recommended intervals for oil
and filter changing, and use a reputable
oil of the specified quality. Neglect of oil
changing, or use of inferior oil, can cause
carbon formation on the turbo shaft,
leading to subsequent failure.*

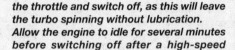

16 Turbocharger – removal,
inspection and refitting

Removal

1.4 litre engines (Stage IV emissions)

1 Remove the catalytic converter as
described in Section 18.

2 Remove the intake air resonator as
described in Section 4.

3 Release the hose clips, and remove the air
duct from the airflow sensor and turbocharger
inlet.

4 Undo the two bolts securing the exhaust
manifold heat shield, and take off the shield.

5 Undo the oil supply pipe banjo union
bolts and recover the sealing washers **(see
illustrations)**.

6 Slacken the retaining clip and disconnect
the oil return pipe from the turbocharger **(see
illustration)**.

16.6 Slacken the oil return hose clip
(arrowed)

7 Remove the two pairs of nuts securing the
turbocharger to the exhaust manifold **(see
illustrations)** and remove the unit.

1.6 litre engines

8 Remove the catalytic converter as
described in Section 18.

9 Slacken the hose clip and disconnect
the air duct from the turbocharger inlet **(see
illustration)**.

10 Unscrew the oil supply pipe banjo bolts
and remove the pipe from the turbocharger
and cylinder block. Recover the sealing
washers.

11 Slacken the hose clip and disconnect the
turbocharger oil return hose from the cylinder
block.

12 Disconnect the vacuum hose from the
turbocharger wastegate capsule.

16.7a Undo the lower nuts (arrowed) ...

16.7b ... and upper nuts (arrowed) securing
the turbocharger to the manifold

16.9 Slacken the hose clip and disconnect
the air duct from the turbocharger inlet

17.2a Disconnect the inlet hose from the intercooler and intake air resonator ...

17.2b ... and outlet hose from the intercooler and intake air shutoff throttle

13 Unscrew the four nuts, and remove the turbocharger from the exhaust manifold.

Inspection

14 With the turbocharger removed, inspect the housing for cracks or other visible damage.
15 Spin the turbine or the compressor wheel, to verify that the shaft is intact and to feel for excessive shake or roughness. Some play is normal, since in use the shaft is 'floating' on a film of oil. Check that the wheel vanes are undamaged.
16 If oil contamination of the exhaust or induction passages is apparent, it is likely that turbo shaft oil seals have failed.
17 No DIY repair of the turbo is possible,

and none of the internal or external parts are available separately. If the turbocharger is suspect in any way, a complete new (or reconditioned) unit must be obtained.

Refitting

18 Refitting is a reverse of the removal procedure, bearing in mind the following points:
a) Renew the turbocharger retaining nuts/bolts and gaskets.
b) If a new turbocharger is being fitted, change the engine oil and filter. Also renew the filter in the oil feed pipe.
c) Prime the turbocharger by injecting clean engine oil through the oil feed pipe union before reconnecting the union.

17 Intercooler – removal and refitting

Note: An intercooler is only fitted to 1.6 litre engines.

Removal

1 The intercooler is located at the front of the car alongside the right-hand side of the radiator.
2 Slacken the retaining clips and disconnect the inlet and outlet hoses from the intercooler, intake air resonator and intake air shutoff throttle **(see illustrations)**.
3 Firmly apply the handbrake, then jack up the front of the vehicle and support it securely on axle stands (see 'Jacking and vehicle support'). Undo the screws and remove the engine undershield.
4 Undo the lower bolt securing the intercooler support frame to the radiator crossmember **(see illustration)**.
5 Undo the two upper retaining bolts and remove the intercooler support frame **(see illustration)**.
6 Using two small screwdrivers, depress the sides of the intercooler upper retaining collar, located on the top centre of the intercooler, to compress the locating lugs each side. With the retaining collar lugs compressed, pull the top of the intercooler towards the engine to disengage the upper retaining collar from its location **(see illustrations)**.
7 Lift the intercooler up to disengage the lower mounting lugs and manipulate the intercooler out from the engine compartment **(see illustration)**.

Refitting

8 Refitting is a reversal of removal.

18 Exhaust system – general information and component renewal

Caution: *Any work on the exhaust system should only be attempted once the system is completely cool – this may take*

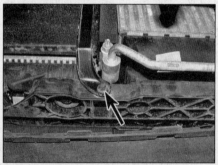

17.4 Undo the lower bolt (arrowed) securing the intercooler support frame to the radiator crossmember

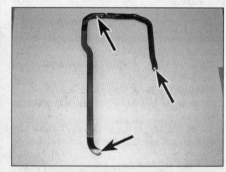

17.5 Intercooler support frame retaining bolt locations (arrowed – shown with frame removed)

17.6a Depress the sides of the intercooler upper retaining collar (shown with intercooler removed) ...

17.6b ... then pull the top of the intercooler towards the engine

17.7 Lift the intercooler up and out from the engine compartment

several hours, especially in the case of the forward sections, such as the manifold and catalytic converter.

General information

1 The exhaust system consists of the catalytic converter and the centre section incorporating the silencer. A flexible ('mesh') section is fitted to allow for engine movement.

2 When fitted in the factory, the exhaust system from the centre section flange joint to the end of the tail pipe is one piece. However, if the silencer is to be renewed, new silencers should be available – check with your parts supplier. It will be necessary to cut through the centre section using a hacksaw if a new rear silencer is to be fitted.

3 The system is suspended throughout its entire length by rubber mountings.

Removal

4 To remove a part of the system, first jack up the front or rear of the car, and support it on axle stands (see *'Jacking and vehicle support'*). Alternatively, position the car over an inspection pit, or on car ramps. Undo the screws and remove the engine undershield.

Catalytic converter/diesel particulate filter – 1.4 litre engines

Note: *The particulate filter is integral with the catalytic converter on Stage V emissions engines.*

5 To prevent damage to the exhaust flexible section, support it by attaching a pair of splints either side (two scrap strips of wood, plant canes, etc) using some cable-ties.

6 Undo the three upper bolts and two lower bolts and remove the turbocharger heat shield.

7 Undo the four bolts securing the catalytic converter to the turbocharger.

8 Unscrew the two nuts securing the exhaust system centre section to the catalytic converter. Unhook the centre section's rubber mounting, then separate the flange joint. Recover the gasket.

9 Undo the two catalytic converter lower mounting bolts from the brackets on the front of the engine, then lower the converter carefully from the engine compartment.

Catalytic converter/diesel particulate filter – 1.6 litre engines

Note: *The particulate filter is integral with the catalytic converter on SOHC 8-valve models (Stage V emissions).*

10 Remove the intake air resonator as described in Section 4.

11 Undo the retaining bolts and remove the turbocharger and catalytic converter heat shields.

12 To prevent damage to the exhaust flexible section, support it by attaching a pair of splints either side (two scrap strips of wood, plant canes, etc) using some cable-ties.

13 Unscrew the two nuts securing the exhaust system centre section to the catalytic converter. Unhook the centre section's rubber mounting, then separate the flange joint. Recover the gasket.

14 Slacken the nut on the retaining clamp, securing the catalytic converter to the turbocharger.

15 Undo the two catalytic converter lower mounting bolts from the brackets on the front of the engine, then lower the converter carefully from the engine compartment.

Flexible section

16 Using a hacksaw, cut the catalytic converter pipe 10 mm in front of the flexible section; the converter can then be connected to the new flexible section with a clamping sleeve (supplied with the new flexible section).

17 Unscrew the two nuts securing the exhaust system centre section to the catalytic converter. Unhook the centre section's rubber mounting, then separate the flange joint. Recover the gasket and remove the cut (flexible) section from under the car.

Centre section

18 To prevent damage to the exhaust flexible section, support it by attaching a pair of splints either side (two scrap strips of wood, plant canes, etc) using some cable-ties. If a new centre section is being fitted, this precaution only applies to the new section of exhaust.

19 From under the car, undo the nuts and remove the underfloor cross-brace beneath the exhaust centre section.

20 Unscrew the nuts securing the centre section to the catalytic converter, and separate the joint. Recover the gasket.

21 Unhook the centre section's rubber mountings, and remove it from under the car.

Rear silencer

22 If the original one-piece exhaust system is still fitted, it will be necessary to cut off the old rear silencer to enable fitment of the new unit. Using the new rear silencer as a pattern, mark the exhaust centre section to determine the cut point. Ensure that the cut point will allow a

sufficient length of centre section to fit into the new rear silencer.

23 Using a hacksaw, cut through the centre section at the marked cut point. Unhook the rear silencer's rubber mountings, and remove it from under the car.

24 If a replacement rear silencer has already been fitted, unbolt the clamp securing the silencer to the centre section, and separate the pipes. Usually, this will require some effort – the most successful method involves twisting the silencer from side to side, to break the joint. Unfortunately, if the pipe at the rear of the centre section has suffered from corrosion, it's very likely that the centre section will be damaged beyond repair in removing the silencer. A less-destructive method of removal involves heating the two pipes, but this carries the risk of damaging the underbody components, and even a risk of fire from the fuel tank and lines.

25 Unhook the silencer rubber mountings, and remove it from under the car.

Heat shields

26 The heat shields are secured to the underside of the body by special nuts. Each shield can be removed separately, but note that they may overlap, making it necessary to loosen another section first. If a shield is being removed to gain access to a component located behind it, it may prove sufficient in some cases to remove the retaining nuts and/or bolts, and simply lower the shield, without disturbing the exhaust system. Otherwise, remove the exhaust section as described earlier.

Refitting

27 In all cases, refitting is a reversal of removal, but note the following points:

a) Always use new gaskets, nuts and clamps (as applicable), and coat all threads with copper grease. Make sure any new clamps are the same size as the original – over-tightening a clamp which is too big will not seal the joint.

b) If any of the exhaust mounting rubbers are in poor condition, fit new ones.

c) Make sure that the exhaust is suspended properly on its mountings, and will not come into contact with the floor or any suspension parts. The rear silencer especially must be aligned correctly before tightening the clamp nuts.

d) Tighten all nuts/bolts to the specified torque, where given.

Chapter 4 Part C
Emission control systems

Contents

Degrees of difficulty

Easy, suitable for novice with little experience	**Fairly easy,** suitable for beginner with some experience	**Fairly difficult,** suitable for competent DIY mechanic	**Difficult,** suitable for experienced DIY mechanic	**Very difficult,** suitable for expert DIY or professional

Specifications

Torque wrench settings	Nm	lbf ft
Petrol engines		
Oxygen (lambda) sensors	48	35
Diesel engines		
EGR valve mounting bolts	10	7

1 General information and precautions

Petrol engines

Crankcase emission control

1 To reduce the emission of unburned hydrocarbons from the crankcase into the atmosphere, the engine is sealed and the blow-by gases and oil vapour are drawn from inside the crankcase, through an oil separator and regulating (PCV – positive crankcase ventilation) valve, into the inlet manifold to be burned by the engine during normal combustion.

2 Under all conditions the gases are forced out of the crankcase by the (relatively) higher crankcase pressure.

Exhaust emission control

3 To minimise the amount of pollutants which escape into the atmosphere, all models are fitted with a catalytic converter in the exhaust system. The system is of the closed-loop type, in which an oxygen (lambda) sensor in the exhaust manifold provides the fuel injection/ignition system Powertrain Control Module (PCM) with constant feedback, enabling the PCM to adjust the mixture to provide the best possible conditions for the converter to operate.

4 The oxygen sensor has a heating element built-in that is controlled by the PCM through a relay to quickly bring the sensor's tip to an efficient operating temperature. The sensor's tip is sensitive to oxygen and sends the PCM a varying voltage depending on the amount of oxygen in the exhaust gases; if the intake air/fuel mixture is too rich, the exhaust gases are low in oxygen so the sensor sends a low-voltage signal, the voltage rising as the mixture weakens and the amount of oxygen rises in the exhaust gases.

5 Peak conversion efficiency of all major pollutants occurs if the intake air/fuel mixture is maintained at the chemically-correct ratio for the complete combustion of petrol of 14.7 parts (by weight) of air to 1 part of fuel (the 'stoichiometric' ratio). The sensor output voltage alters in a large step at this point, the PCM using the signal change as a reference point and correcting the intake air/fuel mixture accordingly by altering the fuel injector pulse width.

6 A second sensor is fitted downstream of the catalytic converter, to monitor the converter's efficiency, and to fine-tune the information being sent back to the PCM, so that emissions are kept even more tightly under control.

Evaporative emission control

7 To minimise the escape into the atmosphere of unburned hydrocarbons, an evaporative emissions control system is also fitted to all models. The fuel tank filler cap is sealed, and a charcoal canister is mounted on the side of the fuel tank. The canister collects the petrol vapours generated in the tank when the car is parked, and stores them until they can be cleared from the canister (under the control of the fuel injection/ignition system PCM) via the purge valve into the inlet tract to be burned by the engine during normal combustion. The purge (or EVAP) valve is located on the inlet manifold.

8 To ensure that the engine runs correctly when it is cold and/or idling and to protect the catalytic converter from the effects of an over-rich mixture, the EVAP valve is not opened by the PCM until the engine has warmed-up, and the engine is under load; the valve solenoid is then modulated on and off to allow the stored vapour to pass into the inlet tract.

Diesel engines

Crankcase emission control

9 To reduce the emission of unburned hydrocarbons from the crankcase into the atmosphere, the engine is sealed and the blow-by gases and oil vapour are drawn from inside the crankcase, through an oil separator and regulating (PCV – positive crankcase ventilation) valve, into the inlet manifold to be burned by the engine during normal combustion.

Exhaust emission control

10 To minimise the level of exhaust pollutants released into the atmosphere, a catalytic converter is fitted in the exhaust system of all models.

11 The catalytic converter consists of a canister containing a fine mesh impregnated with a catalyst material, over which the hot exhaust gases pass. The catalyst speeds up the oxidation of harmful carbon monoxide, unburnt hydrocarbons and soot, effectively reducing the quantity of harmful products released into the atmosphere via the exhaust gases.

12 On 1.4L and 1.6L engines to the highest emission standard, a diesel particulate filter is incorporated in the catalytic converter and contains a silicon carbide honeycomb block containing microscopic channels in which the exhaust gases flow. As the gases flow through the honeycomb channels, soot particles are deposited on the channel walls. To prevent clogging of the honeycomb channels, the soot particles are burned off at regular intervals during what is known as a 'regeneration phase'. Under the control of the engine management system PCM, the injection characteristics are altered to raise the temperature of the exhaust gases to approximately 600°C. At this temperature, the

soot particles are effectively burned off the honeycomb walls as the exhaust gases pass through. A differential pressure sensor and temperature sensor are used to inform the PCM of the condition of the particulate filter, and the temperature of the exhaust gases during the regeneration phase. When the PCM detects that soot build-up is reducing the efficiency of the particulate filter, it will instigate the regeneration process. This occurs at regular intervals under certain driving conditions and will normally not be detected by the driver.

Exhaust gas recirculation system

13 This system is designed to recirculate small quantities of exhaust gas into the inlet tract, and therefore into the combustion process. This process reduces the level of oxides of nitrogen present in the final exhaust gas which is released into the atmosphere.

14 The volume of exhaust gas recirculated is controlled by the engine management PCM.

15 On early 1.4 litre models, a vacuum-operated valve is fitted to the exhaust manifold, to regulate the quantity of exhaust gas recirculated, and the valve is operated by the vacuum supplied by a solenoid valve. On later 1.4 litre and 1.6 litre models, the EGR valve is mounted on the rear of the cylinder head, and is connected by an internal channel to the exhaust manifold on the front of the engine. It incorporates a stepper motor to regulate the quantity of exhaust gas recirculated, and the valve is controlled directly by the engine management PCM.

Catalytic converter precautions

16 For long life and satisfactory operation of the catalytic converter, certain precautions must be observed. These are as follows.

17 For petrol engines, only use unleaded fuel. Leaded fuel will damage the catalyst and the oxygen sensor.

18 Do not run the engine for long periods if it is misfiring. Unburnt fuel entering the catalytic converter can cause it to overheat, resulting in permanent damage. For the same reason,

do not try to start the engine by pushing or towing the car, nor crank it on the starter motor for long periods.

19 Do not strike or drop the catalytic converter. The ceramic honeycomb which forms part of its internal structure may be damaged.

20 Always renew seals and gaskets upstream of the catalytic converter (between the engine and converter) whenever they are disturbed.

> **2 Petrol engine emission control systems** – testing and component renewal

Crankcase emission control

1 The components of this system require no attention, other than to check that the hoses are clear and undamaged at regular intervals.

Evaporative emission control

Testing

2 If the system is thought to be faulty, disconnect the hoses from the charcoal canister and purge control (EVAP) valve and check that they are clear by blowing through them. If the purge control valve or charcoal canister are thought to be faulty, they must be renewed.

Charcoal canister renewal

3 The charcoal canister is located under the rear of the car, in a recess in the side of the fuel tank **(see illustration)**. Referring to Chapter 4A Section 7, remove the fuel tank as far as necessary for access to the canister.

4 Disconnect the hoses and back-pressure valve from the canister, then unscrew the mounting bolt and remove it from the recess in the tank.

5 Fit the new canister using a reversal of the removal procedure.

EVAP purge valve renewal

6 The EVAP purge valve is mounted on the inlet manifold **(see illustration)**.

2.3 The charcoal canister is located in a recess in the side of the fuel tank

2.6 EVAP purge valve location (arrowed) on the inlet manifold

7 To renew the valve, first disconnect the wiring plug.

8 Disconnect the hoses from the valve noting their locations, then detach the valve from its mounting bracket.

9 Fit the new valve using a reversal of the removal procedure.

Exhaust emission control

Testing

10 The performance of the catalytic converter can be checked only by measuring the exhaust gases using a good-quality, carefully-calibrated exhaust gas analyser.

11 If the CO level at the tailpipe is too high, the car should be taken to a Ford dealer so that the complete fuel injection and ignition systems, including the oxygen sensor, can be thoroughly checked using the special diagnostic equipment. Once these have been checked and are known to be free from faults, the fault must be in the catalytic converter, which must be renewed.

Catalytic converter renewal

12 The catalytic converter is integral with the exhaust manifold – refer to Chapter 4A Section 12 for details.

Oxygen (lambda) sensor renewal

Note: *The oxygen sensor is delicate and will not work if it is dropped or knocked, if its power supply is disrupted, or if any cleaning materials are used on it.*

13 Trace the wiring back from the oxygen sensor to the connector and disconnect the wiring – this is typically behind the ignition coil location (**see illustration**).

14 Unscrew the sensor and remove it from the exhaust manifold (**see illustration**). A special slotted socket may be needed (if a spanner cannot be used), to make allowance for the sensor's wiring.

15 Clean the threads of the sensor and the threads in the exhaust manifold.

16 Insert the sensor in the manifold and tighten to the specified torque.

17 Reconnect the wiring, making sure that it is in no danger of contacting the exhaust manifold.

Converter monitor sensor renewal

18 This sensor is very similar to the oxygen sensor, and renewal details are virtually identical. Since the sensor is fitted further down the exhaust manifold than the oxygen sensor, access to the sensor itself will be easier from below (**see illustrations**).

3 Diesel engine emission control systems – testing and component renewal

Crankcase emission control

1 The components of this system require no attention, other than to check that the hoses are clear and undamaged at regular intervals.

2.13 Oxygen sensor wiring connector (arrowed)

2.18a Disconnect the converter monitor sensor wiring plug (arrowed) …

Exhaust emission control

Testing

2 The performance of the catalytic converter can be checked only by measuring the exhaust gases using a good-quality, carefully-calibrated exhaust gas analyser.

3 Before assuming that the catalytic converter is faulty, it is worth checking the problem is not due to a faulty injector. Refer to your Ford dealer for further information.

Catalytic converter renewal

4 Refer to Chapter 4B Section 18.

Exhaust gas recirculation

Testing

5 Testing of the system should be entrusted to a Ford dealer.

EGR valve renewal (early 1.4 litre engine – Emissions level IV)

6 The EGR valve is mounted on the left-hand rear of the cylinder head.

7 Remove the air cleaner as described in Chapter 4B Section 4.

8 Disconnect the wiring connector from the top of the EGR valve.

9 Disengage and release the retaining clamp securing the EGR cooler to the EGR valve.

10 Undo the two bolts and remove the EGR valve and housing assembly from the rear of the engine.

11 Refitting is a reversal of removal. Use a new gasket, and tighten the valve mounting bolts to the specified torque.

2.14 Unscrew the oxygen sensor and remove it from the manifold

2.18b … then unscrew the sensor (arrowed) from the manifold

EGR valve renewal (later 1.4 litre engine – Emissions level V)

12 On these vehicles, the EGR valve is integral with the EGR cooler, as described later in this Section.

EGR cooler renewal (1.4 litre engine)

13 Drain the cooling system as described in Chapter 1B Section 30.

14 Remove the air cleaner as described in Chapter 4B Section 4.

Emissions level IV models

15 Remove the two screws securing the EGR pipe elbow.

16 Release the hose clips, and disconnect the two coolant hoses from the cooler – note their locations for refitting.

17 Disengage and release the retaining clamp securing the EGR cooler to the EGR valve

18 Undo the single bolt securing the assembly, then remove the EGR cooler and pipe. If required, the cooler can be separated from the pipe after removing the clamp.

Emissions level V models

19 The EGR cooler assembly is located on the rear of the engine. Remove the windscreen cowl panel as described in Chapter 11 Section 20.

20 Move any coolant pipes aside to gain access to the EGR cooler assembly.

21 Note their fitted positions, then disconnect the various hoses and wiring plugs from the EGR cooler.

22 Undo the 2 bolts securing the EGR pipe

3.27 Disconnect the wiring from the EGR valve – 1.6 litre engine

3.28a Disengage and release the EGR pipe retaining clamp ...

3.28b ... then undo the EGR pipe support bracket bolt

to the exhaust manifold, and the EGR cooler mounting bolts.

23 Manoeuvre the EGR cooler assembly from place.

All 1.4 litre models

24 Refitting is a reversal of removal. On completion, refill the cooling system as described in Chapter 1B Section 30.

EGR valve renewal (1.6 litre engine Emissions level IV)

25 The EGR valve is mounted on the left-hand rear of the cylinder head.

26 Remove the windscreen cowl panel and bulkhead closure panel as described in Chapter 11 Section 20.

27 Disconnect the wiring from the EGR valve **(see illustration)**.

28 Disengage and release the retaining clamp securing the EGR pipe to the EGR valve, then undo the EGR pipe support bracket bolt **(see illustrations)**.

29 Undo the two bolts and remove the EGR valve and housing assembly from the rear of the engine.

30 Refitting is a reversal of removal. Use a new gasket, and tighten the valve mounting bolts to the specified torque.

EGR valve renewal (1.6 litre engine Emissions level V)

31 On these models, the EGR valve is integral with the EGR cooler assembly as described later in this Section.

EGR valve tube renewal (1.6 litre engine Emissions level IV)

32 The EGR valve tube is mounted on the rear of the engine and connects the EGR valve to the inlet manifold.

33 Remove the windscreen cowl panel and bulkhead closure panel as described in Chapter 11 Section 20.

34 Unscrew the two bolts securing the EGR pipe to the right-hand end of the cylinder head cover/inlet manifold.

35 Disengage and release the retaining clamp securing the EGR pipe to the EGR valve, then undo the EGR pipe support bracket bolt **(see illustrations 3.28a and 3.28b)**.

36 Manipulate the EGR pipe up and out of the engine compartment. Recover the O-ring seal **(see illustrations)**.

37 Examine the O-ring seal and obtain a new one if necessary.

38 Refitting is a reversal of removal.

EGR cooler renewal (1.6 litre engines Emissions level V)

39 The EGR cooler assembly is located on the rear of the engine. Remove the windscreen cowl panel as described in Chapter 11 Section 20.

40 Drain the cooling system as described in Chapter 1B Section 30.

41 Remove the air cleaner assembly as described in Chapter 4B Section 4.

42 Move any coolant pipes aside to gain access to the EGR cooler assembly.

43 Note their fitted positions, then disconnect the various hoses and wiring plugs from the EGR cooler.

44 Undo the 2 bolts securing the EGR pipe to the exhaust manifold, and the EGR cooler mounting bolts.

45 Refitting is a reversal of removal.

---

4   Catalytic converter – general information and precautions

General information

1 The catalytic converter reduces harmful exhaust emissions by chemically converting

3.36a Manipulate the EGR pipe up and out of the engine compartment ...

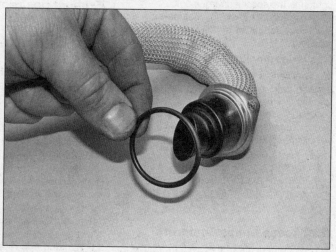

3.36b ... and recover the O-ring seal

the more poisonous gases to ones which (in theory at least) are less harmful. The chemical reaction is known as an 'oxidising' reaction, or one where oxygen is 'added'.

2 Inside the converter is a honeycomb structure, made of ceramic material and coated with the precious metals palladium, platinum and rhodium (the 'catalyst' which promotes the chemical reaction). The chemical reaction generates heat, which itself promotes the reaction – therefore, once the car has been driven several miles, the body of the converter will be very hot.

3 The ceramic structure contained within the converter is understandably fragile, and will not withstand rough treatment. Since the converter runs at a high temperature, driving through deep standing water (in flood conditions, for example) is to be avoided, since the thermal stresses imposed when plunging the hot converter into cold water may well cause the ceramic internals to fracture, resulting in a 'blocked' converter – a common cause of failure. A converter which has been damaged in this way can be checked by shaking it (do not strike it) – if a rattling noise is heard, this indicates probable failure.

Precautions

4 The catalytic converter is a reliable and simple device which needs no maintenance in itself, but there are some facts of which an owner should be aware if the converter is to function properly for its full service life:

Petrol engines

a) *DO NOT use leaded petrol (or lead-replacement petrol, LRP) in a car equipped with a catalytic converter – the lead (or other additives) will coat the precious metals, reducing their converting efficiency and will eventually destroy the converter.*

b) *Always keep the ignition and fuel systems well-maintained in accordance with the manufacturer's schedule (see Chapter 1A).*

c) *If the engine develops a misfire, do not drive the car at all (or at least as little as possible) until the fault is cured.*

d) *DO NOT push- or tow-start the car – this will soak the catalytic converter in unburned fuel, causing it to overheat when the engine does start.*

e) *DO NOT switch off the ignition at high engine speeds – ie, do not 'blip' the throttle immediately before switching off the engine.*

f) *DO NOT use fuel or engine oil additives – these may contain substances harmful to the catalytic converter.*

g) *DO NOT continue to use the car if the engine burns oil to the extent of leaving a visible trail of blue smoke.*

h) *Remember that the catalytic converter operates at very high temperatures. DO NOT, therefore, park the car in dry undergrowth, over long grass or piles of dead leaves after a long run.*

i) *As mentioned above, driving through deep water should be avoided if possible. The sudden cooling effect may fracture the ceramic honeycomb, damaging it beyond repair.*

j) *Remember that the catalytic converter is FRAGILE – do not strike it with tools during servicing work, and take care handling it when removing it from the car for any reason.*

k) *In some cases, a sulphurous smell (like that of rotten eggs) may be noticed from the exhaust. This is common to many catalytic converter-equipped cars, and has more to do with the sulphur content of the brand of fuel being used than the converter itself.*

l) *If a substantial loss of power is experienced, remember that this could be due to the converter being blocked. This can occur simply as a result of high mileage, but may be due to the ceramic element having fractured and collapsed*

internally (see paragraph 3). A new converter is the only cure in this instance.

m) *The catalytic converter, used on a well-maintained and well-driven car, should last at least 100 000 miles – if the converter is no longer effective, it must be renewed.*

Diesel engines

5 The catalytic converter fitted to diesel models is simpler than that fitted to petrol models, but it still needs to be treated with respect to avoid problems:

a) *DO NOT use fuel or engine oil additives – these may contain substances harmful to the catalytic converter.*

b) *DO NOT continue to use the car if the engine burns (engine) oil to the extent of leaving a visible trail of blue smoke.*

c) *Remember that the catalytic converter operates at very high temperatures. DO NOT, therefore, park the car in dry undergrowth, over long grass or piles of dead leaves after a long run.*

d) *As mentioned above, driving through deep water should be avoided if possible. The sudden cooling effect will fracture the ceramic honeycomb, damaging it beyond repair.*

e) *Remember that the catalytic converter is FRAGILE – do not strike it with tools during servicing work, and take care handling it when removing it from the car for any reason.*

f) *If a substantial loss of power is experienced, remember that this could be due to the converter being blocked. This can occur simply as a result of high mileage, but may be due to the ceramic element having fractured and collapsed internally (see paragraph 3). A new converter is the only cure in this instance.*

g) *The catalytic converter, used on a well-maintained and well-driven car, should last at least 100 000 miles – if the converter is no longer effective, it must be renewed.*

Notes

Chapter 5 Part A
Starting and charging systems

Contents

Degrees of difficulty

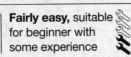

Easy, suitable for novice with little experience

Fairly easy, suitable for beginner with some experience

Fairly difficult, suitable for competent DIY mechanic

Difficult, suitable for experienced DIY mechanic

Very difficult, suitable for expert DIY or professional

Specifications

System type . . . . 12 volt, negative earth

Battery

Type . . . . Low-maintenance or maintenance-free sealed for life
Charge condition:
  Poor . . . . 12.5 volts
  Normal . . . . 12.6 volts
  Good . . . . 12.7 volts

Torque wrench settings	**Nm**	**lbf ft**
Air conditioning compressor mounting bolts (diesel engines)	25	18
Alternator mounting bolts/nuts	45	33
Glow plugs	8	6
Starter motor mounting bolts:		
Petrol engines	35	26
Diesel engines	25	18

1 General information, precautions and battery disconnection

General information

1 The engine electrical system consists mainly of the charging and starting systems. Because of their engine-related functions, these components are covered separately from the body electrical devices such as the lights, instruments, etc (which are covered in Chapter 12). Information on the ignition system is covered in Part B of this Chapter.

2 The electrical system is of 12 volt negative earth type.

3 The battery is of the low-maintenance or 'maintenance-free' (sealed for life) type and is charged by the alternator, which is belt-driven from the crankshaft pulley.

4 The starter motor is of the pre-engaged type incorporating an integral solenoid. On starting, the solenoid moves the drive pinion into engagement with the flywheel ring gear before the starter motor is energised. Once the engine has started, a one-way clutch prevents the motor armature being driven by the engine until the pinion disengages from the flywheel.

Precautions

5 It is necessary to take extra care when working on the electrical system to avoid damage to semi-conductor devices (diodes and transistors), and to avoid the risk of personal injury. In addition to the precautions given in Safety first0,2 ! at the beginning of this manual, observe the following when working on the system:
● Always remove rings, watches, etc, before working on the electrical system. Even with the battery disconnected, capacitive discharge could occur if a component's live terminal is earthed through a metal object. This could cause a shock or nasty burn.
● Do not reverse the battery connections. Components such as the alternator, electronic control units, or any other components having semi-conductor circuitry could be irreparably damaged.
● If the engine is being started using jump leads and a slave battery, connect the batteries positive-to-positive and negative-to-negative (see Jump starting). This also applies when connecting a battery charger.
● Never disconnect the battery terminals, the alternator, any electrical wiring or any test instruments when the engine is running.
● Do not allow the engine to turn the alternator when the alternator is not connected.
● Never 'test' for alternator output by 'flashing' the output lead to earth.
● Never use an ohmmeter of the type incorporating a hand-cranked generator for circuit or continuity testing.

● Always ensure that the battery negative lead is disconnected when working on the electrical system.
● Before using electric-arc welding equipment on the car, disconnect the battery, alternator and components such as the fuel injection/ignition electronic control unit to protect them from the risk of damage.

Battery disconnection

6 Refer to the precautions listed in 'Disconnecting the battery' in the Reference Chapter.

2 Electrical fault finding – general information

1 Refer to Chapter 12 Section 2.

3 Battery – testing and charging

Testing

Standard and low-maintenance battery

1 If the car covers a small annual mileage, it is worthwhile checking the specific gravity of the electrolyte every three months to determine the state of charge of the battery. Use a hydrometer to make the check and compare the results with the following table. Note that the specific gravity readings assume an electrolyte temperature of 15°C; for every 10°C below 15°C subtract 0.007. For every 10°C above 15°C add 0.007.

2 Ambient temperature

	Above 25°C	Below 25°C
Fully-charged	1.210 to 1.230	1.270 to 1.290
70% charged	1.170 to 1.190	1.230 to 1.250
Discharged	1.050 to 1.070	1.110 to 1.130

3 If the battery condition is suspect, first check the specific gravity of electrolyte in each cell. A variation of 0.040 or more between any cells indicates loss of electrolyte or deterioration of the internal plates.

4 If the specific gravity variation is 0.040 or more, the battery should be renewed. If the cell variation is satisfactory but the battery is discharged, it should be charged as described later in this Section.

Maintenance-free battery

5 In cases where a 'sealed for life' maintenance-free battery is fitted, topping-up and testing of the electrolyte in each cell is not possible. The condition of the battery can therefore only be tested using a battery condition indicator or a voltmeter.

6 Certain models are fitted with a maintenance-free battery with a built-in charge condition indicator. The indicator is located in the top of the battery casing, and indicates the condition of the battery from its colour. The charge conditions denoted by the colour of the indicator should be printed on a label attached to the battery – if not, consult a Ford dealer or automotive electrician for advice.

All battery types

7 If testing the battery using a voltmeter, connect the voltmeter across the battery and note the voltage. The test is only accurate if the battery has not been subjected to any kind of charge for the previous six hours. If this is not the case, switch on the headlights for 30 seconds, then wait four to five minutes before testing the battery after switching off the headlights. All other electrical circuits must be switched off, so check that the doors and tailgate are fully shut when making the test.

8 If the voltage reading is less than 12.2 volts, then the battery is discharged, whilst a reading of 12.2 to 12.4 volts indicates a partially-discharged condition.

9 If the battery is to be charged, remove it from the vehicle and charge it as described later in this Section.

Charging

Note: *The following is intended as a guide only. Always refer to the manufacturer's recommendations (often printed on a label attached to the battery) before charging a battery.*

Standard and low-maintenance battery

10 Charge the battery at a rate equivalent to 10% of the battery capacity (eg, for a 45 Ah battery charge at 4.5 A) and continue to charge the battery at this rate until no further rise in specific gravity is noted over a four-hour period.

11 Alternatively, a trickle charger charging at the rate of 1.5 amps can safely be used overnight.

12 Specially rapid boost charges which are claimed to restore the power of the battery in 1 to 2 hours are not recommended, as they can cause serious damage to the battery plates through overheating. If the battery is completely flat, recharging should take at least 24 hours.

13 While charging the battery, note that the temperature of the electrolyte should never exceed 38°C.

Maintenance-free battery

14 This battery type takes considerably longer to fully recharge than the standard type, the time taken being dependent on the extent of discharge, but it can take anything up to three days.

15 A constant voltage type charger is required, to be set, when connected, to 13.9

4.2 Loosen the clamp nut (arrowed) and disconnect the battery negative lead

4.3 Loosen the clamp nut (arrowed) and disconnect the battery positive lead

4.4 Undo the two nuts securing the battery top clamp plate, and lift it off

to 14.9 volts with a charger current below 25 amps. Using this method, the battery should be useable within three hours, giving a voltage reading of 12.5 volts, but this is for a partially-discharged battery and, as mentioned, full charging can take far longer.

16 If the battery is to be charged from a fully-discharged state (condition reading less than 12.2 volts), have it recharged by your Ford dealer or local automotive electrician, as the charge rate is higher, and constant supervision during charging is necessary.

4 Battery and battery tray – removal and refitting

Note: *Refer to the warnings given in 'Safety first!' and in Section 1 of this Chapter before starting work.*

Battery removal

1 The battery is located on the left-hand side of the engine compartment, on a platform above the transmission.
2 Loosen the clamp nut, then detach the earth lead from the battery negative (earth) terminal post **(see illustration)**. This is the terminal to disconnect before working on, or disconnecting, any electrical component on the car. Position the lead away from the battery.
3 Pivot up the plastic cover from the positive terminal, then loosen the positive lead clamp nut **(see illustration)**. Detach the positive lead from the terminal, and position it away from the battery.
4 Undo the two nuts securing the battery top clamp plate, and lift it off **(see illustration)**. On certain models, one or two vacuum hoses may be clipped to the clamp plate – if so, detach them before removal.
5 Lift out the battery, keeping it as level as possible. Take care, as the battery is heavy.

Battery refitting

6 Refitting is a reversal of removal. Reconnect the battery negative lead last. Make sure the battery terminals and clamps are clean before refitting, and that the clamp nuts are tightened securely.

Battery tray removal

7 If required, once the battery has been removed, the battery tray and its support bracket can also be removed, as follows.
8 On all except 1.4 litre diesel engine (Stage IV emissions) models, remove the air cleaner assembly as described in Chapter 4A Section 5 or Chapter 4B Section 4 as applicable.
9 Undo the two bolts and remove the cover over the front of the powertrain control module (PCM) mounted on the side of the battery tray.
10 The battery tray is secured by three bolts at the base. Undo the bolts, and lift the battery tray off its support bracket **(see illustration)**.
11 Undo the bolt at the top and the two bolts on the underside and separate the PCM mounting bracket from the battery tray **(see illustrations)**. Remove the battery tray from the engine compartment.

12 Undo the three nuts securing the battery tray support bracket in position. Release the wiring loom from the support bracket and lift the support bracket out of the engine compartment **(see illustration)**.

Battery tray refitting

13 Refitting is a reversal of removal.

5 Charging system – testing

Note: *Refer to the warnings given in 'Safety first!' and in Section 1 of this Chapter before starting work.*

1 If the ignition warning light fails to illuminate when the ignition is switched on, first check

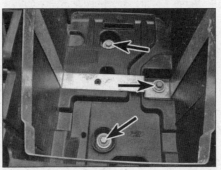

4.10 Undo the three bolts (arrowed) and lift the battery tray off its support bracket

4.11a Undo the bolt at the top (arrowed) ...

4.11b ... and the two bolts on the underside (arrowed) and separate the PCM mounting bracket from the battery tray

4.12 Undo the three nuts, release the wiring loom and lift out the support bracket

the alternator wiring connections for security. If all is satisfactory, the alternator may be at fault and should be renewed or taken to an auto-electrician for testing and repair.

2 If the ignition warning light illuminates when the engine is running, stop the engine and check that the drivebelt is intact and correctly tensioned (see Chapter 1A Section 9 or Chapter 1B Section 10) and that the alternator connections are secure. If all is so far satisfactory, have the alternator checked by an auto-electrician for testing and repair.

3 If the alternator output is suspect even though the warning light functions correctly, the regulated voltage may be checked as follows.

4 Connect a voltmeter across the battery terminals and start the engine.

5 Increase the engine speed until the voltmeter reading remains steady; the reading should be between 13.5 and 14.8 volts.

6 Switch on as many electrical accessories (eg, the headlights, heated rear window and heater blower) as possible, and check that the alternator maintains the regulated voltage between 13.5 and 14.8 volts.

7 If the regulated voltage is not as stated, the fault may be due to worn brushes, weak brush springs, a faulty voltage regulator, a faulty diode, a severed phase winding, or worn or damaged slip-rings. At the time of writing, it would appear that no parts were available for the alternator. If faulty the complete assembly must be renewed. If in doubt, the alternator should be renewed or taken to an auto-electrician for testing.

6 Alternator drivebelt
– removal, refitting and tensioning

1 Refer to the procedure given for the auxiliary drivebelt in Chapter 1A Section 9, 26 or Chapter 1B Section 26, as applicable.

7 Alternator –
removal and refitting

Note: *Refer to the warnings given in 'Safety first!' and in Section 1 of this Chapter before starting work.*

1 Disconnect the battery negative terminal (refer to Disconnecting the battery 14, 6).

Petrol engines

Removal

2 Remove the auxiliary drivebelt as described in Chapter 1A Section 26.

3 Prise up the plastic cap and disconnect the alternator battery cable, then disconnect the field wiring multiplug behind it **(see illustrations)**. Note the fitted positions and routing of the wiring.

4 Undo and remove the alternator upper mounting nut **(see illustration)**.

5 Undo the alternator lower mounting bolt **(see illustration)**.

7.3a Disconnecting the battery positive cable from the alternator terminal

6 Undo the alternator upper mounting bolt, then unscrew the alternator upper mounting stud. This can be done using two nuts locked together on the stud's threads and unscrewing using the inner nut, or pull the alternator forwards a little and use a pair of self-grip pliers to unscrew the stud. Support the alternator as the stud is removed, then lift the alternator from place.

Refitting

7 Refitting is a reversal of removal. Remembering to tighten the various fasteners to their specified torque where given.

Diesel engines

Removal

8 The alternator is located on the left-hand rear of the engine. First, remove the auxiliary drivebelt as described in Chapter 1B Section 26.

9 On the 1.6 litre diesel engine, carry out the following:

7.4 Undo and remove the alternator upper mounting nut (arrowed) ...

7.11 Prise out the cover, then disconnect the alternator wiring and plug

7.3b Disconnecting the field winding wiring

a) Loosen the retaining clips and disconnect the intercooler-to-inlet manifold air hose from the throttle housing and intercooler.

b) Loosen the retaining clips and disconnect the intercooler-to-turbocharger hose from the intercooler and turbocharger outlet pipe.

10 Unbolt and remove the auxiliary drivebelt tensioner.

11 Prise up the plastic cap and disconnect the alternator battery cable, then disconnect the field wiring multiplug next to it **(see illustration)**. Note the fitted positions and routing of the wiring.

12 Where applicable, disconnect the wiring plug from the air conditioning compressor, then remove the four mounting bolts and tie the compressor to one side, without disturbing any of the hose connections.

13 Remove the alternator left-hand mounting bolts **(see illustration)**.

7.5 ... and lower mounting bolt

7.13 Alternator left-hand mounting bolts (arrowed)

7.14 Alternator right-hand mounting bolts (arrowed)

14 Support the alternator, then remove the right-hand mounting bolts **(see illustration)**.

Refitting

15 Refitting is a reversal of removal, noting the following points:
a) Tighten the mounting bolts to the specified torque, including those for the air conditioning compressor, where applicable.
b) Ensure that the wiring is reconnected correctly, and that the retaining nuts are tight.
c) Refit the auxiliary drivebelt as described in Chapter 1B Section 26.

8 Starting system – testing

Note: Refer to the precautions given in 'Safety first!' and in Section 1 of this Chapter before starting work.

1 If the starter motor fails to operate when the ignition key is turned to the appropriate position, the following possible causes may be to blame.
a) The engine immobiliser is faulty.
b) The battery is faulty.
c) The electrical connections between the switch, solenoid, battery and starter motor are somewhere failing to pass the necessary current from the battery through the starter to earth.
d) The solenoid is faulty.
e) The starter motor is mechanically or electrically defective.

2 To check the battery, switch on the headlights. If they dim after a few seconds, this indicates that the battery is discharged – recharge (see Section 3) or renew the battery. If the headlights glow brightly, operate the ignition switch and observe the lights. If they dim, then this indicates that current is reaching the starter motor, therefore the fault must lie in the starter motor. If the lights continue to glow brightly (and no clicking sound can be heard from the starter motor solenoid), this indicates that there is a fault in the circuit or solenoid – see following paragraphs. If the starter motor turns slowly when operated, but the battery is in good condition, then this indicates that either the starter motor is faulty, or there is considerable resistance somewhere in the circuit.

3 If a fault in the circuit is suspected, disconnect the battery leads (including the earth connection to the body), the starter/solenoid wiring and the engine/transmission earth strap. Thoroughly clean the connections, and reconnect the leads and wiring, then use a voltmeter or test lamp to check that full battery voltage is available at the battery positive lead connection to the solenoid, and that the earth is sound. Smear petroleum jelly around the battery terminals to prevent corrosion – corroded connections are amongst the most frequent causes of electrical system faults.

4 If the battery and all connections are in good condition, check the circuit by disconnecting the wire from the solenoid terminal. Connect a voltmeter or test lamp between the wire end and a good earth (such as the battery negative terminal), and check that the wire is live when the ignition switch is turned to the 'start' position. If it is, then the circuit is sound – if not, the circuit wiring can be checked as described in Chapter 12 Section 2.

5 The solenoid contacts can be checked by connecting a voltmeter or test lamp between the battery positive feed connection on the starter side of the solenoid, and earth. When the ignition switch is turned to the 'start' position, there should be a reading or lighted bulb, as applicable. If there is no reading or lighted bulb, the solenoid is faulty and should be renewed.

6 If the circuit and solenoid are proved sound, the fault must lie in the starter motor. In this event, it may be possible to have the starter motor overhauled by a specialist, but check on the cost of spares before proceeding, as it may prove more economical to obtain a new or exchange motor.

9 Starter motor – removal and refitting

Note: Refer to the warnings given in 'Safety first!' and in Section 1 of this Chapter before starting work.

Removal

1 Disconnect the battery negative terminal (refer to 'Disconnecting the battery').

Petrol engines

2 Apply the handbrake, then jack up the front of the car and support on axle stands (see 'Jacking and vehicle support').

3 Working beneath the left-hand front of the engine, unscrew the two nuts and disconnect the wiring assembly from the starter motor **(see illustrations)**. Note the location of each wire, for refitting.

9.3a Unscrew the two nuts ...

9.3b ... and disconnect the starter motor wiring

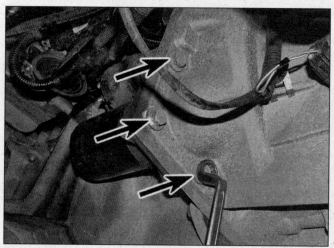

9.4a Unscrew the three bolts ...

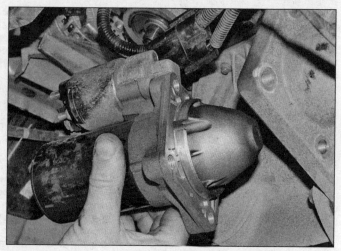

9.4b ... and withdraw the starter motor

4 Support the starter motor, then unscrew and remove the three starter mounting bolts from the transmission bellhousing, and withdraw the motor **(see illustrations)**.

Diesel engines

5 The starter motor is located on the left-hand rear of the engine. First, remove the battery and the battery tray as described on Section 4.
6 Unscrew and remove the two starter motor upper retaining bolts.
7 Apply the handbrake, then jack up the front of the car and support on axle stands (see *'Jacking and vehicle support'*).
8 Working beneath the front of the engine, unscrew the two nuts and disconnect the wiring from the starter motor. Note the location of each wire, for refitting.
9 Support the starter motor, then unscrew and remove the lower mounting bolt, and withdraw the motor.

Refitting

10 Refitting is a reversal of removal, but tighten the mounting bolts to the specified torque.

10 Starter motor – testing and overhaul

1 If the starter motor is thought to be suspect, it should be removed from the car and taken to an auto-electrician for testing. Most auto-electricians will be able to supply and fit brushes at a reasonable cost. However, check on the cost of repairs before proceeding as it may prove more economical to obtain a new or exchange motor.

11 Preheating system – description and testing

Description

1 To assist cold starting, diesel engines are fitted with a preheating system, which consists of four glow plugs (one per cylinder), a glow plug relay, a facia-mounted warning light, the engine management PCM, and the associated electrical wiring.
2 The glow plugs are miniature electric heating elements, encapsulated in a metal case with a probe at one end and electrical connection at the other. Each combustion chamber has one glow plug threaded into it, with the tip of the glow plug probe positioned directly in line with incoming spray of fuel from the injectors. When the glow plug is energised, it heats up rapidly, causing the fuel passing over the glow plug probe to be heated to its optimum temperature, ready for combustion. In addition, some of the fuel passing over the glow plugs is ignited and this helps to trigger the combustion process.
3 The preheating system begins to operate as soon as the ignition key is switched to the second position, but only if the engine coolant temperature is below 20°C and the engine is turned at more than 70 rpm for 0.2 seconds. A facia-mounted warning light informs the driver that preheating is taking place. The light extinguishes when sufficient preheating has taken place to allow the engine to be started, but power will still be supplied to the glow plugs for a further period until the engine is started. If no attempt is made to start the engine, the power supply to the glow plugs is switched off after 10 seconds, to prevent battery drain and glow plug burn-out.
4 With the electronically-controlled diesel injection system fitted to models in this manual, the glow plug relay is controlled by the engine management system PCM, which determines the necessary preheating time based on inputs from the various system sensors. The system monitors the temperature of the intake air, then alters the preheating time (the length for which the glow plugs are supplied with current) to suit the conditions.
5 Post-heating takes place after the ignition key has been released from the 'start' position, but only if the engine coolant temperature is below 20°C, the injected fuel flow is less than a certain rate, and the engine speed is less than 2000 rpm (1.4 litre engine) or 2500 rpm (1.6 litre engine). The glow plugs continue to operate for a maximum of 60 seconds (1.4 litre engine) or 30 seconds (1.6 litre engine), helping to improve fuel combustion whilst the engine is warming-up, resulting in quieter, smoother running and reduced exhaust emissions.

Testing

6 If the system malfunctions, testing is ultimately by substitution of known good units, but some preliminary checks may be made as follows.
7 Connect a voltmeter or 12 volt test light between the glow plug supply cable and earth (engine or car body). Make sure that the live connection is kept clear of the engine and bodywork.
8 Have an assistant switch on the ignition, and check that voltage is applied to the glow plugs. Note the time for which the warning light is lit, and the total time for which voltage is applied before the system cuts out. Switch off the ignition.
9 Warning light time will increase with lower temperatures and decrease with higher temperatures.
10 If there is no supply at all, the module or associated wiring is at fault.
11 To gain access to the glow plugs for further testing, remove the windscreen cowl panel and bulkhead closure panel as

described in Chapter 11 Section 20. On 1.4 litre engines, also remove the inlet manifold (which is integral with the cylinder head cover – see Chapter 2B Section 4).

12 Where applicable, to improve access, remove the engine cover mounting bracket.

13 Disconnect the main supply cable (behind the fuel filter) and the interconnecting wire from the top of the glow plugs. Be careful not to drop the nuts and washers.

14 Use a continuity tester, or a 12 volt test light connected to the battery positive terminal, to check for continuity between each glow plug terminal and earth. The resistance of a glow plug in good condition is very low (less than 1 ohm), so if the test light does not light or the continuity tester shows a high resistance, the glow plug is certainly defective.

15 If an ammeter is available, the current draw of each glow plug can be checked. After an initial surge of 15 to 20 amps, each plug should draw 12 amps. Any plug which draws much more or less than this is probably defective.

16 As a final check, the glow plugs can be removed and inspected as described in the following Section. On completion, refit any components removed for access.

---

12 Glow plugs – removal, inspection and refitting

Caution: If the preheating system has just been energised, or if the engine has been running, the glow plugs will be very hot.

Removal

1 To gain access to the glow plugs, remove the windscreen cowl panel and bulkhead closure panel as described in Chapter 11 Section 20. On 1.4 litre engines (Stage IV emissions), also remove the inlet manifold (which is integral with the cylinder head cover – see Chapter 2B Section 4).

2 Where applicable, to improve access, remove the engine cover mounting bracket.

3 Pull off the wiring connector from the top of each glow plug and move the wiring harness to one side.

4 Where applicable, carefully move any obstructing pipes or wires to one side to enable access to the relevant glow plug(s).

5 Unscrew the glow plug(s) and remove from the cylinder head **(see illustration). Note:** *On 1.4 litre (Stage V emissions) and 1.6 litre models, access to No 4 glow plug is difficult.*

Inspection

6 Inspect each glow plug for physical damage. Burnt or eroded glow plug tips can be caused by a bad injector spray pattern. Have the injectors checked if this sort of damage is found.

7 If the glow plugs are in good physical condition, check them electrically using a 12 volt test light or continuity tester as described in the previous Section.

8 The glow plugs can be energised by applying 12 volts to them, to verify that they heat up evenly and in approximately the same time. Observe the following precautions.

a) *Support the glow plug by clamping it carefully in a vice or self-locking pliers. Remember, it will become red-hot.*

12.5 Glow plug location

b) *Make sure that the power supply or test lead incorporates a fuse or overload trip to protect against damage from a short-circuit.*

c) *After testing, allow the glow plug to cool for several minutes before attempting to handle it.*

9 A glow plug in good condition will start to glow red at the tip after drawing current for 5 seconds or so. Any plug which takes much longer to start glowing, or which starts glowing in the middle instead of at the tip, is defective.

Refitting

10 Refit by reversing the removal operations. Apply a smear of copper-based anti-seize compound to the plug threads, and tighten the glow plugs to the specified torque. Do not overtighten, as this can damage the glow plug element.

11 Refit any components removed for access.

Notes

Chapter 5 Part B
Ignition system – petrol models

Contents

Degrees of difficulty

Easy, suitable for novice with little experience	Fairly easy, suitable for beginner with some experience	Fairly difficult, suitable for competent DIY mechanic	Difficult, suitable for experienced DIY mechanic	Very difficult, suitable for expert DIY or professional

Specifications

General

System type	Electronic distributorless ignition system (DIS) with ignition module controlled by engine management system (Powertrain control module)
Firing order	1-3-4-2
Location of No 1 cylinder	Timing belt end of engine

Torque wrench settings

	Nm	lbf ft
Ignition coil	6	4
Knock sensor	20	15

1 Ignition system – general information and precautions

General information

1 The ignition system is integrated with the fuel injection system to form a combined engine management system under the control of the Powertrain control module (PCM) (see Chapter 4A Section 11 for further information). The main ignition system components include the ignition switch, the battery, the crankshaft speed/position sensor, the ignition coil, and the spark plugs.

2 A Distributorless Ignition System (DIS) is fitted where the main functions of the conventional distributor are superseded by a computerised module within the PCM. The remote ignition coil unit combines a double-ended pair of coils – each time a coil receives an ignition signal, two sparks are produced, one at each end of the secondary windings. One spark goes to a cylinder on its compression stroke and the other goes to the corresponding cylinder on its exhaust stroke. The first will give the correct power stroke, but the second spark will have no effect (a 'wasted spark'), occurring as it does during exhaust conditions.

3 The information contained in this Chapter concentrates on the ignition-related components of the engine management system. Information covering the fuel, exhaust and emission control components can be found in the applicable Parts of Chapter 4A.

Precautions

4 The following precautions must be observed, to prevent damage to the ignition system components and to reduce risk of personal injury.
a) Do not keep the ignition on for more than 10 seconds if the engine will not start.
b) Ensure that the ignition is switched off before disconnecting any of the ignition wiring.
c) Ensure that the ignition is switched off before connecting or disconnecting any ignition test equipment.
d) Do not earth the coil primary or secondary circuits.

⚠ *Warning: Due to the high voltages produced by the electronic ignition system, extreme care must be taken when working on the system with the ignition switched on. Persons with surgically-implanted cardiac pacemaker devices should keep well clear of the ignition circuits, components and test equipment.*

2 Ignition system – testing

1 If a fault appears in the engine management system, first ensure that all the system wiring connectors are securely connected and free of corrosion. Ensure that the fault is not due to poor maintenance; ie, check that the air cleaner filter element is clean, the spark plugs are in good condition and correctly gapped, the cylinder compression pressures are correct and that the engine breather hoses are clear and undamaged, referring to Chapters 1A, 2A and 4C for further information.

2 If these checks fail to reveal the cause of

3.1 The ignition coil is bolted to the left-hand end of the cylinder head

3.2 Disconnecting the coil wiring plug

3.3 Make sure the HT lead positions are marked on the coil before disconnecting

the problem, the car should be taken to a suitably-equipped Ford dealer or engine management diagnostic specialist for testing. A diagnostic socket is incorporated in the engine management circuit into which a fault code reader or other suitable test equipment can be connected (see Chapter 4A). By using the code reader or test equipment, the engine management PCM can be interrogated, and any stored fault codes can be retrieved. This will allow the fault to be quickly and simply traced, alleviating the need to test all the system components individually, which is a time-consuming operation that carries a risk of damaging the PCM.

3 HT coil – removal and refitting

Removal

1 The ignition coil is bolted to the coolant outlet elbow on the left-hand end of the cylinder head **(see illustration)**.
2 Make sure the ignition is switched off, then disconnect the main wiring plug from the coil **(see illustration)**.
3 Identify the HT leads for position (mark the leads and the coil terminals) then carefully

pull them from the terminals on the coil **(see illustration)**.
4 Unscrew the four mounting bolts and remove the ignition coil from the engine compartment. Where applicable, recover the heat shield/mounting plate **(see illustrations)**.

Refitting

5 Refitting is a reversal of removal.

4 Crankshaft position sensor – removal and refitting

1 Refer to Chapter 4A Section 11.

5 Ignition timing – checking and adjustment
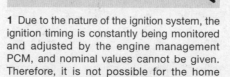

1 Due to the nature of the ignition system, the ignition timing is constantly being monitored and adjusted by the engine management PCM, and nominal values cannot be given. Therefore, it is not possible for the home mechanic to check the ignition timing.
2 The only way in which the ignition timing can be checked is using special electronic test equipment, connected to the engine management system diagnostic socket (refer to Chapter 4A). No adjustment of the ignition

timing is possible. Should the ignition timing be incorrect, then a fault must be present in the engine management system.

6 Knock sensor – removal and refitting

Removal

1 Remove the alternator (see Chapter 5A Section 7).
2 The knock sensor is located on the front facing side of the cylinder block under the inlet manifold.
3 Trace the wiring back from the sensor to the connector, then slide the retaining clip down and disconnect the wiring plug.
4 Note its fitted position, then undo the bolt and remove the sensor **(see illustration)**.

Refitting

5 Refitting is a reversal of removal, noting the following points:
a) *The sensor(s) must be refitted in their original positions, with the wiring harness angle exactly as before.*
b) *Tightening the retaining bolt to the specified torque is absolutely essential. Failure to do so could impair the performance of the sensor, causing engine damage.*

3.4a Unscrew the four mounting bolts ...

3.4b ... then remove the ignition coil and heat shield/mounting plate from the engine

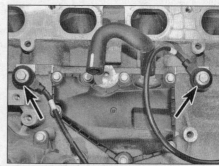

6.4 The knock sensors (arrowed) are located under the inlet manifold – 1.6 litre engine

Chapter 6
Clutch

Contents

Section number

Degrees of difficulty

Easy, suitable for novice with little experience	**Fairly easy,** suitable for beginner with some experience	**Fairly difficult,** suitable for competent DIY mechanic	**Difficult,** suitable for experienced DIY mechanic	**Very difficult,** suitable for expert DIY or professional

Specifications

General
Clutch type . . . . Single dry plate, diaphragm spring, hydraulically-operated release mechanism

Friction disc
Friction material thickness (minimum):
1.25 and 1.4 litre petrol engines . . . . 5.2 mm
1.6 litre petrol engines . . . . 5.6 mm
1.4 litre diesel engines . . . . 4.7 mm
1.6 litre diesel engines . . . . 5.5 mm
1.6 litre diesel engines (Econetic) . . . . 4.7 mm

Torque wrench settings

	Nm	lbf ft
Clutch pedal bracket nuts	25	18
Clutch slave cylinder bolts	10	7
Pressure plate-to-flywheel bolts*	29	21
Steering column shaft universal joint clamp bolt*	35	26

*Use new fasteners

1 General Information

1 The clutch consists of a friction disc, a pressure plate assembly, a release bearing and hydraulic slave cylinder; all of these components are contained in the large cast-aluminium alloy bellhousing, sandwiched between the engine and the transmission.

2 The hydraulic master cylinder is located in the pedal bracket on the bulkhead, and the clutch fluid reservoir is shared with the brake fluid reservoir on the top of the brake master cylinder. Inside the reservoir each circuit has its own compartment, so that in the event of fluid loss in the clutch circuit, the brake circuit remains fully operational.

3 The clutch disc (friction disc) is fitted between the engine flywheel and the clutch pressure plate, and is allowed to slide on the transmission input shaft splines.

4 The pressure plate assembly is bolted to the engine flywheel. When the engine is running, drive is transmitted from the crankshaft, via the flywheel, to the friction disc (these components being clamped securely together by the pressure plate assembly) and from the friction disc to the transmission input shaft.

5 To interrupt the drive, the spring pressure must be relaxed by the hydraulically-operated release mechanism. Depressing the clutch pedal operates the master cylinder which in turn operates the slave cylinder and presses the release bearing against the pressure plate spring fingers. This causes the springs to deform and releases the clamping force on the friction disc.

6 When the pedal is released, the diaphragm spring forces the pressure plate into contact with the friction linings on the friction disc. The disc is now firmly sandwiched between the pressure plate and the flywheel, thus transmitting engine power to the transmission.

7 Wear of the friction material on the friction disc is automatically compensated for by the operation of the hydraulic system. As the friction material on the disc wears, the pressure plate moves towards the flywheel causing the clutch diaphragm spring inner fingers to move outwards. When the clutch pedal is released, excess fluid is expelled through the master cylinder into the fluid reservoir.

2 Clutch master cylinder – removal and refitting

Note: *The clutch master cylinder is an integral part of the clutch pedal assembly and cannot be separated. In the event of a hydraulic system fault, or any sign of visible fluid leakage on or around the master cylinder or clutch pedal, the complete pedal assembly should be renewed.*

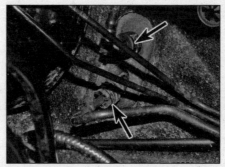

2.2 Hose connections (arrowed) to the master cylinder on the bulkhead

Removal

1 Remove the filler cap from the brake master cylinder reservoir on top of the brake master cylinder, and siphon the hydraulic fluid from the reservoir until it is at the MIN mark (below the outlet to the clutch master cylinder). Alternatively, open the slave cylinder bleed screw, and gently pump the clutch pedal to expel the fluid through a plastic tube connected to the screw; tighten the screw when all the fluid has been removed.

⚠ **Warning: Do not siphon the fluid by mouth, as it is poisonous; use a syringe or an old poultry baster.**

2 Trace the fluid supply hose to the master cylinder connection on the bulkhead. Pull back the collar and disconnect the hose from the master cylinder **(see illustration)**. There will be some loss of fluid as the hose is removed – wipe up any spillage, and rinse any painted surfaces with water (avoid getting water inside the clutch master cylinder, however).

3 Similarly, extract the retaining clip and disconnect the supply pipe to the clutch slave cylinder from the master cylinder connection on the bulkhead (this is the connection below the one just removed).

4 From inside the car, disconnect the wiring connector at the clutch pedal position sensor located at the top of the pedal mounting bracket. Release the wiring from the clips on the pedal bracket.

5 Turn the steering wheel to position the roadwheels in the straight-ahead position,

2.7 Clutch pedal mounting bracket retaining nuts (arrowed)

2.6 Steering column shaft universal joint clamp bolt (arrowed)

then remove the ignition key to engage the steering column lock.

6 Undo the clamp bolt securing the steering column shaft universal joint to the steering gear pinion **(see illustration)**. Pull the shaft upwards and off the pinion and move it to one side, clear of the clutch pedal. Note that a new clamp bolt will be required for refitting.

7 Undo the three nuts and manoeuvre the clutch pedal assembly out from under the facia **(see illustration)**.

Refitting

8 Refitting is a reversal of removal, noting the following points:

a) Use a new clamp bolt when reconnecting the steering column shaft universal joint.

b) Tighten all nuts and bolts to the specified torque, where given.

c) Ensure that all fluid hose connections are clean, and are securely made.

d) Bleed the clutch hydraulic system on completion, as described in Section 4.

3 Clutch slave cylinder – removal and refitting

Removal

1 Remove the transmission as described in Chapter 7A Section 6.

2 Inside the bellhousing, unscrew and remove the three mounting bolts, then withdraw the slave cylinder over the transmission input shaft **(see illustration)**.

3.2 Slave cylinder and mounting bolts (arrowed)

3 With the slave cylinder removed, it is recommended that the transmission input shaft oil seal is renewed. Use a suitable tool to hook it out of the transmission casing and over the input shaft. Refer to Chapter 7A Section 5 if necessary.

4 The release bearing is an interference fit in the slave cylinder, and cannot be renewed separately.

5 If the slave cylinder is faulty it must be renewed, as repair kits are not available.

Refitting

6 Do not apply grease to any part of the slave cylinder or release bearing.

7 Locate a new oil seal over the input shaft and into the transmission housing (refer to Chapter 7A Section 5), then slide the slave cylinder onto the shaft.

8 Insert the mounting bolts and tighten them progressively to the specified torque. As the bolts are tightened, make sure that the oil seal enters the transmission housing correctly.

9 Refit the transmission as described in Chapter 7A Section 6.

10 Refill the master cylinder reservoir with fresh fluid, then bleed the hydraulic system as described in Section 4.

4 Clutch hydraulic system – bleeding

Warning: *Hydraulic fluid is poisonous; wash off immediately and thoroughly in the case of skin contact, and seek immediate medical advice if any fluid is swallowed or gets into the eyes. Certain types of hydraulic fluid are flammable, and may ignite when allowed into contact with hot components; when servicing any hydraulic system, it is safest to assume that the fluid is flammable, and to take precautions against the risk of fire as though it is petrol that is being handled. Hydraulic fluid is also an effective paint stripper, and will attack plastics; if any is spilt, it should be washed off immediately, using copious quantities of fresh water. Finally, it is hygroscopic (it absorbs moisture from the air) – old fluid may be contaminated and unfit for further use. When topping-up or renewing the fluid, always use the recommended type, and ensure that it comes from a freshly-opened sealed container.*

1 The correct operation of any hydraulic system is only possible after removing all air from the components and circuit; this is achieved by bleeding the system.

2 During the bleeding procedure, add only clean, unused hydraulic fluid of the recommended type; never re-use fluid that has already been bled from the system. Ensure that sufficient fluid is available before starting work.

3 If there is any possibility of incorrect fluid being already in the system, the hydraulic circuit must be flushed completely with uncontaminated, correct fluid.

4 If hydraulic fluid has been lost from the system, or air has entered because of a leak, ensure that the fault is cured before continuing further.

5 The bleed screw is screwed into the slave cylinder extension which is positioned on the top of the transmission bellhousing – the bleed screw is behind the fluid supply pipe. Access to the screw is difficult, but may be improved by removing the air cleaner assembly (see Chapter 4A Section 5 or Chapter 4B Section 4).

6 First check that all the hydraulic hoses are securely fitted to the master and slave cylinders. Clean any dirt from around the bleed screw.

7 Unscrew the brake master cylinder fluid reservoir cap, and top-up the fluid level to the upper (MAX) level line; refit the cap loosely, and remember to maintain the fluid level at least above the lower (MIN) level line throughout the procedure, or there is a risk of further air entering the system.

8 There are a number of one-man, do-it-yourself bleeding kits currently available from motor accessory shops. It is recommended that one of these kits is used whenever possible, as they greatly simplify the bleeding operation, and reduce the risk of expelled air and fluid being drawn back into the system. If such a kit is not available, the basic (two-man) method must be used, which is described in detail below.

9 If a kit is to be used, prepare the vehicle as described previously, and follow the kit manufacturer's instructions, as the procedure may vary slightly according to the type being used; generally, they are as outlined below in the relevant sub-section.

Bleeding

Ford method

10 The Ford method for bleeding is to attach a hand vacuum pump and a container of fluid to the slave cylinder bleed screw (in front of the fluid supply pipe on top of the gearbox). Open the bleed screw, and then suck the fluid out of the system until no air bubbles are visible in the connecting tubing (the brake fluid reservoir must be kept topped-up with fluid the whole time). On completion, and before removing the vacuum, close the bleed screw. This is obviously the preferred method if suitable tools are available – if not, the more conventional methods described below should also be successful.

Basic (two-man) method

11 Collect a clean glass jar, a suitable length of plastic or rubber tubing which is a tight fit over the bleed screw. The help of an assistant will also be required. Ensure that the fluid level is maintained at least above the outlet to the clutch master cylinder in the reservoir throughout the procedure.

12 Remove the protective cap from the slave cylinder bleed screw. Fit the tube to the screw, place the other end of the tube in the jar, and pour in sufficient fluid to cover the end of the tube.

13 Loosen the bleed screw (this should be possible by hand) half a turn, then have the assistant slowly depress and release the clutch pedal several times until fluid free of air bubbles emerges. On the final stroke, have the assistant hold the pedal fully depressed. Note that the pedal must be fully depressed and fully released each time.

14 With the pedal held down, tighten the bleed screw and have the assistant fully release the pedal slowly. Check the reservoir fluid level and top-up if necessary, then check the operation of the pedal. After the initial free movement, increased pressure should be felt as the clutch pressure plate diaphragm spring is operated.

15 If the pedal feels spongy, air still remains in the hydraulic system and the bleeding operation must be repeated as described in the previous paragraphs.

16 With the hydraulic system bled, tighten the bleed screw securely, then remove the tube and spanner and refit the dust cap. Do not overtighten the bleed screw.

Using a one-way valve kit

17 As the name implies, these kits consist of a length of tubing with a one-way valve fitted, to prevent expelled air and fluid being drawn back into the system; some kits include a translucent container, which can be positioned so that the air bubbles can be more easily seen flowing from the end of the tube.

18 The kit is connected to the bleed screw, which is then opened (see illustration). The user returns to the driver's seat, depresses the clutch pedal with a smooth, steady stroke, and slowly releases it; this is repeated until the expelled fluid is clear of air bubbles.

19 Note that these kits simplify work so much that it is easy to forget the fluid reservoir level; ensure that this is maintained at least above the outlet to the clutch master cylinder at all times.

Using a pressure-bleeding kit

20 These kits are usually operated by the

4.18 Bleeding the clutch using a one-way valve kit – attach the hose to the bleed screw (arrowed)

reservoir of pressurised air contained in the spare tyre. However, note that it will probably be necessary to reduce the pressure to a lower level than normal; refer to the instructions supplied with the kit.

21 By connecting a pressurised, fluid-filled container to the fluid reservoir, bleeding can be carried out simply by opening the bleed screw and allowing the fluid to flow out until no more air bubbles can be seen in the expelled fluid.

22 This method has the advantage that the large reservoir of fluid provides an additional safeguard against air being drawn into the system during bleeding.

All methods

23 When bleeding is complete, and correct pedal feel is restored, check that the bleed screw is securely tightened and wash off any spilt fluid. Refit the dust cap to the bleed screw.

24 Check the hydraulic fluid level in the reservoir, and top-up if necessary.

25 Discard any hydraulic fluid that has been bled from the system; it will not be fit for re-use.

26 If the clutch is not operating correctly after carrying out the bleeding procedure, the master cylinder or slave cylinder may be faulty.

5 Clutch pedal – removal and refitting

1 The clutch pedal is removed as an assembly with the clutch master cylinder – refer to Section 2.

6 Clutch assembly – removal, inspection and refitting

⚠️ **Warning: Dust created by clutch wear and deposited on the clutch components may contain asbestos, which is a health hazard. DO NOT blow it out with compressed air, or inhale any of it. DO NOT use petrol or petroleum-based solvents to** clean off the dust. Brake system cleaner or methylated spirit should be used to flush the dust into a suitable receptacle. After the clutch components are wiped clean with rags, dispose of the contaminated rags and cleaner in a sealed, marked container.

Removal

1 Unless the complete engine/transmission unit has to be removed from the car (see Chapter 2F Section 4, 5), the clutch can be reached by removing the transmission as described in Chapter 7A Section 6.

2 Before disturbing the clutch, use chalk or a marker pen to mark the relationship of the pressure plate assembly to the flywheel.

3 Hold the flywheel stationary using a suitable tool engaged with the starter ring gear teeth – a piece of metal can be tightened to one of the bolt holes, or alternatively an assistant can use a wide-bladed screwdriver engaged with the teeth **(see illustration)**.

4 Working in a diagonal sequence, slacken the pressure plate bolts by half a turn at a time, until spring pressure is released and the bolts can be unscrewed by hand **(see illustration)**. Discard the bolts – new ones should be used when refitting.

5 Prise the pressure plate assembly off its locating dowels, and collect the friction disc, noting which way round the disc is fitted **(see illustration)**.

Inspection

Note: *Due to the amount of work necessary to remove and refit clutch components, it is usually considered good practice to renew the clutch friction disc, pressure plate assembly and release bearing (slave cylinder) as a matched set, even if only one of these is actually worn enough to require renewal. It is also worth considering the renewal of the clutch components on a preventive basis if the engine and/or transmission have been removed for some other reason.*

6 When cleaning clutch components, read first the warning at the beginning of this Section; remove the dust using a clean, dry cloth, and working in a well-ventilated atmosphere.

7 Check the friction disc linings for signs of wear, damage or oil contamination. If the friction material is cracked, burnt, scored or damaged, or if it is contaminated with oil or grease (shown by shiny black patches), the friction disc must be renewed. Check the depth of the rivets below the friction material surface. If any are at or near the surface of the friction material, then the friction disc must be renewed.

8 If the friction material is still serviceable, check that the centre boss splines are unworn, that the torsion springs are in good condition and securely fastened, and that all the rivets are tight. If any wear or damage is found, the friction disc must be renewed.

9 If the friction material is fouled with oil, this must be due to an oil leak from the crankshaft oil seal, from the sump-to-cylinder block joint, or from the transmission input shaft. Renew the seal or repair the joint, as appropriate, as described in the appropriate part of Chapter 2A or Chapter 7A, before installing the new friction disc.

10 Check the pressure plate assembly for obvious signs of wear or damage; shake it to check for loose rivets or worn or damaged fulcrum rings, and check that the drive straps securing the pressure plate to the cover do not show signs of overheating (such as a deep yellow or blue discoloration). If the diaphragm spring is worn or damaged, or if its pressure is in any way suspect, the pressure plate assembly should be renewed.

11 Examine the machined bearing surfaces of the pressure plate and of the flywheel; they should be clean, completely flat, and free from scratches or scoring. If either is discoloured from excessive heat, or shows signs of cracks, it should be renewed – although minor damage of this nature can sometimes be polished away using emery paper.

12 Check that the release bearing contact surface rotates smoothly and easily, with no sign of noise or roughness. Also check that the surface itself is smooth and unworn, with no signs of cracks, pitting or scoring. If there is any doubt about its condition, the bearing (and slave cylinder) must be renewed.

Refitting

13 On reassembly, ensure that the disc contact surfaces of the flywheel and pressure

6.3 Home-made tool for holding the flywheel stationary

6.4 Slacken and remove the pressure plate bolts

6.5 Prise the pressure plate off its dowels and remove it with the friction disc

6.14a Clutch friction disc FLYWHEEL SIDE markings should face the flywheel

6.14b Fit the friction disc, then use a centralising tool to align it

6.15 Fit the pressure plate onto its dowels

plate are completely clean, smooth, and free from oil or grease. Use solvent to remove any protective grease from new components.

14 Fit the friction disc so that its spring hub assembly faces away from the flywheel; there may also be a marking showing which way round the plate is to be refitted. Depending on the type of centralising tool being used, the friction disc may be held in position at this stage **(see illustrations)**.

15 Refit the pressure plate assembly, aligning the marks made on dismantling (if the original pressure plate is re-used), and locating the pressure plate on its locating dowels **(see illustration)**. Fit the pressure plate bolts, but tighten them only finger-tight, so that the friction disc can still be moved.

16 The friction disc must now be centralised, so that when the transmission is refitted, its input shaft will pass through the splines at the centre of the friction disc.

17 Centralisation can be achieved by passing a screwdriver or other long bar through the friction disc and into the hole in the crankshaft;

the friction disc can then be moved around until it is centred on the crankshaft hole. Alternatively, a clutch-aligning-tool can be used to eliminate the guesswork; these can be obtained from most accessory shops. The normal type consists of a spigot bar with several different adapters, but a more recent type consists of a tool which clamps the friction disc to the pressure plate before locating the two items on the flywheel. A home-made aligning tool can be fabricated from a length of metal rod or wooden dowel which fits closely inside the crankshaft hole, and has insulating tape wound around it to match the diameter of the friction disc splined hole.

18 When the friction disc is centralised, tighten the pressure plate bolts evenly and in a diagonal sequence to the specified torque setting **(see illustration)**.

19 Apply a thin smear of molybdenum disulphide grease to the splines of the friction disc and the transmission input shaft **(see illustration)**.

Caution: Do not apply too much grease, as there is a risk that it will contaminate the friction disc material.

20 Refit the transmission as described in Chapter 7A Section 6.

7 Clutch release bearing – removal, inspection and refitting

Removal

1 For access to the clutch release bearing, the transmission must be removed as described in Chapter 7A Section 6.

2 Remove the slave cylinder as described in Section 3. The release bearing is an interference fit in the slave cylinder, and cannot be renewed separately.

Inspection

3 Note that it is often considered worthwhile to renew the release bearing as a matter of course regardless of its condition, considering the amount of work necessary to access it. Check that the contact surface rotates smoothly and easily, with no sign of noise or roughness, and that the surface itself is smooth and unworn, with no signs of cracks, pitting or scoring. If there is any doubt about its condition, the bearing (and slave cylinder) must be renewed.

Refitting

4 Refit the slave cylinder as described in Section 3.

5 Refit the transmission with reference to Chapter 7A Section 6.

6.18 Tighten the pressure plate bolts to the specified torque

6.19 Apply a little grease to the transmission input shaft splines

Chapter 7 Part A
Manual transmission

Contents

Degrees of difficulty

Easy, suitable for novice with little experience	Fairly easy, suitable for beginner with some experience	Fairly difficult, suitable for competent DIY mechanic	Difficult, suitable for experienced DIY mechanic	Very difficult, suitable for expert DIY or professional

Specifications

General

Transmission type. . . . . Five forward speeds, one reverse. Synchromesh on all forward gears Gearchange linkage operated by twin cables
Transmission code iB5
Transmission oil capacity . . . . See Chapter 1A or 1B Specifications

Gear ratios

All except 1.6 litre petrol engine models:
1st. 3.58: 1
2nd 1.93: 1
3rd 1.28: 1
4th. 0.95: 1
5th. 0.76: 1
Reverse. 3.62: 1
1.6 litre petrol engine models:
1st. 3.85: 1
2nd 2.04: 1
3rd 1.41: 1
4th. 1.11: 1
5th. 0.88: 1
Reverse. 3.62: 1
Final drive ratios:
1.25 litre petrol engine models . . . . 4.06: 1 or 4.25: 1
1.4 litre petrol engine models 4.06: 1
1.6 litre petrol engine models 3.82: 1
Diesel engine models 3.37: 1

Torque wrench settings

	Nm	lbf ft
Exhaust flexible section flange to manifold	48	35
Left-hand engine mounting to transmission	80	59
Oil filler/level plug	35	26
Rear engine mounting bolts	48	35
Reversing light switch	18	13
Selector lever securing bolt	25	18
Slave cylinder pressure pipe bracket	28	21
Transmission to engine	48	35

1 General Information

1 The transmission is contained in a cast-aluminium alloy casing bolted to the engine's left-hand end, and consists of the gearbox and final drive differential – often called a transaxle. The transmission unit type is stamped on a plate attached to the transmission.

2 The iB5 unit is identical to that used in the previous Fiesta range, albeit with improved synchromesh components to improve the quality of gearchange. The transmission is intended to be sealed for life – no oil changes are required, and no drain plug is fitted. Provided that the oil level is maintained as described in Chapter 1A or 1B, no routine maintenance is necessary.

3 Drive is transmitted from the crankshaft via the clutch to the input shaft, which has a splined extension to accept the clutch friction disc. From the input shaft, drive is transmitted to the output shaft, from where the drive is transmitted to the differential crownwheel, which rotates with the differential and planetary gears, thus driving the sun gears and driveshafts. The rotation of the planetary gears on their shaft allows the inner roadwheel to rotate at a slower speed than the outer roadwheel when the car is cornering.

4 The input and output shafts are arranged side-by-side, parallel to the crankshaft and driveshafts, so that their gear pinion teeth are in constant mesh. In the neutral position, the output shaft gear pinions rotate freely, so that drive cannot be transmitted to the crownwheel.

5 Gear selection is via a floor-mounted lever and selector cable mechanism.

6 The transmission selector mechanism causes the appropriate selector fork to move its respective synchro-sleeve along the output shaft, to lock the gear pinion to the synchro-hub. Since the synchro-hubs are splined to the output shaft, this locks the pinion to the shaft, so that drive can be transmitted. To ensure that gearchanging can be made quickly and quietly, a synchromesh system is fitted to all forward gears, consisting of baulk rings and spring-loaded fingers, as well as the gear pinions and synchro-hubs. The synchromesh cones are formed on the mating faces of the baulk rings and gear pinions. The transmission has dual synchromesh on 1st and 2nd gears for even smoother gearchanging.

Transmission overhaul

7 Because of the complexity of the assembly, possible unavailability of new parts and special tools necessary, internal repair procedures for the transmission are not recommended for the home mechanic. The bulk of the information in this Chapter is devoted to removal and refitting procedures.

2.2 Unclip the cover from the front of the transmission

2.4 Unlock the selector cable by pressing the coloured insert (arrowed) towards the engine

2 Gearchange cables – adjustment

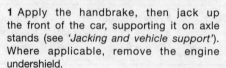

1 Apply the handbrake, then jack up the front of the car, supporting it on axle stands (see 'Jacking and vehicle support'). Where applicable, remove the engine undershield.

2 At the front face of the transmission housing, remove the selector mechanism cover by working around the edge, releasing a total of seven clips (see illustration).

3 Only the selector cable is to be adjusted during this procedure – this is the cable which comes to the lowest point on the front of the transmission, with its end fitting nearest the engine.

4 Unlock the selector cable by pressing the coloured insert towards the engine, then prise the selector cable end fitting from the lever on the transmission (see illustration).

5 Move the shift lever on the transmission (the lever with the other cable still attached) to the 3rd gear position.

6 Move the selector lever on the transmission (the lever with the disconnected selector cable) to the neutral position.

7 Refit the selector cable end fitting to the transmission selector lever, then

lock the selector cable in position by moving the coloured insert away from the engine.

8 Refit the selector mechanism cover, ensuring that the clips engage correctly. Where applicable refit the engine undershield and lower the car to the ground.

9 Start the engine, keeping the clutch pedal depressed, and check for correct gear selection.

3 Gearchange cables and gear lever – removal and refitting

Removal

Gear lever

1 Disconnect the battery negative terminal (refer to 'Disconnecting the battery').

2 Remove the centre console as described in Chapter 11 Section 24.

3 Prise the two gearchange cable end fittings from the levers on the gear lever housing (see illustration).

4 Pull back the retaining collars and detach the gearchange outer cables from their locations on the gear lever housing (see illustration).

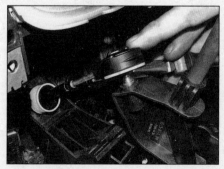

3.3 Prise the two gearchange cable end fittings from the levers on the gear lever housing

3.4 Pull back the retaining collars and detach the gearchange outer cables from the gear lever housing

3.5a Undo the four nuts (arrowed) …

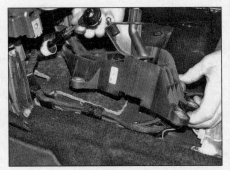

3.5b … and lift out the gear lever housing assembly

3.9 Undo the three bolts (arrowed) securing the battery tray to its support bracket

5 Undo the four nuts and lift out the gear lever housing assembly **(see illustrations)**.

Cables

6 Remove the gear lever as described previously.

7 On all except 1.4 litre diesel engine models, remove the air cleaner assembly as described in Chapter 4A Section 5 or Chapter 4B Section 4 as applicable. On 1.4 litre diesel engine models, remove the plastic air intake duct located at the front left-hand side of the engine compartment.

8 Remove the battery as described in Chapter 5A Section 4.

9 Undo the three bolts securing the battery tray to its support bracket **(see illustration)**. Release the wiring harness from the cable-ties at the front of the battery tray and move the battery tray to one side, as far as the wiring harness will allow.

10 Apply the handbrake, then jack up the front of the car, supporting it on axle stands (see 'Jacking and vehicle support'). Where applicable, remove the engine undershield.

11 At the front face of the transmission housing, remove the selector mechanism cover by working around the edge, releasing a total of seven clips **(see illustration 2.2)**.

12 Prise the shift cable and selector cable end fittings from their levers on the transmission – note their fitted locations. Pull back the retaining collars and detach both cables from the transmission support bracket.

13 From under the car, undo the eight nuts and remove the underfloor cross-brace

beneath the exhaust centre section **(see illustration)**. Release the exhaust system from the rubber mounting block just in front of the cross-brace.

14 Remove the six washer-type fasteners, and slide the exhaust heat shield rearwards.

15 Undo the two nuts securing the cable guide plate to the underbody.

16 Withdraw the cables downwards from the engine compartment, releasing them from their retaining clips and noting how they are routed. Take care not to kink or bend the cables during removal.

17 Undo the bolts and remove the bracket each side between the facia crossmember centre supports and the floor **(see illustration)**. Take care as the edges of the brackets are extremely sharp.

18 The cable entry point into the car should now be visible, but the cables themselves are hidden under the carpet. To gain access to them it will be necessary to cut the carpet and sound-deadening material. Take great care not to cut through the wiring harness when cutting the carpet.

19 Have an assistant unclip the cable guide from the underbody and guide the cables out of the engine compartment. Withdraw the cables into the car, again, taking care not to kink or bend them.

Refitting

20 Refitting is a reversal of removal. On completion, adjust the cables as described in Section 2.

4 Reversing light switch – removal and refitting

Removal

1 The switch is located on the front of the transmission, next to the selector cable front cover. To improve access, jack up the front left-hand side of the car (see 'Jacking and vehicle support'). Where fitted, remove the engine undershield.

2 Disconnect the wiring plug from the switch.

3 Unscrew and remove the switch from the front of the transmission – anticipate a little oil spillage as this is done **(see illustration)**.

Refitting

4 Refitting is a reversal of removal. Tighten the switch to the specified torque.

5 Oil seals – renewal

1 Oil leaks frequently occur due to wear or deterioration of the driveshaft oil seals, or the selector shaft oil seal. Renewal of these seals is relatively easy, since the repairs can be performed without removing the transmission from the vehicle.

3.13 Undo the eight nuts and remove the underfloor cross-brace

3.17 Undo the bolts (arrowed) and remove the facia crossmember support brackets each side

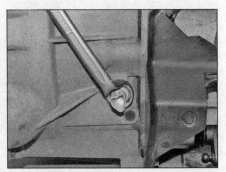

4.3 Unscrew and remove the reversing light switch from the front of the transmission

5.4 Prise out the oil seal using a suitable lever

5.7 Drive the oil seal into place using a tube or socket

6.4 Undo the retaining bolt (arrowed) and disconnect the earth cable from the top of the transmission

Driveshaft oil seals

2 The driveshaft oil seals are located at the sides of the transmission, where the driveshaft or intermediate shaft enters the transmission. If leakage at the seal is suspected, raise the vehicle and support it securely on axle stands. If the seal is leaking, oil will be found on the side of the transmission below the driveshaft/intermediate shaft.

3 Refer to Chapter 8 Section 2 and remove the appropriate driveshaft/intermediate shaft.

4 Using a large screwdriver or lever, carefully prise the oil seal out of the transmission casing, taking care not to damage the transmission casing **(see illustration)**.

5 Wipe clean the oil seal seating in the transmission casing.

6 Dip the new oil seal in clean oil, then press it a little way into the casing by hand, making sure that it is square to its seating.

7 Using suitable tubing or a large socket, carefully drive the oil seal fully into the casing until it contacts the seating **(see illustration)**.

8 When refitting the left-hand driveshaft, use the protective sleeve which should be provided with genuine parts. The sleeve is fitted into the seal, and the driveshaft is then fitted through it – the sleeve is then withdrawn and cut free.

9 Refit the driveshaft/intermediate shaft (see Chapter 8 Section 2).

Selector shaft oil seal

10 Apply the handbrake, then jack up the front of the car, supporting it on axle stands (see 'Jacking and vehicle support'). Where fitted, remove the engine undershield.

11 At the front face of the transmission housing, remove the selector mechanism cover by working around the edge, releasing a total of seven clips.

12 Prise the shift cable and selector cable end fittings from their levers on the transmission – note their fitted locations. Pull back the retaining collars and detach both cables from the transmission support bracket.

13 Unscrew and remove the four bolts securing the selector mechanism rear cover to the transmission housing.

14 Remove the transmission shift lever by prising off the protective cap and extracting

the retaining clip.

15 With the shift lever removed, unscrew the securing bolt and take off the selector lever and dust cover.

16 The selector shaft oil seal can now be prised out of its location. If using a screwdriver or similar sharp tool, take great care not to mark or gouge the selector shaft or the seal housing as this is done, or the new seal will also leak.

17 Before fitting the new oil seal, carefully clean the visible part of the selector shaft, and the oil seal housing. Wrap a little tape around the end of the shaft, to protect the seal lips as they pass over it.

18 Smear the new oil seal with a little oil, then carefully fit it over the end of the selector shaft, lips facing inwards (towards the transmission).

19 Making sure that the seal stays square to the shaft, press it fully along the shaft (if available, a 16 mm ring spanner is ideal for this).

20 Press the seal fully into its housing, again using the ring spanner or perhaps a deep socket. Remove the tape from the end of the shaft.

21 Further refitting is a reversal of removal, tightening the selector lever securing bolt to the specified torque.

22 On completion, check and if necessary adjust the selector cable as described in Section 2.

6 Transmission – removal and refitting

Warning: The hydraulic fluid used in the clutch system is brake fluid, which is poisonous. Take care to keep it off bare skin, and in particular out of your eyes. The fluid also attacks paintwork, and may discolour carpets, etc – keep spillages to a minimum, and wash any off immediately with cold water. Finally, brake fluid is highly inflammable, and should be handled with the same care as petrol.
Note: *Read through this procedure before starting work to see what is involved, particularly in terms of lifting equipment.*

Depending on the facilities available, the home mechanic may prefer to remove the engine and transmission together, then separate them on the bench, as described in Chapter 2F. The help of an assistant is highly recommended if the transmission is to be removed (and later refitted) on its own.

Removal

1 Remove the air cleaner and inlet ducts as described in Chapter 4A Section 5 or Chapter 4B Section 4 as applicable.

2 Remove the battery, battery tray and support bracket as described in Chapter 5A Section 4.

3 Remove the engine management PCM as described in Chapter 4A Section 11 or Chapter 4B Section 12 as applicable.

4 Undo the retaining bolt and disconnect the earth cable from the top of the transmission **(see illustration)**. Release the clutch slave cylinder hydraulic pipe from the support plate and remove the support plate.

5 Disconnect the transmission breather hose from the top of the transmission.

6 Remove the windscreen cowl panel and bulkhead closure panel as described in Chapter 11 Section 20.

7 Undo the transmission-to-engine bolts which are accessible from above.

8 Firmly apply the handbrake, then jack up the front of the vehicle and support it securely on axle stands (see 'Jacking and vehicle support'). Where applicable, remove the engine undershield.

9 Disconnect the gearchange cables from the transmission as described in Section 3. Release the cables from their support bracket.

10 To prevent damage to the exhaust flexible section, support it by attaching a pair of splints either side (two scrap strips of wood, plant canes, etc) using some cable-ties. Undo the nuts securing the flexible section to the exhaust manifold, and separate the joint. Recover the gasket, and discard it. Release the exhaust front rubber mounting block and move the system to one side.

11 Taking adequate precautions against brake fluid spillage (refer to the Warning at the start of this Section), pull out the securing clip, then pull the pipe fitting out of the clutch slave

cylinder at the top of the transmission **(see illustration)**. Plug or tape over the pipe end, to avoid losing fluid, and to prevent dirt entry.

12 Unbolt the engine rear mounting completely from under the car, referring to the relevant Part of Chapter 2A Section 18 if necessary.

13 Disconnect the reversing light switch wiring plug.

14 Remove both driveshafts from the transmission as described in Chapter 8 Section 2.

15 The engine/transmission must now be supported, as the left-hand mounting must be dismantled and removed. Ford technicians use a support bar which locates in the tops of the inner wings – proprietary engine support bars are available from tool outlets.

16 If a support bar is not available, an engine hoist should be used. With an engine hoist, the engine/transmission can be manoeuvred more easily and safely. In the workshop, we found the best solution was to move the engine to the required position, and support it from below – using the hoist on the transmission then gave excellent manoeuvrability, and total control for lowering out.

17 Supporting both the engine and transmission from below should be considered a last resort, and should only be done if a heavy-duty hydraulic ('trolley') jack is used, with a large, flat piece of wood on the jack head to spread the load and avoid damage to the sump. A further jack will be needed to lower the transmission out. **Note:** *Always take care when using a hydraulic jack, as it is possible for this type to collapse under load – generally, a scissor-type jack avoids this problem, but is also less stable, and offers no manoeuvrability.*

18 With the engine securely supported, remove the three bolts from the engine left-hand mounting (on top of the transmission) **(see illustration)**.

19 Taking care that nothing which is still attached to the engine is placed under strain, lower the transmission as far as possible.

20 Remove the lower transmission-to-engine bolts. The bolts are of different lengths, so note their positions carefully for refitting.

21 Swing the transmission forwards, and wedge it in position with a stout piece of wood, about 300 mm long, between the engine and the subframe.

22 Check that, apart from the remaining flange bolts, there is nothing preventing the transmission from being lowered and removed. Make sure that any wiring or hoses lying on top of the transmission are not going to get caught up and stretched as the transmission is lowered.

23 Unscrew the remaining flange bolts. If the transmission does not separate on its own, it must be rocked from side-to-side, to free it from the locating dowels. As the transmission is withdrawn from the engine, make sure its weight is supported at all times – the transmission input shaft (or the clutch) may otherwise be damaged as it is withdrawn through the clutch assembly bolted to the engine flywheel. Recover the adapter plates (where fitted) between the engine and transmission, as they may fall out when the two are separated.

24 Keeping the transmission steady, carefully lower it down and remove it from under the car.

25 The clutch components can now be inspected with reference to Chapter 6, and renewed if necessary. Unless they are virtually new, it is worth renewing the clutch components as a matter of course, even if the transmission has been removed for some other reason.

Refitting

26 If removed, refit the clutch components (see Chapter 6 Section 6). Also ensure that the engine-to-transmission adapter plates (where fitted) are in position on the engine.

27 Apply a very thin smear of high-temperature anti-seize grease to the splines of the transmission input shaft. Take care not

to apply too much or the clutch plates may become contaminated.

28 Where a block of wood was used to wedge the engine forwards for transmission removal, make sure that it is in place for refitting.

29 With the transmission secured to the hoist/trolley jack as on removal, raise it into position, and then carefully slide it onto the engine, at the same time engaging the input shaft with the clutch friction disc splines.

30 Do not use excessive force to refit the transmission – if the input shaft does not slide into place easily, readjust the angle of the transmission so that it is level, and/or turn the input shaft so that the splines engage properly with the disc. If problems are still experienced, check that the clutch disc is correctly centred (Chapter 6 Section 6).

31 Once the transmission is successfully mated to the engine, insert as many of the flange bolts as possible, and tighten them progressively to draw the transmission fully onto the locating dowels.

32 Where applicable, remove the wedge fitted between the engine and subframe. Raise the transmission into position, then refit the engine left-hand mounting bolts. Tighten the bolts to the specified torque.

33 Refit the remaining transmission-to-engine bolts, and tighten all of them to the specified torque.

34 Refit the engine/transmission rear mounting and tighten the bolts to the specified torque.

35 Once the engine/transmission mountings have been refitted, the support bar, engine hoist or supporting jack can be removed.

36 Further refitting is a reversal of removal, noting the following points:

a) *Refit the driveshafts as described in Chapter 8 Section 2.*

b) *Refit the bulkhead closure panel and windscreen cowl panel as described in Chapter 11 Section 20.*

c) *On completion, adjust the gearchange cables as described in Section 2.*

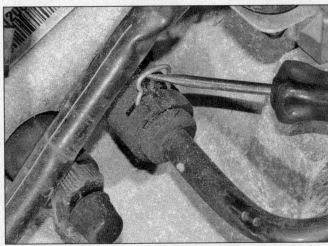

6.11 Extract the retaining clip and disconnect the slave cylinder hydraulic pipe

6.18 Left-hand engine mounting retaining bolts (arrowed)

7 Transmission overhaul – general information

1 The overhaul of a manual transmission is a complex (and often expensive) engineering task for the DIY home mechanic to undertake, which requires access to specialist equipment. It involves dismantling and reassembly of many small components, measuring clearances precisely and if necessary, adjusting them by the selection shims and spacers. Internal transmission components are also often difficult to obtain and in many instances, extremely expensive. Because of this, if the transmission develops a fault or becomes noisy, the best course of action is to have the unit overhauled by a specialist repairer or to obtain an exchange reconditioned unit.

2 Nevertheless, it is not impossible for the more experienced mechanic to overhaul the transmission if the special tools are available and the job is carried out in a deliberate step-by-step manner, to ensure that nothing is overlooked.

3 The tools necessary for an overhaul include internal and external circlip pliers, bearing pullers, a slide hammer, a set of pin punches, a dial test indicator, and possibly a hydraulic press. In addition, a large, sturdy workbench and a vice will be required.

4 During dismantling of the transmission, make careful notes of how each component is fitted to make reassembly easier and accurate.

5 Before dismantling the transmission, it will help if you have some idea of where the problem lies. Certain problems can be closely related to specific areas in the transmission which can make component examination and renewal easier. Refer to Fault finding at the end of this manual for more information.

Chapter 7 Part B
Automatic transmission

Contents

Degrees of difficulty

Easy, suitable for novice with little experience	Fairly easy, suitable for beginner with some experience	Fairly difficult, suitable for competent DIY mechanic	Difficult, suitable for experienced DIY mechanic	Very difficult, suitable for expert DIY or professional

Specifications

General

Transmission type. . . . . Electronically-controlled automatic, four forward speeds and reverse with sequential manual gear selection capability

Transmission code 4F27E

Gear ratios

1st 2.816: 1
2nd 1.498: 1
3rd 1.000: 1
4th 0.726: 1
Reverse 2.649: 1

Torque wrench settings

	Nm	lbf ft
Engine/transmission left-hand mounting to body	80	59
Engine/transmission left-hand mounting to transmission	80	59
Engine/transmission rear mounting bolts.	48	35
Exhaust flexible section flange to manifold	48	35
Fluid pan bolts	10	7
Torque converter to driveplate*	37	27
Transmission lever bolt.	22	16
Transmission range sensor bolts	10	7
Transmission to engine.	48	35

Use new fasteners

1 General Information

1 Optionally available on 1.4 litre petrol engine models, the automatic transmission is controlled electronically by the transmission control module and engine management powertrain control module. The transmission is a four-speed unit with fully automatic gear selection. In addition to the automatic operation, the transmission can also be operated manually with four-speed sequential gear selection.

2 The transmission electronic control system has a fail-safe mode, which gives the transmission limited operation in order to drive the vehicle home or to a repair garage. A warning light on the instrument panel tells the driver when this occurs. The electronic system uses all the information available from the various transmission and engine management-related sensors (also see Chapters 4A and 5B) to determine the optimum gearshift points for smoothness,

performance and economy. Depending on throttle position and vehicle speed, the module can 'lock-up' the torque converter in 3rd and 4th gear, eliminating torque converter 'slip' and improving fuel consumption.

3 The unit has been designed to have a low maintenance requirement, the fluid level being checked periodically (see Chapter 1A Section 29). The fluid is intended to last the life of the transmission, and is cooled by a separate fluid cooler.

4 There is no kickdown switch, as kickdown

is controlled by the throttle position sensor in the engine management system.

5 The gear selector includes the normal P, R, N and D positions together with an additional M position for manual gear selection.

6 As is normally the case with automatic transmissions, a starter inhibitor relay is fitted, which prevents the engine from being started (by interrupting the supply to the starter solenoid) when the selector is in any position other than P or N. The intention is to prevent the car moving, which might otherwise happen if the engine were started in position D, for example. The inhibitor system is electronically controlled, based on signals received from the engine and transmission sensors.

7 As a further safety measure, the ignition key can only be removed from the ignition switch when the selector is in P; it is also necessary for the ignition to be on, and for the brake pedal and selector lever locking button (on the side of the lever) to be depressed in order to move the selector from position P. If the vehicle battery is discharged, the selector lever release solenoid will not function. If it is required to move the vehicle in this state, prise up the flap, and insert a pen or a similar small instrument into the aperture on the right-hand side of the centre console **(see illustration)**. Push the locking lever downwards and move the selector lever to the required position.

2 Fault finding – general

1 In the event of a fault occurring on the transmission, first check that the fluid level is correct (see Chapter 1A Section 29). If there has been a loss of fluid, check the oil seals as described in Section 6. Also check the hoses to the fluid cooler for leaks. The only other tasks possible for the home mechanic are the renewal of the various transmission sensors (Section 5); however, it is not advisable to go ahead and renew any sensor until the fault has been positively identified by reading the transmission fault codes.

2 Any serious fault which occurs will result in the transmission entering the fail-safe mode, and a fault code (or several codes) will be logged in the control module. These codes can be read using an electronic fault code reader. A Ford dealer will obviously have such a reader, but they are also available from other suppliers. It is unlikely to be cost-effective for the private owner to purchase a fault code reader, but a well-equipped local garage or auto-electrical specialist will have one.

3 If the fault still persists, it is necessary to determine whether it is of an electrical, mechanical or hydraulic nature; to do this, special test equipment is required. It is therefore essential to have the work carried out by an automatic transmission specialist or Ford dealer if a transmission fault is suspected.

4 Do not remove the transmission from the vehicle for possible repair before professional fault diagnosis has been carried out, since most tests require the transmission to be in the vehicle.

3 Selector cable – removal, refitting and adjustment

Removal

1 Remove the selector assembly as described in Section 4.

2 Apply the handbrake, then jack up the front of the car, supporting it on axle stands (see 'Jacking and vehicle support').

3 Locate the end of the selector cable, which is on the front of the transmission.

4 Disconnect the cable end fitting by prising it off the transmission selector lever **(see illustration)**.

5 Lift the locking tab, slide up the locking catch, then squeeze together the sides of the clip and slide the cable outer from the bracket on the transmission **(see illustrations)**.

6 From under the car, undo the eight nuts and remove the underfloor cross-brace beneath the exhaust centre section **(see illustration)**. Release the exhaust system from the rubber mounting block just in front of the cross-brace.

7 Remove the six washer-type fasteners, and slide the exhaust heat shield rearwards.

8 Undo the two nuts securing the cable guide plate to the underbody.

9 Withdraw the cable downwards from the

1.7 Press down to release the locking lever

3.4 Prise the cable end fitting from the lever on the transmission

3.5a Prise out the locking catch (arrowed) ...

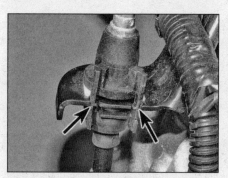

3.5b ... squeeze together the clips (arrowed) ...

3.5c ... and slide the cable from the bracket

3.6 Undo the eight nuts and remove the underfloor cross-brace

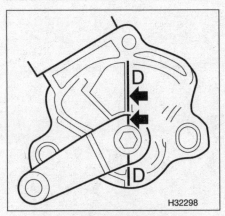

3.14 Range sensor/transmission lever
alignment markings

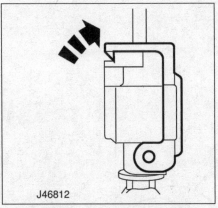

3.15 Prise up the cable locking catch

engine compartment, releasing it from the retaining clips and noting how it is routed. Take care not to kink or bend the cable during removal.

10 From inside the car the cable entry point into the car should be visible, but the cable itself is hidden under the carpet. To gain access it will be necessary to cut the carpet and sound-deadening material. Take great care not to cut through the wiring harness when cutting the carpet.

11 Have an assistant unclip the cable guide from the underbody and guide the cable out of the engine compartment. Withdraw the cable into the car, again, taking care not to kink or bend it.

Refitting

12 Refitting is a reversal of removal, noting the following points:
a) *Once the cable has been reconnected to the selector lever, shift the lever to position D before reconnecting the cable end fitting at the transmission lever.*
b) *Before securing the cable to the transmission bracket or transmission lever, check the cable adjustment as described below.*

Adjustment

13 Inside the vehicle, move the selector lever to position D.

4.2a Prise the end fitting (arrowed) from
the lever

14 With the inner cable disconnected from the lever on the transmission range sensor, check that the transmission lever is in the D position. To do this, it will be necessary to move the lever slightly up and down until it is positioned correctly. A further check can be made by observing that the D mark on the range sensor is correctly aligned with the mark on the transmission lever **(see illustration)**.

15 Unclip the cable locking catch at the transmission end **(see illustration)**.

16 With both the selector levers inside the vehicle and on the side of the transmission in position D, refit the cable end fitting to the transmission lever, then press the catch on the cable into place to lock it.

17 Lower the vehicle to the ground, then carry out a road test to check the operation of the transmission.

4	Selector components – removal and refitting

Selector assembly

Removal

1 Remove the centre console as described in Chapter 11 Section 24.

2 Move the selector lever to P. Working through the front of the selector housing,

4.2b Pull the outer cable collar (arrowed)
forwards

disconnect the cable inner from the lever by prising the end fitting sideways, then pull the collar forwards, and lift the cable outer from the bracket **(see illustrations)**.

3 Disconnect the multiplug wiring connectors at the rear of the assembly, noting their positions, and move the wiring harness clear.

4 Unscrew the four mounting bolts, and withdraw the selector lever assembly **(see illustration)**.

5 If required, the assembly can be further dismantled (after removing the selector lever knob, as described below) by unclipping the top cover and removing the illumination bulb and inner cover.

Refitting

6 Refitting is a reversal of the removal procedure, but adjust the selector cable as described in Section 3.

Selector lever knob

Removal

7 Remove the grub screw at the side of the knob, then pull the knob upwards off the lever.

Refitting

8 Refitting is a reversal of removal.

5	Transmission sensors – removal and refitting	

Transmission range sensor

1 The transmission range sensor is effectively a selector position sensor, the signal from which is used by the control module to modify the operation of the transmission, dependent on which 'gear' is selected. For example, besides controlling gearshift points, depending on the signal received, the module may actuate the starter inhibitor relay, the reversing lights, or the ignition key lock. **Note:** *To set the range sensor in its working position, Ford special tool 307-415 is required. If this tool is not available, the sensor position must be carefully marked before removal.*

2 Access to the range sensor is easiest from below – the sensor is at the front of the transmission, near the transmission selector

4.4 Undo the selector lever housing bolts
(3 arrowed)

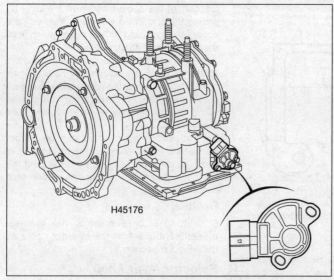

5.2 Transmission range sensor location

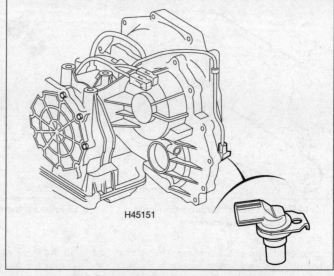

5.15 Output shaft speed sensor location

lever **(see illustration)**. Apply the handbrake, then jack up the front of the car and support it on axle stands (see *'Jacking and vehicle support'*).

3 Prise the selector cable end fitting off the transmission lever, and disconnect the wiring plug from the sensor.

4 Hold the transmission lever against rotation, then unscrew the lever retaining bolt, and remove the lever from the sensor.

5 Caution: If the lever is not held as its bolt is undone, the force required to loosen the bolt will be transmitted to the sensor itself, which may well lead to the sensor being damaged. The same applies when retightening the bolt on completion.

6 Before removing the sensor, make a couple of alignment marks between the sensor and the transmission, for use when refitting.

7 Take precautions against the possible spillage of transmission fluid. Unscrew the two sensor retaining bolts, and withdraw the sensor from the transmission.

8 Clean the sensor location in the transmission, and the sensor itself. If a new sensor is being fitted, transfer the alignment marks from the old unit to the new one – this will provide an approximate setting, which should allow the car to be driven.

9 Refit the sensor, and secure it loosely in position with the two bolts, tightened by hand only at this stage.

10 Ford special tool 307-415 must now be used to set the sensor in its working position. If the tool is not available, realign the marks made prior to removal. When correctly aligned, tighten the two sensor retaining bolts to the specified torque.

11 Refit the transmission lever. Tighten the lever retaining bolt to the specified torque, holding the lever against rotation as the bolt is tightened (refer to the Caution earlier in this Section).

12 Reconnect the selector cable to the transmission lever, and check the cable adjustment as described in Section 3.

13 On completion, lower the car to the ground.

Output shaft speed sensor

14 Access to the speed sensor is easiest from below. Apply the handbrake, then loosen the left-hand front wheel nuts. Jack up the front of the car and support it on axle stands (see *'Jacking and vehicle support'*).

15 Remove the left-hand front wheel and the wheel arch liner – the sensor is located at the rear of the transmission, behind the driveshafts **(see illustration)**.

16 Disconnect the wiring plug from the sensor, then position a suitable container below the sensor to catch any transmission fluid which may be spilt as the sensor is removed.

17 Unscrew the sensor securing bolt, and slowly withdraw the sensor from its location.

18 Check the condition of the O-ring seal fitted to the sensor body – fit a new seal if the old one is in poor condition.

19 Refitting is a reversal of the removal procedure, but clean the sensor location and lightly oil the O-ring before inserting the assembly in the transmission casing. Check the transmission fluid level as described in Chapter 1A Section 29 on completion.

Turbine (input) shaft speed sensor

20 The turbine shaft speed sensor is located on top of the transmission, and is an inductive pick-up sensor which senses the speed of rotation of the input shaft **(see illustration)**. This information is used by the control module to control gearchanging and the

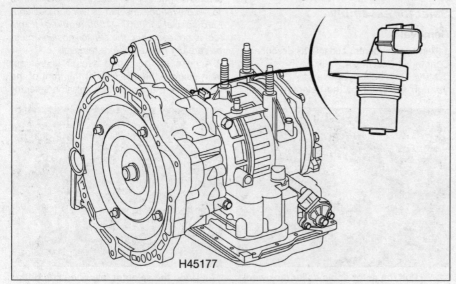

5.20 Turbine (input) shaft speed sensor location

torque converter lock-up clutch. Removal and refitting details are similar to the output shaft speed sensor described previously.

Brake pedal position switch

21 The signal from the switch is used by the control module to disengage the torque converter lock-up, and to allow the selector lever to be moved from the P position when starting the engine. Removal and refitting details for the switch will be the same as for the brake light switch in Chapter 9 Section 17.

Brake pedal shift interlock actuator

22 This unit is part of the system used to lock the selector lever in P when the ignition key is removed, and is incorporated in the selector lever itself.
23 Remove the selector knob as described in Section 4. With the knob removed, the actuator pushrod can be pulled out and removed.
24 Refitting is a reversal of removal. Check the operation of the system on completion.

Selector lever shift interlock solenoid

25 The main solenoid controlling the shift interlock system (used to lock the selector lever in P when the ignition key is removed) is located at the base of the selector lever. For access to the solenoid, remove the centre console as described in Chapter 11 Section 24. At the time of writing, no further removal details were available from Ford.

6 Oil seals – renewal

Driveshaft

1 The procedure is the same as that for the manual transmission (refer to Chapter 7A Section 5).

Output shaft speed sensor

2 The procedure is covered in Section 5.

7 Fluid pan – removal and refitting

Note: This procedure is provided principally to cure any leak developing from the fluid pan joint. It is not advisable for the DIY mechanic to remove the fluid pan for any other reason, since it gives access to internal transmission components, servicing of which is considered beyond the scope of this Manual.

Removal

1 Apply the handbrake, then jack up the front of the car and support it on axle stands (see 'Jacking and vehicle support').
2 Place a suitable container below the pan,

as most of the contents of the transmission will drain when the pan is removed.
3 Progressively unscrew and remove the fluid pan bolts.
4 The fluid pan is 'stuck' to the base of the transmission by a bead of sealant, so it is unlikely that the pan will fall off once the bolts are removed. Care must now be taken to break the sealant without damaging the mating surfaces. Do not prise the pan down, as this may bend it, or damage the sealing surfaces. The most successful method found is to run a sharp knife around the joint – this should cut through sufficiently to make removal possible without excess effort.

Refitting

5 With the fluid pan removed, clean off all traces of sealant from the pan and the mating face on the transmission. Again, take care not to mark either mating surface.
6 Apply a 1.5 mm thick bead of suitable sealant (Ford recommend Loctite 5699, or equivalent) to the fluid pan mating face, running the bead on the inside of the bolt holes. Do not apply excess sealant, or a bead much thicker than suggested, since the excess could end up inside the pan, and contaminate the internal components.
7 Offer the pan up into position, and insert a few of the bolts to locate it. Refit all the remaining bolts, and tighten them progressively to the specified torque.
8 Give the sealant time to cure, then trim off any excess with a knife. Refill the transmission via the dipstick tube, with reference to Chapter 1A Section 29.
9 On completion, take the car for a run of several miles to get the fluid up to operating temperature, then recheck the fluid level, and check for signs of leakage.

8 Fluid cooler – removal and refitting

Removal

1 This procedure should only be attempted when the engine and transmission are completely cool, otherwise there is a great risk of scalding.
2 Apply the handbrake, then jack up the front of the car and support it on axle stands (see 'Jacking and vehicle support').
3 Using suitable hose clamps, clamp the two coolant hoses leading to the fluid cooler.
4 Place a container below the fluid cooler connections to catch the escaping fluid; also note that, if the engine is still warm, the fluid may be extremely hot. Note the positions of the hose connections for refitting, then push the quick-release connector towards the cooler, press together the retaining tabs and pull the hose from the cooler. Tie the hoses up out of the way, and plug the hose ends to prevent the ingress of dirt.

5 Release the retaining clips and disconnect the two coolant hoses from the top of the fluid cooler.
6 Undo the retaining bolt, disengage the two retaining tabs and remove the fluid cooler from its location.

Refitting

7 Clean the fluid cooler fins of any debris as necessary, using a small brush – do not use any other tools, as the fins can easily be damaged.
8 Refitting is a reversal of removal, noting the following points:
a) Top-up the coolant and transmission fluid level using the information contained in Weekly checks0,5 and Chapter 1A Section 29.
b) Start the engine and check for signs of fluid leakage from the disturbed connections.

9 Automatic transmission – removal and refitting

Note: Read through this procedure before starting work to see what is involved, particularly in terms of lifting equipment. Depending on the facilities available, the home mechanic may prefer to remove the engine and transmission together, then separate them on the bench, as described in Chapter 2F. The help of an assistant is highly recommended if the transmission is to be removed (and later refitted) on its own.

Removal

1 Remove the air cleaner and inlet ducts as described in Chapter 4A Section 5.
2 Remove the battery, battery tray and support bracket as described in Chapter 5A Section 4.
3 Remove the engine management PCM as described in Chapter 4A Section 11.
4 Remove the windscreen cowl panel and bulkhead closure panel as described in Chapter 11 Section 20.
5 Undo the transmission-to-engine bolts which are accessible from above.
6 Firmly apply the handbrake, then jack up the front of the vehicle and support it securely on axle stands (see 'Jacking and vehicle support').
7 Disconnect the selector cable from the transmission lever and support bracket as described in Section 3.
8 Undo the bolts and remove the selector cable/fluid filler tube support bracket to the front of the transmission.
9 Remove the starter motor as described in Chapter 5A Section 9.
10 Disconnect the wiring plugs from the vehicle/output shaft speed sensor, turbine shaft speed sensor and transmission range sensor, as described in Section 5.
11 To prevent damage to the exhaust flexible

9.13a Fluid pipe at the left-hand end ...

9.13b ... and right-hand front face of the transmission

section, support it by attaching a pair of splints either side (two scrap strips of wood, plant canes, etc) using some cable-ties. Undo the nuts securing the flexible section to the exhaust manifold, and separate the joint. Recover the gasket, and discard it. Release the exhaust front rubber mounting block and move the system to one side.

12 Wipe clean around the fluid supply and return pipes on the front of the transmission. It is essential that no dirt is introduced into the transmission.

13 Noting their respective positions, disconnect the fluid pipes from the transmission. The connectors are released by pushing the connector towards the transmission, squeezing together the retaining tags, and pulling the connector away **(see illustrations)**. Be prepared for loss of fluid, and cover the pipe ends and transmission pipe fittings to prevent further loss or dirt entry.

14 Undo the fluid cooler mounting bracket retaining bolts and tie the fluid cooler to one side using cable-ties.

15 Locate the transmission fluid filler tube, and remove the screw at its base where it enters the transmission. Pull the tube out of its location, and remove it.

16 Rotate the crankshaft, using a socket on the pulley bolt, until one of the torque converter-to-driveplate retaining nuts becomes accessible through the starter motor opening. Working through the opening, undo the nut. Rotate the crankshaft as necessary and remove the remaining nuts in the same way. Note that new nuts will be required for refitting.

17 Unbolt the engine rear mounting completely from under the car, referring to Chapter 2A Section 18 if necessary.

18 Remove both driveshafts from the transmission as described in Chapter 8 Section 2.

19 The engine/transmission must now be supported, as the left-hand mounting must be removed. Ford technicians use a support bar which locates in the tops of the inner wings – proprietary engine support bars are available from tool outlets.

20 If a support bar is not available, an engine hoist should be used. With an engine hoist, the engine/transmission can be manoeuvred more easily and safely. In the workshop, we found the best solution was to move the engine to the required position, and support it from below – using the hoist on the transmission then gave excellent manoeuvrability, and total control for lowering out.

21 Supporting both the engine and transmission from below should be considered a last resort, and should only be done if a heavy-duty hydraulic ('trolley') jack is used, with a large, flat piece of wood on the jack head to spread the load and avoid damage to the sump. A further jack will be needed to lower the transmission out. **Note:** *Always take care when using a hydraulic jack, as it is possible for this type to collapse under load – generally, a scissor-type jack avoids this problem, but is also less stable, and offers no manoeuvrability.*

22 With the engine securely supported, undo the three nuts securing the left-hand engine/transmission mounting bracket to the transmission and the two bolts securing the mounting to the body sidemember. Remove the mounting from the engine compartment.

23 Swing the transmission forwards, and wedge it in position with a stout piece of wood, about 300 mm long, between the engine and the subframe.

24 Support the transmission from below, ideally using a trolley jack (if one is not available, a sturdy jack with a large, flat piece of wood on top of the jack head will suffice).

25 Have an assistant ready to help steady the transmission as the flange bolts are removed – attempting to remove the transmission single-handed is not recommended, as it is a heavy assembly which can be awkward to handle.

26 Check that, apart from the remaining flange bolts, there is nothing preventing the transmission from being lowered and removed. Make sure that any wiring or hoses lying on top of the transmission are not going to get caught up and stretched as the transmission is lowered.

27 Unscrew and remove the flange bolts – there are three inserted from the transmission side, and six from the engine side **(see illustration)**. Note the bolt locations carefully, as they are of different lengths.

28 If the transmission does not separate on its own, it must be rocked from side-to-side, to free it from the locating dowels. As the transmission is withdrawn from the engine, make sure its weight is supported at all times – care must be taken that the torque converter (which is a large, heavy, circular component) does not fall out.

29 Keeping the transmission steady on the jack head, and maintaining a supporting hand on the torque converter, carefully lower it and remove it from under the car.

30 Once the transmission has been fully lowered and steadied, bolt a strip of wood

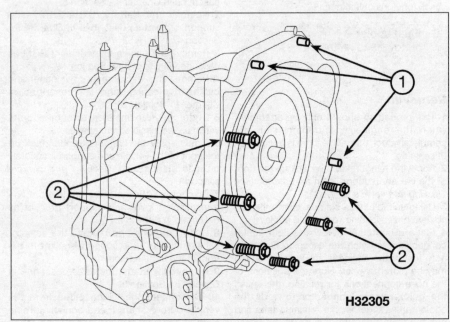

9.27 Engine-to-transmission bolts

1 Three bolts inserted from the transmission side   2 Six bolts inserted from the engine side

or metal across the bellhousing face, with suitable packing, to secure the torque converter firmly in position. The converter centre spigot should be 15 mm below the bellhousing face – this can be determined by placing a straight-edge across the bellhousing, and measuring between it and the centre of the converter.

Refitting

31 Prior to refitting, clean the contact surfaces of the driveplate and torque converter.

32 Check that the torque converter is fully entered in the transmission, as described in paragraph 30.

Caution: This procedure is important, to ensure that the torque converter is engaged with the fluid pump. If it is not fully engaged, serious damage will occur.

33 As for removal, use a block of wood to wedge the engine forwards for refitting.

34 With the help of an assistant, raise the transmission, and locate it on the rear of the driveplate. The torque converter must remain in full engagement during the fitting procedure.

35 Refit the transmission-to-engine flange bolts to the locations noted on removal, and tighten them progressively to draw the transmission fully onto the locating dowels.

36 Align the mark made on removal between the torque converter and driveplate. Refit and tighten the torque converter-to-driveplate nuts to the specified torque – new nuts must be used. Turn the engine as necessary to bring each nut into view, and lock the ring gear to prevent it turning as the nuts are tightened.

37 Remove the wedge fitted between the engine and subframe. Raise the transmission into position, then refit the engine/transmission left-hand mounting. Tighten the nuts/bolts to the specified torque.

38 Working from below, refit the engine/transmission rear mounting, and tighten the bolts to the specified torque.

39 Once the engine/transmission mountings have been refitted, the support bar, engine hoist or supporting jack can be removed.

40 Further refitting is a reversal of removal, noting the following points:

a) Refit the starter motor as described in Chapter 5A Section 9.

b) Refit the driveshafts as described in Chapter 8 Section 2.

c) Tighten all fasteners to the specified torque (where given).

d) On completion, adjust the selector cable as described in Section 3, and top-up the fluid level as described in Chapter 1A Section 29.

e) Recheck the transmission fluid level once the car has been driven.

10 Automatic transmission overhaul – general information

1 Overhaul of the automatic transmission should be left to an automatic transmission specialist or a Ford dealer. Refer to the information given in Section 2 before removing the unit.

2 Note that, if the vehicle is still within the warranty period, in the event of a fault it is important to take it to a Ford dealer who will carry out a comprehensive diagnosis procedure using specialist equipment. Failure to do this will invalidate the warranty.

Notes

Chapter 8
Driveshafts

Contents

Degrees of difficulty

Easy, suitable for novice with little experience	Fairly easy, suitable for beginner with some experience	Fairly difficult, suitable for competent DIY mechanic	Difficult, suitable for experienced DIY mechanic	Very difficult, suitable for expert DIY or professional

Specifications

General
Driveshaft type . . . .   Solid steel shafts with inner and outer constant velocity (CV) joints, both outer joints are of the ball-and-cage type and the inner joints of the tripod (spider-and-yoke) type. Right-hand driveshaft is fitted with a support bearing

Lubricant
Type/specification. . . . .   Special grease (Ford specification WSS-M1C259-A1) supplied in sachets with gaiter kits – joints are otherwise prepacked with grease and sealed

Quantity per joint (approximate):
    Inner joint . . . .   100 g
    Outer joint. . . . .   90 g

Torque wrench settings

	Nm	lbf ft
Anti-roll bar connecting link nuts	48	35
Driveshaft (front hub) nut*.	255	188
Lower arm balljoint clamp bolt nut*	52	38
Right-hand driveshaft support bearing cap nuts*	25	18
Roadwheel nuts	110	81
Suspension strut top mounting nuts	30	22

*Use new fasteners

1 General Information

1 Drive is transmitted from the differential to the front wheels by means of two solid-steel, equal-length driveshafts equipped with constant velocity (CV) joints at their inner and outer ends. Due to the position of the transmission, an intermediate shaft and support bearing are incorporated into the right-hand driveshaft assembly.

2 A ball-and-cage type CV joint is fitted to the outer end of each driveshaft. The joint has an outer member, which is splined at its outer end to accept the wheel hub, and is threaded so that it can be fastened to the hub by a large nut. The joint contains six balls within a cage, which engage with the inner member. The complete assembly is protected by a flexible gaiter secured to the driveshaft and joint outer member.

3 At the inner end, the driveshaft is splined to engage a tripod type CV joint, containing needle roller bearings and cups. On the left-hand side, the driveshaft inner CV joint engages directly with the differential sun wheel. On the right-hand side, the inner joint is integral with the intermediate shaft, the inner end of which engages with the differential sun wheel. As on the outer joints, a flexible gaiter secured to the driveshaft and CV joint outer member protects the complete assembly.

2 Driveshafts – removal and refitting

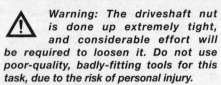

Note: *The driveshaft outer joint splines may be a tight fit in the hub, and it is possible that a puller/extractor will be required to draw the hub assembly off of the driveshaft during removal.*

Removal

1 Firmly apply the handbrake, then jack up the front of the car and support it securely on axle stands (see *'Jacking and vehicle support'*). Remove the relevant front roadwheel. Where applicable, remove the engine undershield.

2 Refit at least two roadwheel nuts to the front hub, and tighten them securely. Have an assistant firmly depress the brake pedal to prevent the front hub from rotating, then using a socket and extension bar, slacken the driveshaft retaining nut. Alternatively, a tool can be fabricated from two lengths of steel strip (one long, one short) and a nut and bolt; the nut and bolt forming the pivot of a forked tool. Attach the tool to the hub using two wheel nuts, and hold the tool to prevent the hub from rotating as the driveshaft retaining nut is slackened **(see illustration)**. Loosen the nut almost to the end of its threads, but do not remove it at this stage.

Warning: The driveshaft nut is done up extremely tight, and considerable effort will be required to loosen it. Do not use poor-quality, badly-fitting tools for this task, due to the risk of personal injury.

3 Remove the windscreen cowl panel and bulkhead closure panel as described in Chapter 11 Section 20.

4 Working in the engine compartment, loosen the three suspension strut top mounting nuts by three turns each on the side concerned **(see illustration)**. Do not loosen the centre nut.

5 Unscrew the bolt and release the brake hydraulic hose from the suspension strut **(see illustration)**.

6 Unscrew and remove the nut securing the anti-roll bar connecting link to the suspension strut, while holding the link stub with an Allen key **(see illustration)**. Release the link from the strut and move it to one side.

7 Unscrew and remove the lower arm balljoint clamp bolt nut, and withdraw the clamp bolt from the swivel hub **(see illustration)**. Note that a new nut and bolt will be required for refitting.

8 Use a chisel or screwdriver as a wedge to expand the lower portion of the swivel hub.

9 Lever down the lower arm to free the balljoint from the swivel hub **(see illustration)**, then move the swivel hub to one side, taking care not to damage the balljoint rubber boot.

2.2 Using a fabricated tool to hold the front hub stationary whilst the driveshaft retaining nut isslackened

2.4 Loosen the three suspension strut nuts (arrowed) by three turns

2.5 Release the brake hydraulic hose from the suspension strut

2.6 Unscrew the nut securing the anti-roll bar connecting link to the suspension strut

2.7 Unscrew the nut and remove the lower arm balljoint clamp bolt

2.9 Home-made method of releasing the lower arm – wood block, long pole and length of chain

2.12 Pull the base of the strut outwards, and pull the driveshaft splines through to the inside

2.14a Use a lever to prise the driveshaft out – this may take some time and effort

2.14b Once the driveshaft comes free, support the inner joint and remove the shaft completely

10 The splined end of the driveshaft now has to be released from its location in the hub. It's likely that the splines will be very tight (corrosion may even be a factor, if the driveshaft has not been disturbed for some time), and considerable force may be needed to push the driveshaft out. Ford recommend using a four-legged puller for this, but if one is not available, the shaft will have to be tapped out with a hammer. If a hammer is used, place a small piece of wood over the end of the driveshaft – in addition to the loosened hub nut, this will protect the threads from damage.

11 Once the splines have been released, remove the hub nut and discard it – a new nut must be used for refitting.

12 The driveshaft can be separated from the hub by having an assistant pull the base of the suspension strut outwards, while the splined end of the shaft is pulled clear of the hub **(see illustration)**. Do not bend the driveshaft excessively at any stage, or the joints may be damaged – the inner and outer joints should not be bent through more than 18° and 45° respectively. Do not let the driveshaft hang down under its own weight – tie it up level if necessary.

13 Proceed as follows, according to which driveshaft is being removed.

Left-hand driveshaft

14 Insert a lever between the driveshaft inner joint and the transmission housing, positioning a thin piece of wood between the lever and housing to protect it. Also position a container below the inner joint, to catch the transmission oil which will be lost as the driveshaft is removed. Carefully lever the driveshaft inner joint out of the differential, taking great care not to damage the transmission housing or the oil seal **(see illustrations)**.

15 Manoeuvre the driveshaft out of position, ensuring that the constant velocity joints are not placed under excessive strain, and remove the driveshaft from underneath the car. Whilst the driveshaft is removed, plug the differential aperture with a clean, lint-free cloth to prevent the entry of dirt.

16 Extract the circlip from the groove on the inner end of the driveshaft, and obtain a new one.

Right-hand driveshaft

17 Unscrew the nuts securing the intermediate shaft support bearing cap to the rear of the cylinder block. On diesel engine models, remove the support bearing cap from the studs. On petrol engine models, lift the support bearing cap and heat shield from the studs and slide it down the intermediate shaft **(see illustration)**. On all models, a new bearing cap and nuts must be used when refitting.

18 Position a container below the transmission, to catch the oil which will be lost as the driveshaft is removed. Withdraw the complete driveshaft from the transmission and from the bearing bracket, and remove it from under the car. On petrol engine models, remove the support bearing cap and heat shield from the intermediate shaft. Whilst the driveshaft is removed, plug the differential aperture with a clean, lint-free cloth to prevent the entry of dirt.

Both driveshafts

19 Check the condition of the differential oil seals, and if necessary renew them as described in Chapter 7A or 7B.

Refitting

Right-hand driveshaft

20 On petrol engine models, fit the new support bearing cap and heat shield to the intermediate shaft.

21 Use a special sleeve to protect the differential oil seal as the intermediate shaft is

inserted. If the sleeve is not used, take great care to avoid damaging the seal. (Installation sleeves are supplied with new oil seals, where required.)

22 Carefully refit the intermediate shaft in the support bearing and into the transmission. Turn the intermediate shaft until it engages the splines on the differential gears.

23 Tighten the new nuts securing the new support bearing cap to the cylinder block to the specified torque. Proceed to paragraph 27.

Left-hand driveshaft

24 Locate the new circlip in the groove on the inner end of the driveshaft **(see illustration)**.

25 Use a special sleeve to protect the differential oil seal as the driveshaft is inserted. If the sleeve is not used, take great care to avoid damaging the seal. (Installation sleeves are supplied with new oil seals, where required.)

26 Insert the driveshaft into the transmission, and push it fully home. Try pulling the shaft out, to make sure the circlip is fully engaged.

Both driveshafts

27 Pull the suspension strut outwards, and insert the outer end of the driveshaft through the hub. Turn the driveshaft to engage the splines in the hub, and fully push on the hub. Ford use a special tool to draw the driveshaft into the hub, but it is unlikely that the splines will be tight. However, if they are, it will be necessary to obtain the tool, or to use a similar home-made tool.

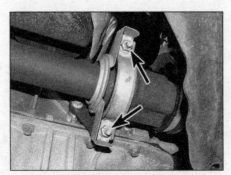

2.17 Unscrew the intermediate shaft bearing cap nuts (arrowed)

2.24 Fit a new circlip to the driveshaft groove

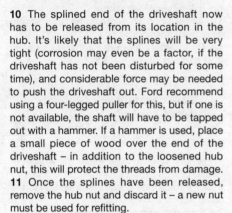

28 Screw on the new driveshaft nut, and use it to draw the driveshaft fully through the hub.
29 Locate the front suspension lower arm balljoint stub in the bottom of the swivel hub. Insert the new clamp bolt in the previously-noted position, screw on the new nut, and tighten it to the specified torque.
30 Locate the anti-roll bar connecting link on the suspension strut, fit a new retaining nut and tighten the nut to the specified torque.
31 Refit the brake hydraulic hose to the suspension strut and tighten the retaining bolt securely.
32 Tighten the suspension strut upper mounting nuts to the specified torque.
33 Using the method employed on removal to prevent rotation, tighten the driveshaft retaining nut to the specified torque.
34 Fill the transmission, and check the level as described in Chapter 1A or Chapter 1B.
35 Where applicable, refit the engine undershield, then refit the wheel, and lower the car to the ground. Tighten the wheel nuts to the specified torque.
36 Refit the bulkhead closure panel and wind- screen cowl panel as described in Chapter 11 Section 20.

3 Outer constant velocity joint gaiter – renewal

1 Dismantle the inner constant velocity joint as described in Section 4.

2 On models with a vibration damper, after removing the inner CV joint, measure and note the distance from the end of the shaft to the edge of the damper. The damper must then be pressed from the shaft, the outer joint boot renewed, then the damper pressed back into its original position using the dimensions previously-noted. If access to a hydraulic press in not available, most engineering workshops (automotive or otherwise) would be prepared to carry out this task for a modest fee.
3 Cut off the gaiter retaining clips, then slide the gaiter down the shaft to expose the outer constant velocity joint **(see illustration)**.
Caution: Do not disassemble the outer CV joint.
4 Scoop out as much grease as possible from the joint.
5 Inspect the ball tracks on the inner and outer members. If the tracks have widened, the balls will no longer be a tight fit. At the same time, check the ball cage windows for wear or cracking between the windows. If the joints appear worn, complete renewal may be the only option – check with a Ford dealer or specialist.
6 If the joint is in satisfactory condition, obtain a repair kit from your Ford dealer, consisting of a new gaiter, retaining clips, driveshaft nut, circlip and grease.
7 Pack the joint with the half of the grease supplied, working it well into the ball tracks,

and into the driveshaft opening in the inner member **(see illustration)**.
8 Slide the rubber gaiter onto the shaft.
9 Apply the remaining grease to the joint and the inside of the gaiter.
10 Locate the outer lip of the gaiter in the groove on the joint outer member, then fit the retaining clip. Remove any slack in the clips by carefully compressing the raised section using a special pair of pincers **(see illustrations)**. **Note:** *Ensure no grease is on the surfaces between the gaiter and the joint housing.*
11 Use a small screwdriver to lift the inner lip of the gaiter, allowing the air pressure inside the gaiter to equalise, then fit the inner clip to the gaiter **(see illustration)**.
12 Where applicable, press the damper into its original position.
13 Reassembly the inner constant velocity joint as described in Section 4.

4 Inner constant velocity joint gaiter – renewal

1 Remove the driveshaft(s) as described in Section 2.
2 Cut through the metal clips, and slide the gaiter from the inner CV joint.
3 Clean out some of the grease from the joint, then make alignment marks between the

3.3 Cut the gaiter retaining clips

3.7 Pack the outer CV joint with about half the grease supplied

3.10a Locate the outer clip on the gaiter ...

3.10b ... then using a special pair of pliers ...

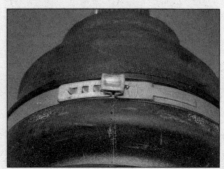
3.10c ... remove any slack in the clip

3.11 Lift the inner edge of the gaiter to equalise the air pressure

4.3 Make alignment marks between the shaft and housing

4.6a Remove the circlip from the end of the shaft ...

4.6b ... then carefully drive the tripod from the shaft

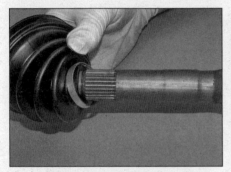

4.7 Slide the new gaiter and smaller diameter clip onto the shaft

4.8a Fit the tripod with the bevelled edge (arrowed) towards the shaft ...

4.8b ... then fit the new circlip

housing and the shaft, to aid reassembly **(see illustration)**.

4 Carefully pull the housing from the tripod, twisting the housing so the tripod rollers come out one at a time. If necessary, use a soft-faced hammer or mallet to tap the housing off.

5 Clean the grease from the tripod and housing.

6 Remove the circlip, and carefully drive the tripod from the end of the shaft **(see illustrations)**. Discard the circlip, a new one (supplied in the repair kit) must be fitted. Remove the gaiter if still on the shaft.

7 Slide the new gaiter onto the shaft along with the smaller clip **(see illustration)**.

8 Refit the tripod with the bevelled edge towards the driveshaft, and drive it fully into place, until the new circlip can be installed **(see illustrations)**.

9 Lubricate the tripod rollers with some of the grease supplied in the gaiter kit, then fill the housing and gaiter with the remainder.

10 Refit the housing to the tripod, tapping it gently into place using a soft-hammer or mallet if necessary.

11 Slide the new gaiter into place ensuring the smaller diameter of the gaiter locates over the grooves in the shaft **(see illustration)**.

12 Fit the new retaining clips **(see illustration)**.

13 Refit the driveshaft(s) as described in Section 2.

5 Driveshaft overhaul – general information

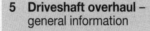

1 Road test the car, and listen for a metallic clicking from the front as the car is driven slowly in a circle with the steering on full-lock. Repeat the check on full-left and full-right lock. This noise may also be apparent when pulling away from a standstill with lock applied. If a clicking noise is heard, this indicates wear in the outer constant velocity joints.

2 If vibration, consistent with roadspeed, is felt through the car when accelerating, there is a possibility of wear in the inner constant velocity joints.

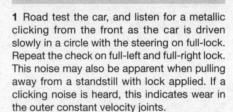

3 If the joints are worn or damaged, it would appear at the time of writing that no parts are available, other than gaiter renewal kits, and the complete driveshaft must be renewed. Exchange driveshafts may be available – check with a Ford dealer or specialist.

4 Continual noise from the right-hand driveshaft, increasing with roadspeed, may indicate wear in the support bearing. To renew this bearing, the driveshaft and intermediate shaft must be removed, and the bearing extracted using a puller.

5 Remove the bearing dust cover, and obtain a new one.

6 Drive or press on the new bearing, applying the pressure to the inner race only. Similarly drive or press on the new dust cover.

4.11 The smaller diameter of the gaiter must locate over the groove in the shaft (arrowed)

4.12 Equalise the air pressure before tightening the gaiter clip

---

Chapter 9
Braking system

Contents

Degrees of difficulty

Easy, suitable for novice with little experience	Fairly easy, suitable for beginner with some experience	Fairly difficult, suitable for competent DIY mechanic	Difficult, suitable for experienced DIY mechanic	Very difficult, suitable for expert DIY or professional

Specifications

Front disc brakes
Type	Ventilated disc, with single-piston sliding caliper
Minimum disc thickness	21.0 mm
Maximum disc thickness variation	0.025 mm
Maximum disc/hub run-out (installed)	0.050 mm
Brake pad friction material minimum thickness	1.5 mm

Rear drum brakes
Type	Leading and trailing shoes, with automatic adjusters
Maximum drum internal diameter	201.5 mm
Brake shoe friction material minimum thickness	1.0 mm

Torque wrench settings
	Nm	lbf ft
ABS hydraulic modulator mounting bracket bolts	23	17
Brake caliper guide pin bolts	28	21
Brake caliper mounting bracket bolts	75	55
Brake fluid pipe unions	18	13
Brake hydraulic hose banjo union bolt	26	19
Brake master cylinder retaining nuts	20	15
Brake pedal mounting bracket nuts	25	18
Engine rear mounting through-bolt	48	35
Engine right-hand mounting to body	48	35
Exhaust flexible section-to-catalytic converter nuts	48	35
Handbrake lever retaining nuts	30	22
Rear wheel cylinder retaining bolt	12	9
Roadwheel nuts	110	81
Steering column shaft universal joint clamp bolt*	34	25
Underfloor cross-brace retaining nuts	40	30
Vacuum pump mounting bolts (diesel engine models)	20	15
Vacuum servo unit to brake pedal mounting bracket	25	18

*Use a new bolt

1 General Information

1 The braking system is of servo-assisted, dual-circuit hydraulic type split diagonally. The arrangement of the hydraulic system is such that each circuit operates one front and one rear brake from a tandem master cylinder. Under normal circumstances, both circuits operate in unison. However, in the event of hydraulic failure in one circuit, full braking force will still be available at two wheels.

2 All models are fitted with front disc and rear drum brakes. The front disc brakes are actuated by single-piston sliding type calipers, which ensure that equal pressure is applied to each disc pad. The rear drum brakes are of the leading and trailing shoe type, and are self-adjusting.

3 The vacuum servo unit uses inlet manifold depression (generated only when a petrol engine is running) to boost the effort applied by the driver at the brake pedal and transmits this increased effort to the master cylinder pistons. Because there is no throttling of the inlet manifold on a diesel engine, it is not a suitable source of vacuum for brake servo operation. Vacuum is therefore derived from a separate camshaft driven vacuum pump.

4 An Anti-lock Braking System (ABS) is fitted as standard equipment. On higher specification models, the ABS may also incorporate traction control or an electronic stability program. Refer to Section 19 for further information on ABS operation.

5 The cable-operated handbrake provides an independent mechanical means of rear brake application.

 Warning: When servicing any part of the system, work carefully and methodically; also observe scrupulous cleanliness when overhauling any part of the hydraulic system. Always renew components (in axle sets, where applicable) if in doubt about their condition, and use only genuine Ford parts, or at least those of known good quality. Note the warnings given in 'Safety first!' and at relevant points in this Chapter concerning the dangers of asbestos dust and hydraulic fluid.

2 Hydraulic system – bleeding

 Warning: Hydraulic fluid is poisonous; wash off immediately and thoroughly in the case of skin contact, and seek immediate medical advice if any fluid is swallowed or gets into the eyes. Certain types of hydraulic fluid are inflammable, and may ignite when allowed into contact with hot components; when servicing any hydraulic system, it is safest to assume that the fluid is inflammable, and to take precautions against the risk of fire as though it is petrol that is being handled. Hydraulic fluid is also an effective paint stripper, and will attack plastics; if any is spilt, it should be washed off immediately, using copious quantities of fresh water. Finally, it is hygroscopic (it absorbs moisture from the air) – old fluid may be contaminated and unfit for further use. When topping-up or renewing the fluid, always use the recommended type, and ensure that it comes from a freshly-opened sealed container.

General

1 The correct operation of any hydraulic system is only possible after removing all air from the components and circuit; this is achieved by bleeding the system.

2 During the bleeding procedure, add only clean, unused hydraulic fluid of the recommended type; never re-use fluid that has already been bled from the system. Ensure that sufficient fluid is available before starting work.

3 If there is any possibility of incorrect fluid being already in the system, the brake components and circuit must be flushed completely with uncontaminated, correct fluid, and new seals should be fitted to the various components.

4 If hydraulic fluid has been lost from the system, or air has entered because of a leak, ensure that the fault is cured before proceeding further.

5 Park the vehicle over an inspection pit or on car ramps. Alternatively, apply the handbrake then jack up the front and rear of the vehicle and support it on axle stands (see 'Jacking and vehicle support'). For improved access with the vehicle jacked up, remove the roadwheels.

6 Check that all pipes and hoses are secure, unions tight and bleed screws closed. Clean any dirt from around the bleed screws.

7 Unscrew the master cylinder reservoir cap, and top the master cylinder reservoir up to the MAX level line; refit the cap loosely, and remember to maintain the fluid level at least above the MIN level line throughout the procedure, otherwise there is a risk of further air entering the system.

8 There are a number of one-man, do-it-yourself brake bleeding kits currently available from motor accessory shops. It is recommended that one of these kits is used whenever possible, as they greatly simplify the bleeding operation, and also reduce the risk of expelled air and fluid being drawn back into the system. If such a kit is not available, the basic (two-man) method must be used, which is described in detail below.

9 If a kit is to be used, prepare the vehicle as described previously, and follow the kit manufacturer's instructions, as the procedure may vary slightly according to the type being used; generally, they are as outlined below in the relevant sub-section.

10 Whichever method is used, the same sequence should be followed (paragraphs 11 and 12) to ensure the removal of all air from the system.

Bleeding sequence

11 If the system has been only partially disconnected, and suitable precautions were taken to minimise fluid loss, it should only be necessary to bleed that part of the system (ie, the primary or secondary circuit). If the master cylinder or main brake lines have been disconnected, then the complete system must be bled.

12 If the complete system is to be bled, then it should be done in the following sequence:
a) Left-hand rear brake.
b) Right-hand rear brake.
c) Left-hand front brake.
d) Right-hand front brake.

Bleeding

Basic (two-man) method

13 Collect together a clean glass jar, a suitable length of plastic or rubber tubing which is a tight fit over the bleed screw, and a ring spanner to fit the screw. The help of an assistant will also be required.

14 Remove the dust cap from the first bleed screw in the sequence (see illustration). Fit the spanner and tube to the screw, place the other end of the tube in the jar, and pour in sufficient fluid to cover the end of the tube.

15 Ensure that the master cylinder reservoir fluid level is maintained at least above the MIN level line throughout the procedure.

16 Have the assistant fully depress the brake pedal several times to build-up pressure, then maintain it on the final downstroke.

17 While pedal pressure is maintained, unscrew the bleed screw (approximately one turn) and allow the compressed fluid and air to flow into the jar. The assistant should maintain pedal pressure, following it down to the floor if necessary, and should not release it until instructed to do so. When the flow stops, tighten the bleed screw again, have the assistant release the pedal slowly, and recheck the reservoir fluid level.

18 Repeat the steps given in paragraphs 16 and 17 until the fluid emerging from the bleed screw is free from air bubbles. If the master cylinder has been drained and refilled, and air is

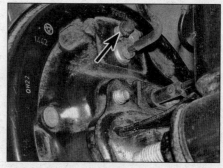

2.14 Rear wheel cylinder bleed screw (arrowed)

being bled from the first screw in the sequence, allow approximately five seconds between cycles for the master cylinder passages to refill.
19 When no more air bubbles appear, securely tighten the bleed screw, remove the tube and spanner, and refit the dust cap. Do not overtighten the bleed screw.
20 Repeat the procedure on the remaining screws in the sequence, until all air is removed from the system and the brake pedal feels firm again.

Using a one-way valve kit

21 As the name implies, these kits consist of a length of tubing with a one-way valve fitted, to prevent expelled air and fluid being drawn back into the system; some kits include a translucent container, which can be positioned so that the air bubbles can be more easily seen flowing from the end of the tube.
22 The kit is connected to the bleed screw, which is then opened. The user returns to the driver's seat, depresses the brake pedal with a smooth, steady stroke, and slowly releases it; this is repeated until the expelled fluid is clear of air bubbles.
23 Note that these kits simplify work so much that it is easy to forget the master cylinder reservoir fluid level; ensure that this is maintained at least above the MIN level line at all times.

Using a pressure-bleeding kit

24 These kits are usually operated by a reservoir of pressurised air contained in the spare tyre. However, note that it will probably be necessary to reduce the pressure to a lower level than normal; refer to the instructions supplied with the kit. You may have to borrow a friend's spare tyre if your car has a puncture kit instead of a spare tyre.
25 By connecting a pressurised, fluid-filled container to the master cylinder reservoir, bleeding can be carried out simply by opening each screw in turn (in the specified sequence), and allowing the fluid to flow out until no more air bubbles can be seen in the expelled fluid.
26 This method has the advantage that the large reservoir of fluid provides an additional safeguard against air being drawn into the system during bleeding.
27 Pressure-bleeding is particularly effective when bleeding 'difficult' systems, or when bleeding the complete system at the time of routine fluid renewal.

All methods

28 When bleeding is complete, and firm pedal feel is restored, wash off any spilt fluid, securely tighten the bleed screws, and refit the dust caps.
29 Check the hydraulic fluid level in the master cylinder reservoir, and top-up if necessary (see *Weekly checks*).
30 Discard any hydraulic fluid that has been bled from the system; it will not be fit for re-use.
31 Check the feel of the brake pedal. If it feels at all spongy, air must still be present in the system, and further bleeding is required.

Failure to bleed satisfactorily after a reasonable repetition of the bleeding procedure may be due to worn master cylinder seals.

3 Hydraulic pipes and hoses – renewal

Note: *Before starting work, refer to the note at the beginning of Section 2 concerning the dangers of hydraulic fluid.*
1 If any pipe or hose is to be renewed, minimise fluid loss by first removing the master cylinder reservoir cap and screwing it down onto a piece of polythene. Alternatively, flexible hoses can be sealed, if required, using a proprietary brake hose clamp. Metal brake pipe unions can be plugged (if care is taken not to allow dirt into the system) or capped immediately they are disconnected. Place a wad of rag under any union that is to be disconnected, to catch any spilt fluid.
2 If a flexible hose is to be disconnected, unscrew the brake pipe union nut before removing the spring clip which secures the hose to its mounting bracket. Where applicable, unscrew the banjo union bolt securing the hose to the caliper and recover the copper washers.
3 To unscrew union nuts, it is preferable to obtain a brake pipe spanner of the correct size; these are available from most motor accessory shops. Failing this, a close-fitting open-ended spanner will be required, though if the nuts are tight or corroded, their flats may be rounded-off if the spanner slips. In such a case, a self-locking wrench is often the only way to unscrew a stubborn union, but it follows that the pipe and the damaged nuts must be renewed on reassembly. Always clean a union and surrounding area before disconnecting it. If disconnecting a component with more than one union, make a careful note of the connections before disturbing any of them.
4 If a brake pipe is to be renewed, it can be obtained, cut to length and with the union nuts and end flares in place, from Ford dealers. All that is then necessary is to bend it to shape, following the line of the original, before fitting it

to the car. Alternatively, most motor accessory shops can make up brake pipes from kits, but this requires very careful measurement of the original, to ensure that the new one is of the correct length. The safest answer is usually to take the original to the shop as a pattern.
5 On refitting, do not overtighten the union nuts.
6 When refitting hoses to the calipers, always use new copper washers and tighten the banjo union bolts to the specified torque. Make sure that the hoses are positioned so that they will not touch surrounding bodywork or the roadwheels.
7 Ensure that the pipes and hoses are correctly routed, with no kinks, and that they are secured in the clips or brackets provided. After fitting, remove the polythene from the reservoir, and bleed the hydraulic system as described in Section 2. Wash off any spilt fluid, and check carefully for fluid leaks.

4 Front brake pads – renewal

⚠️ *Warning: Renew BOTH sets of front brake pads at the same time – NEVER renew the pads on only one wheel, as uneven braking may result. Note that the dust created by wear of the pads may contain asbestos, which is a health hazard. Never blow it out with compressed air, and do not inhale any of it. An approved filtering mask should be worn when working on the brakes. DO NOT use petroleum-based solvents to clean brake parts – use brake cleaner or methylated spirit only.*
1 Apply the handbrake, then jack up the front of the vehicle and support it on axle stands (see *'Jacking and vehicle support'*). Remove the front roadwheels.
2 Follow the accompanying photos **(illustrations 4.2a to 4.2t)** for the pad renewal procedure, bearing in mind the additional points listed below. Be sure to stay in order and read the caption under each illustration. Note that if the old pads are to be refitted, ensure that they are identified so that they can be returned to their original positions.

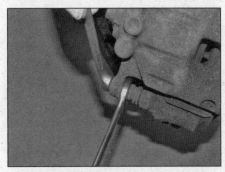
4.2a Unscrew the lower guide pin bolt while holding the guide pin with a second spanner …

4.2b … remove the upper guide pin bolt in the same way

4.2c Unscrew the retaining bolt …

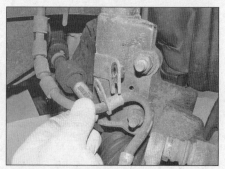
4.2d … and free the brake hose support bracket from the suspension strut

4.2e Lift the caliper off the mounting bracket …

4.2f … and suspend it from the coil spring using wire or a cable-tie

4.2g Remove the outer pad from the caliper mounting bracket …

4.2h … followed by the inner pad

4.2i Remove the anti-rattle plates from the top …

4.2j … and bottom of the caliper mounting bracket

4.2k Measure the thickness of the pad friction material. If any are worn down to the specified minimum, or fouled with oil or grease, all four pads must be renewed

4.2l Brush the dust and dirt from the caliper piston and mounting bracket

4.2m If new pads are to be fitted, before refitting the caliper, push back the caliper piston whilst opening the bleed screw

4.2n Fit the upper anti-rattle plate …

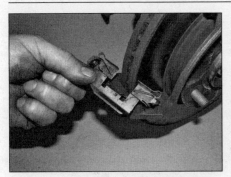
4.2o ... and lower anti-rattle plate to the caliper mounting bracket

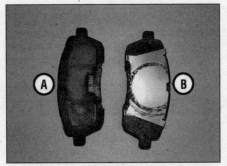
4.2p Note the pad orientation before fitting. Outer pad (A) and inner pad (B)

4.2q Fit the inner and outer pads to the caliper mounting bracket, ensuring that the friction material is facing the brake disc

4.2r Slide the caliper into position in the mounting bracket

4.2s Fit the upper and lower guide pin bolts ...

4.2t ... and tighten the guide pin bolts to the specified torque

3 If the original brake pads are still serviceable, carefully clean them using a clean, fine wire brush or similar, paying particular attention to the sides and back of the metal backing plate. Clean out the grooves in the friction material, and pick out any large embedded particles of dirt or debris. Carefully clean the pad locations in the caliper mounting bracket.

4 Prior to fitting the pads, check that the guide pins are a snug fit in the caliper mounting bracket. Inspect the dust seal around the piston for damage, and the piston for evidence of fluid leaks, corrosion or damage. If attention to any of these components is necessary, refer to Section 5.

5 If new brake pads are to be fitted, the caliper piston must be pushed back into the cylinder to allow for the extra pad thickness. Either use a G-clamp or similar tool, or use suitable pieces of wood as levers. Clamp off the flexible brake hose leading to the caliper then connect a brake bleeding kit to the caliper bleed screw. Open the bleed screw as the piston is retracted, the surplus brake fluid will then be collected in the bleed kit vessel (see illustration 4.2m). Close the bleed screw just before the caliper piston is pushed fully into the caliper. This should ensure no air enters the hydraulic system. Note: The ABS unit contains hydraulic components that are very sensitive to impurities in the brake fluid. Even the smallest particles can cause the system to fail through blockage. The pad retraction

method described here prevents any debris in the brake fluid expelled from the caliper from being passed back to the ABS hydraulic unit, as well as preventing any chance of damage to the master cylinder seals.

6 With the brake pads installed, depress the brake pedal repeatedly, until normal (non-assisted) pedal pressure is restored, and the pads are pressed into firm contact with the brake disc.

7 Repeat the above procedure on the remaining front brake caliper.

8 Refit the roadwheels, then lower the vehicle to the ground and tighten the roadwheel nuts to the specified torque setting.

9 Check the hydraulic fluid level as described in Weekly checks.

Caution: New pads will not give full braking efficiency until they have bedded-in. Be prepared for this, and avoid hard braking as far as possible for the first hundred miles or so after pad renewal.

5 Front brake caliper – removal, overhaul and refitting

Note: New brake hose copper washers will be required when refitting. Before starting work, refer to the warnings at the beginning of Sections 2 and 4 concerning the dangers of hydraulic fluid and asbestos dust.

Removal

1 Apply the handbrake, then jack up the front of the vehicle and support it on axle stands (see 'Jacking and vehicle support'). Remove the roadwheel.

2 Minimise fluid loss by first removing the master cylinder reservoir cap and screwing it down onto a piece of polythene. Alternatively, use a brake hose clamp to clamp the flexible hose leading to the brake caliper.

3 Clean the area around the caliper brake hose union. Unscrew and remove the union bolt, and recover the copper sealing washer from each side of the hose union. Discard the washers; new ones must be used on refitting. Plug the hose end and caliper hole, to minimise fluid loss and prevent the ingress of dust and dirt into the hydraulic system.

4 Undo the caliper upper and lower guide pin bolts then remove the caliper from the mounting bracket (see illustrations 4.2a and 4.2b).

Overhaul

Note: Before starting work, check on the availability of parts (caliper overhaul kit/seals).

5 With the caliper on the bench, brush away all traces of dust and dirt, but take care not to inhale any dust, as it may be harmful to your health.

6 Pull the dust cover rubber seal from the end of the piston.

7 Apply low air pressure to the fluid inlet union, to eject the piston. Only low air pressure

is required for this, such as is produced by a foot-operated tyre pump.
Caution: The piston may be ejected with some force. Position a thin piece of wood between the piston and the caliper body, to prevent damage to the end face of the piston, in the event of it being ejected suddenly.

8 Using a suitable blunt instrument, prise the piston seal from the groove in the cylinder bore. Take care not to scratch the surface of the bore.

9 Clean the piston and caliper body with methylated spirit, and allow to dry. Examine the surfaces of the piston and cylinder bore for wear, damage and corrosion. If the piston alone is unserviceable, a new piston must be obtained, along with seals. If the cylinder bore is unserviceable, the complete caliper must be renewed. The seals must be renewed, regardless of the condition of the other components.

10 Coat the piston and seals with clean brake fluid, then manipulate the piston seal into the groove in the cylinder bore.

11 Push the piston squarely into its bore, taking care not to damage the seal.

12 Fit the dust cover rubber seal onto the piston and caliper, then depress the piston fully.

Refitting

13 Place the caliper in position over the brake pads on the mounting bracket. Fit the upper and lower guide pin bolts and tighten the bolts to the specified torque **(see illustrations 4.2s and 4.2t)**.

14 Position a new copper sealing washer on each side of the hose union, and connect the brake hose to the caliper. Ensure that the hose is correctly positioned against the caliper body lug, then install the union bolt and tighten it to the specified torque setting.

15 Remove the brake hose clamp or polythene, and bleed the hydraulic system as described in Section 2. Note that, providing the precautions described were taken to minimise brake fluid loss, it should only be necessary to bleed the relevant front brake circuit.

16 Refit the roadwheel, then lower the vehicle to the ground and tighten the roadwheel nuts to the specified torque.

6 Front brake disc – inspection, removal and refitting

Note: *Before starting work, refer to the warning at the beginning of Section 4 concerning the dangers of asbestos dust. If either disc requires renewal, both should be renewed at the same time together with new pads, to ensure even and consistent braking.*

Inspection

1 Firmly apply the handbrake, then jack up the front of the vehicle and support it securely on axle stands (see '*Jacking and vehicle support*'). Remove the roadwheel.

2 Unscrew the bolt and release the brake hydraulic hose from the suspension strut **(see illustration)**.

3 Unscrew the bolts securing the brake caliper mounting bracket to the swivel hub, then slide the caliper/bracket assembly from the swivel hub and brake disc (there is no need to remove the brake pads) **(see illustration)**. Suspend the caliper/bracket assembly from the strut coil spring using wire or a cable-tie – do not allow the caliper to hang on the brake hose.

4 Temporarily refit two of the wheel nuts to diagonally-opposite studs, with the flat sides of the nuts against the disc. Tighten the nuts progressively, to hold the disc firmly.

5 Scrape any corrosion from the disc. Rotate the disc, and examine it for deep scoring, grooving or cracks. Using a micrometer, measure the thickness of the disc in several places **(see illustration)**. The minimum thickness is given in the Specifications. Light wear and scoring is normal, but if excessive, the disc should be removed, and either reground by a specialist, or renewed. If regrinding is undertaken, the minimum thickness must be maintained. Obviously, if the disc is cracked, it must be renewed.

6 Using a dial gauge or a flat metal block and feeler gauges, check that the disc run-out 10 mm from the outer edge does not exceed the limit given in the Specifications. To do this, fix the measuring equipment, and rotate the disc, noting the variation in measurement as the disc is rotated **(see illustration)**. The difference between the minimum and maximum measurements recorded is the disc run-out.

7 If the run-out is greater than the specified amount, check for variations of the disc thickness as follows. Mark the disc at eight positions 45° apart then, using a micrometer, measure the disc thickness at the eight positions, 15 mm in from the outer edge. If the variation between the minimum and maximum readings is greater than the specified amount, the disc should be renewed.

8 The hub face run-out can also be checked in a similar way. First remove the disc as described later in this Section, fix the measuring equipment, then slowly rotate the hub, and check that the run-out does not exceed the amount given in the Specifications. If the hub face run-out is excessive, this should be corrected (by renewing the hub bearings – see Chapter 10 Section 3) before rechecking the disc run-out.

Removal

9 With the wheel and caliper removed, remove the wheel nuts which were temporarily refitted in paragraph 4.

10 Mark the disc in relation to the hub, if it is

6.2 Unscrew the bolt and release the brake hydraulic hose from the suspension strut

6.3 Unscrew the bolts (arrowed) securing the brake caliper mounting bracket to the swivel hub

6.5 Using a micrometer to measure the thickness of the brake disc

6.6 Measuring the disc run-out with a dial gauge

6.10 Withdraw the disc from the hub

7.2a Undo the two retaining screws (arrowed) …

7.2b … and withdraw the drum from the wheel hub

to be refitted, then withdraw the disc over the wheel studs **(see illustration)**.

Refitting

11 Make sure that the disc and hub mating surfaces are clean, then locate the disc on the wheel studs. Align the previously-made marks if the original disc is being refitted.

12 Refit the caliper mounting bracket complete with caliper and pads and tighten the bolts to the specified torque.

13 Locate the brake hydraulic hose bracket on the suspension strut, refit the retaining bolt and tighten it securely.

14 Refit the wheel, and lower the car to the ground. Tighten the wheel nuts to the specified torque.

15 Test the brakes carefully before returning the car to normal service.

7 Rear brake drum – removal, inspection and refitting

Note: *Before starting work, refer to the warning at the beginning of Section 8 concerning the dangers of asbestos dust. If either drum requires renewal, both should be renewed at the same time together with new brake shoes, to ensure even and consistent braking.*

Removal

1 Chock the front wheels, then jack up the rear of the vehicle, and support it securely on axle stands (see *'Jacking and vehicle support'*). Remove the roadwheel.

2 Ensure that the handbrake is fully released, then undo the two retaining screws and withdraw the drum from the wheel hub. If the drum is initially tight, screw a suitable bolt into the threaded hole on the front face of the drum. Tighten the bolt to draw off the drum while tapping around the periphery with a copper mallet **(see illustrations)**.

3 If the drum will still not pull off easily due to binding of the brake shoes, proceed as follows.

4 From inside the car, unclip the gear lever or selector lever trim from the base of the gear/ selector lever **(see illustration)**.

5 Pull up the centre console front upper

7.2c If necessary, screw a bolt (arrowed) into the threaded hole and tighten the bolt to draw off the drum

7.4 Unclip the gear lever trim from the base of the gear lever

trim panel, to release the retaining clips. Disconnect the accessory socket wiring connector and remove the panel **(see illustrations)**.

6 Working through the aperture at the base of the handbrake lever, remove the retaining clip from the handbrake adjuster nut on the end of the handbrake cable **(see illustrations)**.

7.5a Pull up the centre console front upper trim panel …

7.5b … then disconnect the accessory socket wiring connector

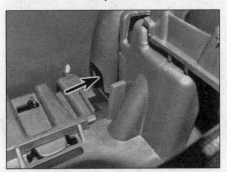

7.6a Working through the aperture (arrowed) at the base of the handbrake lever …

7.6b … remove the retaining clip from the adjuster nut on the end of the handbrake cable

Using a socket and extension bar, slacken the adjuster nut on the handbrake cable six turns to introduce some slack in the cable.

7 It should now be possible to draw off the drum as described in paragraph 2.

8 With the brake drum removed, clean the dust from the drum, brake shoes, wheel cylinder and backplate, using brake cleaner or methylated spirit. Take care not to inhale the dust, as it may contain asbestos.

Inspection

9 Clean the inside surfaces of the brake drum, then examine the internal friction surface for signs of scoring or cracks. If it is cracked, deeply scored, or has worn to a diameter greater than the maximum given in the Specifications, then it should be renewed, together with the drum on the other side.

10 Regrinding of the brake drum is not recommended.

Refitting

11 Refitting is a reversal of removal, noting the following points:

a) If the handbrake adjuster nut was slackened to allow removal of the drum, tighten the adjuster nut six turns to return it to its original position.

b) Adjust the handbrake as described in Section 14.

c) Refit the centre console trim panel and gear/selector lever trim panel after adjusting the handbrake.

d) Test the brakes carefully before returning the car to normal service.

8 Rear brake shoes – renewal

⚠️ **Warning: Brake shoes must be renewed on BOTH rear wheels at the same time – NEVER renew the shoes on only one wheel, as uneven braking may result. The dust created as the shoes wear may contain asbestos, which is a health hazard. Never blow it out with compressed air, and don't inhale any of it. An approved filtering mask should be worn when working on the brakes. DO NOT use petroleum-based solvents to clean brake parts – use brake cleaner or methylated spirit only.**

1 Remove the brake drum as described in Section 7.

2 Working carefully and taking the necessary precautions, remove all traces of brake dust from the brake drum, backplate and shoes.

3 Follow the accompanying photos (illustrations 8.3a to 8.3ac) for the brake shoe renewal procedure, bearing in mind the additional points listed below. Be sure to stay in order and read the caption under each illustration.

4 If both brake assemblies are dismantled at the same time, take care not to mix up the components. Note that the left-hand and right-hand adjuster components are 'handed' and must not be interchanged.

5 Prior to refitting the adjuster mechanism, lift the adjuster lever and turn the adjuster strut wheel to shorten the overall length of the mechanism slightly (see illustration 8.3ac). This will compensate for the additional thickness of the new brake shoes, and allow the brake drum to be fitted easily.

6 On completion, place the brake drum in position over the brake shoes. It is not necessary to refit the two retaining screws at this stage as the drums must be removed again later to adjust the handbrake.

7 Repeat the operation on the remaining brake.

8 Once both sets of rear shoes have been renewed, with the handbrake fully released, adjust the lining-to-drum clearance by

8.3a Measure the thickness of the brake shoe friction material at several points. If any are worn down to the specified minimum, or fouled with oil or grease, all four shoes must be renewed

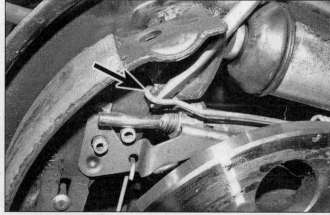

8.3b Using a screwdriver, disengage the upper return spring from the leading shoe (arrowed), then remove it from the trailing shoe

8.3c Depress and pull off the leading shoe retaining spring clip ...

8.3d ... then remove the retainer pin from the rear of the backplate

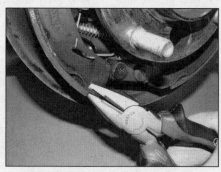

8.3e Pull the lower end of the leading shoe outward and disengage it from the abutment bracket

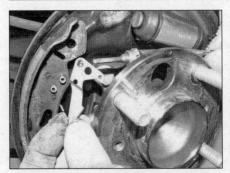

8.3f Disengage the adjuster lever from the brake shoe peg and tension spring then remove the adjuster lever and adjuster strut

8.3g Disengage and remove the tension spring from the leading shoe

8.3h Disengage the lower return spring (arrowed) from the leading shoe and remove the shoe

8.3i Disengage the lower return spring from the trailing shoe and remove the spring

8.3j Depress and pull off the trailing shoe retaining spring clip …

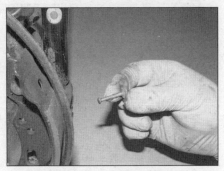

8.3k … then remove the retainer pin from the rear of the backplate

8.3l Pull back the spring and disengage the handbrake cable end from the handbrake lever on the trailing shoe, then remove the shoe

8.3m Use a cable-tie or elastic band to retain the wheel cylinder pistons

8.3n Thoroughly clean the backplate, then apply a smear of high-temperature brake grease to the contact surfaces (arrowed)

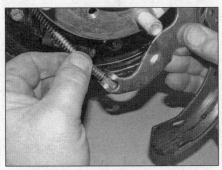

8.3o Engage the handbrake cable with the handbrake lever on the trailing shoe and position the shoe on the backplate

8.3p Insert the trailing shoe retainer pin …

8.3q … then refit the trailing shoe retaining spring clip

8.3r Engage the lower return spring with the trailing shoe …

8.3s … and leading shoe …

8.3t … then engage the leading shoe with the abutment bracket

8.3u Engage the adjuster strut fork (arrowed) with the handbrake lever on the trailing shoe …

8.3v … and over the peg (arrowed) on the leading shoe

8.3w Place the adjuster lever over the peg on the leading shoe and under the adjuster strut fork

8.3x Engage the tension spring with the leading shoe and adjuster lever (arrowed)

8.3y Insert the leading shoe retainer pin …

8.3z … then refit the leading shoe retaining spring clip

8.3aa Engage the upper return spring with the trailing shoe …

8.3ab … then pull it into engagement with the leading shoe (arrowed). Cut off the cable-tie or elastic band used to retain the wheel cylinder pistons

8.3ac Pull adjuster lever away from the adjuster fork and turn the adjuster wheel (arrowed) as necessary until the drum can be refitted

repeatedly depressing the brake pedal 20 to 25 times. Whilst depressing the pedal, have an assistant listen to the rear drums, to check that the adjuster mechanism is functioning correctly; if so, a clicking sound will be emitted by the adjuster as the pedal is depressed.

9 Adjust the handbrake as described in Section 14.

10 Refit the roadwheels, then lower the vehicle to the ground and tighten the roadwheel nuts to the specified torque.

11 Check the hydraulic fluid level as described in *Weekly checks*.

Caution: New brake shoes will not give full braking efficiency until they have bedded-in. Be prepared for this, and avoid hard braking as far as possible for the first hundred miles or so after shoe renewal.

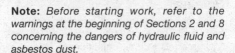

9 Rear wheel cylinder – removal, overhaul and refitting

Note: *Before starting work, refer to the warnings at the beginning of Sections 2 and 8 concerning the dangers of hydraulic fluid and asbestos dust.*

Removal

1 Remove the brake drum as described in Section 7. If the wheel cylinders have been leaking, there will probably be a significant build-up of brake dust on the failed seals (the dust sticks to the leaking fluid). A leak can be confirmed by carefully prising up the outer lip of the seal – any wetness means a new cylinder will be needed.

2 In recent years, the availability of wheel cylinder repair kits has greatly decreased, but it may still be worth asking. Wheel cylinders do not have to be fitted in pairs (providing they are the same size), but if one is leaking, it's reasonable to assume the other one soon will be. If the leak has been going on for some time, it may be serious enough to have contaminated the brake shoes, in which case new shoes should be fitted on BOTH sides.

3 Minimise fluid loss either by removing the master cylinder reservoir cap, and then tightening it down onto a piece of polythene

to obtain an airtight seal, or by using a brake hose clamp, a G-clamp, or similar tool, to clamp the flexible hose at the nearest convenient point to the wheel cylinder.

4 Pull the brake shoes apart at their top ends, so that they are just clear of the wheel cylinder. The automatic adjuster will hold the shoes in this position, so that the cylinder can be withdrawn.

5 Wipe away all traces of dirt around the hydraulic union at the rear of the wheel cylinder, then undo the union nut **(see illustration)**.

6 Unscrew the bolt securing the wheel cylinder to the backplate.

7 Withdraw the wheel cylinder from the backplate so that it is clear of the brake shoes. Plug the open hydraulic unions, to prevent the entry of dirt, and to minimise further fluid loss whilst the cylinder is detached.

Overhaul

8 No overhaul procedures or parts were available at the time of writing – check availability of spares before dismantling. Renewing a wheel cylinder as a unit is recommended.

Refitting

9 Wipe clean the backplate and remove the plug from the end of the hydraulic pipe. Fit the cylinder onto the backplate and screw in the hydraulic union nut by hand, being careful not to cross-thread it.

10 Tighten the mounting bolt, then fully tighten the hydraulic union nut.

11 Retract the automatic brake adjuster mechanism, so that the brake shoes engage with the pistons of the wheel cylinder. To do this, pull adjuster lever away from the adjuster fork and turn the adjuster wheel as necessary until the drum can slide over the brake shoes **(see illustration 8.3ac)**.

12 Remove the clamp from the flexible brake hose, or the polythene from the master cylinder (as applicable).

13 Refit the brake drum (see Section 7).

14 Bleed the hydraulic system as described in Section 2. Providing suitable precautions were taken to minimise loss of fluid, it should only be necessary to bleed the relevant rear brake.

15 Test the brakes carefully before returning the car to normal service.

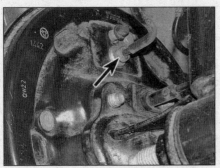

9.5 Undo the brake hydraulic pipe union nut (arrowed) from the wheel cylinder

10 Master cylinder – removal and refitting

Note: *Before starting work, refer to the warning at the beginning of Section 2 concerning the dangers of hydraulic fluid.*

Removal

1 Remove the master cylinder reservoir cap, and siphon the hydraulic fluid from the reservoir. **Note:** *Do not siphon the fluid by mouth, as it is poisonous; use a syringe or an old hydrometer. Alternatively, open any convenient bleed screw in the system, and gently pump the brake pedal to expel the fluid through a plastic tube connected to the screw (see Section 2).*

2 Depress the tabs of the quick-release connector and disconnect the clutch master cylinder hydraulic hose from the rear of the master cylinder reservoir **(see illustration)**.

3 Disconnect the brake fluid level sensor wiring connector from the underside of the reservoir.

4 Place cloth rags beneath the master cylinder to collect escaping brake fluid. Identify the brake lines for position, then unscrew the union nuts and move the lines to one side **(see illustration)**. Tape over or plug the line outlets.

5 Unscrew the mounting nuts and withdraw the master cylinder from the vacuum servo unit **(see illustration)**. Take care not to spill fluid on the vehicle paintwork.

10.2 Clutch hydraulic hose (arrowed) and brake fluid level sensor wiring connector (arrowed) on the master cylinder reservoir

10.4 Brake hydraulic pipe union nuts (arrowed) at the master cylinder

10.5 Master cylinder mounting nuts (arrowed)

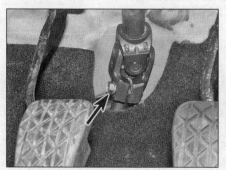

11.4 Undo the clamp bolt (arrowed) securing the steering column shaft universal joint to the steering gearpinion

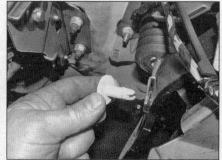

11.6 Prise out the plastic clevis pin securing the brake pedal to the servo unit pushrod

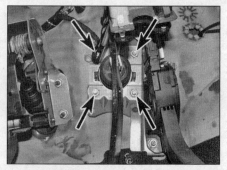

11.7 Brake pedal mounting bracket retaining nuts (arrowed)

6 No further dismantling of the master cylinder is possible as the internal components are not available separately.

Refitting

7 Fit the master cylinder to the servo unit, ensuring that the servo unit pushrod enters the master cylinder piston centrally. Fit the retaining nuts and tighten them to the specified torque setting.

8 Refit the brake lines and tighten the union nuts securely.

9 Reconnect the clutch master cylinder hydraulic hose and the brake fluid level sensor wiring connector to the reservoir.

10 Remove the reservoir filler cap and top-up the reservoir with fresh hydraulic fluid to the MAX mark (see *Weekly checks*).

11 Bleed the hydraulic systems as described in Section 2 and Chapter 6 Section 4 then refit the filler cap. Thoroughly check the operation of the brakes and clutch before using the vehicle on the road.

11 Brake pedal –
removal and refitting

Note: *The brake pedal is an integral part of the pedal mounting bracket assembly and cannot be individually removed. Should renewal of the pedal, due to wear of the pivot bushes or the pedal itself, be required, it will be necessary to renew the complete mounting bracket assembly.*

Removal

1 Disconnect the battery negative terminal (refer to 'Disconnecting the battery').

2 Remove the steering column shrouds as described in Chapter 11 Section 25.

3 Set the front wheels in the straight-ahead position, then lock the steering column in position by removing the ignition key.

4 Working in the driver's footwell, undo the clamp bolt securing the steering column shaft lower universal joint to the steering gear pinion **(see illustration)**. Note that a new clamp bolt will be required for refitting. Pull the shaft upwards and off the pinion.

5 Disconnect the wiring connectors from the brake pedal position switch and brake light switch at the top of the pedal mounting bracket. Release the wiring harness from the clips and ties on the pedal bracket.

6 Using a screwdriver, prise out the plastic clevis pin securing the brake pedal to the servo unit pushrod **(see illustration)**. Note that the clevis pin will be damaged during removal and a new clevis pin will be required for refitting.

7 Undo the nuts securing the accelerator pedal to the brake pedal mounting bracket, and the nuts securing the mounting bracket to the bulkhead **(see illustration)**. Lift off the accelerator pedal and place it to one side.

8 Withdraw the brake pedal mounting bracket off the studs and remove it from inside the car.

Refitting

9 Refitting is a reversal of removal, noting the following points:

a) *Tighten the mounting bracket retaining nuts to the specified torque.*

b) *Reconnect the brake pedal to the servo unit pushrod using a new clevis pin.*

c) *Use a new clamp bolt when reconnecting the steering column shaft universal joint and tighten the clamp bolt to the specified torque.*

12 Vacuum servo unit –
testing, removal and refitting

Testing

1 To test the operation of the servo unit, with the engine off, depress the footbrake several times to exhaust the vacuum. Now start the engine, keeping the pedal firmly depressed. As the engine starts, there should be a noticeable 'give' in the brake pedal as the vacuum builds-up. Allow the engine to run for at least two minutes, then switch it off. The brake pedal should now feel normal, but further applications should result in the pedal feeling firmer, the pedal stroke decreasing with each application.

2 If the servo does not operate as described,

first inspect the servo unit check valve as described in Section 13.

3 If the servo unit still fails to operate satisfactorily, the fault lies within the unit itself. Repairs to the unit are not possible; if faulty, the servo unit must be renewed.

Removal

4 Disconnect the battery negative terminal (refer to 'Disconnecting the battery').

5 On models with air conditioning, have the refrigerant discharged at a dealer service department or an automotive air conditioning repair facility.

6 Remove the brake master cylinder as described in Section 10.

7 Working in the driver's footwell, using a screwdriver, prise out the plastic clevis pin securing the brake pedal to the servo unit pushrod **(see illustration 11.6)**. Note that the clevis pin will be damaged during removal and a new clevis pin will be required for refitting.

8 Undo the four nuts securing the vacuum servo unit to the brake pedal mounting bracket **(see illustration)**.

9 Firmly apply the handbrake, then jack up the front of the vehicle and support it securely on axle stands (see 'Jacking and vehicle support'). Where applicable, remove the engine undershield.

10 To prevent damage to the exhaust flexible section in subsequent operations, support it by attaching a pair of splints either side (two scrap strips of wood, plant canes, etc) using

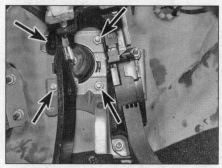

12.8 Vacuum servo unit retaining nuts (arrowed)

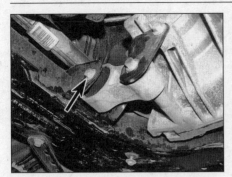

12.11 Unscrew and remove the engine lower mounting link through-bolt (arrowed)

12.12 Undo the nuts (arrowed) securing the refrigerant pipes to the expansion valve on the bulkhead

12.13 Undo the nuts at the refrigerant pipe connector and support bracket (arrowed) and remove the refrigerant pipe

some cable-ties. Undo the nuts securing the flexible section to the catalytic converter, and separate the joint. Recover the gasket, and discard it, a new gasket must be used for refitting.

11 Unscrew and remove the engine lower mounting link through-bolt **(see illustration)**.

12 On models with air conditioning, undo the two nuts securing the refrigerant pipes to the expansion valve on the bulkhead and withdraw the pipes from the valve **(see illustration)**. Discard the O-ring seals – new ones must be used when refitting. Suitably cap the open fittings immediately to keep moisture and contamination out of the system.

13 On models with air conditioning, undo the nut at the upper refrigerant pipe connector adjacent to the brake master cylinder reservoir. Undo the support bracket nut on the front suspension strut tower and remove the refrigerant pipe from the car **(see illustration)**. Discard the refrigerant pipe O-ring seals – new ones must be used when refitting. Suitably cap the open fittings immediately to keep moisture and contamination out of the system.

14 Lift the cooling system expansion tank from its mountings and place it to one side.

15 The engine must now be supported, as the right-hand mounting (right as seen from the driver's seat) must be unbolted from the body. Supporting the engine should ideally be done from above, using an engine crane or a special engine lifting beam. However, in the absence of these tools, the engine can be

supported on the sump, using a trolley jack, providing a piece of wood is used to spread the load.

16 With the engine securely supported, undo the three bolts securing the right-hand engine mounting to the body **(see illustration)**.

17 Carefully ease the vacuum hose out of the servo unit, taking care not to displace the sealing grommet **(see illustration)**.

18 Withdraw the servo unit from the bulkhead as far as the initial working clearance will allow. With the engine securely supported on the jack or crane, pull the engine forward on the right-hand side, until sufficient clearance exists to remove the servo unit from the engine compartment.

Refitting

19 Locate the vacuum servo unit in position on the bulkhead ensuring that the servo unit pushrod locates correctly around the brake pedal.

20 Refit the vacuum hose to the servo grommet, ensuring that the hose is correctly seated.

21 Move the engine back to its fitted position and refit the engine mounting retaining bolts. Tighten the bolts to the specified torque. Remove the jack or crane used to support the engine.

22 Place the cooling system expansion tank back in its mountings.

23 On models with air conditioning, reconnect the refrigerant pipes using new O-ring seals and tighten the pipe retaining

nuts securely. Refit the upper refrigerant pipe support bracket to the suspension strut turret.

24 Using a new gasket, reconnect the exhaust flexible section to the catalytic converter and tighten the retaining nuts to the specified torque. Remove the support splints from the flexible section.

25 Where applicable, refit the engine undershield, then lower the car to the ground.

26 Refit the four nuts securing the vacuum servo unit to the brake pedal mounting bracket and tighten the nuts to the specified torque.

27 Reconnect the brake pedal to the servo unit pushrod using a new clevis pin.

28 Refit the brake master cylinder as described in Section 10, then reconnect the battery negative terminal.

29 On models with air conditioning, have the system evacuated, charged and leak-tested by the specialist who discharged it.

13 Vacuum servo unit check valve and hose – removal, testing and refitting

Removal

1 Carefully ease the vacuum hose out of the servo unit, taking care not to displace the sealing grommet **(see illustration 12.17)**.

2 Disconnect the hose quick-release fitting from the inlet manifold (petrol engines) or vacuum pump (diesel engines).

3 Release the vacuum hose from its clips and support brackets in the engine compartment, then remove the hose and check valve from the car.

Testing

4 Examine the check valve and hose for signs of damage, and renew if necessary. The valve may be tested by blowing through it in both directions. Air should flow through the valve in one direction only – when blown through from the servo unit end. If air flows in both directions, or not at all, renew the valve and hose as an assembly.

5 Examine the servo unit rubber sealing grommet for signs of damage or deterioration, and renew as necessary.

12.16 Undo the three bolts (arrowed) securing the engine mounting to the body

12.17 Ease the vacuum hose (arrowed) out of the servo unit grommet

14.5 Pull adjuster lever away from the adjuster fork and turn the adjuster wheel (arrowed) to shorten the adjuster assembly

14.6 Fit a cable-tie to the trailing shoe to hold the stop-peg (arrowed) on the handbrake lever against the brakeshoe

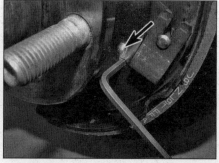

14.7 Insert a 4 mm Allen key between the stop-peg (arrowed) on the handbrake lever, and the edge of the brakeshoe

Refitting

6 Refitting is a reversal of removal ensuring that the quick-release connector audibly locks in position, and that the hose is correctly seated in the servo grommet.

7 On completion, start the engine and check that there are no air leaks.

14 Handbrake – adjustment

1 Remove both rear brake drums as described in Section 7.

2 If not already done when removing the brake drums, unclip the gear lever or selector lever trim from the base of the gear/selector lever **(see illustration 7.4)**.

3 Pull up the centre console front upper trim panel, to release the retaining clips. Disconnect the accessory socket wiring connector and remove the panel **(see illustrations 7.5a and 7.5b)**.

4 Working through the aperture at the base of the handbrake lever, remove the retaining clip from the handbrake adjuster nut on the end of the handbrake cable **(see illustrations 7.6a and 7.6b)**.

5 Working on one side of the car at a time, lift the adjuster lever on each leading brake shoe and slacken the adjuster strut wheel to shorten the overall length of the brake shoe adjuster mechanism slightly **(see illustration)**.

6 Working on the brake shoe assembly on the right-hand side of the car, wrap a cable-tie around the trailing brake shoe and the handbrake operating lever on the brake shoe. Tighten the cable-tie until the stop-peg on the handbrake operating lever is in contact with the edge of the brake shoe **(see illustration)**.

7 Working on the brake shoe assembly on the left-hand side of the car, insert a 4 mm Allen key between the stop-peg on the trailing brake shoe handbrake operating lever, and the edge of the brake shoe **(see illustration)**.

8 Working through the aperture at the base of the handbrake lever, and using a socket and extension bar, tighten the adjuster nut on the handbrake cable until the Allen key falls out **(see illustration)**.

9 Remove the cable-tie from the right-hand brake shoe assembly and refit both brake drums, referring to Section 7 if necessary.

10 With the handbrake fully released, adjust the lining-to-drum clearance by repeatedly depressing the brake pedal at least 10 times. Whilst depressing the pedal, have an assistant listen to the rear drums, to check that the adjuster strut is functioning correctly; if so, a clicking sound will be emitted by the strut as the pedal is depressed.

11 Apply the handbrake and check that the after approximately three to five clicks of the ratchet, both rear brake drums are locked. Now fully release the handbrake lever and check that the drums rotate freely.

12 Place the retaining clip back into position

on the handbrake adjuster nut, then refit the centre console trim panel and gear/selector lever trim panel.

13 Refit the roadwheels and lower the car to the ground.

15 Handbrake lever – removal and refitting

Removal

1 Disconnect the battery negative terminal (refer to 'Disconnecting the battery').

2 Remove the centre console and the front seat on the driver's side as described in Chapter 11.

3 Ensure that the handbrake lever is released (off).

4 Working through the aperture at the base of the handbrake lever, remove the retaining clip from the handbrake adjuster nut on the end of the handbrake cable **(see illustration)**. Using a socket and extension bar, slacken the adjuster nut on the handbrake cable five turns to introduce some slack in the cable.

5 Chock the front wheels, then jack up the rear of the vehicle, and support it securely on axle stands (see 'Jacking and vehicle support').

6 From under the car, undo the eight nuts and remove the underfloor cross-brace beneath the exhaust centre section **(see illustration)**.

14.8 Tighten the adjuster nut on the handbrake cable until the Allen key falls out

15.4 Remove the retaining clip (arrowed) from the adjuster nut on the end of the handbrake cable

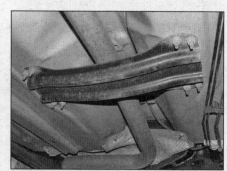

15.6 Undo the eight nuts and remove the underfloor cross-brace

15.9 Depress the retaining tabs (arrowed) and push the handbrake cables out of the support bracket

15.11 Disconnect the wiring connector (arrowed) from the handbrake warning light switch

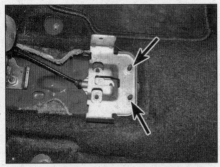

15.12 Undo the two retaining nuts (arrowed) and remove the centre console mounting bracket

7 Release the exhaust system from the centre and rear rubber mountings and allow the system to rest on the rear axle.

8 Undo the washer-type fasteners, and remove the rear and centre exhaust system heat shields.

9 Depress the retaining tabs and push the handbrake cables rearwards out of the support bracket (see illustration).

10 Detach the short (front) handbrake cable from the compensator plate by sliding the end fitting up and out of the elongated hole in the plate.

11 Disconnect the wiring connector from the handbrake lever warning light switch (see illustration).

12 Undo the two retaining nuts and remove the centre console rear mounting bracket from the floor (see illustration).

13 Undo the two retaining nuts and release the handbrake cable guide from the floor.

14 Undo the retaining bolt and two retaining nuts and remove the handbrake lever assembly from inside the car (see illustration).

Refitting

15 Refitting is a reversal of removal, noting the following points:

a) *Tighten all nuts/bolts to the specified torque (where given).*

b) *Adjust the handbrake as described in Section 14.*

c) *Refit the centre console and front seat as described in Chapter 11.*

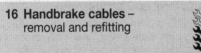

16 Handbrake cables – removal and refitting

Note: *The handbrake cables are supplied as one part, together with the compensator plate.*

Removal

1 From inside the car, unclip the gear lever or selector lever trim from the base of the gear/selector lever (see illustration 7.4).

2 Pull up the centre console front upper trim panel, to release the retaining clips. Disconnect the accessory socket wiring connector and remove the panel (see illustrations 7.5a and 7.5b).

3 Working through the aperture at the base of the handbrake lever, remove the retaining clip from the handbrake adjuster nut on the end of the handbrake cable (see illustrations 7.6a and 7.6b). Using a socket and extension bar, slacken the adjuster nut on the handbrake cable five turns to introduce some slack in the cable.

4 Chock the front wheels, then jack up the rear of the vehicle, and support it securely on axle stands (see *'Jacking and vehicle support'*).

5 From under the car, undo the eight nuts and remove the underfloor cross-brace beneath the exhaust centre section (see illustration 15.6).

6 Release the exhaust system from the centre and rear rubber mountings and allow the system to rest on the rear axle.

15.14 Undo the bolt and two nuts (arrowed) and remove the handbrake lever assembly

7 Undo the washer-type fasteners, and remove the rear and centre exhaust system heat shields.

8 Depress the retaining tabs and push handbrake cables rearwards out of the support bracket (see illustration 15.9).

9 Detach the short (front) handbrake cable from the compensator plate by sliding the end fitting up and out of the elongated hole in the plate.

10 Working on one side of the car at a time, locate the handbrake cable connector link just forward of the rear brake assembly. Using a small screwdriver, depress the tab in the centre of the connector link, then push the handbrake cable end fitting out of the link (see illustrations).

11 Depress the tabs on the handbrake outer cables and pull the disconnected cables out of the support brackets on the trailing arms (see illustration).

16.10a Depress the tab in the centre of the connector link ...

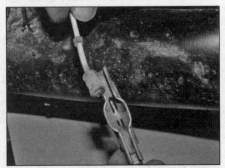

16.10b ... then push the handbrake cable end fitting out of the link

16.11 Depress the tabs (arrowed) and pull the handbrake cable out of the trailing arm support bracket

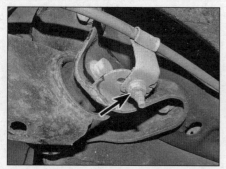

16.12 Undo the nut (arrowed) and release the handbrake cable support bracket from the axle pivot mounting

12 Undo the nut and release the handbrake cable support brackets from the rear axle pivot mountings on each side **(see illustration)**.
13 Release the cables from the underbody retaining clips around the fuel tank and remove the cables from under the car.

Refitting

14 Refitting is a reversal of removal, noting the following points:
a) *Adjust the handbrake as described in Section 14.*
b) *Refit the centre console trim panel and gear/selector lever trim panel after adjusting the handbrake.*

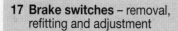

17 Brake switches – removal, refitting and adjustment

Removal

Brake light switch

1 Disconnect the battery negative terminal (refer to *'Disconnecting the battery'*).
2 Working in the driver's footwell, disconnect the wiring connector from the brake light switch, located on the brake pedal mounting bracket. This is the switch on the right-hand side of the pedal mounting bracket, and is coloured black.
3 Rotate the switch clockwise by a quarter-turn, and withdraw it from the pedal bracket **(see illustration)**. Do not depress the brake pedal during the removal or refitting procedure – the pedal must be 'at rest'.

Brake pedal position switch

4 Disconnect the battery negative terminal (refer to *'Disconnecting the battery'*).
5 Working in the driver's footwell, disconnect the wiring connector from the brake pedal position switch, located on the brake pedal mounting bracket. This is the switch on the left-hand side of the pedal mounting bracket, and is coloured blue and white.
6 Rotate the switch anti-clockwise by a quarter-turn, and withdraw it from the pedal bracket. Do not depress the brake pedal during the removal or refitting procedure – the pedal must be 'at rest'.

17.3 Rotate the brake light switch clockwise by a quarter-turn to remove it

Refitting and adjustment

7 Refitting is a reversal of the removal procedure. Both switches are automatically adjusted/calibrated by the vehicle system.

18 Handbrake warning light switch – removal and refitting

Removal

1 Remove the centre console as described in Chapter 11 Section 24.
2 Disconnect the wiring connector from the warning light switch on the side of the handbrake lever **(see illustration 15.11)**.
3 Unscrew the mounting bolt and remove the switch from the handbrake lever bracket.

Refitting

4 Refitting is a reversal of removal.

19 Anti-lock Braking and Traction Control systems – general information

1 ABS is fitted as standard equipment. On higher specification models, the ABS may also incorporate traction control or an electronic stability program as additional safety features.
2 The ABS system comprises a hydraulic modulator and electronic control unit together with four wheel speed sensors. The hydraulic modulator contains the electronic control unit (ECU), the hydraulic solenoid valves (one set for each brake) and the electrically-driven pump. The purpose of the system is to prevent the wheel(s) locking during heavy braking. This is achieved by automatic release of the brake on the relevant wheel, followed by re-application of the brake.
3 The solenoid valves are controlled by the ECU, which itself receives signals from the four wheel speed sensors which monitor the speed of rotation of each wheel. By comparing these signals, the ECU can determine the speed at which the vehicle is travelling. It can then use this speed to determine when a wheel is decelerating at an abnormal rate,

compared to the speed of the vehicle, and therefore predicts when a wheel is about to lock. During normal operation, the system functions in the same way as a conventional braking system.
4 If the ECU senses that a wheel is about to lock, it operates the relevant solenoid valve(s) in the hydraulic unit, which then isolates from the master cylinder the relevant brake(s) on the wheel(s) which is/are about to lock, effectively sealing-in the hydraulic pressure.
5 If the speed of rotation of the wheel continues to decrease at an abnormal rate, the ECU operates the electrically-driven pump which pumps the hydraulic fluid back into the master cylinder, releasing the brake. Once the speed of rotation of the wheel returns to an acceptable rate, the pump stops, and the solenoid valves switch again, allowing the hydraulic master cylinder pressure to return to the caliper, which then re-applies the brake. This cycle can be carried out many times a second.
6 The action of the solenoid valves and return pump creates pulses in the hydraulic circuit. When the ABS system is functioning, these pulses can be felt through the brake pedal.
7 On models with traction control, the ABS hydraulic modulator incorporates an additional set of solenoid valves which operate the traction control system. The system operates at speeds up to approximately 30 mph using the signals supplied by the wheel speed sensors. If the ECU senses that a driving wheel is about to lose traction, it prevents this by momentarily applying the relevant front brake. The ABS ECU also communicates with the engine management powertrain control module during traction control operation. In severe cases of traction loss the engine management ECU will reduce engine power to assist with traction recovery.
8 The electronic stability program (ESP) is a further development of ABS and traction control. Using additional sensors to monitor steering wheel position, vehicle yaw rate, acceleration and deceleration, in conjunction with the ABS sensors, the ECU can intervene under conditions of vehicle instability. Using the signals from the various sensors, the ECU can determine driver intent (steering wheel position, throttle position, vehicle speed and engine speed). From the sensor inputs from the wheel speed sensors, yaw rate sensors and acceleration sensors the ECU can calculate whether the vehicle is responding to driver input, or whether an unstable driving situation is occurring. If instability is detected, the ECU will intervene by applying or releasing the relevant front or rear brake, in conjunction with a power reduction, until vehicle stability returns.
9 The operation of the ABS, traction control, and stability programs is entirely dependent on electrical signals. To prevent the system responding to any inaccurate signals, a built-in safety circuit monitors all signals received by the ECU. If an inaccurate signal

or low battery voltage is detected, the system is automatically shut down, and the relevant warning light on the instrument panel is illuminated, to inform the driver that the system is not operational. Normal braking is still available, however.

10 If a fault develops in the ABS/traction control/ESP system, the vehicle must be taken to a Ford dealer for fault diagnosis and repair.

20 Anti-lock Braking and Traction Control system components – removal and refitting

Note: Faults on the ABS system can only be diagnosed using Ford diagnostic equipment or compatible alternative equipment.

Note: Before starting work, refer to the note at the beginning of Section 2 concerning the dangers of hydraulic fluid.

Hydraulic modulator and ECU

Removal

1 The hydraulic modulator and ECU are located at the rear left-hand corner of the engine compartment. To gain access, remove the battery and battery tray as described in Chapter 5A Section 4.

2 Minimise fluid loss by first removing the master cylinder reservoir cap and screwing it down onto a piece of polythene.

3 Pull out the locking bar and disconnect the wiring harness plug from the ABS ECU on the hydraulic modulator **(see illustration)**. Release the wiring harness from the cable-tie on the modulator mounting bracket.

4 Note and record the fitted position of the brake pipes at the modulator, then unscrew the union nuts and release the pipes. As a precaution, place absorbent rags beneath the brake pipe unions when unscrewing them. Suitably plug or cap the disconnected unions to prevent dirt entry and fluid loss.

5 Unscrew the three mounting bracket retaining bolts and remove the hydraulic modulator together with the mounting bracket.

Refitting

6 Refitting is the reverse of the removal procedure, noting the following points:

a) *Tighten the modulator mounting bracket retaining bolts to the specified torque.*
b) *Refit the brake pipes to their respective locations, and tighten the union nuts to the specified torque.*
c) *Ensure that the wiring is correctly routed, and that the ECU wiring harness plug is firmly pressed into position and secured with the locking bar.*
d) *Refit the battery tray and battery as described in Chapter 5A Section 4.*
e) *On completion, bleed the complete hydraulic system as described in Section 2. Ensure that the system is bled in the correct order, to prevent air entering the modulator return pump.*

Electronic control unit (ECU)

Note: If a new ECU is to be fitted, this work must be entrusted to a Ford dealer or suitably-equipped specialist as it is necessary to programme the new ECU after installation. This work requires the use of dedicated Ford diagnostic equipment or a compatible alternative.

Removal

7 Remove the hydraulic modulator from the car as described previously in this Section.

8 Undo the two retaining bolts and carefully withdraw the ECU from the base of the hydraulic modulator.

9 Thoroughly clean the mating face of the hydraulic modulator and also check the condition of the ECU gasket. If the gasket is damaged it will be necessary to obtain a new ECU.

Refitting

10 Ensuring that the seal is correctly located, carefully place the ECU in position, keeping it square and level.

11 Fit and moderately tighten the two retaining bolts.

12 On completion, refit the hydraulic modulator as described previously in this Section.

Front wheel speed sensors

Removal

13 Disconnect the battery negative terminal (refer to 'Disconnecting the battery').

20.3 ABS ECU wiring harness plug (arrowed)

14 Firmly apply the handbrake, then jack up the front of the car and support it securely on axle stands (see 'Jacking and vehicle support'). Remove the appropriate front roadwheel.

15 Undo the retaining screws, release the clips and remove the wheel arch liner from under the wheel arch.

16 Trace the wheel speed sensor wiring back to its wiring connector on the inner wheel arch, and disconnect the connector. Depress the tab and pull the wiring connector end from the support clip on the wheel arch. Release the wiring harness from the cable-tie and support bracket on the wheel arch.

17 Slide the wheel speed sensor wiring grommet out of the support bracket on the suspension strut **(see illustration)**. Where applicable, also release the wiring from the clip at the base of the strut.

18 Unscrew the wheel speed sensor retaining bolt, then withdraw the wheel speed sensor from the top of the swivel hub **(see illustrations)**. *Note: The sensors can prove difficult to remove, due to corrosion – try soaking the sensor in maintenance spray. Do not use any great force to remove a sensor, or it may be damaged.*

Refitting

19 Ensure that the sensor and swivel hub sealing faces are clean, then fit the sensor to the hub. Refit the retaining bolt, and tighten it securely.

20 Ensure that the sensor wiring is correctly routed, and retained by all the necessary

20.17 Slide the wheel speed sensor wiring grommet (arrowed) out of the strut support bracket

20.18a Unscrew the wheel speed sensor retaining bolt (arrowed) ...

20.18b ... then withdraw the wheel speed sensor from the top of the hub

20.25 Rear wheel speed sensor wiring connector (arrowed) on the inner wheel arch

21.4 Vacuum pump mounting bolts

clips. Reconnect it to its wiring connector, and fit the connector into the retaining clip.

21 Refit the wheel arch liner and roadwheel, then lower the vehicle to the ground and tighten the roadwheel nuts to the specified torque. On completion, reconnect the battery negative terminal.

Rear wheel speed sensors

Removal

22 Disconnect the battery negative terminal (refer to 'Disconnecting the battery').
23 Chock the front wheels, then jack up the rear of the vehicle, and support it securely on axle stands (see 'Jacking and vehicle support'). Remove the appropriate rear roadwheel.
24 Undo the retaining screws and nuts and remove the wheel arch liner from under the wheel arch.
25 Trace the wheel speed sensor wiring back to its wiring connector on the inner wheel arch, and disconnect the connector (see illustration). Depress the tab and pull the wiring connector end from the support clip on the wheel arch. Release the wiring harness from the cable-tie and support bracket on the wheel arch.
26 Release the sensor wiring harness from the grommets and clips on the inner wheel arch and rear suspension trailing arm.
27 Undo the retaining bolt and remove the wheel speed sensor from the rear of the brake backplate.

Refitting

28 Ensure that the sensor and brake

backplate sealing faces are clean, then fit the sensor to the backplate. Refit the retaining bolt, and tighten it securely.
29 Ensure that the sensor wiring is correctly routed, and retained by all the necessary clips. Reconnect it to its wiring connector, and fit the connector into the retaining clip.
30 Refit the wheel arch liner and roadwheel, then lower the vehicle to the ground and tighten the roadwheel nuts to the specified torque. On completion, reconnect the battery negative terminal.

Yaw rate sensor

Note: The yaw rate sensor is only fitted to vehicles with electronic stability control (ESP). The sensor is located beneath the driver's seat on the right-hand side of the car.

Removal

31 Disconnect the battery negative terminal (refer to 'Disconnecting the battery').
32 Remove the driver's seat as described in Chapter 11 Section 21.
33 Disconnect the sensor wiring connector, then undo the three bolts and remove the sensor from the car.

Refitting

34 Refitting is the reverse of the removal procedure.

Steering angle sensor

35 The steering angle sensor is an integral part of the EPS steering column and cannot be individually removed.

21 Vacuum pump (diesel engine models) – removal and refitting

Removal

1.4 litre engines (Stage IV emissions)

1 The vacuum pump is located on the transmission end of the cylinder head and is driven off the end of the camshaft.
2 Remove the air cleaner as described in Chapter 4B Section 4.
3 Depress the locking tabs and release the brake servo vacuum hose from the top of the pump.
4 Unscrew the two mounting bolts, and withdraw the pump from the head (see illustration). Recover the O-ring seals – new ones must be used when refitting.

1.4 litre (Stage V emissions) and 1.6 litre engines

5 The vacuum pump is located on the transmission end of the cylinder head and is driven off the end of the exhaust camshaft.
6 Disengage the retaining clip tabs and disconnect the crankcase ventilation hose from the oil separator (see illustration).
7 Slacken the clips securing the air intake duct to the air cleaner and turbocharger, and remove the duct (see illustration).
8 Depress the locking tabs and release the brake servo vacuum hose from the top of the pump.
9 Unscrew the two mounting bolts, and withdraw the pump from the head (see illustration). Recover the O-ring seals – new ones must be used when refitting.

Refitting

10 Refitting is a reversal of removal, noting the following points:
a) Ensure the pump and cylinder head mating surfaces are clean and dry, and fit new seals.
b) Align the pump's drive dog with the slot in the end of the camshaft, and fit it into place, ensuring the seals are not dislodged in the process.
c) Tighten the pump mounting bolts to the specified torque.

21.6 Disconnect the crankcase ventilation hose from the oil separator

21.7 Slacken the clips securing the intake duct to the air cleaner and turbocharger and remove the duct

21.9 Vacuum pump mounting bolts

Chapter 10
Suspension and steering

Contents

Degrees of difficulty

| **Easy,** suitable for novice with little experience | | **Fairly easy,** suitable for beginner with some experience | | **Fairly difficult,** suitable for competent DIY mechanic | | **Difficult,** suitable for experienced DIY mechanic | | **Very difficult,** suitable for expert DIY or professional | |

Specifications

Front suspension
Type . . . . Independent, with MacPherson struts, gas-filled shock absorbers and anti-roll bar

Rear suspension
Type . . . . Semi-independent torsion beam, with trailing arms, coil springs and telescopic shock absorbers

Steering
Type . . . . Rack-and-pinion with electric power steering (EPS)

Wheel alignment

	Total toe	Caster angle	Camber angle
Front wheel			
Normal suspension	0°9' Toe-in ± 21'	2°26' to 4°26'	-1°56' to 0°34'
Sports suspension	0°13' Toe-in ± 21'	2°19 to 4°19'	-1°57' ± 0°33'
Rear wheel			
Normal suspension	0°21' Toe-in ± 18'		-2°47' to -0°17'
Sports suspension	0°23' Toe-in ± 18'		-2°47' to -0°17'

Torque wrench settings

	Nm	lbf ft
Front suspension		
Anti-roll bar clamp bolts	48	35
Anti-roll bar connecting link nuts	48	35
Brake caliper carrier bracket bolts	75	55
Driveshaft (front hub) nut*	255	188
Lower arm balljoint clamp bolt nut*	52	38
Lower arm mounting bolts: *		
Stage 1	65	48
Stage 2	Angle-tighten a further 180°	
Rear engine mounting through-bolt	48	35
Subframe bolts:		
Front bolts*	60	44
Rear bolts: *		
Stage 1	100	74
Stage 2	Angle-tighten a further 180°	
Subframe brace	52	38
Suspension strut piston rod nut	48	35
Suspension strut top mounting nuts	30	22
Suspension strut to swivel hub: *		
Stage 1	82	61
Stage 2	Angle-tighten a further 90°	
Rear suspension		
Rear axle mounting bolts	125	92
Rear axle pivot through-bolt and nut:		
Stage 1	80	59
Stage 2	Angle-tighten a further 120°	
Rear hub bearing assembly to trailing arm:		
Stage 1	65	48
Stage 2	Slacken by 90°	
Stage 3	65	48
Shock absorber lower mounting bolt	115	85
Shock absorber upper mounting bolts	25	18
Steering		
Steering column retaining nuts*	22	16
Steering column shaft:		
Upper clamp bolt*	32	24
Lower clamp bolt*	34	25
Steering gear securing bolts	90	66
Steering wheel securing bolt	48	35
Track rod end locknuts	79	58
Track rod end-to-swivel hub nuts*	53	39
Roadwheels		
Roadwheel nuts	110	81

Use new fasteners

1 General Information

1 The front suspension is of independent type, with a subframe, MacPherson struts, lower arms, and an anti-roll bar. The struts, which incorporate coil springs and integral shock absorbers, are attached at their upper ends to the reinforced strut mountings on the body shell. The lower end of each strut is bolted to the top of a cast swivel hub, which carries the hub, and the brake disc and caliper. The hubs run within non-adjustable bearings in the swivel hubs. The lower end of each swivel hub is attached, via a balljoint, to a pressed-steel lower arm assembly. The balljoints are integral with the lower arms. Each lower arm is attached at its inboard end to the subframe, via flexible rubber bushes, and controls both lateral and fore-and-aft movement of the front wheels. An anti-roll bar is fitted to all models. The anti-roll bar is mounted on the subframe, and is connected to the suspension struts via vertical connecting links.

2 The rear suspension is of semi-independent type, consisting of a torsion beam and trailing arms, with double-conical coil springs and telescopic shock absorbers. The front ends of the trailing arms are attached to the vehicle underbody by horizontal bushes, and the rear ends are located by the shock absorbers, which are bolted to the underbody at their upper ends. The coil springs are mounted independently of the shock absorbers, and act directly between the trailing arms and the underbody. Each rear wheel bearing, hub and stub axle assembly is manufactured as a sealed unit, and cannot be dismantled.

3 The steering column is linked to the steering gear by a steering column shaft. The shaft has a universal joint fitted to its upper end, and is secured to the column by a clamp bolt. The lower end of the shaft is attached to the steering gear pinion by means of a universal joint and clamp bolts.

4 The rack-and-pinion type steering gear is mounted on the front suspension subframe, and is connected by two track rods, with balljoints at their outer ends, to the steering arms projecting rearwards from the swivel hubs. The track rod ends are threaded, to facilitate adjustment.

5 Electric power-assisted steering is fitted as standard, whereby an electric motor, drive gear assembly and torque sensor incorporated in the steering column provide a variable degree of power assistance according to roadspeed. The system is controlled by an electronic control unit with self-diagnostic capability, integral with the electric motor.

2 Front swivel hub –
removed and refitting

Removal

1 Firmly apply the handbrake, then jack up the front of the car and support it securely on axle stands (see *'Jacking and vehicle support'*). Remove the relevant front roadwheel. Where applicable, remove the engine undershield.

2 Refit at least two roadwheel nuts to the front hub, and tighten them securely. Have an assistant firmly depress the brake pedal to prevent the front hub from rotating, then using a socket and extension bar, slacken the driveshaft retaining nut. Alternatively, a tool can be fabricated from two lengths of steel strip (one long, one short) and a nut and bolt; the nut and bolt forming the pivot of a forked tool. Attach the tool to the hub using two wheel nuts, and hold the tool to prevent the hub from rotating as the driveshaft retaining nut is slackened **(see illustration)**. Loosen the nut almost to the end of its threads, but do not remove it at this stage.

 Warning: The driveshaft nut is done up extremely tight, and considerable effort will be required to loosen it. Do not use poor-quality, badly-fitting tools for this task, due to the risk of personal injury.

3 Unscrew the bolt and release the brake

2.2 Using a fabricated tool to hold the front hub stationary whilst the driveshaft retaining nut is slackened

hydraulic hose from the suspension strut **(see illustration)**.

4 Unscrew the bolts securing the brake caliper carrier bracket to the swivel hub, then slide the caliper/bracket assembly from the swivel hub and brake disc (there is no need to remove the brake pads) **(see illustration)**. Suspend the caliper/bracket assembly from the strut coil spring using wire or string – do not allow the caliper to hang on the brake hose.

5 Mark the brake disc in relation to the hub (assuming it is to be refitted), and withdraw it from the hub **(see illustration)**.

6 On models with ABS, unscrew the wheel speed sensor retaining bolt, then withdraw the wheel speed sensor from the top of the hub **(see illustrations)**. Provided the sensor

2.3 Unscrew the bolt and release the brake hydraulic hose from the suspension strut

is placed out of the way, there is no need to disconnect its wiring. **Note:** *The sensors can prove difficult to remove, due to corrosion – try soaking the sensor in maintenance spray. Do not use any great force to remove a sensor, or it may be damaged.*

7 Slacken the track rod end balljoint nut, and unscrew it as far as the ends of the threads. Counterhold the balljoint pin using a 5 mm Allen key **(see illustration)**.

8 Disconnect the track rod end balljoint from the swivel hub using a balljoint separator tool (leave the nut fitted to protect the threads), taking care not to damage the balljoint rubber seal **(see illustration)**. Once the balljoint has been released, remove the balljoint nut and discard it – a new one should be used for refitting.

2.4 Unscrew the bolts (arrowed) securing the brake caliper carrier bracket to the swivel hub

2.5 Withdraw the brake disc from the hub

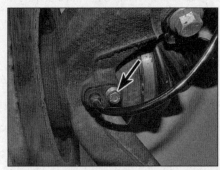

2.6a Unscrew the wheel speed sensor retaining bolt (arrowed) …

2.6b … then withdraw the wheel speed sensor from the top of the hub

2.7 Loosen the track rod end balljoint nut, using an Allen key to stop the pin turning

2.8 Using a balljoint separator tool to free the track rod end

2.9 Unscrew the lower arm balljoint clamp bolt nut, and withdraw the clamp bolt from the swivel hub

2.11 Home-made method of releasing the lower arm – wood block, long pole and length of chain

2.14 Pull the hub outwards, and pull the driveshaft through inside

9 Unscrew and remove the lower arm balljoint clamp bolt nut, and withdraw the clamp bolt from the swivel hub **(see illustration)**. Note that a new nut and bolt will be required for refitting.

10 Use a chisel or screwdriver as a wedge to expand the lower portion of the swivel hub.

11 Lever down the lower arm to free the balljoint from the swivel hub **(see illustration)**, then move the swivel hub to one side, taking care not to damage the balljoint rubber boot.

12 The splined end of the driveshaft now has to be released from its location in the hub. It's likely that the splines will be very tight (corrosion may even be a factor, if the driveshaft has not been disturbed for some time), and considerable force may be needed to push the driveshaft out. Ford recommend using a four-legged puller for this, but if one is not available, the shaft will have to be tapped out with a hammer. If a hammer is used, place a small piece of wood over the end of the driveshaft – in addition to the loosened hub nut, this will protect the threads from damage.

13 Once the splines have been released, remove the driveshaft nut and discard it – a new nut must be used for refitting.

14 The driveshaft can be separated from the hub by having an assistant pull the base of the suspension strut outwards, while the splined end of the shaft is pulled clear of the hub **(see illustration)**. Do not bend the driveshaft

excessively at any stage, or the joints may be damaged – the inner and outer joints should not be bent through more than 18° and 45° respectively. Do not let the driveshaft hang down under its own weight – tie it up level if necessary.

15 Slacken and remove the two nuts and bolts securing the suspension strut to the swivel hub **(see illustration)**. Discard the nuts and bolts; they should be renewed whenever they are disturbed.

16 Pull the upper part of the swivel hub out of the suspension strut and remove it from under the wheel arch.

Refitting

17 Refitting is a reversal of removal, bearing in mind the following points:

a) *Tighten all fixings to the specified torque.*

b) *Use a new driveshaft retaining nut, strut-to-swivel hub nuts and bolts, lower arm balljoint clamp bolt and nut and track rod end nut.*

c) *When inserting the bolts securing the swivel hub to the base of the strut, note that the bolt heads on the left-hand side must be toward the rear of the vehicle and the bolt heads on the right-hand side must be toward the front of the vehicle.*

d) *Use the method employed on removal to prevent rotation of the driveshaft as the retaining nut is tightened.*

3 Front hub bearings – renewal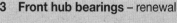

Note: *A press, a suitable puller, or similar improvised tools will be required for this operation. Obtain a bearing overhaul kit before proceeding.*

1 With the swivel hub removed as described in Section 2, proceed as follows.

2 The hub flange must now be removed from the bearing/swivel hub assembly. It is preferable to use a press to do this, but it is possible to drive out the hub using a metal tube of suitable diameter. Alternatively a suitable puller can be used.

3 Securely support the swivel hub, on two metal bars for instance, with the inner face uppermost then, using a metal bar or tube of suitable diameter, press or drive out the hub flange – we used a bolt and large washer (the same diameter as the end of the hub's splined end) **(see illustrations)**. Alternatively, use the puller to separate the hub from the bearing. Note that the bearing inner race will remain on the hub.

4 Now the bearing itself must be removed. Start by extracting the retaining circlip from the swivel hub using circlip pliers. After applying a generous amount of spray lubricant, we were able to drive the bearing out using a suitable

2.15 Slacken and remove the two nuts and bolts securing the suspension strut to the swivel hub

3.3a We used a large bolt and washer ...

3.3b ... and a large hammer to drive out the hub flange

3.4a Extract the retaining circlip from the swivel hub …

3.4b … then using a suitable drift …

3.4c … and several sharp blows from the hammer …

mandrel **(see illustrations)**. Alternatively use another old bearing, together with the same large bolt and hammer used previously. Mount the swivel hub across two large blocks of wood – putting it across the open jaws of a vice might result in damage to the vice, owing to the amount of force which will be necessary.

5   The bearing inner race left on the hub flange must now be removed. To do this, grip the edge of the flange in a vice, and begin tapping the race off with a chisel. Tap the race at the top and both sides (even turn the flange over in the vice) to stop it jamming as it frees. Once the race has moved down the hub flange slightly, a suitable puller, together with a bolt and washer for the puller centre screw to bear against, can be used to draw it off the rest of the way **(see illustrations)**.

6   Using emery paper, clean off any burrs or raised edges from the hub flange and swivel hub, which might stop the components going back together.

7   Apply a light coat of lubricant to the inside of the swivel hub, and to the outside of the new bearing. Start fitting the bearing by offering it squarely into the hub, with the pink-coloured ABS wheel speed sensor ring towards the transmission side of the swivel hub. Give it a few light taps with the hammer all round to locate it – keep the bearing square as this is done, or it will jam **(see illustrations)**.

3.4d … tap out the old bearing

3.5a Mount the hub flange in a vice, and tap the inner race with a chisel …

3.5b … then use a suitable puller to draw it off the rest of the way …

3.5c … until it comes off

3.7a Fit the bearing with the pink-coloured wheel speed sensor ring towards the transmission side of the swivel hub …

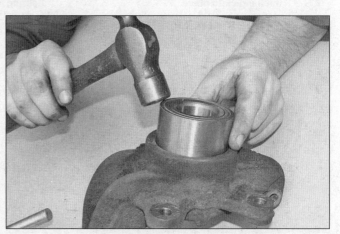

3.7b … then give it a few light taps with the hammer all round to locate it

3.8a Home-made arrangement of threaded rod, nuts and washers ...

3.8b ... used to gradually press the new bearing into place

3.9 Refit the retaining circlip, ensuring that it fully engages with its groove

3.10a Locate the hub flange in the bearing ...

3.10b ... then use the same arrangement of threaded rod, nuts and washers to draw the flange into place ...

3.10c ... ensuring that the washer used to draw in the flange rests against the bearing inner race

8 Fitting the bearing by tapping it in all the way with a hammer will likely damage it. We used a length of threaded bar (available from motor factors, DIY stores, etc) with a nut, some large washers and a drilled plate on the inside of the swivel hub. With another large washer (or the old bearing and a washer) and a nut on the outside, the whole assembly was mounted in a vice, and the nut tightened to press the new bearing in place. The actual method was to tighten the nut slightly, give the old bearing a few taps round its edge, tighten the nut some more, and so on until the bearing was fully home **(see illustrations)**.

9 Once the bearing is fully seated in the swivel hub, refit the retaining circlip, ensuring that it fully engages with its groove **(see illustration)**.

10 The hub flange can be pressed into the new bearing using a very similar method to the one just used. Ensure that the washer used to draw in the flange rests against the bearing inner race **(see illustrations)**.

11 On completion, refit the swivel hub as described in Section 2.

4   Front suspension strut –
     removal, overhaul and refitting

Removal

1 Remove the windscreen cowl panel and bulkhead closure panel as described in Chapter 11 Section 20.

2 Working in the engine compartment, loosen the three suspension strut top mounting nuts by three turns each, on the side concerned **(see illustration)**. Do not loosen the centre nut.

3 Slacken the relevant front wheel nuts, then jack up the front of the car, and support securely on axle stands (see *'Jacking and vehicle support'*). Remove the roadwheel.

4 Unscrew the bolt and release the brake hydraulic hose from the suspension strut **(see illustration 2.3)**.

5 Slide the ABS wheel speed sensor wiring grommet out of the support bracket on the suspension strut **(see illustration)**. Where

4.2 Loosen the three suspension strut top mounting nuts (arrowed) by three turns each

4.5 Slide the wheel speed sensor wiring grommet (arrowed) out of the strut support bracket

4.6a Unscrew the connecting link nut, using an Allen key to stop the pin turning …

4.6b … and separate the top of the connecting link from the strut

4.8 Fully unscrew the three upper mounting nuts, then remove the strut from under the wheel arch

applicable, also release the wiring from the clip at the base of the strut.

6 Unscrew and remove the nut securing the anti-roll bar connecting link to the suspension strut, while holding the link stub with an Allen key. Release the link from the strut and move it to one side **(see illustrations)**.

7 Slacken and remove the two nuts and bolts securing the suspension strut to the swivel hub **(see illustration 2.15)**. Discard the nuts and bolts; they should be renewed whenever they are disturbed.

8 Support the strut from under the wheel arch then, working in the engine compartment, unscrew the suspension strut top mounting nuts. Disengage the base of the strut from the swivel hub, lower the strut out, and remove it under the wheel arch **(see illustration)**.

Overhaul

Note: *A spring compressor tool will be required for this operation. Before overhaul, mark the position of each component in relationship with each other for reassembly.*

4.9 Ensure that the compressor tool is securely located on the spring

9 With the suspension strut resting on a bench, or clamped in a vice, fit a spring compressor tool, and compress the coil spring to relieve the pressure on the spring seats. Ensure that the compressor tool is securely located on the spring, in accordance with the tool manufacturer's instructions **(see illustration)**.

4.10 Counterhold the piston rod with an Allen key or hexagon bit and unscrew the piston rod nut

10 Counterhold the strut piston rod with an Allen key or hexagon bit and unscrew the piston rod nut **(see illustration)**.

11 Remove the piston rod nut, followed by the strut bearing, upper spring seat, dust cover, the spring (with compressor tool still fitted) and the rubber bump stop **(see illustrations)**.

4.11a Remove the piston rod nut …

4.11b … followed by the strut bearing …

4.11c … upper spring seat …

4.11d … dust cover …

4.11e … spring …

4.11f … and the rubber bump stop

4.18 Position the spring so that the lower end (A) is resting against the stop (B) on the lower seat

4.21a Position the upper spring seat and strut bearing so that the lug (arrowed) on the upper spring seat...

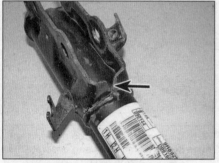
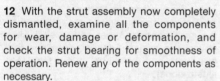

4.21b ... is directly in line with the notch (arrowed) at the base of the strut

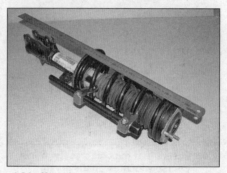

4.21c If necessary, use a straight-edge to check this

12 With the strut assembly now completely dismantled, examine all the components for wear, damage or deformation, and check the strut bearing for smoothness of operation. Renew any of the components as necessary.

13 Examine the strut for signs of fluid leakage. Check the strut piston for signs of pitting along its entire length, and check the strut body for signs of damage. While holding it in an upright position, test the operation of the strut by moving the piston through a full stroke, and then through short strokes of 50 to 100 mm. In both cases, the resistance felt should be smooth and continuous. If the resistance is jerky or uneven or if there is any visible sign of wear or damage to the strut, renewal is necessary.

14 If any doubt exists as to the condition of the coil spring, carefully remove the spring compressors and check the spring for distortion and signs of cracking. Renew the spring if it is damaged or distorted, or if there is any doubt as to its condition.

15 Inspect all other components for damage or deterioration, and renew any that are suspect.

16 Slide the rubber bump stop onto the strut piston.

17 If the spring compressor tool has been removed from the spring, refit it and compress the spring sufficiently to enable it to be refitted to the strut.

18 Slide the spring over the strut, and position it so that the lower end of the spring is resting against the stop on the lower seat **(see illustration)**.

19 Refit the dust cover, upper spring seat and the strut bearing.

20 Refit the piston rod nut, and tighten it to the specified torque. Counterhold the piston rod using an Allen key or hexagon bit as during removal.

21 Position the upper spring seat and strut bearing so that the lug on the upper spring seat is directly in line with the notch at the base of the strut. If necessary, use a straight-edge to check this **(see illustrations)**. Slowly slacken the spring compressor tool to relieve the tension in the spring. Check that the lower end of the spring locates correctly against the stop on the spring seat and the alignment between the lug on the upper seat and notch on the strut is maintained. If necessary, turn the spring and the upper seat so that the components locate correctly before the compressor tool is removed. Remove the compressor tool when the spring is fully seated.

Refitting

22 Refitting is a reversal of removal, bearing in mind the following points:
a) *Tighten all fixings to the specified torque.*
b) *Use new strut-to-swivel hub nuts and bolts.*
c) *When inserting the bolts securing the swivel hub to the base of the strut, note*

that the bolt heads on the left-hand side must be toward the rear of the vehicle and the bolt heads on the right-hand side must be toward the front of the vehicle.
d) *Refit the bulkhead closure panel and windscreen cowl panel as described in Chapter 11 Section 20.*

5 Front anti-roll bar – removal and refitting

Removal

1 Remove the front suspension subframe as described in Section 8.

2 Note the position and orientation of the anti-roll bar mounting clamps, then unscrew the four bolts securing the mounting clamps to the subframe. Lift the anti-roll bar off the subframe.

3 Inspect the mounting clamp rubbers for signs of damage and deterioration, and renew if necessary.

4 If desired, the connecting links can be removed from the anti-roll bar after unscrewing the securing nuts. If necessary, counterhold the drop link pins using a spanner on the flats provided.

Refitting

5 Refitting is a reversal of removal, bearing in mind the following points:
a) *Ensure that the anti-roll bar mounting clamps are refitted with the bevelled side facing the centre of the car.*
b) *Tighten all fixings to the specified torque.*
c) *Refit the front suspension subframe as described in Section 8.*

6 Front lower arm – removal and refitting

Removal

1 Firmly apply the handbrake, then jack up the front of the vehicle and support it securely on axle stands (see *'Jacking and vehicle support'*). Remove the relevant roadwheel.

2 Unscrew and remove the lower arm balljoint clamp bolt nut, and withdraw the clamp bolt from the swivel hub **(see illustration 2.9)**. Note that a new nut and bolt will be required for refitting.

3 Use a chisel or screwdriver as a wedge to expand the lower portion of the swivel hub.

4 Lever down the lower arm to free the balljoint from the swivel hub **(see illustration 2.11)**, then move the swivel hub to one side, taking care not to damage the balljoint rubber boot.

5 Undo the two lower arm mounting bolts and remove the lower arm from the subframe

6.5a Suspension lower arm front mounting bolt (arrowed) ...

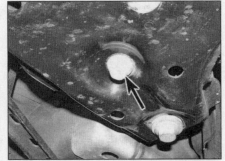

6.5b ... and rear mounting bolt (arrowed)

8.3 Undo the clamp bolt (arrowed) securing the steering column shaft universal joint to the steering gear pinion

(see illustrations). Note that new bolts will be required for refitting.

Overhaul

6 Examine the rubber bushes and the suspension lower balljoint for wear and damage. See Section 7.

Refitting

7 Refitting is a reversal of removal, bearing in mind the following points:
a) Use new lower arm mounting bolts and lower arm balljoint clamp bolt and nut.
b) Tighten all fixings to the specified torque and, where applicable, through the specified angle.

7 Front lower arm balljoint – renewal

1 If the lower arm balljoint is worn, or the rubber seal is damaged, the complete lower arm must be renewed. At the time of writing, the balljoint could not be renewed separately from the lower arm, as it is riveted in place during manufacture. However, balljoint repair kits have become available over time for other similarly-affected models – with these, the original rivets are drilled out, and the new balljoint is bolted onto the arm using the original rivet holes. Check the latest parts availability situation with Ford, and with reputable motor factors, before deciding.

8 Front subframe – removal and refitting

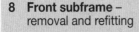

Note: *Special tools (Ford Tool No 205-870) will be required to align the subframe with the body when refitting (see text).*

Removal

1 Disconnect the battery negative terminal (refer to 'Disconnecting the battery').
2 Make sure the front wheels (and steering wheel) are in the straight-ahead position. Lock the steering in this position using the steering column lock.
3 Working in the driver's footwell, undo the clamp bolt securing the steering column shaft universal joint to the steering gear pinion (see illustration). Pull the shaft upwards and off the pinion and move it to one side. Note that a new clamp bolt will be required for refitting.
4 Firmly apply the handbrake, then jack up the front of the vehicle and support it securely on axle stands (see 'Jacking and vehicle support'). Remove both front roadwheels.
5 Slacken the track rod end balljoint nut on each side, and unscrew it as far as the ends of the threads. Counterhold the balljoint pin using a 5 mm Allen key (see illustration 2.7).
6 Disconnect the track rod end balljoint from the swivel hub on each side using a balljoint separator tool (leave the nut fitted to protect the threads), taking care not to damage the

balljoint rubber seal (see illustration 2.8). Once the balljoint has been released, remove the balljoint nut and discard it – a new one should be used for refitting.
7 Working on each side of the car in turn, unscrew and remove the lower arm balljoint clamp bolt nut, and withdraw the clamp bolt from the swivel hub (see illustration 2.9). Note that a new nut and bolt will be required for refitting.
8 Use a chisel or screwdriver as a wedge to expand the lower portion of the swivel hub.
9 Lever down the lower arm to free the balljoint from the swivel hub (see illustration 2.11), then move the swivel hub to one side, taking care not to damage the balljoint rubber boot.
10 Again, working on each side of the car in turn, unscrew the nut securing the anti-roll bar connecting link to the anti-roll bar. If necessary, counterhold the connecting link pin using a 5 mm Allen key.
11 Where applicable, remove the engine undershield.
12 Unscrew and remove the engine lower mounting link through-bolt (see illustration).
13 Unhook the exhaust system front mounting rubber (see illustration).
14 Undo the four retaining bolts and remove the subframe brace on each side (see illustration).
15 If the Ford special tools required for accurate realignment of the subframe are not available, make several accurate marks

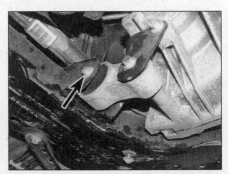

8.12 Unscrew and remove the engine lower mounting link through-bolt (arrowed)

8.13 Unhook the exhaust system front mounting rubber (arrowed)

8.14 Undo the retaining bolts (arrowed) and remove the subframe brace on each side

8.17 Subframe left-hand rear retaining bolt (arrowed)

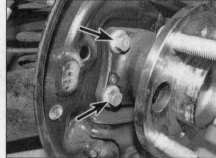

9.7 Rear hub assembly retaining bolts (2 of 4 arrowed)

between the subframe and the car body now, using paint or a sharp tool. If the car has been in service for some time, it may be obvious where the subframe sat, from the clean and dirty paint, but this is a rather hit-and-miss approach. If the subframe is not properly aligned on refitting, the car may steer and handle strangely (pulling to one side), and quickly wear out its tyres.

16 Support the subframe from below, using at least two substantial jacks (one either side).
17 With the subframe securely supported, progressively loosen the four subframe mounting bolts. There are two each side – one at the rear corner and one accessible through a hole in the suspension lower arm **(see illustration)**. Note that new bolts will be required for refitting.
18 When all the bolts have been removed, check once more that nothing is still attached to the subframe, and that nothing is still fitted which would hinder it from being lowered. With the help of an assistant, lower the subframe and remove it from under the car.

Refitting

19 With the help of an assistant, position the subframe on the jacks, then raise the jack to lift the subframe into position under the car. Ensure that the subframe is securely supported.
20 If available, fit the Ford alignment tool into the subframe holes and the holes on each side on the underbody. If not, align the

marks made prior to removal. Fit the four new retaining bolts and tighten them to the specified Stage 1 torque setting, then through the specified Stage 2 angle.
21 The remainder of refitting is a reversal of removal, noting the following points:
a) *Tighten all fixings to the specified torque.*
b) *Have the front wheel toe setting checked, and if necessary adjusted, at the earliest opportunity (see Section 20)*

9 Rear hub and bearings – inspection and renewal

Inspection

1 The rear hub bearings are non-adjustable.
2 To check the bearings for excessive wear, chock the front wheels, then jack up the rear of the vehicle and support it on axle stands. Fully release the handbrake.
3 Grip the rear wheel at the top and bottom, and attempt to rock it. If excessive movement is noted, or if there is any roughness or vibration felt when the wheel is spun, it is indicative that the hub bearings are worn.

Renewal

4 The rear hub bearings cannot be renewed separately, and are supplied with the rear hub as a complete assembly.

5 Remove the brake as described in Chapter 9 Section 7, 8.
6 On models with ABS, undo the bolt and remove the ABS wheel speed sensor from the rear of the brake backplate.
7 Undo the four Torx bolts and withdrawn the bearing assembly from the trailing arm **(see illustration)**.
8 Fit the new assembly to the trailing arm then insert the retaining bolts. Working in a diagonal sequence, tighten the bolts to the specified torque.
9 Refit the ABS wheel speed sensor and brake shoes as described in Chapter 9.

10 Rear shock absorber – removal and refitting

Removal

1 Chock the front wheels, then jack up the rear of the vehicle, and support it securely on axle stands (see *'Jacking and vehicle support'*). Remove the relevant roadwheel.
2 Remove the plastic wheel arch liner for access to the shock absorber upper mounting bolts. The liner is secured by a combination of screws and clips.
3 Support the trailing arm section of the beam axle using a trolley jack, then unscrew the shock absorber lower mounting bolt. Counterhold the bolt using a second spanner as the nut is unscrewed. Withdraw (or tap out) the bolt, then lower the jack supporting the trailing arm. Slide the bottom end of the shock absorber out of its mounting **(see illustrations)**.
4 Support the shock absorber, remove the two upper mounting bolts inside the wheel arch, and remove the unit **(see illustration)**.

Refitting

5 Refitting is a reversal of removal, noting the following points:
a) *Fit the upper mounting bolts first, and tighten them to the specified torque.*
b) *The lower mounting bolt should be fitted hand-tight only, then tightened fully once the roadwheel has been refitted and the car is back on the ground.*

10.3a With the trailing arm supported, unscrew and remove the lower bolt ...

10.3b ... and free the lower end of the shock absorber

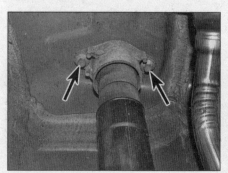

10.4 Shock absorber upper mounting bolts (arrowed)

11.5a Lift the compressed spring off its lower mounting ...

11.5b ... and check that the rubber top mounting comes away with it

12.1 Unclip the gear lever trim from the base of the gear lever

11 Rear spring – removal and refitting

Note: *A spring compressor tool will be required for this operation.*

Removal

1 Chock the front wheels, then jack up the rear of the vehicle, and support it securely on axle stands (see *'Jacking and vehicle support'*). Remove the rear roadwheels.

2 Compress the spring using the spring compressor tool.
3 Place a substantial jack under the end of the trailing arm section of the axle, and lift it slightly, so the shock absorber is just compressed.
4 Unbolt the rear shock absorber lower mounting, and detach the shock absorber from the rear axle (see Section 10).
5 Lower the jack slightly, then lift the (compressed) rear spring off its lower mounting, and remove it from under the car. Recover the rubber top mounting if it sticks to the car (**see illustrations**).

6 If a new spring is being fitted, carefully release the spring compressors, and transfer to the new spring, which should be compressed prior to fitting.

Refitting

7 Refitting is a reversal of removal, noting the following points:
a) *Make sure the spring is properly engaged in the upper and lower mounts.*
b) *Delay fully tightening the shock absorber lower mounting to its specified torque until the car is resting on its wheels.*

12 Rear axle assembly – removal and refitting

Removal

1 From inside the car, unclip the gear lever or selector lever trim from the base of the gear/selector lever (**see illustration**).
2 Pull up the centre console front upper trim panel, to release the retaining clips. Disconnect the accessory socket wiring connector and remove the panel (**see illustrations**).
3 Working through the aperture at the base of the handbrake lever, remove the retaining clip from the handbrake adjuster nut on the end of the handbrake cable (**see illustrations**).

12.2a Pull up the centre console front upper trim panel, to release the retaining clips ...

12.2b ... then disconnect the accessory socket wiring connector and remove the panel

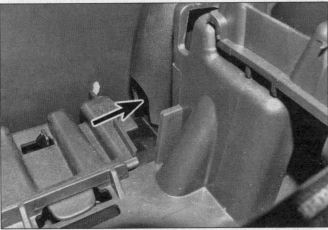

12.3a Working through the aperture (arrowed) at the base of the handbrake lever ...

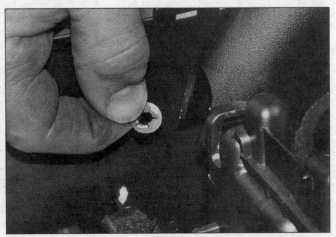

12.3b ... remove the retaining clip from the handbrake adjuster nut on the end of the handbrake cable

12.6a Depress the tab in the centre of the connector link …

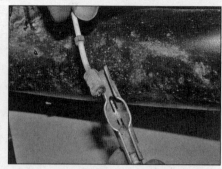

12.6b … then push the handbrake cable end fitting out of the link

12.7 Depress the tabs (arrowed) and pull the handbrake cable out of the trailing arm support bracket

Using a socket and extension bar, slacken the adjuster nut on the handbrake cable five turns to introduce some slack in the cable.

4 Chock the front wheels, then jack up the rear of the vehicle, and support it securely on axle stands (see 'Jacking and vehicle support'). Remove the rear roadwheels.

5 Remove both rear springs as described in Section 11.

6 Working on one side of the car at a time, locate the handbrake cable connector link just forward of the rear brake assembly. Using a small screwdriver, depress the tab in the centre of the connector link, then push the handbrake cable end fitting out of the link (see illustrations).

7 Depress the tabs on the handbrake outer cables and pull the disconnected cables out of the support brackets on the trailing arms (see illustration).

8 Using brake hose clamps, clamp both flexible brake hoses just forward of the brake pipe-to-hose connection on each trailing arm.

9 Clean the area around the brake pipe-to-hose union on each trailing arm, then unscrew the union nuts and disconnect the brake pipes from the brake hoses. Be prepared for fluid spillage. Extract the retaining clips and pull the brake hoses out of the support brackets each side (see illustration).

10 Undo the bolt and remove the ABS wheel speed sensor from the rear of the brake

backplate on each side. Pull out the rubber grommet and detach the ABS wiring from the support brackets.

11 Undo the nut and release the handbrake cable support brackets from the rear axle pivot mountings on each side (see illustration).

12 Support the rear axle using two substantial jacks, one at each side.

13 The rear axle is secured by three bolts each side, around the pivot points (see illustration). Make sure the axle is well-supported (have an assistant on hand to keep the axle steady), then start loosening the bolts. Leave one bolt loosely in place each side until the axle is ready to come down, then support the axle, remove the last bolt each side, and let the axle rest on the jacks. Lower the jacks equally until the axle can be lifted out from under the car.

Refitting

14 Refitting of the axle assembly is a reversal of removal, bearing in mind the following points:

a) Tighten the handbrake adjuster nut five turns to return it to its original position.

b) Do not fully tighten the axle mounting bolts, or the shock absorber lower mounting bolts, until the weight of the car is resting on its wheels.

c) Tighten all fixings to the specified torque.

d) Bleed the brake hydraulic system and adjust the handbrake as described in Chapter 9.

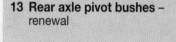

13 Rear axle pivot bushes – renewal

1 Chock the front wheels, then jack up the rear of the vehicle, and support it securely on axle stands (see 'Jacking and vehicle support').

2 Support the rear axle assembly using a jack positioned beneath the axle beam. Use a block of wood between the jack and the axle beam to spread the load.

3 Undo the nut and release the handbrake cable support bracket from the rear axle pivot mounting.

4 Unscrew the through-bolt from the rear axle pivot mounting and withdraw it from the pivot bush. Note that a new pivot bolt will be required for refitting. If necessary, lower the jack slightly and withdraw the pivot bush from the pivot mounting.

5 Make an alignment mark on the bush housing on the trailing arm corresponding to the position of the alignment arrow on the end of the bush. If an alignment arrow is not visible, accurately record the fitted position of the bush in the trailing arm.

6 Using a metal tube of suitable diameter, flat washers and a long bolt and nut, draw the bush out of its location in the trailing arm.

7 Thoroughly clean the bush housing in the trailing arm.

12.9 Brake pipe-to-hose connection (arrowed) on the trailing arm

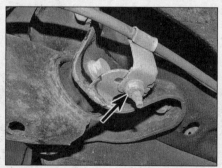

12.11 Undo the nut (arrowed) and release the handbrake cable support bracket from the axle pivot mounting

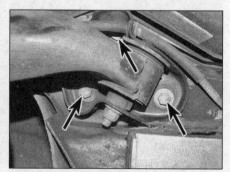

12.13 Rear axle mounting bolts (arrowed)

14.3 Disconnect the wiring connector for the steering wheel switches

14.4 Unscrew and remove the steering wheel securing bolt

8 Lubricate the bush housing, and the new bush, with a soapy solution (eg, washing-up liquid) to aid fitting.

9 Locate the new bush in the trailing arm, ensuring that it is positioned correctly as noted during removal, together with the metal tube, washers, bolt and nut used for removal. Draw the bush into the trailing arm until it is fully engaged.

10 Fit the new pivot through-bolt and tighten by hand only at this stage.

11 If desired, repeat the procedure given in paragraphs 3 to 10 for the remaining bush.

12 Further refitting is a reversal of removal, noting the following points:

a) Do not fully tighten the pivot through-bolts until the weight of the car is resting on its wheels.

b) Tighten all fixings to the specified torque.

14 Steering wheel – removal and refitting

 Warning: Make sure that the airbag safety recommendations given in Chapter 12 Section 22 are followed, to prevent personal injury.

Removal

1 Remove the driver's airbag as described in Chapter 12 Section 23.

2 Set the front wheels in the straight-ahead position, then lock the column in position by removing the ignition key.

3 Disconnect the wiring connector for the steering wheel switches **(see illustration)**.

4 Prevent the steering wheel turning by grasping the rim firmly, then unscrew and remove the steering wheel securing bolt **(see illustration)**. Do not rely on the steering column lock to prevent the wheel turning, as this may damage the lock.

5 Grip the steering wheel with both hands and carefully rock it from side-to-side to release it from the splines on the steering column. As

the steering wheel is being removed, guide the wiring for the airbag through the aperture in the wheel, taking care not to damage the wiring connectors.

6 With the steering wheel removed, place a strip of adhesive tape across the top and front of the airbag rotary connector to prevent the connector rotating.

Refitting

7 Make sure that the front wheels are pointing in the straight-ahead position, then remove the adhesive tape from the airbag rotary connector.

8 Refit the steering wheel, routing the airbag wiring connectors through the steering wheel aperture.

9 Refit the steering wheel securing bolt, and tighten to the specified torque – again, do not rely on the steering column lock to hold the wheel as the bolt is tightened.

10 Reconnect the wiring connector for the steering wheel switches.

11 Release the steering lock, and refit the airbag as described in Chapter 12 Section 23.

15 Steering column shaft – removal and refitting

Removal

1 Make sure the front wheels (and steering wheel) are in the straight-ahead position. Lock the steering in this position using the steering column lock.

2 Working in the driver's footwell, undo the clamp bolt securing the steering column shaft lower universal joint to the steering gear pinion **(see illustration 8.3)**. Note that a new clamp bolt will be required for refitting. Pull the shaft upwards and off the pinion.

3 Similarly, undo the clamp bolt securing steering column shaft upper universal joint to the EPS motor pinion. Note that a new clamp bolt will be required for refitting. Pull the shaft

downwards off the pinion and remove it from the car.

Refitting

4 Refitting is a reversal of removal, using new universal joint clamp bolts, tightened to the specified torque.

16 Steering column – removal and refitting

Note: The steering column comprises the electric power steering (EPS) motor, the EPS electronic control unit and the steering column itself. All these components form one assembly and cannot be individually separated or dismantled.

Note: The steering column is removed together with the complete facia assembly and is then separated from it on the bench. This is an involved and complex operation and it is suggested that the contents of this Section, and the relevant Section in Chapter 11 are studied carefully to gain an understanding of the work involved, before proceeding.

Removal

1 Remove the facia assembly as described in Chapter 11 Section 25.

2 Remove the steering wheel as described in Section 14.

3 On models equipped with a knee airbag on the driver's side, remove the knee airbag as described in Chapter 12 Section 23.

4 On models without a knee airbag on the driver's side, remove the trim panel beneath the steering column by pulling the panel away from the facia to release the three retaining clips each side.

5 Remove the steering column shrouds as described in Chapter 11 Section 23.

6 Disconnect the wiring connectors at the steering column stalk switches, ignition switch, anti-theft immobiliser transceiver unit and

16.7a Undo the clamp bolt (arrowed) securing the steering column stalk switch housing to the column ...

16.7b ... then lift the retaining tab and withdraw the housing from the steering column

16.9 Release the plastic wiring harness trough from the support brackets (arrowed) on the steering column

16.10a Undo the nuts and bolts (arrowed) ...

airbag rotary connector. Release the wiring harness from the cable-ties on the steering column and move the harness to one side.

7 Undo the clamp bolt securing the steering column stalk switch housing to the column.

Using a small screwdriver, lift the retaining tab at the rear of the switch housing and withdraw the housing from the steering column (see illustrations).

8 It is advisable to turn the facia assembly

upside down at this stage to improve access to the steering column attachments on the underside of the facia.

9 Using a small screwdriver, depress the retaining tabs and release the plastic wiring harness trough from the support brackets on the steering column (see illustration).

10 On models equipped with a knee airbag on the driver's side, undo the two nuts and two bolts and remove the support brace from the underside of the facia (see illustrations).

11 Disconnect the three wiring connectors from the side of the EPS motor housing (see illustration).

12 Check that all wiring connectors to the steering column components have been disconnected and that the wiring harness has been released from any remaining cable clips or ties.

13 Undo the two lower nuts and two upper nuts securing the steering column to the facia

16.10b ... and remove the support brace from the underside of the facia

16.11 Disconnect the three wiring connectors (arrowed) from the side of the EPS motor housing

16.13a Steering column lower retaining nuts (arrowed) ...   16.13b ... and upper retaining nuts (arrowed)

crossmember (see illustrations). Note that new nuts will be required for refitting.

14 Lift the steering column assembly off the mounting studs and withdraw it from the underside of the facia (see illustration).

Refitting

15 Refitting is a reversal of removal, bearing in mind the following points:

a) Use new steering column securing nuts.
b) Tighten all fixings to the specified torque, where given.
c) Where applicable, refit the driver's knee airbag as described in Chapter 12 Section 23.
d) Refit the steering wheel as described in Section 14.
e) Refit the facia assembly as described in Chapter 11 Section 25.

17 Steering gear rubber gaiters – renewal

1 Remove the relevant track rod end as described in Section 19.

16.14 Lift the steering column assembly off the mounting studs and withdraw it from the underside of the facia

2 Count and record the number of exposed threads from the track rod end locknut to the end of the track rod, then unscrew the locknut.

3 Remove the inboard and, where fitted, the outboard securing clips, then slide the gaiter off the end of the track rod.

4 Thoroughly clean the track rod, then slide the new gaiter into position.

5 Fit the gaiter securing clip(s), using new clips if necessary, making sure that the gaiter is not twisted.

6 Screw the track rod end locknut back onto the track rod and position it so that the same number of threads are exposed as was noted during removal.

7 Refit the track rod end as described in Section 19.

8 Have the front wheel toe setting checked, and if necessary adjusted, at the earliest opportunity (see Section 20).

18 Steering gear – removal and refitting

Removal

1 Using the information in Section 8, lower the front subframe to access the steering gear. There is no need to disconnect the lower arm balljoints, and the subframe only needs to be lowered approximately 150 mm, not removed completely.

2 Slacken the track rod end balljoint nut each side, and unscrew it as far as the ends of the threads. Counterhold the balljoint pin using a 5 mm Allen key (see illustration 2.7).

3 Disconnect the track rod end balljoint from the swivel hub using a balljoint separator tool (leave the nut fitted to protect the threads), taking care not to damage the balljoint rubber seal (see illustration 2.8). Once the balljoint has been released, remove the balljoint nut

and discard it – a new one should be used for refitting.

4 Unbolt the steering gear from the three mountings on the subframe, and lower it out. Recover the rubber seal from the bulkhead.

Refitting

5 Refitting is a reversal of removal, noting the following points:

a) Tighten all fixings to the specified torque.
b) Refit the subframe as described in Section 8.

19 Track rod end – removal and refitting

Note: *A balljoint separator tool will be required for this operation. Where applicable, Nyloc-type self-locking nuts must be renewed on refitting.*

Removal

1 Firmly apply the handbrake, then jack up the front of the vehicle and support it securely on axle stands (see 'Jacking and vehicle support'). Remove the relevant roadwheel.

2 Slacken the track rod end balljoint nut, and unscrew it as far as the ends of the threads. Counterhold the balljoint pin using a 5 mm Allen key (see illustration 2.7).

3 Disconnect the track rod end balljoint from the swivel hub using a balljoint separator tool (leave the nut fitted to protect the threads), taking care not to damage the balljoint rubber seal (see illustration 2.8). Once the balljoint has been released, remove the balljoint nut and discard it – a new one should be used when refitting.

4 Slacken the track rod end locknut a quarter of a turn, then unscrew the track rod end from

the track rod, counting the number of turns necessary to remove it **(see illustration)**.

Refitting

5 Screw the track rod end onto the track rod the number of turns noted during removal, then tighten the locknut while holding the track rod end in position.

6 Engage the track rod end balljoint pin with the swivel hub, then fit a new securing nut. Tighten the nut to the specified torque, while counterholding the balljoint pin as during removal.

7 Refit the roadwheel, then lower the car to the ground, and tighten the wheel nuts.

8 Have the front wheel toe setting checked, and if necessary adjusted, at the earliest opportunity (see Section 20).

20 Wheel alignment and steering angles – general information

Definitions

1 A car's steering and suspension geometry is defined in four basic settings – all angles are expressed in degrees (toe settings are also expressed as a measurement); the steering axis is defined as an imaginary line drawn through the axis of the suspension strut, extended where necessary to contact the ground.

2 Camber is the angle between each roadwheel and a vertical line drawn through its centre and tyre contact patch, when viewed from the front or rear of the car. Positive camber is when the roadwheels are tilted outwards from the vertical at the top; negative camber is when they are tilted inwards. The camber angle is not adjustable.

3 Castor is the angle between the steering axis and a vertical line drawn through each roadwheel's centre and tyre contact patch,

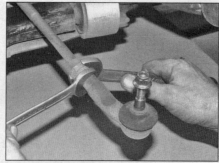

19.4 Slacken the track rod end locknut, and unscrew the track rod end

when viewed from the side of the car. Positive castor is when the steering axis is tilted so that it contacts the ground ahead of the vertical; negative castor is when it contacts the ground behind the vertical. The castor angle is not adjustable.

4 Toe is the difference, viewed from above, between lines drawn through the roadwheel centres and the car's centre-line. 'Toe-in' is when the roadwheels point inwards, towards each other at the front, while 'toe-out' is when they splay outwards from each other at the front.

5 The front wheel toe setting is adjusted by screwing the track rod in or out of its track rod ends, to alter the effective length of the track rod assembly. The rear wheel toe setting is not adjustable.

Checking and adjustment

6 Due to the special measuring equipment necessary to check the wheel alignment and steering angles, and the skill required to use it properly, the checking and adjustment of these settings is best left to a Ford dealer or similar expert. Note that most tyre-fitting shops now possess sophisticated checking equipment.

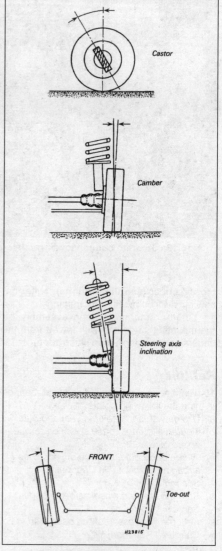

20.5 Wheel alignment details

Chapter 11
Bodywork and fittings

Contents

Degrees of difficulty

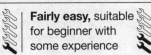

Easy, suitable for novice with little experience | Fairly easy, suitable for beginner with some experience | Fairly difficult, suitable for competent DIY mechanic | Difficult, suitable for experienced DIY mechanic | Very difficult, suitable for expert DIY or professional

Specifications

Torque wrench settings	Nm	lbf ft
Air conditioning refrigerant pipe to expansion valve	10	7
Bonnet hinge nuts	12	9
Bonnet lock bolts	20	15
Door hinge bolts	25	18
Facia retaining bolts	25	18
Facia support strut retaining bolts	2	18
Front seat bolts	35	26
Rear seat bolts	40	30
Seat belts:		
Front seat belt inertia reel lower mounting bolt	25	18
Front seat belt inertia reel upper mounting bolt	8	6
Front seat belt lower anchor rail bolt (3-door models)	40	30
Front seat belt lower anchorage bolt (5-door models)	40	30
Front seat belt stalk retaining bolt	50	37
Front seat belt upper anchorage bolt	40	30
Rear seat belt buckle bolts	55	41
Rear seat belt inertia reel mounting bolt	40	30
Rear seat belt lower anchorage bolt	40	30
Rear seat belt upper anchorage bolt	40	30
Steering column shaft universal joint clamp bolt*	34	25
Tailgate hinge bolts	12	9

*Use a new bolt

1 General Information

1 The bodyshell is of three- and five-door Hatchback (and 3-door Van) configurations, and is made of pressed-steel sections. Most components are welded together, but some use is made of structural adhesives. The front wings are bolted on.

2 The bonnet, doors and some other vulnerable panels are made of zinc-coated metal, and are further protected by being coated with an anti-chip primer prior to being sprayed.

3 Extensive use is made of plastic materials, mainly in the interior, but also in exterior components. The front and rear bumpers and the front grille are injection-moulded from a synthetic material which is very strong, and yet light. Plastic components such as wheel arch liners are fitted to the underside of the car, to improve the body's resistance to corrosion.

2 Maintenance – bodywork and underframe

1 The general condition of a car's bodywork is the one thing that significantly affects its value. Maintenance is easy, but needs to be regular. Neglect, particularly after minor damage, can lead quickly to further deterioration and costly repair bills. It is important also to keep watch on those parts of the car not immediately visible, for instance the underside, inside all the wheel arches, and the lower part of the engine compartment.

2 The basic maintenance routine for the bodywork is washing – preferably with a lot of water, from a hose. This will remove all the loose solids which may have stuck to the car. It is important to flush these off in such a way as to prevent grit from scratching the finish. The wheel arches and underframe need washing in the same way, to remove any accumulated mud which will retain moisture and tend to encourage rust. Paradoxically enough, the best time to clean the underframe and wheel arches is in wet weather, when the mud is thoroughly wet and soft. In very wet weather, the underframe is usually cleaned of large accumulations automatically, and this is a good time for inspection.

3 Periodically, except on models with a wax-based underbody protective coating, it is a good idea to have the whole of the underframe of the car steam-cleaned, engine compartment included, so that a thorough inspection can be carried out to see what minor repairs and renovations are necessary. Steam-cleaning is available at many garages, and is necessary for the removal of the accumulation of oily grime, which sometimes is allowed to become thick in certain areas.

If steam-cleaning facilities are not available, there are one or two excellent grease solvents available, which can be brush-applied; the dirt can then be simply hosed off. Note that these methods should not be used on cars with wax-based underbody protective coating, or the coating will be removed. Such cars should be inspected annually, preferably just prior to Winter, when the underbody should be washed down, and any damage to the wax coating repaired. Ideally, a completely fresh coat should be applied. It would also be worth considering the use of such wax-based protection for injection into door panels, sills, box sections, etc, as an additional safeguard against rust damage, where such protection is not provided by the manufacturer.

4 After washing paintwork, wipe off with a chamois leather to give an unspotted clear finish. A coat of clear protective wax polish will give added protection against chemical pollutants in the air. If the paintwork sheen has dulled or oxidised, use a cleaner/polisher combination to restore the brilliance of the shine. This requires a little effort, but such dulling is usually caused because regular washing has been neglected. Care needs to be taken with metallic paintwork, as special non-abrasive cleaner/polisher is required to avoid damage to the finish. Always check that the door and ventilator opening drain holes and pipes are completely clear, so that water can be drained out. Brightwork should be treated in the same way as paintwork. Windscreens and windows can be kept clear of the smeary film which often appears, by the use of proprietary glass cleaner. Never use any form of wax, or other body or chromium polish, on glass.

3 Maintenance – upholstery and carpets

1 Mats and carpets should be brushed or vacuum-cleaned regularly, to keep them free of grit. If they are badly stained, remove them from the car for scrubbing or sponging, and make quite sure they are dry before refitting. Seats and interior trim panels can be kept clean by wiping with a damp cloth. If they do become stained (which can be more apparent on light-coloured upholstery), use a little liquid detergent and a soft nail brush to scour the grime out of the grain of the material. Do not forget to keep the headlining clean in the same way as the upholstery. When using liquid cleaners inside the car, do not over-wet the surfaces being cleaned. Excessive damp could get into the seams and padded interior, causing stains, offensive odours or even rot. If the inside of the car gets wet accidentally, it is worthwhile taking some trouble to dry it out properly, particularly where carpets are involved. Do not leave oil or electric heaters inside the car for this purpose.

4 Minor body damage – repair

Repair of minor scratches

1 If the scratch is very superficial, and does not penetrate to the metal of the bodywork, repair is very simple. Lightly rub the area of the scratch with a paintwork renovator, or a very fine cutting paste, to remove loose paint from the scratch, and to clear the surrounding bodywork of wax polish. Rinse the area with clean water.

2 In the case of metallic paint, the most commonly-found scratches are not in the paint, but in the lacquer top coat, and appear white. If care is taken, these can sometimes be rendered less obvious by very careful use of paintwork renovator (which would other-wise not be used on metallic paintwork); otherwise, repair of these scratches can be achieved by applying lacquer with a fine brush.

3 Apply touch-up paint to the scratch using a fine paint brush; continue to apply fine layers of paint until the surface of the paint in the scratch is level with the surrounding paintwork. Allow the new paint at least two weeks to harden, then blend it into the surrounding paintwork by rubbing the scratch area with a paintwork renovator or a very fine cutting paste. Finally, apply wax polish.

4 Where the scratch has penetrated right through to the metal of the bodywork, causing the metal to rust, a different repair technique is required. Remove any loose rust from the bottom of the scratch with a penknife, then apply rust-inhibiting paint, to prevent the formation of rust in the future. Using a rubber or nylon applicator, fill the scratch with bodystopper paste. If required, this paste can be mixed with cellulose thinners, to provide a very thin paste which is ideal for filling narrow scratches. Before the stopper-paste in the scratch hardens, wrap a piece of smooth cotton rag around the top of a finger. Dip the finger in cellulose thinners, and quickly sweep it across the surface of the stopper-paste in the scratch; this will ensure that the surface of the stopper-paste is slightly hollowed. The scratch can now be painted over as described earlier in this Section.

Repairs of dents

5 When deep denting of the bodywork has taken place, the first task is to pull the dent out, until the affected bodywork almost attains its original shape. There is little point in trying to restore the original shape completely, as the metal in the damaged area will have stretched on impact, and cannot be reshaped fully to its original contour. It is better to bring the level of the dent up to a point which is about 3 mm below the level of the surrounding bodywork. In cases where the dent is very shallow anyway, it is not worth trying to pull it out at all. If the underside of the dent is accessible,

it can be hammered out gently from behind, using a mallet with a wooden or plastic head. Whilst doing this, hold a suitable block of wood firmly against the outside of the panel, to absorb the impact from the hammer blows and thus prevent a large area of the bodywork from being 'belled-out'.

6 Should the dent be in a section of the bodywork which has a double skin, or some other factor making it inaccessible from behind, a different technique is called for. Drill several small holes through the metal inside the area – particularly in the deeper section. Then screw long self-tapping screws into the holes, just sufficiently for them to gain a good purchase in the metal. Now the dent can be pulled out by pulling on the protruding heads of the screws with a pair of pliers.

7 The next stage of the repair is the removal of the paint from the damaged area, and from an inch or so of the surrounding 'sound' bodywork. This is accomplished most easily by using a wire brush or abrasive pad on a power drill, although it can be done just as effectively by hand, using sheets of abrasive paper. To complete the preparation for filling, score the surface of the bare metal with a screwdriver or the tang of a file, or alternatively, drill small holes in the affected area. This will provide a really good 'key' for the filler paste.

8 To complete the repair, see the Section on filling and respraying.

Repairs of rust holes or gashes

9 Remove all paint from the affected area, and from an inch or so of the surrounding 'sound' bodywork, using an abrasive pad or a wire brush on a power drill. If these are not available, a few sheets of abrasive paper will do the job most effectively. With the paint removed, you will be able to judge the severity of the corrosion, and therefore decide whether to renew the whole panel (if this is possible) or to repair the affected area. New body panels are not as expensive as most people think, and it is often quicker and more satisfactory to fit a new panel than to attempt to repair large areas of corrosion.

10 Remove all fittings from the affected area, except those which will act as a guide to the original shape of the damaged bodywork (eg body side mouldings etc). Then, using tin snips or a hacksaw blade, remove all loose metal and any other metal badly affected by corrosion. Hammer the edges of the hole inwards, in order to create a slight depression for the filler paste.

11 Wire-brush the affected area to remove the powdery rust from the surface of the remaining metal. Paint the affected area with rust-inhibiting paint; if the back of the rusted area is accessible, treat this also.

12 Before filling can take place, it will be necessary to block the hole in some way. This can be achieved by the use of aluminium or plastic mesh, or aluminium tape.

13 Aluminium or plastic mesh, or glass-fibre matting, is probably the best material to use for a large hole. Cut a piece to the approximate size and shape of the hole to be filled, then position it in the hole so that its edges are below the level of the surrounding bodywork. It can be retained in position by several blobs of filler paste around its periphery.

14 Aluminium tape should be used for small or very narrow holes. Pull a piece off the roll, trim it to the approximate size and shape required, then pull off the backing paper (if used) and stick the tape over the hole; it can be overlapped if the thickness of one piece is insufficient. Burnish down the edges of the tape with the handle of a screwdriver or similar, to ensure that the tape is securely attached to the metal underneath.

Filling and respraying

15 Before using this Section, see the Sections on dent, deep scratch, rust holes and gash repairs.

16 Many types of bodyfiller are available, but generally speaking, those proprietary kits which contain a tin of filler paste and a tube of resin hardener are best for this type of repair. A wide, flexible plastic or nylon applicator will be found invaluable for imparting a smooth and well-contoured finish to the surface of the filler.

17 Mix up a little filler on a clean piece of card or board – measure the hardener carefully (follow the maker's instructions on the pack), otherwise the filler will set too rapidly or too slowly. Using the applicator, apply the filler paste to the prepared area; draw the applicator across the surface of the filler to achieve the correct contour and to level the surface. As soon as a contour that approximates to the correct one is achieved, stop working the paste – if you carry on too long, the paste will become sticky and begin to 'pick-up' on the applicator. Continue to add thin layers of filler paste at 20-minute intervals, until the level of the filler is just proud of the surrounding bodywork.

18 Once the filler has hardened, the excess can be removed using a metal plane or file. From then on, progressively-finer grades of abrasive paper should be used, starting with a 40-grade production paper, and finishing with a 400-grade wet-and-dry paper. Always wrap the abrasive paper around a flat rubber, cork, or wooden block – otherwise the surface of the filler will not be completely flat. During the smoothing of the filler surface, the wet-and-dry paper should be periodically rinsed in water. This will ensure that a very smooth finish is imparted to the filler at the final stage.

19 At this stage, the 'dent' should be surrounded by a ring of bare metal, which in turn should be encircled by the finely 'feathered' edge of the good paintwork. Rinse the repair area with clean water, until all of the dust produced by the rubbing-down operation has gone.

20 Spray the whole area with a light coat of – this will show up any imperfections in the surface of the filler. Repair these imperfections with fresh filler paste or bodystopper, and once more smooth the surface with abrasive paper. If bodystopper is used, it can be mixed with cellulose thinners, to form a really thin paste which is ideal for filling small holes. Repeat this spray-and-repair procedure until you are satisfied that the surface of the filler, and the feathered edge of the paintwork, are perfect. Clean the repair area with clean water, and allow to dry fully.

21 The repair area is now ready for final spraying. Paint spraying must be carried out in a warm, dry, windless and dust-free atmosphere. This condition can be created artificially if you have access to a large indoor working area, but if you are forced to work in the open, you will have to pick your day very carefully. If you are working indoors, dousing the floor in the work area with water will help to settle the dust which would otherwise be in the atmosphere. If the repair area is confined to one body panel, mask off the surrounding panels; this will help to minimise the effects of a slight mis-match in paint colours. Bodywork fittings (eg chrome strips, door handles etc) will also need to be masked off. Use genuine masking tape, and several thicknesses of newspaper, for the masking operations.

22 Before commencing to spray, agitate the aerosol can thoroughly, then spray a test area (an old tin, or similar) until the technique is mastered. Cover the repair area with a thick coat of primer; the thickness should be built up using several thin layers of paint, rather than one thick one. Using 400 grade wet-and-dry paper, rub down the surface of the primer until it is really smooth. While doing this, the work area should be thoroughly doused with water, and the wet-and-dry paper periodically rinsed in water. Allow to dry before spraying on more paint.

23 Spray on the top coat, again building up the thickness by using several thin layers of paint. Start spraying at the top of the repair area, and then, using a side-to-side motion, work downwards until the whole repair area and about 2 inches of the surrounding original paintwork is covered. Remove all masking material 10 to 15 minutes after spraying on the final coat of paint.

24 Allow the new paint at least two weeks to harden, then, using a paintwork renovator or a very fine cutting paste, blend the edges of the paint into the existing paintwork. Finally, apply wax polish.

Plastic components

25 With the use of more and more plastic body components by the car manufacturers (eg bumpers. spoilers, and in some cases major body panels), rectification of more serious damage to such items has become a matter of either entrusting repair work to a specialist in this field, or renewing complete components. Repair of such damage by the DIY owner is not really feasible, owing to the cost of the equipment and materials required for effecting such repairs. The basic technique involves making a groove along the line of the crack in the plastic, using a rotary cutter in a power drill. The damaged part is then welded back together, using a hot air gun to heat up and fuse a plastic filler rod into the groove. Any excess plastic is then removed, and the area rubbed down to a smooth finish. It is important that a filler rod of the correct plastic is used, as body components can be made of a variety of different types (eg polycarbonate, ABS, polypropylene).

26 Damage of a less serious nature (abrasions, minor cracks etc) can be repaired by the DIY owner using a two-part epoxy filler repair. Once mixed in equal, this is used in similar fashion to the bodywork filler used on metal panels. The filler is usually cured in twenty to thirty minutes, ready for sanding and painting.

27 If the owner is renewing a complete component himself, or if he has repaired it with epoxy filler, he will be left with the problem of finding a suitable paint for finishing which is compatible with the type of plastic used. At one time, the use of a universal paint was not possible, owing to the complex range of plastics encountered in body component applications. Standard paints, generally speaking, will not bond to plastic or rubber satisfactorily, but suitable paints to match any plastic or rubber finish, can be obtained from dealers. However, it is now possible to

obtain a plastic body parts finishing kit which consists of a preprimer treatment, a primer and coloured top coat. Full instructions are normally supplied with a kit, but basically, the method of use is to first apply the preprimer to the component concerned, and allow it to dry for up to 30 minutes. Then the primer is applied, and left to dry for about an hour before finally applying the special-coloured top coat. The result is a correctly-coloured component, where the paint will flex with the plastic or rubber, a property that standard paint does not normally posses.

5 Major body damage – repair

1 Where serious damage has occurred, or large areas need renewal due to neglect, it means that complete new panels will need welding-in, and this is best left to professionals. If the damage is due to impact, it will also be necessary to check completely the alignment of the bodyshell, and this can only be carried out accurately by a Ford dealer or accident repair specialist, using special jigs. If the body is left misaligned, it is primarily dangerous, as the car will not handle properly, and secondly, uneven stresses will be imposed on the steering, suspension and possibly transmission, causing abnormal wear, or complete failure, particularly to such items as the tyres.

6 Bumpers – removal and refitting

Front bumper
Removal

1 Remove the headlights as described in Chapter 12 Section 7.
2 Firmly apply the handbrake, then jack up the front of the vehicle and support it securely on axle stands (see 'Jacking and vehicle support').
3 Remove the upper plastic rivet each side by prising up the centre section, then withdrawing the rivet body **(see illustrations)**.
4 From within the engine compartment, undo the three bolts each side securing the bumper to the front wing **(see illustration)**.
5 Working under the wheel arch each side, extract the lower plastic rivet, and undo the two screws securing the wheel arch liner to the bumper **(see illustrations)**.
6 On models equipped with front parking sensors, lift the cooling system expansion tank out of its mountings and place it to one side. Trace the parking sensor wiring back to the connectors and disconnect them, then release the wiring from the cable clips and ties.
7 Where applicable, disconnect the wiring plugs from the front foglights.
8 Disengage the two lower plastic retaining

6.3a Remove the upper plastic rivet each side (arrowed) ...

6.3b ... by prising up the centre section ...

6.3c ... then withdrawing the rivet body

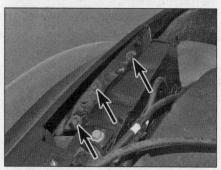
6.4 Undo the three bolts each side (arrowed) securing the bumper to the front wing

6.5a Extract the lower plastic rivet (arrowed) ...

6.5b ... and undo the two screws (arrowed) securing the wheel arch liner to the bumper

6.8a Disengage the two lower plastic retaining tangs (arrowed) ...

6.8b ... then pull the bumper forwards ...

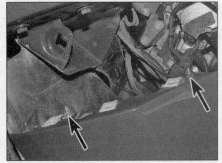

6.8c ... to disengage the side locating pegs (arrowed)

tangs then, with the help of an assistant, pull the bumper forwards to disengage the side locating pegs and lower it to the ground (see illustrations).

Refitting

9 Refitting is a reversal of removal. Have an assistant available to help align the bumper with the side locating pegs, and tighten the six mounting bolts securely.

Rear bumper

Removal

10 Chock the front wheels, then jack up the rear of the vehicle, and support it securely on axle stands (see 'Jacking and vehicle support').
11 On models with mudflaps, remove the mudflaps each side by extracting the three retaining clips, then removing the two plastic rivets by prising up the centre section and withdrawing the rivet body.
12 On models without mudflaps, remove the two plastic rivets each side securing the wheel arch liner to the bumper, by prising up the centre section and withdrawing the rivet body (see illustration).
13 Where fitted, reach in behind the wheel arch liner and disconnect the parking sensor wiring connector under the right-hand wheel arch.
14 Reach in under the right-hand wheel arch and remove the rear foglight bulb holder from the light unit (see illustration). The bulbholder is retained by plastic tabs around its periphery.
15 Undo the bolt each side securing the

upper corner of the bumper to the rear wing (see illustration).
16 Remove the two lower plastic rivets securing the bumper to the body, by prising up the centre section and withdrawing the rivet body (see illustration).
17 Open the tailgate and undo the screw each side in the tailgate aperture (see illustration).
18 With the help of an assistant, pull the bumper rearwards to disengage the side locating tabs and lower it to the ground (see illustration).

Refitting

19 Refitting is a reversal of removal. Have an assistant available to help align the bumper with the side locating tabs, and tighten the mounting bolts securely.

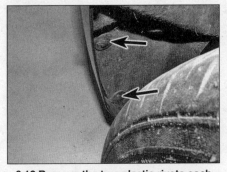

6.12 Remove the two plastic rivets each side (arrowed) securing the wheel arch liner to the rear bumper

6.14 Remove the rear foglight bulb holder from the light unit

6.15 Undo the bolt (arrowed) each side securing the upper corner of the bumper to the rear wing

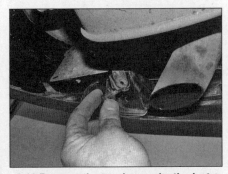

6.16 Remove the two lower plastic rivets securing the bumper to the body

6.17 Undo the screw (arrowed) each side in the tailgate aperture

6.18 Pull the bumper rearwards to disengage the side locating tabs

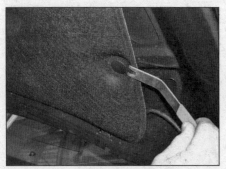

7.3a Prise out the plastic studs and remove the sound deadening pad from inside the bonnet

7.3b Disconnect the windscreen washer fluid hose from the T-piece connector ...

7.3c ... then release the washer hose from the securing clips

7 Bonnet – removal, refitting and adjustment

Removal

1 Open the bonnet, and support it on its stay.
2 Using a marker pen or paint, mark around the hinge positions on the bonnet.
3 Prise out the plastic studs and remove the sound deadening pad from inside the bonnet. Disconnect the windscreen washer fluid hose from the T-piece connector on the passenger side washer jet, then feed the washer hose back to the passenger side corner of the bonnet, releasing it from the securing clips (see illustrations).
4 With the aid of an assistant, support the bonnet, and unscrew the four nuts securing the bonnet to the hinges (see illustration).
5 Lift off the bonnet.

Refitting

6 Align the marks made on the bonnet before removal with the hinges, then refit and tighten the bonnet securing nuts.
7 Feed the washer hose back across the bonnet, and reconnect it to the washer jet T-piece, then refit the sound deadening pad.
8 Check the bonnet adjustment as follows.

Adjustment

9 Close the bonnet, and check that there is an equal gap at each side, between the bonnet and the wing panels. Check that the bonnet sits flush in relation to the surrounding body panels.
10 The bonnet should close smoothly and positively without excessive pressure. If this is not the case, adjustment will be required.
11 To adjust the bonnet alignment, slacken the bonnet securing nuts, and move the bonnet on the studs as required (the holes in the hinges are elongated). To adjust bonnet closure, adjustable bump stops are fitted to the body front panel. These may be raised or lowered by screwing in or out as necessary. If desired, the bonnet lock can be adjusted as described in Section 9.

8 Bonnet release cable – removal and refitting

Removal

1 The bonnet release lever is located under the facia on the right-hand side.
2 Working in the driver's footwell, depress the tab in the centre of the release lever, then slide it to the rear to disengage the locating lugs.
3 Disengage the bonnet release outer cable from the release lever, then slip the inner cable end fitting out of the lever handle (see illustrations).
4 Remove the windscreen cowl panel and bulkhead closure panel as described in Section 20.

5 Undo the three bolts securing the bonnet lock top plate and lift the plate from its location (see illustration 9.2).
6 Prise out the outer cable end fitting from its slot in the bonnet lock, then unhook the inner cable from the lock operating lever.
7 Release the cable from the clips and brackets in the engine compartment, noting its routing.
8 Tie a length of string to the end of the cable at the release lever inside the car, then carefully pull the cable through the bulkhead grommet into the engine compartment.
9 Untie the string from the end of the cable, and leave it in position to aid refitting.

Refitting

10 Refitting is a reversal of removal, but tie the string to the release lever end of the cable, and use the string to pull the cable into position. Ensure that the cable is routed as noted before removal, and make sure that the bulkhead grommet is correctly seated.

9 Bonnet lock – removal and refitting

Removal

1 Open the bonnet and disconnect the two wiring connectors from the bonnet lock, then release the wiring loom from the cable clips on the lock platform.
2 Undo the three bolts securing the bonnet

7.4 Bonnet-to-hinge retaining nuts (arrowed)

8.3a Disengage the bonnet release outer cable from the release lever ...

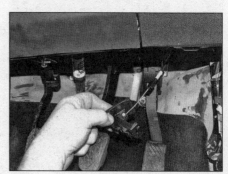

8.3b ... then slip the inner cable end fitting out of the lever handle

lock top plate and lift the plate from its location **(see illustration)**.

3 Prise out the bonnet release outer cable end fitting from its slot in the bonnet lock and unhook the inner cable from the lock operating lever.

4 Depress the four upper retaining tabs and lift up the embellishment panel from the top of the bumper. Depress the four lower retaining tabs and remove the embellishment panel.

5 Undo the two retaining bolts and remove the lock assembly.

Refitting

6 Refitting is a reversal of removal. If necessary, the position of the lock can be altered to adjust the lock operation by moving the lock within the elongated holes.

10 Door – removal and refitting

Removal

1 Release the rubber grommet from the door pillar and withdraw the wiring block connector **(see illustration)**.

2 Extract the connector locking bar, then depress the tabs and disconnect the wiring connectors **(see illustrations)**.

3 Unbolt the door check strap from the door pillar **(see illustration)**.

4 Ensure that the door is adequately supported, with the aid of an assistant, or using wooden blocks or similar under the bottom edge of the door (take care not to damage the paintwork).

5 Mark the position of the hinges on the door, then unscrew the bolts and remove the door from the car **(see illustration)**.

Refitting

6 Refitting is a reversal of removal.

11 Door inner trim panel – removal and refitting

Front door

Removal

1 Using a plastic spatula or similar instrument,

9.2 Undo the three bolts (arrowed) and lift off the bonnet lock top plate

10.2a Extract the connector locking bar ...

10.3 Unbolt the door check strap from the door pillar

10.1 Release the rubber grommet from the door pillar and withdraw the wiring block connector

10.2b ... then depress the tabs and disconnect the wiring connectors

10.5 Door upper hinge bolts (arrowed)

carefully prise up the electric window switch panel and disconnect the wiring connectors **(see illustrations)**.

2 Again, using the plastic spatula or similar, carefully prise free and remove the door pull handle trim surround **(see illustration)**.

11.1a Carefully prise up the electric window switch panel ...

11.1b ... and disconnect the wiring connectors

11.2 Carefully prise free and remove the door pull handle trim surround

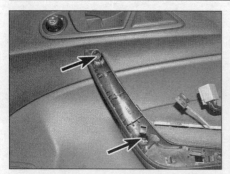

11.3 Undo the two screws (arrowed) securing the door pull handle to the door

11.4a Carefully prise free the electric mirror control switch ...

11.4b ... and disconnect the wiring connector

3 Undo the two screws securing the door pull handle to the door (**see illustration**).

4 Using a small screwdriver, carefully prise free the electric mirror control switch.

Disconnect the wiring connector and remove the switch (**see illustrations**).

5 Remove the circular trim button from the centre of the door interior handle (**see**

illustration). The best way to do this is to stick a small piece of adhesive tape to the trim button and pull on the tape to remove the button.

6 With the trim button removed, undo the panel retaining screw now exposed (**see illustration**).

7 Remove the two lower plastic rivets securing the trim panel to the door, by undoing the retaining screw and withdrawing the rivet body (**see illustration**).

8 Using a wide-bladed screwdriver or removal tool, carefully prise the bottom and sides of the panel away from the door to release the internal clips.

9 Lift the panel upward to release it from the window aperture. From inside the panel, prise open the locking catch using a small screwdriver, and disconnect the interior handle release cable from the panel. Disconnect the wiring connectors and remove the panel (**see illustration**).

Refitting

10 Refitting is a reversal of removal. Before starting, check to see whether any trim clips have been left on the door, and transfer them to the trim panel.

Rear door

Removal

11 Where a manual window regulator is fitted, locate a cloth rag between the handle and the trim panel and pull it back and forth to release the spring clip. Alternatively use a proprietary regulator spring clip removal tool. Remove the handle from the splined shaft then remove the circular spacer (**see illustrations**). Refit the spring clip to the handle.

11.5 Remove the circular trim button from the centre of the door interior handle ...

11.6 ... and undo the panel retaining screw now exposed

11.7 Remove the two lower plastic rivets securing the trim panel to the door

11.9 Disconnect the wiring connectors and remove the trim panel

11.11a Locate a cloth rag between the handle and the trim panel and pull it back and forth to release the spring clip

11.11b Remove the handle from the splined shaft ...

11.11c ... then remove the circular spacer

11.12 Remove the circular trim button from the centre of the door interior handle ...

11.13 ... then undo the panel retaining screw now exposed

11.14 Undo the two screws below the door pull handle

11.15 Carefully prise free the triangular inner trim panel at the rear of the door

11.16 Carefully prise the bottom and sides of the panel away from door

12 Remove the circular trim button from the centre of the door interior handle. The best way to do this is to stick a small piece of adhesive tape to the trim button and pull on the tape to remove the button (see illustration).

13 With the trim button removed, undo the panel retaining screw now exposed (see illustration).

14 Undo the two screws below the door pull handle (see illustration).

15 Carefully prise free the triangular inner trim panel at the rear of the door (see illustration).

16 Using a wide-bladed screwdriver or removal tool, carefully prise the bottom and sides of the panel away from the door to release the internal clips (see illustration).

17 Lift the panel upward to release it from the window aperture. From inside the panel, prise open the locking catch using a small screwdriver, and disconnect the interior

handle release cable from the panel (see illustrations). On models with electrically-operated windows, disconnect the wiring connectors and remove the panel.

Refitting

18 Refitting is a reversal of removal. Before starting, check to see whether any trim clips have been left on the door, and transfer them to the trim panel.

12 Door window glass –
removal and refitting

Front door
3-door models

1 Remove the door inner trim panel as described in Section 11.

2 Carefully prise free the inner and outer waist seals from the door (see illustration).

3 Disconnect the wiring connector, undo the three screws and remove the loudspeaker from the door.

4 Carefully pull off the circular rubber pad from the door panel for access to the window glass-to-regulator rear attachment.

5 Reconnect the door window switch wiring connector.

6 Operate the window switch and align the window glass rear attachment with the aperture exposed by removing the circular rubber pad.

7 Insert a screwdriver through the circular aperture and disengage the regulator rear attachment from the window glass by firmly pushing the regulator locating peg through the glass. Disengage the regulator front attachment from the window glass in the same way, but working through the loudspeaker aperture.

8 Lift the window glass from the door while tilting it up at the rear, and withdraw it from the outside of the door frame.

9 Refitting is a reversal of removal, making sure that the glass is correctly located in the regulator attachments.

5-door models

10 Remove the door inner trim panel as described in Section 11.

11 Carefully prise free the inner and outer waist seals from the door (see illustration 12.2).

12 Carefully pull off the circular rubber pads

11.17a Prise open the locking catch ...

11.17b ... and disconnect the interior handle release cable

12.2 Carefully prise free the inner and outer waist seals from the door

12.12 Pull off the circular rubber pads from the centre of the door panel

12.13 Lower the glass until the window glass clamp bolts (arrowed) are accessible

12.14 Withdraw the window glass from the door while tilting it up at the rear

from the centre of the door panel to access the window glass clamps **(see illustration)**.

13 Reconnect the door window switch wiring connector, and lower the glass until the

window glass clamp bolts are visible in the apertures exposed by removing the circular rubber pads **(see illustration)**.

14 Unscrew the window glass clamp bolts,

then lift the glass to release the plastic locating peg from the regulator clip. Withdraw the window glass from the door while tilting it up at the rear, and withdraw it from the outside of the door frame **(see illustration)**.

15 Refitting is a reversal of removal, noting the following points:

a) *Line up the plastic locating peg in the centre of the regulator guide clip, and push down to locate it.*

b) *Tighten the glass retaining bolts securely.*

Rear door

16 Remove the door inner trim panel as described in Section 11.

17 Temporarily refit the regulator handle, or reconnect the door window switch wiring connector, and lower the window glass all the way.

18 Carefully prise free the inner and outer waist seals from the door **(see illustrations)**.

19 Release the window guide rubber from the door frame and remove it from the door **(see illustration)**.

20 Undo the two screws securing the triangular trim panel to the rear of the door frame. Disengage the lower locating peg and remove the panel from the door **(see illustrations)**.

21 Carefully pull off the circular rubber pads from the centre of the door panel to access the window glass clamps **(see illustration)**.

22 Raise the window until the window glass clamp bolts are visible in the apertures exposed by removing the circular rubber pads **(see illustration)**.

12.18a Carefully prise free the inner waist seal ...

12.18b ... and outer waist seal from the door

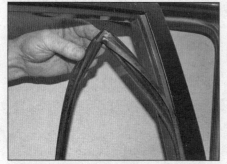

12.19 Release the window guide rubber from the door frame and remove it from the door

12.20a Undo the two screws (arrowed) securing the triangular trim panel to the rear of the door frame ...

12.20b ... then disengage the lower locating peg and remove the panel

12.21 Pull off the circular rubber pads from the centre of the door panel

12.22 Raise the window until the window glass clamp bolts (arrowed) are accessible

23 Unscrew the window glass clamp bolts, then lift the glass to release the plastic locating peg from the regulator clip. Withdraw the window glass upwards from the door, and withdraw it from the outside of the door frame.
24 Refitting is a reversal of removal, noting the following points:
a) Line up the plastic locating peg in the centre of the regulator guide clip, and push down to locate it.
b) Tighten the glass retaining bolts securely.

13 Door window regulator – removal and refitting

Front door

3-door models

1 Remove the door inner trim panel as described in Section 11.
2 Remove the door window glass as described in Section 12 – the glass can be raised and taped to the door frame, as it does not have to be removed completely.
3 Disconnect the wiring connector then undo the three bolts securing the regulator motor to the inner door panel (see illustrations). Release the motor wiring from the cable clips and remove the motor from the door panel.
4 Accurately note and record how the wiring loom is routed over the inner door panel. Disconnect the door mirror wiring connector,

then release all the clips and cable-ties securing the loom to the panel.
5 Undo the twelve bolts securing the inner door panel to the door frame, then pull the panel away from the door at the upper rear corner. Reach in behind the upper rear corner and insert a screwdriver between inner door panel and the door lock support bracket to release the retaining lug. Now slide the inner door panel forward to allow the three securing tabs to disengage through the elongated openings (see illustrations).
6 Prise free the lock interior handle operating cable grommet from the inner door panel (see illustration).
7 Withdraw the inner door panel until sufficient clearance exists to reach behind and disconnect the wiring connector from the door lock (see illustration). Prise free the door lock wiring grommet from the door panel and pull the wiring through to the outside.
8 Remove the inner door panel, feeding the interior handle operating cable through the opening as the panel is removed.
9 From the inside of the door panel, undo the three bolts securing the front lifting channel and the four bolts securing the rear lifting channel and remove the regulator assembly from the panel.
10 Refitting is a reversal of removal, noting the following points:
a) Ensure that the three tabs on the upper rear corner of the inner door panel

correctly engage with the elongated slots on the door lock support bracket.
b) Secure the wiring loom with the clips and cable-ties in the correct positions as noted during removal.
c) Refit the door window glass as described in Section 12.
d) Refit the door inner trim panel as described in Section 11.

5-door models

11 Remove the door inner trim panel as described in Section 11.
12 Remove the door window glass as described in Section 12 – the glass can be raised and taped to the door frame, as it does not have to be removed completely.
13 Disconnect the wiring connector then undo the three bolts securing the regulator motor to the inner door panel (see illustrations 13.3a and 13.3b). Release the motor wiring from the cable clips and remove the motor from the door panel.
14 Accurately note and record how the wiring loom is routed over the inner door panel. Disconnect the door mirror and loudspeaker wiring connectors, then release all the clips and cable-ties securing the loom to the panel.
15 Undo the ten bolts securing the inner door panel to the door frame, then pull the panel away from the door at the upper rear corner. Reach in behind the upper rear corner and insert a screwdriver between inner door panel and the door lock support bracket to release

13.3a Disconnect the wiring connector ...

13.3b ... then undo the three bolts (arrowed) securing the regulator motor to the inner door panel

13.5a Insert a screwdriver between inner door panel and the door lock support bracket ...

13.5b ... to release the retaining lug (arrowed)

13.6 Prise free the interior handle operating cable grommet

13.7 Withdraw the inner door panel and disconnect the wiring connector from the door lock

13.19a Undo the two bolts (arrowed) securing the regulator lifting channel to the door panel ...

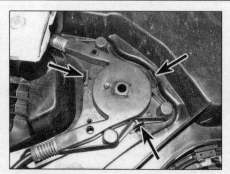

13.19b ... then disengage the front of the regulator from the three retaining lugs (arrowed)

13.24a Disconnect the loudspeaker wiring connector ...

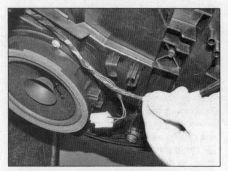

13.24b ... then release the clips and cable-ties securing the wiring loom to the door panel

13.26 Prise free the interior handle operating cable grommet from the inner door panel

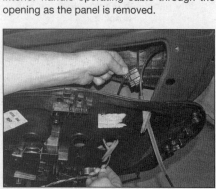

13.27 Disconnect the wiring connector from the door lock then prise free the grommet and pull the wiring through to the outside

13.29 Undo the three screws (arrowed) securing the window regulator to the panel

the retaining lug. Now slide the inner door panel forward to allow the three securing tabs to disengage through the elongated openings **(see illustrations 13.5a and 13.5b)**.

16 Prise free the lock interior handle operating cable grommet from the inner door panel **(see illustration 13.6)**.

17 Withdraw the inner door panel until sufficient clearance exists to reach behind and disconnect the wiring connector from the door lock **(see illustration 13.7)**. Prise free the door lock wiring grommet from the door panel and pull the wiring through to the outside.

18 Remove the inner door panel, feeding the interior handle operating cable through the opening as the panel is removed.

19 From the inside of the door panel, undo the two bolts securing the regulator lifting channel to the panel. Disengage the front of the regulator from the three retaining lugs and remove the regulator assembly from the panel **(see illustrations)**.

20 Refitting is a reversal of removal, noting the following points:

a) Ensure that the three tabs on the upper rear corner of the inner door panel correctly engage with the elongated slots on the door lock support bracket.

b) Secure the wiring loom with the clips and cable-ties in the correct positions as noted during removal.

c) Refit the door window glass as described in Section 12.

d) Refit the door inner trim panel as described in Section 11.

Rear door

21 Remove the door inner trim panel as described in Section 11.

22 Remove the door window glass as described in Section 12 – the glass can be raised and taped to the door frame, as it does not have to be removed completely.

23 On models with electric windows, disconnect the wiring connector then undo the three bolts securing the regulator motor to the inner door panel. Release the motor wiring from the cable clips and remove the motor from the door panel.

24 Accurately note and record how the wiring loom is routed over the inner door panel. Disconnect the loudspeaker wiring connector, then release all the clips and cable-ties securing the loom to the panel **(see illustrations)**.

25 Undo the eight bolts securing the inner door panel to the door frame, then pull the panel away from the door at the upper rear corner. Reach in behind the upper rear corner and insert a screwdriver between inner door panel and the door lock support bracket to release the retaining lug. Now slide the inner door panel forward to allow the three securing tabs to disengage through the elongated openings **(see illustrations 13.5a and 13.5b)**.

26 Prise free the lock interior handle operating cable grommet from the inner door panel **(see illustration)**.

27 Withdraw the inner door panel until sufficient clearance exists to reach behind and disconnect the wiring connector from the door lock. Prise free the door lock wiring grommet from the door panel and pull the wiring through to the outside **(see illustration)**.

28 Remove the inner door panel, feeding the interior handle operating cable through the opening as the panel is removed.

29 From the outside of the door panel on models with manually-operated windows, undo the three screws securing the regulator to the panel **(see illustration)**.

30 From the inside of the door panel, undo

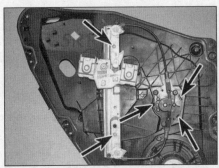

13.30 Undo the bolts (arrowed) securing the lifting channel to the panel then disengage the regulator from the retaining lugs (arrowed)

the two bolts securing the regulator lifting channel to the panel. Disengage the front of the regulator from the three retaining lugs and remove the regulator assembly from the panel **(see illustration)**.

31 Refitting is a reversal of removal, noting the following points:

a) *Ensure that the three tabs on the upper rear corner of the inner door panel correctly engage with the elongated slots on the door lock support bracket.*

b) *Secure the wiring loom with the clips and cable-ties in the correct positions as noted during removal.*

c) *Refit the door window glass as described in Section 12.*

d) *Refit the door inner trim panel as described in Section 11.*

14	Door handles and lock components – removal and refitting

Front door exterior handle

Removal

1 Prise out the rubber grommet from the end of the door adjacent to the exterior handle **(see illustration)**.

2 Working through the aperture, slacken the handle retaining bolt until the lock cylinder can be pulled from the door **(see illustrations)**.

3 Pull the exterior handle rearwards, and

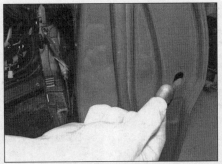

14.1 Prise out the rubber grommet from the end of the door

manoeuvre it from the door. Recover the seal between the handle and the door skin **(see illustrations)**.

4 On models with the Keyless Entry system, gently pull the handle wiring harness until an audible click is heard, and the harness connector is in the horizontal position. Disconnect the wiring plug.

Refitting

5 Refitting is a reversal of removal. When refitting the exterior handle on models with the Keyless Entry system, reconnect the wiring connector and push it into the holder.

Rear door exterior handle

Removal

6 Prise out the rubber grommet from the end of the door adjacent to the exterior handle **(see illustration)**.

14.2a Slacken the handle retaining bolt ...

14.2b ... until the lock cylinder can be pulled from the door

7 Working through the aperture, slacken the handle retaining bolt until the rear portion of the handle can be pulled from the door **(see illustrations)**.

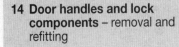

14.3a Pull the exterior handle rearwards, and manoeuvre it from the door ...

14.3b ... then recover the seal between the handle and the door skin

14.6 Prise out the rubber grommet from the end of the door

14.7a Slacken the handle retaining bolt ...

14.7b ... until the rear portion of the handle can be pulled from the door

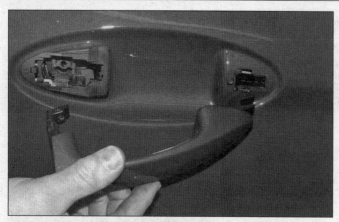

14.8a Pull the exterior handle rearwards, and manoeuvre it from the door ...

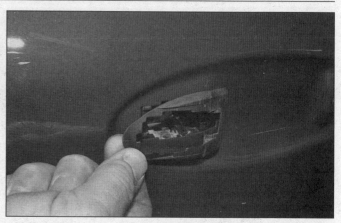

14.8b ... then recover the seal between the handle and the door skin

14.12a Undo the three lock assembly retaining screws (arrowed) at the rear edge of the door ...

8 Pull the exterior handle rearwards, and manoeuvre it from the door. Recover the seal between the handle and the door skin (see illustrations).

Refitting

9 Refitting is a reversal of removal.

Front/rear door lock

Removal

10 Remove the door window regulator as described in Section 13.
11 Remove the door exterior handle as described previously in this Section.
12 Undo the three lock assembly retaining

screws at the rear edge of the door and the single screw in the exterior handle aperture (see illustrations).
13 Slide the door lock assembly towards the front of the car to disengage the locating lugs, then remove the unit from inside the door (see illustrations).
14 Release the exterior handle operating cable from the lock support bracket, then disengage the inner cable end from the lock lever (see illustrations).
15 Remove the plastic retainer over the inner handle operating cable (see illustration).
16 Release the interior handle operating cable from the lock support bracket, then

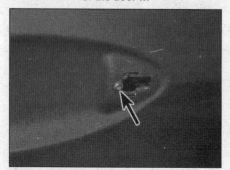

14.12b ... and the single screw (arrowed) in the exterior handle aperture

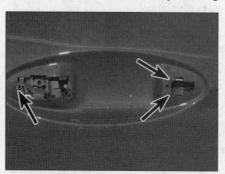

14.13a Slide the door lock assembly towards the front of the car to disengage the locating lugs (arrowed) ...

14.13b ... then remove the unit from inside the door

14.14a Release the exterior handle operating cable from the lock support bracket (arrowed) ...

14.14b ... then disengage the inner cable end from the lock lever

14.15 Remove the plastic retainer over the inner handle operating cable

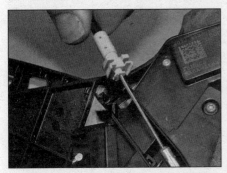

14.16a Release the interior handle operating cable from the lock support bracket …

14.16b … then disengage the inner cable end from the lock lever

14.17 Undo the two screws (arrowed) securing the lock to the support bracket

disengage the inner cable end from the lock lever **(see illustrations)**.

17 Undo the two screws securing the lock to the support bracket **(see illustration)**.

18 Disengage the locating peg on the underside of the lock from the collar on the support bracket, then remove the lock from the bracket **(see illustrations)**.

Refitting

19 Refitting is a reversal of removal.

Front lock cylinder

Removal

20 Prise out the rubber grommet from the end of the door adjacent to the exterior handle **(see illustration 14.1)**.

21 Working through the aperture, slacken the handle retaining bolt until the lock cylinder can be pulled from the door **(see illustrations 14.2a and 14.2b)**. If required, release the clip each side with a small screwdriver, and separate the lock cylinder from the trim

Refitting

22 Refitting is a reversal of removal.

15 Tailgate and support struts – removal, refitting and adjustment

Tailgate

Removal

1 Remove the tailgate trim panel as described in Section 23.

14.18a Disengage the locating peg (arrowed) on the underside of the lock from the collar on the support bracket …

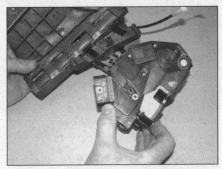

14.18b … then remove the lock from the bracket

2 Remove the high-level brake light as described in Chapter 12 Section 7.

3 Disconnect the tailgate wiring harness at the connector on the left-hand side of the tailgate **(see illustration)**.

4 Prise out the rubber gaiters at the top of the tailgate, and carefully start to pull through the wiring and washer tube **(see illustration)**. If the same tailgate is being refitted, tie on a length of string to the wiring harness and washer tube beforehand – the string can then be untied when it emerges from the top of the tailgate, and left in place to pull the harness and washer tube back through.

5 Using a pencil or marker pen, mark the position of the hinges on the tailgate to aid refitting.

6 Support the tailgate, and disconnect the

support struts as described later in this Section.

7 Ensure that the tailgate is adequately supported, ideally with the aid of an assistant, then unscrew the bolts securing the hinges to the tailgate, and lift the tailgate from the car **(see illustration)**.

Refitting

8 Refitting is a reversal of removal, bearing in mind the following points:
a) *Make sure that the hinges are aligned with the marks made before removal.*
b) *Use the string to pull the wiring harness and the washer fluid hose into position in the tailgate.*
c) *On completion, check the alignment of the tailgate with the surrounding body panels and, if necessary, adjust the position of the*

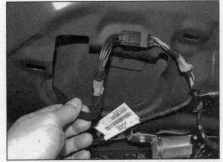

15.3 Disconnect the wiring harness at the connector on the left-hand side of the tailgate

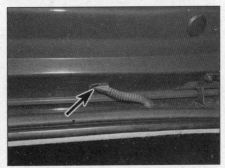

15.4 Prise out the rubber gaiter (arrowed) at the top of the tailgate each side

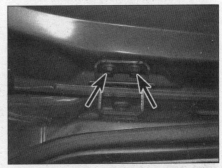

15.7 Unscrew the bolts (arrowed) each side, securing the hinges to the tailgate

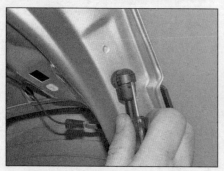

15.10a Lever out the metal clip ...

15.10b ... and prise off the strut

tailgate hinges and/or tailgate lock striker plate within the elongated holes until satisfactory alignment is achieved.

Support struts

Removal

9 Open the tailgate, and support it in the open position, using a wooden prop or similar tool. Note that the tailgate is heavy, and will fall closed if either of the support struts are disconnected.
10 Working at the top end of the strut, lever off the retaining clip, and prise off the end of the strut from the lug on the tailgate **(see illustrations)**.
11 Repeat the procedure at the bottom end of the strut, and withdraw the strut.

Refitting

12 Refitting is a reversal of removal.

---

16 Tailgate lock components – removal and refitting

Lock assembly

Removal

1 Remove the tailgate trim panel as described in Section 23.
2 Disconnect the wiring plug from the lock assembly **(see illustration)**.
3 Unscrew the two lock mounting bolts, and withdraw the lock.

Refitting

4 Refitting is a reversal of removal, but check the operation of the lock mechanism before refitting the tailgate trim panel.

Release switch

Removal

5 Remove the tailgate trim panel as described in Section 23.
6 Undo the six nuts securing the number plate light panel to the tailgate and withdraw the panel **(see illustrations)**.
7 Disconnect the release switch wiring connector **(see illustration)**.
8 Depress the retaining tabs on the side of the release switch and remove the switch from the number plate light panel **(see illustrations)**.

Refitting

9 Refitting is a reversal of removal, but check the operation of the lock mechanism before refitting the tailgate trim panel.

17 Central locking system – testing, reprogramming, removal and refitting

Testing/reprogramming

1 Testing of the central locking/alarm system can only be carried out using Ford diagnostic test equipment.
2 Prior to reprogramming a remote locking transmitter, ensure the vehicle battery is fully-charged, and the alarm is not armed or triggered. Close all doors to ensure conflicting chimes do not sound during programming.
3 Turn the ignition switch from position 0 to position II four times within 6 seconds, then turn it back to position 0 (off).

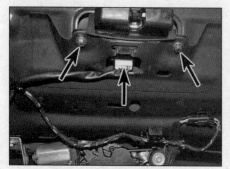

16.2 Tailgate lock wiring plug and mounting bolts (arrowed)

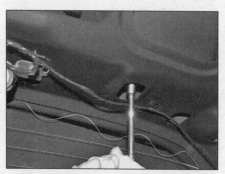

16.6a Undo the six nuts securing the number plate light panel to the tailgate ...

16.6b ... and withdraw the panel

16.7 Disconnect the release switch wiring connector

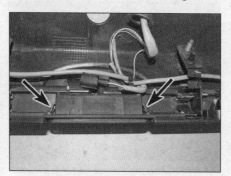

16.8a Depress the tabs (arrowed) on the side of the release switch ...

16.8b ... and remove the switch from the number plate light panel

18.2 Disconnect the mirror wiring connector, then release the wiring grommet from the door panel

18.3 Remove the grommet from the door for access to the mirror retaining nut

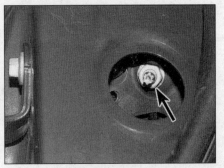

18.4a Undo the mirror retaining nut (arrowed) ...

18.4b ... and withdraw the mirror and wiring harness from the outside of the door

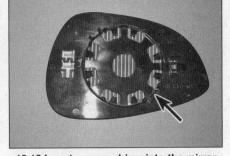

18.10 Insert a screwdriver into the mirror glass retaining clip (arrowed – shown with glass removed)

18.13 Press in the sides of the cover to release the clips and withdraw the cover from the mirror body

4 A chime will be heard to indicate that the 'learning mode' has begun.

5 Within 10 seconds of the previous step, press and hold any button on the remote transmitter until a further chime is heard. This indicates the process has been successful.

6 The system will now return to the 'learning mode' for a further 10 seconds and additional transmitters (up to a maximum of 4) can be programmed as described in paragraph 5. If no further transmitters are programmed, the system will return to normal mode after 10 seconds.

Removal

Generic electronic module (GEM)

Note: If the GEM is to be renewed, the unit settings must be saved prior to removal, then initialised using Ford diagnostic test equipment.

7 Removal and refitting of the GEM is described in Chapter 12 Section 12.

Keyless entry system module

Note: If the module is to be renewed, the unit settings must be saved prior to removal, then initialised using Ford diagnostic test equipment.

8 Disconnect the battery negative terminal (refer to 'Disconnecting the battery').

9 Remove the driver's side front seat as described in Section 21.

10 Undo the 2 retaining bolts, and remove the module. Disconnect the wiring plugs as the module is withdrawn.

Door lock motors

11 The door lock motors are integral with the locks. Refer to Section 14.

Tailgate lock motor

12 The tailgate lock motor is integral with the lock. Refer to Section 16.

Refitting

13 In all cases, refitting is a reversal of removal.

---

18 Exterior mirrors and associated components – removal and refitting

Mirror

Removal

1 Remove the front door inner trim panel as described in Section 11.

2 Disconnect the mirror wiring from the connector on the inside of the door, then release the wiring grommet from the door panel (see illustration). Tie a length of string to the wiring connector – the string can then be untied when it emerges from the top of the door, and left in place to pull the wiring back through when refitting

3 Remove the grommet from the top of the door for access to the mirror retaining nut (see illustration).

4 Undo the mirror retaining nut and withdraw the mirror and wiring harness from the outside of the door (see illustrations).

Refitting

5 Refitting is a reversal of removal.

Mirror motor

6 The motor is integral with the mirror, and cannot be renewed separately. If faulty, the complete mirror assembly must be renewed.

Mirror switch

Removal

7 Using a small screwdriver, carefully prise free the mirror control switch from the door inner trim panel. Disconnect the wiring connector and remove the switch (see illustrations 11.4a and 114b).

Refitting

8 Refitting is a reversal of removal.

Mirror glass

9 Warning: If the mirror glass is broken, wear gloves to protect your hands.

Removal

10 Pull the outer edge of the glass rearwards, insert a flat-bladed screwdriver and gently prise the glass from place (see illustration).

11 Withdraw the mirror glass and, where fitted, disconnect the wiring connectors for the heated mirrors.

Refitting

12 Refitting is a reversal of removal.

Mirror cover

Removal

13 Press in the sides of the cover to release the internal clips and withdraw the cover from the mirror body (see illustration).

Refitting

14 Refitting is a reversal of removal.

Direction indicator side repeater

15 Refer to Chapter 12 Section 7.

19 Windscreen, tailgate and fixed window glass – general information

1 These areas of glass are secured by the tight fit of the weatherseal in the body aperture, and are bonded in position with a special adhesive. Renewal of such fixed glass is a difficult, messy and time-consuming task, which is considered beyond the scope of the home mechanic. It is difficult, unless one has plenty of practice, to obtain a secure, waterproof fit. Furthermore, the task carries a high risk of breakage; this applies especially to the laminated glass windscreen. In view of this, owners are strongly advised to have this sort of work carried out by one of the many specialist windscreen fitters.

20 Body exterior fittings – removal and refitting

Radiator grille panel

Removal

1 Remove the front bumper as described in Section 6.
2 The radiator grille panel and the other detachable panels on the bumper are retained by a series of plastic clips, the location of which will become obvious on visual inspection.
3 Carefully disengage all the relevant clips using a small screwdriver, while at the same time pulling the panel from its location.

Refitting

4 Push the panel carefully into place ensuring that all the retaining clips engage fully.

Bumpers

5 Refer to Section 6.

20.14 Release the vacuum hose support bracket from the bulkhead closure panel

20.7 Prise out the clips securing the windscreen cowl panel to the bulkhead closure panel

Windscreen cowl panel

Removal

6 Remove the windscreen wiper arms as described in Chapter 12 Section 14.
7 Using a small screwdriver prise out the six clips securing the front edge of the windscreen cowl panel to the bulkhead closure panel (see illustration).
8 Lift up the lower corners of the windscreen trim surround to disengage the tabs from the slots in the windscreen cowl panel (see illustration).
9 Lift the cowl panel up and remove it from its location (see illustration).
10 If required, remove the headlights as described in Chapter 12 Section 7, then undo the bolts at each end and remove the fibre panel beneath the scuttle (see illustration).

20.9 Lift the cowl panel up and remove it from its location

20.15 Undo the two bolts (arrowed) each side securing the bulkhead closure panel to the body

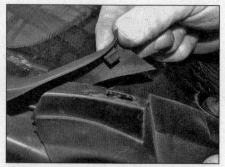
20.8 Lift up the windscreen trim surround to disengage the tabs from the slots in the cowl panel

Refitting

11 Refitting is a reversal of removal.

Bulkhead closure panel

Removal

12 Remove the windscreen cowl panel as described previously.
13 Remove both headlights as described in Chapter 12 Section 7.
14 Release the vacuum hose support bracket from the front of the bulkhead closure panel (see illustration).
15 Undo the two bolts each side securing the bulkhead closure panel to the body (see illustration).
16 Lift the panel up, disengage the four rear retaining tangs and remove the panel from the car (see illustration).

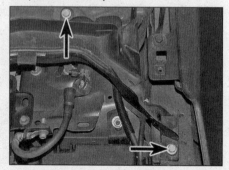
20.10 Undo the bolts at each end and remove the panel

20.16 Lift the panel up, disengage the four rear retaining tangs and remove the panel from the car

21.2 Front seat front retaining bolts (arrowed)

21.3 Front seat rear retaining bolts (arrowed)

Refitting

17 Refitting is a reversal of removal.

Wheel arch liners

18 The wheel arch liners are secured by a combination of self-tapping screws and push-fit clips.

19 The push-pin clips are removed by prising out the centre expanding pin, then prising out the main clip body.

20 The metal star clips used to unscrew from their mounting studs – now the metal tabs have to be prised up at the centre with a small screwdriver to release them.

21 With all the fasteners removed, pull the liner down from the arch and remove it.

Body trim strips and badges

22 The various body trim strips and badges are held in position with a special adhesive. Removal requires the trim/badge to be heated, to soften the adhesive, and then cut away from the surface. Due to the high risk of damage to the paintwork during this operation, it is recommended that this task should be entrusted to a Ford dealer.

21 Seats – removal and refitting

Front seat

Warning: Side airbags may be built into the outer sides of the front seats. Where side airbags are fitted, refer to Chapter 12 Section 22 for the precautions which should be observed when dealing with an airbag system.

1 On models equipped with side airbags, disconnect the battery negative terminal (refer to 'Disconnecting the battery') and wait a minimum of three minutes before proceeding.

2 Slide the seat fully rearwards, then unscrew the two front Torx bolts securing the seat rails to the floor (see illustration).

3 Slide the seat fully forwards, then unscrew the two rear Torx bolts (see illustration).

4 Tilt the seat backwards and disconnect the wiring plug from under the seat (see illustration).

5 Lift the seat, complete with mounting rails, and remove it from the car.

6 Refitting is a reversal of removal, but tighten the seat mounting bolts to the specified torque.

Rear seat
Cushion

7 Lift the seat cushion sharply upwards at the

21.4 Disconnect the wiring plug from under the seat

21.8a Disengage the cushion from the two rear hooks ...

front to disengage the wire retaining hoops from the floor grommets each side (see illustration).

8 Disengage the cushion from the two rear hooks and remove it from the car (see illustrations).

9 Refitting is a reversal of removal, but tighten the seat mounting bolts to the specified torque.

Backrest

10 Remove the rear seat cushion as described previously.

11 Undo the two bolts securing the backrest

21.7 Lift the rear seat cushion upwards at the front to disengage the retaining hoops from the floor grommets

21.8b ... and remove it from the car

21.12a Use a screwdriver to force the locking catch rearwards ...

21.12b ... and lift the outer end of the backrest from the hinge

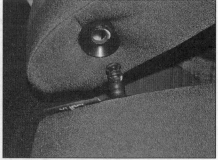

21.13 Pull the backrest from the centre pivot to disengage the mounting pin

centre mounting bracket to the floor, then fold the backrest forward.

12 Use a screwdriver to force the locking catch rearwards, and lift the outer end of the backrest from the hinge **(see illustrations)**.

13 Pull the backrest from the centre pivot to disengage the mounting pin **(see illustration)**.

14 Refitting is a reversal of removal, but tighten the seat mounting bolts to the specified torque.

22 Seat belts – removal and refitting

Front seat belt

1 Disconnect the battery negative terminal (refer to *'Disconnecting the battery'*).

⚠️ *Warning: Before proceeding, wait a minimum of 3 minutes, as a precaution against accidental firing of the seat belt tensioner, incorporated in the inertia reel. This period ensures that any residual electrical energy is dissipated.*

⚠️ *Warning: There is a potential risk of the seat belt tensioning device firing during removal, so it should be handled carefully. Once removed, treat it with care – do not allow use chemicals on or near it, and do not expose it to high temperatures, as it may detonate.*

3-door models

2 Remove the rear quarter trim panel and B-pillar trim panel as described in Section 23.

3 Undo the seat belt upper anchorage bolt **(see illustration)**. Note that the spacer and washer are integral with the bolt.

4 Rotate the seat belt guide loop anti-clockwise and remove it from the B-pillar **(see illustration)**.

5 Undo the two inertia reel mounting bolts and withdraw the reel from the base of the pillar **(see illustration)**. Disconnect the seat belt tensioner wiring connector and remove the belt and reel from the car.

6 Refitting is a reversal of the removal procedure, tightening the mounting bolts to the specified torque.

5-door models

7 Lift up the trim cover and undo the seat belt upper anchorage bolt **(see illustration)**. Note that the spacer and washer are integral with the bolt.

8 Remove the B-pillar lower trim panel as described in Section 23.

9 Rotate the seat belt guide loop anti-clockwise and remove it from the B-pillar.

10 Undo the seat belt lower anchorage bolt **(see illustration)**. Note that the spacer and washer are integral with the bolt.

11 Undo the two inertia reel mounting bolts

22.3 Undo the seat belt upper anchorage bolt (arrowed) – 3-door models

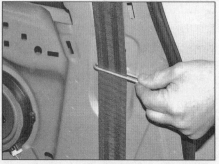

22.4 Rotate the seat belt guide loop anti-clockwise and remove it from the B-pillar – 3-door models

22.5 Undo the inertia reel mounting bolts (arrowed) and withdraw the reel from the base of the pillar – 3-door models

22.7 Lift up the trim cover and undo the seat belt upper anchorage bolt – 5-door models

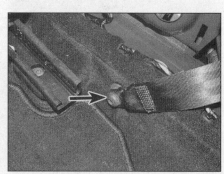

22.10 Undo the seat belt lower anchorage bolt (arrowed) – 5-door models

22.11a Undo the inertia reel upper mounting bolt (arrowed) ...

22.11b ... and lower mounting bolt (arrowed), then withdraw the reel from the base of the pillar – 5-door models

22.14 Undo the rear side seat belt upper anchorage bolt

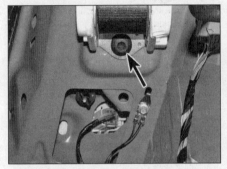

22.15 Undo the inertia reel mounting bolt (arrowed) and withdraw the seat belt and reel from the car

22.19a Push in the clip and pull the headrest guide tube from the backrest

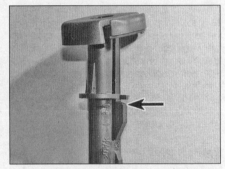

22.19b Depress the headrest guide tube clip (arrowed) – shown with the tube removed

and withdraw the reel from the base of the pillar **(see illustrations)**. Disconnect the seat belt tensioner wiring connector and remove the belt and reel from the car.

12 Refitting is a reversal of the removal procedure, tightening the mounting bolts to the specified torque.

Rear side seat belt

13 Remove the C-pillar trim panel as described in Section 23.

14 Undo the seat belt upper anchorage bolt **(see illustration)**. Note that the spacer and washer are integral with the bolt.

15 Undo the inertia reel mounting bolt and withdraw the seat belt and reel from the car **(see illustration)**.

16 Refitting is a reversal of the removal procedure, tightening the mounting bolts to the specified torque.

Rear centre seat belt

17 The centre rear seat belt reel is attached to the rear seat backrest. Remove the backrest as described in Section 21.

18 Use a screwdriver to prise up the backrest release button surround trim, releasing the clips.

19 Push down the backrest padding and use a screwdriver to depress the clip on the side of the headrest guide tubes **(see illustrations)**. Pull the guide tubes from the backrest.

20 Prise free the front of the seat belt guide trim from the top of the backrest, then

disengage the two rear locating tangs. Feed the seat belt through the slot in the trim **(see illustrations)**.

21 Gently prise out the beading securing

22.20a Prise free the seat belt guide trim from the top of the backrest ...

22.21 Gently prise out the beading securing the top half of the backrest seat fabric

the top half of the backrest seat fabric **(see illustration)**.

22 Undo the bolt securing the inertia reel to the backrest **(see illustration)**.

22.20b ... then feed the seat belt through the slot in the trim

22.22 Undo the bolt securing the inertia reel to the backrest

22.23 Pull the seat foam padding from the backrest and manoeuvre the seat belt reel from the seat backrest

23 Carefully pull the seat foam padding from the top part of the backrest and manoeuvre the seat belt reel from the seat backrest **(see illustration)**. Feed the seat belt through the seat backrest bracket as the reel is withdrawn.
24 Refitting is a reversal of the removal procedure, tightening the mounting bolts to the specified torque.

Front seat belt stalks

25 The front seat belt stalks are bolted to the seat frame and can be removed after removing the front seat as described in Section 21.
26 Refitting is a reversal of the removal procedure, tightening the mounting bolt to the specified torque.

23.3 Prise up the upper shroud to disengage it from the lower shroud tabs (steering wheel removed for clarity)

23.7a Undo the lower shroud upper retaining screws (arrowed) ...

22.28 Rear seat belt buckle retaining bolt

Rear seat belt buckles

27 Remove the rear seat cushion as described in Section 21.
28 Undo the retaining bolt and remove the buckle(s) from the car **(see illustration)**.
29 Refitting is a reversal of the removal procedure, tightening the mounting bolt to the specified torque.

23	Interior trim and fittings – removal and refitting

General

1 The interior trim panels are secured by a combination of clips and screws, with

23.4 Pull the centre plastic section beneath the instrument panel away from the facia, then lift the shroud off

23.7b ... and lower retaining screw ...

easily-broken plastic clips featuring heavily. Removal and refitting is generally self-explanatory, noting that it may be necessary to remove or loosen surrounding panels to allow a particular panel to be removed. The following paragraphs describe the removal and refitting of the major panels in more detail.

Door inner trim panels

2 Refer to Section 11.

Steering column shrouds

Upper shroud

3 Prise up the upper shroud to disengage it from the retaining tabs on the lower shroud **(see illustration)**.
4 Pull the centre plastic section beneath the instrument panel away from the facia, then lift the shroud up and off the steering column **(see illustration)**.
5 Refitting is a reversal of removal.

Lower shroud

6 The lower shroud is clipped to the upper shroud at either side, and is further secured by three screws.
7 Undo the three retaining screws, then lower the steering column height adjuster lever, and remove the lower shroud **(see illustrations)**. If the upper shroud is still in place, the lower shroud will have to be unclipped from it during removal.
8 Refitting is a reversal of removal.

Driver's lower facia trim

⚠️ *Warning: A knee airbag may be incorporated in the lower facia trim panel. Where an airbag is fitted, refer to Chapter 12 Section 22 for the precautions which should be observed when dealing with an airbag system.*

9 On models equipped with a knee airbag, disconnect the battery negative terminal (refer to 'Disconnecting the battery') and wait a minimum of three minutes before proceeding.
10 On models equipped with a knee airbag, reach up under the facia and undo the two nuts securing the airbag to the facia frame.
11 Carefully prise the trim panel away from the facia to release the three retaining clips

23.7c ... then remove the lower shroud

23.11a Carefully prise the panel away from the facia to release the three clips each side ...

23.11b ... then, where applicable, disconnect the airbag wiring connector and remove the panel

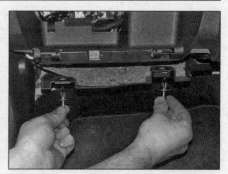

23.13 Remove the two plastic rivets from the passenger's lower facia trim panel

each side. Where applicable, disconnect the airbag wiring connector and remove the panel **(see illustrations)**. Check whether any of the clips pull out of the panel, to be left on the car – transfer them back to the panel before refitting.

12 Refitting is a reversal of removal.

Passenger's lower facia trim

13 Remove the two plastic rivets from the underside of the panel by prising up the centre section, then withdrawing the rivet body **(see illustration)**.

14 Disengage the tabs at the front edge of the panel and remove the panel from under the facia **(see illustration)**.

15 Refitting is a reversal of removal.

Sill trim panels

16 Pull away the rubber door seals in the vicinity of the sill trim panel to be removed.

17 The sill trim panels are clipped in place. Several clips are used, and some are quite stiff to release – start at one end of the panel, and pull the panel back as it is released. Check whether any of the clips pull out of the panel, to be left on the car – transfer them back to the panel before refitting **(see illustration)**.

18 Refitting is a reversal of removal.

A-pillar trim panel

Upper panel

19 Open the door, and carefully prise the rubber door seal from the edge of the door aperture.

20 Pull the panel away from the A-pillar

at the top and work down to disengage the upper retaining clips. Once the panel is free, disengage the two locating tabs at the front and remove the panel **(see illustrations)**. Check whether any of the clips pull out of the panel, to be left on the car – transfer them back to the panel before refitting.

21 Refitting is a reversal of removal.

Lower panel

22 Remove the adjacent sill trim panel as described previously in this Section.

23 Unscrew the plastic retaining stud at the top of the panel **(see illustration)**.

24 Pull the panel up at the rear to release the retaining clips and remove the panel from the car **(see illustration)**.

25 Refitting is a reversal of removal.

23.14 Disengage the tabs at the front and remove the panel from under the facia

23.17 Pull the sill trim panels up to release the clips

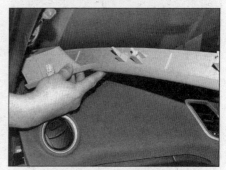

23.20a Pull the trim panel away from the A-pillar at the top and work down to disengage the upper clips...

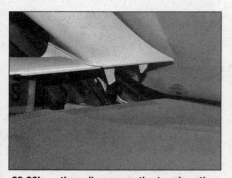

23.20b ... then disengage the two locating tabs at the front and remove the panel

23.23 Unscrew the plastic retaining stud at the top of the A-pillar lower panel

23.24 Pull the panel up at the rear to release the clips and remove the panel from the car

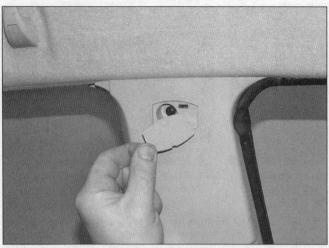

23.28 Prise out the trim cap at the top of the B-pillar and undo the retaining screw – 3-door models

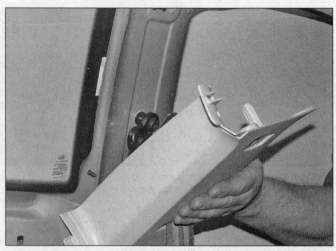

23.29 Pull the panel away to release the clips, then feed the seat belt through the panel slot – 3-door models

B-pillar trim panels

26 Detach the rubber weatherstrip from the B-pillar as necessary to free the edges of the trim panel.

3-door models

27 Remove the rear quarter trim panel as described later in this Section.
28 Carefully prise out the trim cap at the top of the B-pillar and undo the retaining screw now exposed (see illustration).

29 Pull the panel away from the pillar to release the internal clips, then feed the seat belt through the panel and remove the panel from the car (see illustration). Check whether any of the clips pull out of the panel, to be left on the car – transfer them back to the panel before refitting.
30 Refitting is a reversal of removal.

5-door models – lower panel

31 Remove the sill trim panels on either side

of the B-pillar as described previously in this Section.
32 Pull the panel away from the pillar to release the internal clips, then remove the panel from the car (see illustration). Check whether any of the clips pull out of the panel, to be left on the car – transfer them back to the panel before refitting.
33 Refitting is a reversal of removal.

5-door models – upper panel

34 Remove the B-pillar lower panel as described previously in this Section.
35 Lift up the trim cover and undo the seat belt upper anchorage bolt (see illustration). Note that the spacer and washer are integral with the bolt.
36 Carefully prise out the trim cap at the top of the B-pillar and undo the retaining screw now exposed (see illustrations).
37 Pull the panel away from the pillar to release the internal clips, then remove the panel from the car (see illustration). Check whether any of the clips pull out of the panel, to be left on the car – transfer them back to the panel before refitting.
38 Refitting is a reversal of removal. Tighten the seat belt upper anchorage bolt to the specified torque.

23.32 Pull the lower panel away to release the clips, then remove the panel from the car – 5-door models

23.35 Lift up the trim cover and undo the seat belt upper anchorage bolt – 5-door models

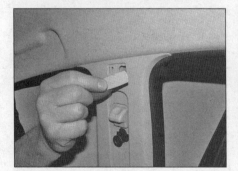

23.36a Prise out the trim cap at the top of the B-pillar ...

23.36b ... and undo the retaining screw now exposed – 5-door models

23.37 Pull the upper panel away to release the clips, then remove the panel from the car – 5-door models

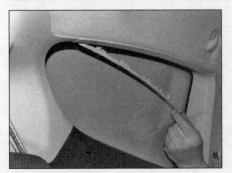

23.39 Prise free and remove the trim covering above the window – 3-door models

23.40a Undo the retaining screws (arrowed) …

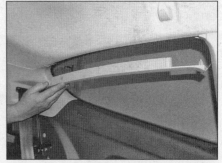

23.40b … and remove the upper trim plate – 3-door models

C-pillar trim panel

3-door models

39 Carefully prise free and remove the trim covering above the window **(see illustration)**.
40 Undo the three retaining screws and remove the upper trim plate **(see illustrations)**.
41 Remove the rear seat cushion as described in Section 21.
42 Undo the seat belt lower anchorage bolt. Note that the spacer and washer are integral with the bolt.
43 Pull the panel away from the pillar to release the internal clips, then feed the seat belt through the panel and remove the panel from the car **(see illustration)**. Check whether any of the clips pull out of the panel, to be left on the car – transfer them back to the panel before refitting.
44 Refitting is a reversal of removal. Tighten the rear seat belt lower anchorage bolt to the specified torque.

5-door models

45 Pull off the rubber seals from the rear door and tailgate apertures, in the area adjoining the trim panel.
46 Remove the rear seat cushion as described in Section 21.

23.43 Pull the C-pillar trim panel away to release the clips, then feed the seat belt through the panel slot – 3-door models

23.47 Undo the rear seat belt lower anchorage bolt (arrowed) – 5-door models

47 Undo the seat belt lower anchorage bolt **(see illustration)**. Note that the spacer and washer are integral with the bolt.
48 Carefully prise out the trim cap at the top of the C-pillar and undo the retaining screw now exposed **(see illustration)**.
49 Pull the panel away from the pillar to release the internal clips, then feed the seat belt through the panel and remove the panel from the car **(see illustration)**. Check whether any of the clips pull out of the panel, to be left

on the car – transfer them back to the panel before refitting.
50 Refitting is a reversal of removal. Tighten the rear seat belt lower anchorage bolt to the specified torque.

Rear quarter trim panel

51 Remove the C-pillar trim panel and the sill trim panel as described previously in this Section.

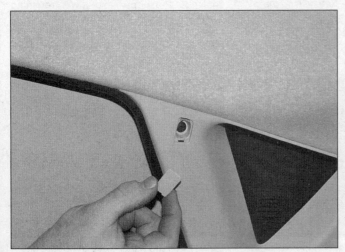

23.48 Prise out the trim cap at the top of the C-pillar and undo the retaining screw now exposed – 5-door models

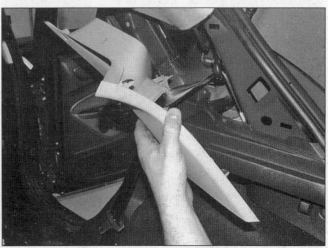

23.49 Pull the panel away to release the clips, then feed the seat belt through the panel slot – 5-door models

23.53 Unscrew the seat belt lower anchor rail bolt, then remove the washer, spacer and bolt from the rail – 3-door models

23.54 Pull the rail out slightly and slide the seat belt off the end of the rail – 3-door models

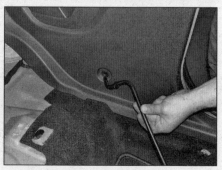

23.55a Disengage the rear end of the rail from its location ...

23.55b ... and collect the locating collar – 3-door models

23.56 Prise out the plastic fastener at the lower rear corner of the panel – 3-door models

52 Pull off the rubber seal from the door aperture, in the area adjoining the trim panel.
53 Unscrew the bolt at the front of the seat belt lower anchor rail, remove the washer and spacer from the bolt, then remove the bolt from the rail (**see illustration**).
54 Pull the front of the rail out slightly and slide the seat belt off the end of the rail (**see illustration**).
55 Disengage the rear end of the rail from its location and collect the locating collar (**see illustrations**).
56 Prise out the plastic fastener at the lower rear corner of the panel (**see illustration**).

57 Unclip the side trim panel at the base, then work round the edges of the panel, freeing the remaining clips until the panel can be lifted out (**see illustration**). Check whether any of the clips pull out of the panel, to be left on the car – transfer them back to the panel before refitting.
58 Refitting is a reversal of removal, noting the following points:
a) Make sure the seat belt anchor rail locating collar is in position before refitting the anchor rail.
b) Refit the spacer and washer to the anchor rail retaining bolt.

c) Tighten the mounting bolts to the specified torque.

Rear door aperture trim panel

59 Remove the C-pillar trim panel and the sill trim panel as described previously in this Section.
60 Prise out the plastic fastener at the lower rear corner of the panel (**see illustration**).
61 Pull the panel away from the door aperture to release the internal clips, then remove the panel from the car (**see illustration**). Check whether any of the clips pull out of the panel, to be left on the car – transfer them back to the panel before refitting.
62 Refitting is a reversal of removal.

Parcel shelf support

3-door models

63 Remove the rear quarter trim panel as described previously in this Section.
64 Pull off the rubber seal from the tailgate aperture, in the area adjoining the parcel shelf support.
65 Undo the upper and lower retaining screws, then pull the support away from the body to release the internal clips, and remove the support from the car (**see**

23.57 Starting at the base, unclip the trim panel, then work round the edges until the panel can be lifted out –3-door models

23.60 Prise out the plastic fastener at the lower rear corner of the panel – 5-door models

23.61 Pull the panel away to release the clips, then remove the panel from the car – 5-door models

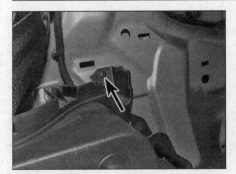

23.65a Undo the parcel shelf support upper retaining screw (arrowed) …

23.65b … and lower retaining screw (arrowed) …

23.65c … then pull the support away to release the clips, and remove the support from the car – 3-door models

23.69a Undo the parcel shelf support upper retaining screw (arrowed) …

23.69b … and lower retaining screw (arrowed) – 5-door models

23.70 Pull the parcel shelf support away to release the clips – 5-door models

illustrations). Check whether any of the clips pull out of the support, to be left on the car – transfer them back to the support before refitting.

66 Refitting is a reversal of removal.

5-door models

67 Remove the C-pillar trim panel as described previously in this Section.

68 Pull off the rubber seal from the tailgate aperture, in the area adjoining the parcel shelf support.

69 Undo the parcel shelf support upper and lower retaining screws (see illustrations).

70 Pull the rear door aperture trim panel out slightly, then pull the parcel shelf support away from the body to release the internal

retaining clips (see illustration). Where applicable, release the interior light bulbholder then remove the support from the car. Check whether any of the clips pull out of the support, to be left on the car – transfer them back to the support before refitting.

71 Refitting is a reversal of removal.

Tailgate aperture lower trim

72 Pull off the rubber seal from the tailgate aperture, in the area adjoining the trim panel.

73 Prise out the plastic fasteners at each inner side of the trim panel (see illustration).

74 Pull the panel away from the tailgate aperture to release the internal clips, then remove the panel from the car (see

illustration). Check whether any of the clips pull out of the panel, to be left on the car – transfer them back to the panel before refitting.

75 Refitting is a reversal of removal.

Loadspace side trim

76 Remove the parcel shelf support and tailgate aperture trim panel as described previously in this Section.

77 Lift the trim from its location and remove it from the car (see illustration).

78 Refitting is a reversal of removal.

Tailgate trim panel

79 Disengage the parcel shelf lifting cords from the studs on the upper trim panel sides.

23.73 Prise out the plastic fasteners at each inner side of the tailgate aperture trim panel

23.74 Pull the panel away to release the clips, then remove the panel from the car

23.77 Lift the loadspace side trim from its location and remove it from the car

23.88 Depress the retaining tabs and withdraw the two hinge pins from the base of the glovebox

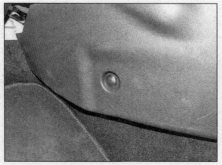

24.1a Extract the plastic rivets securing the inner trim panels to the base of the facia ...

24.1b ... then pull the panels away to release the retaining clips and remove the panels

80 Undo the retaining screw each side and pull the upper trim panel sides away from the tailgate to release the internal clips.
81 Undo the trim panel retaining screw in the grab handle recess.
82 Pull the main panel away from the tailgate to release the internal retaining clips and remove the panel from the car. Check whether any of the clips pull out of the panel, to be left on the car – transfer them back to the panel before refitting.
83 Refitting is a reversal of removal.

Carpets

84 The passenger compartment floor carpet is in several pieces, and is secured along the edges by various types of clips.
85 Carpet removal and refitting is reasonably straightforward, but time-consuming, due to the fact that all adjoining trim panels must be released, and the seats and centre console must be removed.

Headlining

86 The headlining is clipped to the roof, and can be withdrawn only once all fittings such as the grab handles, sunvisors, front, centre and rear pillar trim panels, and associated components have been removed. The door and tailgate weatherseals will also have to be prised clear.
87 Note that headlining removal requires considerable skill and experience if it is to be carried out without damage, and is therefore best entrusted to an expert.

Glovebox

88 Depress the retaining tabs and withdraw the two hinge pins from the base of the glovebox **(see illustration)**.
89 Press the sides of the glovebox inwards and remove the glovebox from the facia.
90 Refitting is a reversal of removal.

24 Centre console – removal and refitting

Removal

1 Working in the footwell on the driver's and passenger's side, pull out the centre pins and extract the plastic rivets securing the inner trim panels to the base of the facia. Pull the panels away to release the three retaining clips at the rear and remove the trim panels **(see illustrations)**.
2 On manual transmission models, hold the gear lever and unscrew the gear lever knob from the lever. Unclip the gear lever gaiter surround from the centre console and remove it up and over the gear lever **(see illustrations)**.
3 On automatic transmission models, carefully prise up the selector lever trim panel and surround from the centre console **(see illustrations)**.
4 Undo the centre screw, then pull out the expanding plastic rivet from each side of the centre console at the rear **(see illustration)**.

24.2a On manual transmission models, hold the gear lever and unscrew the gear lever knob ...

24.2b ... unclip the gaiter surround from the centre console and remove it up and over the gear lever

24.3a On automatic transmission models, carefully prise up the selector lever trim panel ...

24.3b ... and surround from the centre console

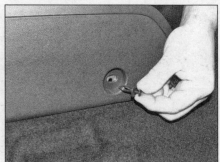

24.4 Undo the centre screw, then pull out the expanding plastic rivet from each side of the centre console at the rear

24.5 Undo the two screws (arrowed) securing the front of the centre console to the facia

24.6a Pull the console to the rear to disengage the two front locating lugs ...

24.6b ... then disconnect the wiring connectors at the accessory socket and audio socket/switch panel

5 Undo the two screws securing the front of the centre console to the facia **(see illustration)**.

6 Pull the console to the rear to disengage the two front locating lugs. Disconnect the wiring connectors at the accessory socket and audio socket/switch panel, then lift the console up and over the handbrake lever and remove it from the car **(see illustrations)**.

Refitting

7 Refitting is a reversal of removal.

25 Facia assembly – removal and refitting

Note: *This is an involved procedure which entails removal of the facia in virtually its totally assembled condition, containing the steering column, heater/air conditioning assembly and all the main facia attachments and controls. Once the facia is removed, it can be dismantled by referring to the procedures contained in Chapters 3, 10 and 12 of this manual. It is strongly recommended that this Section is read through thoroughly before starting the procedure.*

Removal

1 On models equipped with air conditioning, have the refrigerant discharged at a dealer service department or an automotive air conditioning repair facility.

2 Set the steering wheel and roadwheels in the straight-ahead position, then remove the ignition key and engage the steering lock. On vehicles with keyless entry, make sure the passive key is outside the vehicle to allow the steering lock to engage.

3 Disconnect the battery negative terminal (refer to *'Disconnecting the battery'*) and wait a minimum of three minutes before proceeding.

⚠ *Warning: Driver's and passenger's airbags are incorporated in the steering wheel and facia. Refer to Chapter 12 Section 22 for the precautions which should be observed when dealing with an airbag system.*

4 Drain the cooling system as described in Chapter 1A Section 31 or Chapter 1B Section 30.

5 Remove the centre console as described in Section 24.

6 Remove the windscreen cowl panel and bulkhead closure panel as described in Section 20.

7 Remove the windscreen wiper motor and linkage as described in Chapter 12 Section 15.

8 Undo the bolt behind the windscreen wiper location securing the facia crossmember to the bulkhead **(see illustration)**.

9 Release the retaining clip and disconnect the upper coolant hose from the heater matrix pipe stub on the engine compartment bulkhead. Disconnect the lower coolant hose from the matrix pipe stub by pressing together the tabs on the side of the quick-release fitting **(see illustration)**.

10 On models with air conditioning, undo the retaining nuts and disconnect the refrigerant pipe connector blocks from the expansion valve on the engine compartment bulkhead **(see illustration)**. Discard the seals – new ones must be used when refitting. Suitably cap the open fittings immediately to keep moisture and contamination out of the system.

11 Unscrew the plastic nut adjacent to the heater matrix coolant hose attachments on the engine compartment bulkhead **(see illustration)**.

12 Remove the driver's side front door and

25.8 Undo the bolt (arrowed) behind the windscreen wiper location securing the facia crossmember to the bulkhead

25.9 Coolant hose connections at the heater matrix pipe stubs

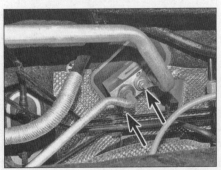

25.10 Refrigerant pipe connector block retaining nuts (arrowed) at the expansion valve

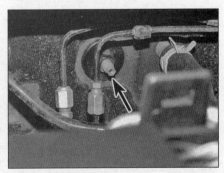

25.11 Unscrew the plastic nut (arrowed) adjacent to the heater matrix coolant hose attachments

25.16 Disconnect the three wiring connectors (arrowed) from the generic electronics module

25.17 Undo the retaining bolt and disconnect the wiring harness connector on the passenger's side lower A-pillar

the driver's seat as described in Sections 10 and 21 respectively.

13 On models with manual transmission, remove the gear lever housing assembly as described in Chapter 7A, Section 3.

14 On models with automatic transmission, remove the gear selector assembly as described in Chapter 7B, Section 4.

15 Remove the passenger's lower facia trim panel, and the upper and lower A-pillar trim panels each side, as described in Section 23.

16 Working under the facia on the passenger's side, disconnect the three wiring connectors from the generic electronics module **(see illustration)**.

17 Undo the retaining bolt and disconnect the wiring harness connector on the passenger's side lower A-pillar **(see illustration)**.

18 Lift up the locking bar and disconnect the wiring harness connector on the driver's side lower A-pillar **(see illustration)**.

19 Using a plastic spatula or similar tool, carefully prise off the facia end panels on each side to release the four internal clips **(see illustrations)**.

20 Working under the facia on the driver's side, depress the tab in the centre of the bonnet release lever, then slide the lever to the rear to disengage the locating lugs.

21 Undo the clamp bolt securing the steering column shaft lower universal joint to the steering gear pinion **(see illustration)**. Note that a new clamp bolt will be required for refitting. Pull the shaft upwards and off the pinion.

22 Disconnect the wiring from the warning light switch on the side of the handbrake lever **(see illustration)**. Free the wiring from the clips on the plastic cover over the airbag control unit.

23 Lift off the cover over the airbag control

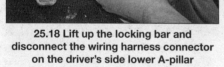

25.18 Lift up the locking bar and disconnect the wiring harness connector on the driver's side lower A-pillar

25.19a Carefully prise off the facia end panels on each side ...

25.19b ... to release the four internal clips

25.21 Undo the clamp bolt (arrowed) securing the steering column shaft lower universal joint to the steering gear pinion

25.22 Disconnect the wiring connector from the warning light switch on the side of the handbrake lever

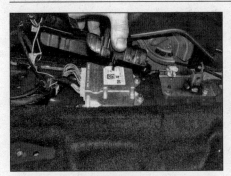

25.23a Lift off the cover over the airbag control unit ...

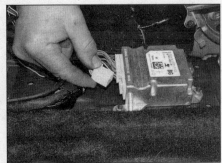

25.23b ... and disconnect the three airbag wiring connectors

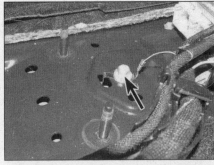

25.24 Undo the earth lead retaining bolt (arrowed) located in front of the airbag control unit

unit and disconnect the three airbag wiring connectors **(see illustrations)**.

24 Undo the earth lead retaining bolt located in front of the airbag control unit **(see illustration)**.

25 Open the tabs on the plastic wiring trough and lift out the upper wiring harness so that it's free to be removed with the facia **(see illustrations)**.

26 Undo the two bolts each side and remove the two facia support struts **(see illustration)**.

27 Insert a small screwdriver into the slot in the front face of the overhead reading light. Depress the clip and carefully prise the light unit from its location. Disconnect the wiring connectors and remove the light unit **(see illustrations)**.

28 Using a small screwdriver, open the

25.25a Open the tabs on the plastic wiring trough ...

25.25b ... and lift out the upper wiring harness so that it's free to be removed with the facia

locking flap and remove the driver's side sunvisor. Now carefully open the trim tab,

undo the retaining screw and remove the sunvisor pivot mounting **(see illustrations)**.

25.26 Undo the two bolts each side (arrowed) and remove the two facia support struts

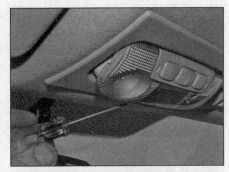

25.27a Using a small screwdriver, depress the clip and carefully prise the light unit from its location...

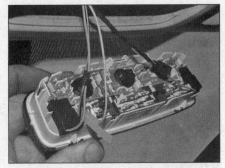

25.27b ... disconnect the wiring connectors and remove the light unit

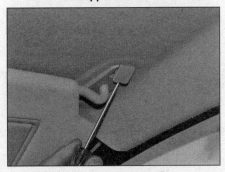

25.28a Open the locking flap ...

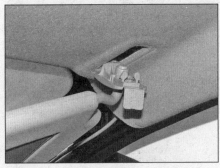

25.28b ... and remove the driver's side sunvisor ...

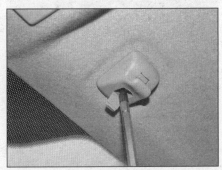

25.28c ... then open the trim tab, undo the retaining screw, and remove the sunvisor pivot mounting

25.29 Undo the screw securing the radio aerial and aerial cable to the roof panel

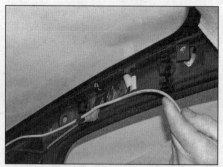

25.32 Release the aerial lead from the clips on the A-pillar so that the lead is free to be removed with thefacia

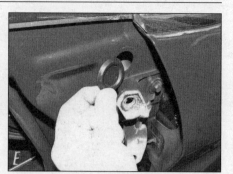

25.33a Extract the rubber grommet from the A-pillar on the driver's side ...

25.33b ... then using a socket and extension bar, undo the facia side retaining bolt ...

25.33c ... and remove the bolt from the A-pillar

25.34 Make an alignment mark on the pillar in the centre of the oval hole (arrowed) on the facia mounting bracket

29 Working through the reading light aperture, undo the screw securing the radio aerial and aerial cable to the roof panel, then remove the aerial (see illustration).

30 Tie a suitable length of string to the end of the aerial lead to aid refitting. Carefully pull the headliner down slightly at the front, then reach in and release the aerial lead from the clips on the roof. Take great care not to crease the headliner.

31 Pull the aerial lead out from its roof location until the string emerges at the top of the A-pillar. Untie the string and leave it in place to enable the lead to be drawn back through when refitting.

32 Release the aerial lead from the clips on the A-pillar so that the lead is free to be removed with the facia (see illustration).

33 Extract the rubber grommet from the A-pillar on the driver's side, then using a socket and extension bar, undo and remove the facia side retaining bolt (see illustrations).

34 Using a suitable marker pen, make an alignment mark on the pillar in the centre of the oval hole on the facia mounting bracket each side (see illustration).

35 Undo the two bolts each side securing the facia to the A-pillars (see illustration).

36 With the help of an assistant, carefully lift the facia from its location. Check that all wiring has been disconnected, then remove the facia out from the driver's side of the car (see illustration).

Refitting

37 Refitting is a reversal of removal, noting the following points:

a) Tighten all retaining bolts to the specified torque (where given).

b) Use a new clamp bolt when reconnecting the steering column shaft universal joint and tighten the clamp bolt to the specified torque.

c) Refill the cooling system as described in Chapter 1A Section 31 or Chapter 1B Section 30.

d) On models equipped with air conditioning, use new O-rings, coated with refrigerant oil, when reconnecting the refrigerant lines.

e) On models equipped with air conditioning, have the system evacuated, charged and leak-tested by the specialist that discharged it.

25.35 Undo the two bolts (arrowed) each side securing the facia to the A-pillars

25.36 With the help of an assistant, carefully lift the facia from its location and remove it from the car

Chapter 12
Body electrical system

Contents

Degrees of difficulty

Easy, suitable for novice with little experience 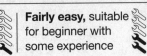 | **Fairly easy,** suitable for beginner with some experience | **Fairly difficult,** suitable for competent DIY mechanic | **Difficult,** suitable for experienced DIY mechanic | **Very difficult,** suitable for expert DIY or professional

Specifications

General
System type . . . . 12 volt, negative earth

Fuses
. . . . *Refer to label on fuse/relay box cover and back of glovebox*

Bulbs
	Wattage
Front direction indicator light	21
Front direction indicator side repeater light	5
Front foglight	55
Front sidelight	5
Glovebox light	5
Headlight dipped beam	55
Headlight main beam	55
Interior light	6
Luggage compartment light	5
Map reading lights	5
Number plate light	5
Rear direction indicator light	21
Rear foglight	21
Reversing light	16
Brake/tail light	21/5

1 General information and precautions

⚠️ **Warning: Before carrying out any work on the electrical system, read through the precautions given in 'Safety first!' at the beginning of this manual, and in Chapter 5A.**

1 The electrical system is of the 12 volt negative earth type. Power for the lights and all electrical accessories is supplied by a lead-acid type battery, which is charged by the engine-driven alternator.

2 This Chapter covers repair and service procedures for the various electrical components not associated with the engine. Information on the battery, alternator and starter motor can be found in Chapter 5A.

3 It should be noted that, prior to working on any component in the electrical system, the battery negative terminal should first be disconnected, to prevent the possibility of electrical short-circuits and/or fires.
Caution: Before proceeding, refer to 'Disconnecting the battery' for further information.

2 Electrical fault finding – general information

Note: *Refer to the precautions given in 'Safety first!' and in Section 1 before starting work. The following tests relate to testing of the main electrical circuits, and should not be used to test delicate electronic circuits (such as the anti-lock braking system or fuel injection system), particularly where an electronic control unit is used.*

General

1 A typical electrical circuit consists of an electrical component, any switches, relays, motors, fuses, fusible links or circuit breakers related to that component, and the wiring and connectors which link the component to both the battery and the vehicle body. To help to pinpoint a problem in an electrical circuit, wiring diagrams are shown at the end of this Chapter.

2 Before attempting to diagnose an electrical fault, first study the appropriate wiring diagram to obtain a complete understanding of the components included in the particular circuit concerned. The possible sources of a fault can be narrowed down by noting if other components related to the circuit are operating properly. If several components or circuits fail at one time, the problem is likely to be related to a shared fuse or earth connection.

3 Electrical problems usually stem from simple causes, such as loose or corroded connections, a faulty earth connection, a blown fuse, a melted fusible link, or a faulty relay. Inspect the condition of all fuses, wires and connections in a problem circuit before testing the components. Use the wiring diagrams to determine which terminal connections will need to be checked in order to pinpoint the trouble-spot.

4 The basic tools required for electrical fault finding include a circuit tester or voltmeter (a 12 volt bulb with a set of test leads can also be used for certain tests); a self-powered test light (sometimes known as a continuity tester); an ohmmeter (to measure resistance); a battery and set of test leads; and a jumper wire, preferably with a circuit breaker or fuse incorporated, which can be used to bypass suspect wires or electrical components. Before attempting to locate a problem with test instruments, use the wiring diagram to determine where to make the connections.

5 To find the source of an intermittent wiring fault (usually due to a poor or dirty connection, or damaged wiring insulation), a 'wiggle' test can be performed on the wiring. This involves wiggling the wiring by hand to see if the fault occurs as the wiring is moved. It should be possible to narrow down the source of the fault to a particular section of wiring. This method of testing can be used in conjunction with any of the tests described in the following sub-Sections.

6 Apart from problems due to poor connections, two basic types of fault can occur in an electrical circuit – open-circuit, or short-circuit.

7 Open-circuit faults are caused by a break somewhere in the circuit, which prevents current from flowing. An open-circuit fault will prevent a component from working, but will not cause the relevant circuit fuse to blow.

8 Short-circuit faults are caused by a 'short' somewhere in the circuit, which allows the current flowing in the circuit to 'escape' along an alternative route, usually to earth. Short-circuit faults are normally caused by a breakdown in wiring insulation, which allows a feed wire to touch either another wire, or an earthed component such as the bodyshell. A short-circuit fault will normally cause the relevant circuit fuse to blow.

Finding an open-circuit

9 To check for an open-circuit, connect one lead of a circuit tester or voltmeter to either the negative battery terminal or a known good earth.

10 Connect the other lead to a connector in the circuit being tested, preferably nearest to the battery or fuse.

11 Switch on the circuit, bearing in mind that some circuits are live only when the ignition switch is turned to a particular position.

12 If voltage is present (indicated either by the tester bulb lighting or a voltmeter reading, as applicable), this means that the section of the circuit between the relevant connector and the battery is problem-free.

13 Continue to check the remainder of the circuit in the same fashion.

14 When a point is reached at which no voltage is present, the problem must lie between that point and the previous test point with voltage. Most problems can be traced to a broken, corroded or loose connection.

Finding a short-circuit

15 To check for a short-circuit, first disconnect the load(s) from the circuit (loads are the components which draw current from a circuit, such as bulbs, motors, heating elements, etc).

16 Remove the relevant fuse from the circuit, and connect a circuit tester or voltmeter to the fuse connections.

17 Switch on the circuit, bearing in mind that some circuits are live only when the ignition switch is turned to a particular position.

18 If voltage is present (indicated either by the tester bulb lighting or a voltmeter reading, as applicable), this means that there is a short-circuit.

19 If no voltage is present, but the fuse still blows with the load(s) connected, this indicates an internal fault in the load(s).

Finding an earth fault

20 The battery negative terminal is connected to 'earth' – the metal of the engine/transmission unit and the car body – and most systems are wired so that they only receive a positive feed, the current returning via the metal of the car body. This means that the component mounting and the body form part of that circuit. Loose or corroded mountings can therefore cause a range of electrical faults, ranging from total failure of a circuit, to a puzzling partial fault. In particular, lights may shine dimly (especially when another circuit sharing the same earth point is in operation), motors (eg, wiper motors or the radiator cooling fan motor) may run slowly, and the operation of one circuit may have an apparently-unrelated effect on another. Note that on many vehicles, earth straps are used between certain components, such as the engine/transmission and the body, usually where there is no metal-to-metal contact between components, due to flexible rubber mountings, etc.

21 To check whether a component is properly earthed, disconnect the battery, and connect one lead of an ohmmeter to a known good earth point. Connect the other lead to the wire or earth connection being tested. The resistance reading should be zero; if not, check the connection as follows.

22 If an earth connection is thought to be faulty, dismantle the connection, and clean back to bare metal both the bodyshell and the wire terminal or the component earth connection mating surface. Be careful to remove all traces of dirt and corrosion, then use a knife to trim away any paint, so that a clean metal-to-metal joint is made. On reassembly, tighten the joint fasteners

3.2 Unclip and remove the cover for access to the engine compartment fuse/relay box

3.3 Additional fuses are located in the passenger compartment fuse/relay box located behind the glovebox

securely; if a wire terminal is being refitted, use serrated washers between the terminal and the bodyshell, to ensure a clean and secure connection. When the connection is remade, prevent the onset of corrosion in the future by applying a coat of petroleum jelly or silicone-based grease. Alternatively, at regular intervals, spray on a proprietary ignition sealer or a water-dispersant lubricant.

3 Fuses, relays and Generic Electronic Module (GEM) – general information

Fuses

1 Fuses are designed to break a circuit when a predetermined current is reached, in order to protect the components and wiring which could be damaged by excessive current flow. Any excessive current flow will be due to a fault in the circuit, usually a short-circuit (see Section 2).
2 The main fuses are located in the engine compartment fuse/relay box on the left-hand side of the engine compartment. Unclip and remove the cover for access **(see illustration)**. Refer to the information on the fuse/relay box lid and to the wiring diagrams at the end of Chapter 12 for details of the fuse locations and circuits protected.
3 Additional fuses are located in the passenger compartment fuse/relay box located behind the glovebox. Open the glovebox and press the sides inwards to release it from the facia **(see illustration)**.
4 A blown fuse can be recognised from its melted or broken wire **(see illustration)**.
5 To remove a fuse, first ensure that the relevant circuit is switched off – for maximum safety, disconnect the battery (see 'Disconnecting the battery').
6 Pull the fuse from its location, using thin-nosed pliers if necessary **(see illustration)**.
7 Before renewing a blown fuse, trace and

3.4 The fuses can be checked visually to determine if they have blown

GOOD   BLOWN

rectify the cause, and always use a fuse of the correct rating. Never substitute a fuse of a higher rating, or make temporary repairs using wire or metal foil; more serious damage, or even fire, could result.
8 If a new fuse blows immediately, find the cause before renewing it again; a short to earth as a result of faulty insulation is most likely. Where a fuse protects more than one circuit, try to isolate the defect by switching on each circuit in turn (if possible) until the fuse blows again. Always carry a supply of spare fuses of each relevant rating on the vehicle, a spare of each rating should be clipped into the base of the fuse/relay box.

Relays

9 The main relays are located in the engine compartment fuse/relay box on the left-hand side of the engine compartment, and in the passenger compartment fuse/relay box located behind the glovebox. Refer to paragraphs 2 and 3 for further information.
10 If a circuit or system controlled by a relay develops a fault, and the relay is suspect, operate the system. If the relay is functioning, it should be possible to hear it 'click' as it is energised. If this is the case, the fault lies with the components or wiring of the system.

3.6 Pull the fuse from its location, using thin-nosed pliers if necessary

If the relay is not being energised, then either the relay is not receiving a main supply or a switching voltage, or the relay itself is faulty. Testing is by the substitution of a known good unit, but be careful – while some relays are identical in appearance and in operation, others look similar but perform different functions.
11 To remove a relay, first ensure that the relevant circuit is switched off. The relay can then simply be pulled out from the socket, and pushed back into position.

Generic Electronic Module (GEM)

12 This module, which is fitted behind the facia on the passenger's side, controls many of the car's electrical functions:
a) *Direction indicators and hazard lights.*
b) *Interior lighting, including battery saver function (the interior lights and chimes are automatically shut off after a predetermined period of inactivity).*
c) *Heated windscreen and rear window.*
d) *Electric mirrors.*
e) *Wipers and washers.*
f) *Lights-on and door-ajar warnings.*
g) *Central locking.*
h) *Tailgate release.*
i) *Alarm system.*
j) *Autolamp system.*

13 Removal and refitting of the module is described in Section 12.

14 The module has a self-test facility (service mode), which can be used without specialist diagnostic equipment. Although ultimately, any problem with the GEM may have to be referred to a Ford dealer, this procedure may help in tracking down the cause of any particular problem. For instance, in the event of a fault with the wipers, if they 'pass' the GEM test, the switch and the GEM are proved okay, and the fault must lie elsewhere.

15 Before starting the test, switch off the ignition and all electrical equipment. The handbrake should be applied, the gear lever in neutral, and all doors closed.

16 To activate the service mode, press and hold the heated rear window switch (on models with a heated windscreen, the rear window switch is the lower of the two). Turn on the ignition, release the heated rear window switch, then operate the switch 8 times within 6 seconds. A signal should sound, and the indicators will flash. If the car's alarm sounds, service mode cannot be activated.

17 Except when testing the wipers, make sure the wiper switch is in the 'off' position to test the input signals listed below. Operate each item in turn, and a signal should sound, together with a flash of the indicators.

a) *Direction indicators (right, left, hazard lights).*
b) *Lights-on warning.*
c) *Windscreen wipers (intermittent).*
d) *Windscreen washers.*
e) *Rear wiper.*
f) *Rear washer.*
g) *Doors open/closed.*
h) *Central locking.*
i) *Bonnet open/closed.*
j) *Front foglight switch.*
k) *Rear foglight switch.*
l) *Heated rear window.*
m) *Heated windscreen.*

18 Now move the wiper switch to the 'intermittent' position to test the output signals listed below. Pressing the heated rear window switch activates each of the following signals, in the following order:

a) *Windscreen wipers (a signal sounds and direction indicators flash when the wiper 'park' position is reached).*

4.3 Disconnect the wiring plug and unclip the immobiliser unit

b) *Heated rear window.*
c) *Interior lights (switches must be on).*
d) *Rear wiper.*
e) *Heated windscreen (only with the engine running).*

19 The GEM will automatically end the service mode after 20 seconds. To end the service mode manually, press and hold the heated rear window switch, switch off the ignition, and release the heated rear window switch. There will be three sound signals, and the direction indicators will flash, to confirm the end of the service mode.

4 Switches – removal and refitting

1 Disconnect the battery negative terminal (refer to '*Disconnecting the battery*') before removing any switch, and reconnect the terminal after refitting.

Ignition switch/steering lock

Steering column lock cylinder

2 Remove the steering column shrouds as described in Chapter 11, Section 23.

3 Disconnect the wiring plug, then unclip and withdraw the anti-theft immobiliser transceiver unit from the ignition switch/steering lock assembly **(see illustration)**.

4 Insert the ignition key, and turn it to position I.

5 Using a small screwdriver, depress the

4.5 Depress the locking pin at the front of the lock housing, and pull out the lock cylinder using the key

locking pin at the front of the lock housing, and pull out the lock cylinder using the key **(see illustration)**.

6 To refit the lock cylinder, push the assembly into the lock housing, until the locking pin engages, then turn the ignition key to position 0 and withdraw the key.

Ignition switch

7 Caution: Do not remove the ignition switch whilst the steering column lock cylinder is removed.

8 Remove the steering column shrouds as described in Chapter 11, Section 23.

9 Use a small screwdriver to lift the locking tab on the wiring connector at the back of the switch, then disconnect it.

10 The same screwdriver can now be used to release the switch retaining tabs at the top and bottom, then the switch is withdrawn from the steering column **(see illustration)**.

11 Refitting is a reversal of removal, but make sure that the switch engages correctly.

Steering column switches

12 Remove the steering column shrouds as described in Chapter 11, Section 23.

13 Disconnect the wiring connector from the underside of the relevant switch **(see illustration)**.

14 Using a screwdriver if necessary, release the plastic catch at the top of the relevant switch, then slide the switch upwards to remove it **(see illustration)**.

15 Refitting is a reversal of removal.

4.10 Release the switch retaining tabs then withdraw the ignition switch from the steering column

4.13 Disconnect the wiring connector from the underside of the relevant switch

4.14 Release the plastic catch at the top of the relevant switch, then slide the switch upwards to remove it

4.16a Using a plastic spatula or similar tool, carefully prise off the facia end panel …

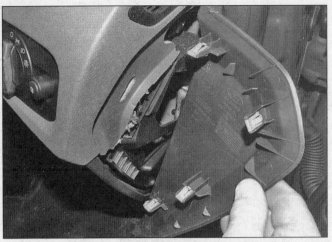

4.16b … to release the four internal clips

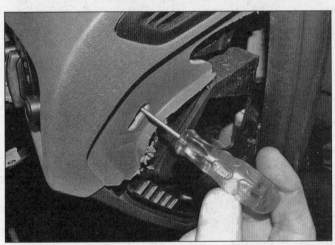

4.17a Insert a screwdriver through the slot in the side of the facia …

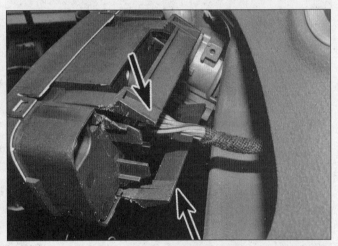

4.17b … and push the light switch retaining bars (arrowed) to release the switch

Exterior light switch

16 Using a plastic spatula or similar tool, carefully prise off the facia end panel on the driver's side to release the four internal clips **(see illustrations)**.

17 Insert a screwdriver through the slot in the side of the facia and push down the light switch upper retaining bar. Pull the switch out slightly at the top to stop the retaining bar re-engaging, then push up on the lower retaining bar **(see illustrations)**.

18 Withdraw the light switch from the facia, disconnect the wiring connector and remove the switch **(see illustration)**.

19 Refitting is a reversal of removal.

Facia centre switch/vent panel

20 Using a plastic spatula or similar tool, carefully prise up and remove the multifunction display trim panel in the centre of the facia **(see illustration)**.

21 Undo the two screws securing the upper centre switch/vent panel to the facia **(see illustration)**.

4.18 Withdraw the light switch from the facia and disconnect the wiring connector

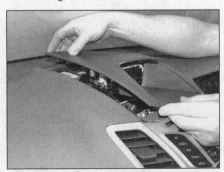

4.20 Carefully prise up and remove the multifunction display trim panel

4.21 Undo the two screws (arrowed) securing the upper centre switch/vent panel to the facia

4.22a Carefully prise free the top of the blanking plate ...

4.22b ... then disengage the two lower pegs and remove the blanking plate

4.23a Pull the upper centre switch/vent panel away from the facia to release the lower clips ...

4.23b ... then disconnect the wiring connector and remove the panel

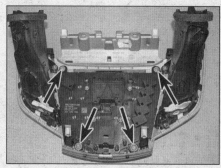

4.24 The switch pack can be removed from the panel by undoing the four screws (arrowed)

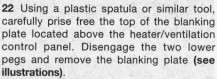

22 Using a plastic spatula or similar tool, carefully prise free the top of the blanking plate located above the heater/ventilation control panel. Disengage the two lower pegs and remove the blanking plate (see illustrations).

23 Pull the upper centre switch/vent panel away from the facia to release the lower retaining clips, then disconnect the wiring connector and remove the panel (see illustrations).

24 If required, the switch pack can be removed from the panel by undoing the four screws at the rear (see illustration).

25 Refitting is a reversal of removal.

Heated rear window and windscreen switches

26 The switches are part of the heater control panel, which is removed as described in Chapter 3 Section 9.

Air conditioning and recirculation switches

27 The switches are part of the heater control panel, which is removed as described in Chapter 3 Section 9.

Electric window switches

28 Using a plastic spatula or similar instrument, carefully prise up the electric window switch panel from the door inner trim panel and disconnect the wiring connectors (see illustrations).

29 Refitting is a reversal of removal.

4.28a Carefully prise up the electric window switch panel ...

4.28b ... and disconnect the wiring connectors

Electric mirror switch

30 Using a small screwdriver, carefully prise free the electric mirror control switch from the door trim panel. Disconnect the wiring connector and remove the switch (see illustrations).

31 Refitting is a reversal of removal.

Steering wheel switches

32 Remove the driver's airbag as described in Section 23.

33 Turn the steering wheel as necessary for

4.30a Carefully prise free the electric mirror control switch ...

4.30b ... and disconnect the wiring connector

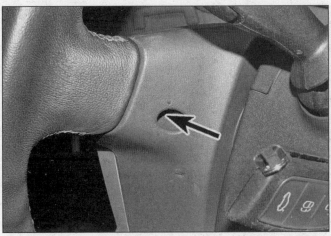

4.33a Undo the screw (arrowed) on each side of the steering wheel horizontal spoke ...

4.33b ... and at the base of the vertical spoke

access, then undo the three screws securing the switch panel to the steering wheel **(see illustrations)**.

34 Disconnect the steering wheel switch wiring connectors, then undo the earth lead retaining screw. Lift the switch panel off the steering wheel **(see illustrations)**.

35 Disconnect the wiring connector from the relevant switch module, then undo the three screws and remove the relevant module from the switch panel **(see illustrations)**.

36 Refitting is a reversal of removal.

Handbrake-on warning switch

37 Remove the centre console as described in Chapter 11, Section 24.

38 Disconnect the wiring connector, then undo the retaining bolt and remove the switch from the side of the handbrake lever **(see illustration)**.

39 Refitting is a reversal of removal.

Brake light switch

40 Refer to Chapter 9, Section 17.

Brake pedal position switch

41 Refer to Chapter 9, Section 17.

Clutch pedal position switch

42 Refer to Chapter 4A, Section 11.

5	Bulbs (exterior lights) – renewal	

1 Whenever a bulb is renewed, note the following points:

a) *Make sure the switch is in the OFF position, for the bulb you are working on.*

4.34a Disconnect the steering wheel switch wiring connectors, then undo the earth lead retaining screw (arrowed)

4.34b Lift the switch panel off the steering wheel

4.35a Disconnect the wiring connector from the relevant switch module ...

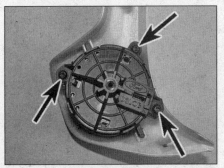

4.35b ... then undo the three screws (arrowed) ...

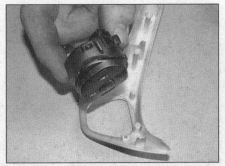

4.35c ... and remove the relevant module from the switch panel

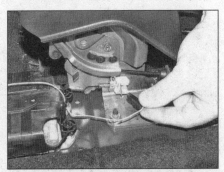

4.38 Disconnect the wiring connector, then undo the bolt and remove the handbrake-on warning switch

b) Remember that if the light has just been in use, the bulb may be extremely hot.
c) Always check the bulb contacts and holder, ensuring that there is clean metal-to-metal contact between the bulb and its live(s) and earth. Clean off any corrosion or dirt before fitting a new bulb.
d) Wherever bayonet-type bulbs are fitted, ensure that the live contact(s) bear firmly against the bulb contact.
e) Always ensure that the new bulb is of the correct rating, and that it is completely clean before fitting it; this applies particularly to headlight/foglight bulbs.

Headlight

2 Remove the relevant headlight as described in Section 7.

Dipped beam bulb

3 Remove the cover from the rear of the headlight unit **(see illustration)**.
4 Turn the bulbholder anti-clockwise and release it from the light unit **(see illustration)**.
5 Insert a screwdriver between the bulb base and bulbholder and prise them apart, then withdraw the bulb from the bulbholder **(see illustrations)**.
6 When handling the new bulb, use a tissue or clean cloth, to avoid touching the glass with the fingers; moisture and grease from the skin can cause blackening and rapid failure of this type of bulb. If the glass is accidentally touched, wipe it clean using methylated spirit.
7 Install the new bulb into the bulbholder, ensuring it is fully seated.

5.3 Remove the cover from the rear of the headlight unit

8 Refit the bulbholder and turn it clockwise to lock it in position, then refit the cover to the rear of the light unit.
9 Refit the headlight as described in Section 7.

Main beam bulb

10 Remove the cover from the rear of the headlight unit **(see illustration)**.
11 Release the bulb's wire retaining clip by unhooking it at the top, then pivot the clip down. Withdraw the bulb **(see illustrations)**.
12 Pull the wiring plug from the rear of the bulb **(see illustration)**.
13 When handling the new bulb, use a tissue or clean cloth, to avoid touching the glass with the fingers; moisture and grease from the skin can cause blackening and rapid failure of this type of bulb. If the glass is accidentally

5.4 Turn the dipped beam bulbholder anti-clockwise and release it from the light unit

touched, wipe it clean using methylated spirit.
14 Reconnect the wiring plug to the new bulb, then install the bulb, ensuring that its locating tabs are correctly seated in the light cut-outs. Secure the bulb in position with the spring clip.
15 Refit the cover to the rear of the light unit.
16 Refit the headlight as described in Section 7.

Front sidelight

17 Remove the headlight as described in Section 7.
18 Remove the cover from the rear of the headlight unit **(see illustration 5.10)**.
19 Using a small screwdriver, prise free the

5.5a Insert a screwdriver between the bulb base and bulbholder and prise them apart ...

5.5b ... then withdraw the bulb from the bulbholder

5.10 Remove the cover from the rear of the headlight unit

5.11a Release the main beam bulb's wire retaining clip ...

5.11b ... then withdraw the bulb

5.12 Pull the wiring plug from the rear of the bulb

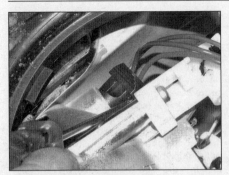

5.19 Using a small screwdriver, prise free the sidelight bulbholder from the light unit

5.20 Pull out the capless bulb from the holder

5.24 Twist the direction indicator bulbholder anti-clockwise and withdraw it from the headlight

sidelight bulbholder from the light unit **(see illustration)**.

20 Pull out the capless bulb from the holder, and fit a new one firmly into place **(see illustration)**.

21 Refit the bulbholder and rear cover, then refit the headlight as described in Section 7.

Front direction indicator light

22 Remove the headlight as described in Section 7.

23 Remove the cover from the rear of the headlight unit **(see illustration 5.10)**.

24 Using the raised rib on the back of the indicator bulbholder, twist the holder anti-clockwise and withdraw it from the headlight **(see illustration)**.

25 Depress and twist the bulb anti-clockwise to remove it **(see illustration)**.

26 Fit the new bulb, then twist the bulbholder clockwise into the back of the headlight – the raised rib should be vertical when the bulbholder is fully located.

27 Refit the headlight as described in Section 7.

Front foglight

28 Firmly apply the handbrake, then jack up the front of the vehicle and support it securely on axle stands (see *'Jacking and vehicle support'*).

29 Remove the front bumper as described in Chapter 11, Section 6.

30 Twist the bulb anti-clockwise to remove it from the back of the light unit **(see illustration)**.

31 The H11 bulb is unusual in having its wiring socket integrated with it – for this reason, this type of bulb may only be readily obtainable from Ford dealers.

32 When handling the new bulb, use a tissue or clean cloth, to avoid touching the glass with the fingers; moisture and grease from the skin can cause blackening and rapid failure of this type of bulb. If the glass is accidentally touched, wipe it clean using methylated spirit.

33 Fit the new bulb, twisting it clockwise into the back of the light unit to secure. Refit the front bumper as described in Chapter 11, Section 6.

Indicator side repeater light

34 Press in the sides of the exterior mirror cover to release the internal clips and withdraw the cover from the mirror body **(see illustration)**.

35 Pull the bulbholder from the mirror lens **(see illustration)**.

36 Pull out the capless bulb, and press a new one into place **(see illustration)**.

37 Refit the bulbholder then clip the mirror cover back into position.

Rear lights

38 Open the tailgate, and remove the two cross-head screws in the tailgate aperture securing the light unit **(see illustration)**.

39 Carefully prise the rubber seal from the

5.25 Depress and twist the bulb anti-clockwise to remove it

5.30 Twist the foglight bulb anti-clockwise to remove it from the light unit

5.34 Press in the sides of the cover to release the clips and withdraw the cover from the mirror body

5.35 Pull the bulbholder from the mirror lens

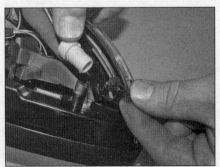

5.36 Pull out the capless bulb from the bulbholder

5.38 Remove the two rear light unit retaining screws (arrowed)

5.40 Pull away the loadspace trim for access to the rear of the light unit

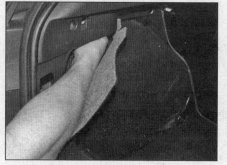

5.41a Reach in behind the light unit ...

5.41b ... and unscrew the plastic wing nut securing the light unit to the body

edge of the tailgate aperture in the vicinity of the light unit.

40 Pull away the loadspace trim for access to the rear of the light unit **(see illustration)**.

41 Reach in behind the light unit and unscrew the plastic wing nut securing the light unit to the body **(see illustrations)**.

42 Withdraw the light unit from the rear wing, disconnect the wiring connector and remove the light unit **(see illustration)**.

43 Squeeze together the two tabs on the bulbholder and withdraw the bulbholder from the light unit **(see illustration)**.

44 Any of the bayonet-fitting bulbs can now be removed by pressing and turning them anti-clockwise **(see illustration)**. The capless reversing light bulb can be simply pulled from its location and a new bulb pressed in.

45 Fit the new bulb(s), then clip the bulbholder back onto the light unit, making sure that the clips engage securely.

46 Reconnect the wiring connector then offer the light unit back into place, engaging the two pegs on the rear with the holes in the car. Refit the wingnut and tighten it securely.

47 Fit the loadspace trim back into position then re-engage the rubber seal in the tailgate aperture.

48 Refit the two outer screws and tighten them securely.

Number plate light

49 To make access easier, open the tailgate and hold it approximately half-open.

50 Insert a small screwdriver into the slot on the side of the light unit and carefully prise the light unit from the tailgate **(see illustration)**.

51 Remove the bulbholder from the light unit **(see illustration)**.

52 Pull out the capless bulb, and press a new one into place **(see illustration)**.

53 Refitting is a reversal of removal.

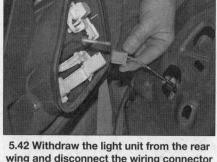

5.42 Withdraw the light unit from the rear wing and disconnect the wiring connector

5.43 Squeeze together the two tabs and withdraw the bulbholder from the light unit

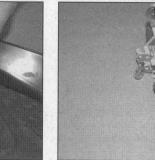

5.44 Remove the bayonet-fitting bulbs by pressing and turning them anti-clockwise

5.50 Insert a small screwdriver into the slot and carefully prise the number plate light unit from the tailgate

5.51 Remove the bulbholder from the light unit

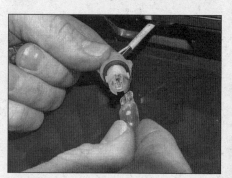

5.52 Pull out the capless bulb from the bulbholder

5.56 Remove the two plastic rivets (arrowed) securing the wheel arch liner to the bumper

5.57 Reach in under the wheel arch and remove the rear foglight bulbholder

5.58 Remove the bulb by pressing and turning anti-clockwise

High-level brake light

54 The high-level brake light bulbs are of the LED (light emitting diode) type and cannot be individually renewed. Remove the complete light unit as described in Section 7.

Rear foglight

55 On models with rear mudflaps, remove them by extracting the three retaining clips, then removing the two plastic rivets by prising up the centre section and withdrawing the rivet body.

56 On models without mudflaps, remove the two plastic rivets securing the wheel arch liner to the bumper by prising up the centre section and withdrawing the rivet body **(see illustration)**.

57 Reach in under the right-hand wheel arch and remove the rear foglight bulb holder from the light unit **(see illustration)**. The bulbholder is retained by plastic tabs around its periphery.

58 Remove the bulb by pressing and turning anti-clockwise **(see illustration)**.

59 Refitting is a reversal of removal.

6 Bulbs (interior lights) – renewal

General

1 Refer to Section 5, paragraph 1.

Interior and map reading lights

2 Insert a small screwdriver into the slot in the front face of the light unit. Depress the clip and carefully prise the light unit from its location **(see illustrations)**.

3 Turn the relevant bulbholder anti-clockwise and remove it from the light unit.

4 Pull out the capless bulb, and press a new one into place.

5 Refitting is a reversal of removal.

Luggage compartment light

6 Carefully prise the light unit out from the trim panel **(see illustration)**.

7 Pull out the capless bulb from the bulbholder **(see illustration)**.

8 Fit the new bulb using a reversal of the removal procedure.

Instrument panel illumination

9 It is not possible to renew the instrument panel bulbs individually as they are of LED

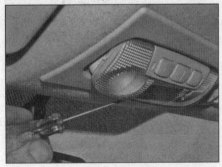

6.2a Using a small screwdriver, depress the clip ...

design and soldered to a printed circuit board. Where an LED is not functioning, the complete instrument panel must be renewed.

Switch illumination

10 The switches are illuminated by LEDs, and cannot be renewed separately. Refer to Section 4 and remove the relevant switch.

Heater control unit illumination

11 The control panel is illuminated by non-renewable LEDs. If defective, the control panel may need to be renewed.

Footwell illumination

12 Release the bulbholder from its location under the facia **(see illustration)**.

13 Pull out the bulb from the bulbholder.

14 Fit the new bulb using a reversal of the removal procedure.

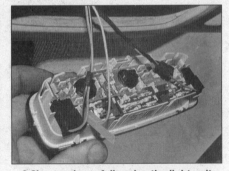

6.2b ... and carefully prise the light unit from its location

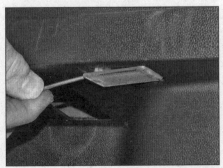

6.6 Carefully prise the light unit out from the trim panel

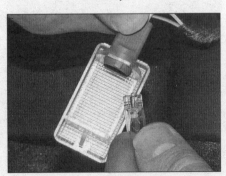

6.7 Pull out the capless bulb from the bulbholder

6.12 Release the footwell illumination bulbholder from its location under the facia

7.1a Remove the plastic rivets by prising up the centre section ...

7.1b ... and withdrawing the rivet body

7.2a Undo the headlight upper retaining screw ...

7.2b ... and lower retaining screw

7.3 Disconnect the wiring connector at the rear of the headlight

7 Exterior light units – removal and refitting

Headlight

1 Open the bonnet and remove the plastic rivets securing the front bumper upper edge by prising up the centre section and withdrawing the rivet body **(see illustrations)**.
2 Undo the headlight upper and lower retaining screws **(see illustrations)**.
3 Disconnect the wiring connector at the rear of the headlight **(see illustration)**.
4 Lift the headlight up to release the lower mounting lug and remove the headlight from the car **(see illustrations)**.
5 Refitting is a reversal of removal.

Front foglight

6 Remove the front bumper as described in Chapter 11, Section 6.
7 Undo the two screws and remove the light unit from the rear of the bumper **(see illustration)**.
8 Refitting is a reversal of removal.

Rear foglight

9 Remove the rear bumper as described in Chapter 11, Section 6.
10 Undo the two screws and remove the light unit from the rear of the bumper **(see illustrations)**.
11 Refitting is a reversal of removal.

7.4a Lift the headlight up ...

7.4b ... to release the lower mounting lug (arrowed) and remove the headlight

7.7 Undo the two screws (arrowed) and remove the front foglight from the bumper

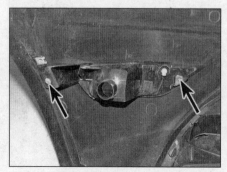

7.10a Undo the two screws (arrowed) ...

7.10b ... and remove the rear foglight from the bumper

7.15 Undo the two screws (arrowed) and withdraw the high-level brake light from the tailgate

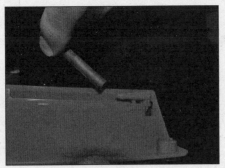

7.16 Pull off the washer hose

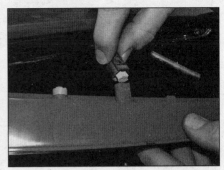

7.17 Disconnect the wiring connector and remove the light unit

Indicator side repeater light

12 The procedure is described as part of the bulb renewal procedure in Section 5.

Rear lights

13 The procedure is described as part of the bulb renewal procedure in Section 5.

Rear number plate light

14 The procedure is described as part of the bulb renewal procedure in Section 5.

High-level brake light

15 Undo the two screws securing the light unit to the tailgate and withdraw the unit from its location (see illustration).
16 Pull off the washer hose, and tape the end of the hose up to the tailgate, end upwards, to reduce fluid spillage (see illustration).
17 Disconnect the wiring connector and remove the light unit from the car (see illustration).
18 Refitting is a reversal of removal.

8 Headlight adjuster components – removal and refitting

Adjuster switch

1 Refer to Section 4, paragraphs 14 to 17.

Adjuster motor

2 The motor is integral with the headlight, and is not available separately. The headlight is removed as described in Section 7.

9 Headlight beam alignment – general information

1 All models are equipped with an electrical vertical beam adjuster unit – this can be used to adjust the headlight beam, to compensate for the relevant load which the car is carrying. An adjuster switch is provided on the facia. Refer to the car's handbook for further information.
2 Accurate adjustment of the headlight beam is only possible using optical beam-setting

equipment, and this work should therefore be carried out by a Ford dealer or suitably-equipped workshop.
3 For reference, the headlights can be finely adjusted by rotating the adjuster screws fitted to the top of each light unit.

10 Instrument panel – removal and refitting

Note: If a new instrument panel is to be fitted, the configuration information stored within the unit must be uploaded to Ford diagnostic equipment prior to removal, and downloaded to the new unit once installed. Entrust this task to a Ford dealer or suitably-equipped specialist.

10.2 Use a small piece of adhesive tape to pull off the circular trim button

10.4 Undo the two screws (arrowed) at the base of the instrument panel, then withdraw it from the facia

Removal

1 Disconnect the battery negative terminal (refer to 'Disconnecting the battery').
2 Remove the circular trim button from the upper centre of the instrument panel. The best way to do this is to stick a small piece of adhesive tape to the trim button and pull on the tape to remove the button (see illustration).
3 With the trim button removed, undo the panel retaining screw now exposed (see illustration).
4 Remove the two screws at the base of the instrument panel, then withdraw it from the facia (see illustration).
5 Release the hinged locking catch on the single wiring plug at the rear, disconnect the plug, and remove the instrument panel (see illustration).

Refitting

6 Refitting is a reversal of removal.

10.3 Undo the instrument panel upper retaining screw now exposed

10.5 Release the hinged locking catch and disconnect the wiring plug

11.2 Undo the two screws securing multifunction display to the top of the facia

11.3a Withdraw the unit from the facia ...

11.3b ... and disconnect the wiring connector

11 Multifunction display – removal and refitting

Removal

1 Using a plastic spatula or similar tool, carefully prise up and remove the multifunction display trim panel in the centre of the facia (**see illustration 4.20**).
2 Undo the two screws securing multifunction display to the top of the facia (**see illustration**).
3 Withdraw the unit from the facia, disconnect the wiring connector and remove the unit from the car (**see illustrations**).

Refitting

4 Refitting is a reversal of removal.

12 Generic Electronic Module (GEM) – removal and refitting

Note: *If a new module is to be fitted, the configuration information stored within the unit must be uploaded to Ford diagnostic equipment prior to removal, and downloaded to the new unit once installed. Entrust this task to a Ford dealer or suitably-equipped specialist.*

Removal

1 Disconnect the battery negative terminal (refer to *'Disconnecting the battery'*).
2 The generic electronic module is located behind the facia on the passenger's side (**see illustration**). To gain access, remove the passenger's lower facia trim panel as described in Chapter 11, Section 23.

3 Lift up the locking bars, where necessary, and disconnect the wiring harness connectors from the front of the GEM.
4 Undo the two nuts securing the GEM mounting bracket to the floor, then remove the GEM and mounting bracket from the car.
5 Release the two tabs on the rear of the unit and separate the GEM from the mounting bracket.

Refitting

6 Refitting is a reversal of removal.

13 Horn – removal and refitting

Removal

1 The horn is located under the front bumper on the right-hand side.
2 Remove the front bumper as described in Chapter 11, Section 6.
3 Disconnect the wiring plug from the horn.
4 Unscrew the securing nut, and remove the horn from its mounting bracket (**see illustration**).

Refitting

5 Refitting is a reversal of removal.

14 Wiper arm – removal and refitting

Removal

1 Operate the wiper motor, then switch it off so that the wiper arm returns to the park position.
2 Before removing an arm, mark its parked position on the glass with a strip of adhesive tape.
3 Prise up the wiper arm spindle nut cover, then slacken and remove the spindle nut (**see illustration**). Recover the washer.
4 Lift the blade off the glass, and pull the wiper arm off its spindle. Note that on some models, the wiper arms may be very tight on the spindle splines – it should be possible to lever the arm off the spindle, using a flat-bladed screwdriver (take care not to damage the windscreen cowl panel). In extreme cases, it may even be necessary to use a small puller to free the arm (**see illustration**).

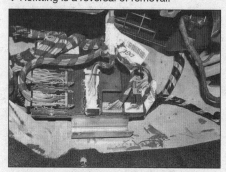

12.2 The generic electronic module is located behind the facia on the passenger's side

13.4 Unscrew the securing nut (arrowed) and remove the horn from its mounting bracket

14.3 Prise up the wiper arm spindle nut cover, then remove the spindle nut

14.4 Using a small puller to free the wiper arm from the spindle

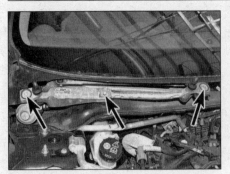

15.2 Undo the three bolts (arrowed) securing the wiper motor and linkage assembly to the scuttle

15.3 Withdraw the motor and linkage assembly from its location

15.4a Extract the two wiring harness support clips from the linkage frame …

Refitting

5 Ensure that the wiper arm and spindle splines are clean and dry, then refit the arm to the spindle. Align the wiper blade with the tape fitted on removal.
6 Refit the spindle nut, tightening it securely, and clip the nut cover back into position.

15 Windscreen wiper motor and linkage – removal and refitting

Removal

1 Remove the windscreen cowl panel and bulkhead closure panel as described in Chapter 11, Section 20.
2 Undo the three bolts securing the wiper motor and linkage assembly to the scuttle **(see illustration)**.
3 Withdraw the motor and linkage assembly from its location, disengage the locating grommet as the assembly is withdrawn **(see illustration)**.
4 Extract the two wiring harness support clips from the linkage frame, then disconnect the wiring connector from the motor **(see illustrations)**. Remove the assembly from the car.
5 Note the fitted position of the wiper motor arm (typically, it will be horizontally aligned,

15.4b … then disconnect the wiring connector from the motor

along the axis of the linkage frame). Undo the motor arm retaining nut and lift off the arm, then unscrew the three bolts and remove the motor from the frame **(see illustration)**.

Refitting

6 Refitting is a reversal of removal, bearing in mind the following points:
a) Ensure that the motor is in the 'parked' position before refitting.
b) Set the motor arm to the position noted prior to removal, then refit the arm and tighten the retaining nut securely.
c) Refit the bulkhead closure panel and

15.5 Unscrew the motor arm retaining nut and the motor retaining bolts (arrowed)

windscreen cowl panel as described in Chapter 11, Section 20.

16 Tailgate wiper motor – removal and refitting

Removal

1 Remove the tailgate trim panel as described in Chapter 11, Section 23.
2 Remove the wiper arm as described in Section 14 **(see illustrations)**.
3 Disconnect the wiper motor wiring plug **(see illustration)**.

16.2a Unscrew the retaining nut …

16.2b … and remove the wiper arm

16.3 Disconnect the wiper motor wiring plug

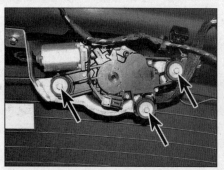

16.4 Remove the three motor mounting bolts (arrowed)

4 Remove the three motor mounting bolts, recover the washers, and withdraw the motor from the tailgate (see illustration).

Refitting

5 Refitting is a reversal of removal. Ensure that the wiper motor spindle grommet stays in place in the tailgate as the spindle is fitted back through.

17 Windscreen/tailgate washer system components – removal and refitting

Washer fluid reservoir

Removal

1 The windscreen washer fluid reservoir is located behind the front bumper on the left-

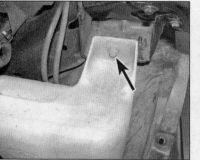

17.4a Undo the reservoir upper retaining bolt (arrowed) ...

17.14 Pull the T-piece hose connector off the end of the washer jet

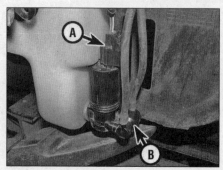

17.3 Disconnect the wiring plug (A) and the washer hoses (B) from the washer pump

hand side.
2 Remove the front bumper as described in Chapter 11, Section 6.
3 Disconnect the wiring plug and the washer hoses from the washer pump (see illustration). Anticipate some spillage of washer fluid (have a suitable container ready).
4 Undo the two reservoir retaining bolts, disengage the locating peg and remove the reservoir from the car (see illustrations).

Refitting

5 Refitting is a reversal of removal. Make sure the washer hoses are securely reconnected to their original positions.

Washer fluid pump

Removal

6 If possible, siphon the fluid from the reservoir into a suitable container using a long

17.4b ... and lower retaining bolt (arrowed)

17.15a Depress the tab (arrowed) at the top of the jet body ...

tube inserted through the filler neck.
7 Refer to the previous sub-Section and carry out the relevant work to gain access to the fluid reservoir.
8 Prise the pump from the reservoir, and recover the rubber sealing grommet. If all the fluid was not removed, position a container beneath the reservoir.

Refitting

9 Examine the rubber sealing grommet, and renew if necessary.
10 Refitting is a reversal of removal, but take care not to push the grommet into the reservoir when refitting the pump. Make sure that the pump is securely fitted in its sealing grommet, and make sure that the fluid hose(s) are securely reconnected.

Windscreen washer jet

Removal

11 Open the bonnet, and support it on its stay.
12 Using a marker pen or paint, mark around the hinge positions on the bonnet.
13 Prise out the plastic studs and remove the sound deadening pad from inside the bonnet (see illustration).
14 Pull the T-piece hose connector off the end of the washer jet (see illustration).
15 Depress the tab at the top of the jet body, then remove the jet from the outside of the bonnet (see illustrations).

Refitting

16 Refitting is a reversal of removal.

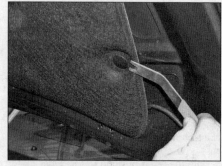

17.13 Prise out the plastic studs and remove the sound deadening pad from inside the bonnet

17.15b ... then remove the jet from the outside of the bonnet

Tailgate washer jet

17 The washer jet is an integral part of the high-level brake light and cannot be individually removed. Removal of the high-level brake light is described in Section 7.

18 Radio/CD player – removal and refitting

Note: *If a Ford 'Keycode' unit is fitted, and the battery is disconnected, the unit will not function again on reconnection until the correct security code is entered.*

Removal

1 Remove the facia upper centre switch/vent panel as described in Section 4.
2 Lift the radio/CD player from its location in the facia for access to the rear wiring and aerial **(see illustration)**.
3 Disconnect the wiring connectors and aerial lead then remove the unit from the car **(see illustration)**.

Refitting

4 Refitting is a reversal of removal.

19 Loudspeakers – removal and refitting

Removal

1 Remove the relevant door inner trim panel (or rear side trim panel), as described in Chapter 11. Removal of the small treble speaker is contained in the trim panel removal procedure.
2 Unscrew the three main loudspeaker securing screws, then withdraw the loudspeaker and disconnect the wiring plug **(see illustration)**.

Refitting

3 Refitting is a reversal of removal.

20 Radio aerial – removal and refitting

Removal

1 If only the aerial mast is to be removed, this can be unscrewed from the aerial base. To remove the base, proceed as follows.
2 Remove the interior light as described in Section 6.
3 Working through the interior light aperture, unscrew the bolt, and disconnect the aerial cable **(see illustration)**. Remove the aerial from the roof, and recover the sealing grommet.

Refitting

4 Refitting is a reversal of removal.

18.2 Lift the radio/CD player from its location in the facia

18.3 Disconnect the wiring connectors and aerial lead at the rear

21 Anti-theft alarm system and engine immobiliser – general information

1 Certain models are equipped with an anti-theft alarm system, in addition to the engine immobiliser fitted to all models. Various types of system may be fitted, depending on specification and market.
2 The anti-theft alarm system is automatically activated by the central locking system (manually, or via the remote control, where applicable). The engine immobiliser system is operated by a coded unit in the ignition key – the engine can only be started using one of the ignition keys originally supplied with the car when new.
3 The alarm system uses the courtesy light switches built into the door lock assemblies.
4 Any faults with the system should be referred to a Ford dealer.

Immobiliser system

5 An engine immobiliser system is fitted as standard to all models, and the system is operated automatically every time the ignition key is inserted/removed.
6 The immobiliser system ensures that the car can only be started using the original Ford ignition key. The key contains an electronic chip (transponder) which is programmed with a code. When the key is inserted into the ignition switch, it uses the current present in the sensor coil (which is fitted to the switch housing) to send a signal to the Generic Electronic Module (GEM). The GEM checks

this code every time the ignition is switched on. If the key code does not match the GEM code, the GEM will disable the starter circuit to prevent the engine being started.
7 If the ignition key is lost, a new one can be obtained from a Ford dealer. They have access to the correct key code for the immobiliser system of your car, and will be able to supply a new coded key.
8 If you have any spare keys cut, if they are not coded correctly, they will only open the doors, etc, and will not be capable of starting the engine. For this reason, it may be best to have any spare keys supplied by your Ford dealer, who will also be able to advise you on coding the keys. The key coding procedure for new keys is given in the car's handbook.

22 Airbag system – general information, precautions and system de-activation

General information

1 Driver's and front seat passenger's airbags are fitted as standard equipment on all models. The driver's airbag is fitted to the steering wheel centre pad, while the passenger's unit is fitted to the top of the facia.
2 Models equipped with higher specification equipment packages also have side airbags, which fire from modules built into the front seats, side curtain airbags, which are deployed from modules in the headlining and a driver's knee airbag deployed from a module under the facia.

19.2 Loudspeaker securing screws (arrowed)

20.3 Unscrew the aerial base retaining bolt and disconnect the aerial cable

3 The system is armed only when the ignition is switched on, however, a reserve power source maintains a power supply to the system in the event of a break in the main electrical supply. The system is activated by a 'g' sensor (deceleration sensor), incorporated in the electronic control unit. Note that the electronic control unit also controls the front seat belt tensioners, fitted to all models.

4 The airbags are inflated by gas generators, which force the bags out from their locations. Although these are safety items, their deployment is violently rapid, and this may cause injury if they are triggered unintentionally.

Precautions

⚠️ *Warning: The following precautions must be observed when working on vehicles equipped with an airbag system, to prevent the possibility of personal injury.*

General precautions

5 The following precautions must be observed when carrying out work on a vehicle equipped with an airbag:

a) *Do not disconnect the battery with the engine running.*

b) *Before carrying out any work in the vicinity of the airbag, removal of any of the airbag components, or any welding work on the*

car, de-activate the system as described in the following sub-Section.

c) *Do not attempt to test any of the airbag system circuits using test meters or any other test equipment.*

d) *If the airbag warning light comes on, or any fault in the system is suspected, consult a Ford dealer without delay. Do not attempt to carry out fault diagnosis, or any dismantling of the components.*

Precautions when handling an airbag

a) *Transport the airbag by itself, bag upward.*

b) *Do not put your arms around the airbag.*

c) *Carry the airbag close to the body.*

d) *Do not drop the airbag or expose it to impacts.*

e) *Do not attempt to dismantle the airbag unit.*

f) *Do not connect any form of electrical equipment to any part of the airbag circuit.*

Precautions when storing an airbag

a) *Store the unit in a cupboard with the airbag upward.*

b) *Do not expose the airbag to temperatures above 80°C.*

c) *Do not expose the airbag to flames.*

d) *Do not attempt to dispose of the airbag – consult a Ford dealer.*

e) *Never refit an airbag which is known to be faulty or damaged.*

De-activation of airbag system

6 The system must be de-activated as follows, before carrying out any work on the airbag components or surrounding area.

a) *Switch off the ignition.*

b) *Remove the ignition key.*

c) *Switch off all electrical equipment.*

d) *Disconnect the battery negative lead (see 'Disconnecting the battery' in the Reference Chapter).*

e) *Insulate the battery negative terminal and the end of the battery negative lead to prevent any possibility of contact.*

f) *Wait for at least three minutes before carrying out any further work.*

23 Airbag system components – removal and refitting

⚠️ *Warning: Refer to the precautions given in Section 22 before attempting to carry out work on the airbag components.*

Driver's airbag unit

Removal

1 De-activate the airbag system as described in Section 22. The airbag unit is an integral part of the steering wheel centre pad.

2 Locate the two airbag retaining wire spring access points on the back of the steering wheel. These will be visible as a slight mark or indentation in the steering wheel hub **(see illustration)**.

3 Using a sharp knife, make a slit at the access point on each side, then enlarge the slit using a 3 mm diameter punch **(see illustrations)**.

4 Using a 3 mm diameter screwdriver inserted through the hole now created, engage the end of the screwdriver with the airbag retaining wire spring. Push up on the wire spring while at the same time pulling the airbag module to release it from the steering wheel **(see illustration)**. Once the airbag is released on

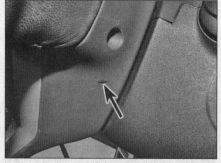

23.2 Airbag retaining wire spring access point (arrowed) on the back of the steering wheel

23.3a Using a sharp knife, make a slit at the access point on each side …

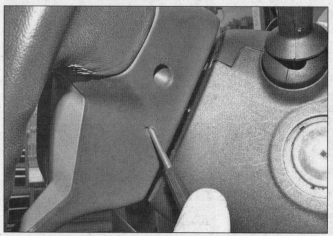

23.3b … then enlarge the slit using a 3 mm diameter punch

23.4 Engage the end of a screwdriver with the airbag retaining wire spring (shown with airbag released)

23.5a Disconnect the airbag wiring plug …

23.5b … and the two earth leads

one side, repeat the procedure on the other side.

5 Once the airbag retaining wire springs have been released, withdraw the airbag from the steering wheel and disconnect the main wiring plug and the two earth leads **(see illustrations)**. Remove the airbag and store it in a safe place, with reference to the precautions in Section 22.

Refitting

6 Refitting is a reversal of removal, noting the following points:

a) *The battery must still be disconnected when reconnecting the airbag wiring.*
b) *Ensure that the airbag wiring plug is securely reconnected.*
c) *The airbag must be firmly pressed into place to secure the retaining wire spring.*

Passenger's airbag unit

Removal

7 De-activate the airbag system as described in Section 22.
8 Remove the glovebox as described in Chapter 11, Section 23.
9 Disconnect the airbag wiring connector,

then undo the two nuts securing the airbag support bracket to the facia crossmember **(see illustration)**.
10 Undo the remaining retaining nuts securing the airbag to the facia and remove the unit from below.

Refitting

11 Refitting is a reversal of removal, bearing in mind the following points:

a) *The battery must still be disconnected when reconnecting the airbag wiring.*
b) *Make sure that the wiring connector is securely reconnected.*
c) *Tighten the mounting bolts securely.*

Driver's knee airbag unit

12 De-activate the airbag system as described in Section 22.
13 Remove the driver's lower facia trim panel as described in Chapter 11, Section 23. The knee airbag is an integral part of the lower facia trim panel and cannot be individually removed.

Airbag control unit

Removal

14 De-activate the airbag system as described in Section 22.

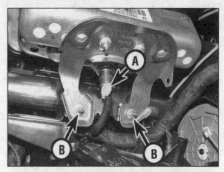

23.9 Passenger's airbag wiring connector (A) and airbag support bracket retaining nuts (B)

15 Remove the centre console as described in Chapter 11, Section 24.
16 Free the handbrake warning switch wiring from the clips on the plastic cover over the airbag control unit.
17 Lift off the cover over the airbag control unit and disconnect the three airbag wiring connectors **(see illustrations)**.
18 Undo the three retaining nuts and remove the control unit from the car.

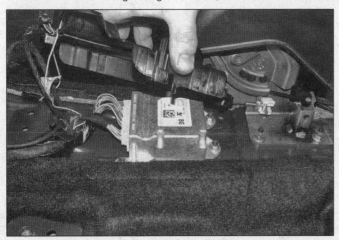

23.17a Lift off the cover over the airbag control unit …

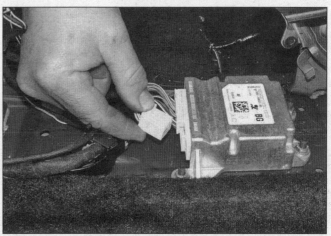

23.17b … and disconnect the three airbag wiring connectors

Refitting

19 Refitting is a reversal of removal.

Airbag clockspring (rotary connector)

Removal

20 De-activate the airbag system as described in Section 22.

21 Remove the steering wheel as described in Chapter 10 Section 14.

22 Remove the steering column shrouds as described in Chapter 11, Section 23.

23 Disconnect the wiring connector from the base of the clockspring **(see illustration)**.

24 Using a small screwdriver, lift the three locating tabs and withdraw the unit from the steering column.

Refitting

25 Refitting is a reversal of removal.

26 Before refitting the steering column shrouds, the clockspring unit should be centralised (unless it is known absolutely that the steering wheel was centralised before removal, and that the clockspring has not been turned during or since its removal).

27 The procedure for centralising should be written on the clockspring itself. If this procedure conflicts significantly with what appears below, consult a Ford dealer for the latest information.

28 First, turn the clockspring anti-clockwise gently, until resistance is felt. Now turn the clockspring about two and a half turns clockwise, until the arrow marking on the front face aligns with the raised V marking on the clockspring's outer cover.

29 Refit the steering column shrouds and steering wheel as described in Chapters 11 and 10.

Side airbags

30 The side airbags are located internally within the front seat backrest, and no attempt should be made to remove them. Any suspected problems with the side airbag system should be referred to a Ford dealer.

23.23 Disconnect the wiring connector from the base of the airbag clockspring

Side curtain airbags

31 The modules for the side curtain airbags are located at the sides of the headlining. It is strongly recommended that any work which requires even just the removal of the headlining, never mind any work on the side curtain airbags, be referred to a Ford dealer.

Ford Fiesta wiring diagrams

Diagram 1

 WARNING: *This vehicle is fitted with a supplemental restraint system (SRS) consisting of a combination of driver (and passenger) airbag(s), side impact protection airbags and seatbelt pre-tensioners. The use of electrical test equipment on any SRS wiring systems may cause the seatbelt pre-tensioners to abruptly retract and airbags to explosively deploy, resulting in potentially severe personal injury. Extreme care should be taken to correctly identify any circuits to be tested to avoid choosing any of the SRS wiring in error.*

For further information see airbag system precautions in body electrical systems chapter.

Note: The SRS wiring harness can normally be identified by yellow and/or orange harness or harness connectors.

Key to symbols

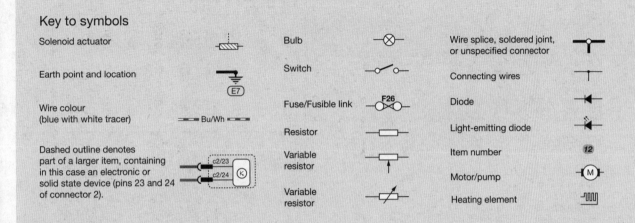

Solenoid actuator	Bulb	Wire splice, soldered joint, or unspecified connector
Earth point and location	Switch	Connecting wires
Wire colour (blue with white tracer)	Fuse/Fusible link	Diode
	Resistor	Light-emitting diode
Dashed outline denotes part of a larger item, containing in this case an electronic or solid state device (pins 23 and 24 of connector 2).	Variable resistor	Item number
		Motor/pump
	Variable resistor	Heating element

Engine fusebox 5

F1	40A	ABS control unit
F1	30A	ABS/ESP control unit
F2	60A	Cooling fan high speed
F3	40A	Cooling system fan
F3	30A	Cooling system fan low speed
F4	30A	Heater blower
F5	60A	Passenger compartment fusebox supply (battery)
F6	30A	Generic control unit
F7	60A	Passenger compartment fusebox supply (ignition)
F8	60A	Glow plugs
F9	60A	Heated windscreen
F10	-	Spare
F11	30A	Starter relay
F12	10A	LH main beam relay
F13	10A	RH main beam relay
F14	10A	LH dip beam relay
F15	10A	RH dip beam relay
F16	15A	Engine management control unit, high and low speed cooling fan
F17	15A	Oxygen sensors (petrol)
F17	20A	Power supply control unit (Diesel)
F18	10A	Engine management control unit
F19	-	Spare
F20	-	Spare
F21	-	Spare
F22	15A	Lighting control battery supply
F23	15A	Front foglights
F24	15A	Direction indicators
F25	10A	Daytime running lights
F26	7.5A	Mirror control switch, folding mirrors, driver's electric window
F27	7.5A	Engine management
F28	20A	ABS/ESP control unit
F29	10A	Air conditioning clutch
F30	-	Spare
F31	-	Spare
F32	20A	Horn, battery saver, keyless vehicle control unit
F33	20A	Heated rear window
F34	20A	Fuel pump relay
F35	-	Spare
F36	-	Spare
F37	-	Spare
F38	-	Spare
F39	-	Spare
F40	-	Spare

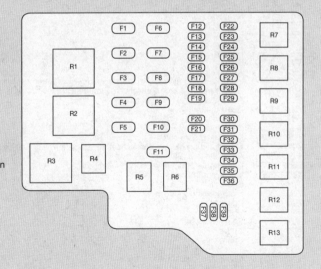

R1	Engine cooling fan
R2	Glow plugs
R3	Engine management
R4	Main beam
R5	Dipped beam
R6	Daytime running lights
R7	Engine cooling fan
R8	Starter
R9	Air conditioning conpressor clutch
R10	Front fog lights
R11	Fuel pump, fuel heater
R12	Reversing light
R13	Heater blower

H47240

Ford Fiesta wiring diagrams

Diagram 2

Passenger fusebox 6
(low specification models)

F1	7.5A	Ignition, rain sensor, heated windscreen
F2	10A	Stop lights
F3	7.5A	Reversing lights
F4	7.5A	Headlight levelling
F5	20A	Windscreen wipers
F6	15A	Rear windscreen wiper
F7	10A	Washer pump
F8	15A	Parking aid
F9	-	Spare
F10	7.5A	Heated seats
F11	-	Spare
F12	10A	Airbag control unit
F13	10A	Ignition, power steering, instrument cluster, anti-theft system, ABS
F14	7.5A	Engine management control unit, gear selector lever, fuel pump
F15	7.5A	Audio system, instrument cluster
F16	7.5A	Heated mirrors
F17	15A	Ignition switch
F18	7.5A	Instrument cluster
F19	15A	Diagnostic connector
F20	7.5A	Multi-function display, clock, heating ventilation, air conditioning
F21	15A	Audio system, Bluetooth
F22	20A	Cigar lighter, front accessory socket
F23	20A	Trailer control unit
F24	-	Spare
F25	30A	Front electric windows
F26	-	Spare
F27	-	Spare

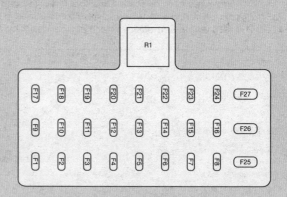

R1   Ignition

Passenger fusebox 6
(High specification models)

F1	7.5A	Ignition, rain sensor, heated windscreen
F2	10A	Stop lights
F3	7.5A	Reversing lights
F4	7.5A	Headlight levelling
F5	20A	Windscreen wipers
F6	15A	Rear windscreen wiper
F7	10A	Washer pump
F8	15A	Parking aid
F9	10	Parking aid
F10	7.5A	Heated seats
F11	-	Spare
F12	10A	Airbag control unit
F13	10A	Ignition, power steering, instrument cluster, anti-theft system, ABS
F14	7.5A	Engine management control unit, gear selector lever, fuel pump
F15	7.5A	Audio system, instrument cluster
F16	7.5A	Heated mirrors
F17	15A	Ignition switch
F18	7.5A	Instrument cluster
F19	15A	Diagnostic connector
F20	7.5A	Multi-function display, clock, heating ventilation, air conditioning
F21	15A	Audio system, Bluetooth
F22	20A	Cigar lighter, front accessory socket
F23	20A	Trailer control unit
F24	-	Spare
F25	30A	Front electric windows
F26	-	Spare
F27	-	Spare
F28	-	Spare
F29	-	Spare
F30	-	Spare
F31	30A	Rear electric windows
F32	30A	LH heated windscreen
F33	30A	RH heated windscreen
F34	20A	Keyless entry
F35	20A	Keyless entry
F36	15A	Rear accessory socket, battery saver
F37	15A	Luggage compartment accessory socket
F38	-	Spare
F39	-	Spare
F40	-	Spare
F41	7.5	Ignition switch position 1
F42	-	Spare
F43	-	Spare
F44	7.5A	Ignition switch position 2
F45	-	Spare
F46	-	Spare
F47	-	Spare
F48	-	Spare
F49	-	Spare

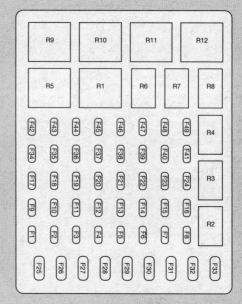

R1	Ignition
R2	Folding mirror 1
R3	Folding mirror 2
R4	Spare
R5	Heated front screen
R6	Keyless entry (accessory)
R7	Keyless entry (ignition)
R8	Battery saver
R9	Spare
R10	Spare
R11	Spare
R12	Spare

H47241

Colour codes

Wh	White	Og	Orange
Bu	Blue	Rd	Red
Gy	Grey	Pk	Pink
Ye	Yellow	Gn	Green
Bn	Brown	Vt	Violet
Bk	Black	Sr	Silver
Na	Natural	Lg	Light green

Key to items

1 Battery
2 Battery fusebox
3 Starter motor
4 Alternator
5 Engine fusebox
  R8 = starter relay
6 Passenger fusebox
7 Ignition switch
8 Transmission range switch (automatic transmission)
9 Keyless vehicle control unit
10 Start control unit
11 Generic control unit
12 Horn
13 Steering wheel clock springs
14 Horn switch

Diagram 3

H47242

Earth Locations

E1 Battery support
E2 Left cross car beam centre
E3 Right cross car beam
E4 LH rocker panel
E5 Left cross car beam centre
E6 LH front bumper
E7 RH 'B' pillar
E8 LH 'B' pillar
E9 LH 'C' pillar
E10 LH strut tower
E11 RH front bumper
E12 Left cross car beam centre
E13 RH rocker panel
E14 LH 'A' pillar
E15 Right cross car beam

Horn

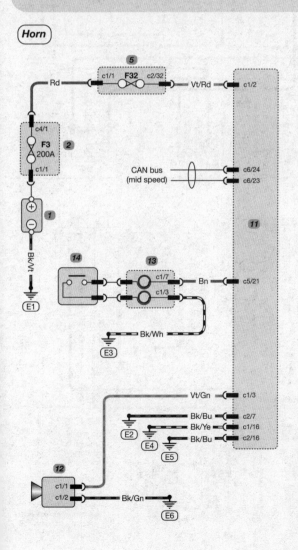

Starting & charging (without keyless system)

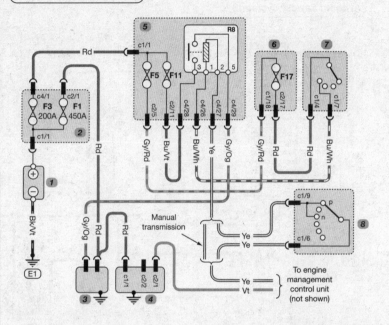

Starting & charging (with keyless system)

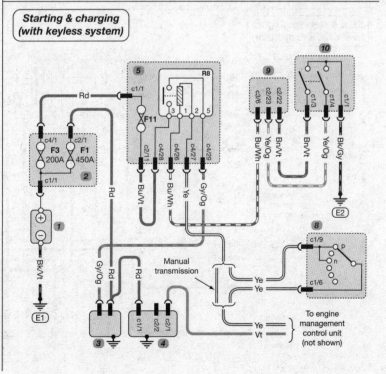

Colour codes

Wh	White	Og	Orange
Bu	Blue	Rd	Red
Gy	Grey	Pk	Pink
Ye	Yellow	Gn	Green
Bn	Brown	Vt	Violet
Bk	Black	Sr	Silver
Na	Natural	Lg	Light green

Key to items

1 Battery
2 Battery fusebox
5 Engine fusebox
  R12 = reversing light relay
        (auto. transmission)
6 Passenger fusebox
  R1 = ignition relay
  R7 = keyless entry ignition relay
7 Ignition switch

9 Keyless vehicle control unit
10 Start control unit
11 Generic control unit
17 Stop light switch
18 Reversing light switch
   (manual transmission)
19 LH rear light unit
   a = stop/tail light
   b = reversing light

20 RH rear light unit
   a = stop/tail light
   b = reversing light
21 High level stop light

Diagram 4

H47243

Stop & reversing lights (without keyless system)

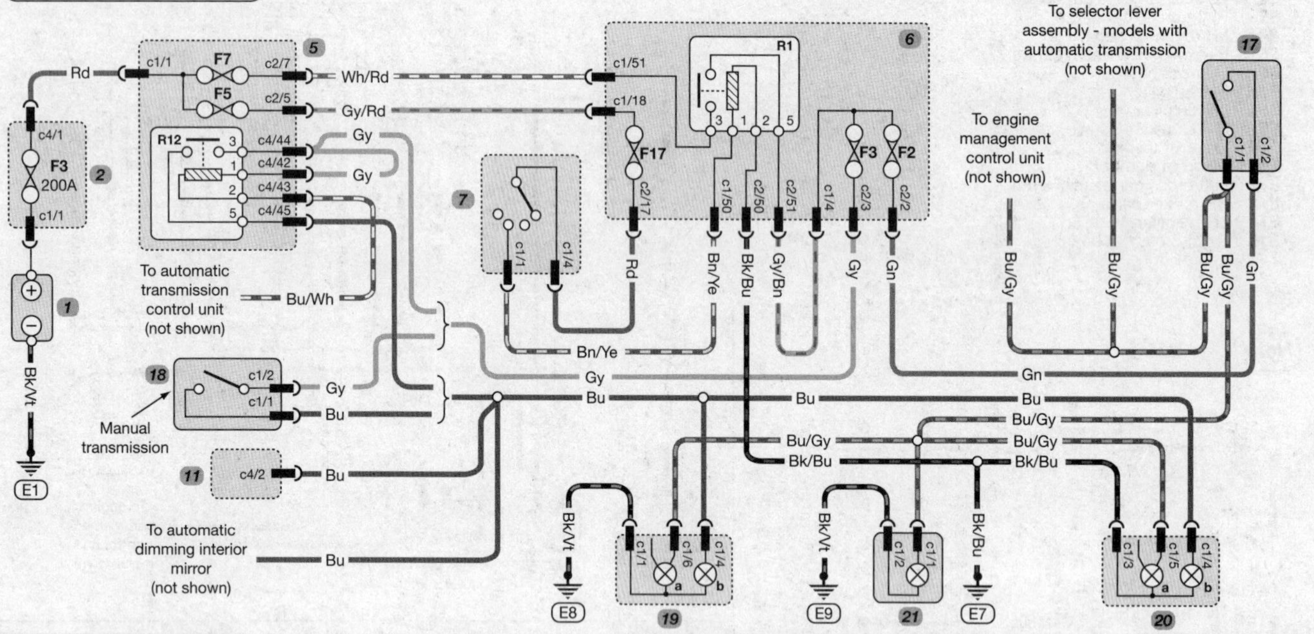

Stop & reversing lights (with keyless system)

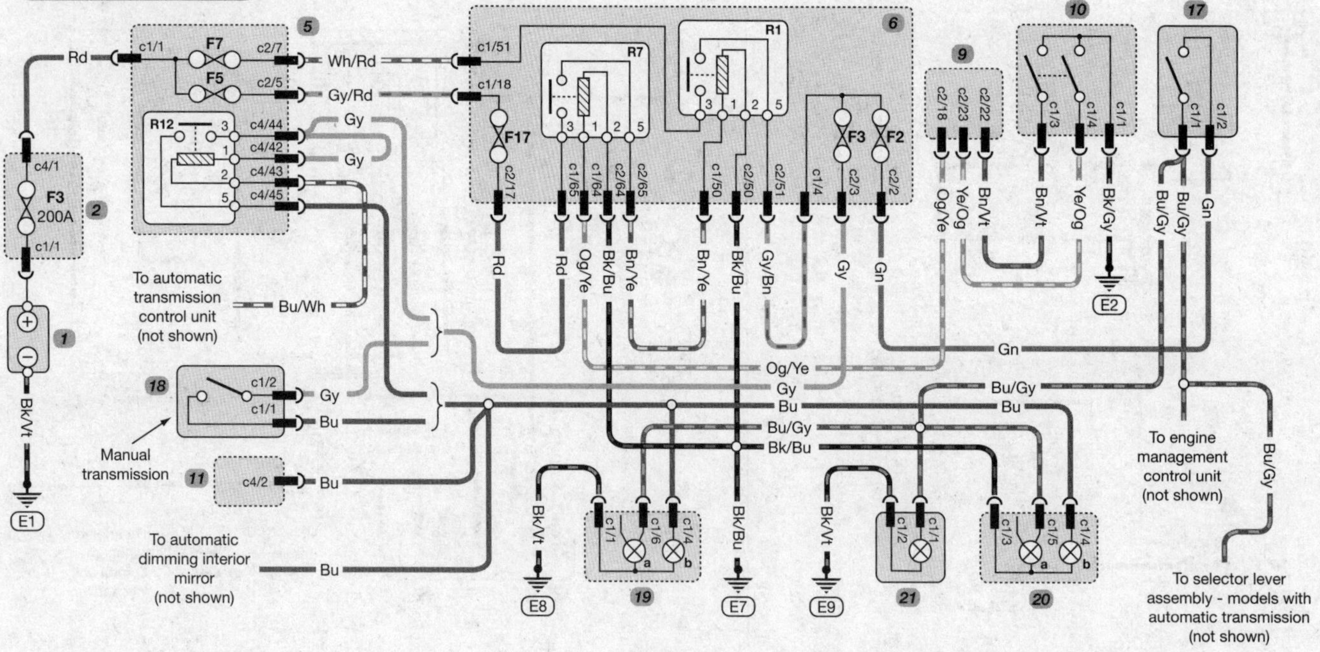

Side & headlights (without keyless system)

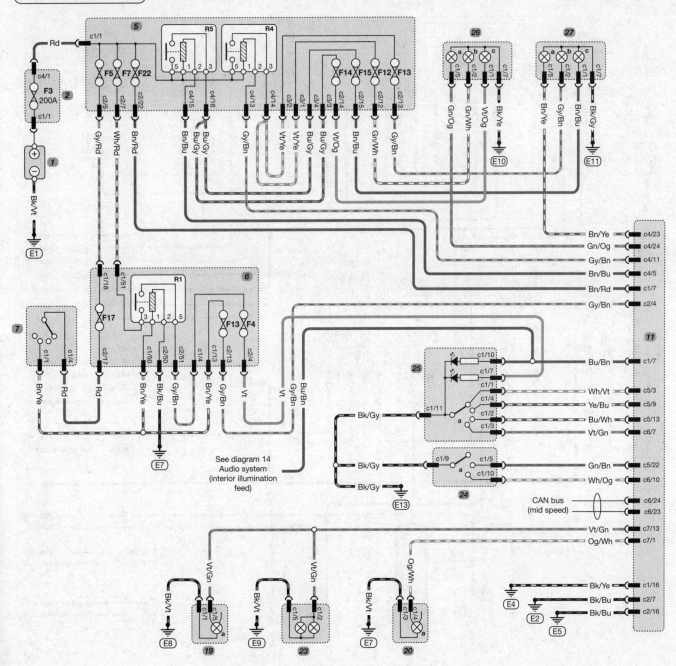

Colour codes

Wh	White	**Og**	Orange
Bu	Blue	**Rd**	Red
Gy	Grey	**Pk**	Pink
Ye	Yellow	**Gn**	Green
Bn	Brown	**Vt**	Violet
Bk	Black	**Sr**	Silver
Na	Natural	**Lg**	Light green

Key to items

1 Battery
2 Battery fusebox
5 Engine fusebox
  R4 = main beam relay
  R5 = dip beam relay
6 Passenger fusebox
  R1 = ignition relay
  R7 = keyless entry ignition relay
9 Keyless vehicle control unit
10 Start control unit
11 Generic control unit

19 LH rear light unit
  a = stop/tail light
20 RH rear light unit
  a = stop/tail light
23 Tailgate release switch/
  number plate light
24 Steering column multifunction switch
  a = headlight flash/main beam switch
25 Lighting switch
  a = side/headlight/auto switch

26 LH headlight unit
  a = sidelight
  b = main beam
  c = dip beam
27 RH headlight unit
  a = sidelight
  b = main beam
  c = dip beam

Diagram 6

H47245

**Side & headlights
(with keyless system)**

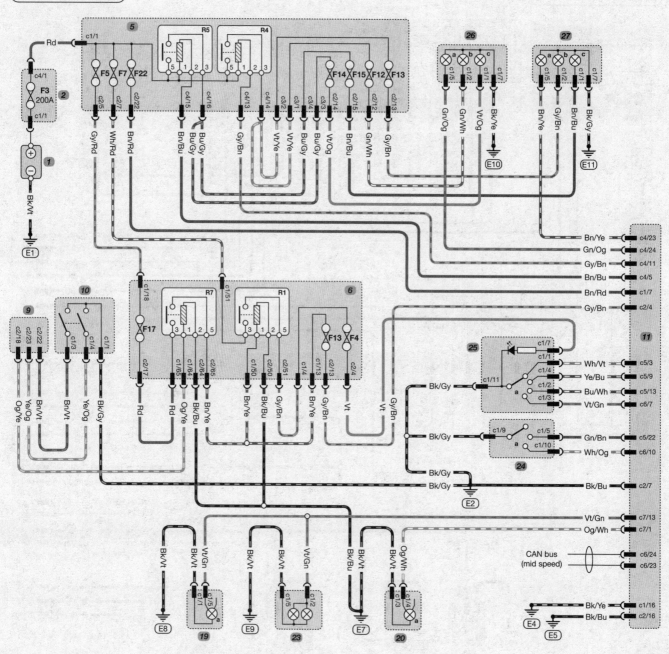

Diagram 7

Colour codes

Wh	White	**Og**	Orange
Bu	Blue	**Rd**	Red
Gy	Grey	**Pk**	Pink
Ye	Yellow	**Gn**	Green
Bn	Brown	**Vt**	Violet
Bk	Black	**Sr**	Silver
Na	Natural	**Lg**	Light green

Key to items

1 Battery
2 Battery fusebox
5 Engine fusebox
  R10 = front foglight relay
6 Passenger fusebox
  R7 = keyless entry ignition relay
7 Ignition switch
9 Keyless vehicle control unit

10 Start control unit
11 Generic control unit
25 Lighting switch
  b = front foglight switch
  c = rear foglight switch
30 LH front foglight
31 RH front foglight
32 Rear foglight

H47246

Foglights (without keyless system)

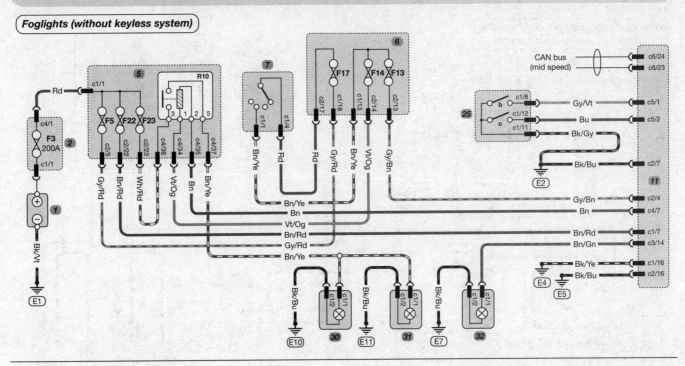

Foglights (with keyless system)

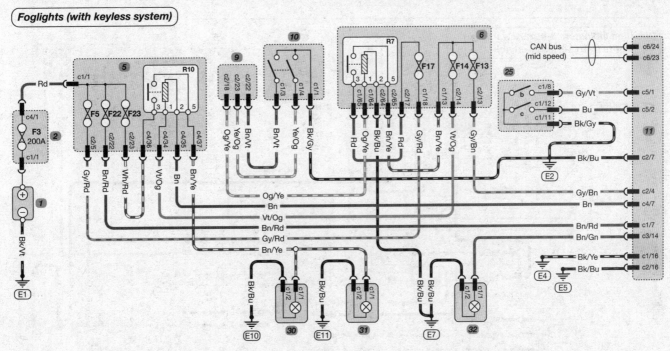

Colour codes

Wh White	**Og** Orange
Bu Blue	**Rd** Red
Gy Grey	**Pk** Pink
Ye Yellow	**Gn** Green
Bn Brown	**Vt** Violet
Bk Black	**Sr** Silver
Na Natural	**Lg** Light green

Key to items

1 Battery
2 Battery fusebox
5 Engine fusebox
6 Passenger fusebox
   R7 = keyless entry ignition relay
7 Ignition switch
9 Keyless vehicle control unit
10 Start control unit

11 Generic control unit
19 LH rear light unit
   c = direction indicator
20 RH rear light unit
   c = direction indicator
24 Steering column multifunction switch
   c = direction indicator switch
26 LH front light unit
   d = direction indicator

27 RH front light unit
   d = direction indicator
35 Information and entertainment panel
   a = hazard warning switch
36 LH mirror assembly
   a = indicator side repeater
37 RH mirror assembly
   a = indicator side repeater

Diagram 8

H47247

Direction indicators & hazard warning lights (without keyless system)

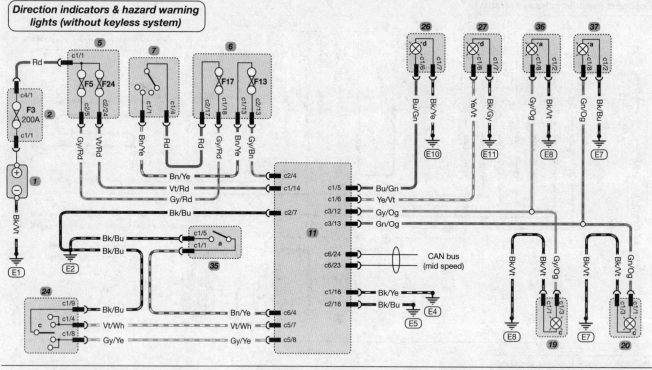

Direction indicators & hazard warning lights (with keyless system)

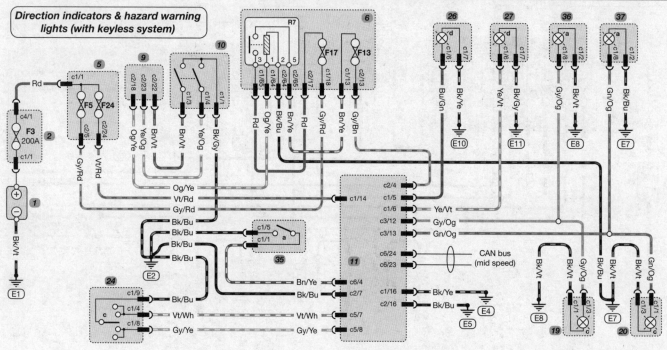

Colour codes

Wh	White	Og	Orange
Bu	Blue	Rd	Red
Gy	Grey	Pk	Pink
Ye	Yellow	Gn	Green
Bn	Brown	Vt	Violet
Bk	Black	Sr	Silver
Na	Natural	Lg	Light green

Key to items

1 Battery
2 Battery fusebox
5 Engine fusebox
6 Passenger fusebox
R1 = ignition relay
R7 = keyless entry ignition relay
7 Ignition switch
9 Keyless vehicle control unit
10 Start control unit
25 Lighting switch
 d = headlight levelling adjuster
26 LH headlight unit
 d = headlight levelling asembly
27 RH headlight unit
 d = headlight levelling assembly
40 Power steering control unit

Diagram 9

H47248

Headlight levelling (without keyless system)
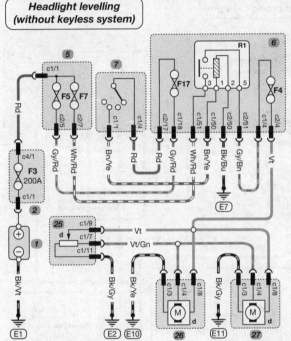

Headlight levelling (with keyless system)
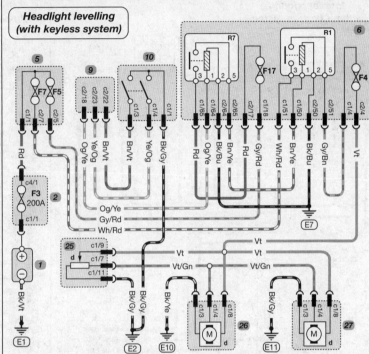

Power steering (without keyless system)
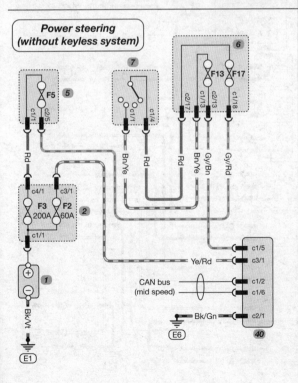

Power steering (with keyless system)
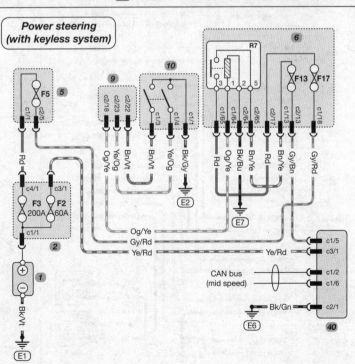

Colour codes

Wh White	**Og** Orange		
Bu Blue	**Rd** Red		
Gy Grey	**Pk** Pink		
Ye Yellow	**Gn** Green		
Bn Brown	**Vt** Violet		
Bk Black	**Sr** Silver		
Na Natural	**Lg** Light green		

Key to items

1 Battery
2 Battery fusebox
5 Engine fusebox
6 Passenger fusebox
R1 = ignition relay
R7 = keyless entry ignition relay
7 Ignition switch
9 Keyless vehicle control unit
10 Start control unit
11 Generic control unit
43 Interior light
44 LH footwell light
45 RH footwell light
46 Luggage compartment light
47 Tailgate lock assembly
48 LH rear door lock assembly
49 RH rear door lock assembly
50 Driver's door lock assembly
51 Passenger's door lock assembly
52 LH dashboard ambient light
53 RH dashboard ambient light

Diagram 10

H47249

Interior lighting (without keyless system)

Interior lighting (without keyless system)

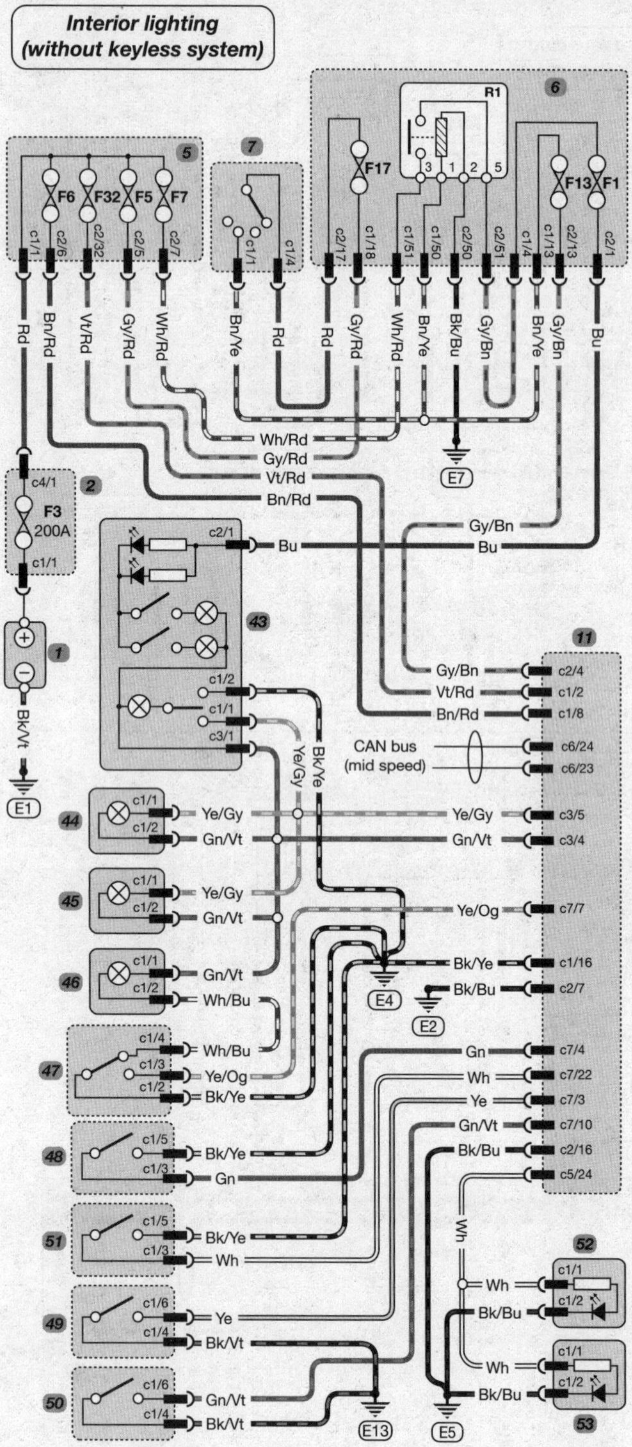

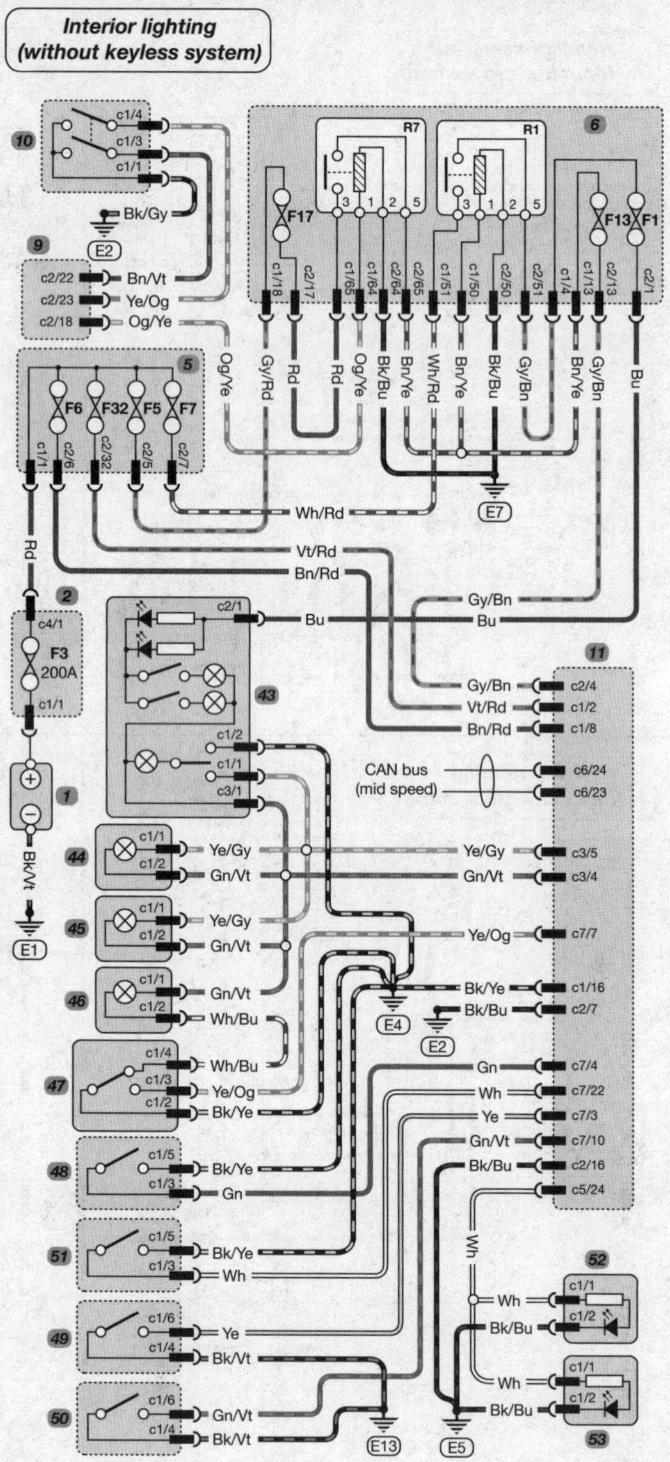

Colour codes

Wh	White	Og	Orange
Bu	Blue	Rd	Red
Gy	Grey	Pk	Pink
Ye	Yellow	Gn	Green
Bn	Brown	Vt	Violet
Bk	Black	Sr	Silver
Na	Natural	Lg	Light green

Key to items

1 Battery
2 Battery fusebox
5 Engine fusebox
6 Passenger fusebox
   R6 = keyless entry accessory relay
   R7 = keyless entry ignition relay
7 Ignition switch
9 Keyless vehicle control unit
10 Start control unit
24 Steering column multifunction switch
   d = MFD switch
56 Instrument cluster
57 Clutch pedal switch
58 Brake pedal switch
59 Low brake fluid switch
60 Ambient air temperature switch
61 Evaporator sensor temperature
62 Handbrake switch
63 Fuel pump/fuel gauge sender unit

Diagram 11

H47250

Instrument cluster (without keyless system)

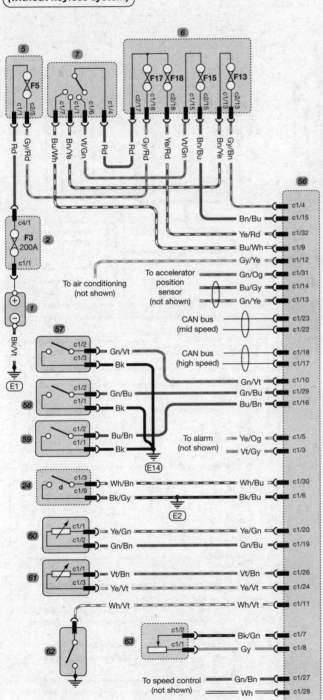

Instrument cluster (with keyless system)

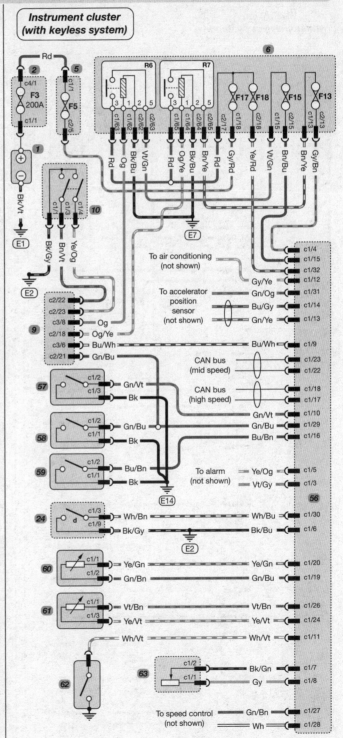

Colour codes

Wh	White	**Og**	Orange
Bu	Blue	**Rd**	Red
Gy	Grey	**Pk**	Pink
Ye	Yellow	**Gn**	Green
Bn	Brown	**Vt**	Violet
Bk	Black	**Sr**	Silver
Na	Natural	**Lg**	Light green

Key to items

1 Battery
2 Battery fusebox
5 Engine fusebox
6 Passenger fusebox
R1 = ignition relay
R7 = keyless entry ignition relay
7 Ignition switch
9 Keyless vehicle control unit
10 Start control unit
11 Generic control unit
66 Wash/wipe switch
67 Front wiper motor
68 Rear wiper motor
69 Washer pump
70 Rain sensor

Diagram 12

H47251

Wash/wipe (without keyless system)

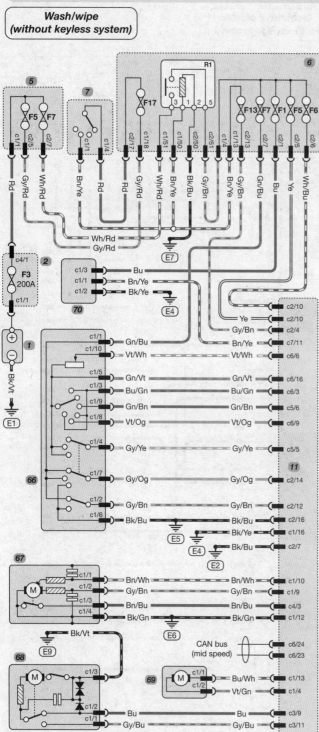

Wash/wipe (with keyless system)

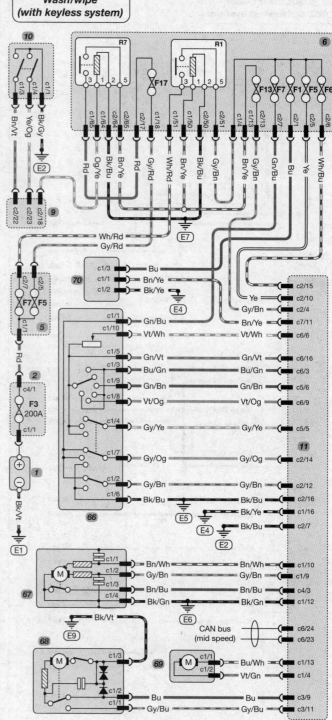

Colour codes

Wh	White	**Og**	Orange
Bu	Blue	**Rd**	Red
Gy	Grey	**Pk**	Pink
Ye	Yellow	**Gn**	Green
Bn	Brown	**Vt**	Violet
Bk	Black	**Sr**	Silver
Na	Natural	**Lg**	Light green

Key to items

1 Battery
2 Battery fusebox
5 Engine fusebox
  R13 = heater blower relay
6 Passenger fusebox
  R1 = ignition relay
  R7 = keyless entry ignition relay

7 Ignition switch
9 Keyless vehicle control unit
10 Start control unit
11 Generic control unit
75 Heated rear window
76 Climate control module
  a = heater blower switch

77 Heater blower motor
78 Heater blower resistors
79 Heater blower control unit

Diagram 13

H47252

Heated rear window (without keyless system)

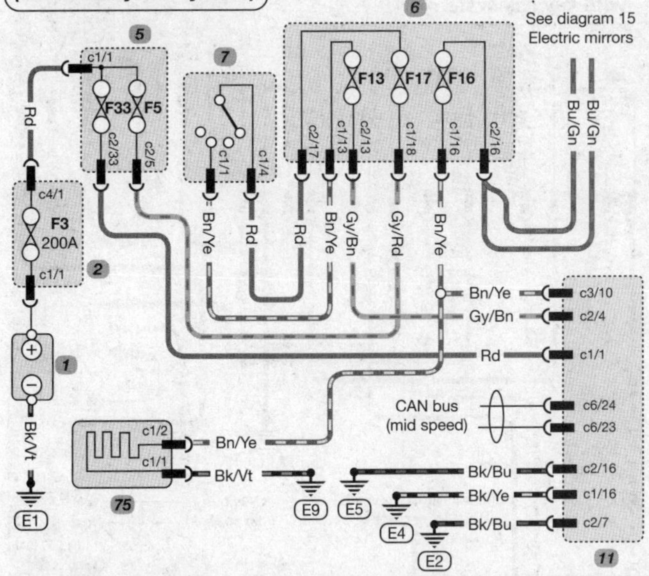

Typical heater blower (without climate control)

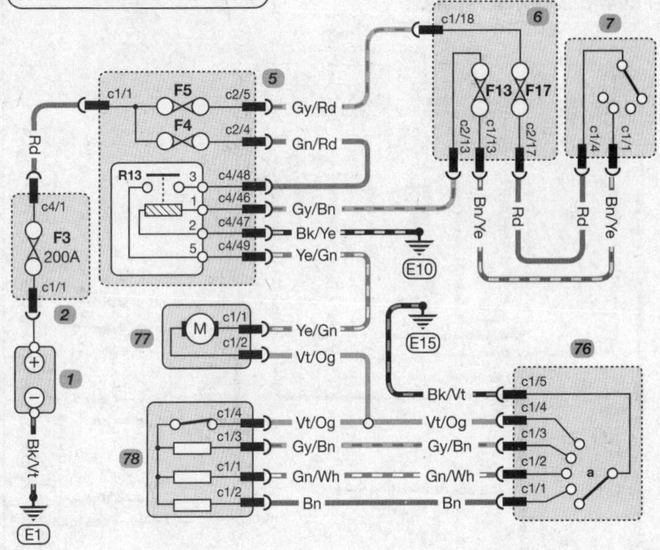

Heated rear window (with keyless system)

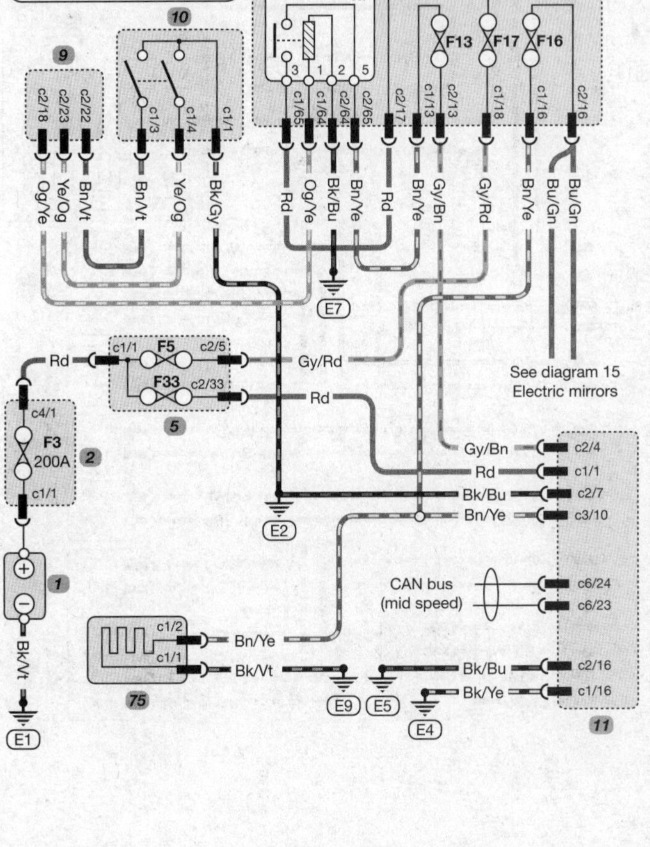

Typical heater blower (with climate control)

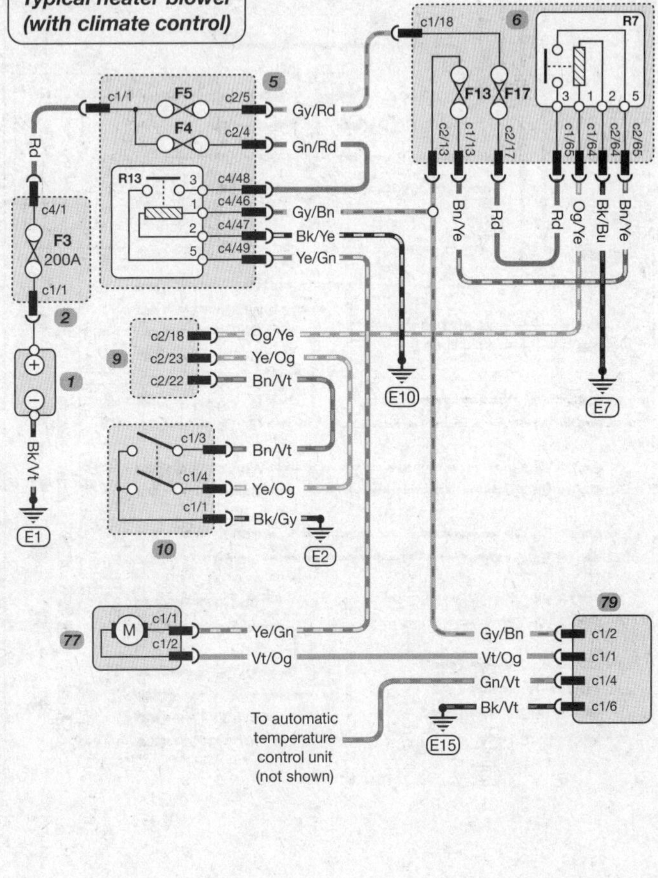

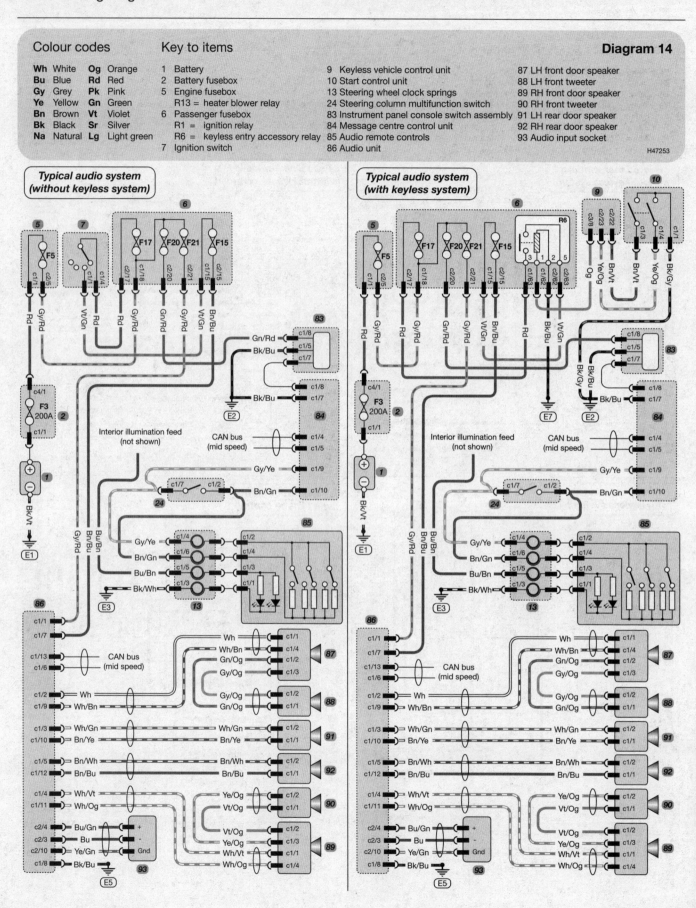

Colour codes

Wh	White	**Og**	Orange
Bu	Blue	**Rd**	Red
Gy	Grey	**Pk**	Pink
Ye	Yellow	**Gn**	Green
Bn	Brown	**Vt**	Violet
Bk	Black	**Sr**	Silver
Na	Natural	**Lg**	Light green

Key to items

1 Battery
2 Battery fusebox
5 Engine fusebox
  R13 = heater blower relay
6 Passenger fusebox
  R1 = ignition relay
  R6 = keyless entry accessory relay
7 Ignition switch
9 Keyless vehicle control unit
10 Start control unit
13 Steering wheel clock springs
24 Steering column multifunction switch
83 Instrument panel console switch assembly
84 Message centre control unit
85 Audio remote controls
86 Audio unit
87 LH front door speaker
88 LH front tweeter
89 RH front door speaker
90 RH front tweeter
91 LH rear door speaker
92 RH rear door speaker
93 Audio input socket

Diagram 14

H47253

Typical audio system (without keyless system)

Typical audio system (with keyless system)

Colour codes

Wh	White	**Og**	Orange
Bu	Blue	**Rd**	Red
Gy	Grey	**Pk**	Pink
Ye	Yellow	**Gn**	Green
Bn	Brown	**Vt**	Violet
Bk	Black	**Sr**	Silver
Na	Natural	**Lg**	Light green

Key to items

1 Battery
2 Battery fusebox
5 Engine fusebox
  R13 = heater blower relay
6 Passenger fusebox
  R1 = ignition relay
  R6 = keyless entry accessory relay
11 Generic control unit
23 Tailgate release switch/number
    plate light

36 LH mirror assembly
  b = mirror heater
  c = up/down motor
  d = left/right motor
  e = retraction motor
37 RH mirror assembly
  (as above)
47 Tailgate lock assembly
48 LH rear door lock assembly

49 RH rear door lock assembly
50 Driver's door lock assembly
51 Passenger's door lock assembly
83 Message centre control unit
95 Mirror control switch

Diagram 15

H47254

Electric mirrors

Central locking – without keyless entry

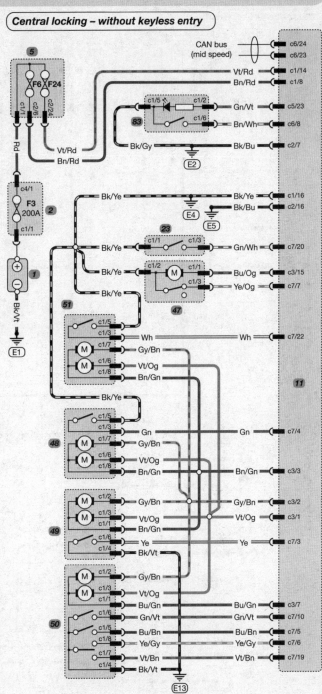

See diagram 13
Heated rear window

Colour codes

Wh	White	**Og**	Orange
Bu	Blue	**Rd**	Red
Gy	Grey	**Pk**	Pink
Ye	Yellow	**Gn**	Green
Bn	Brown	**Vt**	Violet
Bk	Black	**Sr**	Silver
Na	Natural	**Lg**	Light green

Key to items

1 Battery
2 Battery fusebox
5 Engine fusebox
6 Passenger fusebox
    R1 = ignition relay
    R6 = keyless entry accessory relay
7 Ignition switch

9 Keyless vehicle control unit
10 Start control unit
97 Driver's window switch
98 Passenger's window switch
99 LH rear window switch

100 RH rear window switch
101 Driver's window motor
102 Passenger's window motor
103 LH rear window motor
104 RH rear window motor

Diagram 16

H47255

Electric windows

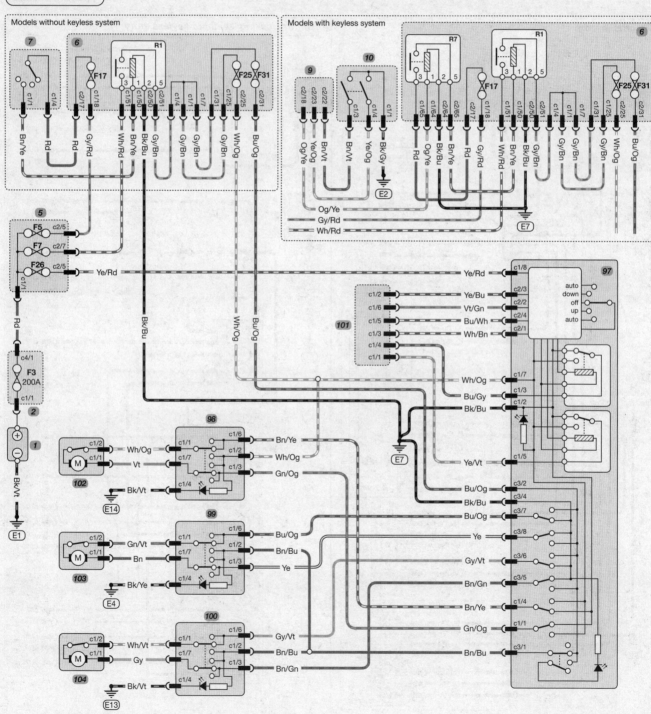

Note: *All figures are approximate and may vary according to model. Refer to manufacturer's data for exact figures.*

Dimensions

Overall length	3958 mm
Overall width (including door mirrors)	1973 mm
Overall height (unladen)	1481 mm
Wheelbase	2489 mm
Front track	1493 mm
Rear track.	1480 mm

Weights

Kerb weight	Refer to information contained on the vehicle identification plate
Gross vehicle weight	Refer to information contained on the vehicle identification plate
Maximum roof load (including weight of rack)	50 kg

Fuel economy

Although depreciation is still the biggest part of the cost of motoring for most car owners, the cost of fuel is more immediately noticeable. These pages give some tips on how to get the best fuel economy.

Working it out

Manufacturer's figures

Car manufacturers are required by law to provide fuel consumption information on all new vehicles sold. These 'official' figures are obtained by simulating various driving conditions on a rolling road or a test track. Real life conditions are different, so the fuel consumption actually achieved may not bear much resemblance to the quoted figures.

How to calculate it

Many cars now have trip computers which will

display fuel consumption, both instantaneous and average. Refer to the owner's handbook for details of how to use these.

To calculate consumption yourself (and maybe to check that the trip computer is accurate), proceed as follows.

1. Fill up with fuel and note the mileage, or zero the trip recorder.
2. Drive as usual until you need to fill up again.
3. Note the amount of fuel required to refill the tank, and the mileage covered since the previous fill-up.
4. Divide the mileage by the amount of fuel used to obtain the consumption figure.

For example:

    Mileage at first fill-up (a) = 27,903
    Mileage at second fill-up (b) = 28,346
    Mileage covered (b - a) = 443
    Fuel required at second fill-up = 48.6 litres

The half-completed changeover to metric units in the UK means that we buy our fuel

in litres, measure distances in miles and talk about fuel consumption in miles per gallon. There are two ways round this: the first is to convert the litres to gallons before doing the calculation (by dividing by 4.546, or see Table 1). So in the example:

    48.6 litres ÷ 4.546 = 10.69 gallons
    443 miles ÷ 10.69 gallons = 41.4 mpg

The second way is to calculate the consumption in miles per litre, then multiply that figure by 4.546 (or see Table 2).

So in the example, fuel consumption is:

    443 miles ÷ 48.6 litres = 9.1 mpl
    9.1 mpl x 4.546 = 41.4 mpg

The rest of Europe expresses fuel consumption in litres of fuel required to travel 100 km (l/100 km). For interest, the conversions are given in Table 3. In practice it doesn't matter what units you use, provided you know what your normal consumption is and can spot if it's getting better or worse.

Table 1: conversion of litres to Imperial gallons

litres	1	2	3	4	5	10	20	30	40	50	60	70
gallons	0.22	0.44	0.66	0.88	1.10	2.24	4.49	6.73	8.98	11.22	13.47	15.71

Table 2: conversion of miles per litre to miles per gallon

miles per litre	5	6	7	8	9	10	11	12	13	14
miles per gallon	23	27	32	36	41	46	50	55	59	64

Table 3: conversion of litres per 100 km to miles per gallon

litres per 100 km	4	4.5	5	5.5	6	6.5	7	8	9	10
miles per gallon	71	63	56	51	47	43	40	35	31	28

Maintenance

A well-maintained car uses less fuel and creates less pollution. In particular:

Filters

Change air and fuel filters at the specified intervals.

Oil

Use a good quality oil of the lowest viscosity specified by the vehicle manufacturer (see *Lubricants and fluids*). Check the level often and be careful not to overfill.

Spark plugs

When applicable, renew at the specified intervals.

Tyres

Check tyre pressures regularly. Under-inflated tyres have an increased rolling resistance. It is generally safe to use the higher pressures specified for full load conditions even when not fully laden, but keep an eye on the centre band of tread for signs of wear due to over-inflation.

When buying new tyres, consider the 'fuel saving' models which most manufacturers include in their ranges.

Driving style

Acceleration

Acceleration uses more fuel than driving at a steady speed. The best technique with modern cars is to accelerate reasonably briskly to the desired speed, changing up through the gears as soon as possible without making the engine labour.

Air conditioning

Air conditioning absorbs quite a bit of energy from the engine – typically 3 kW (4 hp) or so. The effect on fuel consumption is at its worst in slow traffic. Switch it off when not required.

Anticipation

Drive smoothly and try to read the traffic flow so as to avoid unnecessary acceleration and braking.

Automatic transmission

When accelerating in an automatic, avoid depressing the throttle so far as to make the transmission hold onto lower gears at higher speeds. Don't use the 'Sport' setting, if applicable.

When stationary with the engine running, select 'N' or 'P'. When moving, keep your left foot away from the brake.

Braking

Braking converts the car's energy of motion into heat – essentially, it is wasted. Obviously some braking is always going to be necessary, but with good anticipation it is surprising how much can be avoided, especially on routes that you know well.

Carshare

Consider sharing lifts to work or to the shops. Even once a week will make a difference.

Electrical loads

Electricity is 'fuel' too; the alternator which charges the battery does so by converting some of the engine's energy of motion into electrical energy. The more electrical accessories are in use, the greater the load on the alternator. Switch off big consumers like the heated rear window when not required.

Freewheeling

Freewheeling (coasting) in neutral with the engine switched off is dangerous. The effort required to operate power-assisted brakes and steering increases when the engine is not running, with a potential lack of control in emergency situations.

In any case, modern fuel injection systems automatically cut off the engine's fuel supply on the overrun (moving and in gear, but with the accelerator pedal released).

Gadgets

Bolt-on devices claiming to save fuel have been around for nearly as long as the motor car itself. Those which worked were rapidly adopted as standard equipment by the vehicle manufacturers. Others worked only in certain situations, or saved fuel only at the expense of unacceptable effects on performance, driveability or the life of engine components.

The most effective fuel saving gadget is the driver's right foot.

Journey planning

Combine (eg) a trip to the supermarket with a visit to the recycling centre and the DIY store, rather than making separate journeys.

When possible choose a travelling time outside rush hours.

Load

The more heavily a car is laden, the greater the energy required to accelerate it to a given speed. Remove heavy items which you don't need to carry.

One load which is often overlooked is the contents of the fuel tank. A tankful of fuel (55 litres / 12 gallons) weighs 45 kg (100 lb) or so. Just half filling it may be worthwhile.

Lost?

At the risk of stating the obvious, if you're going somewhere new, have details of the route to hand. There's not much point in achieving record mpg if you also go miles out of your way.

Parking

If possible, carry out any reversing or turning manoeuvres when you arrive at a parking space so that you can drive straight out when you leave. Manoeuvering when the engine is cold uses a lot more fuel.

Driving around looking for free on-street parking may cost more in fuel than buying a car park ticket.

Premium fuel

Most major oil companies (and some supermarkets) have premium grades of fuel which are several pence a litre dearer than the standard grades. Reports vary, but the consensus seems to be that if these fuels improve economy at all, they do not do so by enough to justify their extra cost.

Roof rack

When loading a roof rack, try to produce a wedge shape with the narrow end at the front. Any cover should be securely fastened – if it flaps it's creating turbulence and absorbing energy.

Remove roof racks and boxes when not in use – they increase air resistance and can create a surprising amount of noise.

Short journeys

The engine is at its least efficient, and wear is highest, during the first few miles after a cold start. Consider walking, cycling or using public transport.

Speed

The engine is at its most efficient when running at a steady speed and load at the rpm where it develops maximum torque. (You can find this figure in the car's handbook.) For most cars this corresponds to between 55 and 65 mph in top gear.

Above the optimum cruising speed, fuel consumption starts to rise quite sharply. A car travelling at 80 mph will typically be using 30% more fuel than at 60 mph.

Supermarket fuel

It may be cheap but is it any good? In the UK all supermarket fuel must meet the relevant British Standard. The major oil companies will say that their branded fuels have better additive packages which may stop carbon and other deposits building up. A reasonable compromise might be to use one tank of branded fuel to three or four from the supermarket.

Switch off when stationary

Switch off the engine if you look like being stationary for more than 30 seconds or so. This is good for the environment as well as for your pocket. Be aware though that frequent restarts are hard on the battery and the starter motor.

Windows

Driving with the windows open increases air turbulence around the vehicle. Closing the windows promotes smooth airflow and

reduced resistance. The faster you go, the more significant this is.

And finally . . .

Driving techniques associated with good fuel economy tend to involve moderate acceleration and low top speeds. Be considerate to the needs of other road users who may need to make brisker progress; even if you do not agree with them this is not an excuse to be obstructive.

Safety must always take precedence over economy, whether it is a question of accelerating hard to complete an overtaking manoeuvre, killing your speed when confronted with a potential hazard or switching the lights on when it starts to get dark.

Length (distance)

Inches (in)	x 25.4	= Millimetres (mm)	x 0.0394	= Inches (in)
Feet (ft)	x 0.305	= Metres (m)	x 3.281	= Feet (ft)
Miles	x 1.609	= Kilometres (km)	x 0.621	= Miles

Volume (capacity)

Cubic inches (cu in; in³)	x 16.387	= Cubic centimetres (cc; cm³)	x 0.061	= Cubic inches (cu in; in³)
Imperial pints (Imp pt)	x 0.568	= Litres (l)	x 1.76	= Imperial pints (Imp pt)
Imperial quarts (Imp qt)	x 1.137	= Litres (l)	x 0.88	= Imperial quarts (Imp qt)
Imperial quarts (Imp qt)	x 1.201	= US quarts (US qt)	x 0.833	= Imperial quarts (Imp qt)
US quarts (US qt)	x 0.946	= Litres (l)	x 1.057	= US quarts (US qt)
Imperial gallons (Imp gal)	x 4.546	= Litres (l)	x 0.22	= Imperial gallons (Imp gal)
Imperial gallons (Imp gal)	x 1.201	= US gallons (US gal)	x 0.833	= Imperial gallons (Imp gal)
US gallons (US gal)	x 3.785	= Litres (l)	x 0.264	= US gallons (US gal)

Mass (weight)

Ounces (oz)	x 28.35	= Grams (g)	x 0.035	= Ounces (oz)
Pounds (lb)	x 0.454	= Kilograms (kg)	x 2.205	= Pounds (lb)

Force

Ounces-force (ozf; oz)	x 0.278	= Newtons (N)	x 3.6	= Ounces-force (ozf; oz)
Pounds-force (lbf; lb)	x 4.448	= Newtons (N)	x 0.225	= Pounds-force (lbf; lb)
Newtons (N)	x 0.1	= Kilograms-force (kgf; kg)	x 9.81	= Newtons (N)

Pressure

Pounds-force per square inch (psi; lbf/in²; lb/in²)	x 0.070	= Kilograms-force per square centimetre (kgf/cm²; kg/cm²)	x 14.223	= Pounds-force per square inch (psi; lbf/in²; lb/in²)
Pounds-force per square inch (psi; lbf/in²; lb/in²)	x 0.068	= Atmospheres (atm)	x 14.696	= Pounds-force per square inch (psi; lbf/in²; lb/in²)
Pounds-force per square inch (psi; lbf/in²; lb/in²)	x 0.069	= Bars	x 14.5	= Pounds-force per square inch (psi; lbf/in²; lb/in²)
Pounds-force per square inch (psi; lbf/in²; lb/in²)	x 6.895	= Kilopascals (kPa)	x 0.145	= Pounds-force per square inch (psi; lbf/in²; lb/in²)
Kilopascals (kPa)	x 0.01	= Kilograms-force per square centimetre (kgf/cm²; kg/cm²)	x 98.1	= Kilopascals (kPa)
Millibar (mbar)	x 100	= Pascals (Pa)	x 0.01	= Millibar (mbar)
Millibar (mbar)	x 0.0145	= Pounds-force per square inch (psi; lbf/in²; lb/in²)	x 68.947	= Millibar (mbar)
Millibar (mbar)	x 0.75	= Millimetres of mercury (mmHg)	x 1.333	= Millibar (mbar)
Millibar (mbar)	x 0.401	= Inches of water (inH₂O)	x 2.491	= Millibar (mbar)
Millimetres of mercury (mmHg)	x 0.535	= Inches of water (inH₂O)	x 1.868	= Millimetres of mercury (mmHg)
Inches of water (inH₂O)	x 0.036	= Pounds-force per square inch (psi; lbf/in²; lb/in²)	x 27.68	= Inches of water (inH₂O)

Torque (moment of force)

Pounds-force inches (lbf in; lb in)	x 1.152	= Kilograms-force centimetre (kgf cm; kg cm)	x 0.868	= Pounds-force inches (lbf in; lb in)
Pounds-force inches (lbf in; lb in)	x 0.113	= Newton metres (Nm)	x 8.85	= Pounds-force inches (lbf in; lb in)
Pounds-force inches (lbf in; lb in)	x 0.083	= Pounds-force feet (lbf ft; lb ft)	x 12	= Pounds-force inches (lbf in; lb in)
Pounds-force feet (lbf ft; lb ft)	x 0.138	= Kilograms-force metres (kgf m; kg m)	x 7.233	= Pounds-force feet (lbf ft; lb ft)
Pounds-force feet (lbf ft; lb ft)	x 1.356	= Newton metres (Nm)	x 0.738	= Pounds-force feet (lbf ft; lb ft)
Newton metres (Nm)	x 0.102	= Kilograms-force metres (kgf m; kg m)	x 9.804	= Newton metres (Nm)

Power

Horsepower (hp)	x 745.7	= Watts (W)	x 0.0013	= Horsepower (hp)

Velocity (speed)

Miles per hour (miles/hr; mph)	x 1.609	= Kilometres per hour (km/hr; kph)	x 0.621	= Miles per hour (miles/hr; mph)

Fuel consumption*

Miles per gallon, Imperial (mpg)	x 0.354	= Kilometres per litre (km/l)	x 2.825	= Miles per gallon, Imperial (mpg)
Miles per gallon, US (mpg)	x 0.425	= Kilometres per litre (km/l)	x 2.352	= Miles per gallon, US (mpg)

Temperature

Degrees Fahrenheit = (°C x 1.8) + 32   Degrees Celsius (Degrees Centigrade; °C) = (°F - 32) x 0.56

It is common practice to convert from miles per gallon (mpg) to litres/100 kilometres (l/100km), where mpg x l/100 km = 282

Spare parts are available from many sources, including maker's appointed garages, accessory shops, and motor factors. To be sure of obtaining the correct parts, it will sometimes be necessary to quote the vehicle identification number (see Vehicle identification). If possible, it can also be useful to take the old parts along for positive identification. Items such as starter motors and alternators may be available under a service exchange scheme – any parts returned should always be clean.

Our advice regarding spare part sources is as follows.

Officially-appointed garages

This is the best source of parts which are peculiar to your car, and which are not otherwise generally available (eg badges, interior trim, certain body panels, etc). It is also the only place at which you should buy parts if the car is still under warranty.

Accessory shops

These are very good places to buy materials and components needed for the maintenance of your car (oil, air and fuel filters, spark plugs, light bulbs, drivebelts, oils and greases, brake pads, touch-up paint, etc). Components of this nature sold by a reputable shop are of the same standard as those used by the car manufacturer.

Besides components, these shops also sell tools and general accessories, usually have convenient opening hours, charge lower prices, and can often be found not far from home. Some accessory shops have parts counters where the components needed for almost any repair job can be purchased or ordered.

Motor factors

Good factors will stock all the more important components which wear out comparatively quickly, and can sometimes supply individual components needed for the overhaul of a larger assembly (eg brake seals and hydraulic parts, bearing shells, pistons, valves, alternator brushes). They may also handle work such as cylinder block reboring, crankshaft regrinding and balancing, etc.

Tyre and exhaust specialists

These outlets may be independent, or members of a local or national chain. They frequently offer competitive prices when compared with a main dealer or local garage, but it will pay to obtain several quotes before making a decision. When researching prices, also ask what 'extras' may be added – for instance, fitting a new valve and balancing the wheel are both commonly charged on top of the price of a new tyre.

Other sources

Beware of parts or materials obtained from market stalls, car boot sales or similar outlets. Such items are not invariably sub-standard, but there is little chance of compensation if they do prove unsatisfactory. In the case of safety-critical components such as brake pads, there is the risk not only of financial loss but also of an accident causing injury or death.

Second-hand components or assemblies obtained from a car breaker can be a good buy in some circumstances, but this sort of purchase is best made by the experienced DIY mechanic.

Vehicle identification numbers

Modifications are a continuing and unpublicised process in car manufacture, quite apart from major model changes. Spare parts manuals and lists are compiled upon a numerical basis, the individual vehicle identification numbers being essential to correct identification of the component concerned.

When ordering spare parts, always give as much information as possible. Quote the car model, year of manufacture, body and engine numbers as appropriate.

The vehicle identification plate is located at the base of the driver's door B-pillar, and can be viewed with the door open (see illustration). In addition to many other details, it carries the Vehicle Identification Number (VIN), maximum vehicle weight information, and codes for interior trim and body colours.

The Vehicle Identification Number (VIN) is given on the vehicle identification plate. It is also stamped into the driver's-side floor panel beside the front seat, and may also be viewed through the base of the windscreen on the passenger's side (see illustration).

The engine number is stamped in the following locations, according to engine type:

☐ On petrol engines, it appears at the transmission end of the engine, below the throttle housing (see illustration).

☐ On diesel engines, the number is stamped at the top of the engine, below and in line with the oil filler cap (see illustration).

VIN plate at the base of the driver's door pillar

VIN is visible on the passenger side of the windscreen

On petrol engines, the engine number is under the throttle housing

Engine number location on diesel engines

Whenever servicing, repair or overhaul work is carried out on the car or its components, observe the following procedures and instructions. This will assist in carrying out the operation efficiently and to a professional standard of workmanship.

Joint mating faces and gaskets

When separating components at their mating faces, never insert screwdrivers or similar implements into the joint between the faces in order to prise them apart. This can cause severe damage which results in oil leaks, coolant leaks, etc upon reassembly. Separation is usually achieved by tapping along the joint with a soft-faced hammer in order to break the seal. However, note that this method may not be suitable where dowels are used for component location.

Where a gasket is used between the mating faces of two components, a new one must be fitted on reassembly; fit it dry unless otherwise stated in the repair procedure. Make sure that the mating faces are clean and dry, with all traces of old gasket removed. When cleaning a joint face, use a tool which is unlikely to score or damage the face, and remove any burrs or nicks with an oilstone or fine file.

Make sure that tapped holes are cleaned with a pipe cleaner, and keep them free of jointing compound, if this is being used, unless specifically instructed otherwise.

Ensure that all orifices, channels or pipes are clear, and blow through them, preferably using compressed air.

Oil seals

Oil seals can be removed by levering them out with a wide flat-bladed screwdriver or similar implement. Alternatively, a number of self-tapping screws may be screwed into the seal, and these used as a purchase for pliers or some similar device in order to pull the seal free.

Whenever an oil seal is removed from its working location, either individually or as part of an assembly, it should be renewed.

The very fine sealing lip of the seal is easily damaged, and will not seal if the surface it contacts is not completely clean and free from scratches, nicks or grooves. If the original sealing surface of the component cannot be restored, and the manufacturer has not made provision for slight relocation of the seal relative to the sealing surface, the component should be renewed.

Protect the lips of the seal from any surface which may damage them in the course of fitting. Use tape or a conical sleeve where possible. Where indicated, lubricate the seal lips with oil before fitting and, on dual-lipped seals, fill the space between the lips with grease.

Unless otherwise stated, oil seals must be fitted with their sealing lips toward the lubricant to be sealed.

Use a tubular drift or block of wood of the appropriate size to install the seal and, if the seal housing is shouldered, drive the seal down to the shoulder. If the seal housing is unshouldered, the seal should be fitted with its face flush with the housing top face (unless otherwise instructed).

Screw threads and fastenings

Seized nuts, bolts and screws are quite a common occurrence where corrosion has set in, and the use of penetrating oil or releasing fluid will often overcome this problem if the offending item is soaked for a while before attempting to release it. The use of an impact driver may also provide a means of releasing such stubborn fastening devices, when used in conjunction with the appropriate screwdriver bit or socket. If none of these methods works, it may be necessary to resort to the careful application of heat, or the use of a hacksaw or nut splitter device. Before resorting to extreme methods, check that you are not dealing with a left-hand thread!

Studs are usually removed by locking two nuts together on the threaded part, and then using a spanner on the lower nut to unscrew the stud. Studs or bolts which have broken off below the surface of the component in which they are mounted can sometimes be removed using a stud extractor.

Always ensure that a blind tapped hole is completely free from oil, grease, water or other fluid before installing the bolt or stud. Failure to do this could cause the housing to crack due to the hydraulic action of the bolt or stud as it is screwed in.

For some screw fastenings, notably cylinder head bolts or nuts, torque wrench settings are no longer specified for the latter stages of tightening, "angle-tightening" being called up instead. Typically, a fairly low torque wrench setting will be applied to the bolts/nuts in the correct sequence, followed by one or more stages of tightening through specified angles.

When checking or retightening a nut or bolt to a specified torque setting, slacken the nut or bolt by a quarter of a turn, and then retighten to the specified setting. However, this should not be attempted where angular tightening has been used.

Locknuts, locktabs and washers

Any fastening which will rotate against a component or housing during tightening should always have a washer between it and the relevant component or housing.

Spring or split washers should always be renewed when they are used to lock a critical component such as a big-end bearing retaining bolt or nut. Locktabs which are folded over to retain a nut or bolt should always be renewed.

Self-locking nuts can be re-used in non-critical areas, providing resistance can be felt when the locking portion passes over the bolt or stud thread. However, it should be noted that self-locking stiffnuts tend to lose their effectiveness after long periods of use, and should then be renewed as a matter of course.

Split pins must always be replaced with new ones of the correct size for the hole.

When thread-locking compound is found on the threads of a fastener which is to be re-used, it should be cleaned off with a wire brush and solvent, and fresh compound applied on reassembly.

Special tools

Some repair procedures in this manual entail the use of special tools such as a press, two or three-legged pullers, spring compressors, etc. Wherever possible, suitable readily-available alternatives to the manufacturer's special tools are described, and are shown in use. In some instances, where no alternative is possible, it has been necessary to resort to the use of a manufacturer's tool, and this has been done for reasons of safety as well as the efficient completion of the repair operation. Unless you are highly-skilled and have a thorough understanding of the procedures described, never attempt to bypass the use of any special tool when the procedure described specifies its use. Not only is there a very great risk of personal injury, but expensive damage could be caused to the components involved.

Environmental considerations

When disposing of used engine oil, brake fluid, antifreeze, etc, give due consideration to any detrimental environmental effects. Do not, for instance, pour any of the above liquids down drains into the general sewage system, or onto the ground to soak away, as this is likely to pollute your local environment. Many local council refuse tips provide a facility for waste oil disposal, as do some garages. You can find your nearest disposal point by calling the Environment Agency on 03708 506 506 or by visiting www.oilbankline.org.uk.

Note: It is illegal and anti-social to dump oil down the drain. To find the location of your local oil recycling bank, call 03708 506 506 or visit www.oilbankline.org.uk.

The jack supplied with the car's tool kit should only be used for changing the roadwheels – see Wheel changing at the front of this manual. When carrying out any other kind of work, raise the car using a hydraulic (or 'trolley') jack, and always supplement the jack with axle stands positioned under the jacking/support points (see illustration). If the roadwheels do not have to be removed, consider using wheel ramps – if wished, these can be placed under the wheels once the car has been raised using a hydraulic jack, and then lowered onto the ramps so that it is resting on its wheels.

Only ever jack the car up on a solid, level surface. If there is even a slight slope, take great care that the car cannot move as the wheels are lifted off the ground. Jacking up on an uneven or gravelled surface is not recommended, as the weight of the car will not be evenly distributed, and the jack may slip as the car is raised.

As far as possible, do not leave the car unattended once it has been raised, particularly if children are playing nearby.

Before jacking up the front of the car, ensure that the handbrake is firmly applied. When jacking up the rear of the car, place wooden chocks in front of the front wheels, and engage first gear.

To raise the front and/or rear of the car, use the jacking/support points at the front and rear ends of the door sills, which are located at the places marked by a notch in the sill's lower flange (see illustration). Position a block of wood with a groove cut in it on the jack head to prevent the car's weight resting on the sill edge; align the sill edge with the groove in the wood so that the car's weight is spread evenly over the surface of the block. Supplement the jack with axle stands (also with slotted blocks of wood) positioned as close as possible to the jacking points.

When using a hydraulic jack or axle stands,

always try to position the jack head or axle stand head under one of the relevant jacking points.

Providing care is taken (and a block of wood is used to spread the load), the centre of the front subframe and centre of the rear axle beam, may be used as support points. It may be safe also to use reinforced areas of the floor pan ('chassis legs'), particularly those in the region of suspension mountings, as support points – consult a Ford dealer for advice before using anything other than the approved jacking points, however.

Do not jack the car under any other part of the sill, sump, floor pan, or directly under any of the steering or suspension components.

⚠️ *Warning: Never work under, around, or near a raised vehicle, unless it is adequately supported on stands. Do not rely on a jack alone, as even a hydraulic jack could fail under load.*

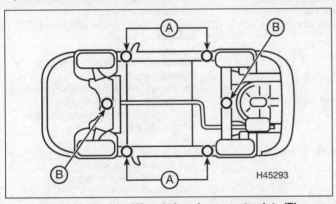

Sill jacking points (A) and chassis support points (B)

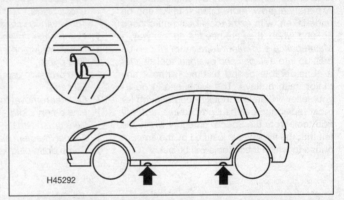

Jacking points on sill flanges are indicated by notches

Disconnecting the battery

1 Numerous systems fitted to the vehicle require battery power to be available at all times, either to ensure their continued operation (such as the clock) or to maintain control unit memories which would be erased if the battery were to be disconnected. Whenever the battery is to be disconnected therefore, first note the following, to ensure that there are no unforeseen consequences of this action:

a) First, on any vehicle with central locking, it is a wise precaution to remove the key from the ignition, and to keep it with you, so that it does not get locked in, if the central locking should engage accidentally when the battery is reconnected.

b) If the battery is disconnected while the alarm system is armed or activated, the alarm will remain in the same state when the battery is reconnected. The same applies to the engine immobiliser system.

c) If a Ford 'Keycode' audio unit is fitted, and the unit and/or the battery is disconnected, the unit will not function again on reconnection until the correct

security code is entered. Details of this procedure, which varies according to the unit and model year, are given in the 'Ford Audio Systems Operating Guide' supplied with the car when new, with the code itself being given in a 'Radio Passport' and/or a 'Keycode Label' at the same time. Ensure you have the correct code before you disconnect the battery. For obvious security reasons, the procedure is not given in this manual. If you do not have the code or details of the correct procedure, but can supply proof of ownership and a legitimate reason for wanting this information, the car's selling dealer may be able to help.

d) The engine management powertrain control module (PCM) is of the 'self-learning' type, meaning that as it operates, it also monitors and stores the settings which give optimum engine performance under all operating conditions. When the battery is disconnected, these settings are lost and the PCM reverts to the base settings

programmed into its memory at the factory. On restarting, this may lead to the engine running/idling roughly for a short while, until the PCM has re-learned the optimum settings. This process is best accomplished by taking the vehicle on a road test (for approximately 15 minutes), covering all engine speeds and loads, concentrating mainly in the 2500 to 3500 rpm region,

e) On models with electric windows, it will be necessary to reprogramme the motors to restore the one-touch function of the buttons, after reconnection of the battery. To do this, fully close both front windows. With the windows closed, depress the up button of the driver's side window for approximately 5 seconds, then release it and depress the passenger side window up button for approximately 5 seconds.

f) On all models, when reconnecting the battery after disconnection, switch on the ignition and wait 10 seconds to allow the electronic vehicle systems to stabilise and re-initialise.

Introduction

A selection of good tools is a fundamental requirement for anyone contemplating the maintenance and repair of a motor vehicle. For the owner who does not possess any, their purchase will prove a considerable expense, offsetting some of the savings made by doing-it-yourself. However, provided that the tools purchased meet the relevant national safety standards and are of good quality, they will last for many years and prove an extremely worthwhile investment.

To help the average owner to decide which tools are needed to carry out the various tasks detailed in this manual, we have compiled three lists of tools under the following headings: *Maintenance and minor repair*, *Repair and overhaul*, and *Special*. Newcomers to practical mechanics should start off with the *Maintenance and minor repair* tool kit, and confine themselves to the simpler jobs around the vehicle. Then, as confidence and experience grow, more difficult tasks can be undertaken, with extra tools being purchased as, and when, they are needed. In this way, a *Maintenance and minor repair* tool kit can be built up into a *Repair and overhaul* tool kit over a considerable period of time, without any major cash outlays. The experienced do-it-yourselfer will have a tool kit good enough for most repair and overhaul procedures, and will add tools from the *Special* category when it is felt that the expense is justified by the amount of use to which these tools will be put.

Maintenance and minor repair tool kit

The tools given in this list should be considered as a minimum requirement if routine maintenance, servicing and minor repair operations are to be undertaken. We recommend the purchase of combination spanners (ring one end, open-ended the other); although more expensive than open-ended ones, they do give the advantages of both types of spanner.

☐ *Combination spanners:*
Metric - 8 to 19 mm inclusive
☐ *Adjustable spanner - 35 mm jaw (approx.)*
☐ *Spark plug spanner (with rubber insert) - petrol models*
☐ *Spark plug gap adjustment tool - petrol models*
☐ *Set of feeler gauges*
☐ *Brake bleed nipple spanner*
☐ *Screwdrivers:*
Flat blade - 100 mm long x 6 mm dia
Cross blade - 100 mm long x 6 mm dia
Torx - various sizes (not all vehicles)
☐ *Combination pliers*
☐ *Hacksaw (junior)*
☐ *Tyre pump*
☐ *Tyre pressure gauge*
☐ *Oil can*
☐ *Oil filter removal tool (if applicable)*
☐ *Fine emery cloth*
☐ *Wire brush (small)*
☐ *Funnel (medium size)*
☐ *Sump drain plug key (not all vehicles)*

Repair and overhaul tool kit

These tools are virtually essential for anyone undertaking any major repairs to a motor vehicle, and are additional to those given in the *Maintenance and minor repair* list. Included in this list is a comprehensive set of sockets. Although these are expensive, they will be found invaluable as they are so versatile - particularly if various drives are included in the set. We recommend the half-inch square-drive type, as this can be used with most proprietary torque wrenches.

The tools in this list will sometimes need to be supplemented by tools from the *Special* list:

☐ *Sockets to cover range in previous list (including Torx sockets)*
☐ *Reversible ratchet drive (for use with sockets)*
☐ *Extension piece, 250 mm (for use with sockets)*
☐ *Universal joint (for use with sockets)*
☐ *Flexible handle or sliding T "breaker bar" (for use with sockets)*
☐ *Torque wrench (for use with sockets)*
☐ *Self-locking grips*
☐ *Ball pein hammer*
☐ *Soft-faced mallet (plastic or rubber)*
☐ *Screwdrivers:*
Flat blade - long & sturdy, short (chubby), and narrow (electrician's) types
Cross blade – long & sturdy, and short (chubby) types
☐ *Pliers:*
Long-nosed
Side cutters (electrician's)
Circlip (internal and external)
☐ *Cold chisel - 25 mm*
☐ *Scriber*
☐ *Scraper*
☐ *Centre-punch*
☐ *Pin punch*
☐ *Hacksaw*
☐ *Brake hose clamp*
☐ *Brake/clutch bleeding kit*
☐ *Selection of twist drills*
☐ *Steel rule/straight-edge*
☐ *Allen keys (inc. splined/Torx type)*
☐ *Selection of files*
☐ *Wire brush*
☐ *Axle stands*
☐ *Jack (strong trolley or hydraulic type)*
☐ *Light with extension lead*
☐ *Universal electrical multi-meter*

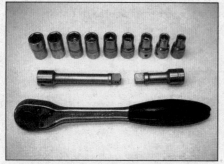

Sockets and reversible ratchet drive

Brake bleeding kit

Torx key, socket and bit

Hose clamp

Angular-tightening gauge

Special tools

The tools in this list are those which are not used regularly, are expensive to buy, or which need to be used in accordance with their manufacturers' instructions. Unless relatively difficult mechanical jobs are undertaken frequently, it will not be economic to buy many of these tools. Where this is the case, you could consider clubbing together with friends (or joining a motorists' club) to make a joint purchase, or borrowing the tools against a deposit from a local garage or tool hire specialist.

The following list contains only those tools and instruments freely available to the public, and not those special tools produced by the vehicle manufacturer specifically for its dealer network. You will find occasional references to these manufacturers' special tools in the text of this manual. Generally, an alternative method of doing the job without the vehicle manufacturers' special tool is given. However, sometimes there is no alternative to using them. Where this is the case and the relevant tool cannot be bought or borrowed, you will have to entrust the work to a dealer.

☐ Angular-tightening gauge
☐ Valve spring compressor
☐ Valve grinding tool
☐ Piston ring compressor
☐ Piston ring removal/installation tool
☐ Cylinder bore hone
☐ Balljoint separator
☐ Coil spring compressors (where applicable)
☐ Two/three-legged hub and bearing puller
☐ Impact screwdriver
☐ Micrometer and/or vernier calipers
☐ Dial gauge
☐ Tachometer
☐ Fault code reader
☐ Cylinder compression gauge
☐ Hand-operated vacuum pump and gauge
☐ Clutch plate alignment set
☐ Brake shoe steady spring cup removal tool
☐ Bush and bearing removal/installation set
☐ Stud extractors
☐ Tap and die set
☐ Lifting tackle

Buying tools

Reputable motor accessory shops and superstores often offer excellent quality tools at discount prices, so it pays to shop around.

Remember, you don't have to buy the most expensive items on the shelf, but it is always advisable to steer clear of the very cheap tools. Beware of 'bargains' offered on market stalls, on-line or at car boot sales. There are plenty of good tools around at reasonable prices, but always aim to purchase items which meet the relevant national safety standards. If in doubt, ask the proprietor or manager of the shop for advice before making a purchase.

Care and maintenance of tools

Having purchased a reasonable tool kit, it is necessary to keep the tools in a clean and serviceable condition. After use, always wipe off any dirt, grease and metal particles using a clean, dry cloth, before putting the tools away. Never leave them lying around after they have been used. A simple tool rack on the garage or workshop wall for items such as screwdrivers and pliers is a good idea. Store all normal spanners and sockets in a metal box. Any measuring instruments, gauges, meters, etc, must be carefully stored where they cannot be damaged or become rusty.

Take a little care when tools are used. Hammer heads inevitably become marked, and screwdrivers lose the keen edge on their blades from time to time. A little timely attention with emery cloth or a file will soon restore items like this to a good finish.

Working facilities

Not to be forgotten when discussing tools is the workshop itself. If anything more than routine maintenance is to be carried out, a suitable working area becomes essential.

It is appreciated that many an owner-mechanic is forced by circumstances to remove an engine or similar item without the benefit of a garage or workshop. Having done this, any repairs should always be done under the cover of a roof.

Wherever possible, any dismantling should be done on a clean, flat workbench or table at a suitable working height.

Any workbench needs a vice; one with a jaw opening of 100 mm is suitable for most jobs. As mentioned previously, some clean dry storage space is also required for tools, as well as for any lubricants, cleaning fluids, touch-up paints etc, which become necessary.

Another item which may be required, and which has a much more general usage, is an electric drill with a chuck capacity of at least 8 mm. This, together with a good range of twist drills, is virtually essential for fitting accessories.

Last, but not least, always keep a supply of old newspapers and clean, lint-free rags available, and try to keep any working area as clean as possible.

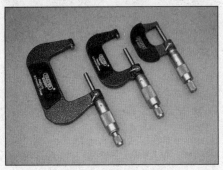

Micrometers

Dial test indicator ("dial gauge")

Oil filter removal tool (strap wrench type)

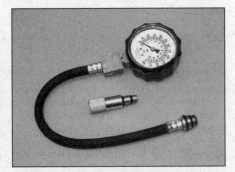

Compression tester

Bearing puller

This is a guide to getting your vehicle through the MOT test. Obviously it will not be possible to examine the vehicle to the same standard as the professional MOT tester. However, working through the following checks will enable you to identify any problem areas before submitting the vehicle for the test.

It has only been possible to summarise the test requirements here, based on the regulations in force at the time of printing. Test standards are becoming increasingly stringent, although there are some exemptions for older vehicles.

An assistant will be needed to help carry out some of these checks.

The checks have been sub-divided into four categories, as follows:

1 Checks carried out **FROM THE DRIVER'S SEAT**

2 Checks carried out **WITH THE VEHICLE ON THE GROUND**

3 Checks carried out **WITH THE VEHICLE RAISED AND THE WHEELS FREE TO TURN**

4 Checks carried out on **YOUR VEHICLE'S EXHAUST EMISSION SYSTEM**

1 Checks carried out **FROM THE DRIVER'S SEAT**

Handbrake (parking brake)

☐ Test the operation of the handbrake. Excessive travel (too many clicks) indicates incorrect brake or cable adjustment.
☐ Check that the handbrake cannot be released by tapping the lever sideways. Check the security of the lever mountings.

☐ If the parking brake is foot-operated, check that the pedal is secure and without excessive travel, and that the release mechanism operates correctly.
☐ Where applicable, test the operation of the electronic handbrake. The brake should engage and disengage without excessive delay. If the warning light does not extinguish when the brake is disengaged, this could indicate a fault which will need further investigation.

Footbrake

☐ Depress the brake pedal and check that it does not creep down to the floor, indicating a master cylinder fault. Release the pedal,

wait a few seconds, then depress it again. If the pedal travels nearly to the floor before firm resistance is felt, brake adjustment or repair is necessary. If the pedal feels spongy, there is air in the hydraulic system which must be removed by bleeding.

☐ Check that the brake pedal is secure and in good condition. Check also for signs of fluid leaks on the pedal, floor or carpets, which would indicate failed seals in the brake master cylinder.
☐ Check the servo unit (when applicable) by operating the brake pedal several times, then keeping the pedal depressed and starting the engine. As the engine starts, the pedal will move down slightly. If not, the vacuum hose or the servo itself may be faulty.

Steering wheel and column

☐ Examine the steering wheel for fractures or looseness of the hub, spokes or rim.
☐ Move the steering wheel from side to side and then up and down. Check that the steering wheel is not loose on the column, indicating wear or a loose retaining nut. Continue moving the steering wheel as before, but also turn it slightly from left to right.

☐ Check that the steering wheel is not loose on the column, and that there is no abnormal movement of the steering wheel, indicating wear in the column support bearings or couplings.
☐ Check that the ignition lock (where fitted) engages and disengages correctly.
☐ Steering column adjustment mechanisms (where fitted) must be able to lock the column securely in place with no play evident.

Windscreen, mirrors and sunvisor

☐ The windscreen must be free of cracks or other significant damage within the driver's field of view. (Small stone chips are acceptable.) Rear view mirrors must be secure, intact, and capable of being adjusted.

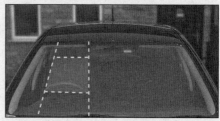

☐ The driver's sunvisor must be capable of being stored in the "up" position.

Seat belts and seats

Note: *The following checks are applicable to all seat belts, front and rear.*

☐ Examine the webbing of all the belts (including rear belts if fitted) for cuts, serious fraying or deterioration. Fasten and unfasten each belt to check the buckles. If applicable, check the retracting mechanism. Check the security of all seat belt mountings accessible from inside the vehicle, ensuring any height adjustable mountings lock securely in place.

☐ Seat belts with pre-tensioners, once activated, have a "flag" or similar showing on the seat belt stalk. This, in itself, is not a reason for test failure.

☐ The front seats themselves must be securely attached and the backrests must lock in the upright position.

Doors

☐ Both front doors must be able to be opened and closed from outside and inside, and must latch securely when closed.

Bonnet and boot/tailgate

☐ The bonnet and boot/tailgate must latch securely when closed.

2 Checks carried out WITH THE VEHICLE ON THE GROUND

Vehicle identification

☐ Number plates must be in good condition, secure and legible, with letters and numbers correctly spaced – spacing at (A) should be 33 mm and at (B) 11 mm. At the front, digits must be black on a white background and at the rear black on a yellow background. Other background designs (such as honeycomb) are not permitted.

☐ The VIN plate and/or homologation plate must be permanently displayed and legible.

Electrical equipment

☐ Switch on the ignition and check the operation of the horn.

☐ Check the windscreen washers and wipers, examining the wiper blades; renew damaged or perished blades. Also check the operation of the stop-lights.

☐ Check the operation of the sidelights and number plate lights. The lenses and reflectors must be secure, clean and undamaged.

☐ Check the operation and alignment of the headlights. The headlight reflectors must not be tarnished and the lenses must be undamaged.

☐ Switch on the ignition and check the operation of the direction indicators (including the instrument panel tell-tale) and the hazard warning lights. Operation of the sidelights and stop-lights must not affect the indicators - if it does, the cause is usually a bad earth at the rear light cluster. Indicators should flash at a rate of between 60 and 120 times per minute – faster or slower than this could indicate a fault with the flasher unit or a bad earth at one of the light units.

☐ Check the operation of the rear foglight(s), including the warning light on the instrument panel or in the switch.

☐ The warning lights must illuminate in accordance with the manufacturer's design. For most vehicles, the ABS and other warning lights should illuminate when the ignition is switched on, and (if the system is operating properly) extinguish after a few seconds. Refer to the owner's handbook.

Footbrake

☐ Examine the master cylinder, brake pipes and servo unit for leaks, loose mountings, corrosion or other damage. If ABS is fitted, this unit should also be examined for signs of leaks or corrosion.

☐ The fluid reservoir must be secure and the fluid level must be between the upper (**A**) and lower (**B**) markings.

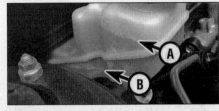

☐ Inspect both front brake flexible hoses for cracks or deterioration of the rubber. Turn the steering from lock to lock, and ensure that the hoses do not contact the wheel, tyre, or any part of the steering or suspension mechanism. With the brake pedal firmly depressed, check the hoses for bulges or leaks under pressure.

Steering and suspension

☐ Have your assistant turn the steering wheel from side to side slightly, up to the point where the steering gear just begins to transmit this movement to the roadwheels. Check for excessive free play between the steering wheel and the steering gear, indicating wear or insecurity of the steering column joints, the column-to-steering gear coupling, or the steering gear itself.

☐ Have your assistant turn the steering wheel more vigorously in each direction, so that the roadwheels just begin to turn. As this is done, examine all the steering joints, linkages, fittings and attachments. Renew any component that shows signs of wear or damage. On vehicles with power steering, check the security and condition of the steering pump, drivebelt and hoses.

☐ Check that the vehicle is standing level, and at approximately the correct ride height.

Shock absorbers

☐ Depress each corner of the vehicle in turn, then release it. The vehicle should rise and then settle in its normal position. If the vehicle continues to rise and fall, the shock absorber is defective. A shock absorber which has seized will also cause the vehicle to fail.

Exhaust system

☐ Start the engine. With your assistant holding a rag over the tailpipe, check the entire system for leaks. Repair or renew leaking sections.

3 Checks carried out **WITH THE VEHICLE RAISED AND THE WHEELS FREE TO TURN**

Jack up the front and rear of the vehicle, and securely support it on axle stands. Position the stands clear of the suspension assemblies. Ensure that the wheels are clear of the ground and that the steering can be turned from lock to lock.

Steering mechanism

☐ Have your assistant turn the steering from lock to lock. Check that the steering turns smoothly, and that no part of the steering mechanism, including a wheel or tyre, fouls any brake hose or pipe or any part of the body structure.
☐ Examine the steering rack rubber gaiters for damage or insecurity of the retaining clips. If power steering is fitted, check for signs of damage or leakage of the fluid hoses, pipes or connections. Also check for excessive stiffness or binding of the steering, a missing split pin or locking device, or severe corrosion of the body structure within 30 cm of any steering component attachment point.

Front and rear suspension and wheel bearings

☐ Starting at the front right-hand side, grasp the roadwheel at the 3 o'clock and 9 o'clock positions and rock gently but firmly. Check for free play or insecurity at the wheel bearings, suspension balljoints, or suspension mount-ings, pivots and attachments.
☐ Now grasp the wheel at the 12 o'clock and 6 o'clock positions and repeat the previous inspection. Spin the wheel, and check for roughness or tightness of the front wheel bearing.

☐ If excess free play is suspected at a component pivot point, this can be confirmed by using a large screwdriver or similar tool and levering between the mounting and the component attachment. This will confirm whether the wear is in the pivot bush, its retaining bolt, or in the mounting itself (the bolt holes can often become elongated).

☐ Carry out all the above checks at the other front wheel, and then at both rear wheels.

Springs and shock absorbers

☐ Examine the suspension struts (when applicable) for serious fluid leakage, corrosion, or damage to the casing. Also check the security of the mounting points.
☐ If coil springs are fitted, check that the spring ends locate in their seats, and that the spring is not corroded, cracked or broken.
☐ If leaf springs are fitted, check that all leaves are intact, that the axle is securely attached to each spring, and that there is no deterioration of the spring eye mountings, bushes, and shackles.

☐ The same general checks apply to vehicles fitted with other suspension types, such as torsion bars, hydraulic displacer units, etc. Ensure that all mountings and attachments are secure, that there are no signs of excessive wear, corrosion or damage, and (on hydraulic types) that there are no fluid leaks or damaged pipes.
☐ Inspect the shock absorbers for signs of serious fluid leakage. Check for wear of the mounting bushes or attachments, or damage to the body of the unit.

Driveshafts
(fwd vehicles only)

☐ Rotate each front wheel in turn and inspect the constant velocity joint gaiters for splits or damage. Also check that each driveshaft is straight and undamaged.

Braking system

☐ If possible without dismantling, check brake pad wear and disc condition. Ensure that the friction lining material has not worn excessively, (A) and that the discs are not fractured, pitted, scored or badly worn (B).

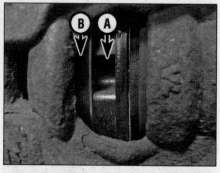

☐ Examine all the rigid brake pipes underneath the vehicle, and the flexible hose(s) at the rear. Look for corrosion, chafing or insecurity of the pipes, and for signs of bulging under pressure, chafing, splits or deterioration of the flexible hoses.
☐ Look for signs of fluid leaks at the brake calipers or on the brake backplates. Repair or renew leaking components.
☐ Slowly spin each wheel, while your assistant depresses and releases the footbrake. Ensure that each brake is operating and does not bind when the pedal is released.

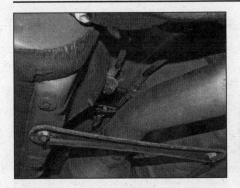

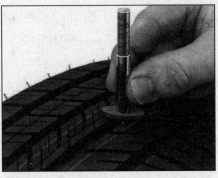

☐ Examine the handbrake mechanism, checking for frayed or broken cables, excessive corrosion, or wear or insecurity of the linkage. Check that the mechanism works on each relevant wheel, and releases fully, without binding.

☐ It is not possible to test brake efficiency without special equipment, but a road test can be carried out later to check that the vehicle pulls up in a straight line.

Fuel and exhaust systems

☐ Inspect the fuel tank (including the filler cap), fuel pipes, hoses and unions. All components must be secure and free from leaks. Locking fuel caps must lock securely and the key must be provided for the MOT test.

☐ Examine the exhaust system over its entire length, checking for any damaged, broken or missing mountings, security of the retaining clamps and rust or corrosion.

Wheels and tyres

☐ Examine the sidewalls and tread area of each tyre in turn. Check for cuts, tears, lumps, bulges, separation of the tread, and exposure of the ply or cord due to wear or damage. Check that the tyre bead is correctly seated on the wheel rim, that the valve is sound and properly seated, and that the wheel is not distorted or damaged.

☐ Check that the tyres are of the correct size for the vehicle, that they are of the same size and type on each axle, and that the pressures are correct.

☐ Check the tyre tread depth. The legal minimum at the time of writing is 1.6 mm over the central three-quarters of the tread width. Abnormal tread wear may indicate incorrect front wheel alignment or wear in steering or suspension components.

☐ If the spare wheel is fitted externally or in a separate carrier beneath the vehicle, check that mountings are secure and free of excessive corrosion.

Body corrosion

☐ Check the condition of the entire vehicle structure for signs of corrosion in load-bearing areas. (These include chassis box sections, side sills, cross-members, pillars, and all suspension, steering, braking system and seat belt mountings and anchorages.) Any corrosion which has seriously reduced the thickness of a load-bearing area (or is within 30 cm of safety-related components such as steering or suspension) is likely to cause the vehicle to fail. In this case professional repairs are likely to be needed.

☐ Damage or corrosion which causes sharp or otherwise dangerous edges to be exposed will also cause the vehicle to fail.

Towbars

☐ Check the condition of mounting points (both beneath the vehicle and within boot/hatchback areas) for signs of corrosion, ensuring that all fixings are secure and not worn or damaged. There must be no excessive play in detachable tow ball arms or quick-release mechanisms.

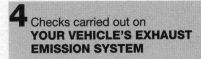

4 Checks carried out on **YOUR VEHICLE'S EXHAUST EMISSION SYSTEM**

Petrol models

☐ The engine should be warmed up, and running well (ignition system in good order, air filter element clean, etc).

☐ Before testing, run the engine at around 2500 rpm for 20 seconds. Let the engine drop to idle, and watch for smoke from the exhaust. If the idle speed is too high, or if dense blue or black smoke emerges for more than 5 seconds, the vehicle will fail. Typically, blue smoke signifies oil burning (engine wear); black smoke means unburnt fuel (dirty air cleaner element, or other fuel system fault).

☐ An exhaust gas analyser for measuring carbon monoxide (CO) and hydrocarbons (HC) is now needed. If one cannot be hired or borrowed, have a local garage perform the check.

CO emissions (mixture)

☐ The MOT tester has access to the CO limits for all vehicles. The CO level is measured at idle speed, and at 'fast idle' (2500 to 3000 rpm). The following limits are given as a general guide:

At idle speed – Less than 0.5% CO
At 'fast idle' – Less than 0.3% CO
Lambda reading – 0.97 to 1.03

☐ If the CO level is too high, this may point to poor maintenance, a fuel injection system problem, faulty lambda (oxygen) sensor or catalytic converter. Try an injector cleaning treatment, and check the vehicle's ECU for fault codes.

HC emissions

☐ The MOT tester has access to HC limits for all vehicles. The HC level is measured at 'fast idle' (2500 to 3000 rpm). The following limits are given as a general guide:

At 'fast idle' – Less then 200 ppm

☐ Excessive HC emissions are typically caused by oil being burnt (worn engine), or by a blocked crankcase ventilation system ('breather'). If the engine oil is old and thin, an oil change may help. If the engine is running badly, check the vehicle's ECU for fault codes.

Diesel models

☐ The only emission test for diesel engines is measuring exhaust smoke density, using a calibrated smoke meter. The test involves accelerating the engine at least 3 times to its maximum unloaded speed.

Note: *On engines with a timing belt, it is VITAL that the belt is in good condition before the test is carried out.*

☐ With the engine warmed up, it is first purged by running at around 2500 rpm for 20 seconds. A governor check is then carried out, by slowly accelerating the engine to its maximum speed. After this, the smoke meter is connected, and the engine is accelerated quickly to maximum speed three times. If the smoke density is less than the limits given below, the vehicle will pass:

Non-turbo vehicles: 2.5m-1
Turbocharged vehicles: 3.0m-1

☐ If excess smoke is produced, try fitting a new air cleaner element, or using an injector cleaning treatment. If the engine is running badly, where applicable, check the vehicle's ECU for fault codes. Also check the vehicle's EGR system, where applicable. At high mileages, the injectors may require professional attention.

Engine

- ☐ Engine fails to rotate when attempting to start
- ☐ Engine rotates, but will not start
- ☐ Engine difficult to start when cold
- ☐ Engine difficult to start when hot
- ☐ Starter motor noisy or excessively-rough in engagement
- ☐ Engine starts, but stops immediately
- ☐ Engine idles erratically
- ☐ Engine misfires at idle speed
- ☐ Engine misfires throughout the driving speed range
- ☐ Engine hesitates on acceleration
- ☐ Engine stalls
- ☐ Engine lacks power
- ☐ Engine backfires
- ☐ Oil pressure warning light illuminated with engine running
- ☐ Engine runs-on after switching off
- ☐ Engine noises

Cooling system

- ☐ Overheating
- ☐ Overcooling
- ☐ External coolant leakage
- ☐ Internal coolant leakage
- ☐ Corrosion

Fuel and exhaust systems

- ☐ Excessive fuel consumption
- ☐ Fuel leakage and/or fuel odour
- ☐ Excessive noise or fumes from exhaust system

Clutch

- ☐ Pedal travels to floor – no pressure or very little resistance
- ☐ Clutch fails to disengage (unable to select gears)
- ☐ Clutch slips (engine speed increases, with no increase in vehicle speed)
- ☐ Judder as clutch is engaged
- ☐ Noise when depressing or releasing clutch pedal

Manual transmission

- ☐ Noisy in neutral with engine running
- ☐ Noisy in one particular gear
- ☐ Difficulty engaging gears
- ☐ Jumps out of gear
- ☐ Vibration
- ☐ Lubricant leaks

Automatic transmission

- ☐ Fluid leakage
- ☐ General gear selection problems
- ☐ Transmission will not downshift (kickdown) with accelerator pedal fully depressed
- ☐ Engine will not start in any gear, or starts in gears other than Park or Neutral
- ☐ Transmission slips, shifts roughly, is noisy, or has no drive in forward or reverse gears

Driveshafts

- ☐ Vibration when accelerating or decelerating
- ☐ Clicking or knocking noise on turns (at slow speed on full-lock)

Braking system

- ☐ Vehicle pulls to one side under braking
- ☐ Noise (grinding or high-pitched squeal) when brakes applied
- ☐ Excessive brake pedal travel
- ☐ Brake pedal feels spongy when depressed
- ☐ Excessive brake pedal effort required to stop vehicle
- ☐ Judder felt through brake pedal or steering wheel when braking
- ☐ Brakes binding
- ☐ Rear wheels locking under normal braking

Suspension and steering

- ☐ Vehicle pulls to one side
- ☐ Wheel wobble and vibration
- ☐ Excessive pitching and/or rolling around corners, or during braking
- ☐ Wandering or general instability
- ☐ Excessively-stiff steering
- ☐ Excessive play in steering
- ☐ Lack of power assistance
- ☐ Tyre wear excessive

Electrical system

- ☐ Battery will not hold a charge for more than a few days
- ☐ Ignition/no-charge warning light remains illuminated with engine running
- ☐ Ignition/no-charge warning light fails to come on
- ☐ Lights inoperative
- ☐ Instrument readings inaccurate or erratic
- ☐ Horn inoperative, or unsatisfactory in operation
- ☐ Windscreen wipers inoperative, or unsatisfactory in operation
- ☐ Windscreen washers inoperative, or unsatisfactory in operation
- ☐ Electric windows inoperative, or unsatisfactory in operation
- ☐ Window glass fails to move
- ☐ Central locking system inoperative, or unsatisfactory in operation

Introduction

The vehicle owner who does his or her own maintenance according to the recommended service schedules should not have to use this section of the manual very often. Modern component reliability is such that, provided those items subject to wear or deterioration are inspected or renewed at the specified intervals, sudden failure is comparatively rare. Faults do not usually just happen as a result of sudden failure, but develop over a period of time. Major mechanical failures in particular are usually preceded by characteristic symptoms over hundreds or even thousands of miles. Those components which do

occasionally fail without warning are often small and easily carried in the vehicle.

With any fault-finding, the first step is to decide where to begin investigations. Sometimes this is obvious, but on other occasions, a little detective work will be necessary. The owner who makes half a dozen haphazard adjustments or replacements may be successful in curing a fault (or its symptoms), but will be none the wiser if the fault recurs, and ultimately may have spent more time and money than was necessary. A calm and logical approach will be found to be more satisfactory in the long run.

Always take into account any warning signs or abnormalities that may have been noticed in the period preceding the fault – power loss, high or low gauge readings, unusual smells, etc – and remember that failure of components such as fuses or spark plugs may only be pointers to some underlying fault.

The pages which follow provide an easy-reference guide to the more common problems which may occur during the operation of the vehicle. These problems and their possible causes are grouped under headings denoting various components or systems, such as Engine, Cooling system, etc. The general Chapter which deals with the problem is also shown in brackets; refer to the relevant part of that Chapter for system-specific information. Whatever the fault, certain basic principles apply. These are as follows:

Verify the fault. This is simply a matter of being sure that you know what the symptoms are before starting work. This is particularly important if you are investigating a fault for someone else, who may not have described it very accurately.

Don't overlook the obvious. For example, if the vehicle won't start, is there fuel in the tank? (Don't take anyone else's word on this particular point, and don't trust the fuel gauge either!) If an electrical fault is indicated, look for loose or broken wires before digging out the test gear.

Cure the disease, not the symptom. Substituting a flat battery with a fully-charged one will get you off the hard shoulder, but if the underlying cause is not attended to, the new battery will go the same way. Similarly, changing oil-fouled spark plugs for a new set will get you moving again, but remember that the reason for the fouling (if it wasn't simply an incorrect grade of plug) will have to be established and corrected.

Don't take anything for granted. Particularly, don't forget that a 'new' component may itself be defective (especially if it's been rattling around in the boot for months), and don't leave components out of a fault diagnosis sequence just because they are new or recently-fitted. When you do finally diagnose a difficult fault, you'll probably realise that all the evidence was there from the start.

Consider what work, if any, has recently been carried out. Many faults arise through careless or hurried work. For instance, if any work has been performed under the bonnet, could some of the wiring have been dislodged or incorrectly routed, or a hose trapped? Have all the fasteners been properly tightened? Were new, genuine parts and new gaskets used? There is often a certain amount of detective work to be done in this case, as an apparently-unrelated task can have far-reaching consequences.

Diesel fault diagnosis

The majority of starting problems on small diesel engines are electrical in origin. The mechanic who is familiar with petrol engines but less so with diesel may be inclined to view the diesel's injectors and pump in the same light as the spark plugs and distributor, but this is generally a mistake.

When investigating complaints of difficult starting for someone else, make sure that the correct starting procedure is understood and is being followed. Some drivers are unaware of the significance of the preheating warning light – many modern engines are sufficiently forgiving for this not to matter in mild weather, but with the onset of winter, problems begin. Glow plugs in particular are often neglected – just one faulty plug will make cold-weather starting very difficult.

As a rule of thumb, if the engine is difficult to start but runs well when it has finally got going, the problem is electrical (battery, starter motor or preheating system). If poor performance is combined with difficult starting, the problem is likely to be in the fuel system. The low-pressure (supply) side of the fuel system should be checked before suspecting the injectors and high-pressure pump. The most common fuel supply problem is air getting into the system, and any pipe from the fuel tank forwards must be scrutinised if air leakage is suspected.

Engine

Engine fails to rotate when attempting to start
- [ ] Battery terminal connections loose or corroded (see *Weekly checks*)
- [ ] Battery discharged or faulty (Chapter 5A Section 3)
- [ ] Broken, loose or disconnected wiring in the starting circuit (Chapter 5A Section 10)
- [ ] Defective starter solenoid or ignition switch (Chapter 5A or 12)
- [ ] Defective starter motor (Chapter 5A Section 9)
- [ ] Starter pinion or flywheel ring gear teeth loose or broken (Chapter 2A, 2B, 2D, 2E or 5A)
- [ ] Engine earth strap broken or disconnected (Chapter 5A Section 8)
- [ ] Engine suffering "hydraulic lock" (eg from water drawn into the engine after traversing flooded roads, or from a serious internal coolant leak) – consult a main dealer for advice

Engine rotates, but will not start
- [ ] Fuel tank emptyBattery discharged (engine rotates slowly) (Chapter 5A Section 3)
- [ ] Battery terminal connections loose or corroded (see *Weekly checks*)
- [ ] Ignition components damp or damaged – petrol models (Chapter 1A or 5B)
- [ ] Immobiliser fault, or "uncoded" ignition key being used (Chapter 12 or *Roadside repairs*)
- [ ] Broken, loose or disconnected wiring in the ignition circuit – petrol models (Chapter 1A or 5B)
- [ ] Worn, faulty or incorrectly-gapped spark plugs – petrol models (Chapter 1A Section 21)
- [ ] Preheating system faulty – diesel models (Chapter 5A Section 11)
- [ ] Fuel injection/engine management system fault (Chapter 4A, 4B or 4C)
- [ ] Air in fuel system – diesel models (Chapter 4B Section 3)
- [ ] Major mechanical failure (eg timing belt snapped) (Chapter 2A, 2B, 2D, 2E or 2F)

Engine difficult to start when cold
- [ ] Battery discharged (Chapter 5A Section 3)
- [ ] Battery terminal connections loose or corroded (see *Weekly checks*)
- [ ] Worn, faulty or incorrectly-gapped spark plugs – petrol models (Chapter 1A Section 21)

- [ ] Other ignition system fault – petrol models (Chapter 1A or 5B)
- [ ] Preheating system faulty – diesel models (Chapter 5A Section 11)
- [ ] Fuel injection/engine management system fault (Chapter 4A, 4B or 4C)
- [ ] Wrong grade of engine oil used (*Weekly checks*, Chapter 1A or 1B)
- [ ] Low cylinder compression (Chapter 2A, 2B, 2D or 2E)

Engine difficult to start when hot
- [ ] Air filter element dirty or clogged (Chapter 1A or 1B)
- [ ] Fuel injection/engine management system fault (Chapter 4A, 4B or 4C)
- [ ] Low cylinder compression (Chapter 2A, 2B, 2D or 2E)

Starter motor noisy or excessively-rough in engagement
- [ ] Starter pinion or flywheel ring gear teeth loose or broken (Chapter 2A, 2B, 2D, 2E or 5A)
- [ ] Starter motor mounting bolts loose or missing (Chapter 5A Section 9)
- [ ] Starter motor internal components worn or damaged (Chapter 5A Section 10)

Engine starts, but stops immediately
- [ ] Loose or faulty electrical connections in the ignition circuit – petrol models (Chapter 1A or 5B)
- [ ] Vacuum leak at the throttle housing or inlet manifold – petrol models (Chapter 4A or 4B)
- [ ] Blocked injectors/fuel injection system fault (Chapter 4A or 4B)

Engine idles erratically
- [ ] Air filter element clogged (Chapter 1A or 1B)
- [ ] Vacuum leak at the throttle housing, inlet manifold or associated hoses – petrol models (Chapter 4A or 4C)
- [ ] Worn, faulty or incorrectly-gapped spark plugs – petrol models (Chapter 1A Section 21)
- [ ] Uneven or low cylinder compression (Chapter 2A, 2B or 2D)
- [ ] Camshaft lobes worn (Chapter 2A, 2B or 2D)
- [ ] Blocked injectors/fuel injection system fault (Chapter 4A, or 4B)

Engine (continued)

Engine misfires at idle speed

- ☐ Worn, faulty or incorrectly-gapped spark plugs – petrol models (Chapter 1A Section 21)
- ☐ Vacuum leak at the throttle housing, inlet manifold or associated hoses – petrol models (Chapter 4A or 4C)
- ☐ Blocked injectors/fuel injection system fault (Chapter 4A, 4B or 4C)
- ☐ Faulty injector(s) – diesel models (Chapter 4B Section 11)
- ☐ Uneven or low cylinder compression (Chapter 2A, 2B, 2D or 2E)
- ☐ Disconnected, leaking, or perished crankcase ventilation hoses (Chapter 4C)

Engine misfires throughout the driving speed range

- ☐ Fuel filter choked (Chapter 1B Section 22)
- ☐ Fuel pump faulty, or delivery pressure low – petrol models (Chapter 4A Section 8)
- ☐ Fuel tank vent blocked, or fuel pipes restricted (Chapter 4A or 4B)
- ☐ Vacuum leak at the throttle housing, inlet manifold or associated hoses – petrol models (Chapter 4A or 4C)
- ☐ Worn, faulty or incorrectly-gapped spark plugs – petrol models (Chapter 1A Section 21)
- ☐ Faulty injector(s) – diesel models (Chapter 4B Section 11)
- ☐ Faulty ignition module – petrol models (Chapter 5B Section 2)
- ☐ Uneven or low cylinder compression (Chapter 2A, 2B, 2D or 2E)
- ☐ Blocked injector/fuel injection system fault (Chapter 4A or 4B)
- ☐ Blocked catalytic converter (Chapter 4A, 4B or 4C)
- ☐ Engine overheating (Chapter 3)

Engine hesitates on acceleration

- ☐ Worn, faulty or incorrectly-gapped spark plugs – petrol models (Chapter 1A Section 21)
- ☐ Vacuum leak at the throttle housing, inlet manifold or associated hoses – petrol models (Chapter 4A or 4C)
- ☐ Blocked injectors/fuel injection system fault (Chapter 4A or 4B)
- ☐ Faulty injector(s) – diesel models (Chapter 4B Section 11)

Engine stalls

- ☐ Vacuum leak at the throttle housing, inlet manifold or associated hoses – petrol models (Chapter 4A or 4C)
- ☐ Fuel filter choked (Chapter 1B Section 22)
- ☐ Fuel pump faulty, or delivery pressure low – petrol models (Chapter 4A Section 8)
- ☐ Fuel tank vent blocked, or fuel pipes restricted (Chapter 4A or 4B)
- ☐ Blocked injectors/fuel injection system fault (Chapter 4A or 4B)
- ☐ Faulty injector(s) – diesel models (Chapter 4B Section 11)

Engine lacks power

- ☐ Air filter element blocked (Chapter 1A or 1B)
- ☐ Fuel filter choked (Chapter 1B Section 22)
- ☐ Fuel pipes blocked or restricted (Chapter 4A or 4B)
- ☐ Worn, faulty or incorrectly-gapped spark plugs – petrol models (Chapter 1A Section 21)
- ☐ Engine overheating (Chapter 3)
- ☐ Fuel tank level low – diesel models (Chapter 4B Section 7)
- ☐ Accelerator pedal position sensor faulty (Chapter 4A or 4B)
- ☐ Vacuum leak at the throttle housing, inlet manifold or associated hoses – petrol models (Chapter 4A or 4C)
- ☐ Blocked injectors/fuel injection system fault (Chapter 4A or 4B)
- ☐ Faulty injector(s) – diesel models (Chapter 4B Section 11)
- ☐ Fuel pump faulty, or delivery pressure low – petrol models (Chapter 4A Section 8)
- ☐ Uneven or low cylinder compression (Chapter 2A, 2B, 2D or 2E)
- ☐ Blocked catalytic converter (Chapter 4A, 4B or 4C)
- ☐ Brakes binding (Chapter 1A, 1B or 9)
- ☐ Clutch slipping (Chapter 6 Section 6)

Engine backfires

- ☐ Vacuum leak at the throttle housing, inlet manifold or associated hoses – petrol models (Chapter 4A)
- ☐ Blocked injectors/fuel injection system fault (Chapter 4A or 4B)
- ☐ Blocked catalytic converter (Chapter 4A, 4B or 4C)
- ☐ Faulty ignition module – petrol models (Chapter 5B Section 2)

Oil pressure warning light illuminated with engine running

- ☐ Low oil level, or incorrect oil grade (see *Weekly checks*)
- ☐ Faulty oil pressure switch, or wiring damaged (Chapter 2A, 2B, 2D or 2E)
- ☐ Worn engine bearings and/or oil pump (Chapter 2A, 2B, 2D, 2E or 2F)
- ☐ High engine operating temperature (Chapter 3)
- ☐ Oil pump pressure relief valve defective (Chapter 2A, 2B, 2D or 2E)
- ☐ Oil pump pick-up strainer clogged (Chapter 2A, 2B, 2D or 2E)

Engine runs-on after switching off

- ☐ Excessive carbon build-up in engine (Chapter 2A, 2B, 2D or 2E)
- ☐ High engine operating temperature (Chapter 3)
- ☐ Fuel injection/engine management system fault (Chapter 4A, 4B or 4C)

Engine noises

- ☐ Pre-ignition (pinking) or knocking during acceleration or under load
- ☐ Ignition timing incorrect/ignition system fault – petrol models (Chapter 1A or 5B)
- ☐ Incorrect grade of spark plug – petrol models (Chapter 1A Section 21)
- ☐ Incorrect grade of fuel (Chapter 4A or 4B)
- ☐ Knock sensor faulty – petrol models (Chapter 5B Section 6)
- ☐ Vacuum leak at the throttle housing, inlet manifold or associated hoses – petrol models (Chapter 4A or 4C)
- ☐ Excessive carbon build-up in engine (Chapter 2A, 2B, 2D ro 2E)
- ☐ Fuel injection/engine management system fault (Chapter 4A, 4B or 4C)
- ☐ Faulty injector(s) – diesel models (Chapter 4B Section 11)

Whistling or wheezing noises

- ☐ Leaking inlet manifold or throttle housing gasket – petrol models (Chapter 4A)
- ☐ Leaking exhaust manifold gasket or pipe-to-manifold joint (Chapter 4A or 4B)
- ☐ Leaking vacuum hose (Chapter 4A, 4B, 4C or 9)
- ☐ Blowing cylinder head gasket (Chapter 2A, 2B, 2D or 2E)
- ☐ Partially blocked or leaking crankcase ventilation system (Chapter 4C)

Tapping or rattling noises

- ☐ Worn valve gear or camshaft (Chapter 2A, 2B, 2D or 2E)
- ☐ Ancillary component fault (coolant pump, alternator, etc) (Chapter 3, 5A, etc)

Knocking or thumping noises

- ☐ Worn big-end bearings (regular heavy knocking, perhaps less under load) (Chapter 2F Section 13)
- ☐ Worn main bearings (rumbling and knocking, perhaps worsening under load) (Chapter 2F Section 15)
- ☐ Piston slap – most noticeable when cold, caused by piston/bore wear (Chapter 2F Section 13)
- ☐ Ancillary component fault (coolant pump, alternator, etc) (Chapter 3, 5A, etc)
- ☐ Engine mountings worn or defective (Chapter 2A, 2B, 2D or 2F)
- ☐ Front suspension or steering components worn (Chapter 10)

Cooling system

Overheating

- [ ] Insufficient coolant in system (see *Weekly checks*)
- [ ] Thermostat faulty (Chapter 3 Section 4)
- [ ] Radiator core blocked, or grille restricted (Chapter 3 Section 3)
- [ ] Cooling fan faulty, or resistor pack fault (Chapter 3 Section 5)
- [ ] Inaccurate coolant temperature sensor (Chapter 3 Section 6)
- [ ] Airlock in cooling system (Chapter 1A, 1B or 3)
- [ ] Expansion tank pressure cap faulty (Chapter 3 Section 1)
- [ ] Engine management system fault (Chapter 4A, 4B or 4C)

Overcooling

- [ ] Thermostat faulty (Chapter 3 Section 4)
- [ ] Inaccurate coolant temperature sensor (Chapter 3 Section 6)
- [ ] Cooling fan faulty (Chapter 3 Section 5)
- [ ] Engine management system fault (Chapter 4A, 4B or 4C)

External coolant leakage

- [ ] Deteriorated or damaged hoses or hose clips (Chapter 1A or 1B)
- [ ] Radiator core or heater matrix leaking (Chapter 3 Section 3)
- [ ] Expansion tank pressure cap faulty (Chapter 1A or 1B)
- [ ] Coolant pump internal seal leaking (Chapter 3 Section 7)
- [ ] Coolant pump gasket leaking (Chapter 3 Section 7)
- [ ] Boiling due to overheating (Chapter 3 Section 1)
- [ ] Cylinder block core plug leaking (Chapter 2F Section 12)

Internal coolant leakage

- [ ] Leaking cylinder head gasket (Chapter 2A, 2B or 2D)
- [ ] Cracked cylinder head or cylinder block (Chapter 2A, 2B, 2D or 2F)

Corrosion

- [ ] Infrequent draining and flushing (Chapter 1A or 1B)
- [ ] Incorrect coolant mixture or inappropriate coolant type (see *Weekly checks*)

Fuel and exhaust systems

Excessive fuel consumption

- [ ] Air filter element dirty or clogged (Chapter 1A or 1B)
- [ ] Fuel injection system fault (Chapter 4A, 4B or 4C)
- [ ] Engine management system fault (Chapter 4A, 4B or 4C)
- [ ] Crankcase ventilation system blocked (Chapter 4C)
- [ ] Tyres under-inflated (see *Weekly checks*)
- [ ] Brakes binding (Chapter 1A, 1B or 9)
- [ ] Fuel leak, causing apparent high consumption (Chapter 1A, 1B, 4A or 4B)

Fuel leakage and/or fuel odour

- [ ] Damaged or corroded fuel tank, pipes or connections (Chapter 4A, 4B or 4C)
- [ ] Evaporative emissions system fault – petrol models (Chapter 4C Section 2)

Excessive noise or fumes from exhaust system

- [ ] Leaking exhaust system or manifold joints (Chapter 1A, 1B, 4A or 4B)
- [ ] Leaking, corroded or damaged silencers or pipe (Chapter 1A, 1B, 4A, 4B or 4C)
- [ ] Broken mountings causing body or suspension contact (Chapter 1A or 1B)

Clutch

Pedal travels to floor – no pressure or very little resistance

- [ ] Air in hydraulic system/faulty master or slave cylinder (Chapter 6)
- [ ] Faulty hydraulic release system (Chapter 6 Section 4)
- [ ] Clutch pedal return spring detached or broken (Chapter 6 Section 5)
- [ ] Broken diaphragm spring in clutch pressure plate (Chapter 6 Section 6)

Clutch fails to disengage (unable to select gears)

- [ ] Air in hydraulic system/faulty master or slave cylinder (Chapter 6 Section 4)
- [ ] Faulty hydraulic release system (Chapter 6 Section 3)
- [ ] Clutch disc sticking on transmission input shaft splines (Chapter 6 Section 6)
- [ ] Clutch disc sticking to flywheel or pressure plate (Chapter 6 Section 6)
- [ ] Faulty pressure plate assembly (Chapter 6 Section 6)
- [ ] Clutch release mechanism worn or incorrectly assembled (Chapter 6 Section 7)

Clutch slips (engine speed increases, with no increase in vehicle speed)

- [ ] Faulty hydraulic release system (Chapter 6 Section 4)
- [ ] Clutch disc linings excessively worn (Chapter 6 Section 6)
- [ ] Clutch disc linings contaminated with oil or grease (Chapter 6 Section 6)
- [ ] Faulty pressure plate or weak diaphragm spring (Chapter 6 Section 6)

Judder as clutch is engaged

- [ ] Clutch disc linings contaminated with oil or grease (Chapter 6 Section 6)
- [ ] Clutch disc linings excessively worn (Chapter 6 Section 6)
- [ ] Faulty or distorted pressure plate or diaphragm spring (Chapter 6 Section 6)
- [ ] Worn or loose engine or transmission mountings (Chapter 2A, 2B, 2D or 2E)
- [ ] Clutch disc hub or transmission input shaft splines worn (Chapter 6)

Noise when depressing or releasing clutch pedal

- [ ] Faulty hydraulic release system (Chapter 6 Section 4)
- [ ] Worn or dry clutch pedal bushes (Chapter 6 Section 5)
- [ ] Worn or dry clutch master cylinder piston (Chapter 6 Section 2)
- [ ] Faulty pressure plate assembly (Chapter 6 Section 6)
- [ ] Pressure plate diaphragm spring broken (Chapter 6 Section 6)
- [ ] Broken clutch disc cushioning springs (Chapter 6 Section 6)

Manual transmission

Noisy in neutral with engine running

- ☐ Lack of oil (Chapter 1A Section 28 or 1B Section 28)
- ☐ Input shaft bearings worn (noise apparent with clutch pedal released, but not when depressed) (Chapter 7A)*
- ☐ Clutch release bearing system (noise apparent with clutch pedal depressed, possibly less when released) (Chapter 6 Section 7)

Noisy in one particular gear

- ☐ Worn, damaged or chipped gear teeth (Chapter 7A Section 7)*

Difficulty engaging gears

- ☐ Clutch fault (Chapter 6)
- ☐ Worn, damaged, or poorly-adjusted gearchange (Chapter 7A Section 2)
- ☐ Lack of oil (Chapter 7A)
- ☐ Worn synchroniser units (Chapter 7A Section 7)*

Jumps out of gear

- ☐ Worn, damaged, or poorly-adjusted gearchange (Chapter 7A Section 2)
- ☐ Worn synchroniser units (Chapter 7A Section 7)*
- ☐ Worn selector forks (Chapter 7A Section 7)*

Vibration

- ☐ Lack of oil (Chapter 7A)
- ☐ Worn bearings (Chapter 7A Section 7)*

Lubricant leaks

- ☐ Leaking driveshaft or selector shaft oil seal (Chapter 7A Section 5)
- ☐ Leaking housing joint (Chapter 7A Section 7)*
- ☐ Leaking input shaft oil seal (Chapter 7A Section 5)*

Automatic transmission

Fluid leakage

Note: *Due to the complexity of the automatic transmission, it is difficult for the home mechanic to properly diagnose and service this unit. For problems other than the following, the vehicle should be taken to a dealer service department or automatic transmission specialist. Do not be too hasty in removing the transmission if a fault is suspected, as most of the testing is carried out with the unit still fitted.*

- ☐ Automatic transmission fluid is usually dark in colour. Fluid leaks should not be confused with engine oil, which can easily be blown onto the transmission by airflow.
- ☐ To determine the source of a leak, first remove all built-up dirt and grime from the transmission housing and surrounding areas using a degreasing agent, or by steam-cleaning. Drive the vehicle at low speed, so airflow will not blow the leak far from its source. Raise and support the vehicle, and determine where the leak is coming from.

General gear selection problems

- ☐ Chapter 7B deals with checking and adjusting the selector mechanism on automatic transmissions. The following are common problems which may be caused by a poorly-adjusted mechanism:

    Engine starting in gears other than Park or Neutral.
    Indicator panel indicating a gear other than the one actually being used.
    Vehicle moves when in Park or Neutral.
    Poor gear shift quality or erratic gear changes.

Refer to Chapter 7B Section 3 for the selector mechanism adjustment procedure.

Transmission will not downshift (kickdown) with accelerator pedal fully depressed

- ☐ Low transmission fluid level (Chapter 1A Section 29).
- ☐ Incorrect selector mechanism adjustment (Chapter 7B Section 3).

Engine will not start in any gear, or starts in gears other than Park or Neutral

- ☐ Incorrect selector mechanism adjustment (Chapter 7B Section 3).

Transmission slips, shifts roughly, is noisy, or has no drive in forward or reverse gears

- ☐ There are many probable causes for the above problems, but unless there is a very obvious reason (such as a loose or corroded wiring plug connection on or near the transmission), the car should be taken to a franchise dealer or specialist for the fault to be diagnosed. The transmission control unit incorporates a self-diagnosis facility, and any fault codes can quickly be read and interpreted by a dealer with the proper diagnostic equipment.

Driveshafts

Vibration when accelerating or decelerating
- [ ] Worn inner constant velocity joint (Chapter 8 Section 4, 5)
- [ ] Bent or distorted driveshaft (Chapter 8 Section 5)
- [ ] Worn intermediate bearing (Chapter 8 Section 5)

Clicking or knocking noise on turns (at slow speed on full-lock)
- [ ] Worn outer constant velocity joint (Chapter 8 Section 5)
- [ ] Lack of constant velocity joint lubricant, possibly due to damaged gaiter (Chapter 8)

Braking system

Vehicle pulls to one side under braking
Note: *Before assuming that a brake problem exists, make sure that the tyres are in good condition and correctly inflated, that the front wheel alignment is correct, and that the vehicle is not loaded with weight in an unequal manner. Apart from checking the condition of all pipe and hose connections, any faults occurring on the anti-lock braking system should be referred to a Ford dealer for diagnosis.*
- [ ] Worn, defective, damaged or contaminated brake pads/shoes on one side (Chapter 1A, 1B or 9)
- [ ] Seized or partially-seized brake caliper or wheel cylinder piston (Chapter 1A, 1B or 9)
- [ ] A mixture of brake pad/shoe lining materials fitted between sides (Chapter 1A, 1B or 9)
- [ ] Brake caliper or backplate mounting bolts loose (Chapter 9 Section 5)
- [ ] Worn or damaged steering or suspension components (Chapter 1A, 1B or 10)

Noise (grinding or high-pitched squeal) when brakes applied
- [ ] Brake pad/shoe friction lining material worn down to metal backing (Chapter 1A, 1B or 9)
- [ ] Excessive corrosion of brake disc/drum (may be apparent after the vehicle has been standing for some time (Chapter 1A, 1B or 9)
- [ ] Foreign object (stone chipping, etc)
- [ ] trapped between brake disc and shield (Chapter 1A, 1B or 9)

Excessive brake pedal travel
- [ ] Faulty master cylinder (Chapter 9 Section 10)
- [ ] Air in hydraulic system (Chapter 9 Section 2)
- [ ] Faulty vacuum servo unit (Chapter 9 Section 12)

Brake pedal feels spongy when depressed
- [ ] Air in hydraulic system (Chapter 9 Section 2)
- [ ] Deteriorated flexible rubber brake hoses (Chapter 1A, 1B or 9)

- [ ] Master cylinder mounting nuts loose (Chapter 9 Section 10)
- [ ] Faulty master cylinder (Chapter 9 Section 10)

Excessive brake pedal effort required to stop vehicle
- [ ] Faulty vacuum servo unit (Chapter 9 Section 12, 13)
- [ ] Faulty vacuum pump – diesel models (Chapter 9 Section 21)
- [ ] Disconnected, damaged or insecure brake servo vacuum hose (Chapter 9 Section 13)
- [ ] Primary or secondary hydraulic circuit failure (Chapter 9)
- [ ] Seized brake caliper or wheel cylinder piston (Chapter 9)
- [ ] Brake pads/shoes incorrectly fitted (Chapter 9)
- [ ] Incorrect grade of brake pads/shoes fitted (Chapter 9)
- [ ] Brake pad/shoe linings contaminated (Chapter 1A, 1B or 9)

Judder felt through brake pedal or steering wheel when braking
Note: *Under heavy braking on models equipped with ABS, vibration may be felt through the brake pedal. This is a normal feature of ABS operation, and does not constitute a fault.*
- [ ] Excessive run-out or distortion of discs/drums (Chapter 9)
- [ ] Brake pad/shoe linings worn (Chapter 1A, 1B or 9)
- [ ] Brake caliper/backplate mounting bolts loose (Chapter 9)
- [ ] Wear in suspension or steering components or mountings (Chapter 1A, 1B or 10)
- [ ] Front wheels out of balance (see *Weekly checks*)

Brakes binding
- [ ] Seized brake caliper or wheel cylinder piston (Chapter 9)
- [ ] Incorrectly-adjusted handbrake mechanism (Chapter 9 Section 14)
- [ ] Faulty master cylinder (Chapter 9 Section 10)

Rear wheels locking under normal braking
- [ ] Rear brake shoe linings contaminated or damaged (Chapter 1A or 9)
- [ ] Rear brake drums warped (Chapter 1A, 1B or 9)

Suspension and steering

Vehicle pulls to one side

Note: *Before diagnosing suspension or steering faults, be sure that the trouble is not due to incorrect tyre pressures, mixtures of tyre types, or binding brakes.*

☐ Defective tyre (see *Weekly checks*)
☐ Excessive wear in suspension or steering components (Chapter 1A, 1B or 10)
☐ Incorrect front wheel alignment (Chapter 10 Section 20)
☐ Accident damage to steering or suspension components (Chapter 1A or 1B)

Wheel wobble and vibration

☐ Front wheels out of balance (vibration felt mainly through the steering wheel) (see *Weekly checks*)
☐ Rear wheels out of balance (vibration felt throughout the vehicle) (see *Weekly checks*)
☐ Roadwheels damaged or distorted (see *Weekly checks*)
☐ Faulty or damaged tyre (see *Weekly checks*)
☐ Worn steering or suspension joints, bushes or components (Chapter 1A, 1B or 10)
☐ Wheel nuts loose (Chapter 1A or 1B)

Excessive pitching and/or rolling around corners, or during braking

☐ Defective shock absorbers (Chapter 1A, 1B or 10)
☐ Broken or weak spring and/or suspension component (Chapter 1A, 1B or 10)
☐ Worn or damaged anti-roll bar or mountings (Chapter 1A, 1B or 10)

Wandering or general instability

☐ Incorrect front wheel alignment (Chapter 10 Section 20)
☐ Worn steering or suspension joints, bushes or components (Chapter 1A, 1B or 10)
☐ Roadwheels out of balance (see *Weekly checks*)
☐ Faulty or damaged tyre (see *Weekly checks*)
☐ Wheel nuts loose (Chapter 1A or 1B)
☐ Defective shock absorbers (Chapter 1A, 1B or 10)
☐ Electric power steering system fault (Chapter 10 Section 16)

Excessively-stiff steering

☐ Seized steering linkage balljoint or suspension balljoint (Chapter 1A, 1B or 10)
☐ Incorrect front wheel alignment (Chapter 10 Section 20)
☐ Steering rack damaged (Chapter 10 Section 18)
☐ Electric power steering system fault (Chapter 10 Section 15)

Excessive play in steering

☐ Worn steering column/intermediate shaft joints (Chapter 10 Section 15)
☐ Worn track rod end balljoints (Chapter 1A, 1B or 10)
☐ Worn steering rack (Chapter 10 Section 18)
☐ Worn steering or suspension joints, bushes or components (Chapter 1A, 1B or 10)

Lack of power assistance

☐ Electric power steering system fault (Chapter 10 Section 15)
☐ Faulty steering rack (Chapter 10 Section 18)

Tyre wear excessive

Tyres worn on inside or outside edges

☐ Tyres under-inflated (wear on both edges) (see *Weekly checks*)
☐ Incorrect camber or castor angles (wear on one edge only) (Chapter 10 Section 20)
☐ Worn steering or suspension joints, bushes or components (Chapter 1A, 1B or 10)
☐ Excessively-hard cornering or brakingAccident damage

Tyre treads exhibit feathered edges

☐ Incorrect toe-setting (Chapter 10 Section 20)

Tyres worn in centre of tread

☐ Tyres over-inflated (see *Weekly checks*)

Tyres worn on inside and outside edges

☐ Tyres under-inflated (see *Weekly checks*)

Tyres worn unevenly

☐ Tyres/wheels out of balance (see *Weekly checks*)
☐ Excessive wheel or tyre run-out
☐ Worn shock absorbers (Chapter 1A, 1B or 10)
☐ Faulty tyre (see *Weekly checks*)

Electrical system

Battery will not hold a charge for more than a few days

Note: *For problems associated with the starting system, refer to the faults listed under "Engine" earlier in this Section.*

☐ Battery defective internally (Chapter 5A Section 3)
☐ Battery terminal connections loose or corroded (see *Weekly checks*)
☐ Auxiliary drivebelt worn or incorrectly adjusted (Chapter 1A or 1B)
☐ Alternator not charging at correct output (Chapter 5A Section 5)
☐ Alternator or voltage regulator faulty (Chapter 5A Section 5)
☐ Short-circuit causing continual battery drain (Chapter 5A or 12)

Ignition/no-charge warning light remains illuminated with engine running

☐ Auxiliary drivebelt broken, worn, or incorrectly adjusted (Chapter 1A or 1B)
☐ Internal fault in alternator or voltage regulator (Chapter 5A Section 5)
☐ Broken, disconnected, or loose wiring in charging circuit (Chapter 5A or 12)

Ignition/no-charge warning light fails to come on

☐ Broken, disconnected, or loose wiring in warning light circuit (Chapter 5A or 12)
☐ Alternator faulty (Chapter 5A Section 5)

Electrical system (continued

Lights inoperative

- [ ] Bulb blown (Chapter 12)
- [ ] Corrosion of bulb or bulbholder contacts (Chapter 12)
- [ ] Blown fuse (Chapter 12 Section 3)
- [ ] Faulty relay (Chapter 12 Section 3)
- [ ] Broken, loose, or disconnected wiring (Chapter 12)
- [ ] Faulty switch (Chapter 12 Section 4)

Instrument readings inaccurate or erratic

Fuel or temperature gauges give no reading

- [ ] Faulty gauge sender unit (Chapter 3, 4A or 4B)
- [ ] Wiring open-circuit (Chapter 12 Section 2)
- [ ] Faulty gauge (Chapter 12 Section 10)

Fuel or temperature gauges give continuous maximum reading

- [ ] Faulty gauge sender unit (Chapter 3, 4A or 4B)
- [ ] Wiring short-circuit (Chapter 12 Section 2)
- [ ] Faulty gauge (Chapter 12 Section 10)

Horn inoperative, or unsatisfactory in operation

Horn operates all the time

- [ ] Horn push either earthed or stuck down (Chapter 12 Section 4)
- [ ] Horn cable-to-horn push earthed (Chapter 12 Section 2)

Horn fails to operate

- [ ] Blown fuse (Chapter 12 Section 3)
- [ ] Cable or connections loose, broken or disconnected (Chapter 12 Section 2)
- [ ] Faulty horn (Chapter 12 Section 13)

Horn emits intermittent or unsatisfactory sound

- [ ] Cable connections loose (Chapter 12 Section 2)
- [ ] Horn mountings loose (Chapter 12 Section 13)
- [ ] Faulty horn (Chapter 12 Section 13)

Windscreen wipers inoperative, or unsatisfactory in operation

Wipers fail to operate, or operate very slowly

- [ ] Wiper blades stuck to screen, or linkage seized or binding (Chapter 12 Section 15)
- [ ] Blown fuse (Chapter 12 Section 3)
- [ ] Battery discharged (Chapter 5A Section 3)
- [ ] Cable or connections loose, broken or disconnected (Chapter 12 Section 2)
- [ ] Faulty relay (Chapter 12 Section 3)
- [ ] Faulty wiper motor (Chapter 12 Section 15)

Wiper blades sweep over too large or too small an area of the glass

- [ ] Wiper blades incorrectly fitted, or wrong size used (see *Weekly checks*)
- [ ] Wiper arms incorrectly positioned on spindles (Chapter 12 Section 14)
- [ ] Excessive wear of wiper linkage (Chapter 12 Section 15)
- [ ] Wiper motor or linkage mountings loose or insecure (Chapter 12 Section 15)

Wiper blades fail to clean the glass effectively

- [ ] Wiper blade rubbers dirty, worn or perished (see *Weekly checks*)
- [ ] Wiper blades incorrectly fitted, or wrong size used (see *Weekly checks*)
- [ ] Wiper arm tension springs broken, or arm pivots seized (Chapter 12 Section 14)
- [ ] Insufficient windscreen washer additive to adequately remove road film (see Weekly checks)

Windscreen washers inoperative, or unsatisfactory in operation

One or more washer jets inoperative

- [ ] Blocked washer jetDisconnected, kinked or restricted fluid hose (Chapter 12)
- [ ] Insufficient fluid in washer reservoir (see *Weekly checks*)

Washer pump fails to operate

- [ ] Broken or disconnected wiring or connections (Chapter 12 Section 2)
- [ ] Blown fuse (Chapter 12 Section 3)
- [ ] Faulty washer switch (Chapter 12 Section 4)
- [ ] Faulty washer pump (Chapter 12 Section 17)

Washer pump runs for some time before fluid is emitted from jets

- [ ] Faulty one-way valve in fluid supply hose (Chapter 12)

Electric windows inoperative, or unsatisfactory in operation

Window glass will only move in one direction

- [ ] Faulty switch (Chapter 12 Section 4)

Window glass slow to move

- [ ] Battery discharged (Chapter 5A Section 3)
- [ ] Regulator seized or damaged, or in need of lubrication (Chapter 11 Section 13)
- [ ] Door internal components or trim fouling regulator (Chapter 11 Section 13)
- [ ] Faulty motor (Chapter 11 Section 13)

Window glass fails to move

- [ ] Blown fuse (Chapter 12 Section 3)
- [ ] Faulty relay (Chapter 12 Section 3)
- [ ] Broken or disconnected wiring or connections (Chapter 12 Section 2)
- [ ] Faulty motor (Chapter 11 Section 13)

Central locking system inoperative, or unsatisfactory in operation

Complete system failure

- [ ] Remote handset battery discharged, where applicable (Chapter 1A or 1B)
- [ ] Blown fuse (Chapter 12 Section 3)
- [ ] Faulty relay (Chapter 12 Section 3)
- [ ] Broken or disconnected wiring or connections (Chapter 12)
- [ ] Faulty motor (Chapter 11 Section 14)

Latch locks but will not unlock, or unlocks but will not lock

- [ ] Remote handset battery discharged, where applicable (Chapter 1A or 1B)
- [ ] Faulty master switch (Chapter 12 Section 4)
- [ ] Broken or disconnected latch operating rods or levers (Chapter 11 Section 14)
- [ ] Faulty relay (Chapter 12 Section 3)
- [ ] Faulty motor (Chapter 11 Section 17)

One solenoid/motor fails to operate

- [ ] Broken or disconnected wiring or connections (Chapter 12 Section 2)
- [ ] Faulty operating assembly (Chapter 11 Section 17)
- [ ] Broken, binding or disconnected latch operating rods or levers (Chapter 11 Section 14)
- [ ] Fault in door latch (Chapter 11 Section 14)

A

ABS (Anti-lock brake system) A system, usually electronically controlled, that senses incipient wheel lockup during braking and relieves hydraulic pressure at wheels that are about to skid.

Air bag An inflatable bag hidden in the steering wheel (driver's side) or the dash or glovebox (passenger side). In a head-on collision, the bags inflate, preventing the driver and front passenger from being thrown forward into the steering wheel or windscreen.

Air cleaner A metal or plastic housing, containing a filter element, which removes dust and dirt from the air being drawn into the engine.

Air filter element The actual filter in an air cleaner system, usually manufactured from pleated paper and requiring renewal at regular intervals.

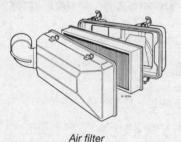

Air filter

Allen key A hexagonal wrench which fits into a recessed hexagonal hole.

Alligator clip A long-nosed spring-loaded metal clip with meshing teeth. Used to make temporary electrical connections.

Alternator A component in the electrical system which converts mechanical energy from a drivebelt into electrical energy to charge the battery and to operate the starting system, ignition system and electrical accessories.

Ampere (amp) A unit of measurement for the flow of electric current. One amp is the amount of current produced by one volt acting through a resistance of one ohm.

Anaerobic sealer A substance used to prevent bolts and screws from loosening. Anaerobic means that it does not require oxygen for activation. The Loctite brand is widely used.

Antifreeze A substance (usually ethylene glycol) mixed with water, and added to a vehicle's cooling system, to prevent freezing of the coolant in winter. Antifreeze also contains chemicals to inhibit corrosion and the formation of rust and other deposits that would tend to clog the radiator and coolant passages and reduce cooling efficiency.

Anti-seize compound A coating that reduces the risk of seizing on fasteners that are subjected to high temperatures, such as exhaust manifold bolts and nuts.

Asbestos A natural fibrous mineral with great heat resistance, commonly used in the composition of brake friction materials.

Asbestos is a health hazard and the dust created by brake systems should never be inhaled or ingested.

Axle A shaft on which a wheel revolves, or which revolves with a wheel. Also, a solid beam that connects the two wheels at one end of the vehicle. An axle which also transmits power to the wheels is known as a live axle.

Axleshaft A single rotating shaft, on either side of the differential, which delivers power from the final drive assembly to the drive wheels. Also called a driveshaft or a halfshaft.

B

Ball bearing An anti-friction bearing consisting of a hardened inner and outer race with hardened steel balls between two races.

Bearing The curved surface on a shaft or in a bore, or the part assembled into either, that permits relative motion between them with minimum wear and friction.

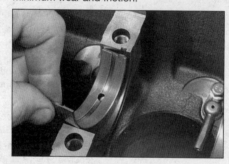

Bearing

Big-end bearing The bearing in the end of the connecting rod that's attached to the crankshaft.

Bleed nipple A valve on a brake wheel cylinder, caliper or other hydraulic component that is opened to purge the hydraulic system of air. Also called a bleed screw.

Brake bleeding Procedure for removing air from lines of a hydraulic brake system.

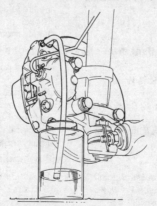

Brake bleeding

Brake disc The component of a disc brake that rotates with the wheels.

Brake drum The component of a drum brake that rotates with the wheels.

Brake linings The friction material which contacts the brake disc or drum to retard the vehicle's speed. The linings are bonded or riveted to the brake pads or shoes.

Brake pads The replaceable friction pads that pinch the brake disc when the brakes are applied. Brake pads consist of a friction material bonded or riveted to a rigid backing plate.

Brake shoe The crescent-shaped carrier to which the brake linings are mounted and which forces the lining against the rotating drum during braking.

Braking systems For more information on braking systems, consult the *Haynes Automotive Brake Manual*.

Breaker bar A long socket wrench handle providing greater leverage.

Bulkhead The insulated partition between the engine and the passenger compartment.

C

Caliper The non-rotating part of a disc-brake assembly that straddles the disc and carries the brake pads. The caliper also contains the hydraulic components that cause the pads to pinch the disc when the brakes are applied. A caliper is also a measuring tool that can be set to measure inside or outside dimensions of an object.

Camshaft A rotating shaft on which a series of cam lobes operate the valve mechanisms. The camshaft may be driven by gears, by sprockets and chain or by sprockets and a belt.

Canister A container in an evaporative emission control system; contains activated charcoal granules to trap vapours from the fuel system.

Canister

Carburettor A device which mixes fuel with air in the proper proportions to provide a desired power output from a spark ignition internal combustion engine.

Castellated Resembling the parapets along the top of a castle wall. For example, a castellated balljoint stud nut.

Castor In wheel alignment, the backward or forward tilt of the steering axis. Castor is positive when the steering axis is inclined rearward at the top.

Catalytic converter A silencer-like device in the exhaust system which converts certain pollutants in the exhaust gases into less harmful substances.

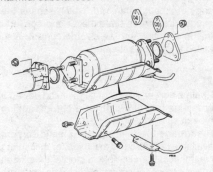

Catalytic converter

Circlip A ring-shaped clip used to prevent endwise movement of cylindrical parts and shafts. An internal circlip is installed in a groove in a housing; an external circlip fits into a groove on the outside of a cylindrical piece such as a shaft.

Clearance The amount of space between two parts. For example, between a piston and a cylinder, between a bearing and a journal, etc.

Coil spring A spiral of elastic steel found in various sizes throughout a vehicle, for example as a springing medium in the suspension and in the valve train.

Compression Reduction in volume, and increase in pressure and temperature, of a gas, caused by squeezing it into a smaller space.

Compression ratio The relationship between cylinder volume when the piston is at top dead centre and cylinder volume when the piston is at bottom dead centre.

Constant velocity (CV) joint A type of universal joint that cancels out vibrations caused by driving power being transmitted through an angle.

Core plug A disc or cup-shaped metal device inserted in a hole in a casting through which core was removed when the casting was formed. Also known as a freeze plug or expansion plug.

Crankcase The lower part of the engine block in which the crankshaft rotates.

Crankshaft The main rotating member, or shaft, running the length of the crankcase, with offset "throws" to which the connecting rods are attached.

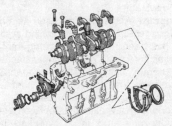

Crankshaft assembly

Crocodile clip See Alligator clip

D

Diagnostic code Code numbers obtained by accessing the diagnostic mode of an engine management computer. This code can be used to determine the area in the system where a malfunction may be located.

Disc brake A brake design incorporating a rotating disc onto which brake pads are squeezed. The resulting friction converts the energy of a moving vehicle into heat.

Double-overhead cam (DOHC) An engine that uses two overhead camshafts, usually one for the intake valves and one for the exhaust valves.

Drivebelt(s) The belt(s) used to drive accessories such as the alternator, water pump, power steering pump, air conditioning compressor, etc. off the crankshaft pulley.

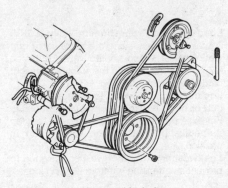

Accessory drivebelts

Driveshaft Any shaft used to transmit motion. Commonly used when referring to the axleshafts on a front wheel drive vehicle.

Drum brake A type of brake using a drum-shaped metal cylinder attached to the inner surface of the wheel. When the brake pedal is pressed, curved brake shoes with friction linings press against the inside of the drum to slow or stop the vehicle.

E

EGR valve A valve used to introduce exhaust gases into the intake air stream.

Electronic control unit (ECU) A computer which controls (for instance) ignition and fuel injection systems, or an anti-lock braking system. For more information refer to the *Haynes Automotive Electrical and Electronic Systems Manual.*

Electronic Fuel Injection (EFI) A computer controlled fuel system that distributes fuel through an injector located in each intake port of the engine.

Emergency brake A braking system, independent of the main hydraulic system, that can be used to slow or stop the vehicle if the primary brakes fail, or to hold the vehicle stationary even though the brake pedal isn't depressed. It usually consists of a hand lever that actuates either front or rear brakes mechanically through a series of cables and linkages. Also known as a handbrake or parking brake.

Endfloat The amount of lengthwise movement between two parts. As applied to a crankshaft, the distance that the crankshaft can move forward and back in the cylinder block.

Engine management system (EMS) A computer controlled system which manages the fuel injection and the ignition systems in an integrated fashion.

Exhaust manifold A part with several passages through which exhaust gases leave the engine combustion chambers and enter the exhaust pipe.

F

Fan clutch A viscous (fluid) drive coupling device which permits variable engine fan speeds in relation to engine speeds.

Feeler blade A thin strip or blade of hardened steel, ground to an exact thickness, used to check or measure clearances between parts.

Feeler blade

Firing order The order in which the engine cylinders fire, or deliver their power strokes, beginning with the number one cylinder.

Flywheel A heavy spinning wheel in which energy is absorbed and stored by means of momentum. On cars, the flywheel is attached to the crankshaft to smooth out firing impulses.

Free play The amount of travel before any action takes place. The "looseness" in a linkage, or an assembly of parts, between the initial application of force and actual movement. For example, the distance the brake pedal moves before the pistons in the master cylinder are actuated.

Fuse An electrical device which protects a circuit against accidental overload. The typical fuse contains a soft piece of metal which is calibrated to melt at a predetermined current flow (expressed as amps) and break the circuit.

Fusible link A circuit protection device consisting of a conductor surrounded by heat-resistant insulation. The conductor is smaller than the wire it protects, so it acts as the weakest link in the circuit. Unlike a blown fuse, a failed fusible link must frequently be cut from the wire for replacement.

G

Gap The distance the spark must travel in jumping from the centre electrode to the side electrode in a spark plug. Also refers to the spacing between the points in a contact breaker assembly in a conventional points-type ignition, or to the distance between the reluctor or rotor and the pickup coil in an electronic ignition.

Adjusting spark plug gap

Gasket Any thin, soft material - usually cork, cardboard, asbestos or soft metal - installed between two metal surfaces to ensure a good seal. For instance, the cylinder head gasket seals the joint between the block and the cylinder head.

Gasket

Gauge An instrument panel display used to monitor engine conditions. A gauge with a movable pointer on a dial or a fixed scale is an analogue gauge. A gauge with a numerical readout is called a digital gauge.

H

Halfshaft A rotating shaft that transmits power from the final drive unit to a drive wheel, usually when referring to a live rear axle.

Harmonic balancer A device designed to reduce torsion or twisting vibration in the crankshaft. May be incorporated in the crankshaft pulley. Also known as a vibration damper.

Hone An abrasive tool for correcting small irregularities or differences in diameter in an engine cylinder, brake cylinder, etc.

Hydraulic tappet A tappet that utilises hydraulic pressure from the engine's lubrication system to maintain zero clearance (constant contact with both camshaft and valve stem). Automatically adjusts to variation in valve stem length. Hydraulic tappets also reduce valve noise.

I

Ignition timing The moment at which the spark plug fires, usually expressed in the number of crankshaft degrees before the piston reaches the top of its stroke.

Inlet manifold A tube or housing with passages through which flows the air-fuel mixture (carburettor vehicles and vehicles with throttle body injection) or air only (port fuel-injected vehicles) to the port openings in the cylinder head.

J

Jump start Starting the engine of a vehicle with a discharged or weak battery by attaching jump leads from the weak battery to a charged or helper battery.

L

Load Sensing Proportioning Valve (LSPV) A brake hydraulic system control valve that works like a proportioning valve, but also takes into consideration the amount of weight carried by the rear axle.

Locknut A nut used to lock an adjustment nut, or other threaded component, in place. For example, a locknut is employed to keep the adjusting nut on the rocker arm in position.

Lockwasher A form of washer designed to prevent an attaching nut from working loose.

M

MacPherson strut A type of front suspension system devised by Earle MacPherson at Ford of England. In its original form, a simple lateral link with the anti-roll bar creates the lower control arm. A long strut - an integral coil spring and shock absorber - is mounted between the body and the steering knuckle. Many modern so-called MacPherson strut systems use a conventional lower A-arm and don't rely on the anti-roll bar for location.

Multimeter An electrical test instrument with the capability to measure voltage, current and resistance.

N

NOx Oxides of Nitrogen. A common toxic pollutant emitted by petrol and diesel engines at higher temperatures.

O

Ohm The unit of electrical resistance. One volt applied to a resistance of one ohm will produce a current of one amp.

Ohmmeter An instrument for measuring electrical resistance.

O-ring A type of sealing ring made of a special rubber-like material; in use, the O-ring is compressed into a groove to provide the sealing action.

Overhead cam (ohc) engine An engine with the camshaft(s) located on top of the cylinder head(s).

Overhead valve (ohv) engine An engine with the valves located in the cylinder head, but with the camshaft located in the engine block.

Oxygen sensor A device installed in the engine exhaust manifold, which senses the oxygen content in the exhaust and converts this information into an electric current. Also called a Lambda sensor.

P

Phillips screw A type of screw head having a cross instead of a slot for a corresponding type of screwdriver.

Plastigage A thin strip of plastic thread, available in different sizes, used for measuring clearances. For example, a strip of Plastigage is laid across a bearing journal. The parts are assembled and dismantled; the width of the crushed strip indicates the clearance between journal and bearing.

Plastigage

Propeller shaft The long hollow tube with universal joints at both ends that carries power from the transmission to the differential on front-engined rear wheel drive vehicles.

Proportioning valve A hydraulic control valve which limits the amount of pressure to the rear brakes during panic stops to prevent wheel lock-up.

R

Rack-and-pinion steering A steering system with a pinion gear on the end of the steering shaft that mates with a rack (think of a geared wheel opened up and laid flat). When the steering wheel is turned, the pinion turns, moving the rack to the left or right. This movement is transmitted through the track rods to the steering arms at the wheels.

Radiator A liquid-to-air heat transfer device designed to reduce the temperature of the coolant in an internal combustion engine cooling system.

Refrigerant Any substance used as a heat transfer agent in an air-conditioning system. R-12 has been the principle refrigerant for many years; recently, however, manufacturers have begun using R-134a, a non-CFC substance that is considered less harmful to the ozone in the upper atmosphere.

Rocker arm A lever arm that rocks on a shaft or pivots on a stud. In an overhead valve engine, the rocker arm converts the upward movement of the pushrod into a downward movement to open a valve.

Rotor In a distributor, the rotating device inside the cap that connects the centre electrode and the outer terminals as it turns, distributing the high voltage from the coil secondary winding to the proper spark plug. Also, that part of an alternator which rotates inside the stator. Also, the rotating assembly of a turbocharger, including the compressor wheel, shaft and turbine wheel.

Runout The amount of wobble (in-and-out movement) of a gear or wheel as it's rotated. The amount a shaft rotates "out-of-true." The out-of-round condition of a rotating part.

S

Sealant A liquid or paste used to prevent leakage at a joint. Sometimes used in conjunction with a gasket.

Sealed beam lamp An older headlight design which integrates the reflector, lens and filaments into a hermetically-sealed one-piece unit. When a filament burns out or the lens cracks, the entire unit is simply replaced.

Serpentine drivebelt A single, long, wide accessory drivebelt that's used on some newer vehicles to drive all the accessories, instead of a series of smaller, shorter belts. Serpentine drivebelts are usually tensioned by an automatic tensioner.

Serpentine drivebelt

Shim Thin spacer, commonly used to adjust the clearance or relative positions between two parts. For example, shims inserted into or under bucket tappets control valve clearances. Clearance is adjusted by changing the thickness of the shim.

Slide hammer A special puller that screws into or hooks onto a component such as a shaft or bearing; a heavy sliding handle on the shaft bottoms against the end of the shaft to knock the component free.

Sprocket A tooth or projection on the periphery of a wheel, shaped to engage with a chain or drivebelt. Commonly used to refer to the sprocket wheel itself.

Starter inhibitor switch On vehicles with an automatic transmission, a switch that prevents starting if the vehicle is not in Neutral or Park.

Strut See MacPherson strut.

T

Tappet A cylindrical component which transmits motion from the cam to the valve stem, either directly or via a pushrod and rocker arm. Also called a cam follower.

Thermostat A heat-controlled valve that regulates the flow of coolant between the cylinder block and the radiator, so maintaining optimum engine operating temperature. A thermostat is also used in some air cleaners in which the temperature is regulated.

Thrust bearing The bearing in the clutch assembly that is moved in to the release levers by clutch pedal action to disengage the clutch. Also referred to as a release bearing.

Timing belt A toothed belt which drives the camshaft. Serious engine damage may result if it breaks in service.

Timing chain A chain which drives the camshaft.

Toe-in The amount the front wheels are closer together at the front than at the rear. On rear wheel drive vehicles, a slight amount of toe-in is usually specified to keep the front wheels running parallel on the road by offsetting other forces that tend to spread the wheels apart.

Toe-out The amount the front wheels are closer together at the rear than at the front. On front wheel drive vehicles, a slight amount of toe-out is usually specified.

Tools For full information on choosing and using tools, refer to the *Haynes Automotive Tools Manual*.

Tracer A stripe of a second colour applied to a wire insulator to distinguish that wire from another one with the same colour insulator.

Tune-up A process of accurate and careful adjustments and parts replacement to obtain the best possible engine performance.

Turbocharger A centrifugal device, driven by exhaust gases, that pressurises the intake air. Normally used to increase the power output from a given engine displacement, but can also be used primarily to reduce exhaust emissions (as on VW's "Umwelt" Diesel engine).

U

Universal joint or U-joint A double-pivoted connection for transmitting power from a driving to a driven shaft through an angle. A U-joint consists of two Y-shaped yokes and a cross-shaped member called the spider.

V

Valve A device through which the flow of liquid, gas, vacuum, or loose material in bulk may be started, stopped, or regulated by a movable part that opens, shuts, or partially obstructs one or more ports or passageways. A valve is also the movable part of such a device.

Valve clearance The clearance between the valve tip (the end of the valve stem) and the rocker arm or tappet. The valve clearance is measured when the valve is closed.

Vernier caliper A precision measuring instrument that measures inside and outside dimensions. Not quite as accurate as a micrometer, but more convenient.

Viscosity The thickness of a liquid or its resistance to flow.

Volt A unit for expressing electrical "pressure" in a circuit. One volt that will produce a current of one ampere through a resistance of one ohm.

W

Welding Various processes used to join metal items by heating the areas to be joined to a molten state and fusing them together. For more information refer to the *Haynes Automotive Welding Manual*.

Wiring diagram A drawing portraying the components and wires in a vehicle's electrical system, using standardised symbols. For more information refer to the *Haynes Automotive Electrical and Electronic Systems Manual*.

Note: *References throughout this index are in the form "Chapter number" • "Page number". So, for example, 2C•15 refers to page 15 of Chapter 2C.*

Note: *References throughout this index are in the form "Chapter number" • "Page number". So, for example, 2C•15 refers to page 15 of Chapter 2C.*

Note: *References throughout this index are in the form* **"Chapter number"** • **"Page number"**. *So, for example, 2C•15 refers to page 15 of Chapter 2C.*

Note: *References throughout this index are in the form* "**Chapter number**" • "**Page number**". *So, for example, 2C•15 refers to page 15 of Chapter 2C.*

Preserving Our Motoring Heritage

< *The Model J Duesenberg Derham Tourster. Only eight of these magnificent cars were ever built – this is the only example to be found outside the United States of America*

Almost every car you've ever loved, loathed or desired is gathered under one roof at the Haynes Motor Museum. Over 300 immaculately presented cars and motorbikes represent every aspect of our motoring heritage, from elegant reminders of bygone days, such as the superb Model J Duesenberg to curiosities like the bug-eyed BMW Isetta. There are also many old friends and flames. Perhaps you remember the 1959 Ford Popular that you did your courting in? The magnificent 'Red Collection' is a spectacle of classic sports cars including AC, Alfa Romeo, Austin Healey, Ferrari, Lamborghini, Maserati, MG, Riley, Porsche and Triumph.

A Perfect Day Out

Each and every vehicle at the Haynes Motor Museum has played its part in the history and culture of Motoring. Today, they make a wonderful spectacle and a great day out for all the family. Bring the kids, bring Mum and Dad, but above all bring your camera to capture those golden memories for ever. You will also find an impressive array of motoring memorabilia, a comfortable 70 seat video cinema and one of the most extensive transport book shops in Britain. The Pit Stop Cafe serves everything from a cup of tea to wholesome, home-made meals or, if you prefer, you can enjoy the large picnic area nestled in the beautiful rural surroundings of Somerset.

John Haynes O.B.E., Founder and Chairman of the museum at the wheel of a Haynes Light 12. >

< *Graham Hill's Lola Cosworth Formula 1 car next to a 1934 Riley Sports.*

The Museum is situated on the A359 Yeovil to Frome road at Sparkford, just off the A303 in Somerset. It is about 40 miles south of Bristol, and 25 minutes drive from the M5 intersection at Taunton.
Open 9.30am - 5.30pm (10.00am - 4.00pm Winter) 7 days a week, *except Christmas Day, Boxing Day and New Years Day*
Special rates available for schools, coach parties and outings Charitable Trust No. 292048